maran

illustrated™

Microsoft®

Office 2003

Download the examples used in this book from www.maran.com/office2003

maranGraphics®
&
THOMSON
COURSE TECHNOLOGY™
Professional ■ Technical ■ Reference

Distributed in the U.S. and Canada by Thomson Course Technology PTR. For enquiries about Maran Illustrated™ books outside the U.S. and Canada, please contact maranGraphics at international@maran.com

For U.S. orders and customer service, please contact Thomson Course Technology at 1-800-354-9706. For Canadian orders, please contact Thomson Course Technology at 1-800-268-2222 or 416-752-9448.

ISBN-13: 978-1-59200-890-2
ISBN-10: 1-59200-890-9

Library of Congress Catalog Card Number: 2005921495

Printed in the United States of America

07 08 09 BU 10 9 8 7 6

Trademarks

maranGraphics is a registered trademark of maranGraphics Inc. Maran Illustrated, the Maran Illustrated logos and any trade dress related to or associated with the contents or cover of this book are trademarks of maranGraphics Inc. and may not be used without written permission.

The Thomson Course Technology PTR logo is a trademark of Course Technology and may not be used without written permission.

All other trademarks are the property of their respective owners.

Permissions

Microsoft
©2003 Microsoft Corporation. All rights reserved.

Important

maranGraphics and Thomson Course Technology PTR cannot provide software support. Please contact the appropriate software manufacturer's technical support line or Web site for assistance.

maranGraphics and Thomson Course Technology PTR have attempted throughout this book to distinguish proprietary trademarks by following the capitalization style used by the source. However, we cannot attest to the accuracy of the style, and the use of a word or term in this book is not intended to affect the validity of any trademark.

Copies

Educational facilities, companies, and organizations located in the U.S. and Canada that are interested in multiple copies of this book should contact Thomson Course Technology PTR for quantity discount information. Training manuals, CD-ROMs, and portions of this book are also available individually or can be tailored for specific needs.

maranGraphics®

maranGraphics Inc.
5755 Coopers Avenue
Mississauga, Ontario
L4Z 1R9
www.maran.com

THOMSON
COURSE TECHNOLOGY
Professional ■ Technical ■ Reference

Thomson Course Technology PTR, a division of Thomson Course Technology
25 Thomson Place ■ Boston, MA 02210 ■ http://www.courseptr.com

maranGraphics is a family-run business.

At **maranGraphics**, we believe in producing great computer books—one book at a time.

Each maranGraphics book uses the award-winning communication process that we have been developing over the last 30 years. Using this process, we organize screen shots, text and illustrations in a way that makes it easy for you to learn new concepts and tasks.

We spend hours deciding the best way to perform each task, so you don't have to! Our clear, easy-to-follow screen shots and instructions walk you through each task from beginning to end.

Our detailed illustrations go hand-in-hand with the text to help reinforce the information. Each illustration is a labor of love—some take up to a week to draw!

We want to thank you for purchasing what we feel are the best computer books money can buy. We hope you enjoy using this book as much as we enjoyed creating it!

Sincerely,

The Maran Family

We would love to hear from you! Send your comments and feedback about our books to family@maran.com

Please visit us on the Web at:

www.maran.com

CREDITS

Authors:
Ruth Maran
Kelleigh Johnson

Copy Development and Editing:
Raquel Scott

Project Manager:
Judy Maran

Editing and Screen Captures:
Roxanne Van Damme
Roderick Anatalio
Adam Giles
Megan Robinson

Layout Designer:
Steven Schaerer

Illustrator:
Russ Marini

Illustrator, Screen Artist and Assistant Layout Designer:
Richard Hung

Indexer:
Raquel Scott

Post Production:
Robert Maran

President, Thomson Course Technology:
David R. West

Senior Vice President of Business Development, Thomson Course Technology:
Andy Shafran

Publisher and General Manager, Thomson Course Technology PTR:
Stacy L. Hiquet

Associate Director of Marketing, Thomson Course Technology PTR:
Sarah O'Donnell

National Sales Manager, Thomson Course Technology PTR:
Amy Merrill

Manager of Editorial Services, Thomson Course Technology PTR:
Heather Talbot

ACKNOWLEDGMENTS

maranGraphics®

Thanks to the dedicated staff of maranGraphics, including Roderick Anatalio, Adam Giles, Richard Hung, Kelleigh Johnson, Wanda Lawrie, Jill Maran, Judy Maran, Robert Maran, Ruth Maran, Russ Marini, Steven Schaerer, Raquel Scott and Roxanne Van Damme.

Finally, to Richard Maran who originated the easy-to-use graphic format of this guide. Thank you for your inspiration and guidance.

TABLE OF CONTENTS

GETTING STARTED

1) Getting Started

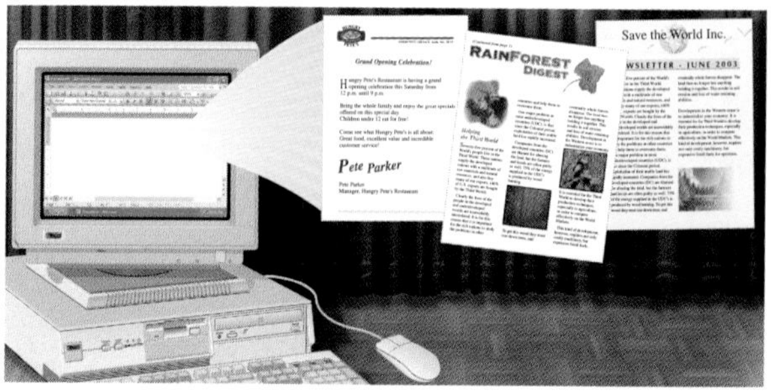

USING WORD

1) Getting Started

2) Save, Open and Print a Document

3) Edit a Document

4) Format Text

5) Format Pages

GLOBAL REPORT
Helping the Third World Countries
Seventy-five percent of the world's people live in the Third World. These nations supply the developed nations with a multitude of raw materials and natural resources, and also buy many of our exports, (40% of U.S. exports are bought by the Third World). Clearly the lives of the people in the developed and underdeveloped worlds are unavoidably interrelated. It is for this reason that it is important for the rich nations to study the problems in other countries and help them to overcome them.
One major problem in most underdeveloped countries (UDC), is that since the Colonial period, exploitation of their arable land has rapidly increased. Companies from the developed countries (DC) are blamed for abusing the land, but the farmers and locals are often guilty as well. 75% of the energy supplied in the UDCs is produced by wood burning. To get this wood they must tear down trees, and eventually whole forests disappear. The land then no longer has anything holding it together. This results in soil erosion and loss of water retaining abilities.
Development in the Western sense is to industrialize your economy. It is essential for the Third World to develop their production techniques, especially in agriculture, in order to compete effectively on the World Markets. This kind of development, however, requires not only costly machinery, but expensive fossil fuels for operation. For countries already billions in debt this is obviously not economically possible.
1
2
3
4
5

TABLE OF CONTENTS

USING EXCEL

1) Getting Started

2) Save and Open a Workbook

3) Edit a Worksheet

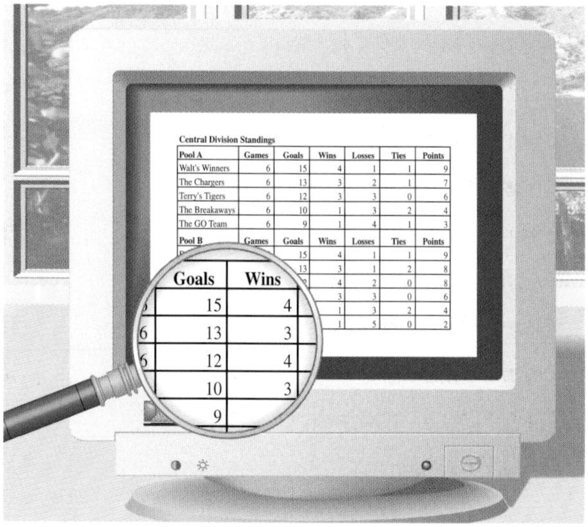

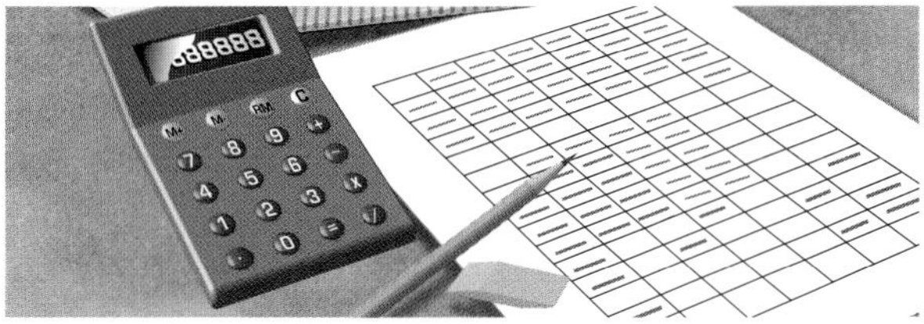

4) Using Formulas and Functions

5) Format a Worksheet

6) Print a Worksheet

7) Working With Charts

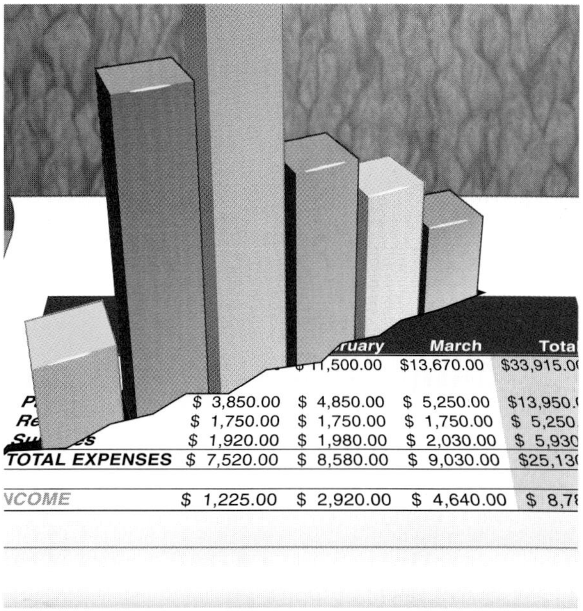

TABLE OF CONTENTS

USING POWERPOINT

1) Getting Started

2) Edit Slides

3) Add Objects to Slides

4) Enhance a Presentation

5) Fine-Tune a Presentation

USING PUBLISHER

1) Getting Started

2) Save, Print & Open a Publication

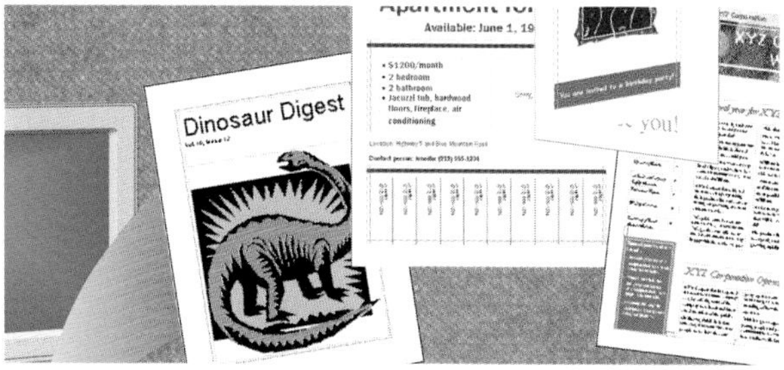

TABLE OF CONTENTS

3) Enhance a Publication

4) Create and Work With Objects

USING OUTLOOK

1) Exchange E-mail

2) Manage Information

3) Outlook With Business Contact Manager

OFFICE AND THE INTERNET

1) Office and the Internet

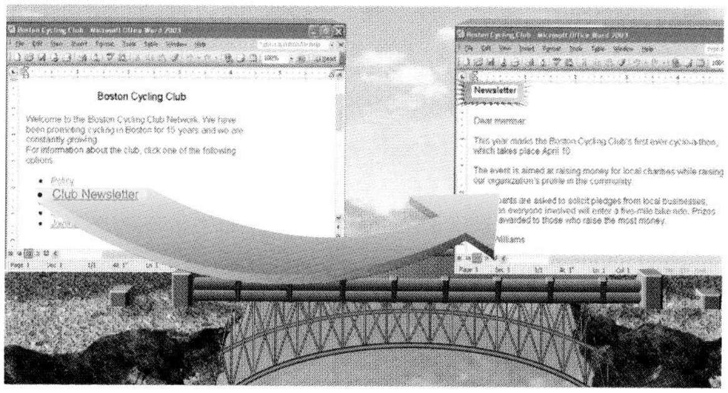

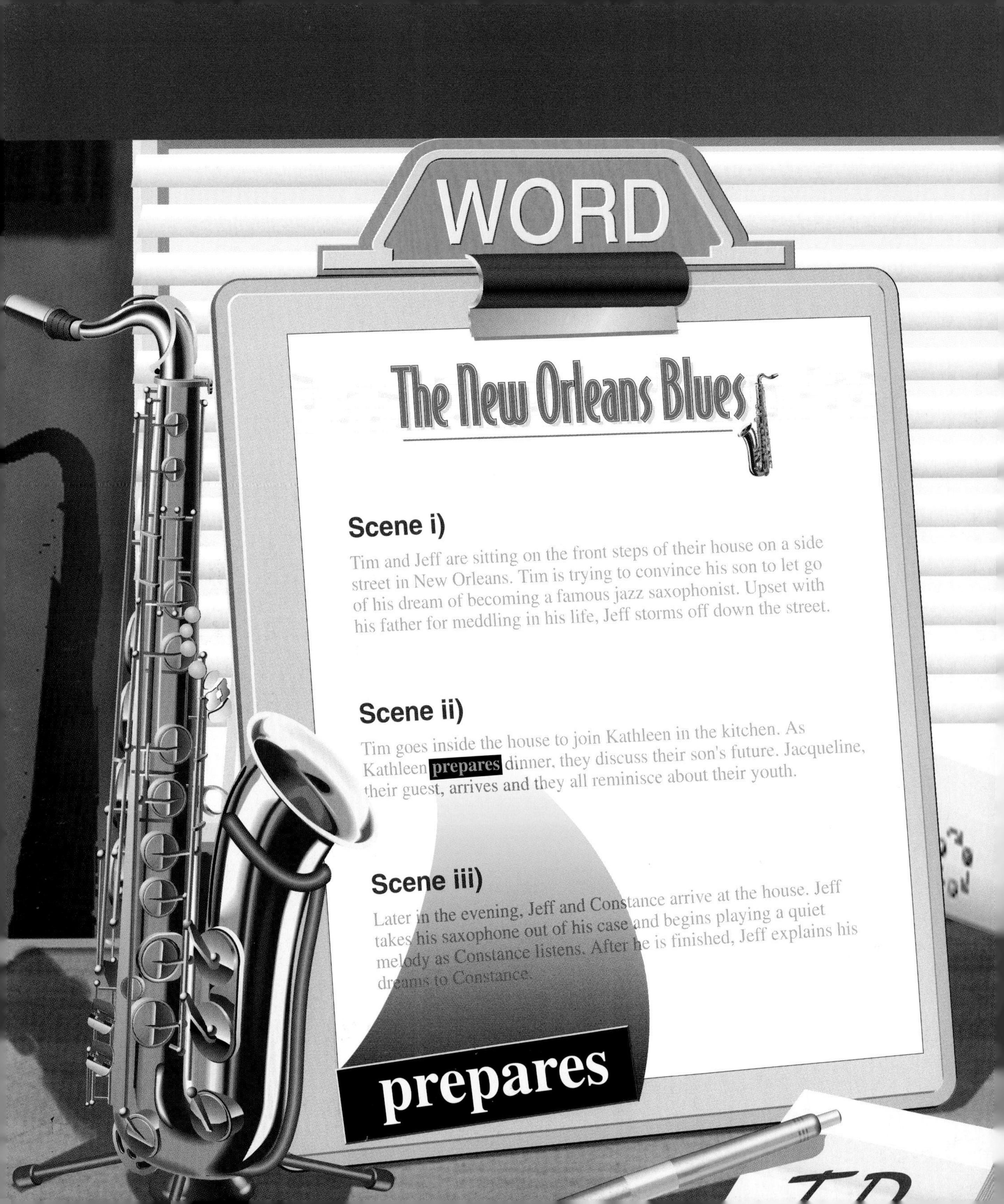
WORD
The New Orleans Blues
Scene i)
Tim and Jeff are sitting on the front steps of their house on a side street in New Orleans. Tim is trying to convince his son to let go of his dream of becoming a famous jazz saxophonist. Upset with his father for meddling in his life, Jeff storms off down the street.
Scene ii)
Tim goes inside the house to join Kathleen in the kitchen. As Kathleen prepares dinner, they discuss their son's future. Jacqueline, their guest, arrives and they all reminisce about their youth.
Scene iii)
Later in the evening, Jeff and Constance arrive at the house. Jeff takes his saxophone out of his case and begins playing a quiet melody as Constance listens. After he is finished, Jeff explains his dreams to Constance.
prepares

Getting Started

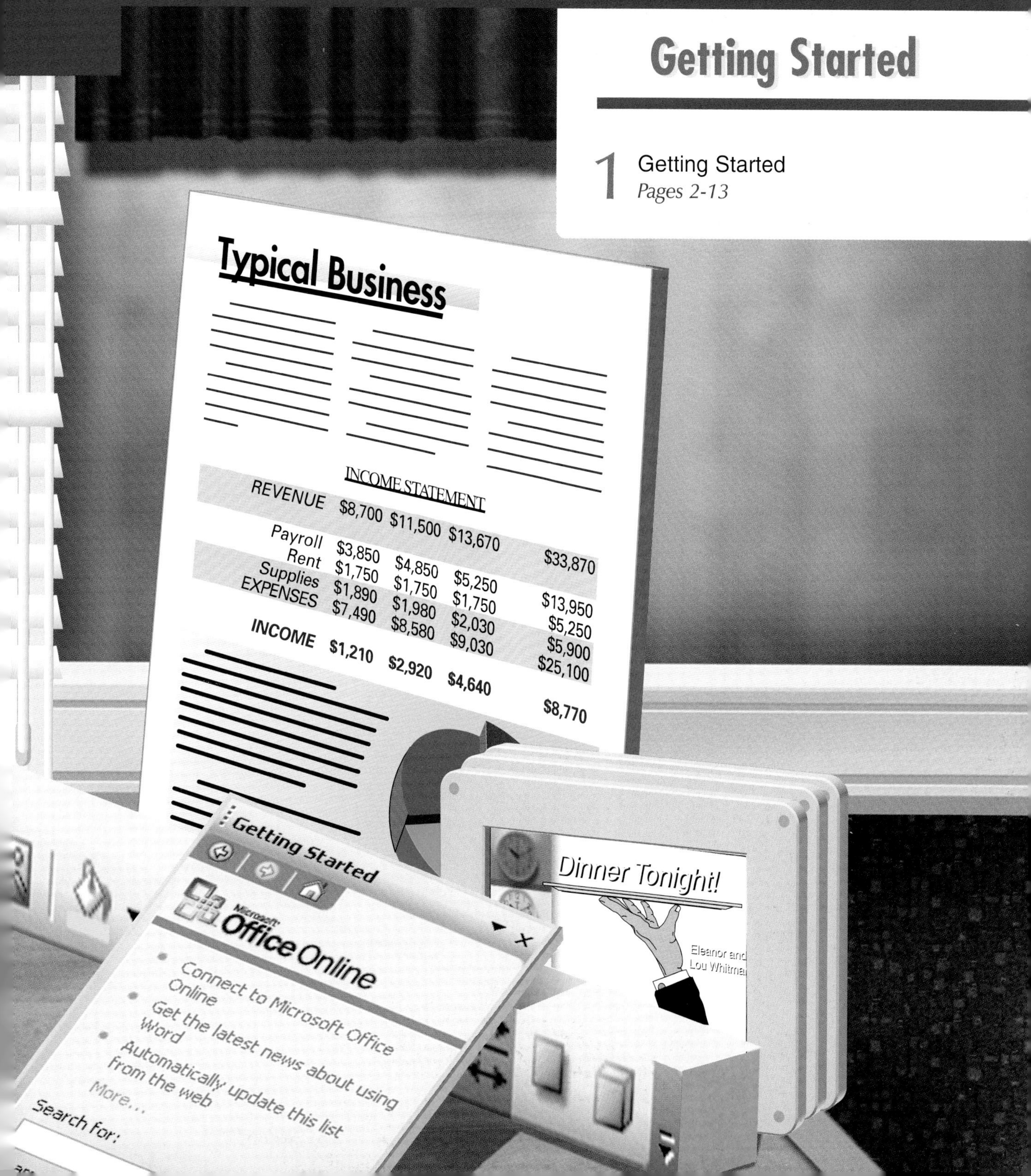

Microsoft® Office 2003 is a suite of programs that you can use to accomplish various tasks.

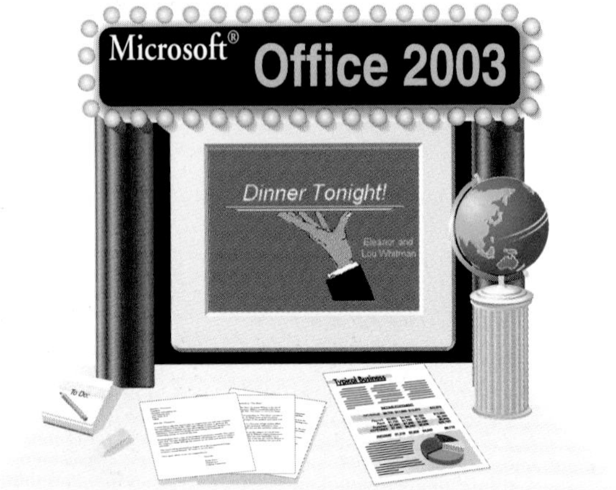

All Microsoft Office 2003 programs share a common design and work in a similar way. Once you learn one program, you can easily learn the others.

Office Editions

There are several editions of Microsoft Office 2003 available. Each edition contains a different combination of programs. In this book, we focus on the programs that are included in the Small Business Edition of Microsoft Office 2003. This edition is suited to home and small business users who require basic Office programs to accomplish day-to-day tasks.

Word

Word is a word processing program that you can use to quickly and efficiently create documents such as letters, memos and reports. Word offers many features that make it easy to edit and format your documents.

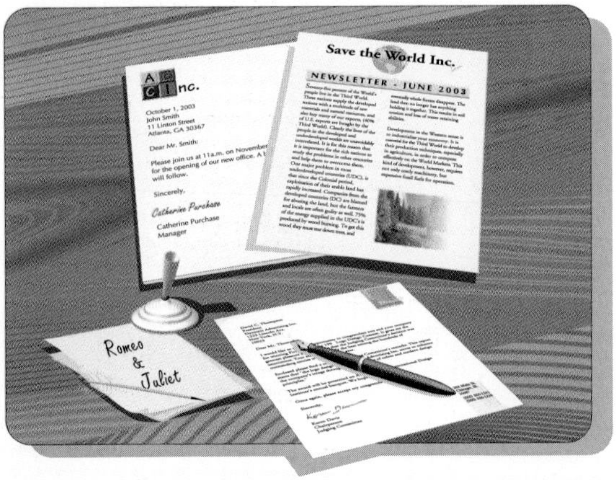

Excel

Excel is a spreadsheet program that allows you to organize and analyze data, such as a budget or sales report. Excel can also help you create colorful charts to attractively present data.

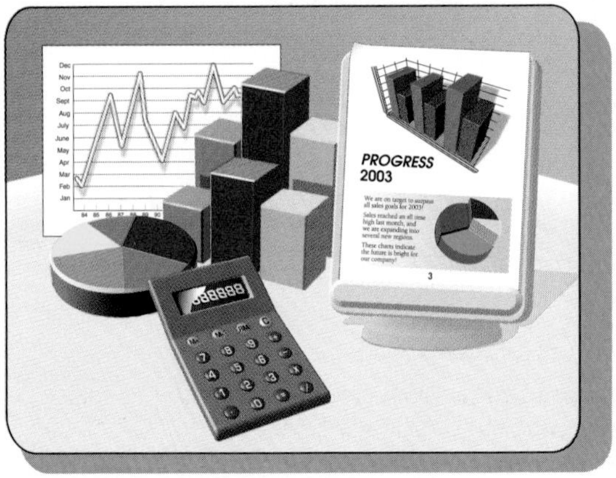

PowerPoint

PowerPoint is a program that helps you plan, organize and design professional presentations. You can add objects such as pictures, charts and diagrams to your presentations to add visual interest to the presentations.

Publisher

Publisher is a desktop publishing program that helps you design professional publications, such as banners, brochures, catalogs, flyers, invitation cards and newsletters.

Outlook

Outlook is an information management program that allows you to exchange e-mail messages and organize information, including appointments, contacts, tasks and notes.

Business Contact Manager

Business Contact Manager is an add-on to Outlook that allows small business users to more effectively keep track of their accounts, business contacts and sales leads.

Office and the Internet

Each Office program provides features that allow you to take advantage of the Internet. You can create a hyperlink in an Office file to link the file to a Web page or to another file on your computer or network. You can also save Office files as Web pages, which allows you to place your files on the Internet.

START A PROGRAM

You can start an Office program to perform a task, such as writing a letter, analyzing financial data, creating a presentation or designing a brochure.

START A PROGRAM

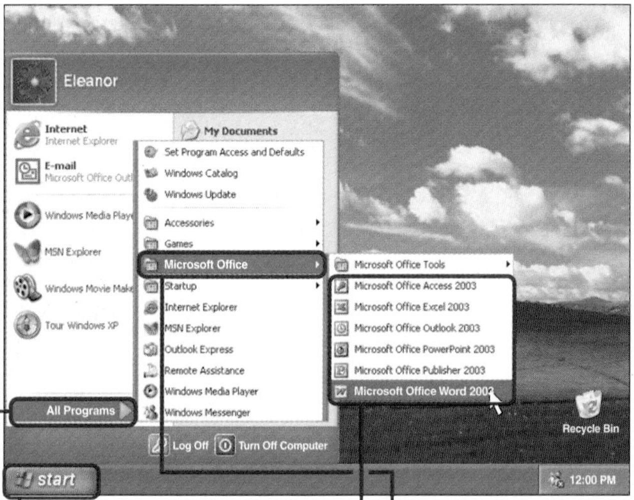

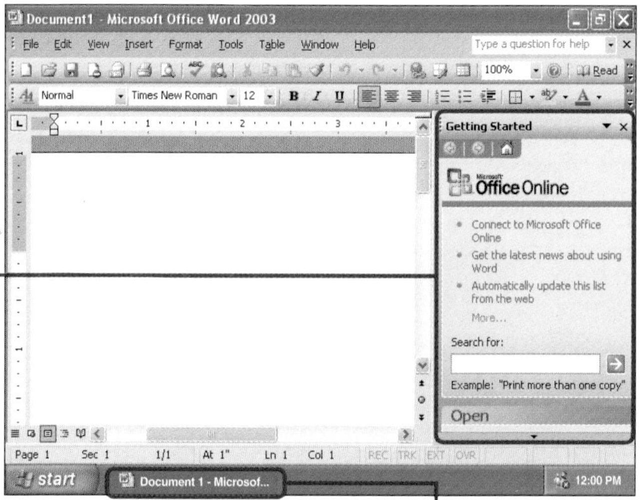

1 Click **start**.

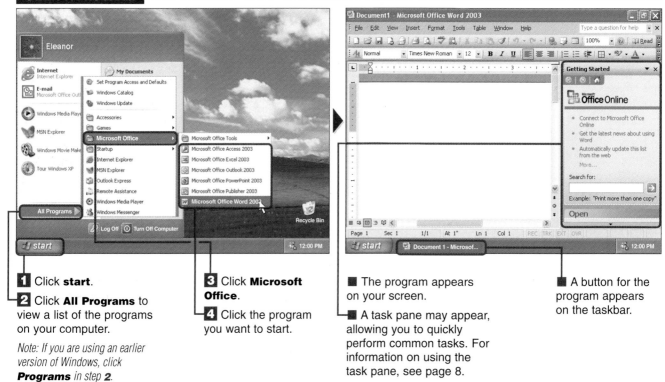

2 Click **All Programs** to view a list of the programs on your computer.

Note: If you are using an earlier version of Windows, click ***Programs*** *in step* ***2****.*

3 Click **Microsoft Office**.

4 Click the program you want to start.

■ The program appears on your screen.

■ A task pane may appear, allowing you to quickly perform common tasks. For information on using the task pane, see page 8.

■ A button for the program appears on the taskbar.

EXIT A PROGRAM

When you finish using a program, you can exit the program.

You should always exit all programs before turning off your computer.

EXIT A PROGRAM

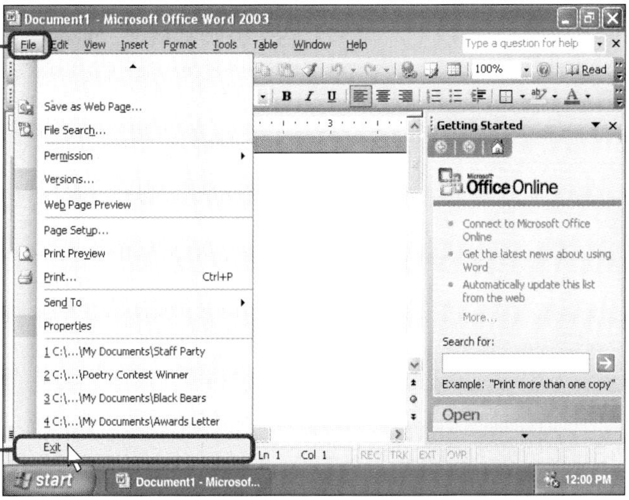

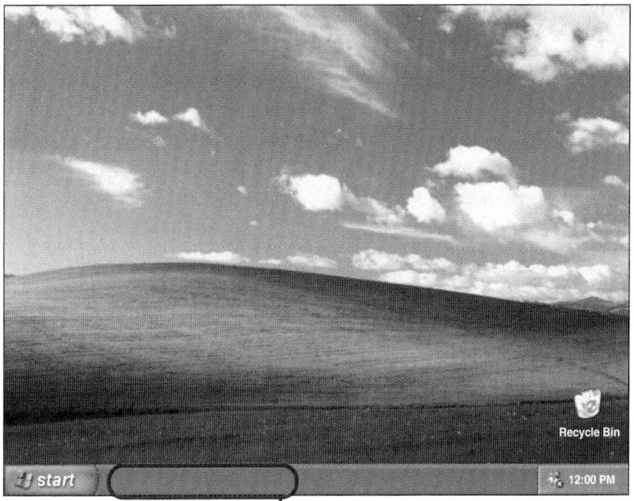

1 Click **File**.

2 Click **Exit** to shut down the program.

Note: If Exit does not appear on the menu, position the mouse over the bottom of the menu to display the menu option.

■ The program disappears from your screen.

■ The button for the program disappears from the taskbar.

SELECT COMMANDS

You can select a command from a menu or toolbar to perform a task in an Office program. Each command performs a different task.

When you first start an Office program, the most commonly used commands and buttons appear on the short version of each menu and toolbar. As you work, the program customizes the menus and toolbars to display the commands and buttons you use most often.

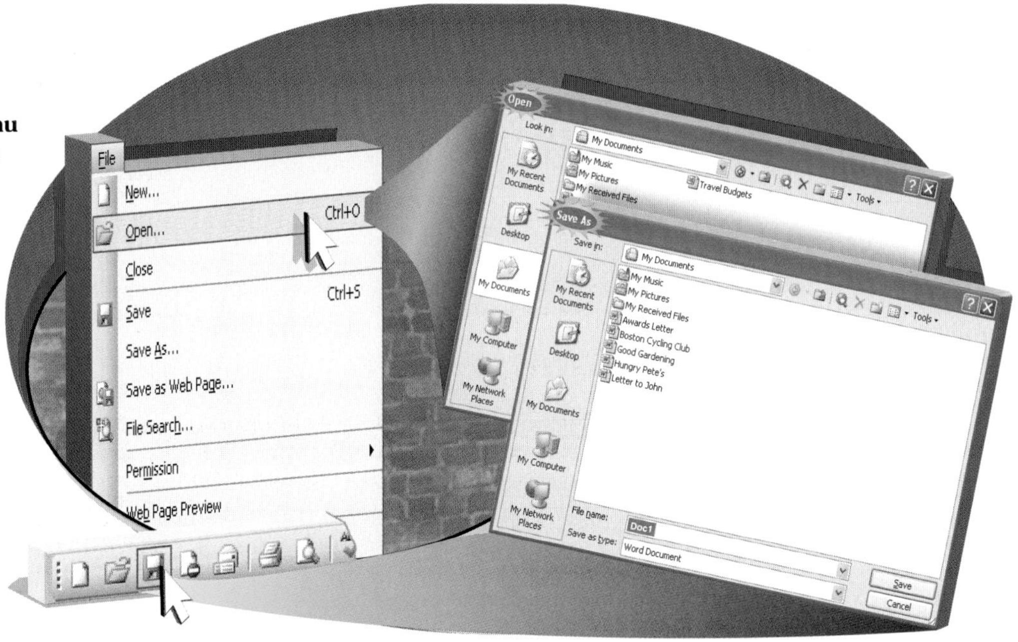

SELECT COMMANDS

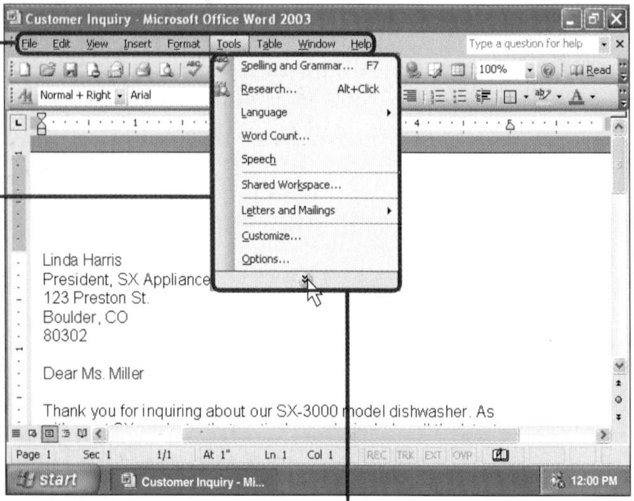

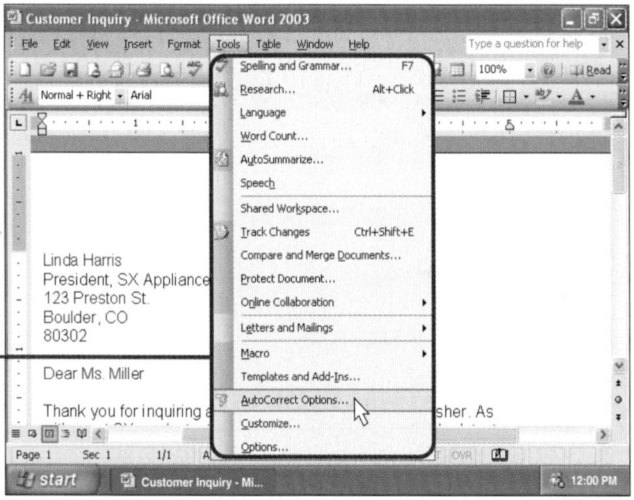

USING MENUS

1 Click the name of the menu you want to display.

■ A short version of the menu appears, displaying the most commonly used commands.

2 To expand the menu and display all the commands, position the mouse over ».

■ The expanded menu appears, displaying all the commands.

3 Click the command you want to use.

■ To close a menu without selecting a command, click outside the menu.

Tip

How can I quickly select a command?

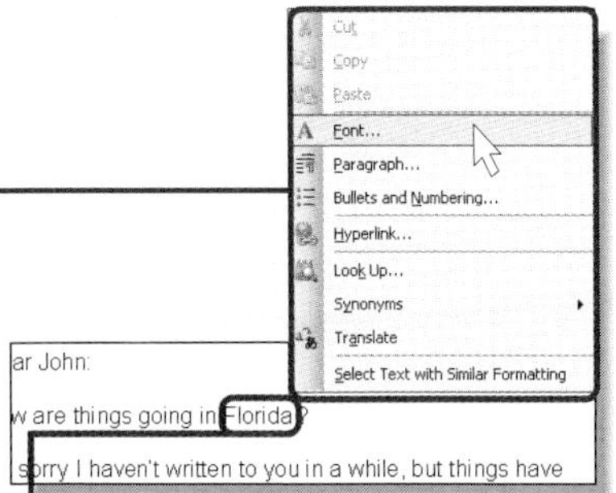

1 Right-click an item to display a shortcut menu containing the most frequently used commands for the item.

2 Click the command you want to use.

■ To close a shortcut menu without selecting a command, click outside the menu.

Tip

Why do some commands or buttons have a dimmed appearance?

Menu commands or buttons that have a dimmed appearance are currently not available. You must perform a specific task before you can select the commands or buttons. For example, you must select text to make the Cut and Copy commands in the Edit menu available in Word.

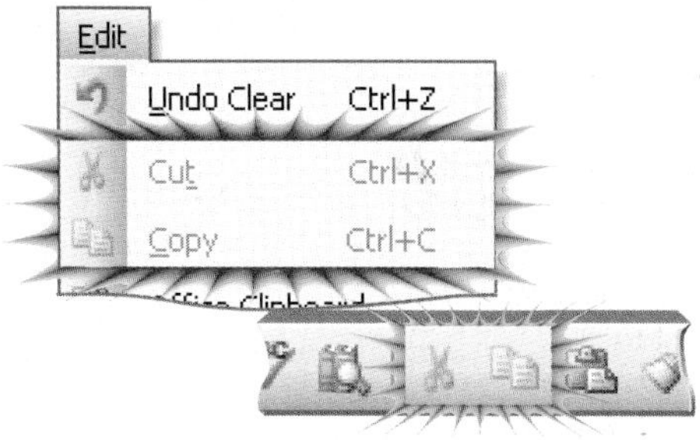

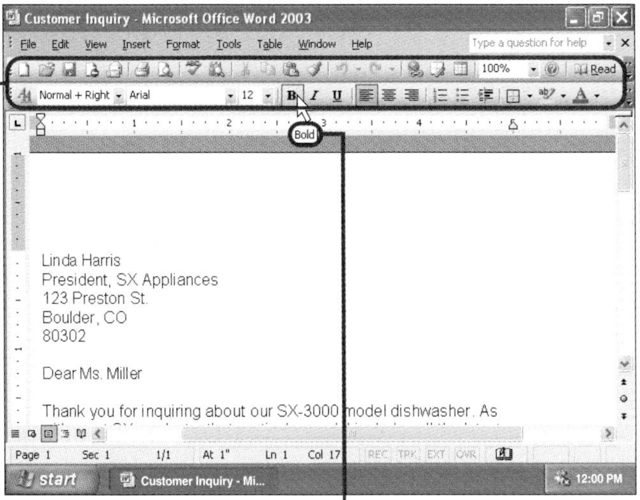

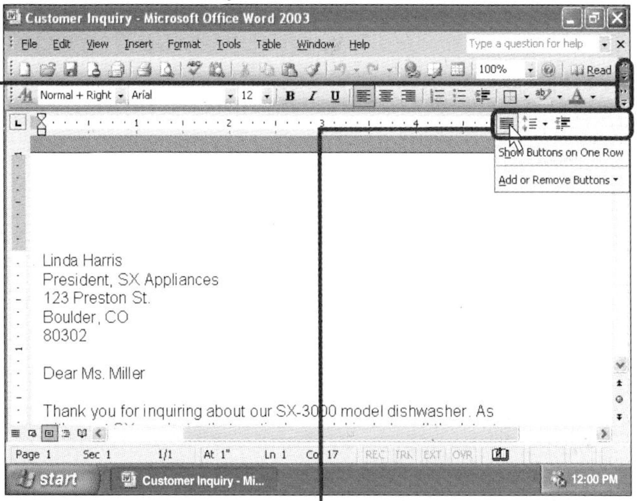

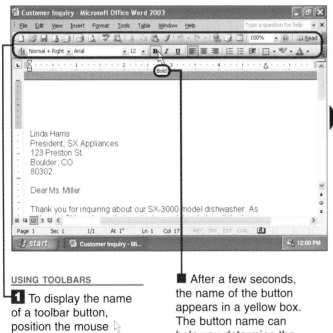

USING TOOLBARS

1 To display the name of a toolbar button, position the mouse over the button.

■ After a few seconds, the name of the button appears in a yellow box. The button name can help you determine the task the button performs.

2 A toolbar may not be able to display all its buttons. Click to display additional buttons for the toolbar.

■ Additional buttons for the toolbar appear.

3 To use a toolbar button to select a command, click the button.

USING THE TASK PANE

Most Office programs offer task panes that you can use to perform common tasks.

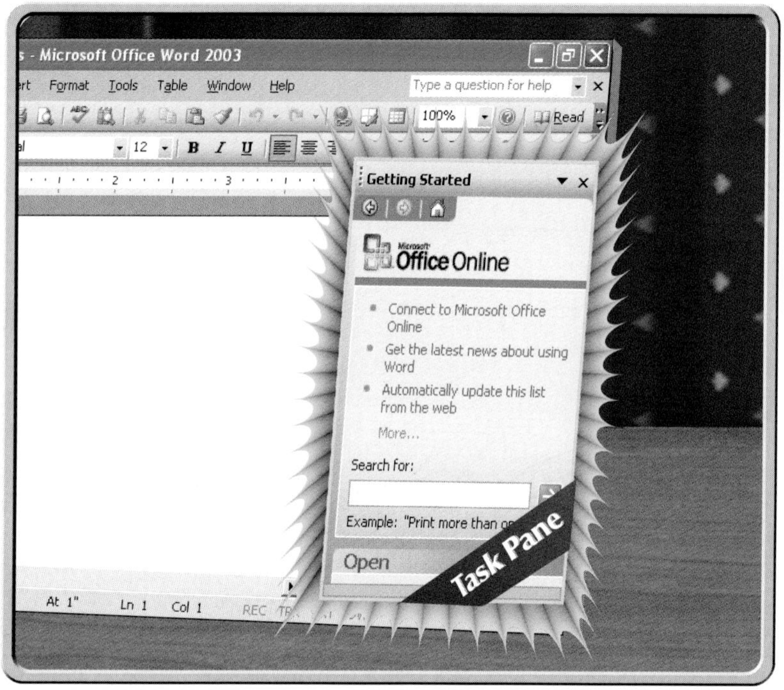

You can display or hide a task pane at any time. When you start an Office program or perform a task, a task pane may automatically appear.

USING THE TASK PANE

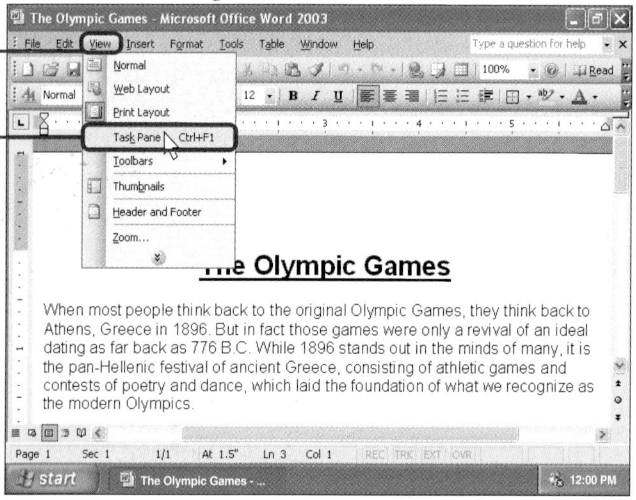

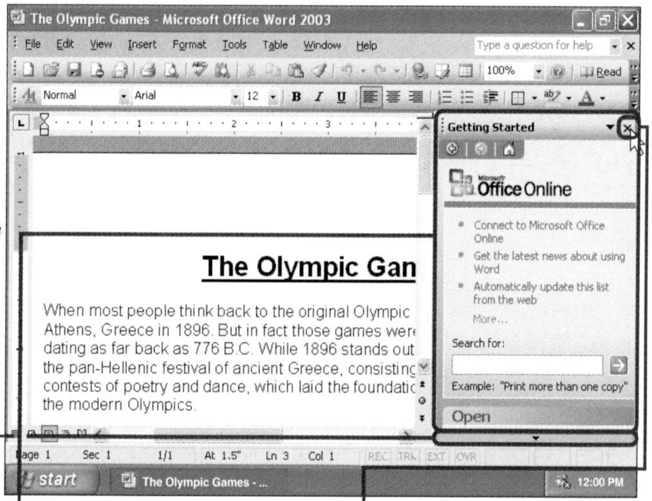

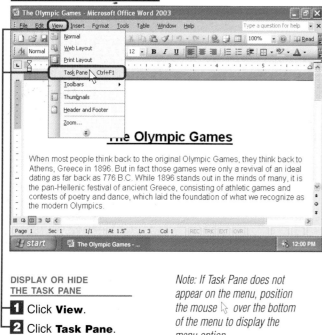

DISPLAY OR HIDE THE TASK PANE

1 Click **View**.

2 Click **Task Pane**.

Note: If Task Pane does not appear on the menu, position the mouse over the bottom of the menu to display the menu option.

■ The task pane appears or disappears.

■ You can click ▲ or ▼ to browse through the information in a task pane.

■ To quickly hide the task pane at any time, click ☒.

Tip

What task panes are available in Office?

The available task panes depend on the Office program you are working in. Some common task panes are listed below.

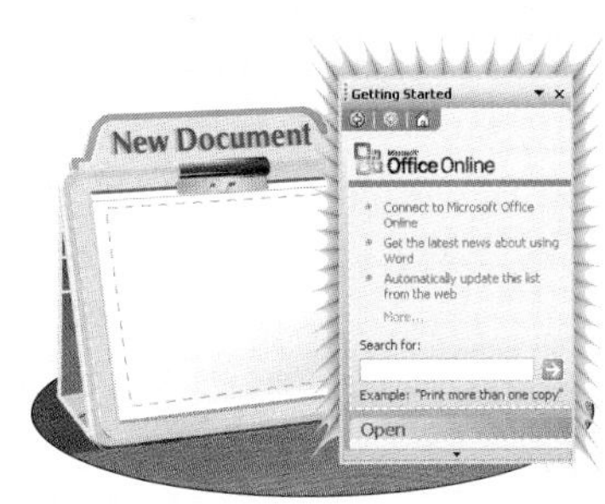

Getting Started

Allows you to perform tasks such as creating a new document and opening a file.

Help

Allows you to obtain help information from the program's help feature and the Internet.

Clipboard

Displays each item you have selected to move or copy.

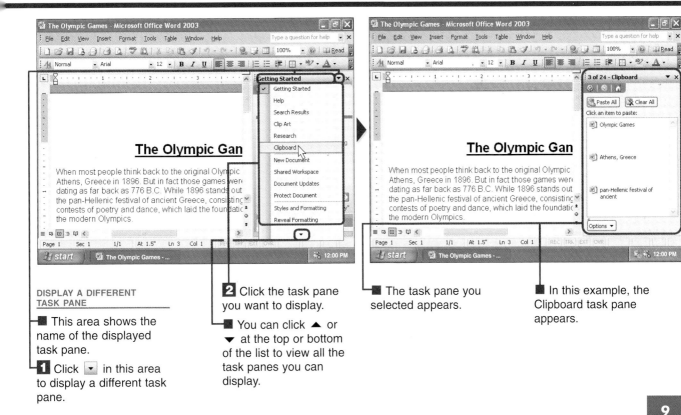

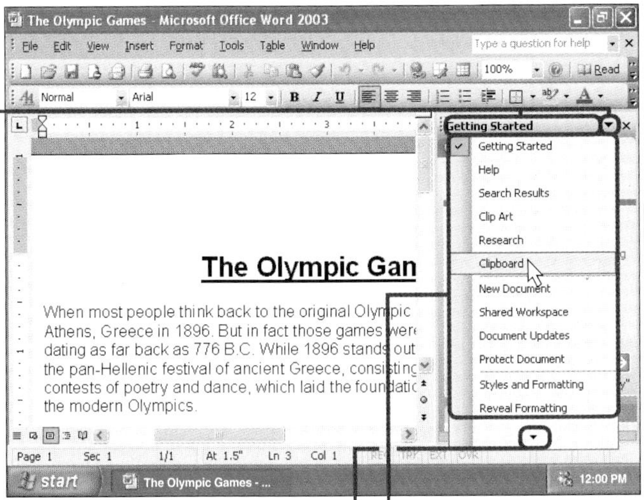

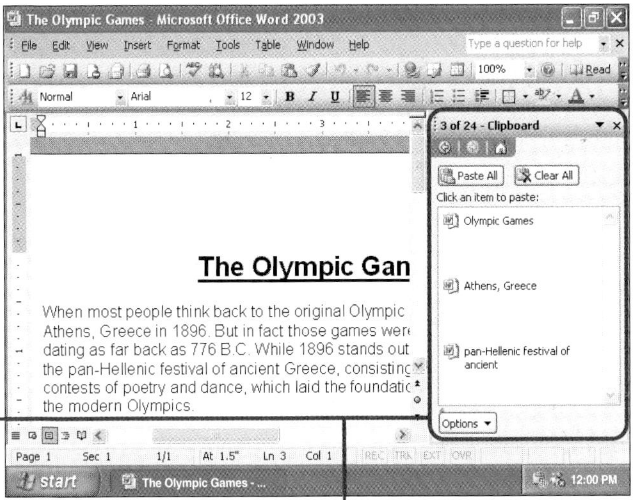

DISPLAY A DIFFERENT TASK PANE

- This area shows the name of the displayed task pane.

1 Click ▾ in this area to display a different task pane.

2 Click the task pane you want to display.

- You can click ▲ or ▼ at the top or bottom of the list to view all the task panes you can display.

- The task pane you selected appears.

- In this example, the Clipboard task pane appears.

WORK WITH TOOLBARS

Each Microsoft Office program offers several toolbars that you can work with on your screen. Each toolbar contains buttons that help you quickly perform common tasks.

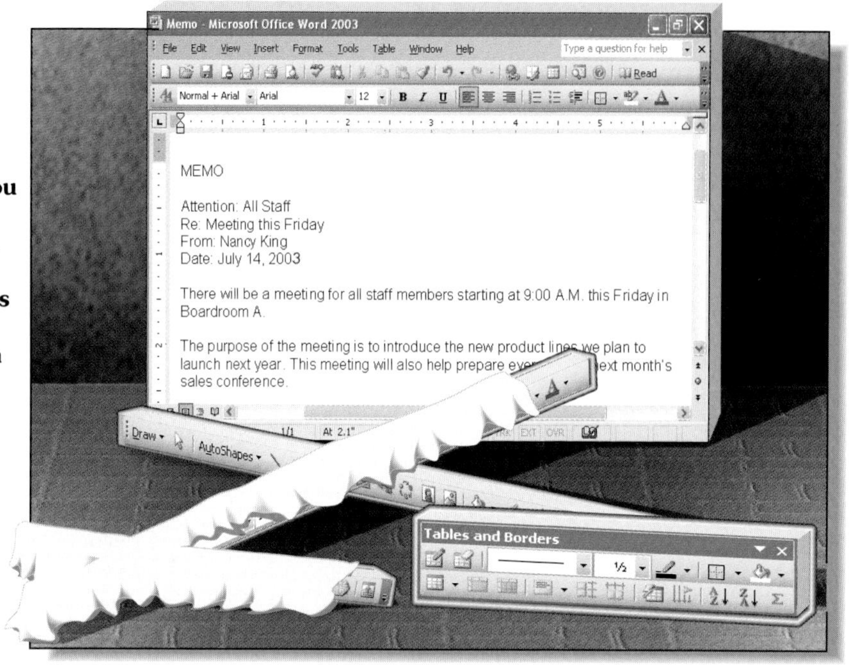

When you first start an Office program, one or more toolbars automatically appear on your screen. You can choose which toolbars to display based on the tasks you perform most often. You can also move toolbars to a new location to better suit the way you work.

DISPLAY OR HIDE A TOOLBAR

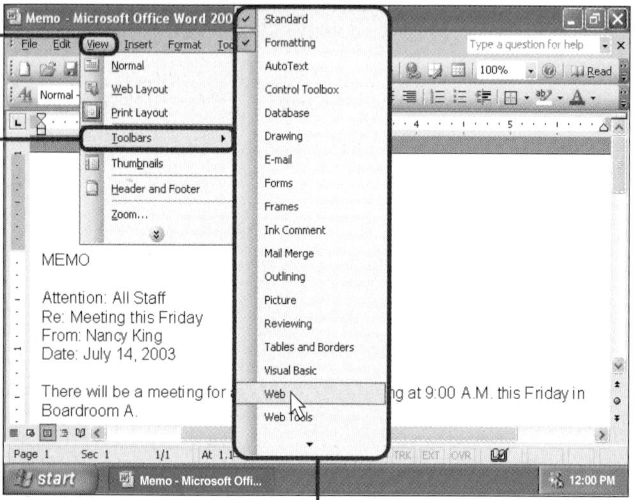

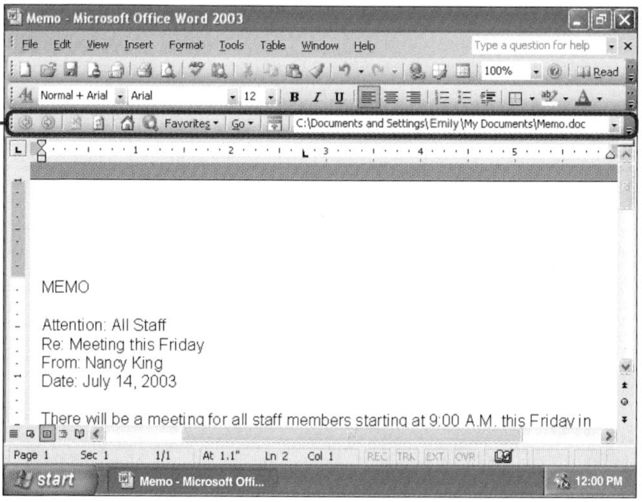

1 To display or hide a toolbar, click **View**.

2 Click **Toolbars**.

■ A list of toolbars appears. A check mark (✓) beside a toolbar name tells you the toolbar is currently displayed.

3 Click the name of the toolbar you want to display or hide.

■ The program displays or hides the toolbar you selected.

Tip

Can I increase the size of a toolbar on my screen?

You can increase the size of a toolbar to display more buttons on the toolbar. This is useful when a toolbar appears on the same row as another toolbar and cannot display all of its buttons. You cannot resize a toolbar that appears on its own row.

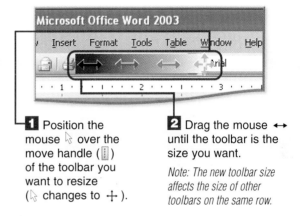

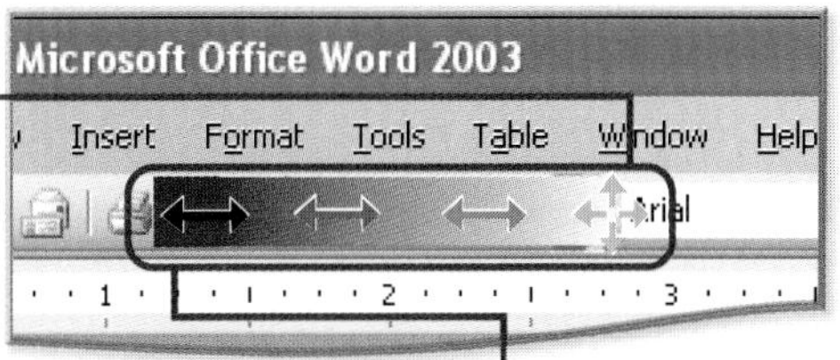

1 Position the mouse (☐) over the move handle (☐) of the toolbar you want to resize (☐ changes to ✥).

2 Drag the mouse ↔ until the toolbar is the size you want.

Note: The new toolbar size affects the size of other toolbars on the same row.

MOVE A TOOLBAR

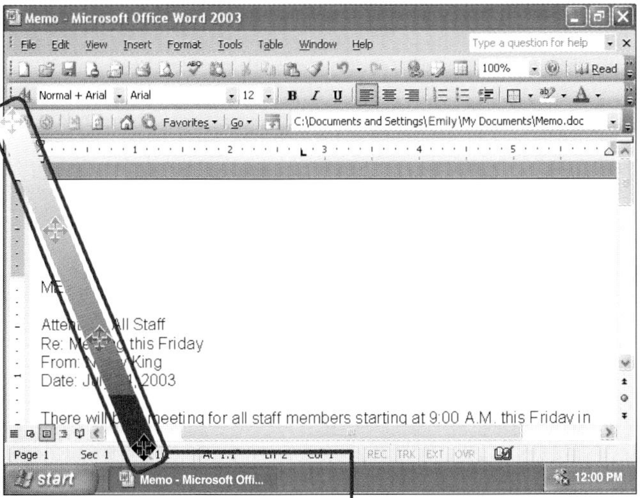

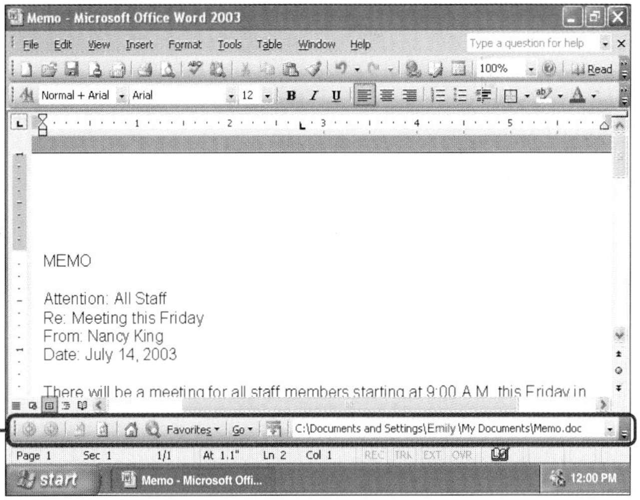

1 Position the mouse (☐) over the move handle (☐) of the toolbar you want to move (☐ changes to ✥).

2 Drag the toolbar to a new location.

Note: You can move a toolbar to the same row as another toolbar or to its own row at the top, bottom, right or left edge of your screen.

■ The toolbar appears in the new location.

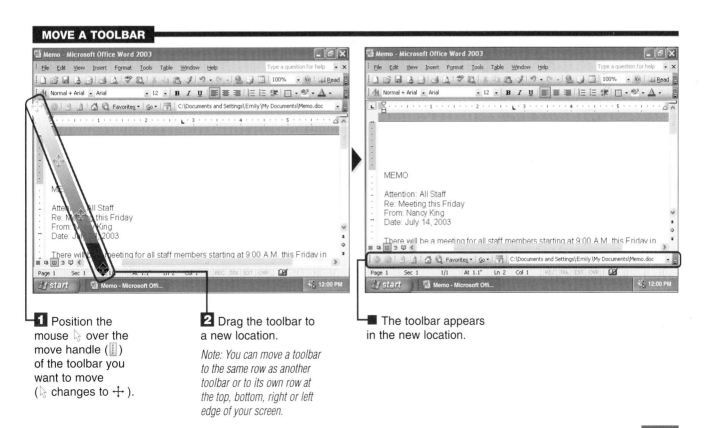

GETTING HELP

If you do not know how to perform a task in a Microsoft Office program, you can search for help information on the task.

Some help information is only available on the Internet. You must be connected to the Internet to access online help information.

GETTING HELP

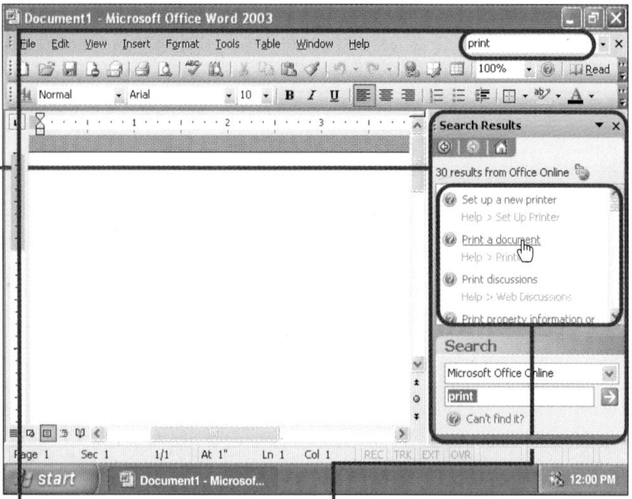

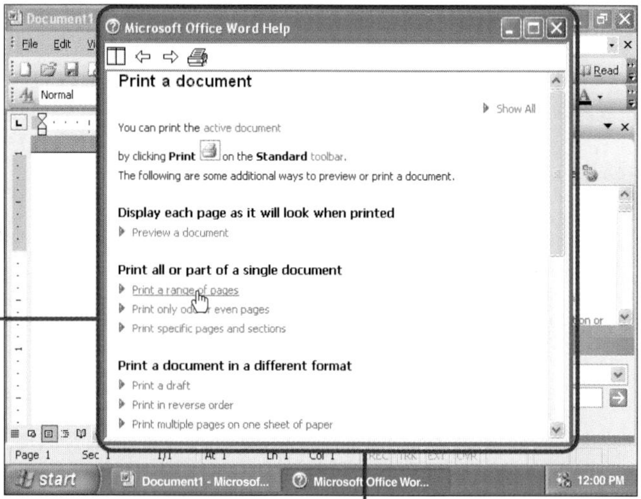

1 Click this area and type the task you want to get help information on. Then press the Enter key.

■ The Search Results task pane appears.

■ This area displays a list of related help topics. You can use the scroll bar to browse through the available topics.

2 Click the help topic of interest.

■ A window appears, displaying information about the help topic you selected.

3 To display additional information for a word or phrase that appears in color, click the word or phrase.

Tip

What do the icons beside each help topic represent?

Here are some icons you will see beside help topics.

	Displays a help topic.
	Opens a Web page that takes you through step-by-step training for the task.
	Displays a pre-designed template, such as a calendar, invoice or resume.
	Opens a Web page that offers a product or service to enhance Microsoft Office.
	Opens a Web page that displays an article on a specific topic.

Tip

How can I get help information when working with a dialog box?

You can click ? in the top right corner of a dialog box. A window will appear, displaying help information for the dialog box.

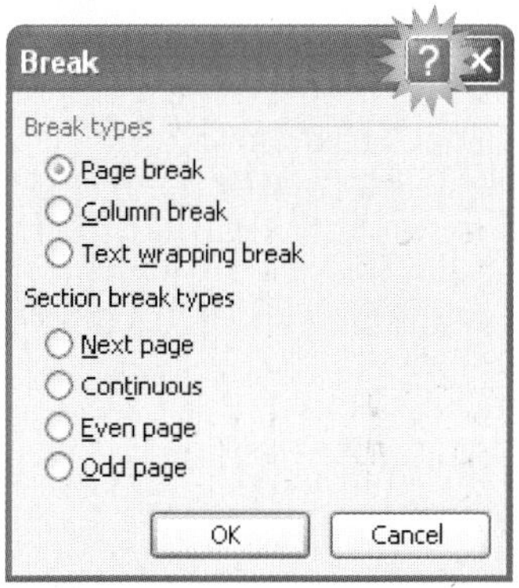

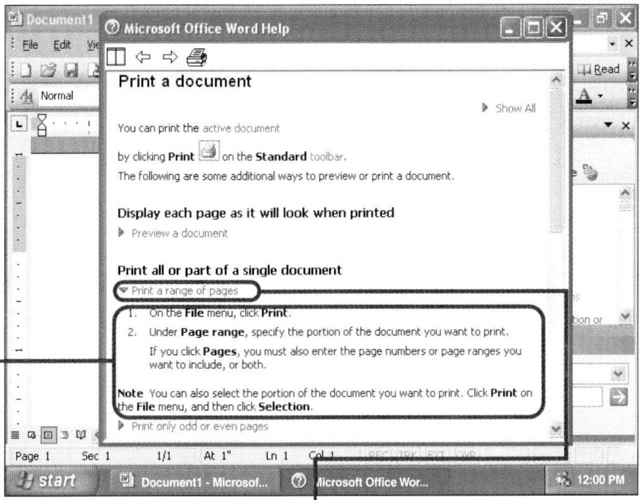

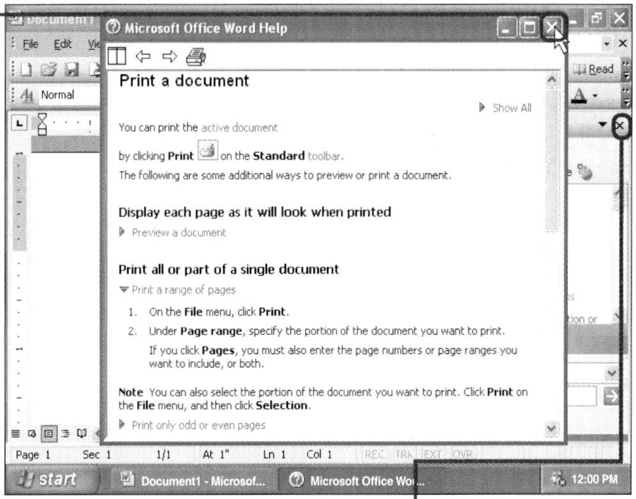

■ The additional information appears.

Note: Selecting a colored word or phrase will display information such as a definition, tip or a list of steps.

■ To once again hide the information, click the colored word or phrase.

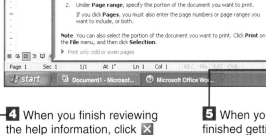

4 When you finish reviewing the help information, click ☒ to close the window.

■ To display the information for another help topic, click the help topic.

5 When you are finished getting help, click ☒ to close the Search Results task pane.

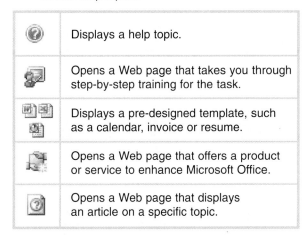

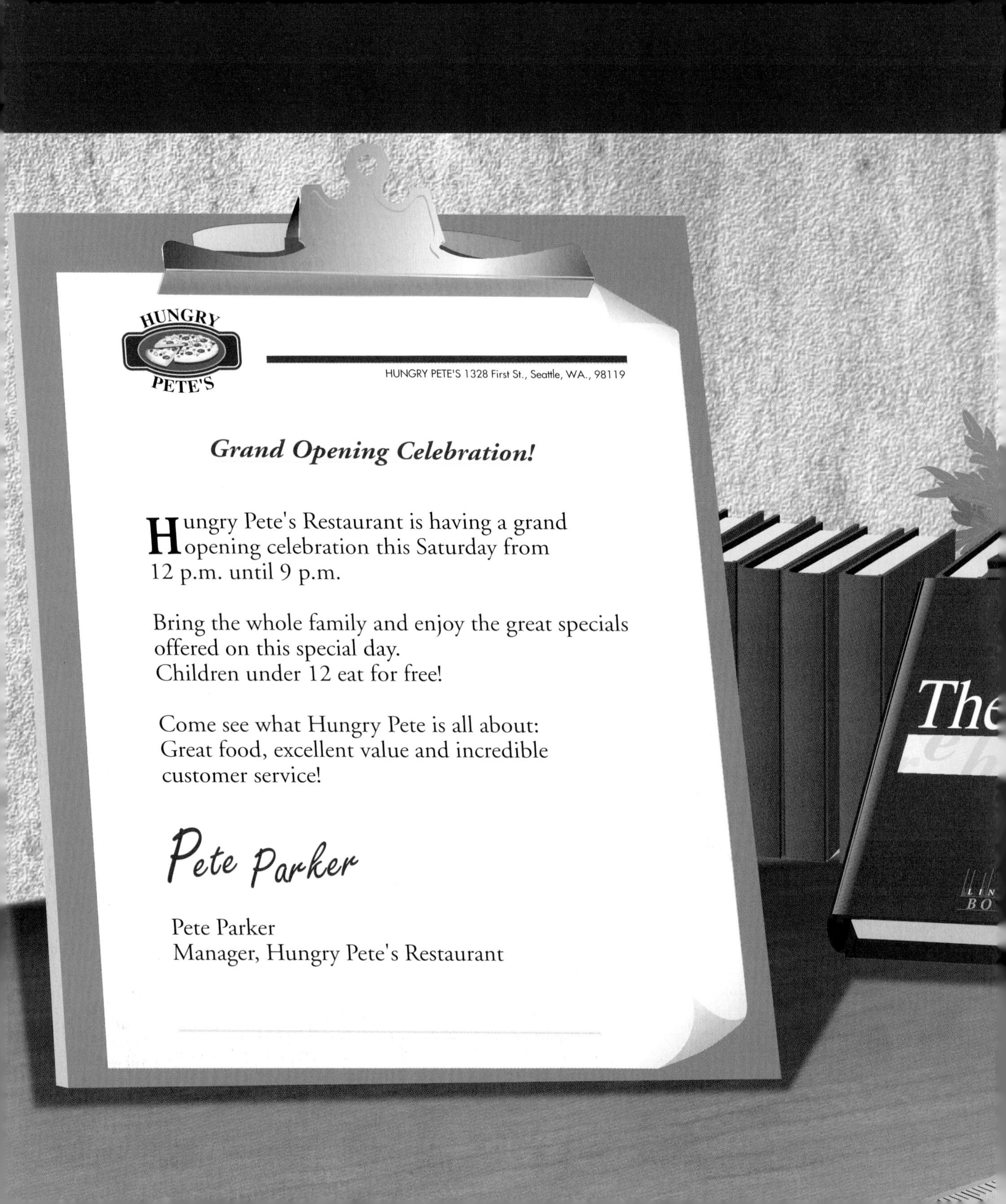

HUNGRY PETE'S

HUNGRY PETE'S 1328 First St., Seattle, WA., 98119

Grand Opening Celebration!

Hungry Pete's Restaurant is having a grand opening celebration this Saturday from 12 p.m. until 9 p.m.

Bring the whole family and enjoy the great specials offered on this special day.
Children under 12 eat for free!

Come see what Hungry Pete is all about:
Great food, excellent value and incredible customer service!

Pete Parker

Pete Parker
Manager, Hungry Pete's Restaurant

Using Word

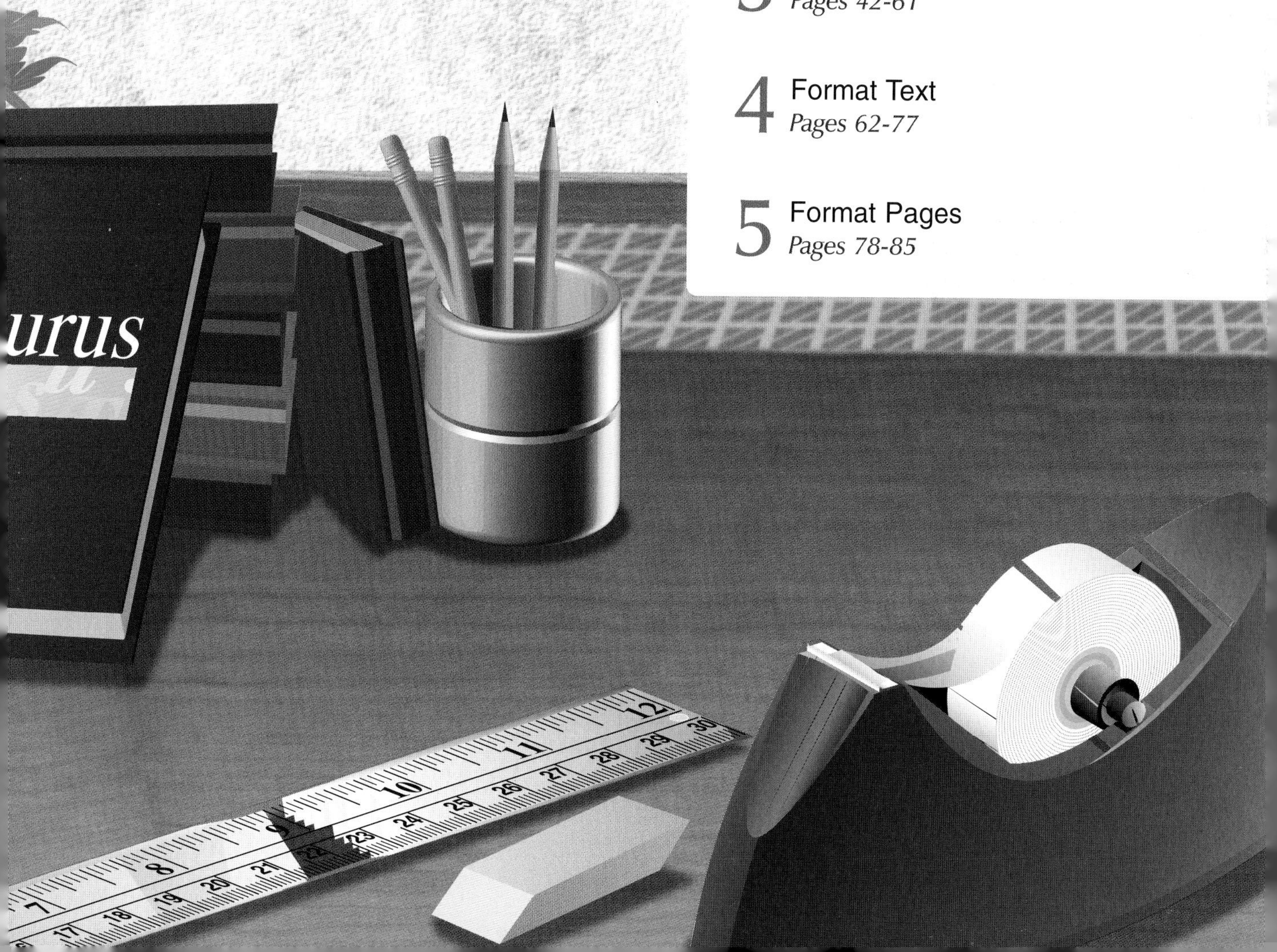

Word is a word processing program you can use to efficiently produce professional-looking documents, such as letters, reports and essays.

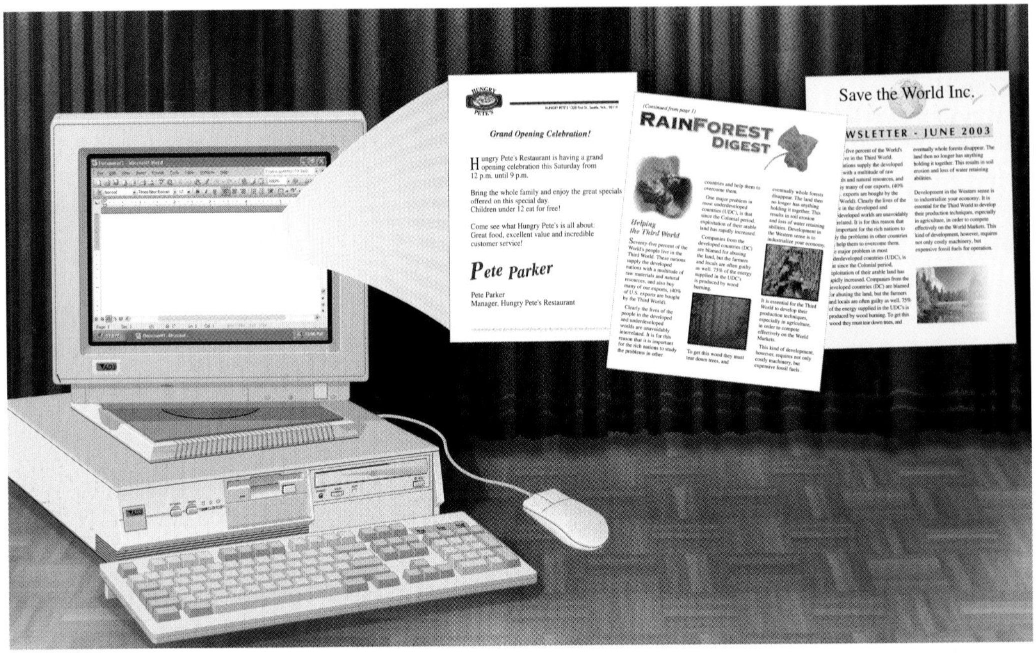

Edit Documents

Word offers many time-saving features to help you edit text in a document. You can add, delete and rearrange text. You can also quickly count the number of words in a document, check your document for spelling and grammar errors and use Word's thesaurus to find more suitable words.

Format Documents

You can format a document to enhance the appearance of the document. You can use various font sizes, styles and colors to emphasize important text. You can also add page numbers, change the margins and use bullets to separate items in a list.

Print Documents

You can produce a paper copy of a document you create. Before printing, you can preview how the document will appear on a printed page.

PARTS OF THE WORD WINDOW

The Word window displays many items you can use to create and work with your documents.

Title Bar

Shows the name of the displayed document.

Menu Bar

Provides access to lists of commands available in Word and displays an area where you can type a question to get help information.

Standard Toolbar

Contains buttons you can use to select common commands, such as Save and Print.

Formatting Toolbar

Contains buttons you can use to select common formatting commands, such as Bold and Italic.

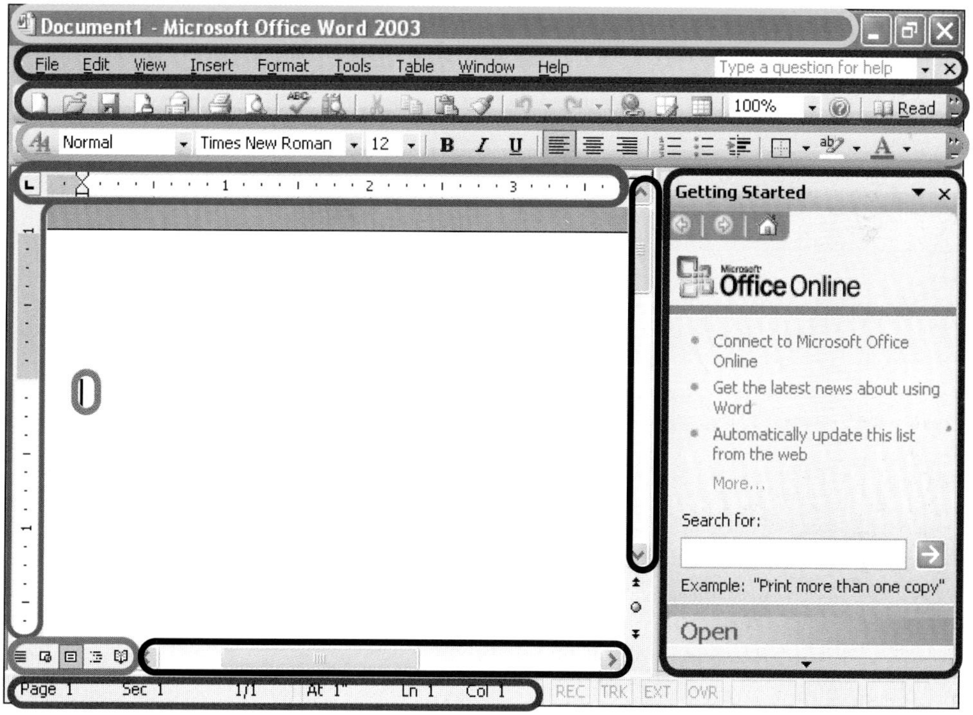

Ruler

Allows you to change tab and indent settings for your documents.

Task Pane

Contains options you can select to perform common tasks, such as opening a document.

Insertion Point

The flashing line on the screen that indicates where the text you type will appear.

Document Views

Provides access to five different views of your documents.

Scroll Bars

Allow you to browse through a document.

Status Bar

Provides information about the area of the document displayed on the screen and the position of the insertion point.

Page 1

The page displayed on the screen.

Sec 1

The section of the document displayed on the screen.

1/1

The page displayed on the screen and the total number of pages in the document.

At 1"

The distance from the top of the page to the insertion point.

Ln 1

The number of lines from the top margin to the insertion point.

Col 1

The number of characters from the left margin to the insertion point, including spaces.

ENTER TEXT

Word allows you to type text into your document quickly and easily.

The sample documents used in each chapter of this book are available on the Web at www.maran.com/office2003. You can download the sample documents so you can perform the tasks in this book without having to type the documents yourself.

ENTER TEXT

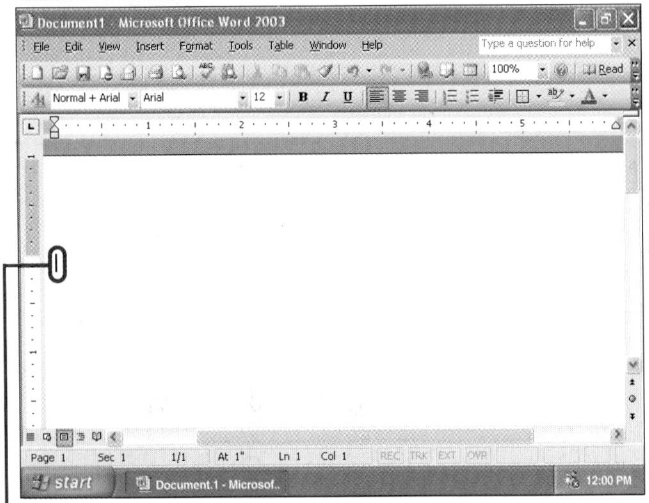

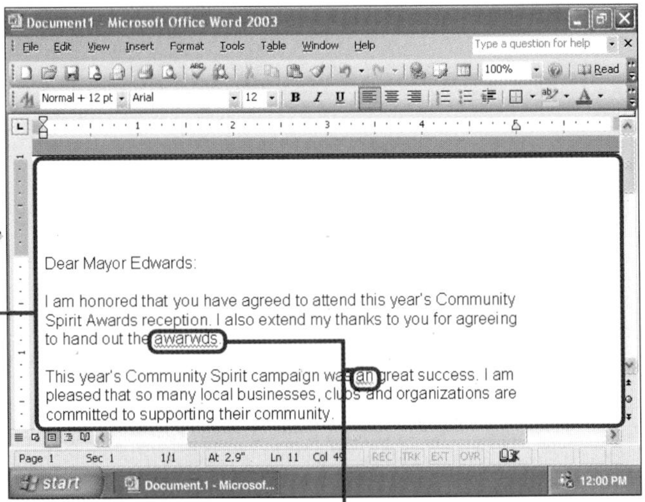

■ The text you type will appear where the insertion point flashes on your screen.

1 Type the text for your document.

Note: In this book, the font of text was changed to Arial to make the examples easier to read. To change the font of text, see page 62.

■ When you reach the end of a line, Word automatically wraps the text to the next line. You only need to press the **Enter** key when you want to start a new paragraph.

■ Word automatically underlines misspelled words in red and grammar errors in green. The underlines will not appear when you print your document. To correct misspelled words and grammar errors, see page 50.

Tip

Can I enter text anywhere in my document?

Word's Click and Type feature allows you to quickly position the insertion point in a new location so you can enter text. Double-click a blank area where you want to position the insertion point and then type the text you want to enter. The Click and Type feature is available in the Web Layout, Print Layout and Reading Layout views. To change the view, see page 24.

Tip

Why does Word automatically change the text I am typing?

Word's AutoCorrect feature automatically corrects common spelling errors as you type. You can stop Word from automatically correcting the text you type.

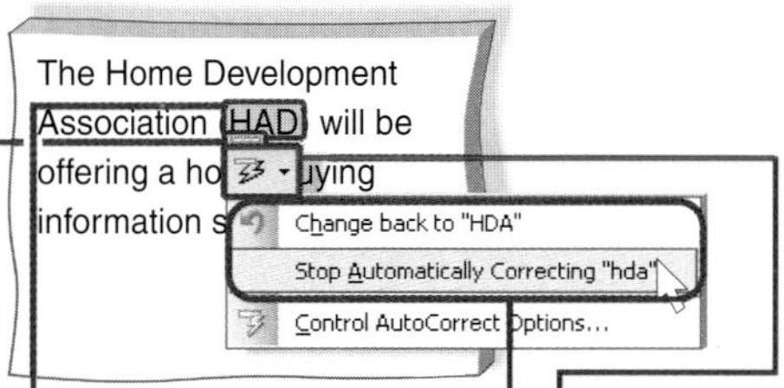

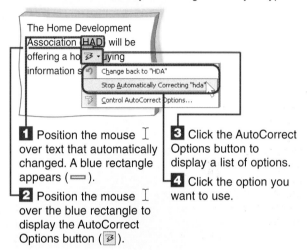

1 Position the mouse over text that automatically changed. A blue rectangle appears (▭).

2 Position the mouse over the blue rectangle to display the AutoCorrect Options button (⚡).

3 Click the AutoCorrect Options button to display a list of options.

4 Click the option you want to use.

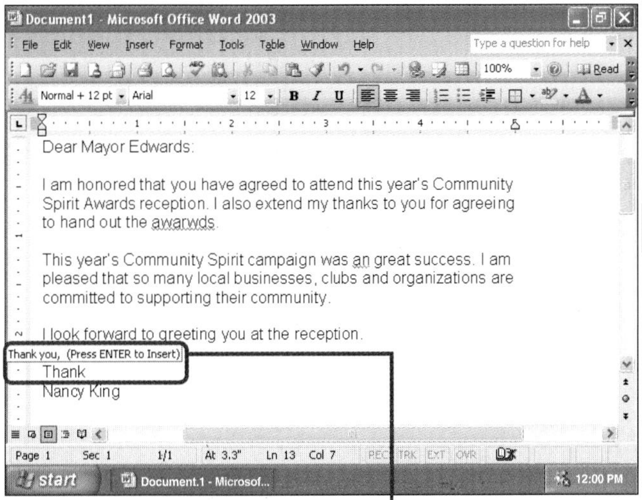

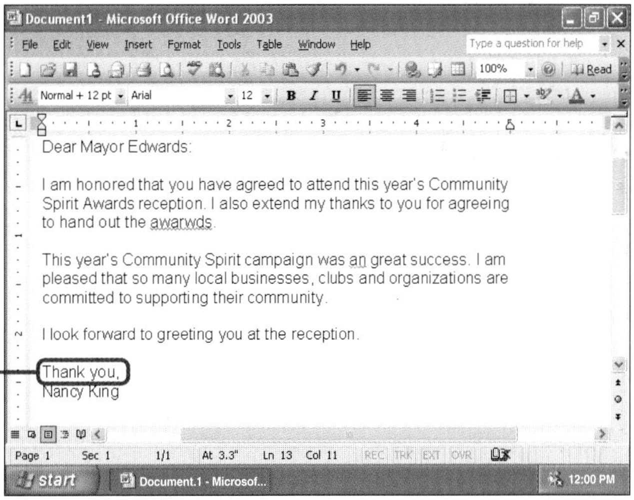

ENTER TEXT AUTOMATICALLY

■ Word's AutoText feature helps you quickly enter common words and phrases.

■ When you type the first few characters of a common word or phrase, a yellow box appears, displaying the text.

1 To insert the text, press the Enter key.

■ To ignore the text, continue typing.

SELECT TEXT

Before performing many tasks in Word, you must select the text you want to work with. Selected text appears highlighted on your screen.

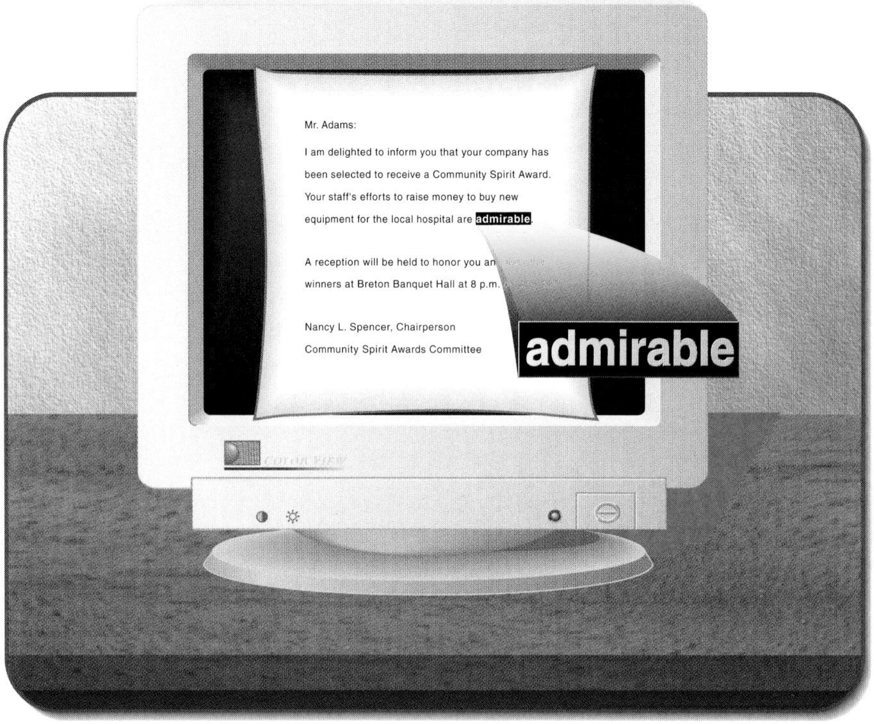

SELECT TEXT

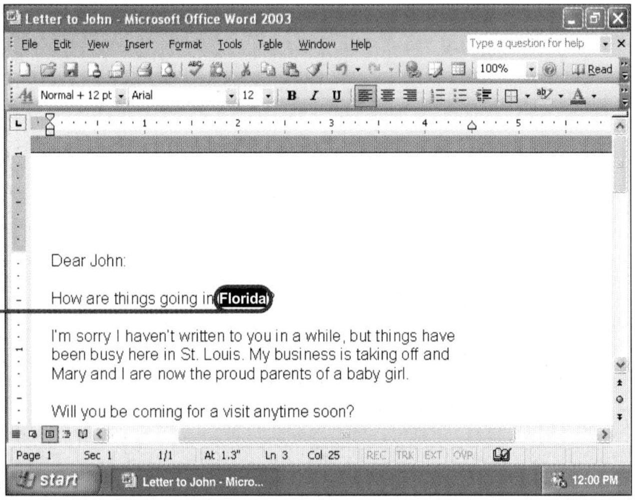

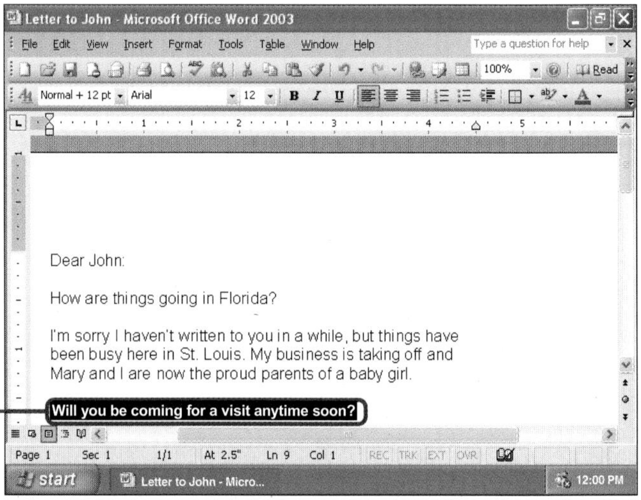

SELECT A WORD

1 Double-click the word you want to select. The word is highlighted.

■ To deselect text, click outside the selected area.

SELECT A SENTENCE

1 Press and hold down the Ctrl key as you click the sentence you want to select.

Tip

How do I select a paragraph or a large area of text?

To select a paragraph, position the mouse I over the paragraph you want to select and then quickly click **three** times.

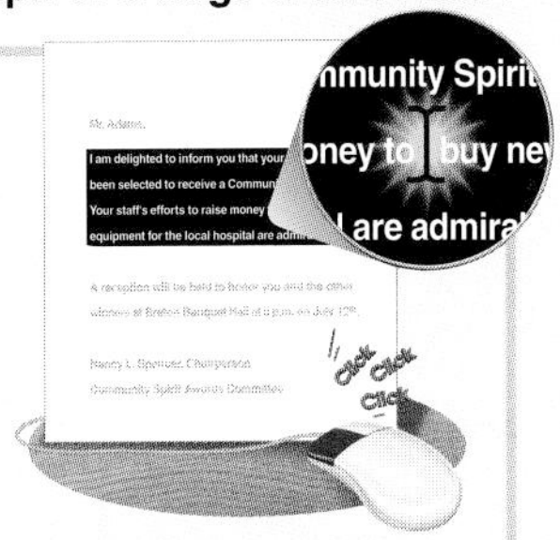

To select a large area of text, click at the beginning of the text. Then press and hold down the Shift key as you click at the end of the text.

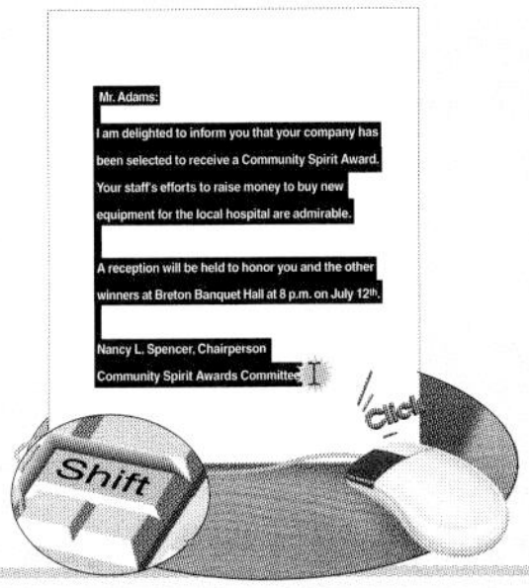

Tip

Can I select multiple areas of text in my document?

Yes. To select multiple areas of text, press and hold down the Ctrl key as you select each area.

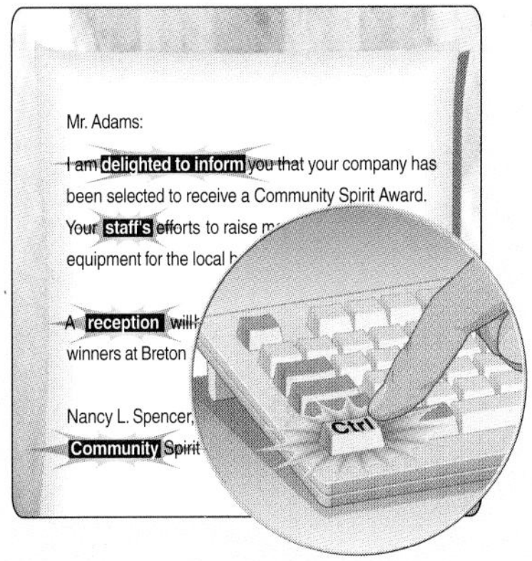

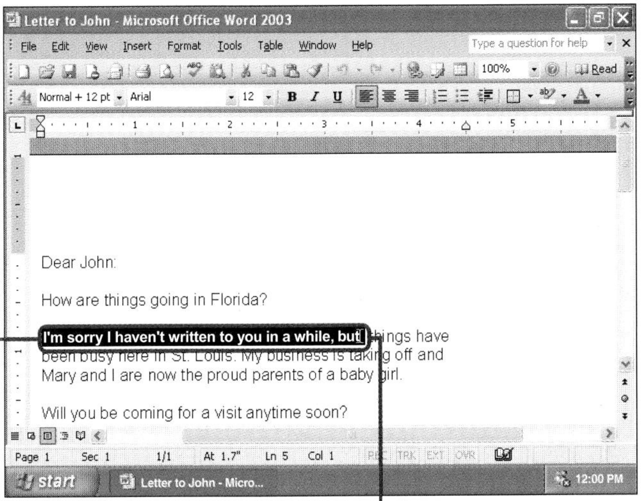

SELECT ANY AMOUNT OF TEXT

1 Position the mouse I over the first word you want to select.

2 Drag the mouse I over the text you want to select.

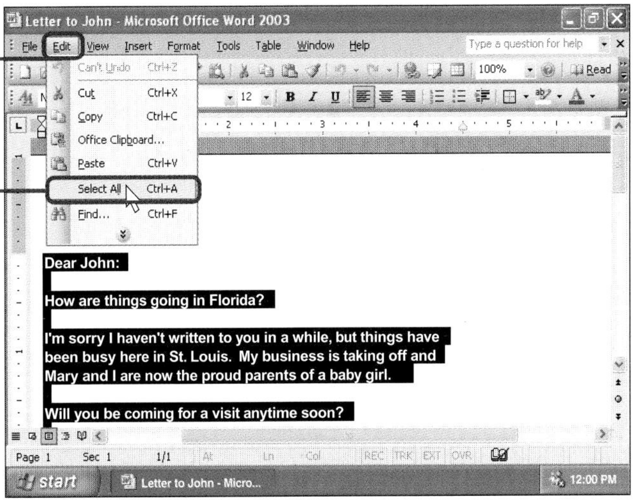

SELECT ENTIRE DOCUMENT

1 Click **Edit**.

2 Click **Select All** to select all the text in your document.

Note: You can also press and hold down the Ctrl key as you press the A key to select all the text in your document.

MOVE THROUGH A DOCUMENT

You can easily move to another location in your document.

If your document contains a lot of text, your computer screen may not be able to display all the text at once. You must scroll through your document to view other parts of the document.

MOVE THROUGH A DOCUMENT

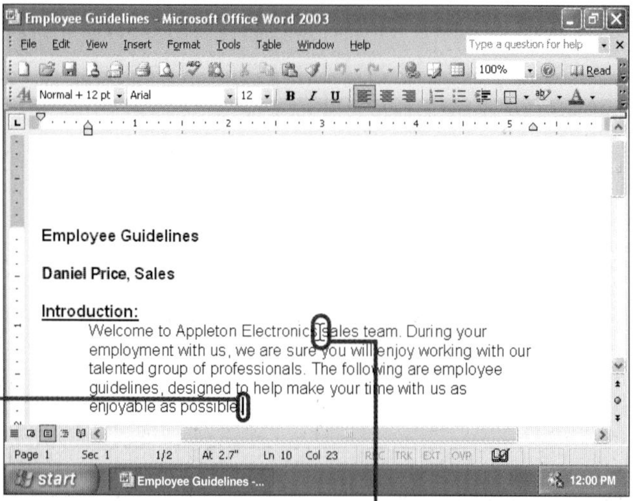

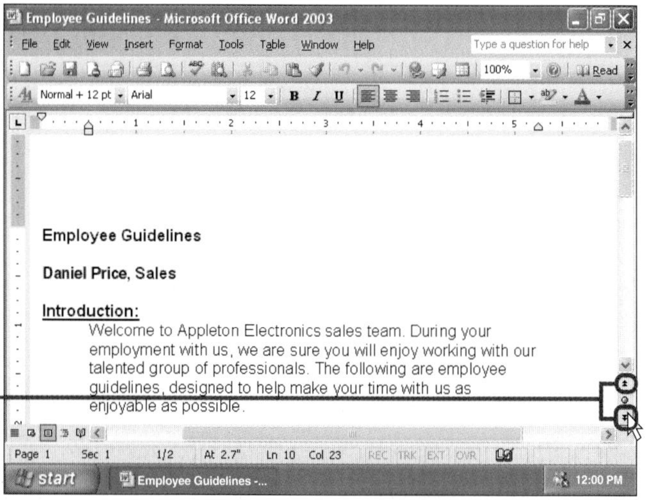

MOVE THE INSERTION POINT

■ The flashing line on your screen, called the insertion point, indicates where the text you type will appear.

1 Click the location in your document where you want to place the insertion point.

DISPLAY PREVIOUS OR NEXT PAGE

1 To display the previous or next page, click one of the following buttons.

- Display previous page
- Display next page

Tip

How can I use my keyboard to move through a document?

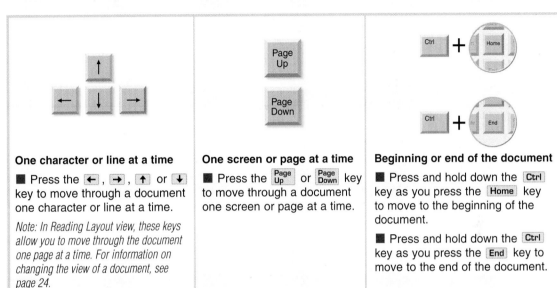

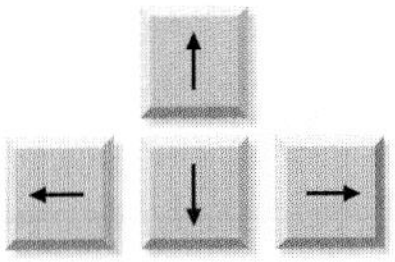

One character or line at a time

■ Press the ←, →, ↑ or ↓ key to move through a document one character or line at a time.

Note: In Reading Layout view, these keys allow you to move through the document one page at a time. For information on changing the view of a document, *see page 24.*

One screen or page at a time

■ Press the Page Up or Page Down key to move through a document one screen or page at a time.

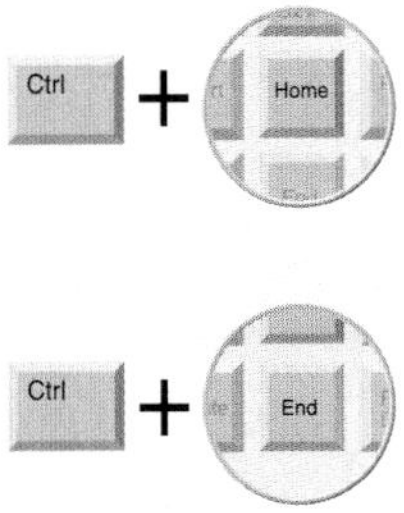

Beginning or end of the document

■ Press and hold down the Ctrl key as you press the Home key to move to the beginning of the document.

■ Press and hold down the Ctrl key as you press the End key to move to the end of the document.

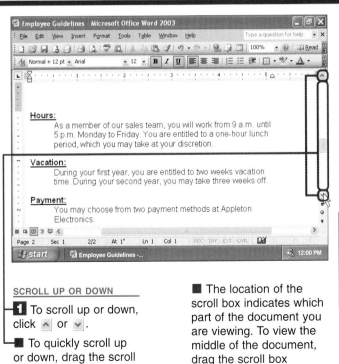

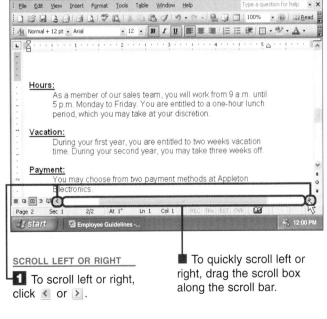

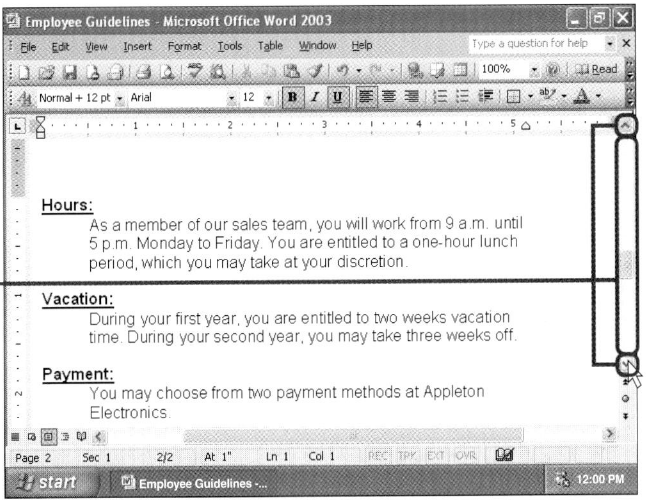

SCROLL UP OR DOWN

1 To scroll up or down, click ˄ or ˅.

■ To quickly scroll up or down, drag the scroll box along the scroll bar.

■ The location of the scroll box indicates which part of the document you are viewing. To view the middle of the document, drag the scroll box halfway down the scroll bar.

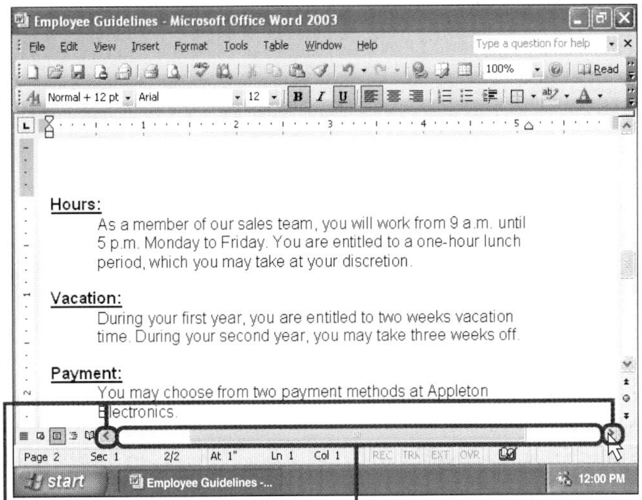

SCROLL LEFT OR RIGHT

1 To scroll left or right, click ‹ or ›.

■ To quickly scroll left or right, drag the scroll box along the scroll bar.

CHANGE THE VIEW OF A DOCUMENT

Word offers five different views that you can use to display your document. You can choose the view that best suits your needs.

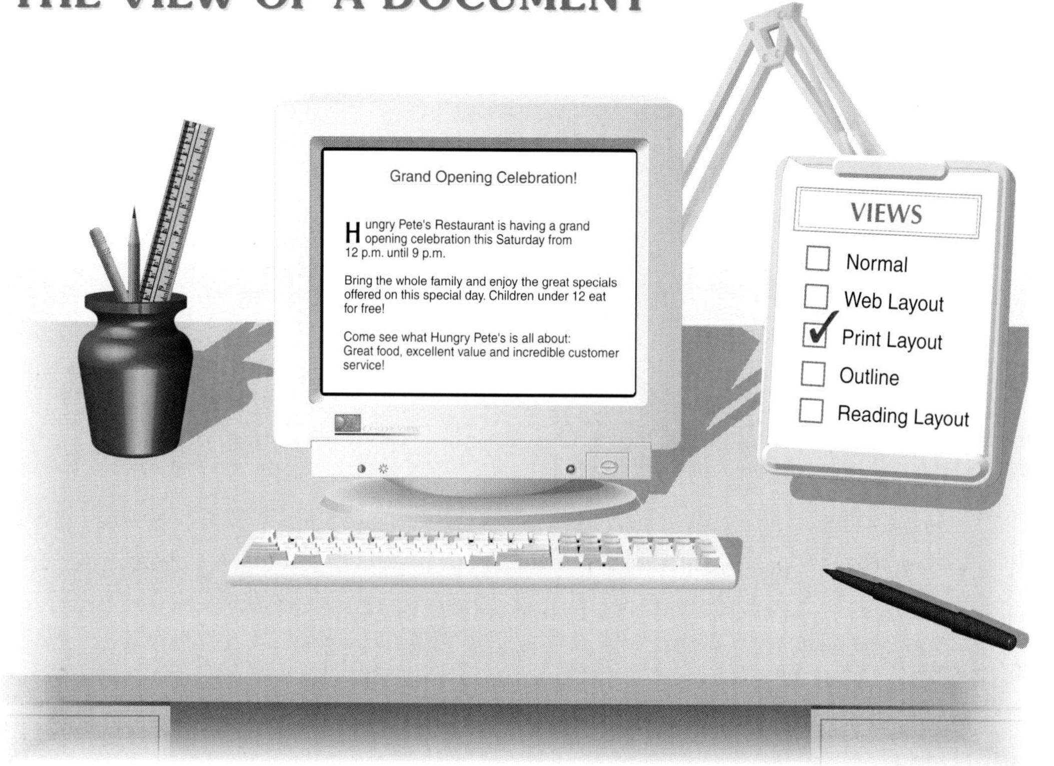

CHANGE THE VIEW OF A DOCUMENT

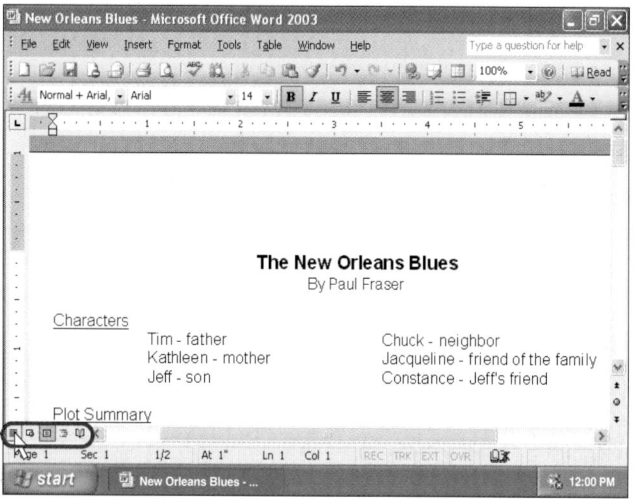

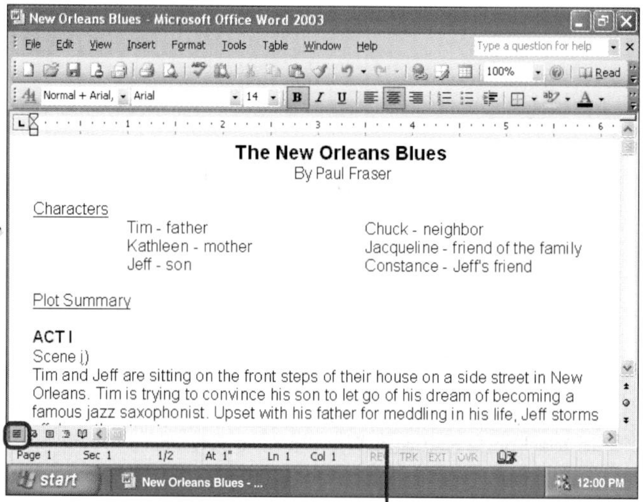

1 To change the view of your document, click one of the following buttons.

- Normal
- Web Layout
- Print Layout
- Outline
- Reading Layout

■ Your document appears in the view you selected.

■ The button for the view you selected appears orange.

THE DOCUMENT VIEWS

Normal View

The Normal view simplifies the layout of your document so you can quickly enter, edit and format text. This view does not display certain elements in your document, such as margins and page numbers.

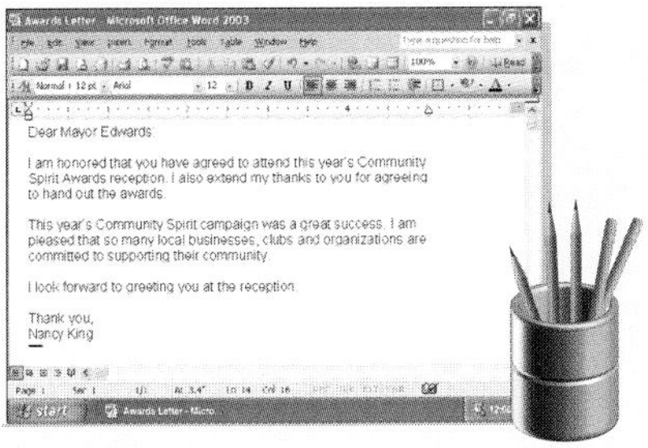

Web Layout View

Working in the Web Layout view is useful when you are creating a Web page or a document that you plan to view only on a computer screen.

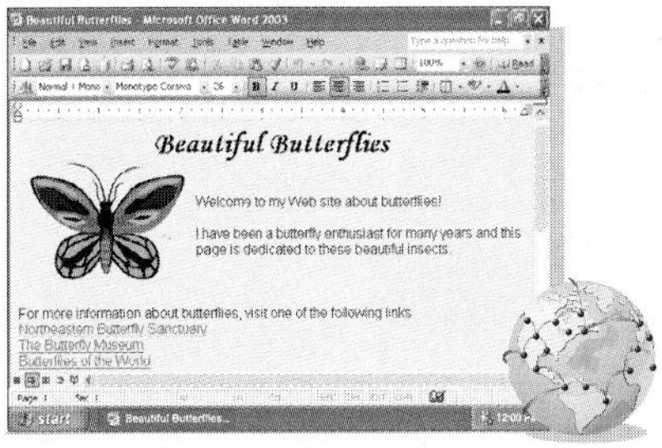

Print Layout View

You can work in the Print Layout view when you want to see how your document will appear on a printed page. This view displays all the elements in your document, such as margins and page numbers.

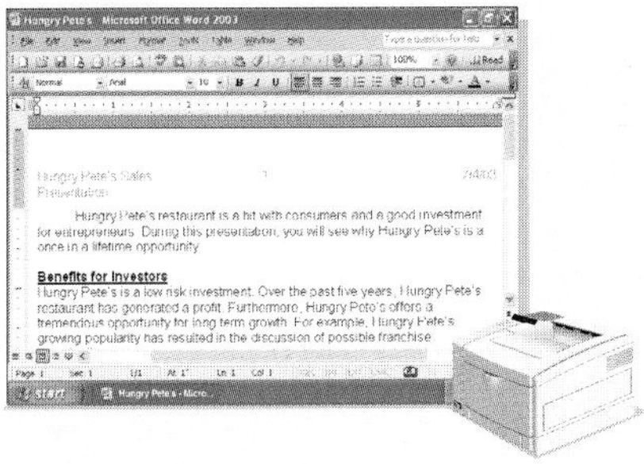

Outline View

The Outline view is useful when you want to review and work with the structure of a long document. This view allows you to collapse a document to see only the headings or expand a document to see all the headings and text.

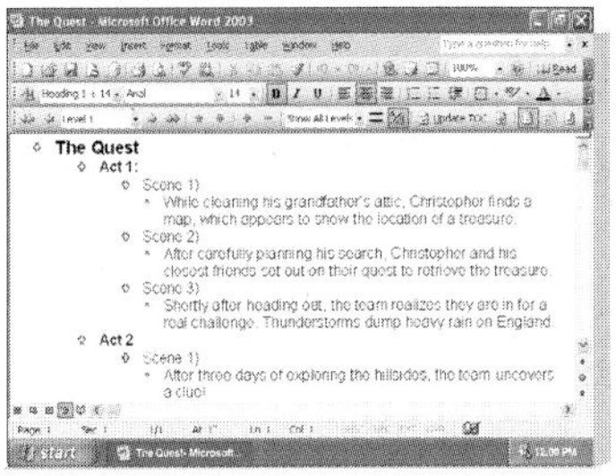

Reading Layout View

The Reading Layout view is useful when you are reading a document on screen. This view removes distracting elements and makes adjustments to the document to make it easy to read on the screen. For more information on the Reading Layout view, see page 38.

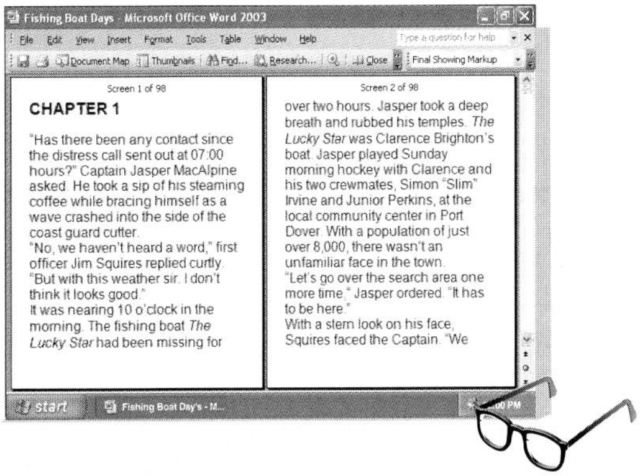

SAVE A DOCUMENT

You can save your document to store it for future use. Saving a document allows you to later review and edit the document.

You should regularly save changes you make to a document to avoid losing your work.

When you finish working with the document you saved, you can close the document to remove it from your screen.

SAVE A DOCUMENT

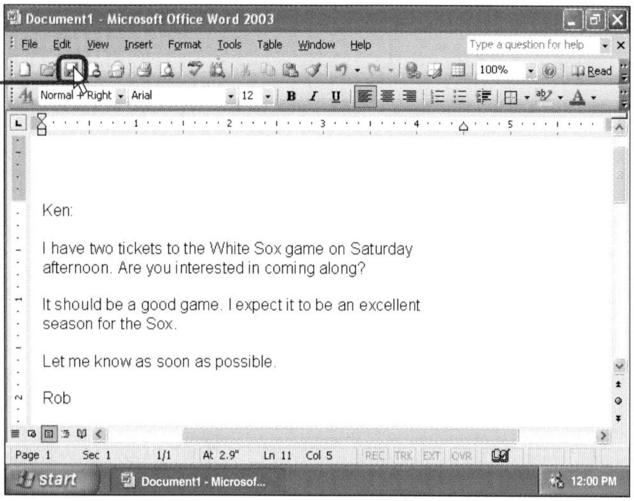

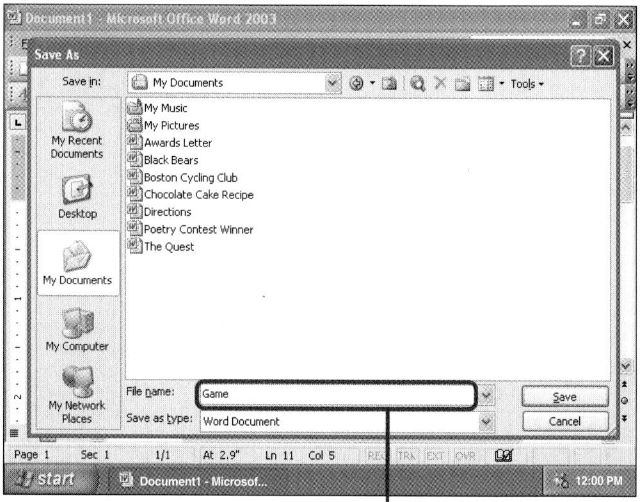

1 Click to save your document.

Note: If is not displayed, click on the Standard toolbar to display the button.

■ The Save As dialog box appears.

Note: If you previously saved your document, the Save As dialog box will not appear since you have already named the document.

2 Type a name for the document.

Tip

What are the commonly used locations that I can access?

Provides access to documents and folders you recently worked with.	Allows you to store a document on the Windows desktop.	Provides a convenient place to store a document.	Allows you to store a document on a drive on your computer, such as a floppy or external hard drive.	Allows you to store a document on your network.

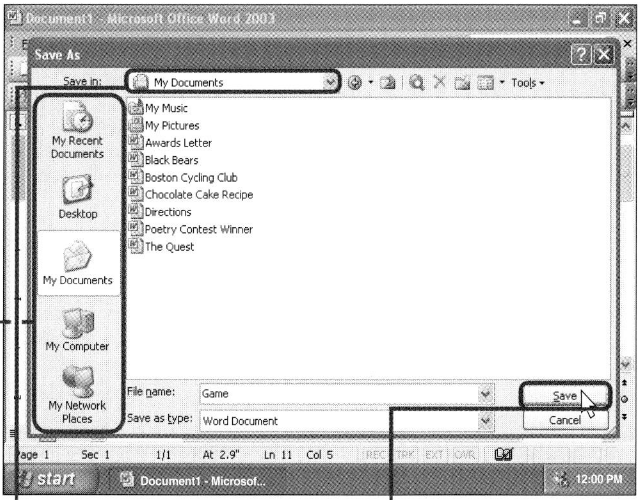

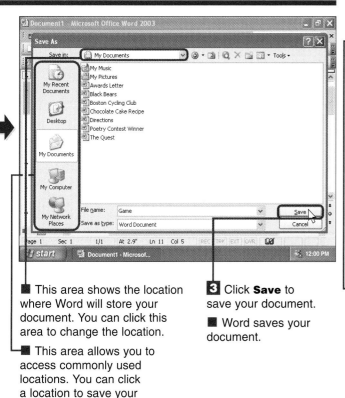

■ This area shows the location where Word will store your document. You can click this area to change the location.

■ This area allows you to access commonly used locations. You can click a location to save your document in the location.

3 Click **Save** to save your document.

■ Word saves your document.

CLOSE A DOCUMENT

1 When you finish working with a document, click ☒ to close the document.

■ The document disappears from your screen.

■ If you had more than one document open, the second last document you worked with appears on your screen.

OPEN A DOCUMENT

You can open a saved document to view the document on your screen. This allows you to review and make changes to the document.

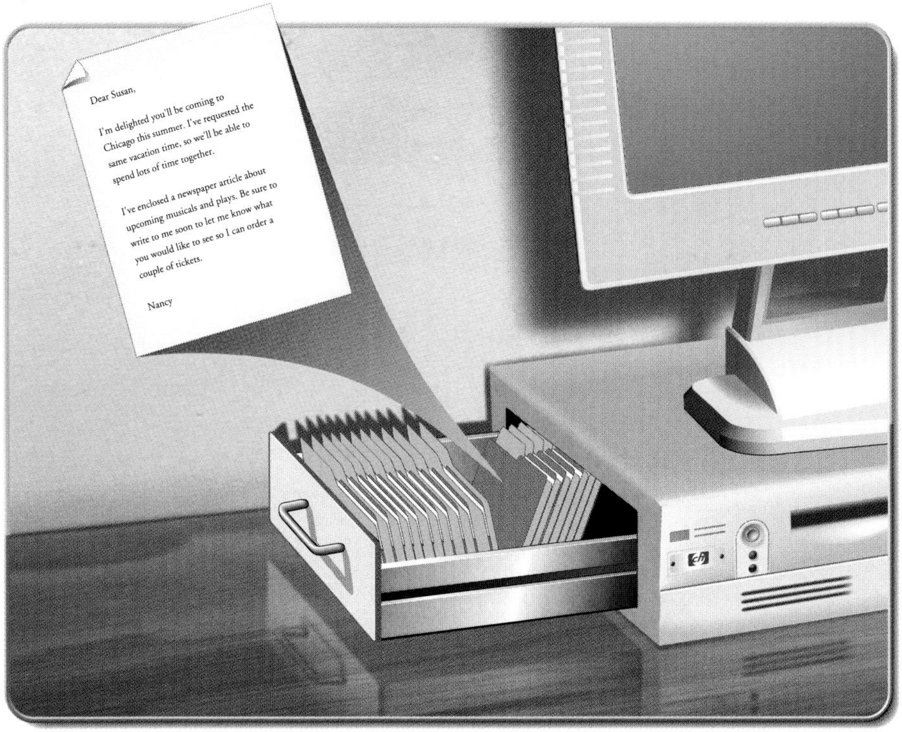

OPEN A DOCUMENT

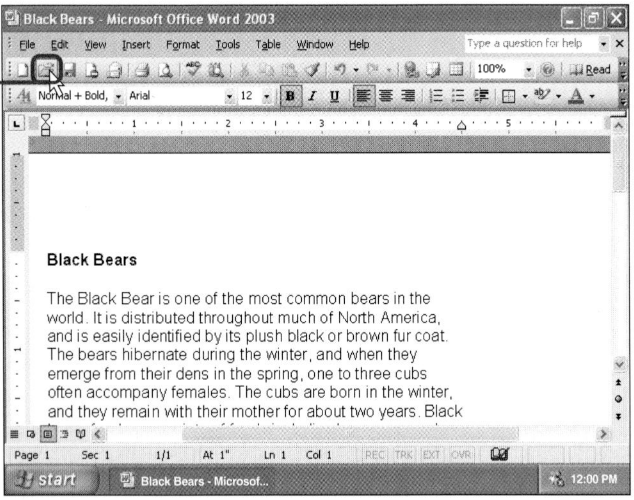

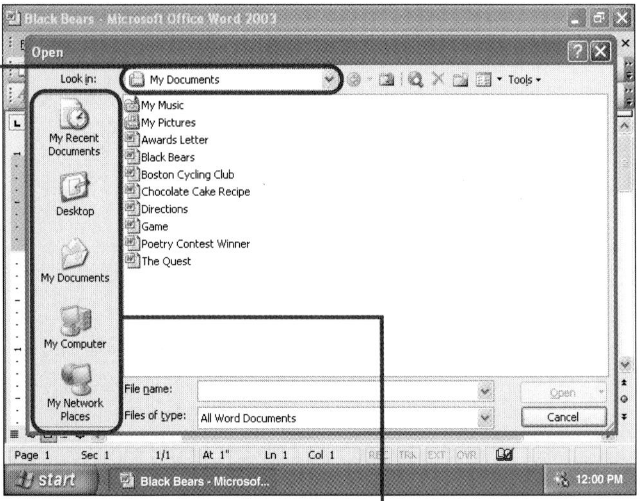

1 Click to open a document.

Note: If does not appear, click on the Standard toolbar to display the button.

■ The Open dialog box appears.

■ This area shows the location of the displayed documents. You can click this area to change the location.

■ This area allows you to access documents in commonly used locations. You can click a location to display the documents stored in the location.

Note: For information on the commonly used locations, see the top of page 27.

Tip

How can I quickly open a document I recently worked with?

Word remembers the names of the last four documents you worked with. You can use the Getting Started task pane or the File menu to quickly open any of these documents.

Note: The Getting Started task pane appears each time you start Word. To display the Getting Started task pane, see page 8.

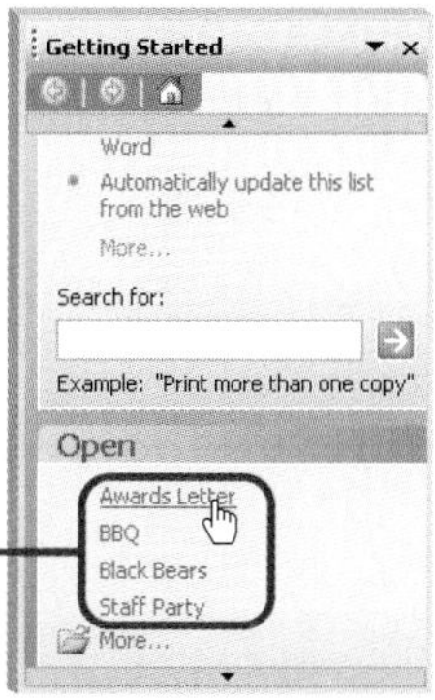

Use the Task Pane

1 Click the name of the document you want to open.

Note: If the name of the document is not displayed, position the mouse over the bottom of the task pane to display the name.

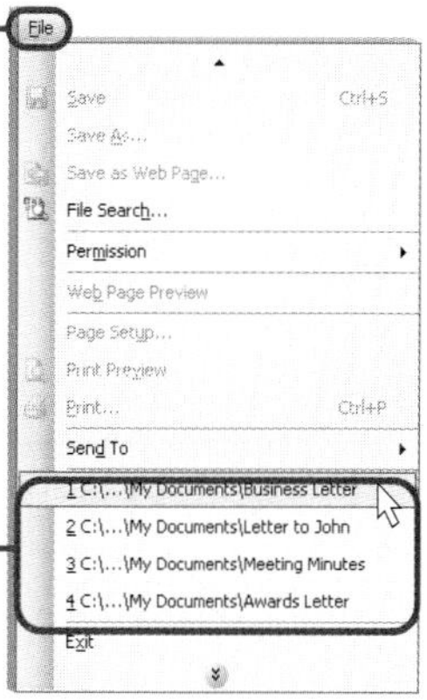

Use the File Menu

1 Click **File**.

2 Click the name of the document you want to open.

Note: If the name of the document you want is not displayed, position the mouse over the bottom of the menu to display the name.

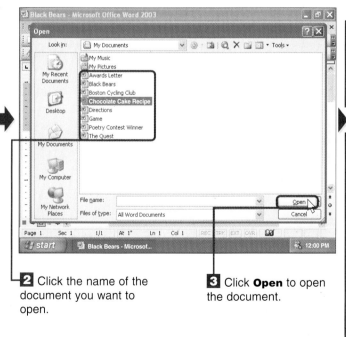

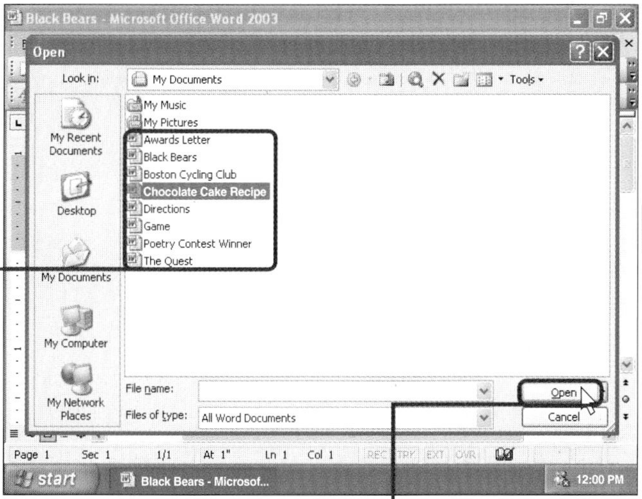

2 Click the name of the document you want to open.

3 Click **Open** to open the document.

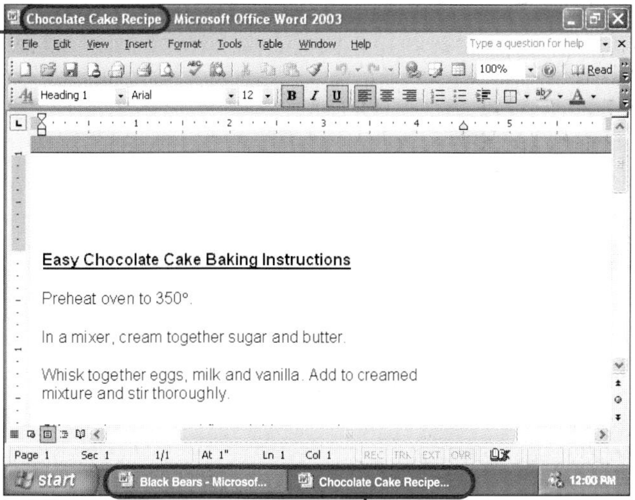

■ The document opens and appears on your screen. You can now review and make changes to the document.

■ This area displays the name of the document.

■ If you already had a document open, the new document appears in a new Microsoft Word window. You can click the buttons on the taskbar to switch between the open documents.

PREVIEW A DOCUMENT BEFORE PRINTING

You can use the Print Preview feature to see how your document will look when printed.

The Print Preview feature allows you to confirm that the document will print the way you want.

PREVIEW A DOCUMENT BEFORE PRINTING

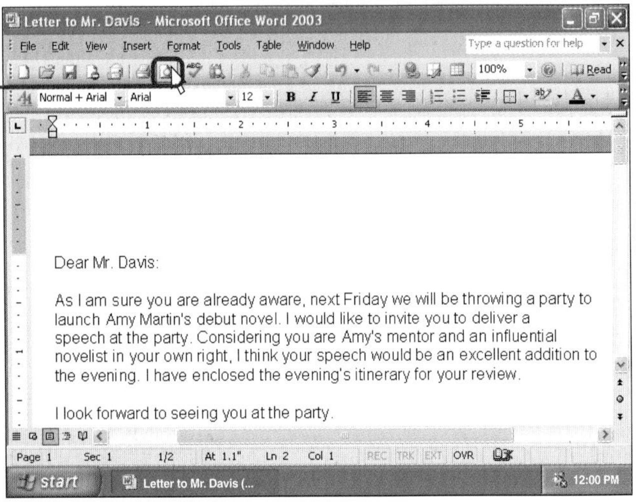

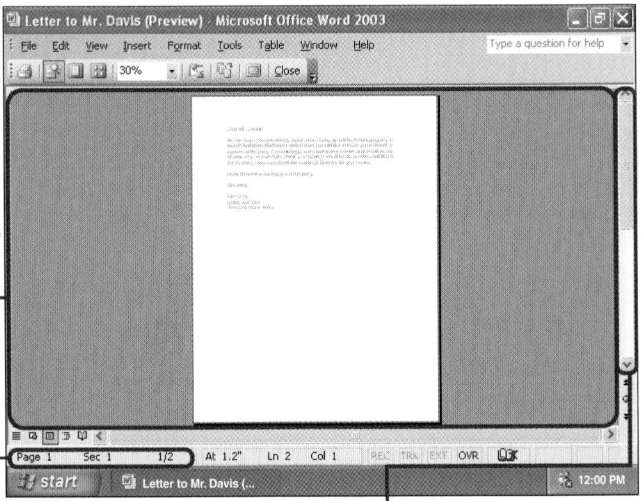

1 Click to preview your document before printing.

Note: If is not displayed, click on the Standard toolbar to display the button.

■ The Print Preview window appears.

■ This area displays a page from your document.

■ This area indicates which page is displayed and the total number of pages in your document.

■ If your document contains more than one page, you can use the scroll bar to view the other pages.

Tip

Can I edit my document in the Print Preview window?

Yes. If the mouse pointer looks like I when over your document, you can edit the document. If the mouse pointer looks like (magnify) or (reduce) when over your document, you can enlarge or reduce the size of the page displayed on your screen. To change the appearance of the mouse pointer, click the Magnifier button ( ).

Tip

Can I shrink the text in my document to fit on one less page?

If the last page in your document contains only a few lines of text, Word can shrink the text in your document to fit on one less page. In the Print Preview window, click the Shrink to Fit button ( ) to shrink the text in your document.

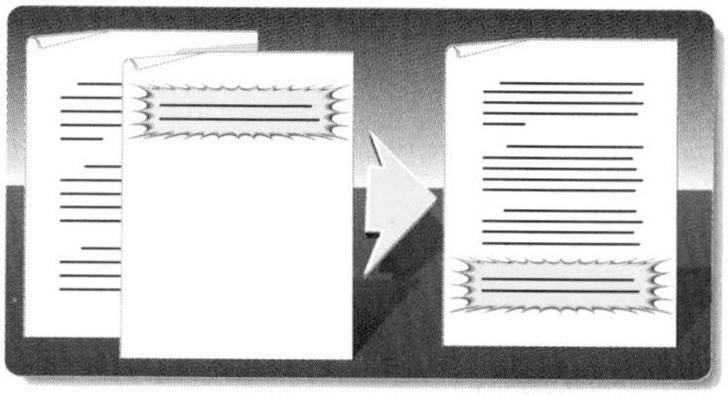

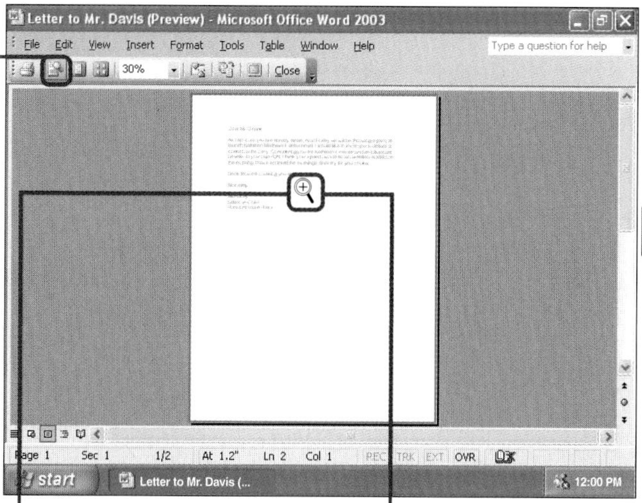

2 To magnify an area of the page, position the mouse over the area you want to magnify (changes to).

■ If the mouse pointer looks like I when over the page, click .

3 Click the area to magnify the area.

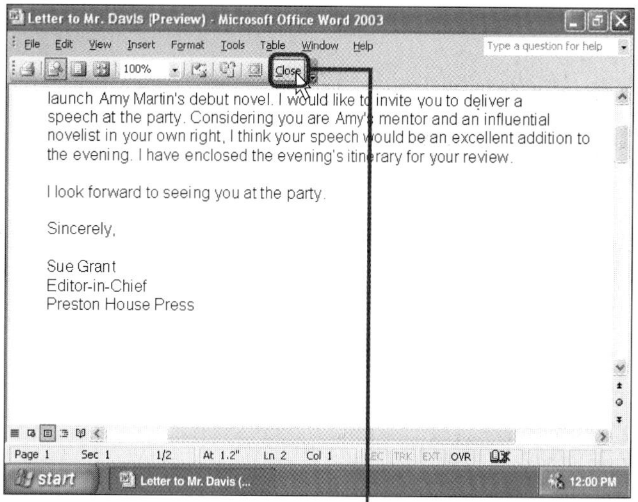

■ A magnified view of the area appears.

4 To once again display the entire page, click anywhere on the page.

5 When you finish previewing your document, click **Close** to close the Print Preview window.

PRINT A DOCUMENT

You can produce a paper copy of the document displayed on your screen.

Before printing your document, make sure the printer is turned on and contains an adequate supply of paper.

PRINT A DOCUMENT

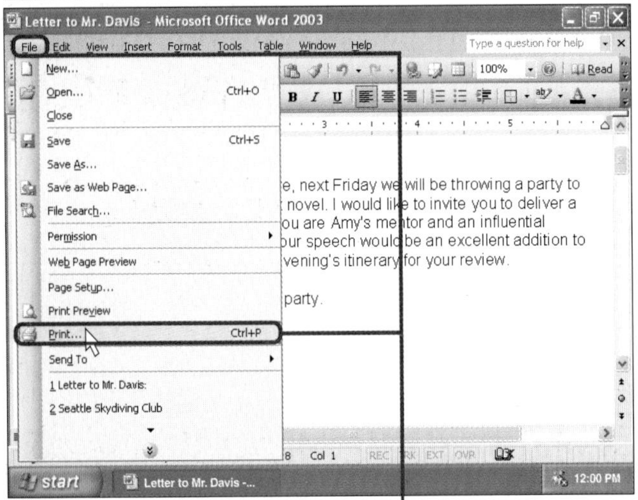

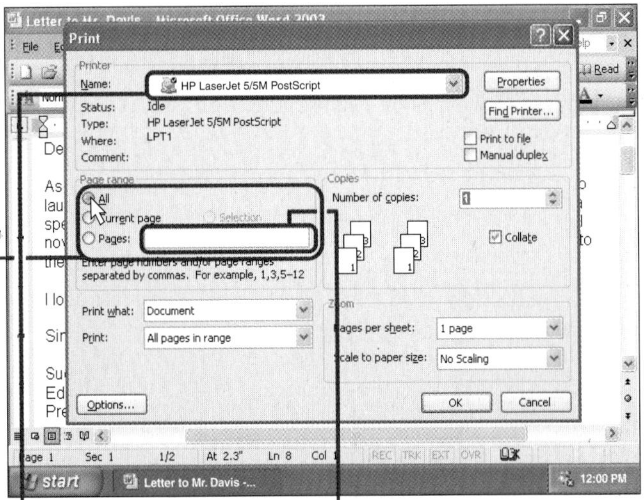

1 Click anywhere in the document or page you want to print.

■ To print only some of the text in the document, select the text you want to print. To select text, see page 20.

2 Click **File**.

3 Click **Print**.

■ The Print dialog box appears.

■ This area displays the printer that will print your document. You can click this area to select a different printer.

4 Click the print option you want to use (○ changes to ◉).

Note: For more information on the print options, see the top of page 33.

■ If you selected **Pages** in step **4**, type the pages you want to print in this area (example: 1,3,5 or 2-4).

Tip

Which print option should I use?

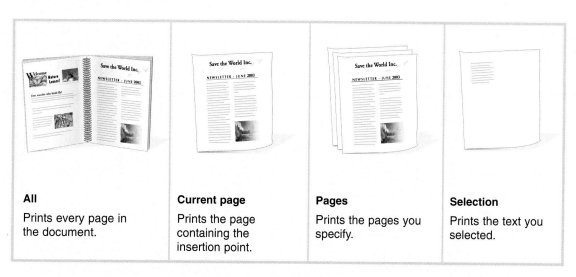

All Prints every page in the document.	**Current page** Prints the page containing the insertion point.	**Pages** Prints the pages you specify.	**Selection** Prints the text you selected.

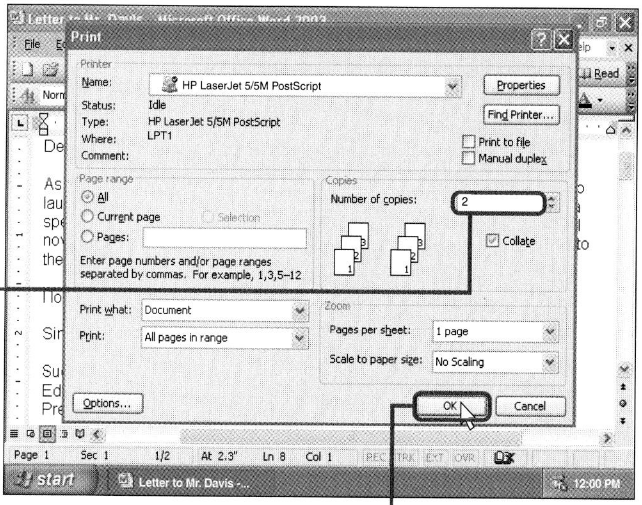

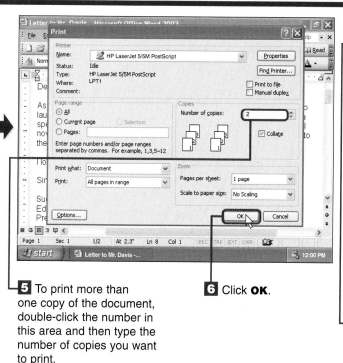

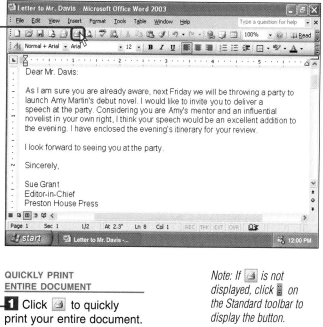

5 To print more than one copy of the document, double-click the number in this area and then type the number of copies you want to print.

6 Click **OK**.

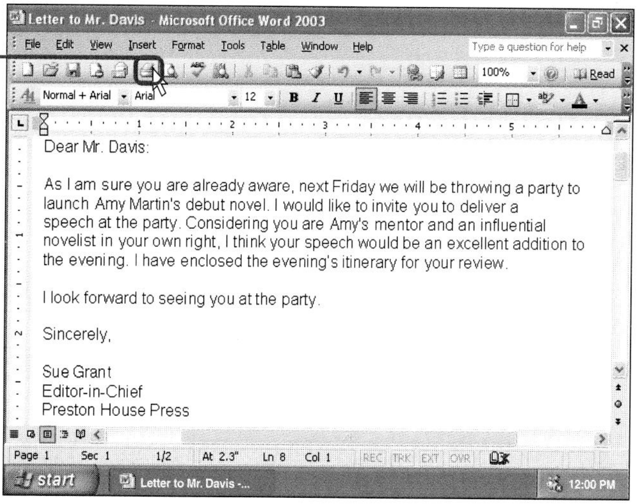

QUICKLY PRINT ENTIRE DOCUMENT

1 Click [print icon] to quickly print your entire document.

Note: If [print icon] is not displayed, click [toolbar options icon] on the Standard toolbar to display the button.

CREATE A NEW DOCUMENT

You can create a new document to start writing a new letter, memo or report.

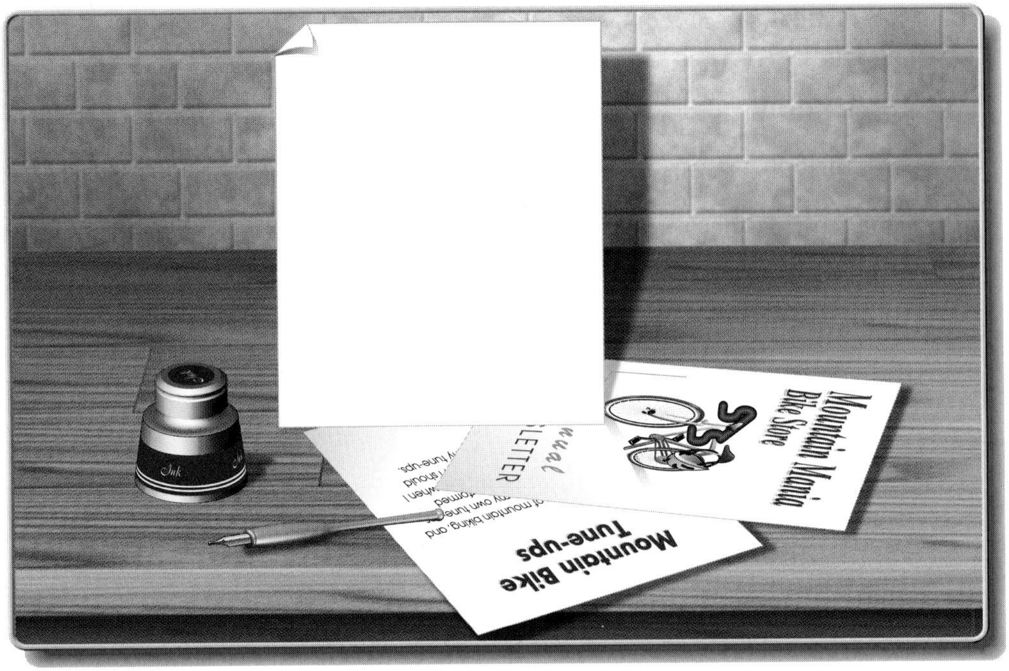

Each document is like a separate piece of paper. Creating a new document is like placing a new piece of paper on your screen.

CREATE A NEW DOCUMENT

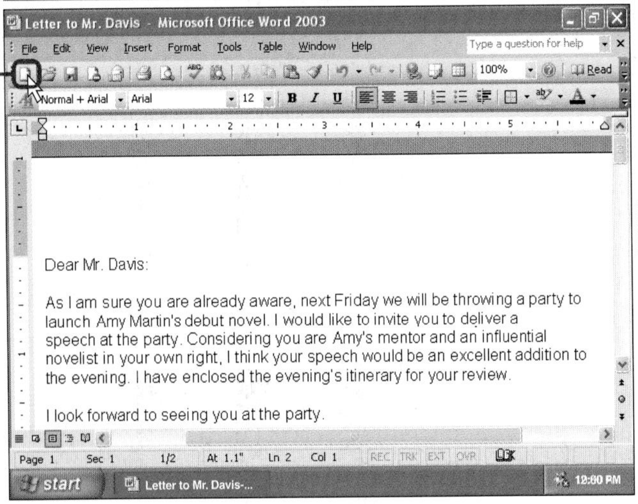

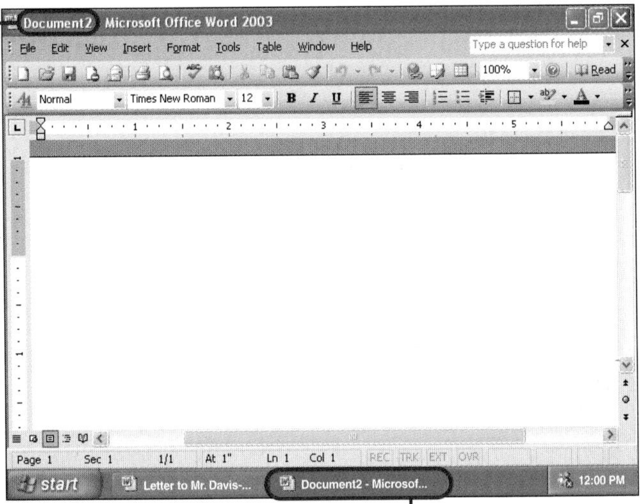

1 Click to create a new document.

Note: If is not displayed, click on the Standard toolbar to display the button.

■ The new document appears. The previous document is now hidden behind the new document.

■ Word gives the new document a temporary name, such as Document2, until you save the document. To save a document, see page 26.

■ A button for the new document appears on the taskbar.

SWITCH BETWEEN DOCUMENTS

You can have several documents open at once. Word allows you to easily switch from one open document to another.

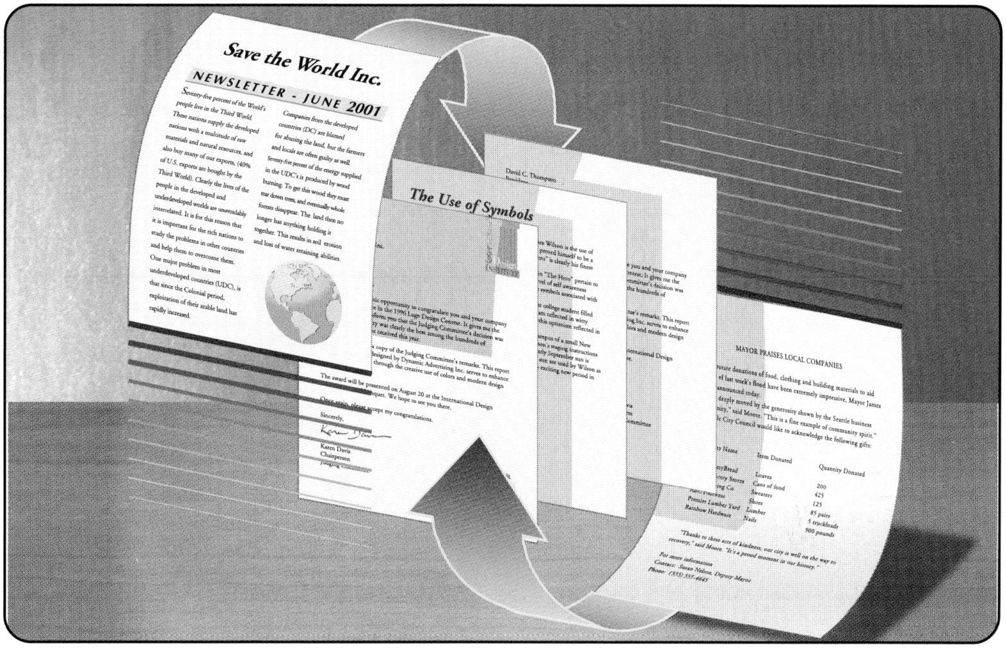

Switching between documents is useful when you want to review the contents of more than one document at a time. For example, you may want to simultaneously review a recipe and a shopping list for the recipe's ingredients.

SWITCH BETWEEN DOCUMENTS

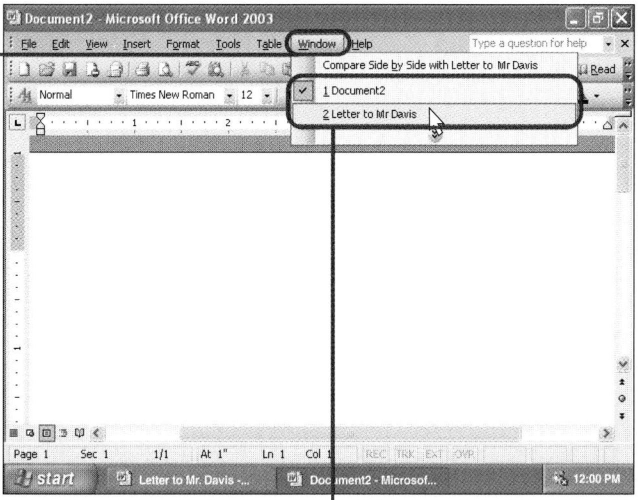

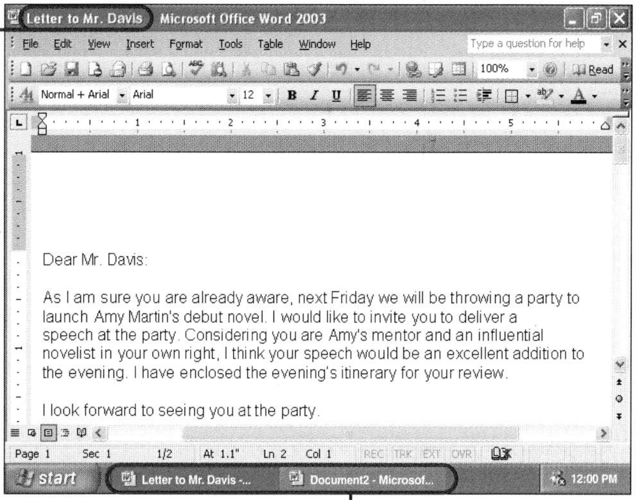

1 Click **Window** to display a list of all the documents you have open.

2 Click the name of the document you want to switch to.

■ The document appears.

■ This area shows the name of the displayed document.

■ The taskbar displays a button for each open document. You can also click the buttons on the taskbar to switch between the open documents.

COMPARE DOCUMENTS SIDE BY SIDE

You can display two documents side by side on your screen. Comparing documents side by side is useful if you want to compare an edited document to an original version of the document.

When you scroll through one document, Word automatically scrolls through the other document for you, so you can easily compare the contents of the two documents.

COMPARE DOCUMENTS SIDE BY SIDE

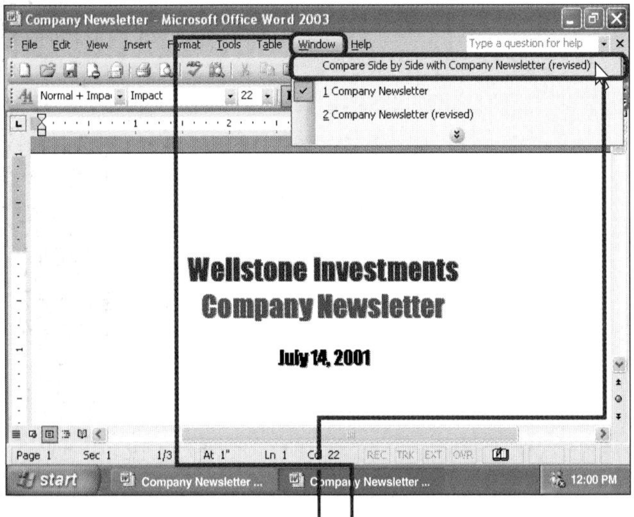

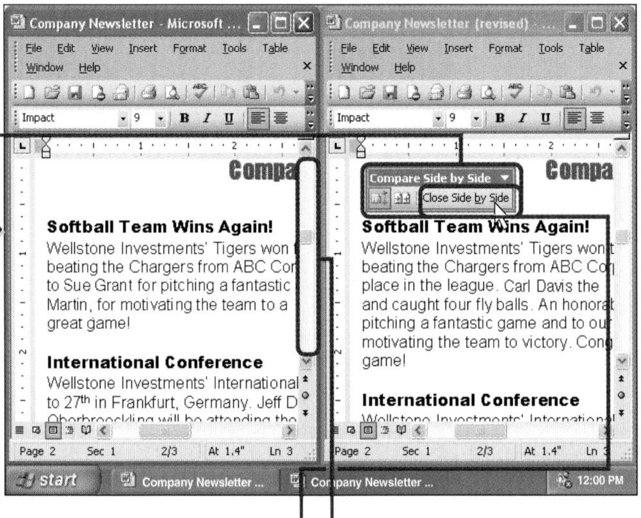

1 Open the two documents you want to compare side by side.

Note: To open a document, see page 28.

2 Click **Window** in the current document.

3 Click **Compare Side by Side with** to compare the current document with the other open document.

■ Word displays the documents side by side on your screen.

■ The Compare Side by Side toolbar also appears.

4 To scroll through the documents, drag the scroll box up or down in one document. Word automatically scrolls through the other document for you.

5 When you finish comparing the documents on your screen, click **Close Side by Side**.

ZOOM IN OR OUT

Word allows you to enlarge or reduce the display of text on your screen.

You can increase the zoom setting to view an area of your document in more detail or decrease the zoom setting to view more of your document at once.

The available zoom settings depend on the current view of your document. For information on the document views, see page 24.

ZOOM IN OR OUT

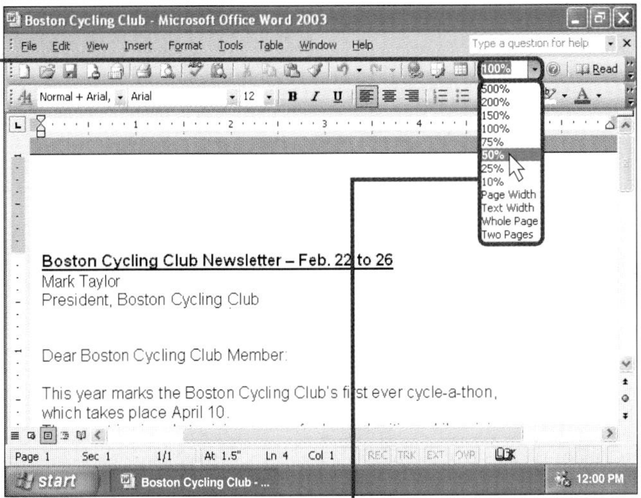

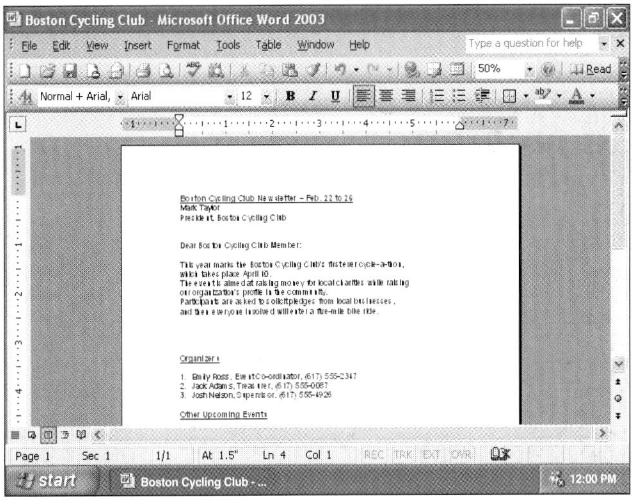

1 Click ▾ in this area to display a list of zoom settings.

Note: If the Zoom area is not displayed, click ⁝ on the Standard toolbar to display the area.

2 Click the zoom setting you want to use.

*Note: Select **Page Width** or **Text Width** to fit the page or the text across the width of your screen. Select **Whole Page** or **Two Pages** to display one or two full pages across your screen.*

■ The document appears in the new zoom setting. You can edit the document as usual.

■ Changing the zoom setting will not affect the way text appears on a printed page.

■ To return to the normal zoom setting, repeat steps **1** and **2**, selecting **100%** in step **2**.

READ A DOCUMENT ON SCREEN

You can use the Reading Layout view to make a document easier to read on your screen. However, your document will no longer accurately represent how it will appear when printed.

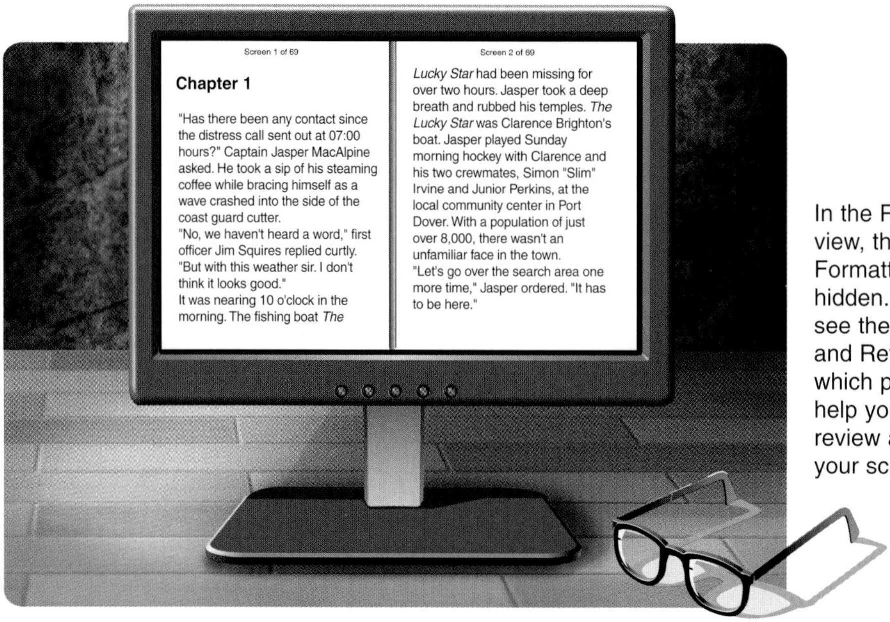

In the Reading Layout view, the Standard and Formatting toolbars are hidden. Instead, you will see the Reading Layout and Reviewing toolbars, which provide tools to help you read and review a document on your screen.

READ A DOCUMENT ON SCREEN

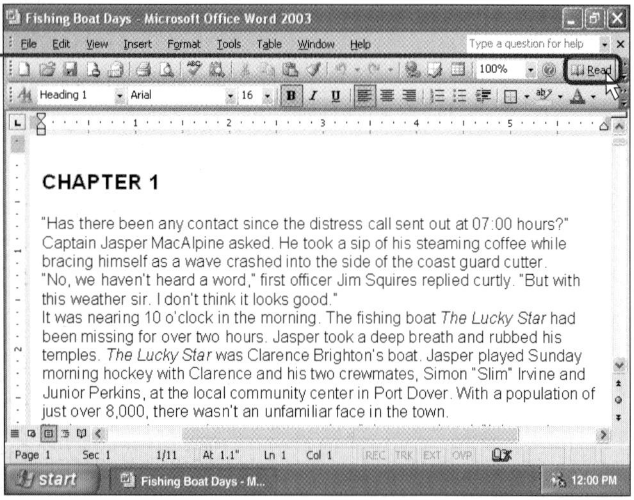

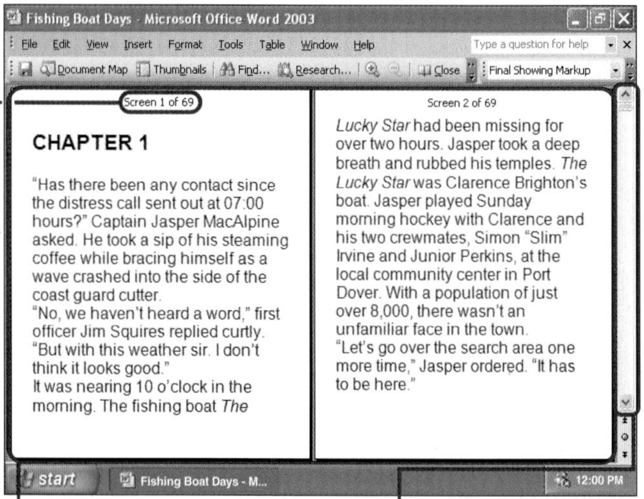

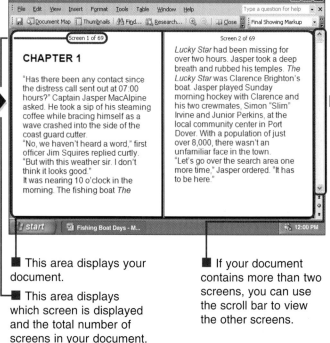

1 Click **Read** to view your document in the Reading Layout view.

Note: If the Read button is not displayed, click on the Standard toolbar to display the button.

■ The document appears in the Reading Layout view.

■ This area displays your document.

■ This area displays which screen is displayed and the total number of screens in your document.

■ If your document contains more than two screens, you can use the scroll bar to view the other screens.

Tip

Will Word ever automatically switch to the Reading Layout view?

When someone sends you a Word document as an attachment to an e-mail message and you open the attachment in Outlook, Word will automatically switch to the Reading Layout view. For information on attaching a file to a message, see page 316.

Tip

Is the Reading Layout view suitable for all my documents?

The Reading Layout view may not be suitable for all your documents. For example, tables, columns or WordArt may not appear correctly. If you need to view these types of items, you should view your document in the Print Layout view instead. For more information on the Print Layout view, see page 24.

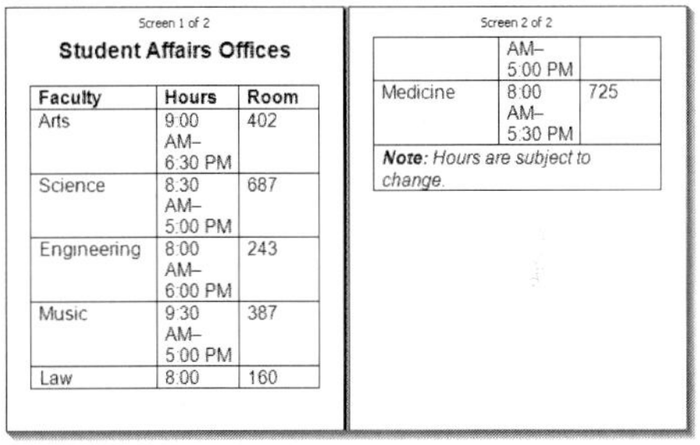
Screen 1 of 2
Student Affairs Offices
Faculty | Hours | Room
Arts | 9:00 AM–6:30 PM | 402
Science | 8:30 AM–5:00 PM | 687
Engineering | 8:00 AM–6:00 PM | 243
Music | 9:30 AM–5:00 PM | 387
Law | 8:00 | 160
Screen 2 of 2
AM–5:00 PM
Medicine | 8:00 AM–5:30 PM | 725
Note: Hours are subject to change.

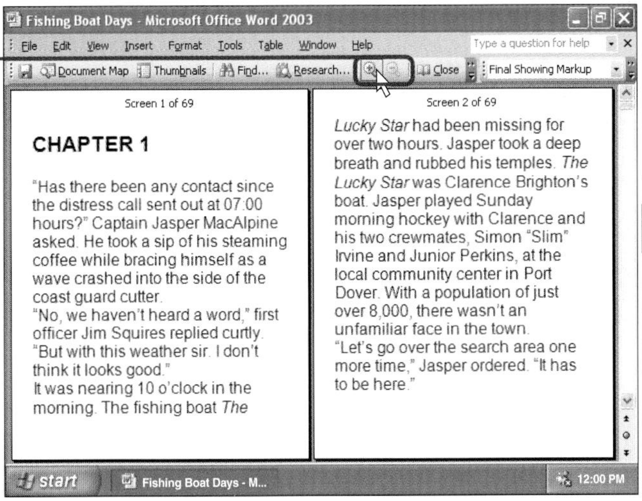

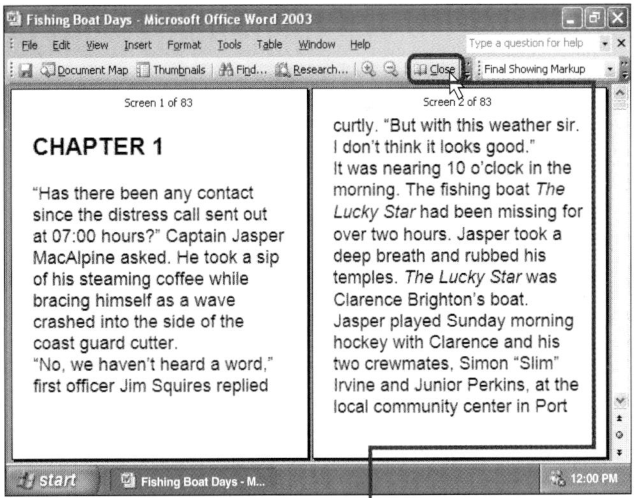

2 To change the size of the text on your screen, click one of the following buttons.

- Increase the size of text
- Decrease the size of text

Note: If or is not displayed, click on the Reading Layout toolbar to display the buttons.

■ You can edit the document in the Reading Layout view as you would in any other view.

Note: For information on the other document views, see page 24.

3 When you finish reading your document, click **Close** to return to the previous view.

Note: If the Close button is not displayed, click on the Reading Layout toolbar to display the button.

E-MAIL A DOCUMENT

You can e-mail the document displayed on your screen to a friend, family member or colleague.

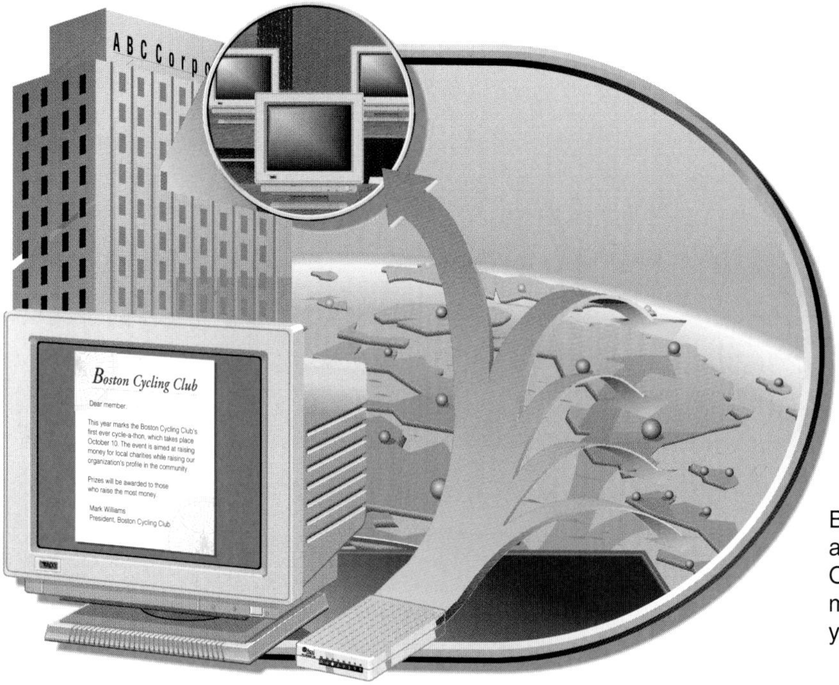

Before you can e-mail a document, Microsoft Office Outlook 2003 must be set up on your computer.

E-MAIL A DOCUMENT

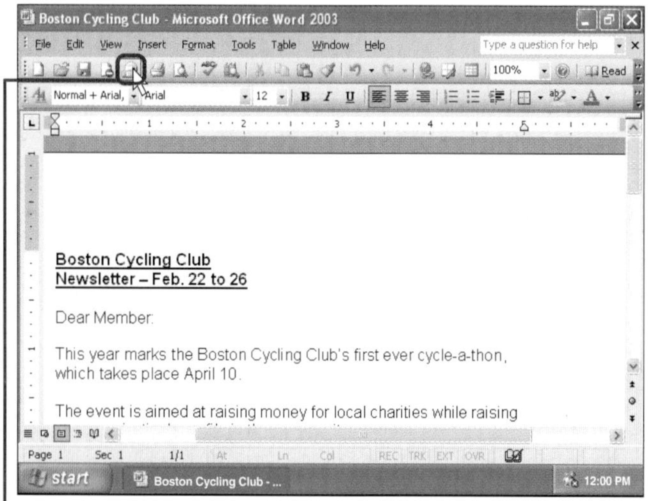

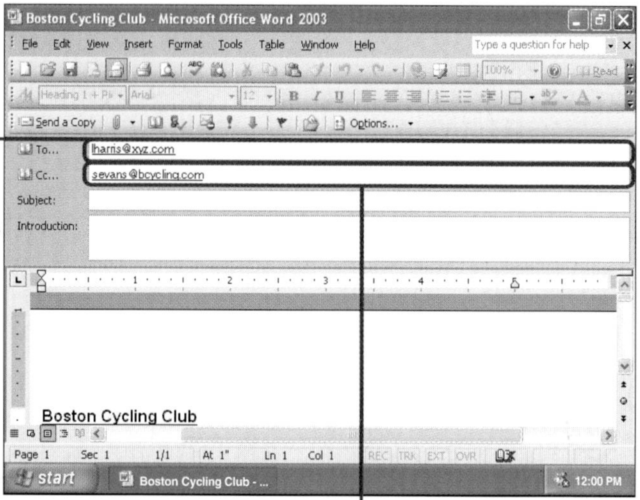

1 Click [button] to e-mail the displayed document.

Note: If [button] is not displayed, click [button] on the Standard toolbar to display the button.

■ An area appears for you to address the message.

2 Click this area and type the e-mail address of the person you want to receive the message.

3 To send a copy of the message to another person, click this area and type their e-mail address.

*Note: To enter more than one e-mail address in step **2** or **3**, separate each e-mail address with a semicolon (;).*

Tip

How can I address an e-mail message?

To

Sends the message to the person you specify.

Carbon Copy (Cc)

Sends an exact copy of the message to a person who is not directly involved, but would be interested in the message.

Tip

Why would I include an introduction for the document I am e-mailing?

Including an introduction allows you to provide the recipient of the message with additional information about the document. For example, the recipient may require instructions or an explanation of the content of the document.

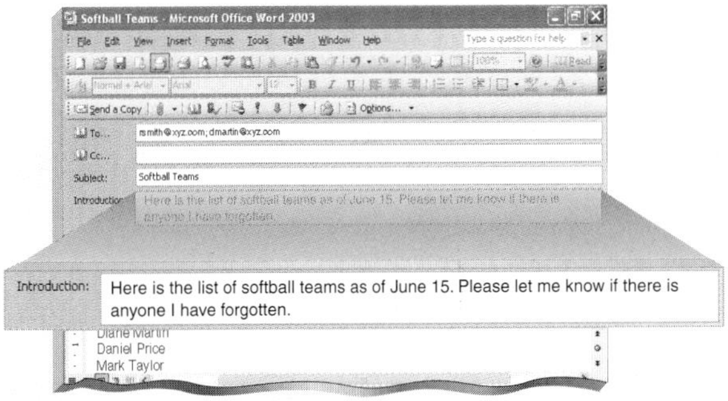

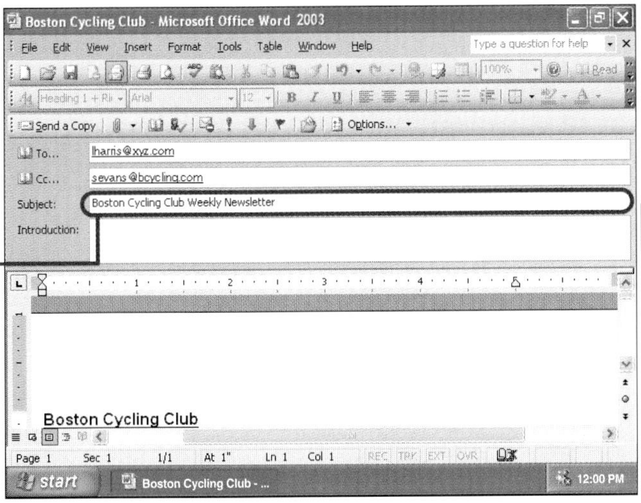

4 Click this area and type a subject for the message.

Note: If a subject already exists, you can drag the mouse I over the existing subject and then type a new subject.

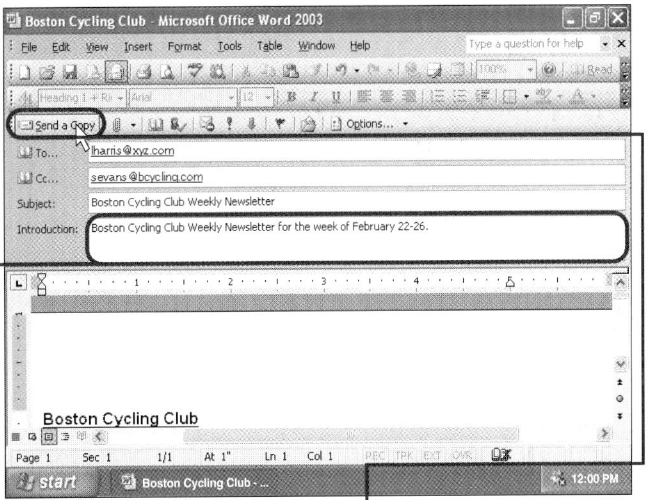

5 To include an introduction for the document you are e-mailing, click this area and type the introduction.

6 Click **Send a Copy** to send the message.

INSERT AND DELETE TEXT

You can easily add new text to your document and remove text you no longer need.

Word is an efficient editing tool. When you insert new text, the existing text moves to make room for the new text. When you remove text, the remaining text moves to fill the empty space.

INSERT TEXT

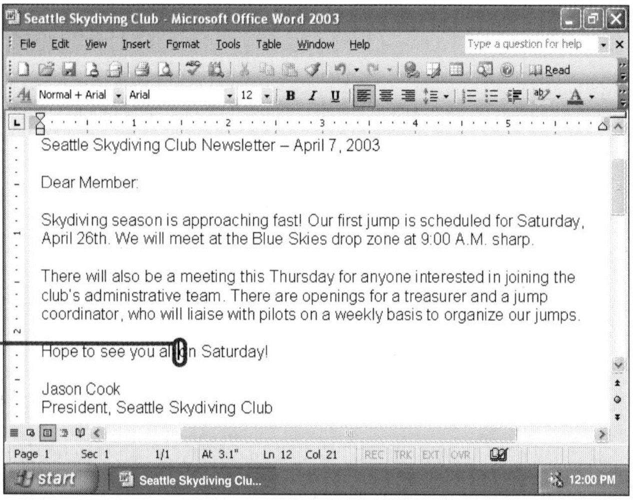

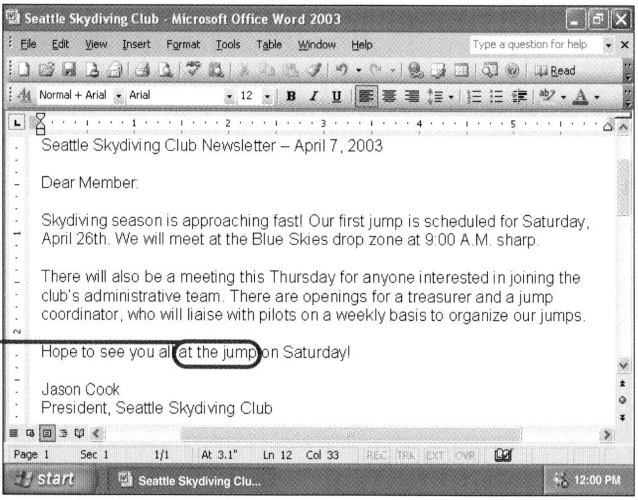

1 Click the location in your document where you want to insert new text.

■ The text you type will appear where the insertion point flashes on your screen.

Note: You can press the ←, →, ↓ or ↑ key to move the insertion point one character or line in any direction.

2 Type the text you want to insert.

■ To insert a blank space, press the **Spacebar**.

■ The words to the right of the new text move forward.

Tip

How can I insert symbols that are not available on my keyboard?

When you type one of the following sets of characters, Word automatically replaces the characters with a symbol.

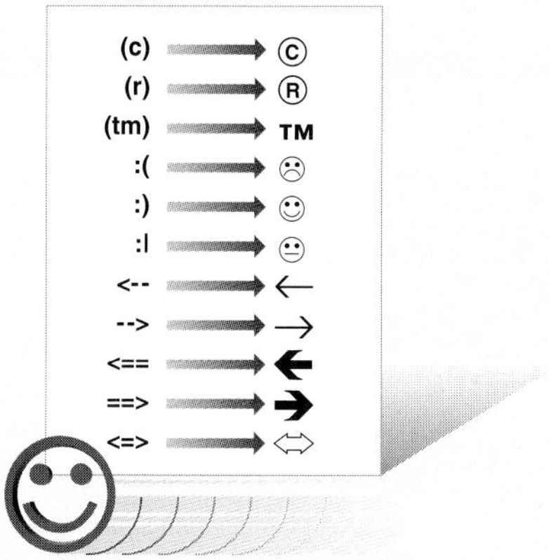

Tip

Why does the existing text in my document disappear when I insert new text?

You may have turned on the Overtype feature, which will replace existing text with the text you type. When the Overtype feature is on, the **OVR** status indicator at the bottom of your screen is **bold**. To turn the Overtype feature on or off, press the Insert key.

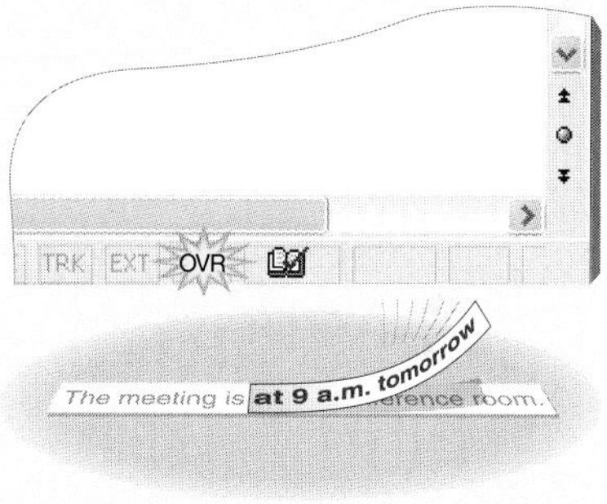

DELETE TEXT

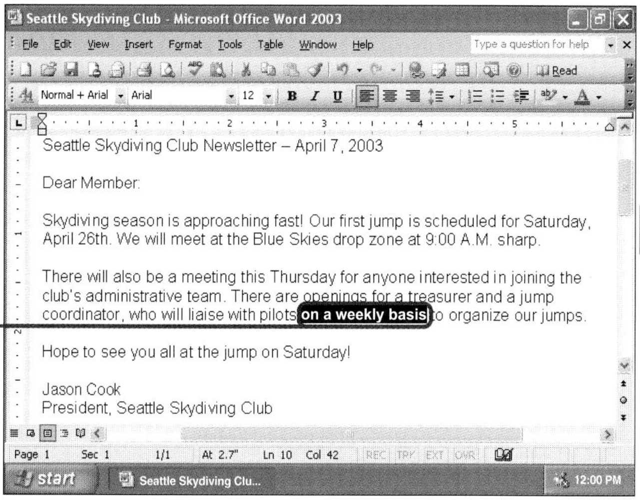

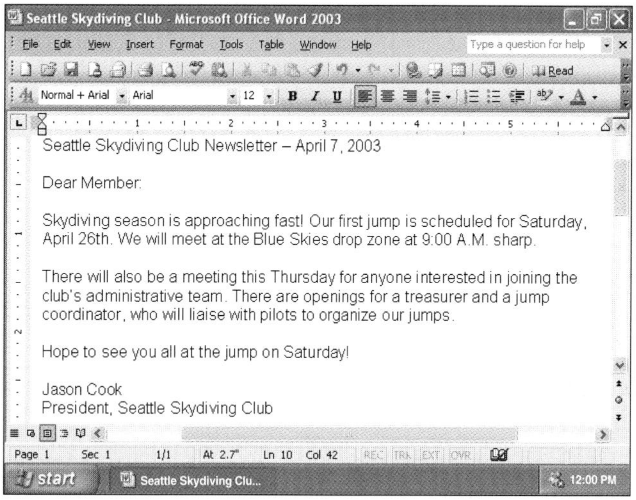

1 Select the text you want to delete. To select text, see page 20.

2 Press the Delete key to remove the text.

■ The text disappears. The remaining text in the line or paragraph moves to fill the empty space.

■ To delete a single character, click to the right of the character you want to delete and then press the Backspace key. Word deletes the character to the left of the flashing insertion point.

MOVE OR COPY TEXT

You can move or copy text to a new location in your document.

Moving text allows you to rearrange text in your document. When you move text, the text disappears from its original location.

Copying text allows you to repeat information in your document without having to retype the text. When you copy text, the text appears in both the original and new locations.

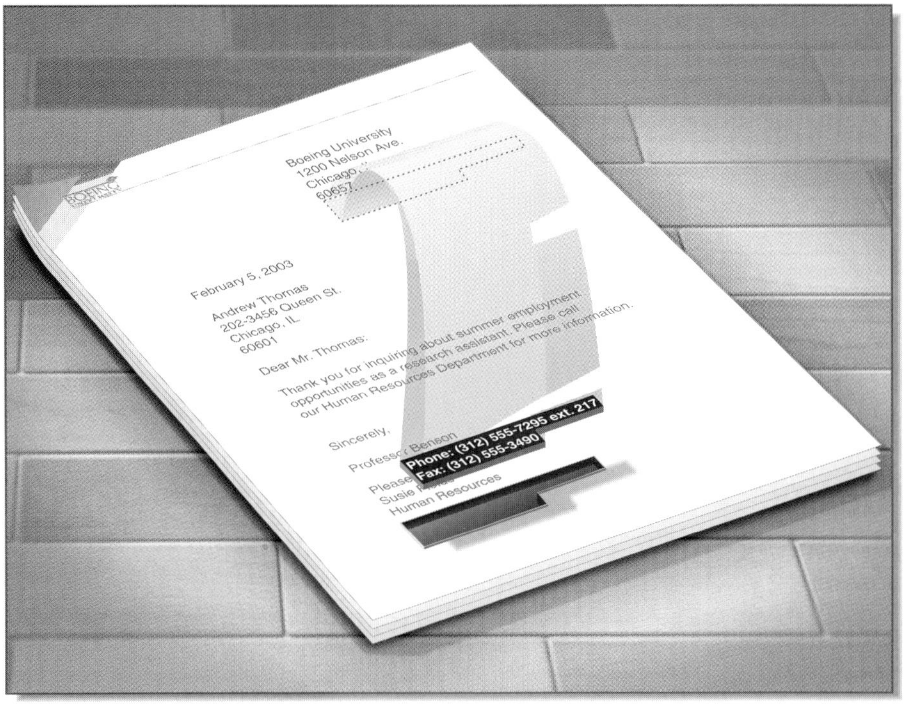

MOVE OR COPY TEXT

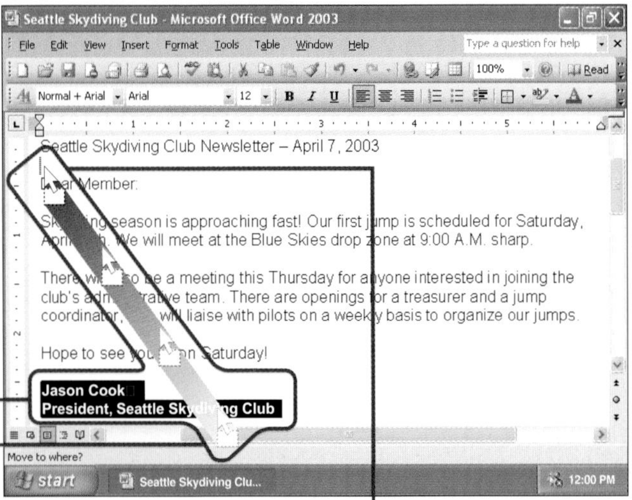

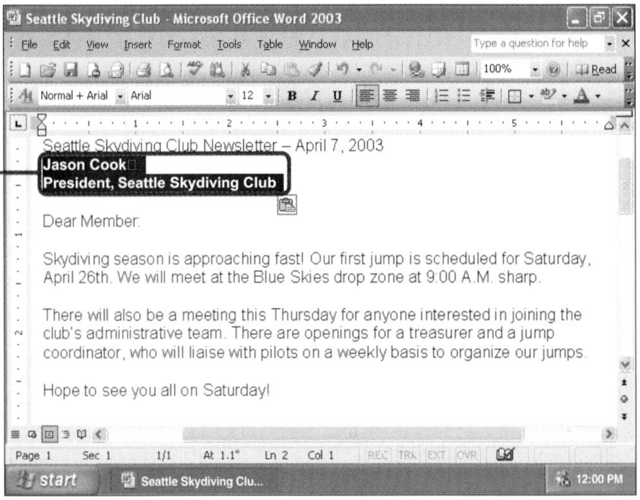

USING DRAG AND DROP

1 Select the text you want to move. To select text, see page 20.

2 Position the mouse over the selected text (I changes to ↖).

3 To move the text, drag the mouse to where you want to place the text.

Note: The text will appear where you position the dotted insertion point on your screen.

■ The text moves to the new location.

■ To copy text, perform steps **1** to **3**, except press and hold down the Ctrl key as you perform step **3**.

Tip

How can I use the Clipboard task pane to move or copy text?

The Clipboard task pane displays up to the last 24 items you have selected to move or copy. To place an item that appears on the Clipboard task pane in your document, click the location in your document where you want the item to appear and then click the item in the task pane. For information about task panes, see page 8.

Tip

Why does the Paste Options button appear when I move or copy text?

The Paste Options button allows you to change the format of text you moved or copied. For example, you can choose to keep the original formatting of the text or change the formatting of the text to match the text in the new location. Click the Paste Options button to display a list of options and then select the option you want to use. The Paste Options button is available only until you perform another task.

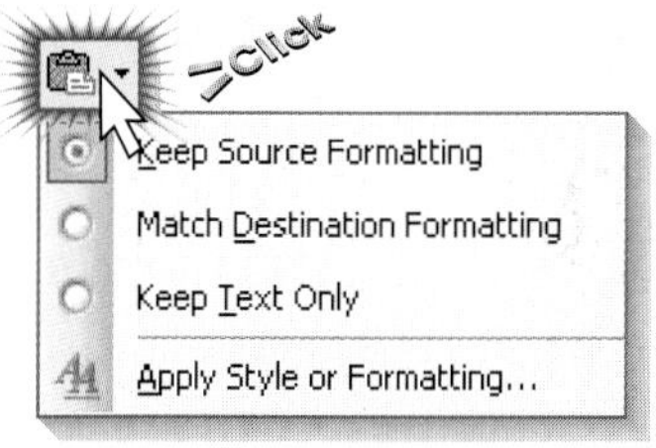

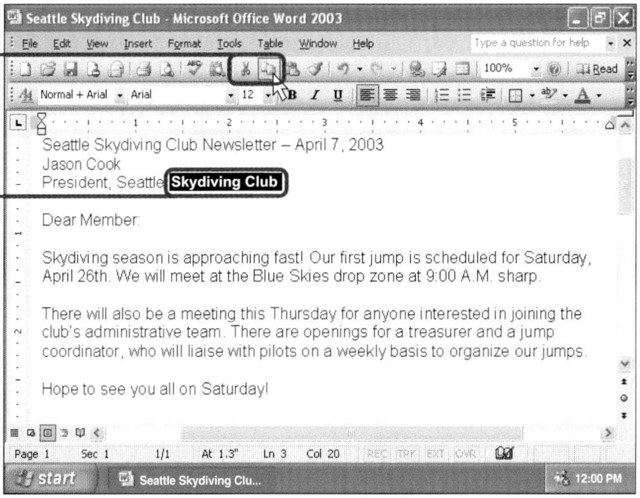

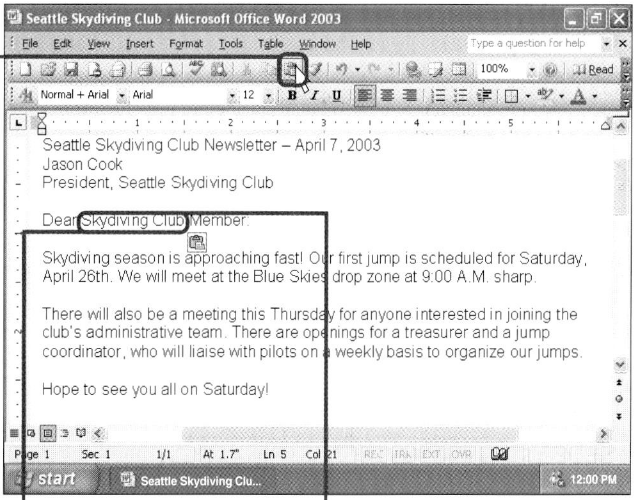

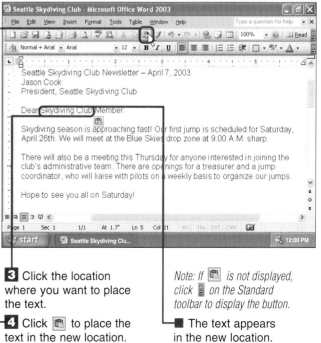

USING THE TOOLBAR BUTTONS

1 Select the text you want to move or copy. To select text, see page 20.

2 Click one of the following buttons.

- Move text
- Copy text

Note: If the button you want is not displayed, click on the Standard toolbar to display the button.

■ The Clipboard task pane may appear. To use the Clipboard task pane, see the top of this page.

3 Click the location where you want to place the text.

4 Click to place the text in the new location.

Note: If is not displayed, click on the Standard toolbar to display the button.

■ The text appears in the new location.

UNDO CHANGES

Word remembers the last changes you made to your document. If you regret these changes, you can cancel them by using the Undo feature.

The Undo feature can cancel your last editing and formatting changes. For example, you can cancel editing changes such as deleting a paragraph and cancel formatting changes such as underlining a word.

UNDO CHANGES

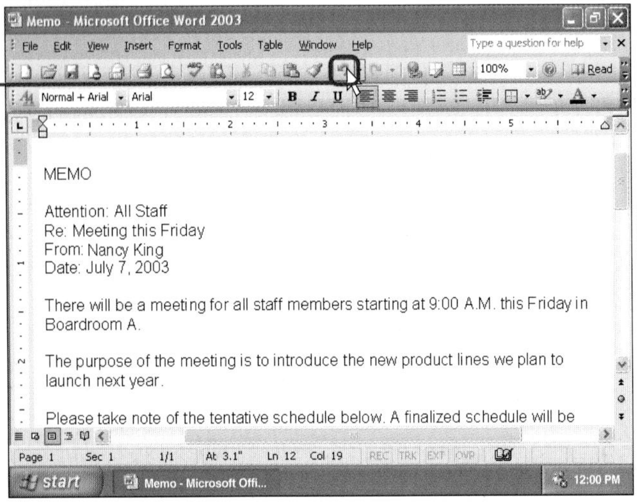

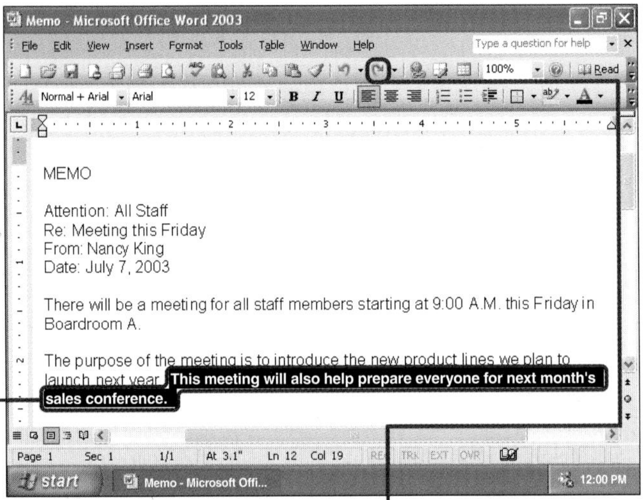

1 Click [Undo] to undo the last change you made to your document.

Note: If [Undo] is not displayed, click [Toolbar Options] on the Standard toolbar to display the button.

■ Word cancels the last change you made to your document.

■ You can repeat step **1** to cancel previous changes you made.

■ To reverse the results of using the Undo feature, click [Redo].

Note: If [Redo] is not displayed, click [Toolbar Options] on the Standard toolbar to display the button.

COUNT WORDS IN A DOCUMENT

You can have Word count the number of words in your document. Counting words is useful if you have a document that must contain a specific number of words, such as a magazine submission.

Dear Susan:
Trafalgar High School celebrates its 50th anniversary this year. We will be celebrating on September 22nd with an Open House, followed by a buffet dinner.
Please bring your school photos and memorabilia for our display table.
Word Count
38

When counting the number of words in your document, Word also counts the number of pages, characters, paragraphs and lines in your document.

COUNT WORDS IN A DOCUMENT

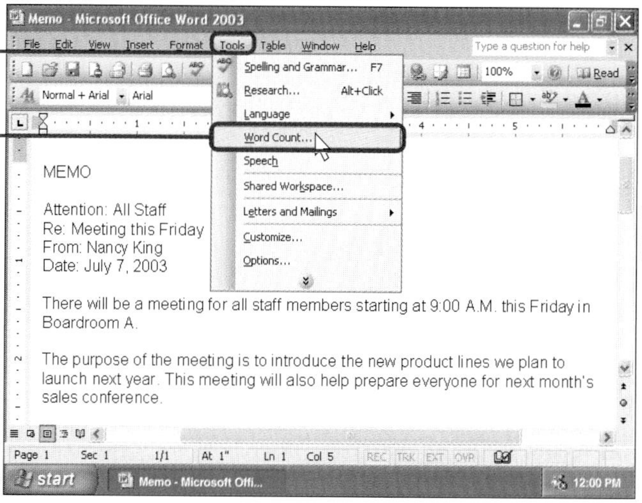

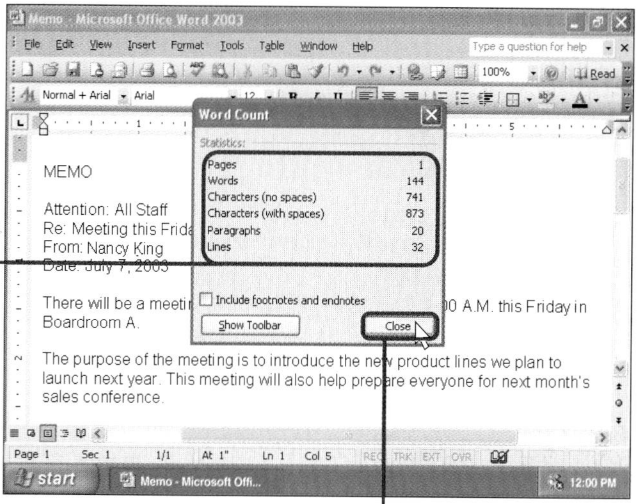

1 Click **Tools**.

2 Click **Word Count**.

*Note: To count the number of words in only part of your document, select the text before performing step **1**. To select text, see page 20.*

■ The Word Count dialog box appears.

■ This area displays the total number of pages, words, characters, paragraphs and lines in your document.

3 When you finish reviewing the information, click **Close** or **Cancel** to close the Word Count dialog box.

FIND AND REPLACE TEXT

You can find and replace every occurrence of a word or phrase in your document. This is useful if you have frequently misspelled a name.

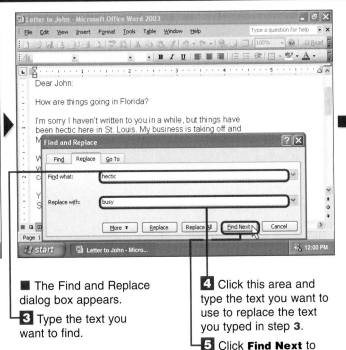

FIND AND REPLACE TEXT

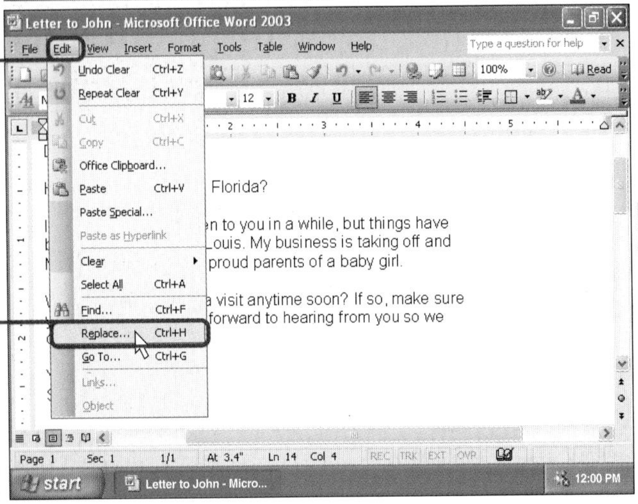

1 Click **Edit**.

2 Click **Replace**.

Note: If Replace does not appear on the menu, position the mouse over the bottom of the menu to display the menu option.

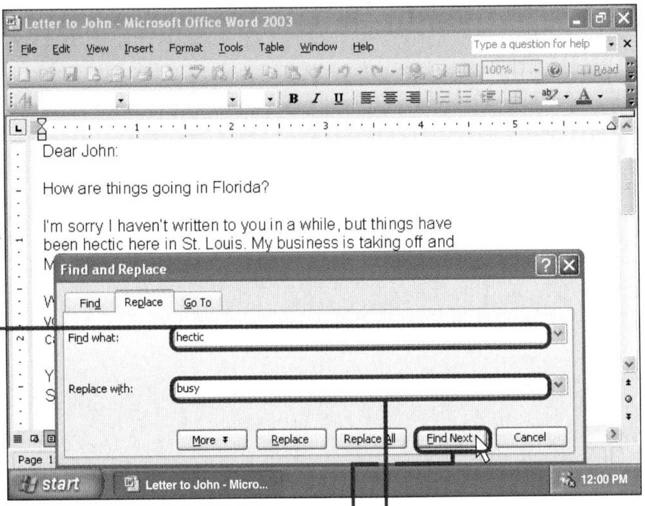

■ The Find and Replace dialog box appears.

3 Type the text you want to find.

4 Click this area and type the text you want to use to replace the text you typed in step **3**.

5 Click **Find Next** to start the search.

Tip

How can the Find and Replace feature help me quickly enter text?

When you need to type a long word or phrase, such as University of Massachusetts, many times in a document, you can use the Replace feature to simplify the task. You can type a short form of the word or phrase, such as UM, throughout your document and then have Word replace the short form with the full word or phrase.

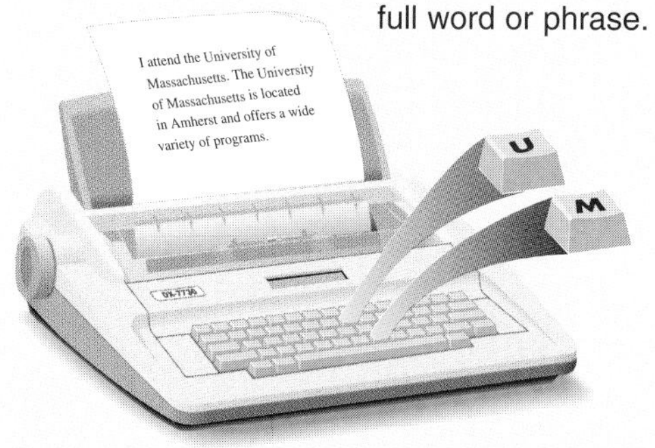

Tip

Can I find text in my document without replacing the text?

Yes. You can use the Find and Replace feature to locate a word or phrase in your document. To find text in your document, perform steps **1** to **3** below. Then perform step **5** until you find the text. To close the dialog box, press the Esc key.

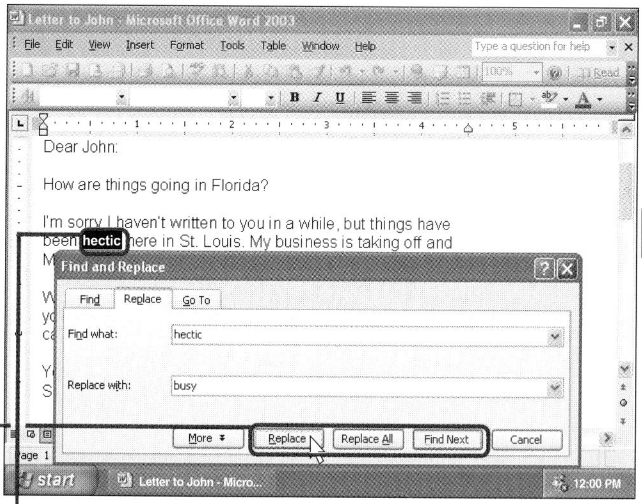

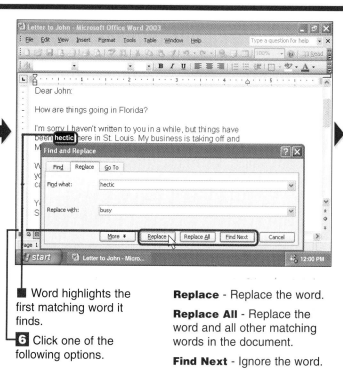

■ Word highlights the first matching word it finds.

6 Click one of the following options.

Replace - Replace the word.

Replace All - Replace the word and all other matching words in the document.

Find Next - Ignore the word.

Note: To cancel the search at any time, press the Esc *key.*

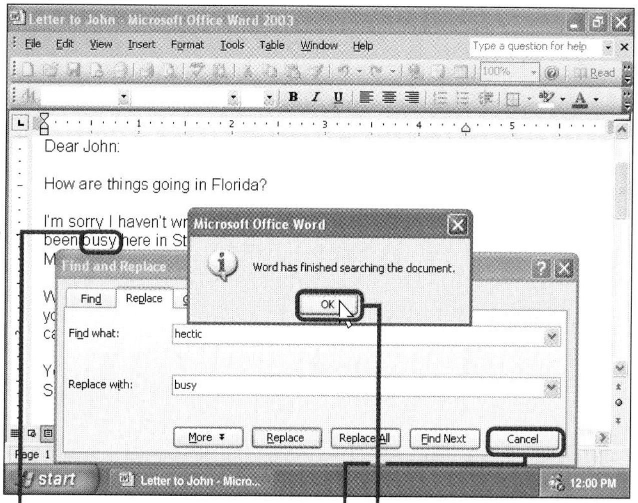

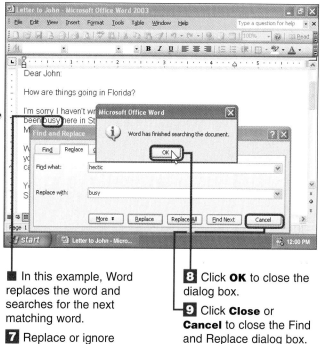

■ In this example, Word replaces the word and searches for the next matching word.

7 Replace or ignore matching words until a dialog box appears, telling you the search is complete.

8 Click **OK** to close the dialog box.

9 Click **Close** or **Cancel** to close the Find and Replace dialog box.

CHECK SPELLING AND GRAMMAR

You can find and correct all the spelling and grammar errors in your document.

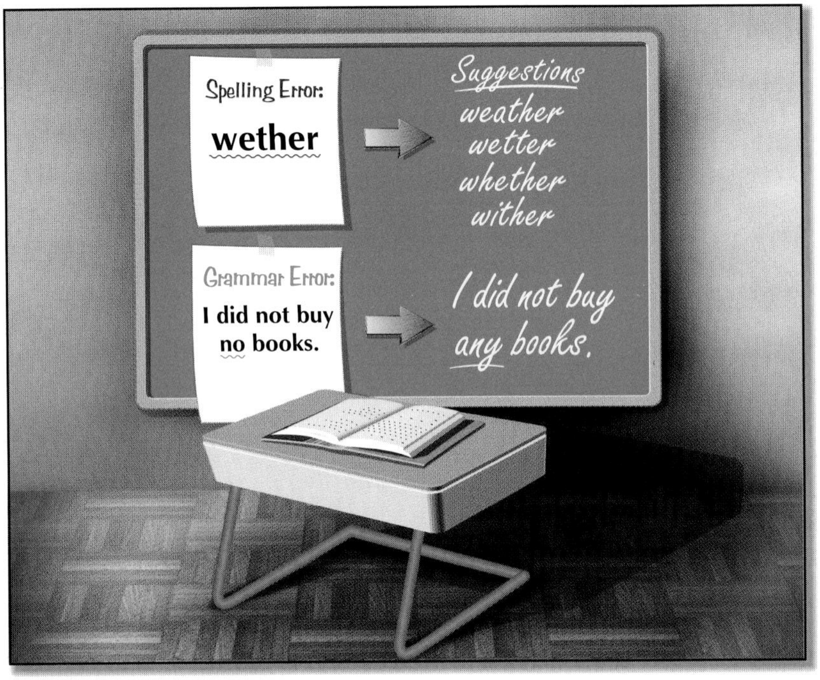

Word compares every word in your document to words in its dictionary. If a word does not exist in the dictionary, the word is considered misspelled.

Word will not find a correctly spelled word used in the wrong context, such as "My niece is **sit** years old." You should carefully review your document to find this type of error.

CHECK SPELLING AND GRAMMAR

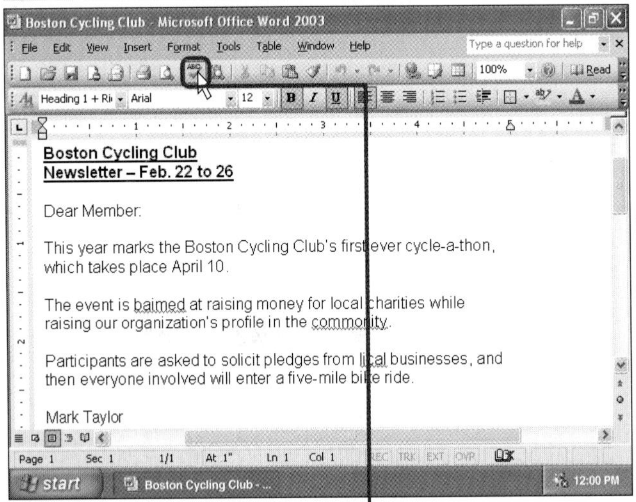

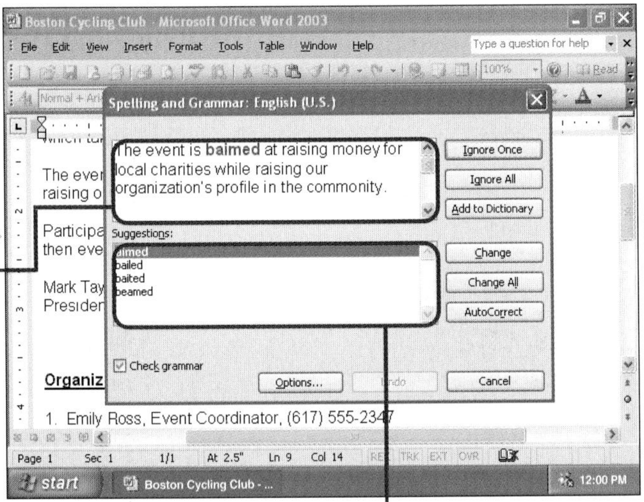

■ Word automatically underlines misspelled words in red and grammar errors in green. The underlines will not appear when you print your document.

1 Click to start checking your document for spelling and grammar errors.

Note: If is not displayed, click on the Standard toolbar to display the button.

■ The Spelling and Grammar dialog box appears if Word finds an error in your document.

■ This area displays the first misspelled word or grammar error.

■ This area displays suggestions for correcting the error.

Tip

Why did Word underline a correctly spelled word?

The word does not exist in Word's dictionary. You can add the word to the dictionary so Word will recognize the word during future spell checks.

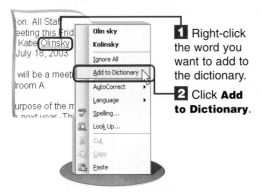

1 Right-click the word you want to add to the dictionary.

2 Click **Add to Dictionary**.

Tip

How can I quickly correct a single misspelled word or grammar error in my document?

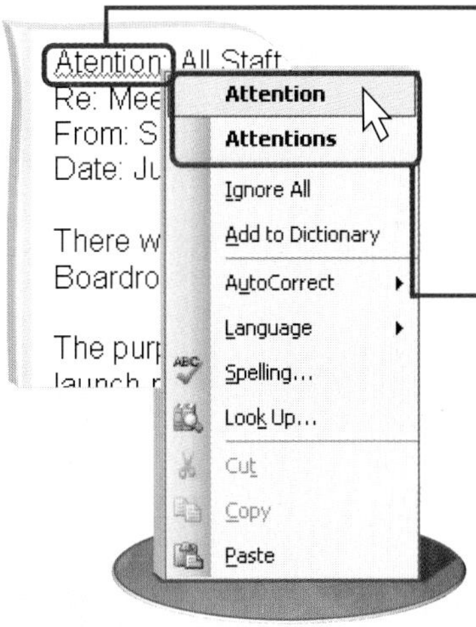

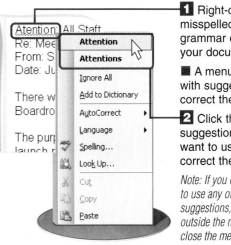

1 Right-click the misspelled word or grammar error in your document.

■ A menu appears with suggestions to correct the error.

2 Click the suggestion you want to use to correct the error.

Note: If you do not want to use any of the suggestions, click outside the menu to close the menu.

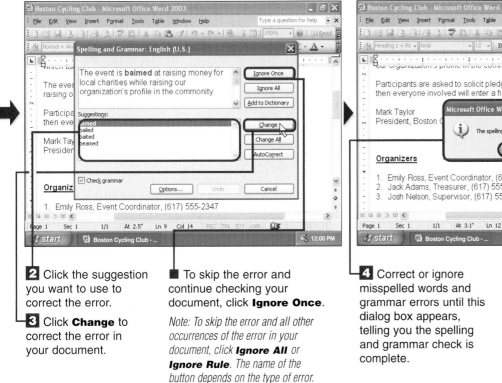

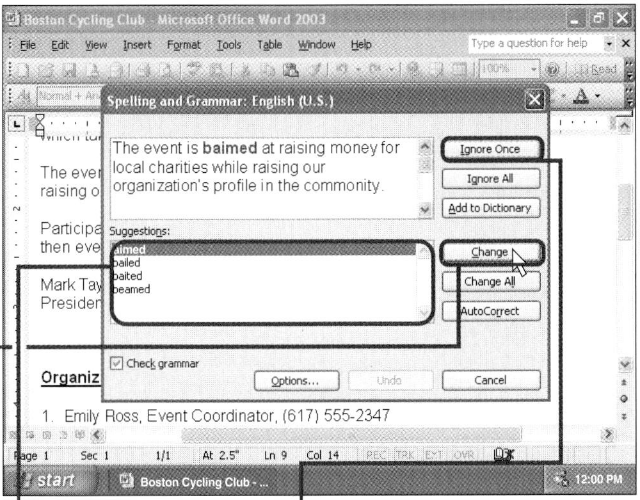

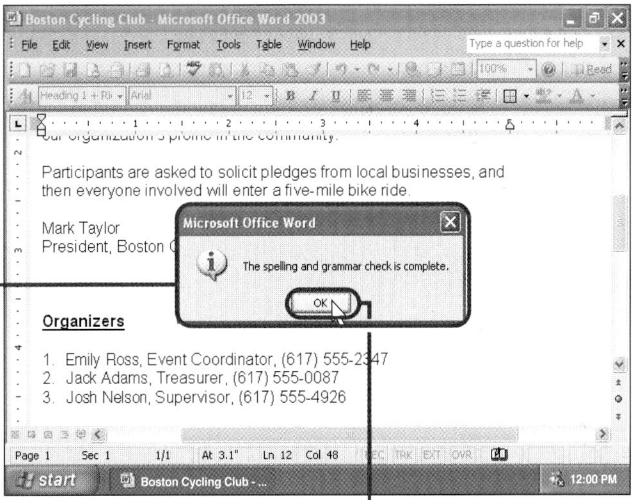

2 Click the suggestion you want to use to correct the error.

3 Click **Change** to correct the error in your document.

■ To skip the error and continue checking your document, click **Ignore Once**.

*Note: To skip the error and all other occurrences of the error in your document, click **Ignore All** or **Ignore Rule**. The name of the button depends on the type of error.*

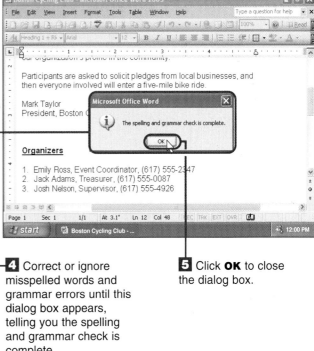

4 Correct or ignore misspelled words and grammar errors until this dialog box appears, telling you the spelling and grammar check is complete.

5 Click **OK** to close the dialog box.

USING THE THESAURUS

You can use the thesaurus on Word's Research task pane to replace a word in your document with a more suitable word.

The thesaurus can replace a word in your document with a word that shares the same meaning, called a synonym.

Using the thesaurus included with Word is faster and more convenient than searching through a printed thesaurus.

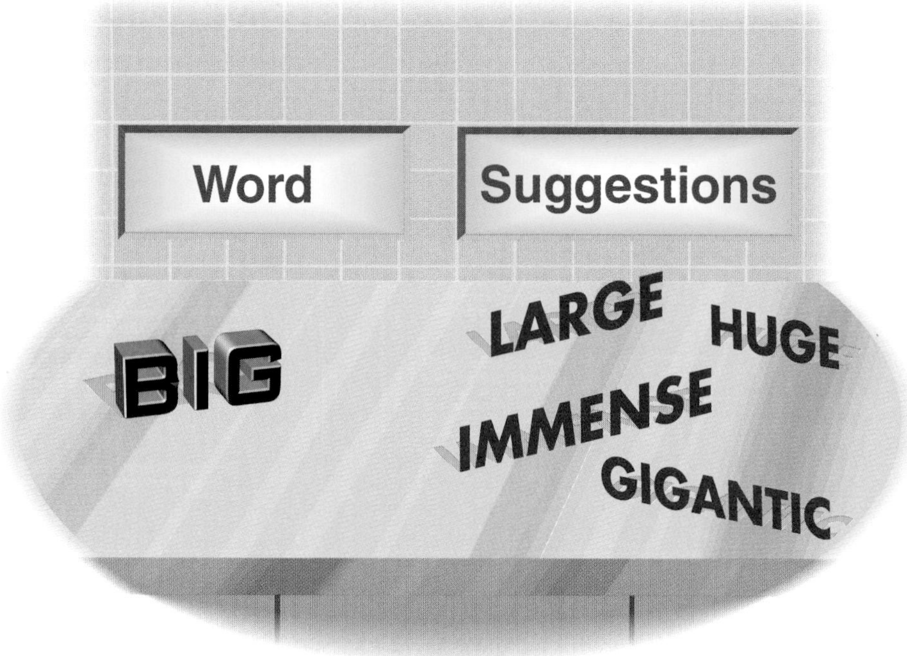

USING THE THESAURUS

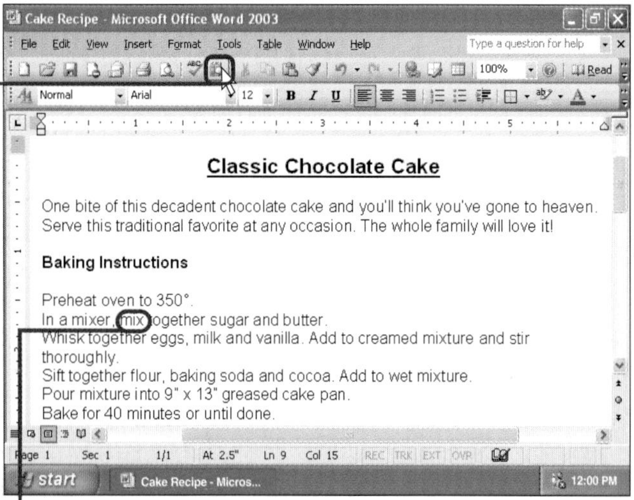

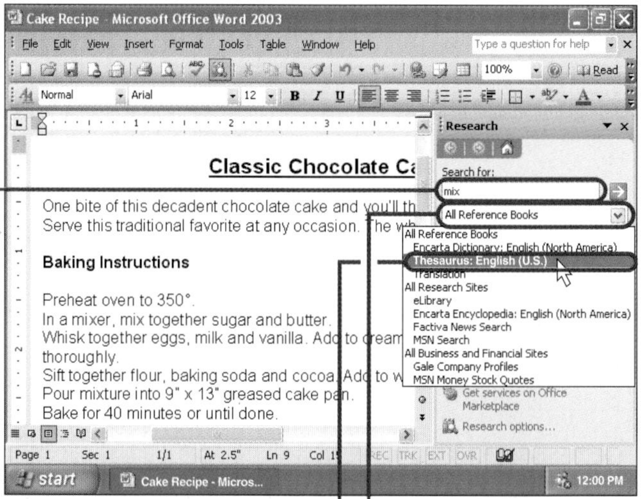

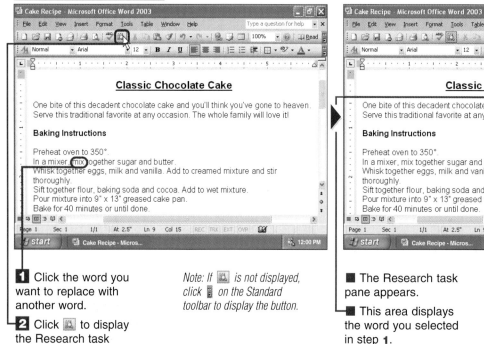

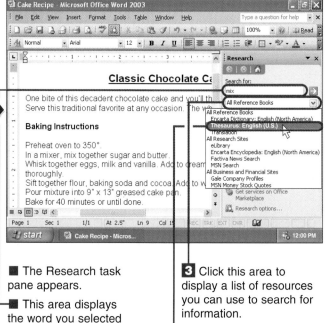

1 Click the word you want to replace with another word.

2 Click to display the Research task pane.

Note: If is not displayed, click on the Standard toolbar to display the button.

■ The Research task pane appears.

■ This area displays the word you selected in step **1**.

3 Click this area to display a list of resources you can use to search for information.

4 Click **Thesaurus**.

Tip

What if the Research task pane does not display a word I want to use?

You can look up synonyms for the words displayed in the Research task pane to find a more suitable word. Click a word in the task pane to display synonyms for the word.

*Note: If you click a **bold** word in the task pane, you will hide or display the list of synonyms for the bold word.*

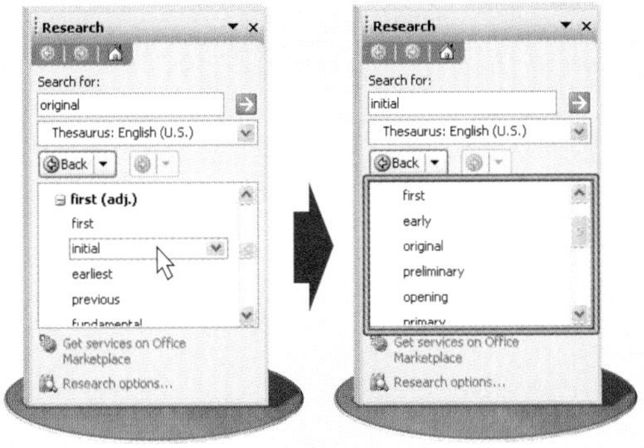

Tip

How can I quickly replace a word in my document with a synonym?

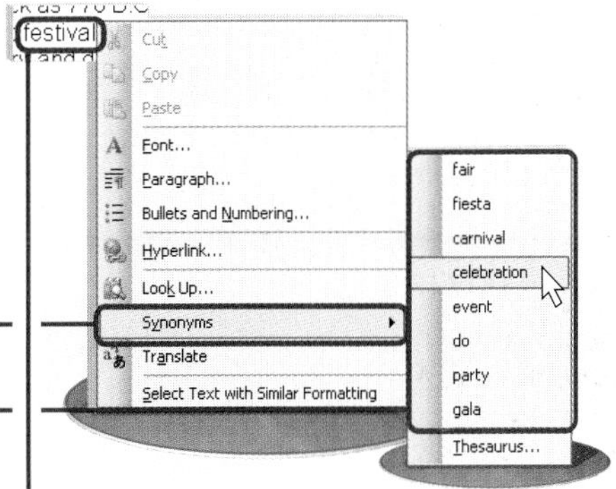

1 Right-click the word you want to replace with another word. A menu appears.

2 Click **Synonyms** to view a list of words with similar meanings.

3 Click the word you want to replace the word in your document.

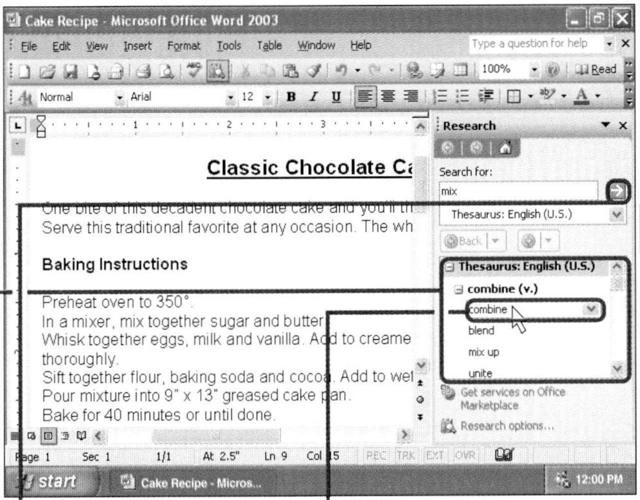

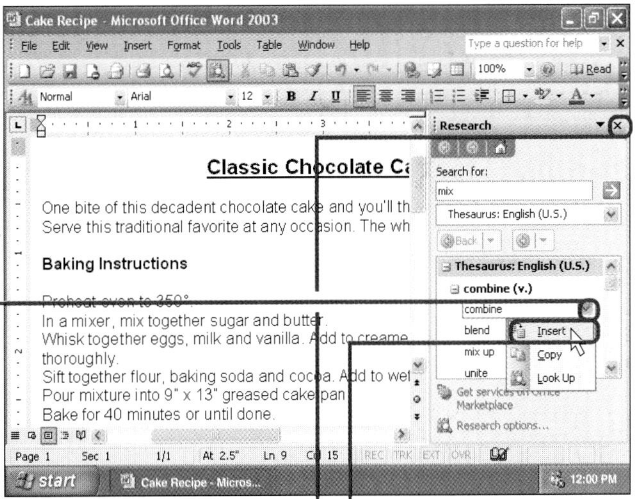

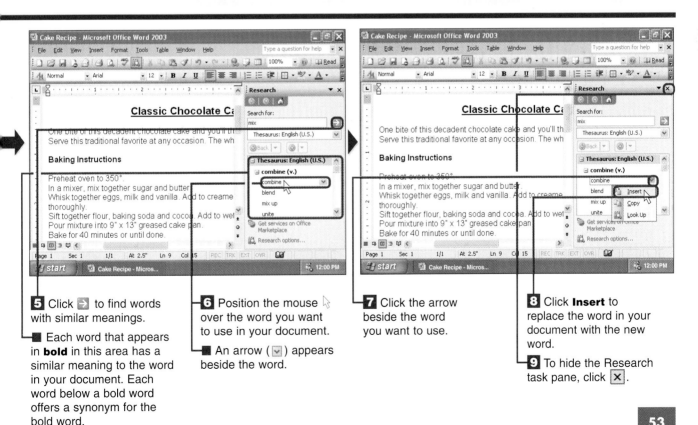

5 Click ➡ to find words with similar meanings.

■ Each word that appears in **bold** in this area has a similar meaning to the word in your document. Each word below a bold word offers a synonym for the bold word.

6 Position the mouse over the word you want to use in your document.

■ An arrow (▼) appears beside the word.

7 Click the arrow beside the word you want to use.

8 Click **Insert** to replace the word in your document with the new word.

9 To hide the Research task pane, click ☒.

USING THE RESEARCH TASK PANE

You can use the Research task pane to gather reference material without ever having to leave your Word document. For example, you can look up a word in a dictionary or search through an encyclopedia on the Web.

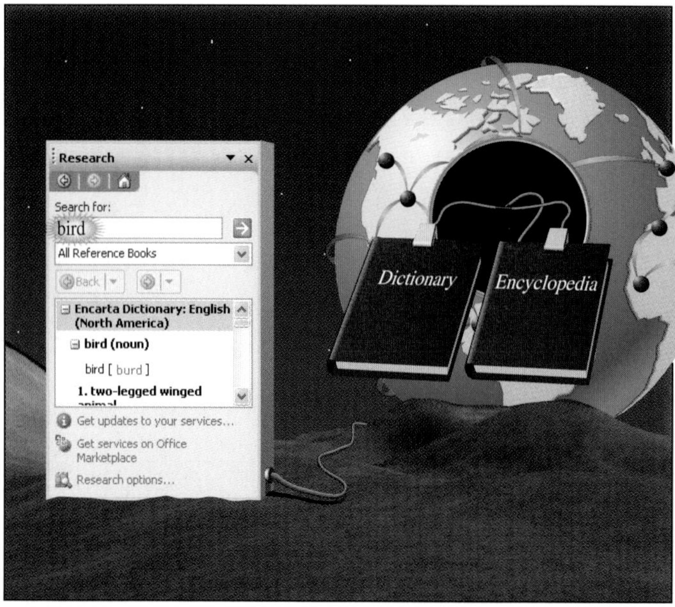

To use some of the resources offered in the Research task pane, your computer must be connected to the Internet.

Links to Web sites in the Research task pane that are preceded by a dollar symbol ( ) require you to register and pay before you can view the information.

USING THE RESEARCH TASK PANE

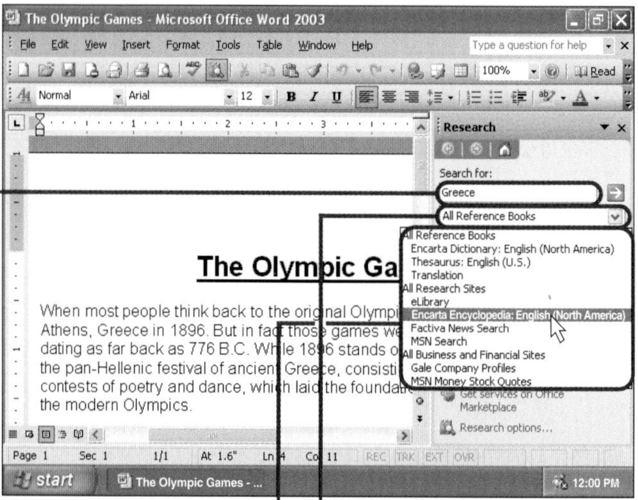

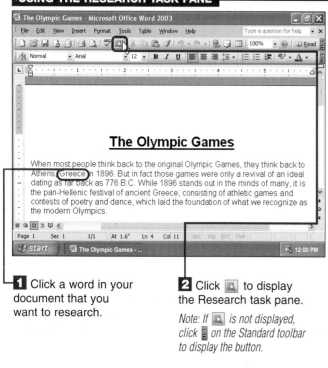

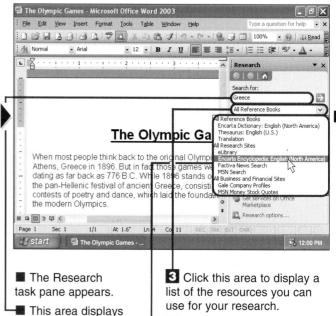

1 Click a word in your document that you want to research.

2 Click to display the Research task pane.

Note: If is not displayed, click on the Standard toolbar to display the button.

■ The Research task pane appears.

■ This area displays the word you selected in step **1**.

3 Click this area to display a list of the resources you can use for your research.

4 Click the resource you want to use to find information.

Note: In this example, we select Encarta Encyclopedia. The following screens depend on the resource you select.

Tip

What types of resources can I search using the Research task pane?

Reference Books

You can choose to look up terms in reference books, such as the Encarta Dictionary or a thesaurus. For information on using the thesaurus, see page 52.

Research Sites

You can research information online using eLibrary, Encarta Encyclopedia, Factiva News Search or MSN Search.

Business and Financial Sites

You can access company and stock market information through Gale Company Profiles or MSN Money Stock Quotes.

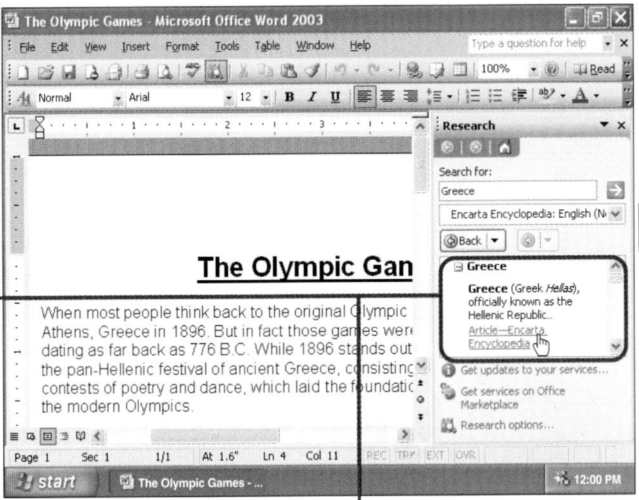

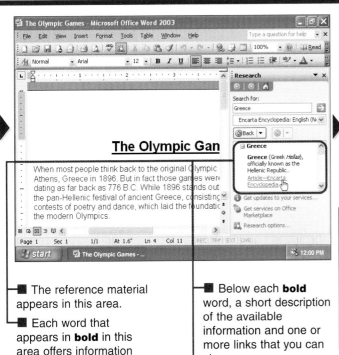

■ The reference material appears in this area.

■ Each word that appears in **bold** in this area offers information about the word you specified in step **1**.

■ Below each **bold** word, a short description of the available information and one or more links that you can choose appear.

5 Click a link to view the information.

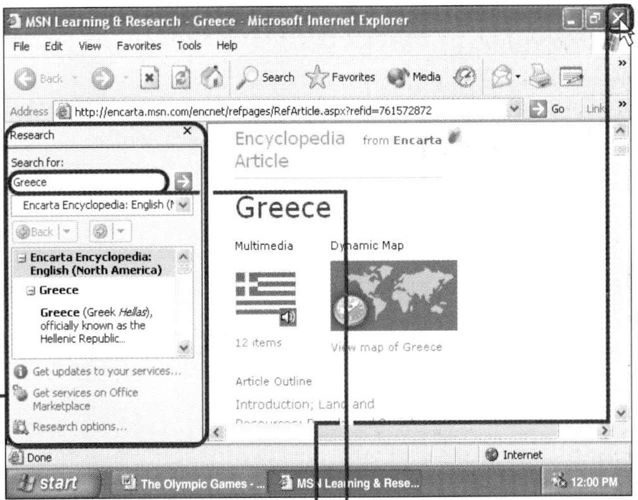

■ A Web browser window opens and displays the information you selected.

■ The Research task pane also appears in the Web browser window.

■ To research a different word at any time, double-click this area and type the word. Then press the Enter key.

6 To return to your document, click ☒.

USING SMART TAGS

Word labels certain types of information, such as dates and addresses, with smart tags. You can use a smart tag to perform an action, such as scheduling a meeting on a specific date or displaying a map for an address.

You can change the options for smart tags to specify the types of information you want Word to recognize and label with a smart tag.

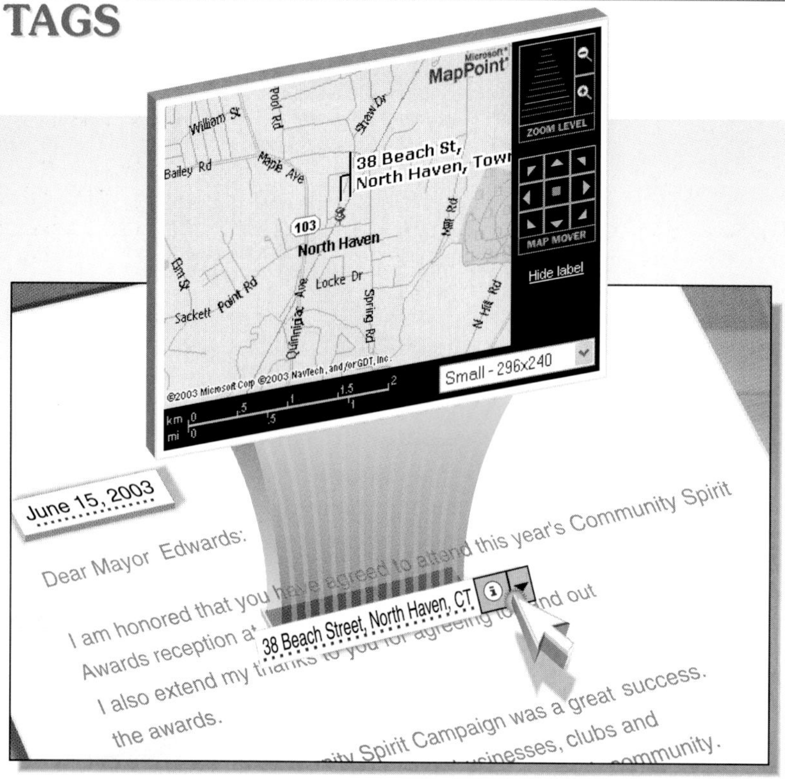

USING SMART TAGS

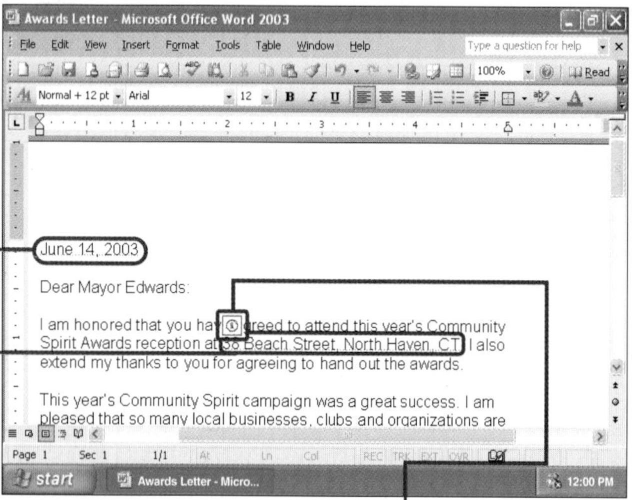

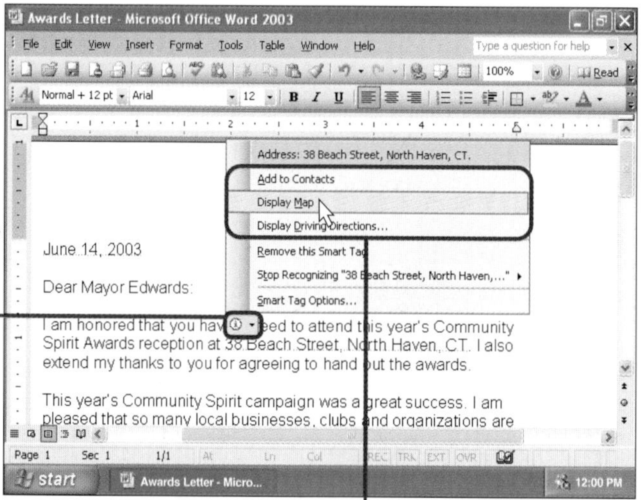

■ A dotted, purple underline appears below text Word has labeled as a smart tag.

1 To perform an action using a smart tag, position the mouse I over the text labeled as a smart tag.

■ The Smart Tag Actions button (ⓘ) appears.

2 Click the Smart Tag Actions button (ⓘ) to display a list of actions you can perform using the smart tag.

3 Click the action you want to perform.

■ The program that allows you to perform the action will appear on your screen.

Tip

How can I remove a smart tag from text in my document?

To remove a smart tag from text in your document, perform steps **1** to **3** on page 56, selecting **Remove this Smart Tag** in step **3**.

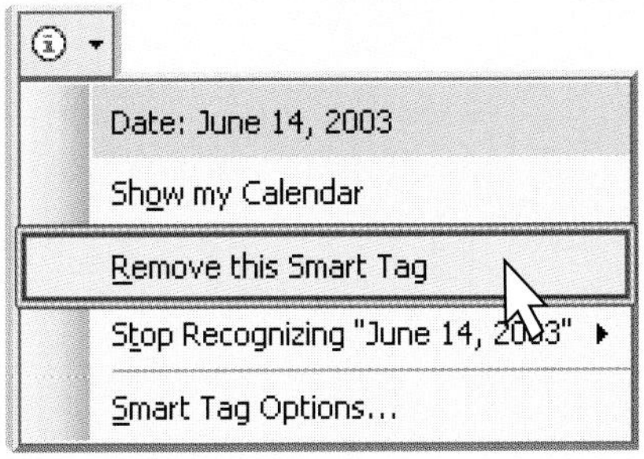

Tip

What types of information can Word label with smart tags?

Word can label people's names, dates, times, addresses, places and telephone numbers with smart tags. Word can also label e-mail addresses of people to whom you sent messages using Microsoft Office Outlook and financial symbols you type in capital letters, such as MSFT.

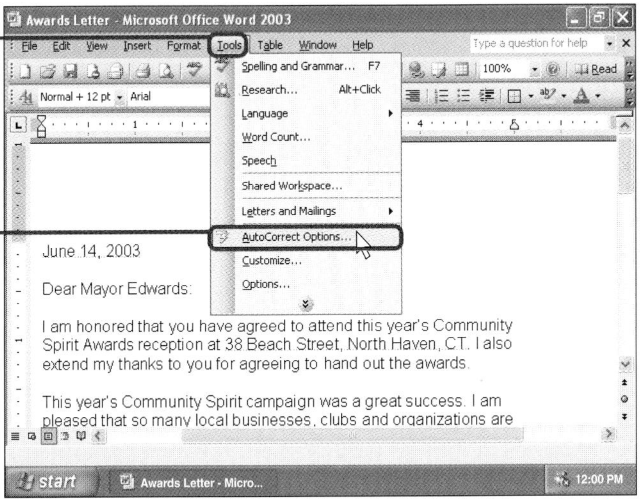

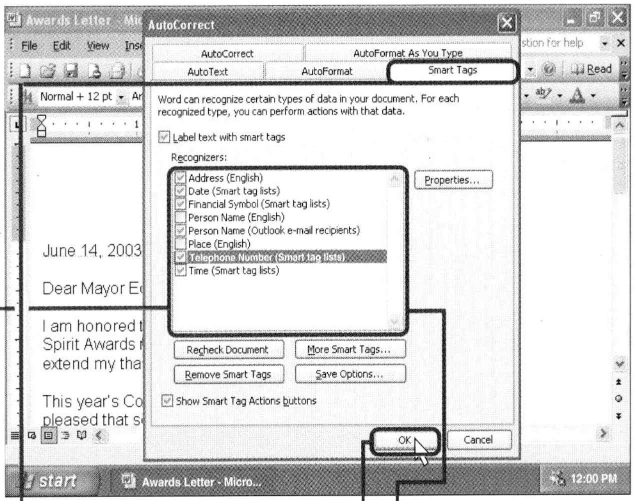

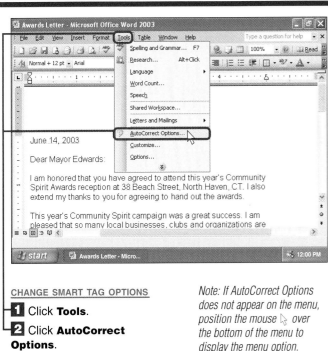

CHANGE SMART TAG OPTIONS

1 Click **Tools**.

2 Click **AutoCorrect Options**.

Note: If AutoCorrect Options does not appear on the menu, position the mouse over the bottom of the menu to display the menu option.

■ The AutoCorrect dialog box appears.

3 Click the **Smart Tags** tab to display the smart tag options.

■ This area displays the types of information Word can label as smart tags. Smart tags are currently turned on for each type of information that displays a check mark (✓).

4 You can click the check box beside a type of information to turn smart tags on (☑) or off (☐) for the information.

5 Click **OK** to confirm your changes.

ADD A CLIP ART IMAGE

You can add professionally designed clip art images to your document. Clip art images can help illustrate concepts and make your document more interesting.

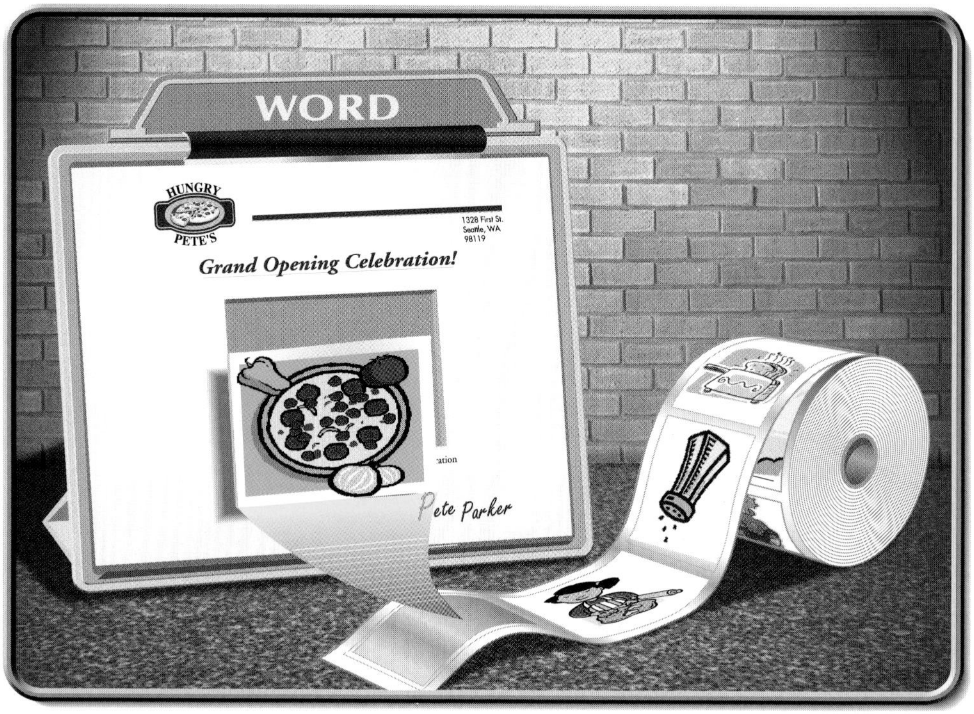

ADD A CLIP ART IMAGE

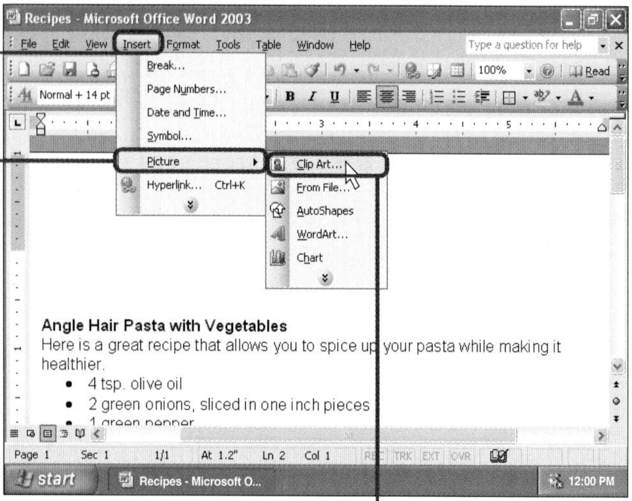

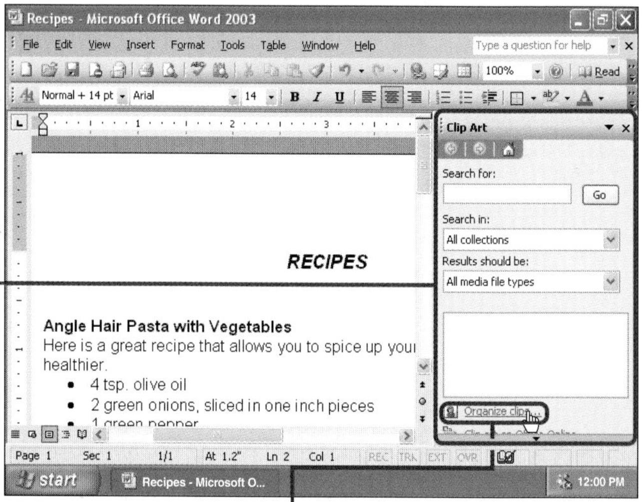

1 Click **Insert**.

2 Click **Picture**.

3 Click **Clip Art**.

■ The Clip Art task pane appears.

4 Click **Organize clips** to view all the available clip art images in the Microsoft Clip Organizer.

*Note: The first time you add a clip art image to a document, the Add Clips to Organizer dialog box appears. To catalog the clip art images and other media files on your computer, click **Now** in the dialog box.*

Tip

In the Microsoft Clip Organizer, what type of clip art images will I find in each collection?

My Collections

Displays images that came with Microsoft Windows and images you created or obtained on your own.

Office Collections

Displays the images that came with Microsoft Office.

Web Collections

Displays the images that are available at Microsoft's Web site and at Web sites in partnership with Microsoft.

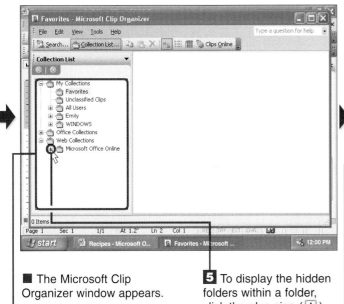

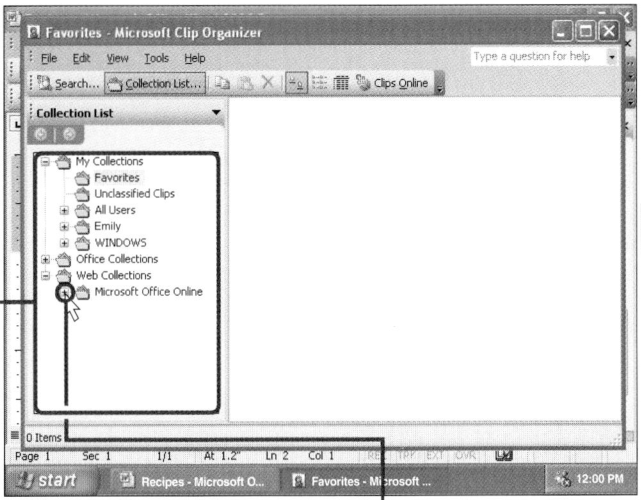

■ The Microsoft Clip Organizer window appears.

■ This area displays the folders that contain the clip art images you can add to your document. A folder displaying a plus sign (+) contains hidden folders.

5 To display the hidden folders within a folder, click the plus sign (+) beside the folder (+ changes to −).

Note: You must be connected to the Internet to view the contents of the Web Collections folder.

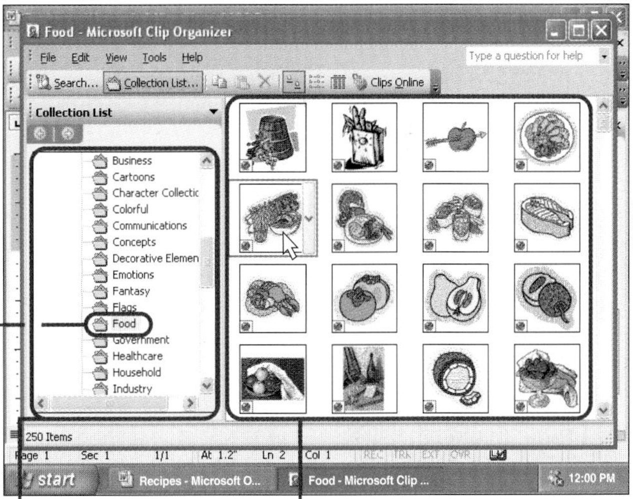

■ The hidden folders appear.

6 Click a folder of interest.

■ This area displays the clip art images in the folder you selected.

7 Click the clip art image you want to add to your document.

CONTINUED

After you locate an image you want to add to your document, you can copy the image to the clipboard and then place the image in your document.

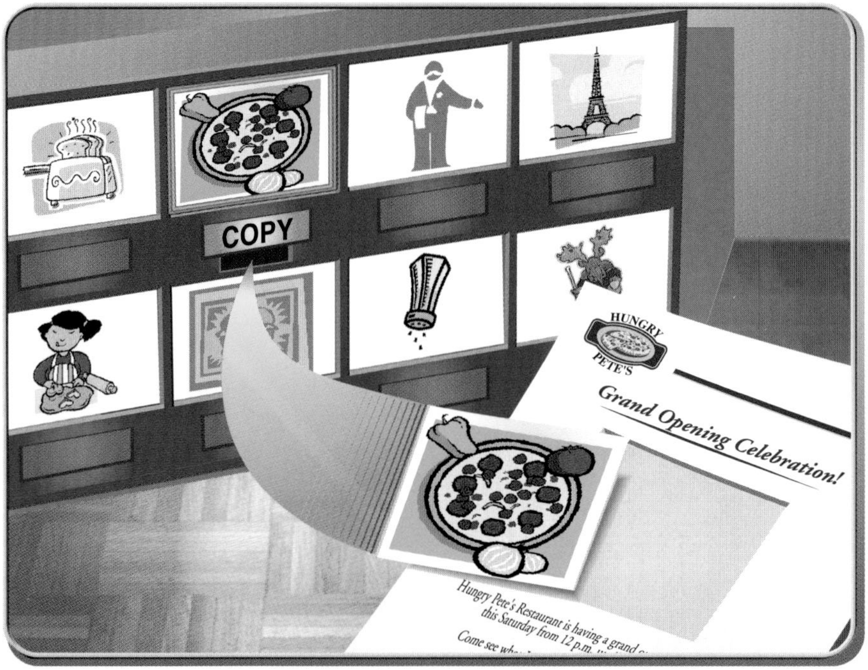

The clipboard temporarily stores information you have selected to move or copy.

ADD A CLIP ART IMAGE (CONTINUED)

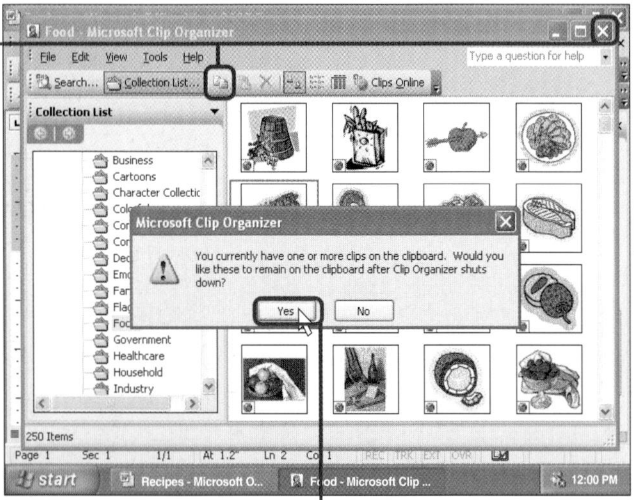

8 Click [copy icon] to copy the image you selected to the clipboard.

9 Click [close icon] to close the Microsoft Clip Organizer.

■ A dialog box appears, stating that you have one or more clip art images on the clipboard.

10 Click **Yes** to continue.

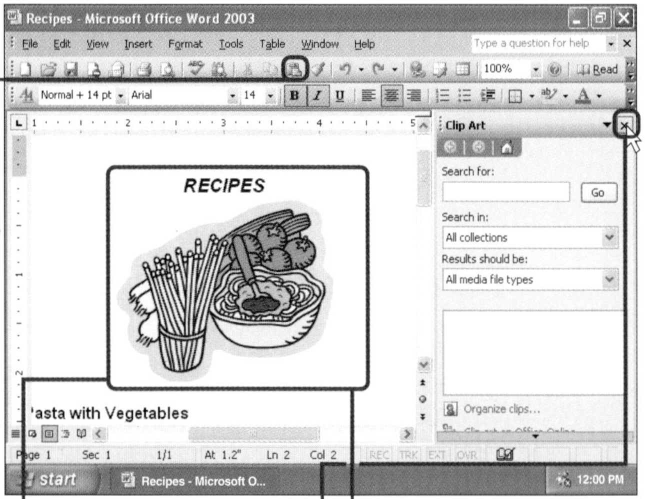

11 Click the location in your document where you want to add the image.

12 Click [paste icon] to place the image in your document.

■ The image appears in your document.

13 To close the Clip Art task pane, click [close icon].

Tip

How do I resize a clip art image?

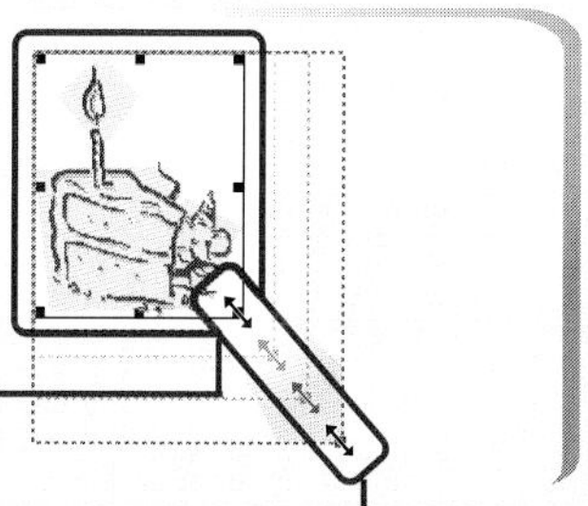

1 Click the image you want to resize. Handles (■) appear around the image.

2 Position the mouse over one of the handles (pointer changes to ↖, ↗, ↕ or ↔).

3 Drag the handle until the image is the size you want.

■ A dashed line shows the new size.

Tip

How do I delete a clip art image?

Click the clip art image you want to delete. Handles (■) appear around the image. Press the **Delete** key to delete the image.

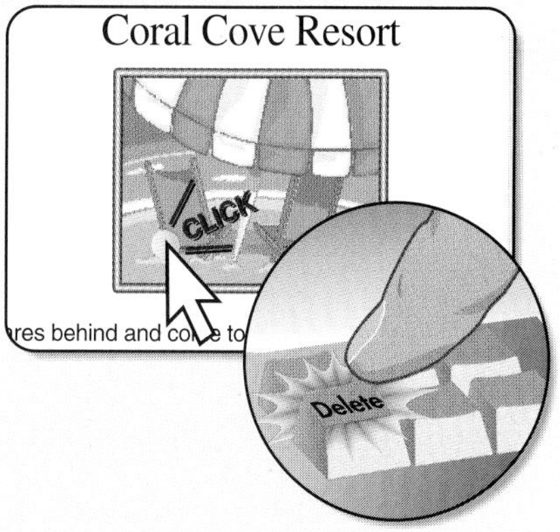

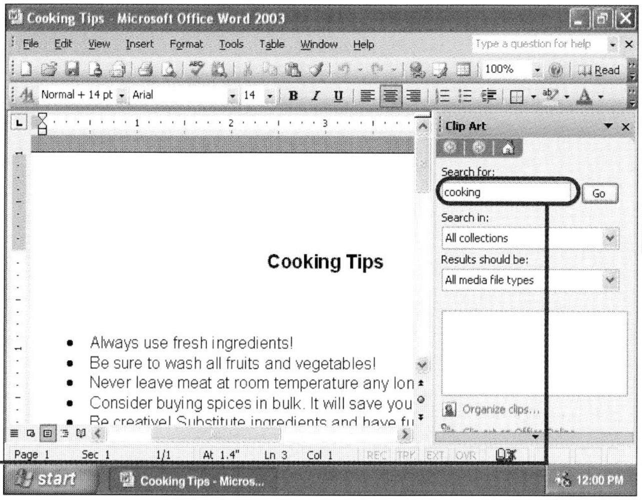

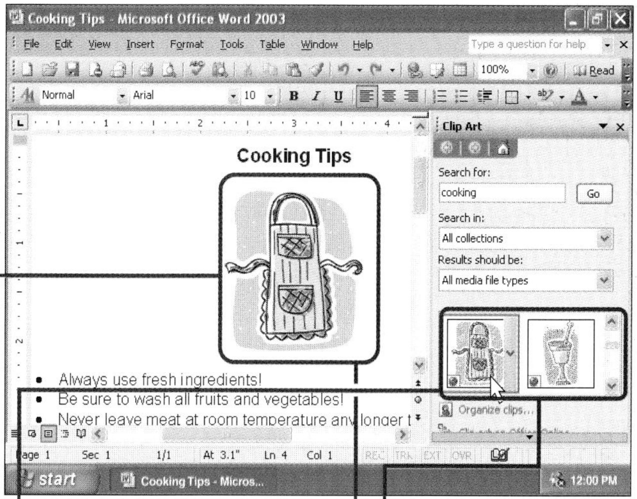

SEARCH FOR CLIP ART IMAGES

You can search for clip art images by specifying one or more words of interest in the Clip Art task pane.

1 Double-click this area and type one or more words that describe the image you want to find. Then press the **Enter** key.

*Note: To display the Clip Art task pane, perform steps **1** to **3** on page 58.*

■ Clip art images that match the words you specified appear in this area.

2 Click the location in your document where you want to add an image.

3 Click the image you want to add to your document.

■ The image appears in your document.

CHANGE FONT OF TEXT

You can change the font of text to enhance the appearance of your document.

CHANGE FONT OF TEXT

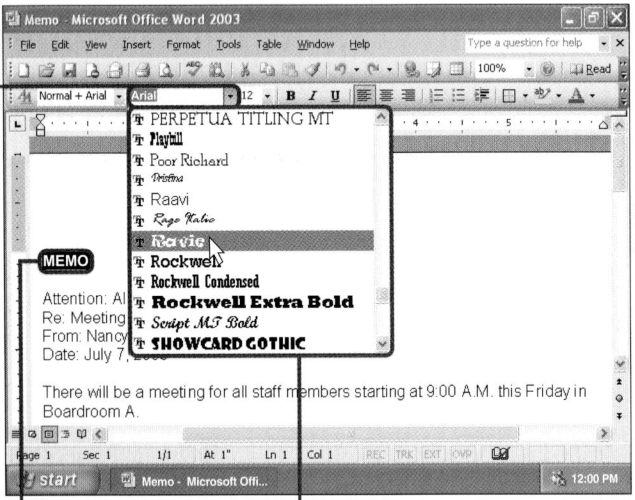

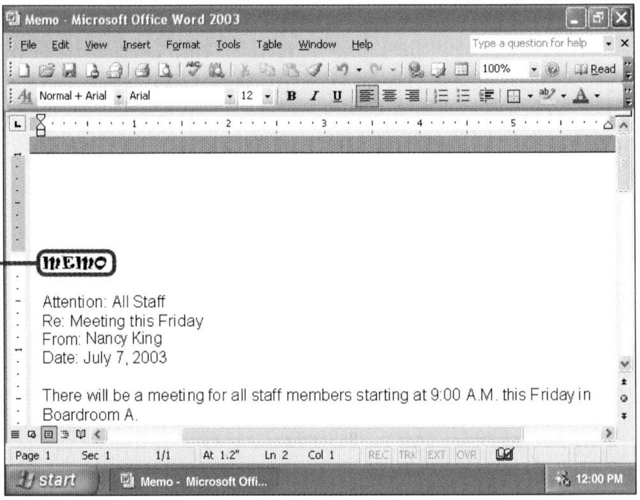

1 Select the text you want to change to a different font. To select text, see page 20.

2 Click ▾ in this area to display a list of the available fonts.

Note: If the Font area is not displayed, click ⁝ on the Formatting toolbar to display the area.

3 Click the font you want to use.

Note: Word displays the fonts you have most recently used at the top of the list.

■ The text you selected changes to the new font.

■ To deselect text, click outside the selected area.

CHANGE SIZE OF TEXT

You can increase or decrease the size of text in your document.

Larger text is easier to read, but smaller text allows you to fit more information on a page.

CHANGE SIZE OF TEXT

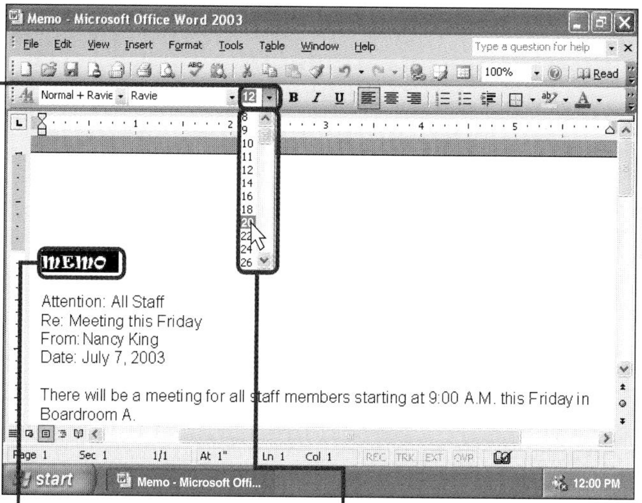

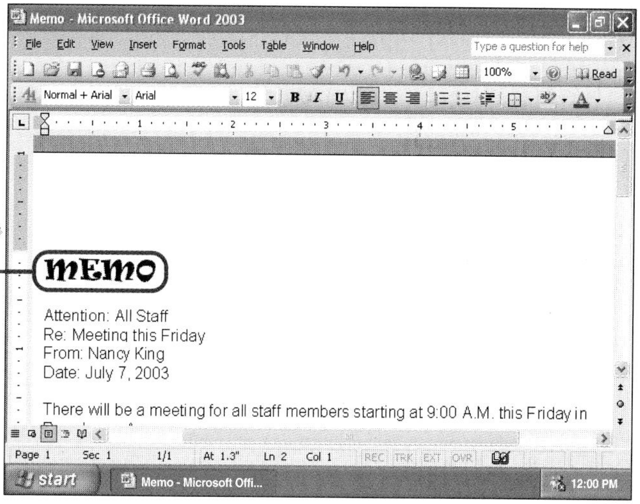

1 Select the text you want to change to a new size. To select text, see page 20.

2 Click ▾ in this area to display a list of the available sizes.

Note: If the Font Size area is not displayed, click ⁝ on the Formatting toolbar to display the area.

3 Click the size you want to use.

■ The text you selected changes to the new size.

■ To deselect text, click outside the selected area.

CHANGE TEXT COLOR

You can change the color of text to draw attention to headings or important information in your document.

Keep in mind that when you print a document that contains colored text on a black-and-white printer, the colored text will appear in shades of gray.

CHANGE TEXT COLOR

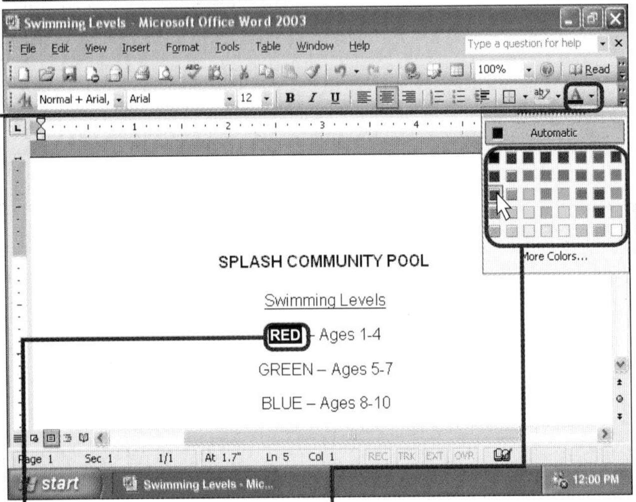

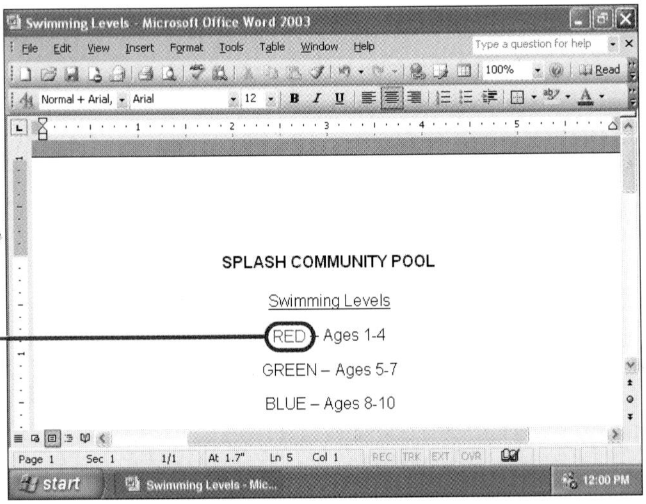

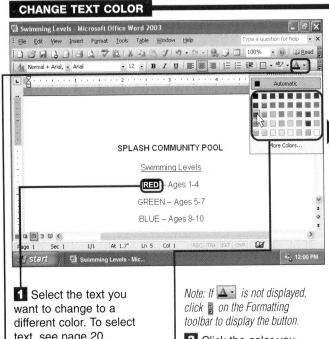

1 Select the text you want to change to a different color. To select text, see page 20.

2 Click in this area to display the available colors.

Note: If is not displayed, click on the Formatting toolbar to display the button.

3 Click the color you want to use.

■ The text you selected appears in the new color.

■ To deselect text, click outside the selected area.

■ To return text to its original color, repeat steps **1** to **3**, selecting **Automatic** in step **3**.

HIGHLIGHT TEXT

You can highlight text that you want to stand out in your document. Highlighting text is useful for marking information you want to review or verify later.

If you plan to print your document on a black-and-white printer, use a light highlight color so you will be able to easily read the printed text.

HIGHLIGHT TEXT

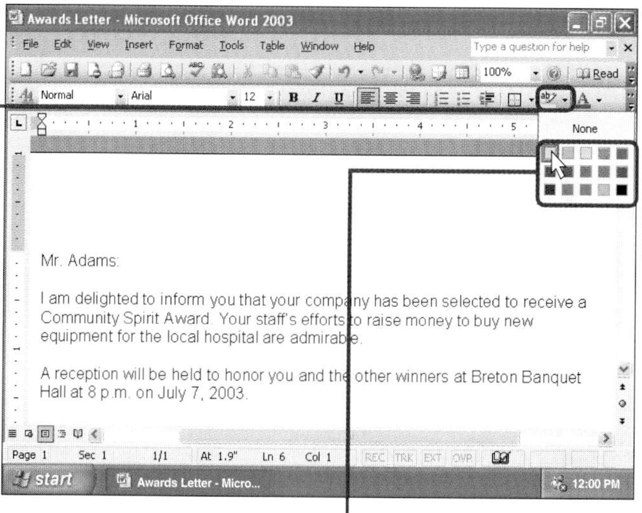

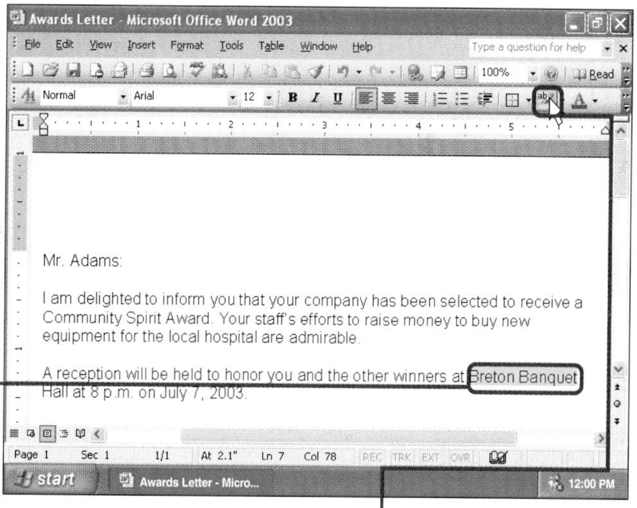

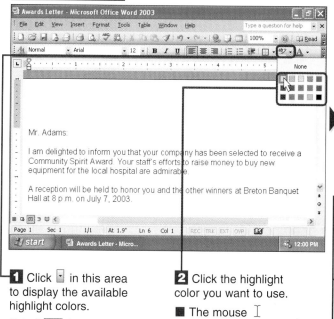

1 Click ▾ in this area to display the available highlight colors.

Note: If ab▾ *is not displayed, click* ⁝ *on the Formatting toolbar to display the button.*

2 Click the highlight color you want to use.

■ The mouse I changes to ✎ when over your document.

3 Select each area of text you want to highlight. To select text, see page 20.

■ The text you select appears highlighted.

4 When you finish highlighting text, click ab or press the Esc key.

■ To remove a highlight from text, repeat steps **1** to **4**, selecting **None** in step **2**.

BOLD, ITALICIZE OR UNDERLINE TEXT

You can bold, italicize or underline text to emphasize information in your document.

You can use one feature at a time or any combination of the three features to change the style of text.

BOLD, ITALICIZE OR UNDERLINE TEXT

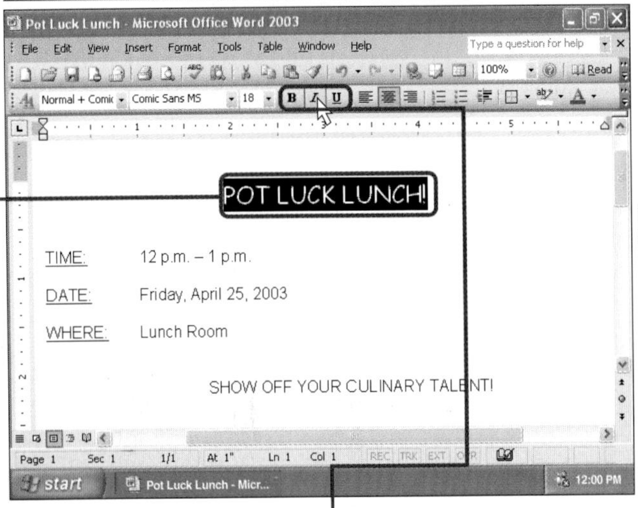

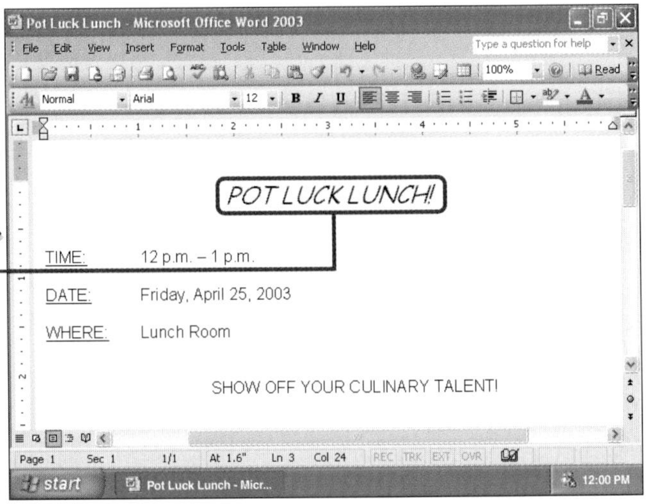

1 Select the text you want to bold, italicize or underline. To select text, see page 20.

2 Click one of the following buttons.

- **B** Bold
- *I* Italic
- U Underline

Note: If the button you want is not displayed, click on the Formatting toolbar to display the button.

■ The text you selected appears in the new style.

■ To deselect text, click outside the selected area.

■ To remove a bold, italic or underline style, repeat steps **1** and **2**.

COPY FORMATTING

You can copy the formatting of text to make one area of text in your document look exactly like another.

You may want to copy the formatting of text to make all the headings or important words in your document look the same. This will give the text in your document a consistent appearance.

COPY FORMATTING

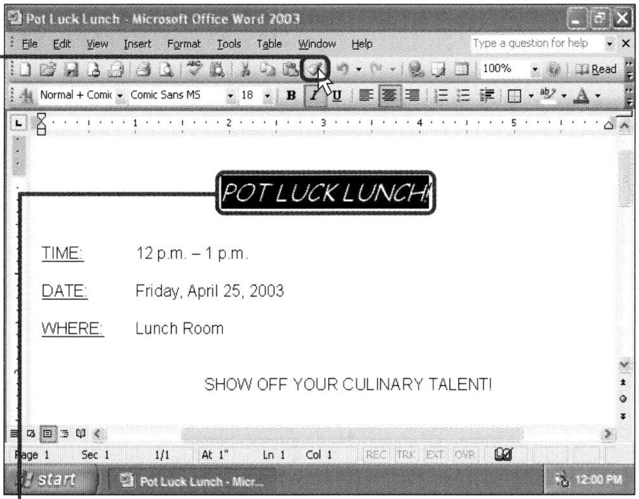

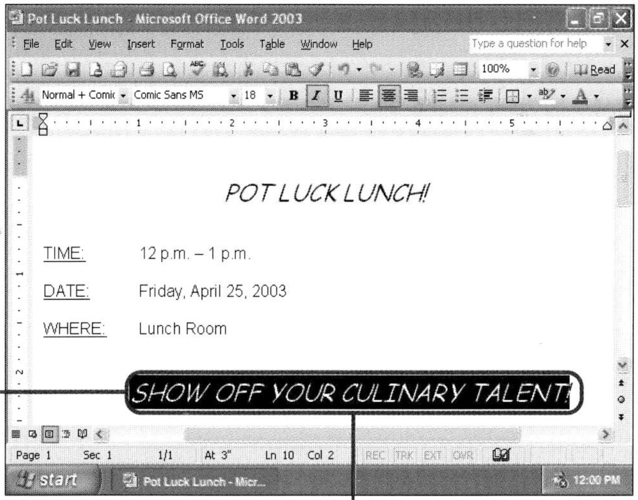

1 Select the text that displays the formatting you want to copy. To select text, see page 20.

2 Click the Format Painter button to copy the formatting of the text.

Note: If the Format Painter button is not displayed, click the Toolbar Options button on the Standard toolbar to display the button.

■ The mouse I changes to the Format Painter pointer when over your document.

3 Select the text you want to display the same formatting.

■ The text you selected displays the formatting.

■ To deselect text, click outside the selected area.

CREATE A BULLETED OR NUMBERED LIST

You can separate items in a list by beginning each item with a bullet or number.

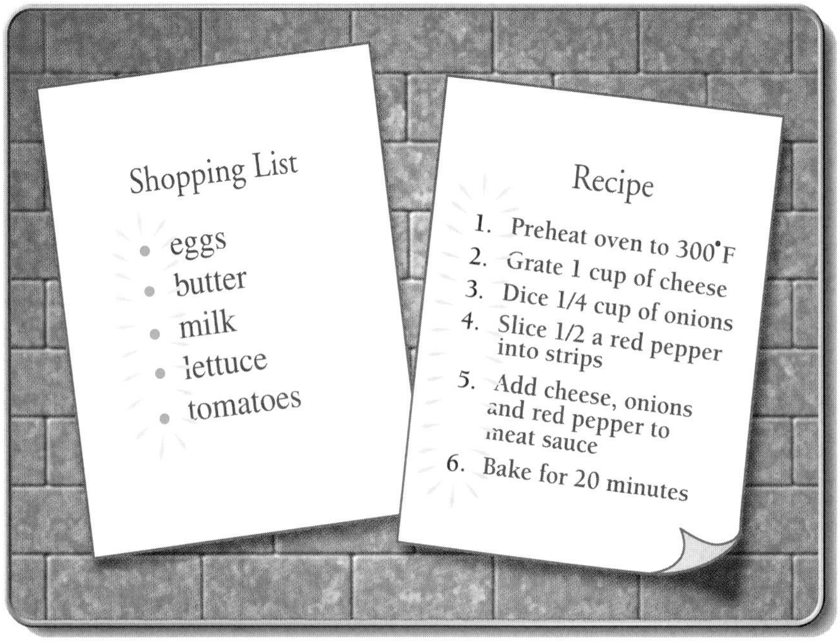

Bulleted lists are useful for items in no particular order, such as items in a shopping list.

Numbered lists are useful for items in a specific order, such as instructions in a recipe.

CREATE A BULLETED OR NUMBERED LIST

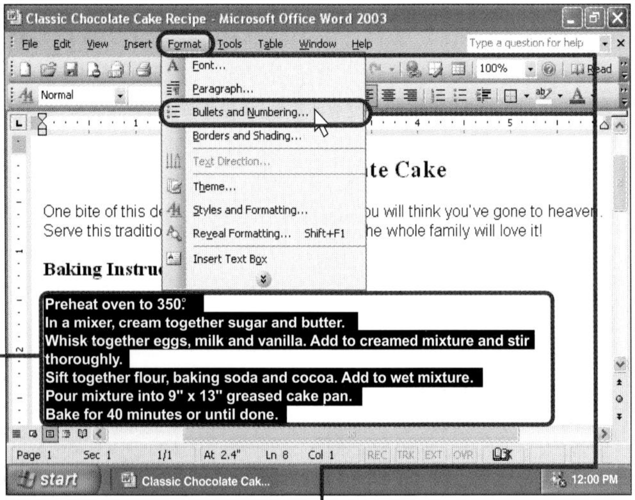

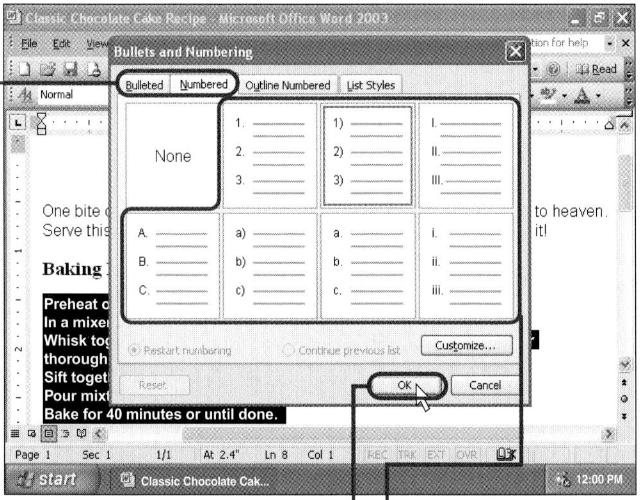

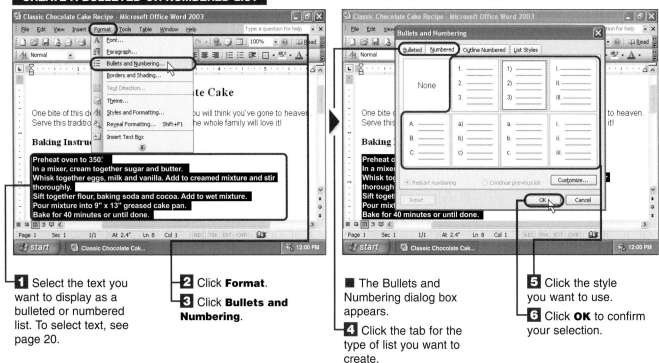

1 Select the text you want to display as a bulleted or numbered list. To select text, see page 20.

2 Click **Format**.

3 Click **Bullets and Numbering**.

■ The Bullets and Numbering dialog box appears.

4 Click the tab for the type of list you want to create.

5 Click the style you want to use.

6 Click **OK** to confirm your selection.

Tip

How can I create a bulleted or numbered list as I type?

1 Type * to create a bulleted list or type **1.** to create a numbered list. Then press the Spacebar .

2 Type the first item in the list and then press the Enter key. Word automatically adds a bullet or number for the next item.

3 Repeat step **2** for each item in the list.

4 To finish the list, press the Enter key twice.

Note: When you create a bulleted or numbered list as you type, the AutoCorrect Options button ( ) appears. You can click this button and select ***Undo Automatic Bullets/Numbering*** *to specify that you do not want Word to create a bulleted or numbered list in this instance.*

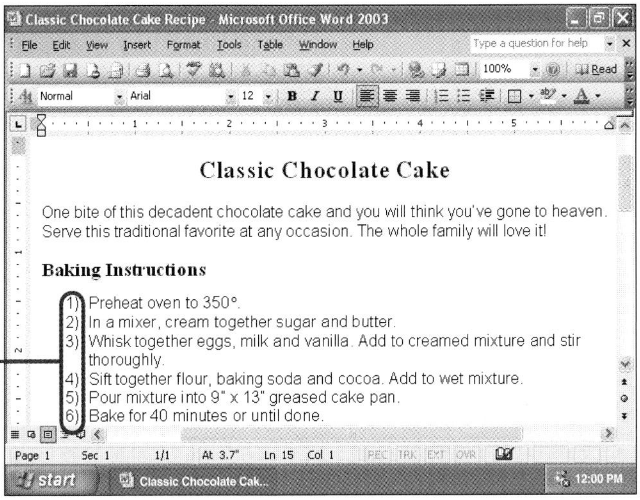

■ A bullet or number appears in front of each item in the list.

■ To deselect the text in the list, click outside the selected area.

■ To remove bullets or numbers from a list, repeat steps **1** to **6**, selecting **None** in step **5**.

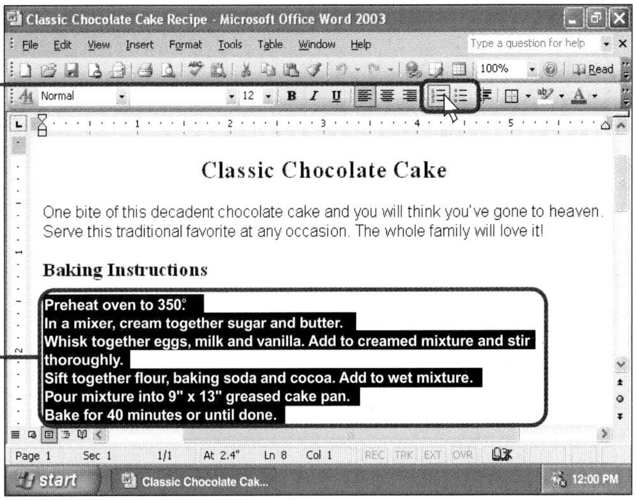

USING THE TOOLBAR BUTTONS

1 Select the text you want to display as a list. To select text, see page 20.

2 Click one of the following buttons.

Add numbers

Add bullets

Note: If the button you want is not displayed, click on the Formatting toolbar to display the button.

CHANGE ALIGNMENT OF TEXT

You can enhance the appearance of your document by aligning text in different ways.

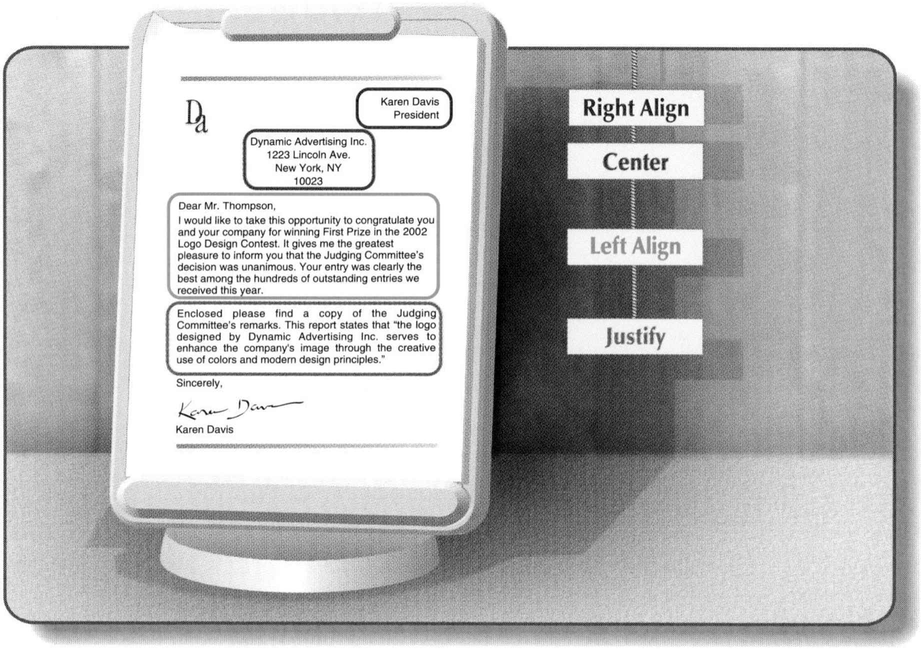

By default, Word aligns text along the left margin.

CHANGE ALIGNMENT OF TEXT

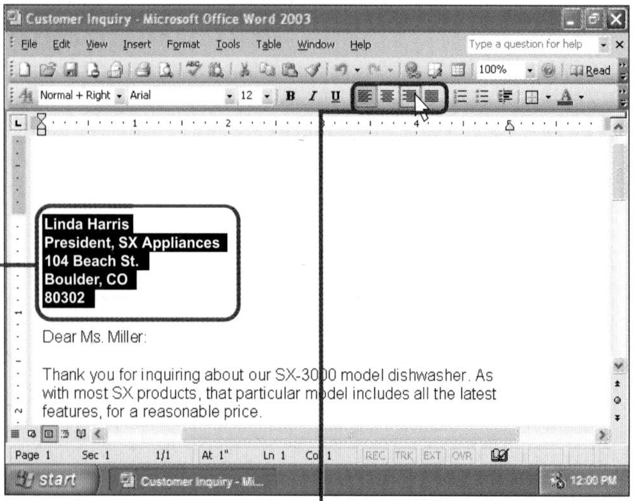

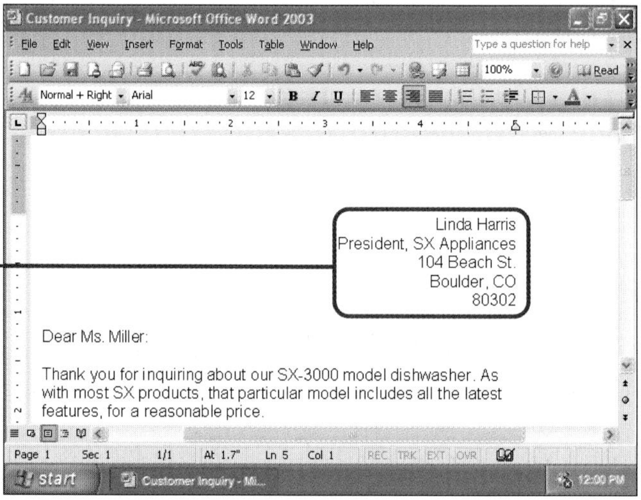

1 Select the text you want to align differently. To select text, see page 20.

2 Click one of the following buttons.

- Left align
- Center
- Right align
- Justify

Note: If the button you want is not displayed, click on the Formatting toolbar to display the button.

■ The text displays the new alignment.

■ To deselect text, click outside the selected area.

CHANGE LINE SPACING

You can change the amount of space between the lines of text in your document.

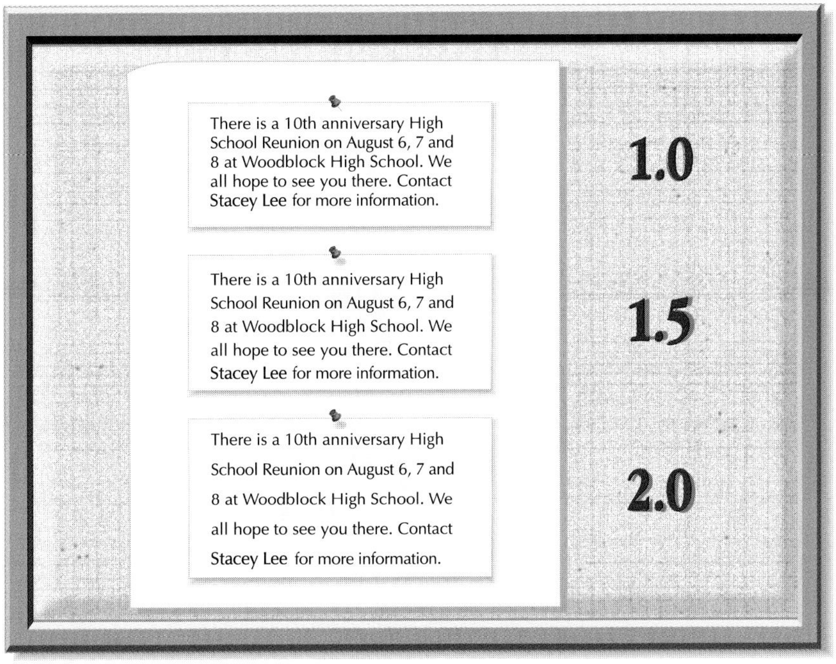

Changing the line spacing can make a document easier to review and edit.

CHANGE LINE SPACING

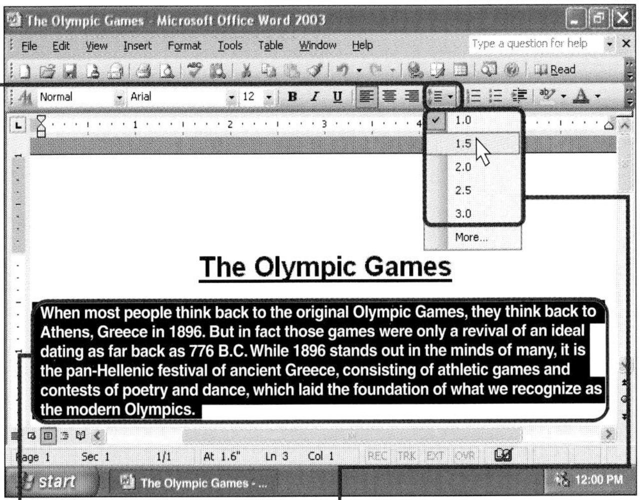

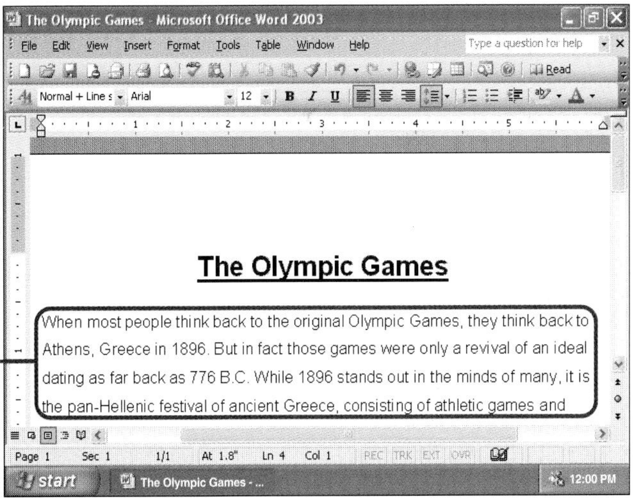

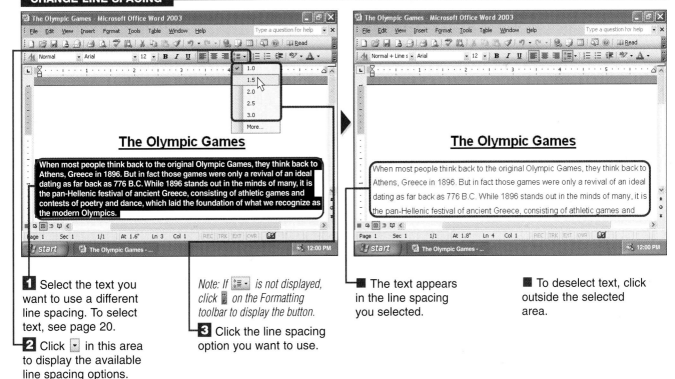

1 Select the text you want to use a different line spacing. To select text, see page 20.

2 Click ▾ in this area to display the available line spacing options.

Note: If the line spacing button is not displayed, click the toolbar options button on the Formatting toolbar to display the button.

3 Click the line spacing option you want to use.

■ The text appears in the line spacing you selected.

■ To deselect text, click outside the selected area.

INDENT PARAGRAPHS

You can indent text to make paragraphs in your document stand out.

INDENT PARAGRAPHS

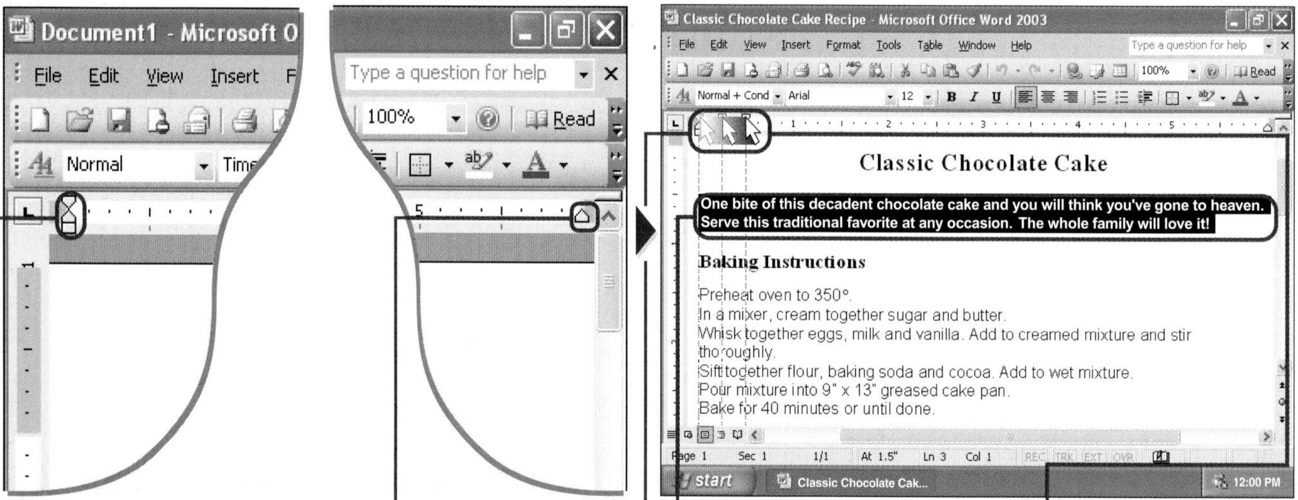

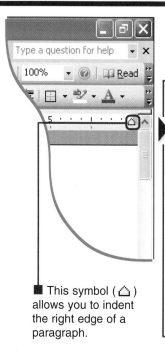

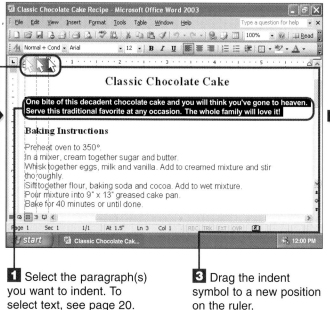

■ These symbols allow you to indent the left edge of a paragraph.

▽ Indent first line

△ Indent all but the first line

☐ Indent all lines

■ This symbol (△) allows you to indent the right edge of a paragraph.

1 Select the paragraph(s) you want to indent. To select text, see page 20.

2 Position the mouse ↖ over the indent symbol you want to use.

3 Drag the indent symbol to a new position on the ruler.

■ A dotted line shows the new indent position.

Tip

What types of indents can I create?

First Line Indent

Indents only the first line of a paragraph. First line indents are often used to mark the beginning of paragraphs in letters and professional documents.

Hanging Indent

Indents all but the first line of a paragraph. Hanging indents are useful when you are creating a glossary or bibliography.

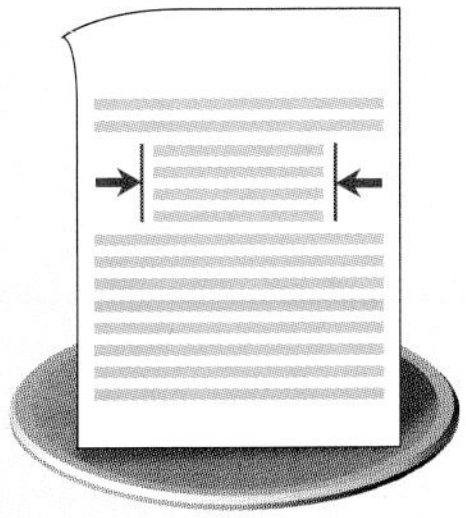

Indent Both Sides

Indenting both the left and right sides of a paragraph is useful when you want to set text, such as a quotation, apart from the rest of the text in your document.

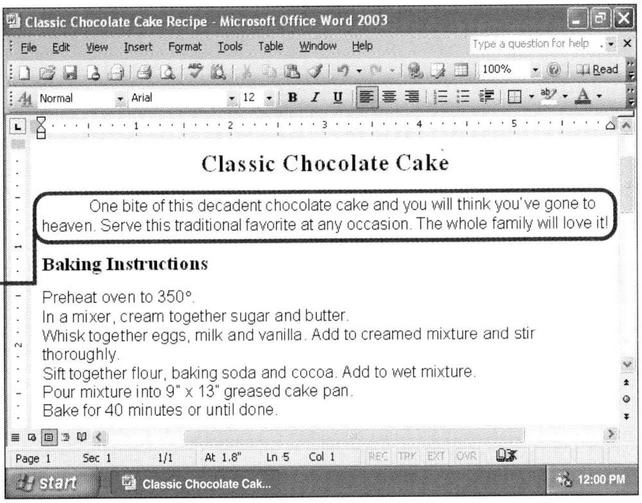

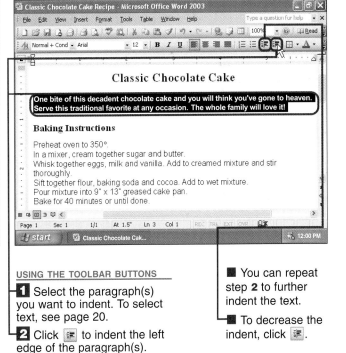

■ Word indents the paragraph(s) you selected.

■ To deselect text, click outside the selected area.

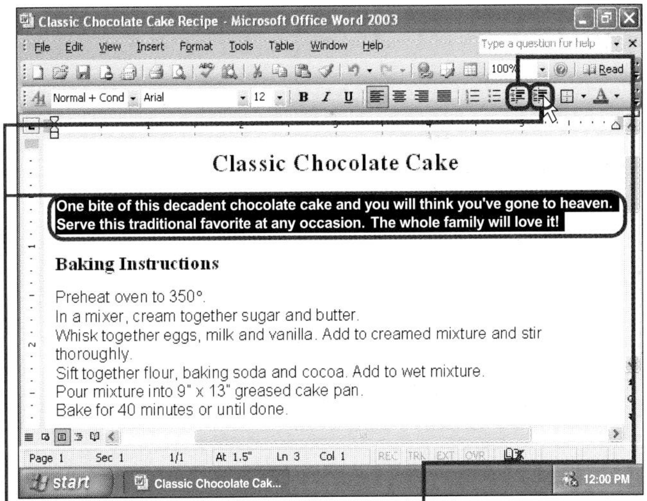

USING THE TOOLBAR BUTTONS

1 Select the paragraph(s) you want to indent. To select text, see page 20.

2 Click [icon] to indent the left edge of the paragraph(s).

Note: If [icon] is not displayed, click [icon] on the Formatting toolbar to display the button.

■ You can repeat step **2** to further indent the text.

■ To decrease the indent, click [icon].

You can use tabs to line up information in your document. Word offers several types of tabs that you can choose from.

Word automatically places a tab every 0.5 inches across a page.

You should use tabs instead of spaces to line up information. If you use spaces, the information may not be lined up when you print your document.

CHANGE TAB SETTINGS

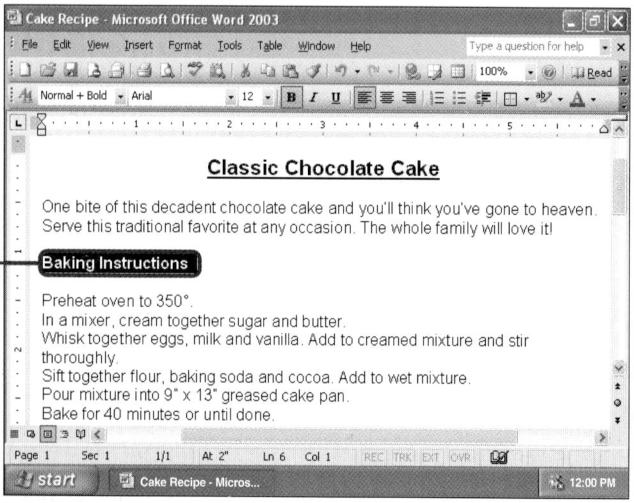

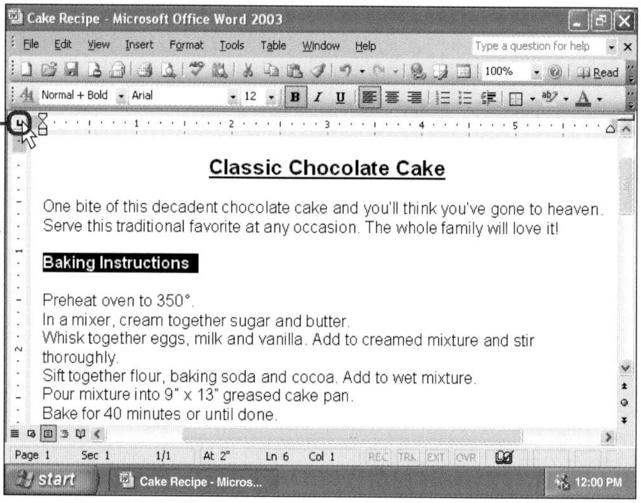

ADD A TAB

1 Select the text you want to use the new tab. To select text, see page 20.

■ To add a tab to text you are about to type, click the location in your document where you want to type the text.

2 Click this area until the type of tab you want to add appears.

- Left tab
- Center tab
- Right tab
- Decimal tab

Tip

How do I move a tab?

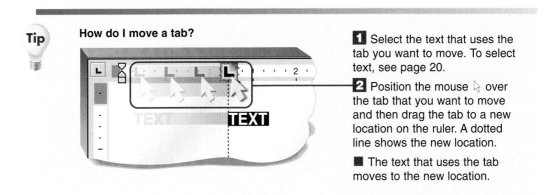

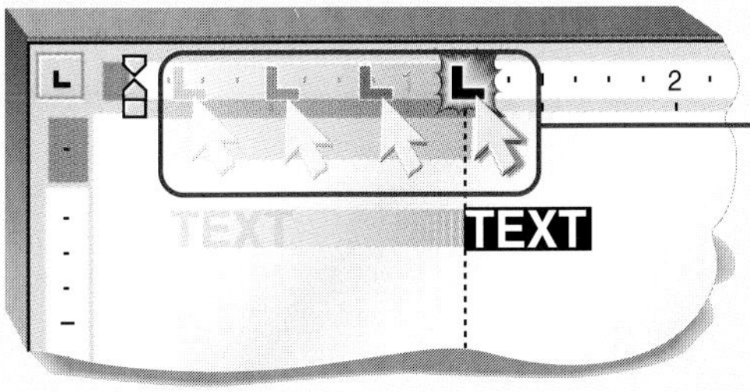

1 Select the text that uses the tab you want to move. To select text, see page 20.

2 Position the mouse over the tab that you want to move and then drag the tab to a new location on the ruler. A dotted line shows the new location.

■ The text that uses the tab moves to the new location.

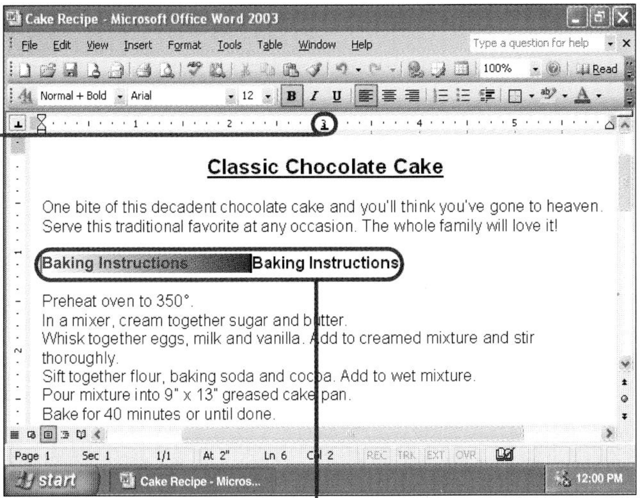

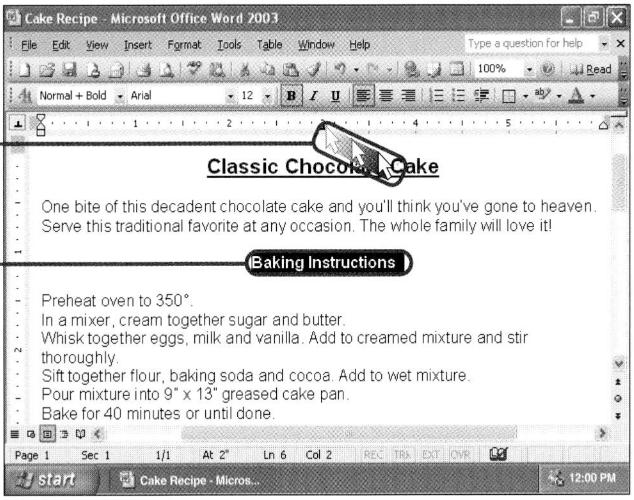

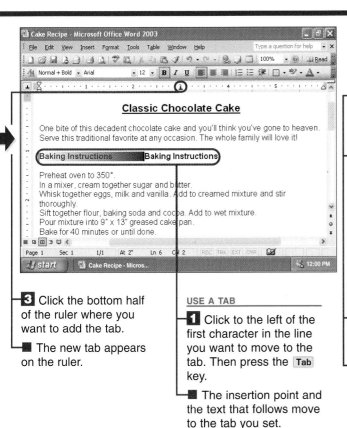

3 Click the bottom half of the ruler where you want to add the tab.

■ The new tab appears on the ruler.

USE A TAB

1 Click to the left of the first character in the line you want to move to the tab. Then press the Tab key.

■ The insertion point and the text that follows move to the tab you set.

REMOVE A TAB

1 Select the text that uses the tab you want to remove. To select text, see page 20.

2 Position the mouse over the tab you want to remove and then drag the tab downward off the ruler.

■ The tab disappears from the ruler.

■ To move the text back to the left margin, click to the left of the first character. Then press the ←Backspace key.

CREATE A TABLE

You can create a table to neatly display information in your document.

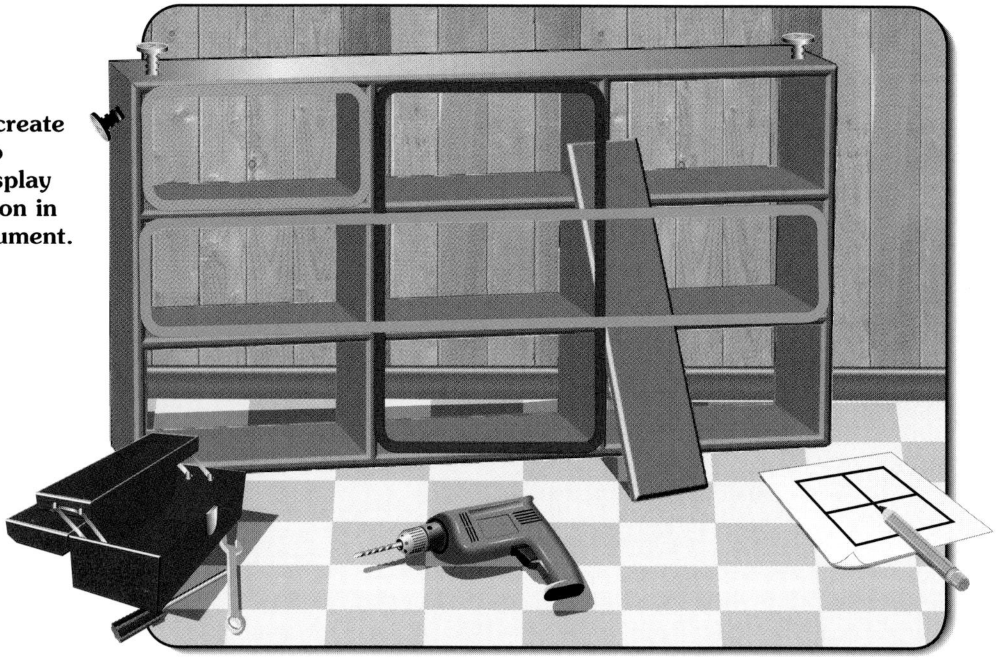

A table consists of rows, columns and cells.

Row

Column

Cell

CREATE A TABLE

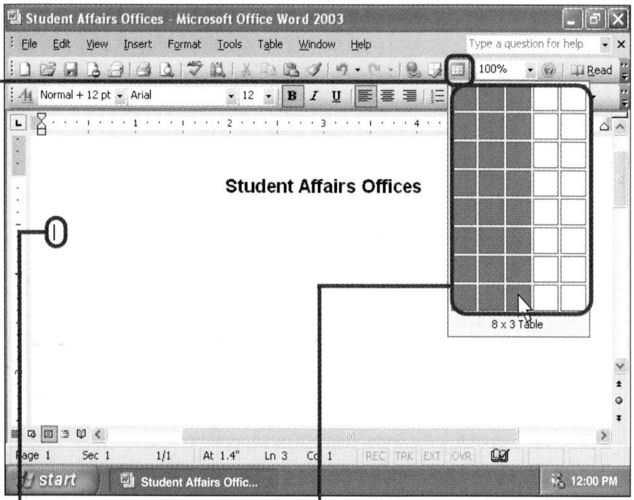

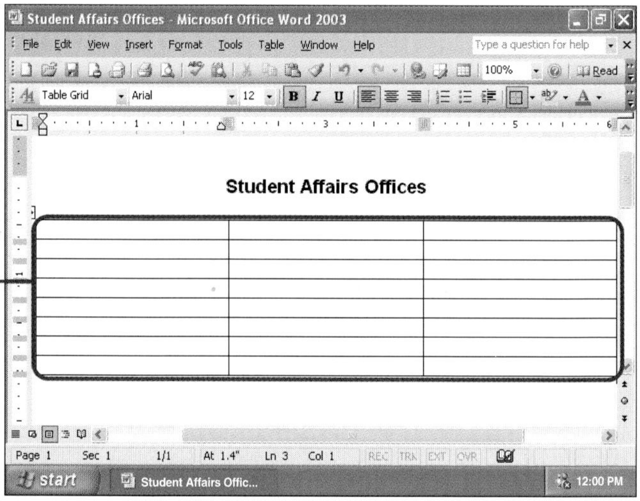

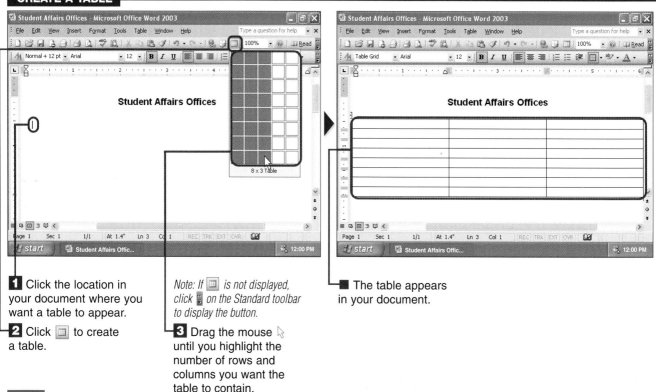

1 Click the location in your document where you want a table to appear.

2 Click to create a table.

Note: If is not displayed, click on the Standard toolbar to display the button.

3 Drag the mouse until you highlight the number of rows and columns you want the table to contain.

■ The table appears in your document.

Tip

Can I change the appearance of text in a table?

Yes. You can format text in a table as you would format any text in your document. For example, you can change the font, size, color and alignment of text in a table. To format text, see pages 62 to 70.

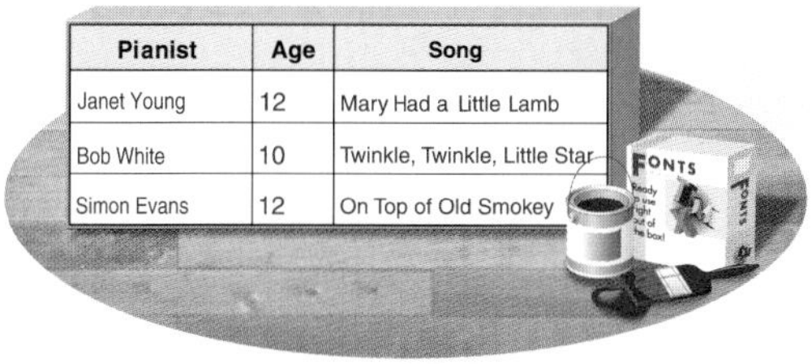
Pianist
Age
Song
Janet Young
12
Mary Had a Little Lamb
Bob White
10
Twinkle, Twinkle, Little Star
Simon Evans
12
On Top of Old Smokey
FONTS

Tip

How do I delete a table I no longer need?

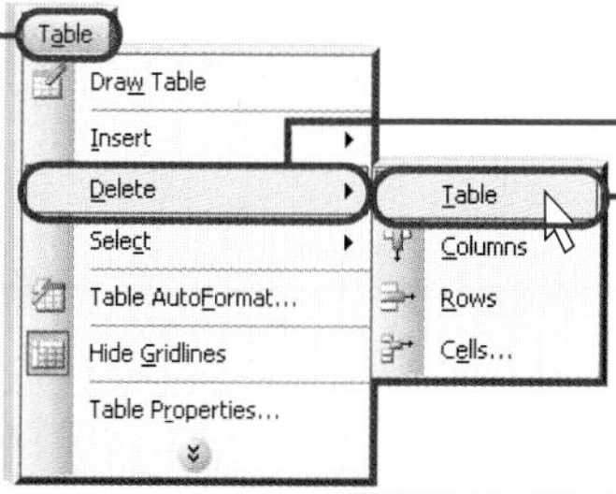

1 Click anywhere in the table you want to delete.

2 Click **Table**.

3 Click **Delete**.

4 Click **Table** to remove the table from your document.

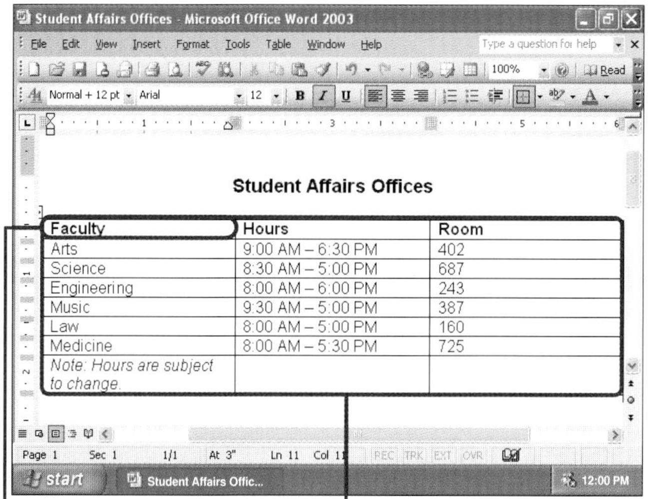

ENTER TEXT IN A TABLE

1 Click the cell in the table where you want to enter text. Then type the text.

2 Repeat step **1** until you finish entering all the text you want the table to display.

Note: When you enter text in a table, Word automatically increases the row height or column width to accommodate the text you type.

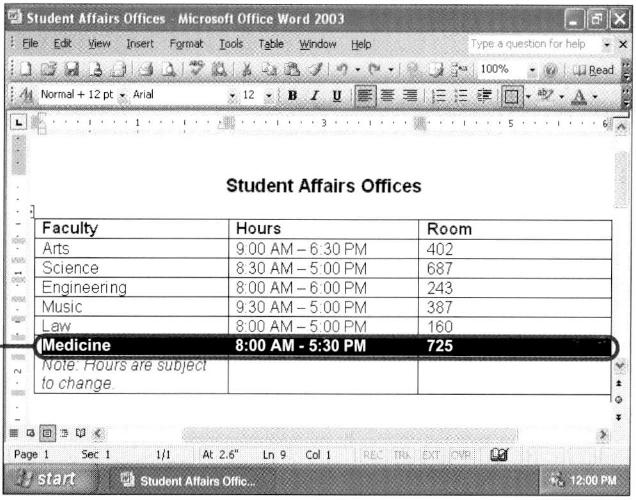

DELETE TEXT FROM A TABLE

1 Drag the mouse I over the cells displaying the text you want to delete until the cells are highlighted.

2 Press the Delete key to remove the text from the cells.

INSERT A PAGE BREAK

You can insert a page break to start a new page at a specific location in your document. A page break indicates where one page ends and another begins.

Inserting a page break is useful when you want a heading to appear at the top of a new page.

INSERT A PAGE BREAK

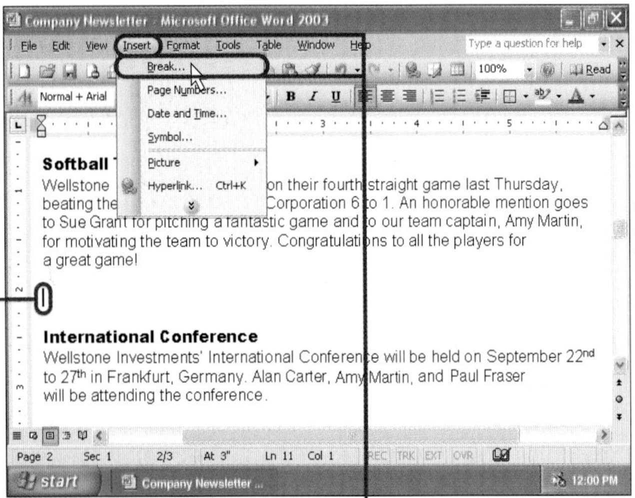

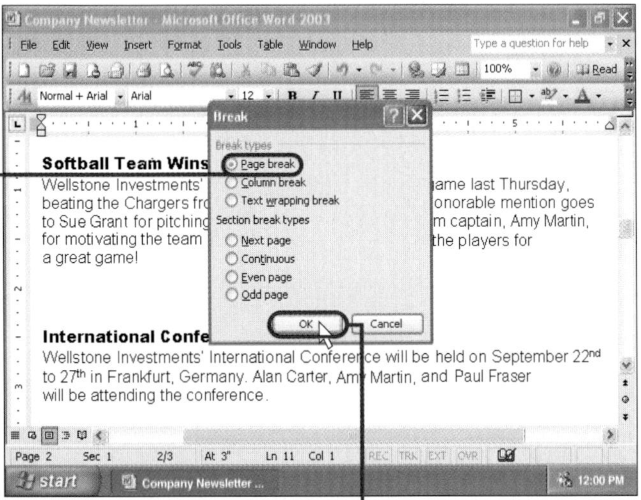

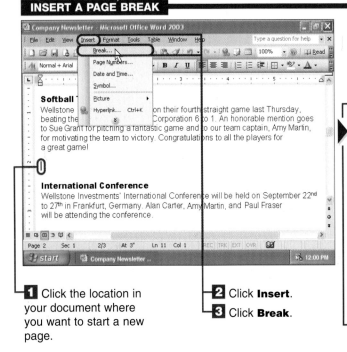

1 Click the location in your document where you want to start a new page.

2 Click **Insert**.

3 Click **Break**.

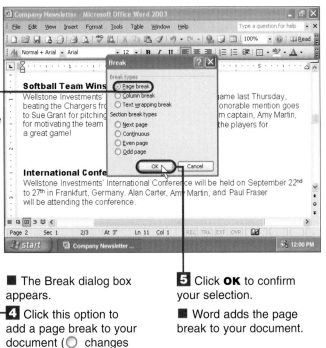

■ The Break dialog box appears.

4 Click this option to add a page break to your document (○ changes to ◉).

5 Click **OK** to confirm your selection.

■ Word adds the page break to your document.

Will Word ever insert a page break automatically?

When you fill a page with information, Word automatically starts a new page by inserting a page break to start a new page. The length of the pages in your document is determined by the paper size and margin settings you are using. For information on margins, see page 83.

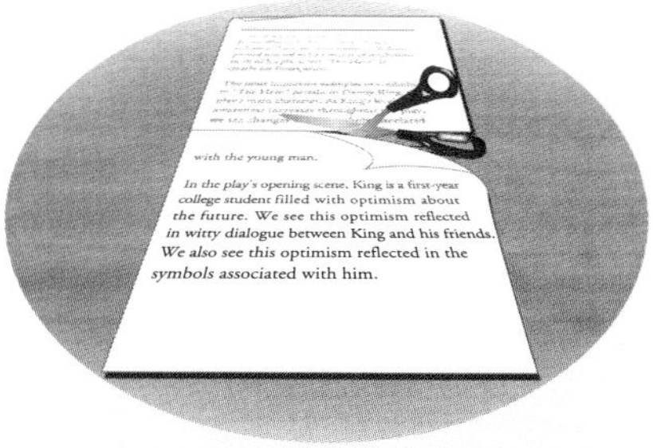

How can I quickly insert a page break?

1 Click the location in your document where you want to insert a page break.

2 Press and hold down the Ctrl key as you press the Enter key.

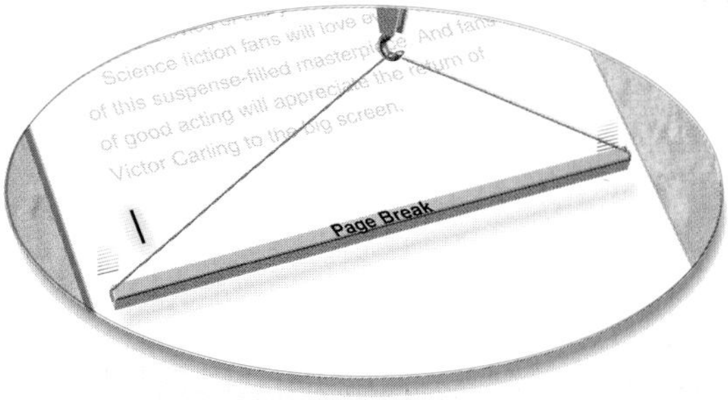

DELETE A PAGE BREAK

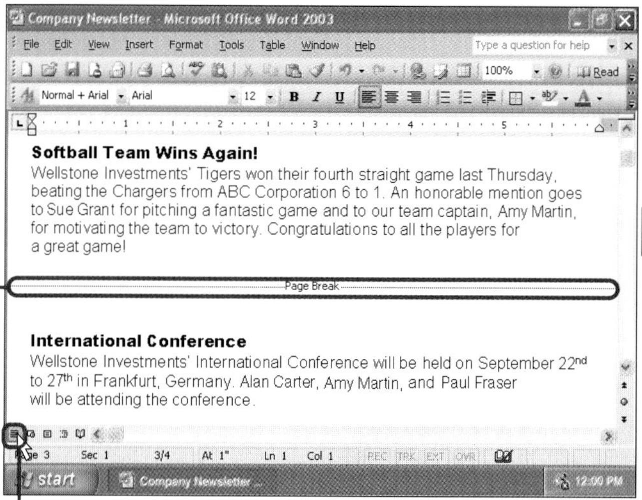

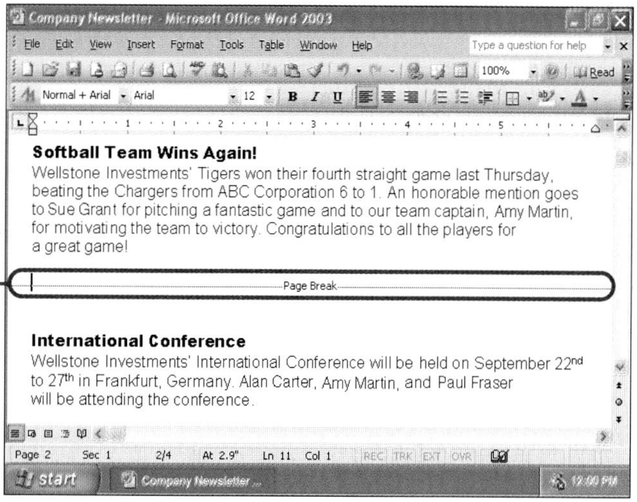

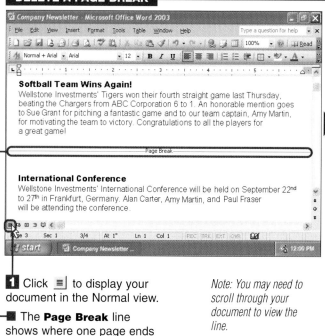

1 Click ≡ to display your document in the Normal view.

■ The **Page Break** line shows where one page ends and another begins. The line will not appear when you print your document.

Note: You may need to scroll through your document to view the line.

2 Click the **Page Break** line.

3 Press the Delete key to remove the page break.

INSERT A SECTION BREAK

You can insert section breaks to divide your document into sections.

Dividing your document into sections allows you to apply formatting to only part of your document. For example, you may want to vertically center text or change the margins for only part of your document.

INSERT A SECTION BREAK

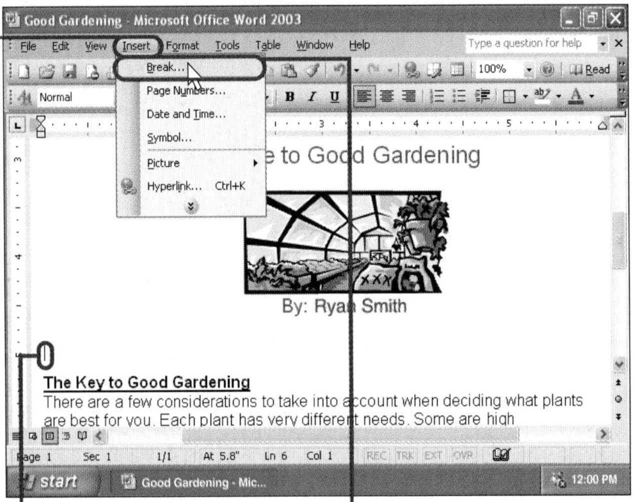

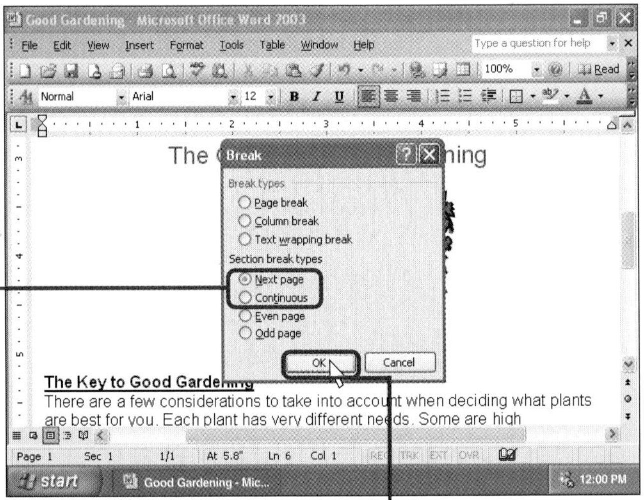

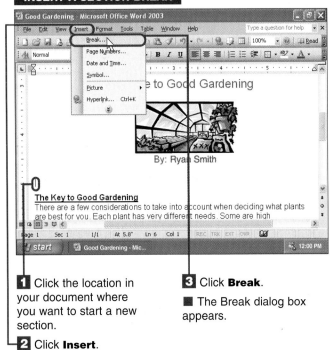

1 Click the location in your document where you want to start a new section.

2 Click **Insert**.

3 Click **Break**.

■ The Break dialog box appears.

4 Click the type of section break you want to add (○ changes to ◉).

Next page - Starts a new section on a new page.

Continuous - Starts a new section on the current page.

5 Click **OK** to confirm your selection.

■ Word adds the section break to your document.

Tip

Will the appearance of my document change when I delete a section break?

When you delete a section break, the text above the break assumes the appearance of the text below the break. For example, if you changed the margins for the text below a section break, the text above the break will also display the new margins when you delete the break.

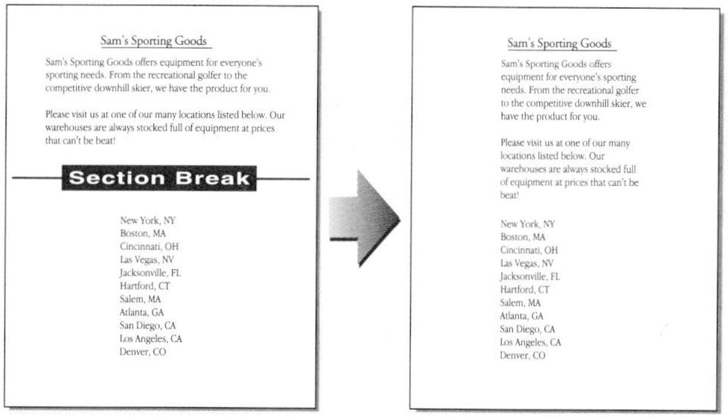

DELETE A SECTION BREAK

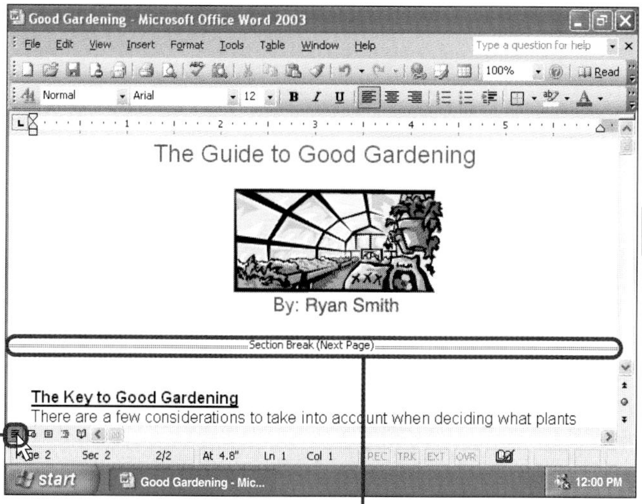

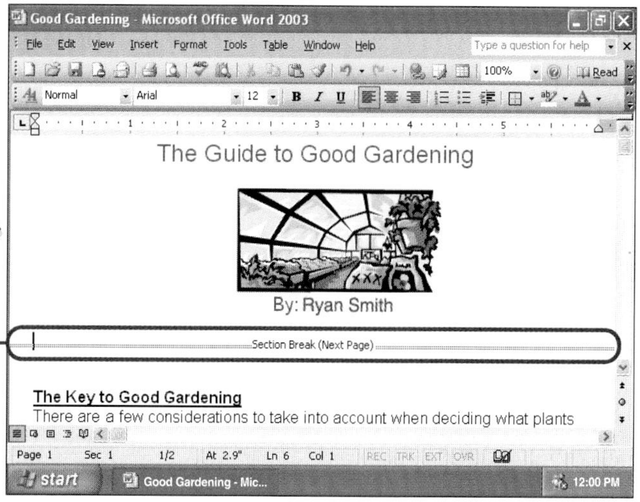

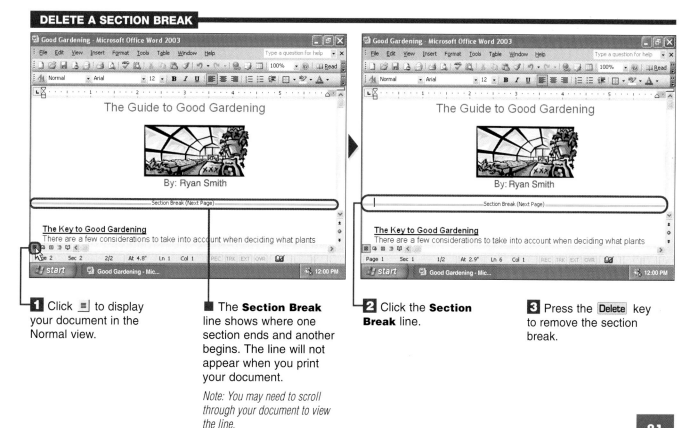

1 Click ≡ to display your document in the Normal view.

■ The **Section Break** line shows where one section ends and another begins. The line will not appear when you print your document.

Note: You may need to scroll through your document to view the line.

2 Click the **Section Break** line.

3 Press the Delete key to remove the section break.

CENTER TEXT ON A PAGE

You can vertically center the text on each page in your document. Vertically centering text is useful when creating title pages and short memos.

When you vertically center text on a page, Word centers the text between the top and bottom margins of the page. For information on margins, see page 83.

After vertically centering text, you can use the Print Preview feature to see how the centered text will appear on a printed page. For information on the Print Preview feature, see page 30.

CENTER TEXT ON A PAGE

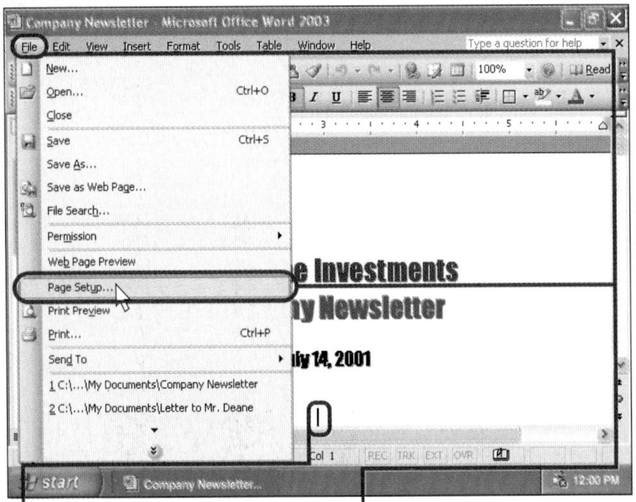

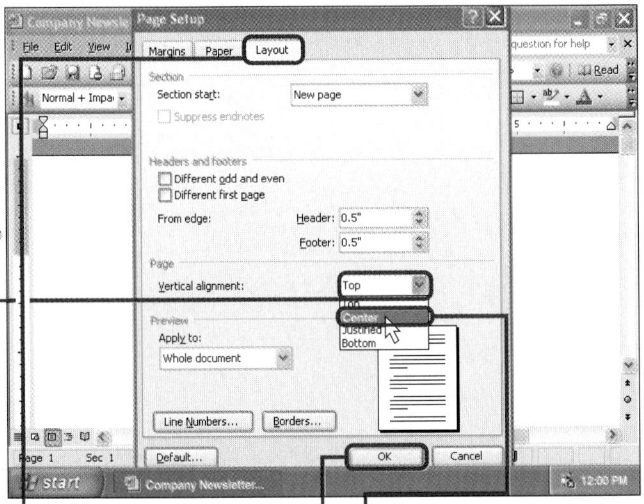

1 Click anywhere in the document or section you want to vertically center.

Note: To vertically center only some of the text in a document, you must divide the document into sections. For more information, see page 80.

2 Click **File**.

3 Click **Page Setup**.

■ The Page Setup dialog box appears.

4 Click the **Layout** tab.

5 Click this area to display the vertical alignment options.

6 Click **Center** to vertically center the text on the page.

7 Click **OK** to confirm the change.

■ To remove the centering, repeat steps **1** to **7**, except select **Top** in step **6**.

CHANGE MARGINS

You can change the margins in your document to suit your needs. A margin is the amount of space between the text in your document and the edge of your paper.

Word automatically sets the top and bottom margins to 1 inch and the left and right margins to 1.25 inches.

Changing the margins allows you to fit more or less information on a page and can help you accommodate letterhead and other specialty paper.

CHANGE MARGINS

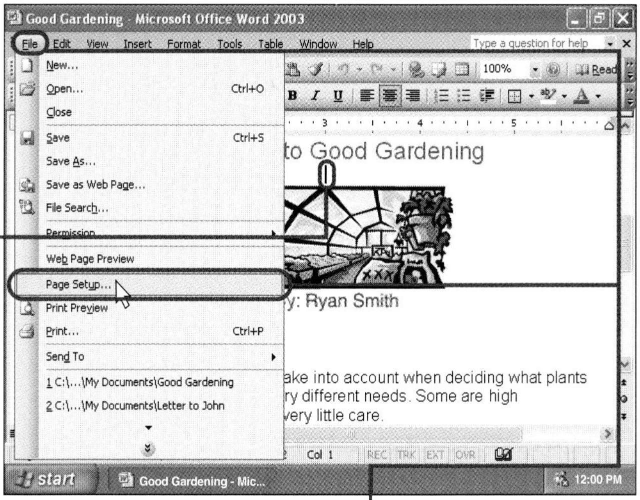

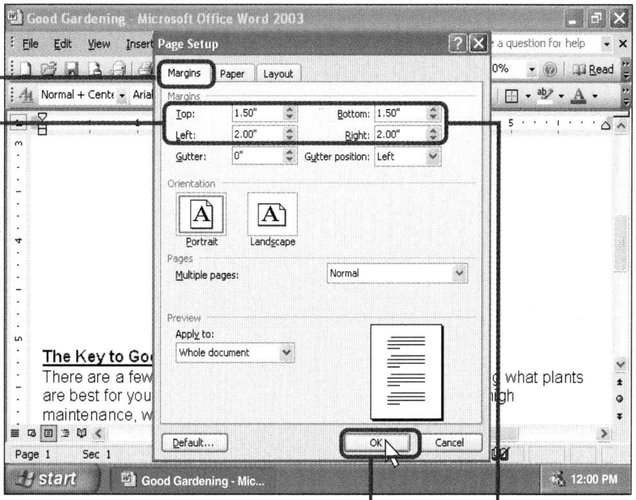

1 Click anywhere in the document or section where you want to change the margins.

Note: To change the margins for part of a document, you must divide the document into sections. For more information, see page 80.

2 Click **File**.

3 Click **Page Setup**.

■ The Page Setup dialog box appears.

4 Click the **Margins** tab.

■ This area displays the current margins for the document or section.

5 Double-click the margin size you want to change and then type a new size.

■ Repeat step **5** for each margin you want to change.

6 Click **OK** to confirm the change.

ADD PAGE NUMBERS

You can have Word number the pages in your document. Numbering pages can help make a long document easier to organize when printed.

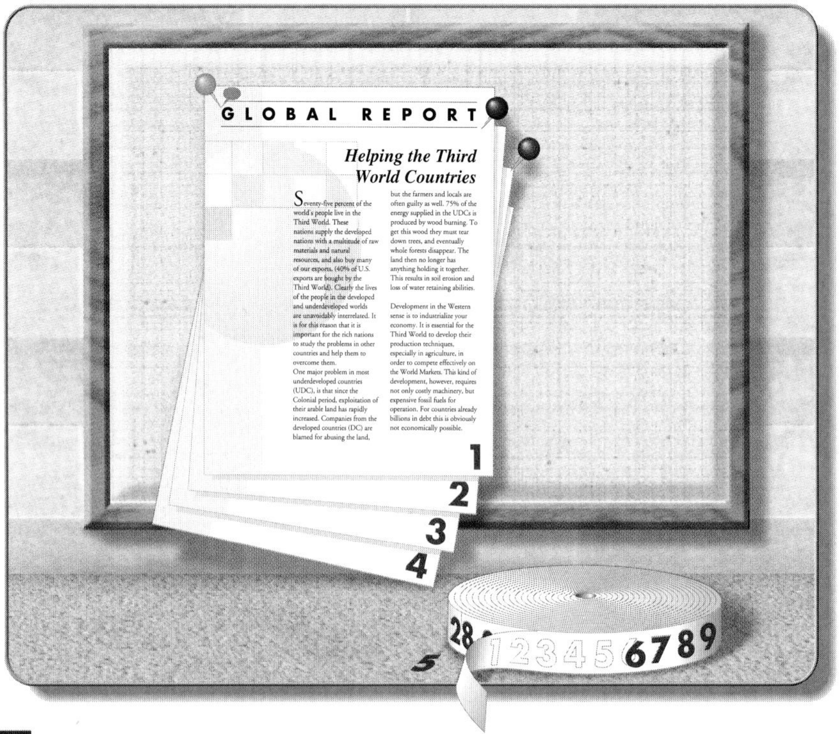

To view the page numbers on your screen, your document must be displayed in the Print Layout view. For information on changing the view of a document, see page 24.

ADD PAGE NUMBERS

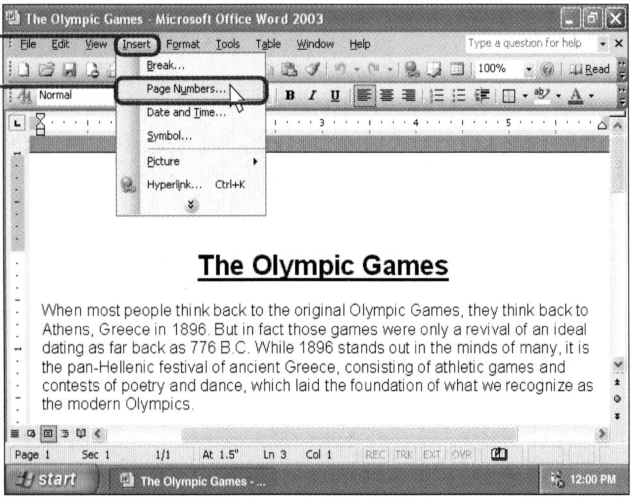

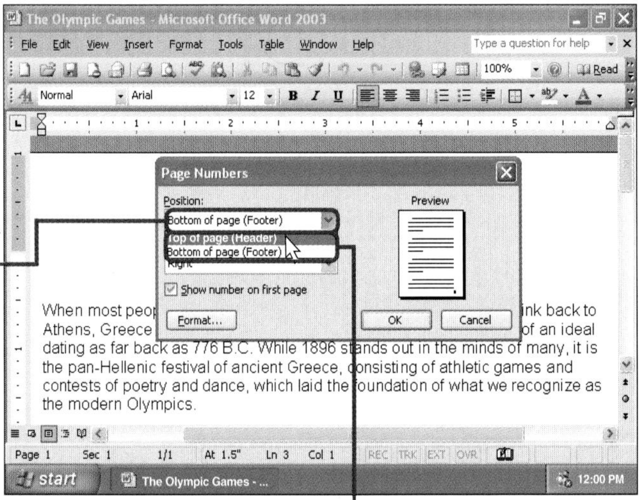

1 Click **Insert**.

2 Click **Page Numbers**.

■ The Page Numbers dialog box appears.

3 Click this area to select a position for the page numbers.

4 Click the position where you want the page numbers to appear.

Tip

How do I remove page numbers from my document?

Deleting a page number from your document's header or footer will remove all the page numbers from your document.

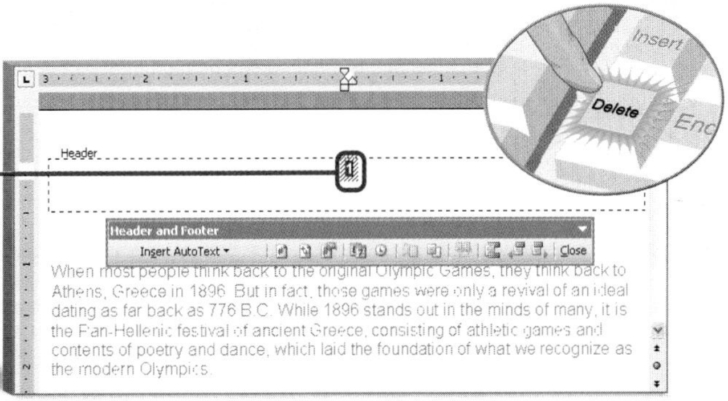

1 Double-click a page number to display the Header or Footer area.

2 Double-click the page number to select the number.

3 Press the Delete key to delete the page number.

Note: To close the Header or Footer area, click ***Close*** *on the Header and Footer toolbar.*

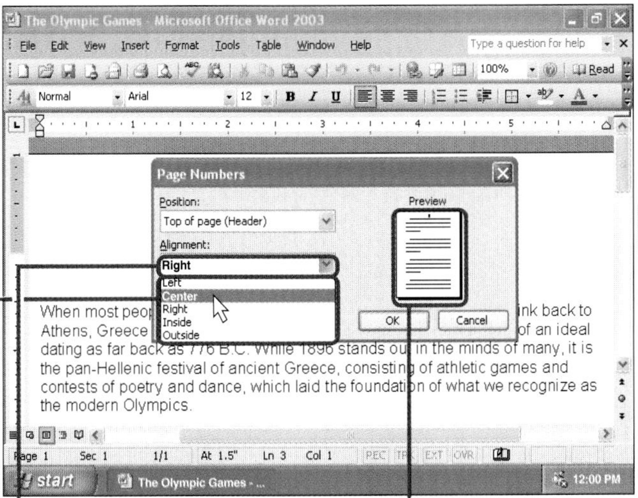

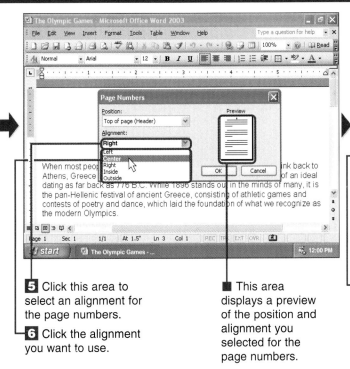

5 Click this area to select an alignment for the page numbers.

6 Click the alignment you want to use.

■ This area displays a preview of the position and alignment you selected for the page numbers.

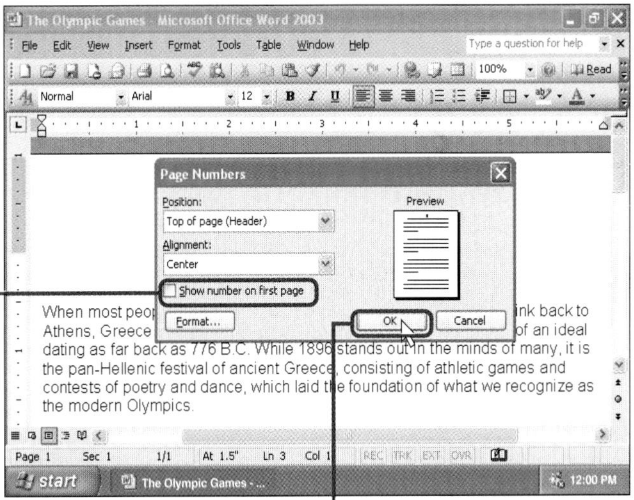

7 If you want to hide the page number on the first page of your document, click this option (☑ changes to ☐).

Note: This option is useful if the first page in your document is a title page.

8 Click **OK** to add the page numbers to your document.

■ If you later make changes that affect the pages in your document, such as adding or removing text, Word will automatically adjust the page numbers for you.

Team B
Player
Goals
Assists
Points
F. Hill
M. Cole
E. Baker
M. Wilson
H. Reed
D. Jones
L. Bell
N. King
D. Morris
K. Turner
5 1 6
2 5 7
3 2 5
7 1 8
1 4 5
0 3 3
6 2 8
4 4 8
2 5 7
9 0 9
Team C
Player
Goals
Assists
Points
M. Wilson 6 1 7
S. Grant 5 2 7
M. Taylor
B. White
E. Ross
D. Morris
S. Miller
A. Martin
S. Lee
S. Evans
Workbook
REVENUE
Payroll
TOTAL EXPENS
Jan

SUM

Using Excel

$1200
$1100
$1000
$900
$800
$700
$600
$500
$400
$300
$200
$100
84 85 86 87 88 89 90

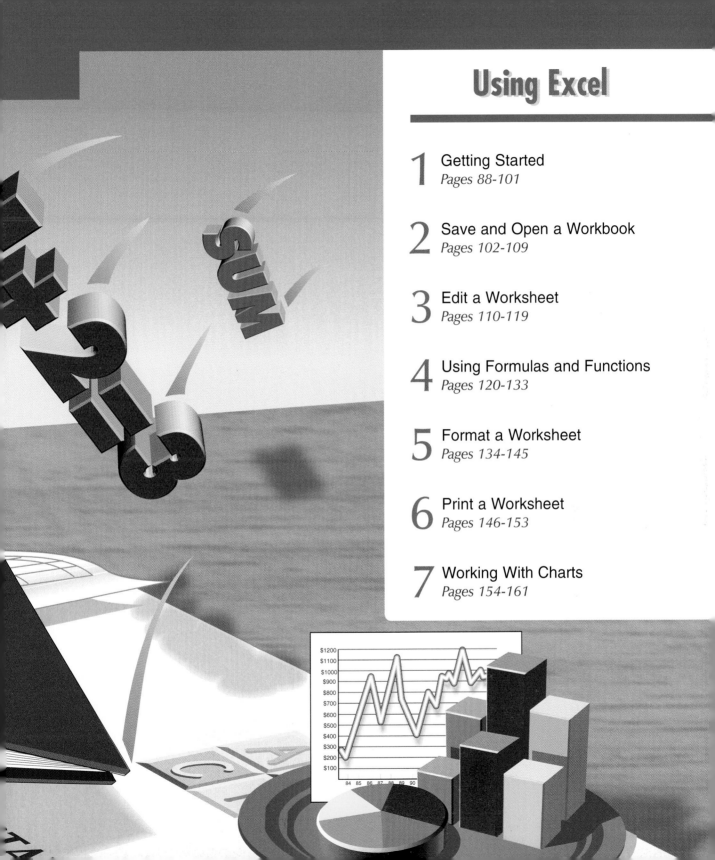

Excel is a spreadsheet program you can use to organize, analyze and attractively present data, such as a budget or sales report.

Each Excel file, called a workbook, contains several worksheets that you can use to store your data and charts.

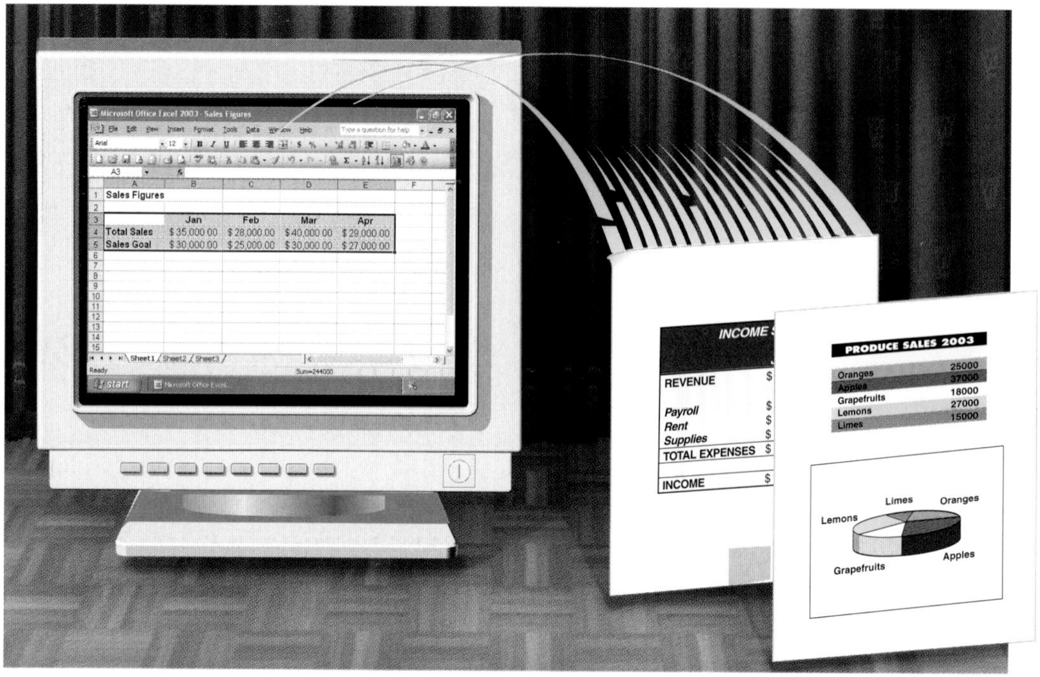

Editing and Formatting

Excel allows you to efficiently enter, edit and format data in a worksheet. You can quickly enter a series of numbers, insert new rows or change the width of columns. You can also emphasize data by changing the font, color and style of data.

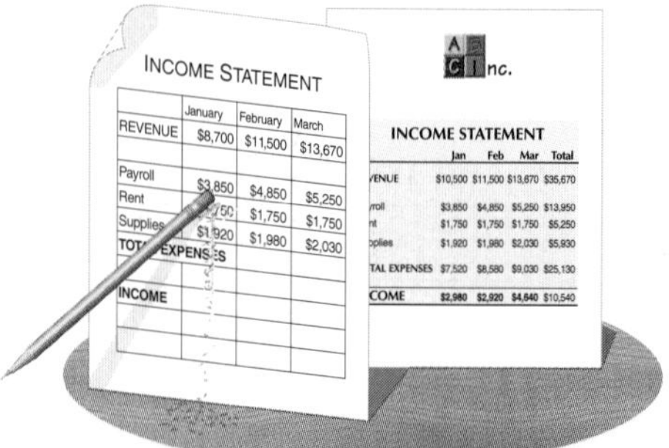

Using Formulas and Functions

Formulas and functions allow you to perform calculations and analyze data in a worksheet. Common calculations include finding the sum, average or total number of values in a list.

Creating Charts

Excel helps you create colorful charts to visually display worksheet data. If you change the data in your worksheet, Excel will automatically update the chart to display the changes. You can also move and resize a chart to suit your needs.

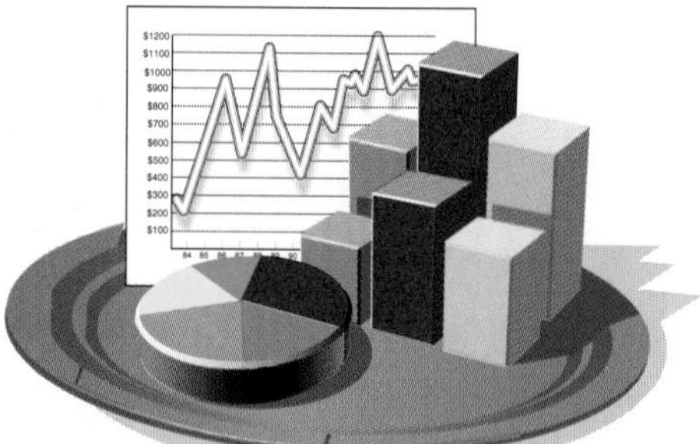

PARTS OF THE EXCEL WINDOW

The Excel window displays many items you can use to work with your data.

Title Bar

Shows the name of the displayed workbook.

Menu Bar

Provides access to lists of commands available in Excel and displays an area where you can type a question to get help information.

Standard Toolbar

Contains buttons you can use to select common commands, such as Save and Print.

Formatting Toolbar

Contains buttons you can use to select common formatting commands, such as Bold and Underline.

Formula Bar

Displays the cell reference and the contents of the active cell. A cell reference identifies the location of each cell in a worksheet and consists of a column letter followed by a row number, such as **A1**.

Active Cell

Displays a thick border. You enter data into the active cell.

Cell

The area where a row and column intersect.

Column

A vertical line of cells. A letter identifies each column.

Row

A horizontal line of cells. A number identifies each row.

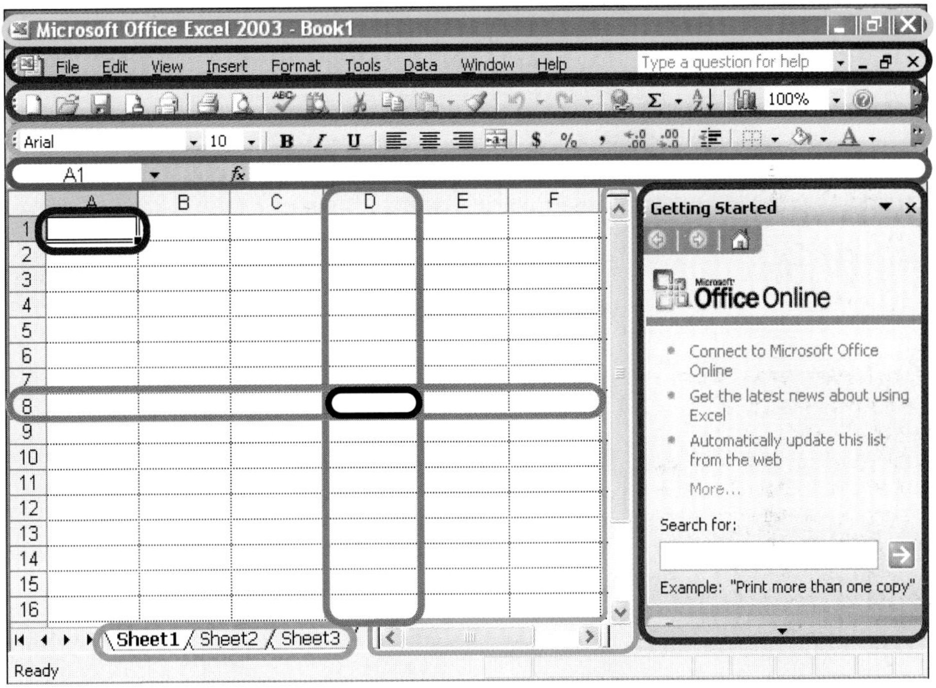

Worksheet Tabs

Each Excel file, called a workbook, is divided into several worksheets. Excel displays a tab for each worksheet.

Scroll Bars

Allow you to browse through a worksheet.

Task Pane

Contains options you can select to perform common tasks, such as creating a new workbook.

CHANGE THE ACTIVE CELL

You can use the mouse or keyboard to make any cell in your worksheet the active cell. You enter data into the active cell.

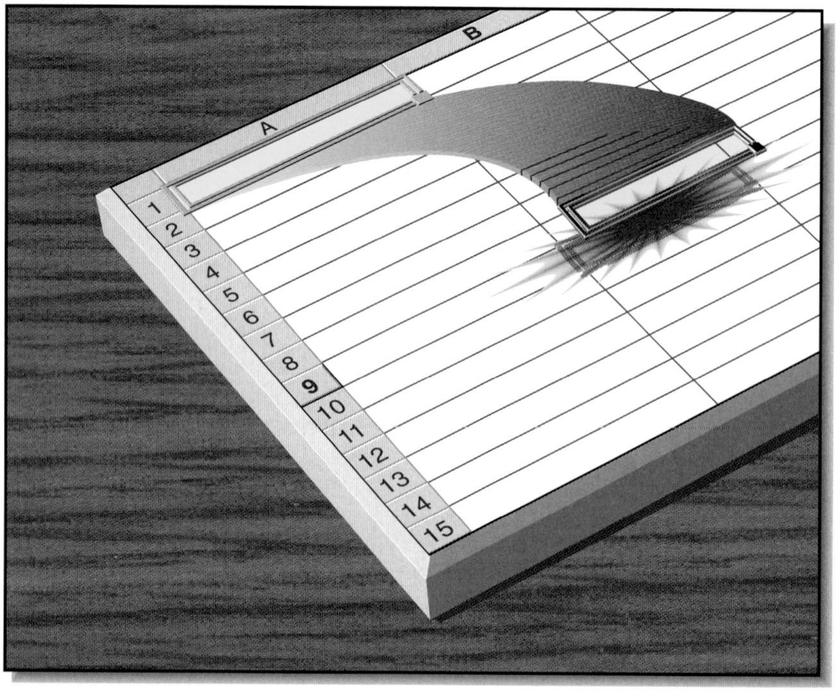

You can only make one cell in your worksheet active at a time.

CHANGE THE ACTIVE CELL

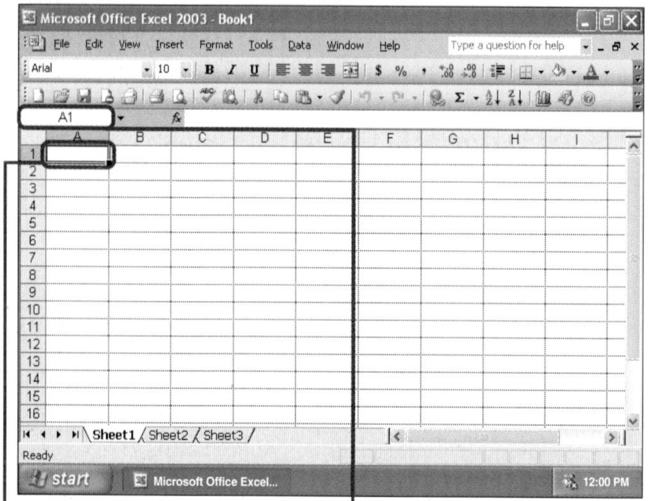

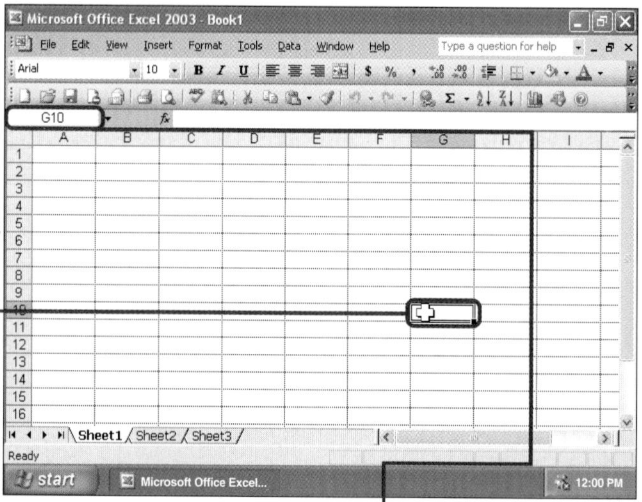

■ The active cell displays a thick border.

■ The cell reference for the active cell appears in this area. A cell reference identifies the location of each cell in a worksheet and consists of a column letter followed by a row number (example: **A1**).

1 Click the cell you want to make the active cell.

Note: You can also press the ←, →, ↑ or ↓ key to change the active cell.

■ The cell reference for the new active cell appears in this area.

SCROLL THROUGH A WORKSHEET

You can scroll through your worksheet to view other areas of the worksheet. This is useful when your worksheet contains a lot of data and your computer screen cannot display all the data at once.

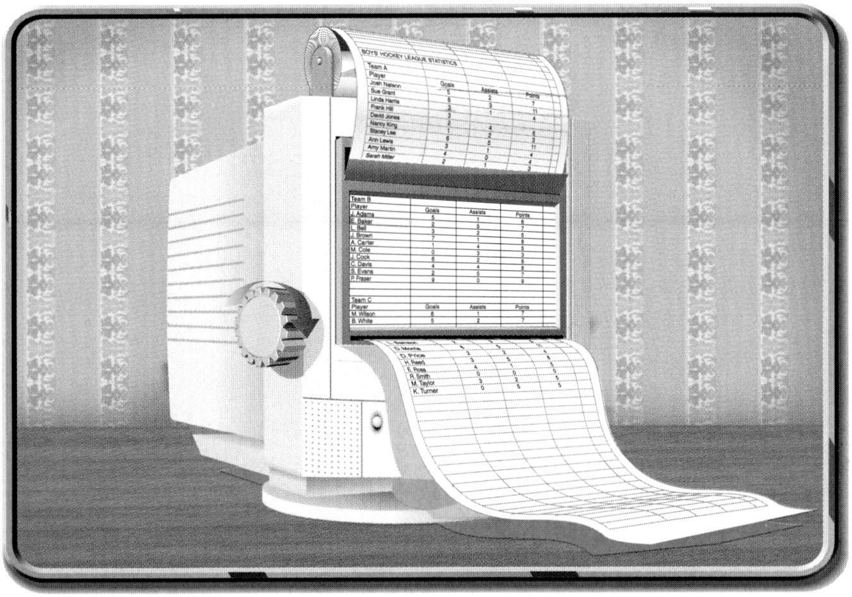

You can use a scroll bar to scroll up and down or left and right. The location of the scroll box on the scroll bar indicates which area of the worksheet you are viewing.

SCROLL THROUGH A WORKSHEET

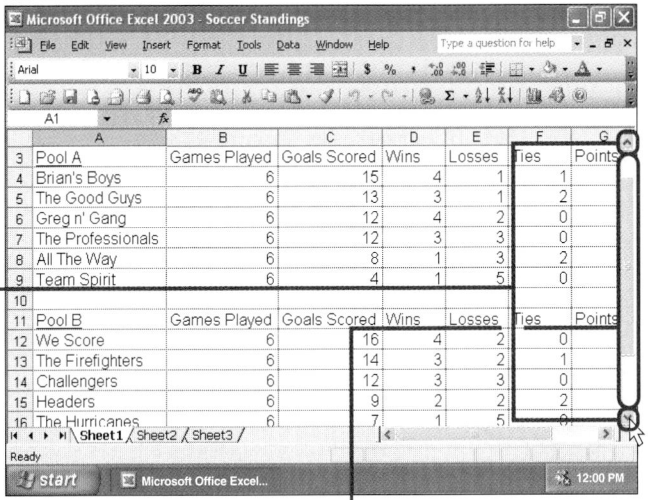

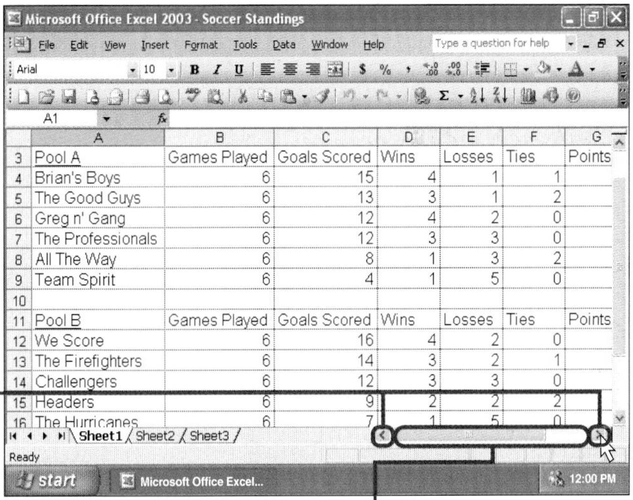

SCROLL UP OR DOWN

1 To scroll up or down one row, click ▲ or ▼.

■ To quickly scroll to any row in your worksheet, position the mouse over the scroll box and then drag the scroll box along the scroll bar until the row you want to view appears.

SCROLL LEFT OR RIGHT

1 To scroll left or right one column, click ◄ or ►.

■ To quickly scroll to any column in your worksheet, position the mouse over the scroll box and then drag the scroll box along the scroll bar until the column you want to view appears.

ENTER DATA

You can enter data, such as text, numbers and dates, into your worksheet quickly and easily.

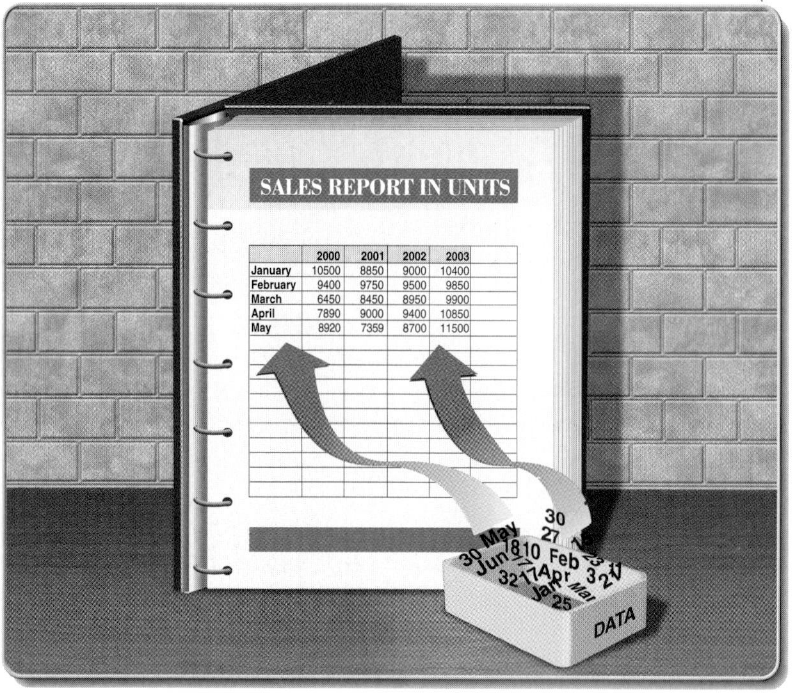

Excel automatically left aligns text and right aligns numbers and dates you enter in cells.

ENTER DATA

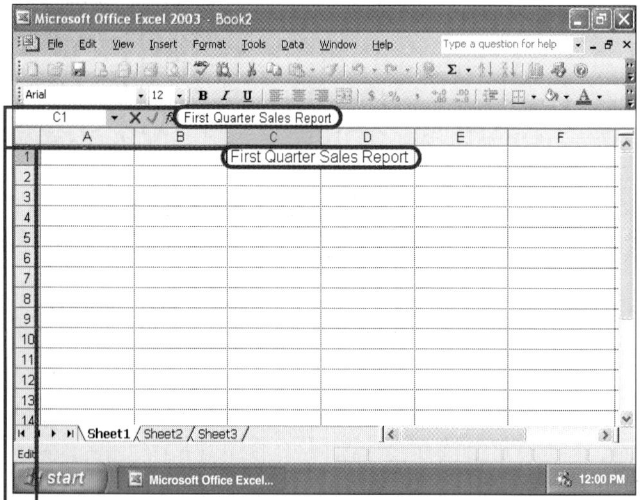

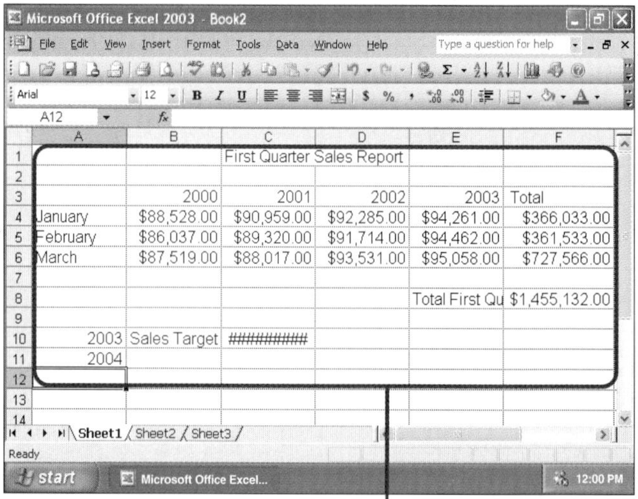

■1 Click the cell where you want to enter data. Then type the data.

■ The data you type appears in the active cell and in the formula bar.

■ If you make a typing mistake while entering data, press the Backspace key to remove the incorrect data. Then type the correct data.

■2 Press the Enter key to enter the data and move down one cell.

Note: To enter the data and move one cell in any direction, press the ←, →, ↑ or ↓ key.

■3 Repeat steps **1** and **2** until you finish entering all your data.

Note: In this book, the size of data was changed to 12 points to make the data easier to read. To change the size of data, see page 137.

Tip

How can I quickly enter numbers?

You can use the number keys on the right side of your keyboard to quickly enter numbers into your worksheet. To be able to use these number keys, **NUM** must be displayed at the bottom of your screen. You can press the Num Lock key to display **NUM** on your screen.

Tip

Why did Excel change the appearance of a date I entered?

When you enter a date into your worksheet, Excel may change the format of the date to one of the following formats: 3/14/2003, 14-Mar or 14-Mar-03. To change the format of dates, see page 138.

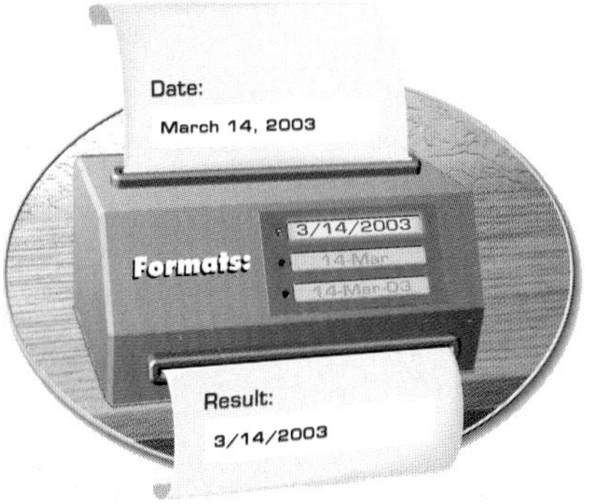

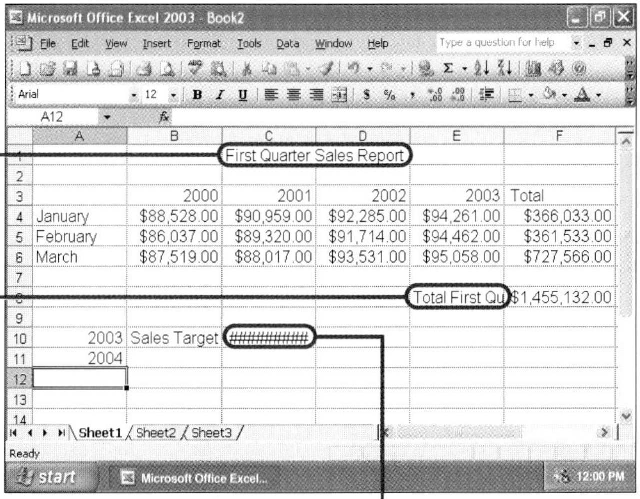

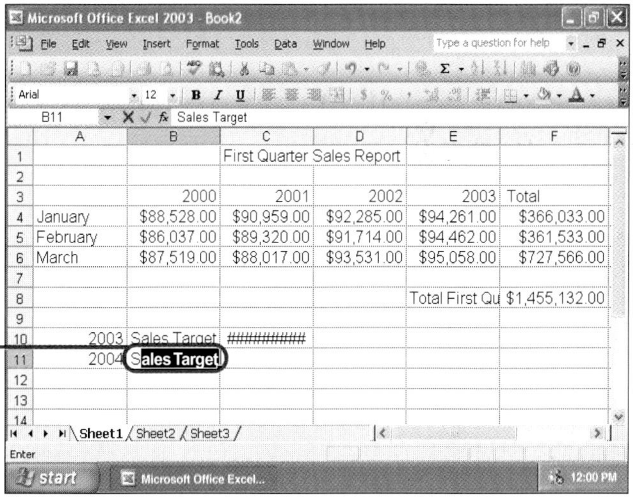

■ If the text is too long to fit in a cell, the text will spill into the neighboring cell. If the neighboring cell contains data, Excel will display as much of the text as the column width will allow.

■ If a number is too large to fit in a cell, Excel will display the number in scientific notation or as number signs (#).

Note: To change the width of a column to display text or a number, see page 134.

AUTOCOMPLETE

■ If the first few letters you type match the text in another cell in the same column, Excel will complete the text for you.

1 To enter the text Excel provides, press the Enter key.

■ To enter different text, continue typing.

SELECT CELLS

Before performing many tasks in Excel, you must select the cells you want to work with. Selected cells appear highlighted on your screen. This makes cells you select stand out from the rest of the cells in your worksheet.

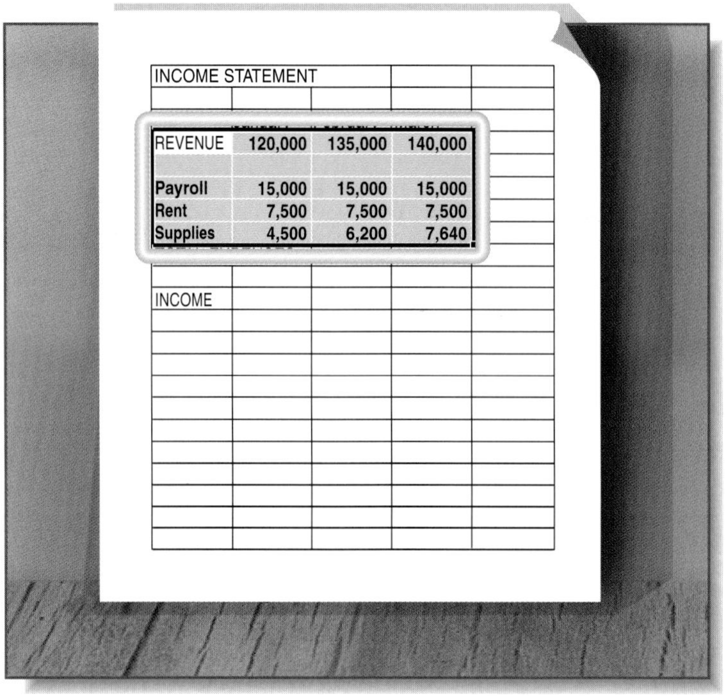

You must select the cells containing data you want to move or copy to another location in your worksheet or to change to a different font or size. To move or copy data, see page 112. To change the font or size of data, see pages 136 and 137.

SELECT CELLS

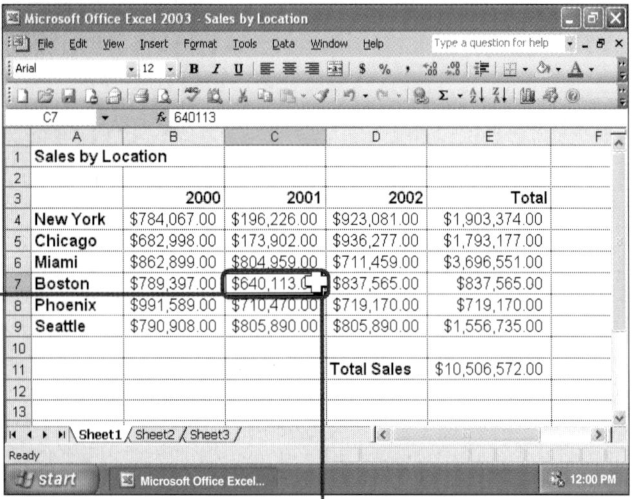

SELECT A CELL

1 Click the cell you want to select.

■ The cell becomes the active cell and displays a thick border.

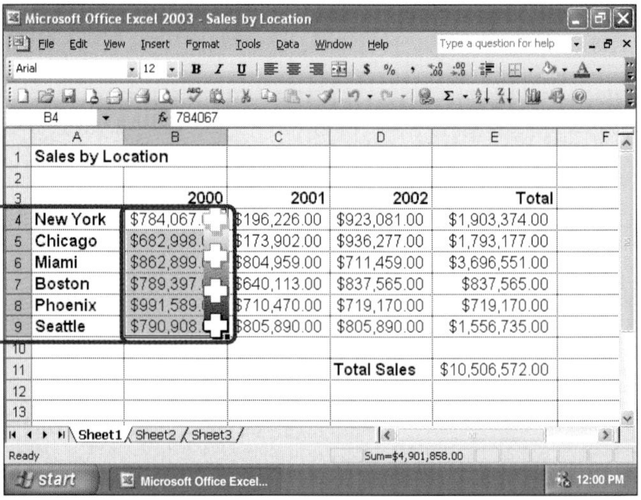

SELECT A GROUP OF CELLS

1 Position the mouse ✥ over the first cell you want to select.

2 Drag the mouse ✥ until you highlight all the cells you want to select.

■ To select multiple groups of cells, press and hold down the **Ctrl** key as you repeat steps **1** and **2** for each group of cells you want to select.

■ To deselect cells, click any cell.

Tip

How do I select all the cells in my worksheet?

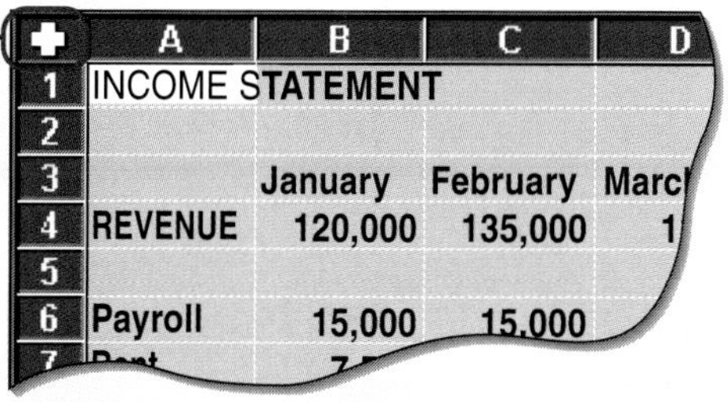

■ To select all the cells in your worksheet, click the box ( ) at the top left corner of your worksheet, where the row numbers and column letters meet.

Tip

How do I select data in a cell?

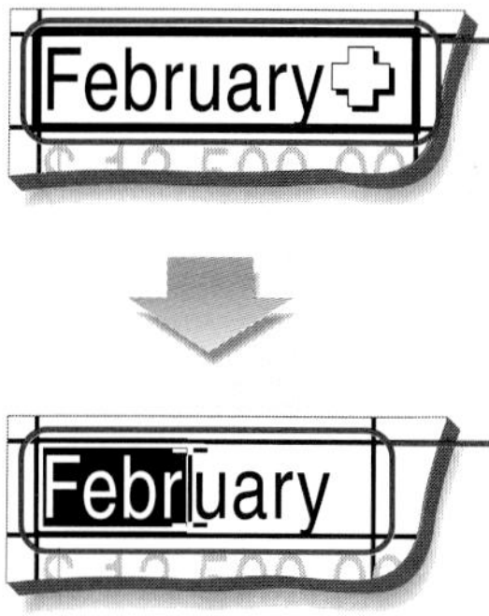

1 To select data in a cell, double-click the cell that contains the data.

2 Drag the mouse I over the data in the cell until you highlight all the data you want to select.

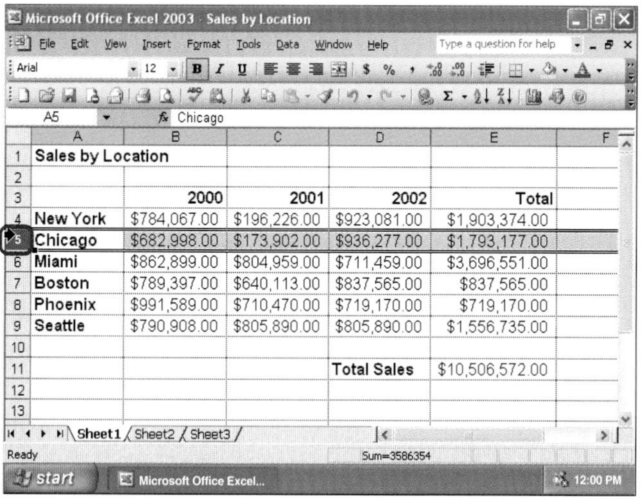

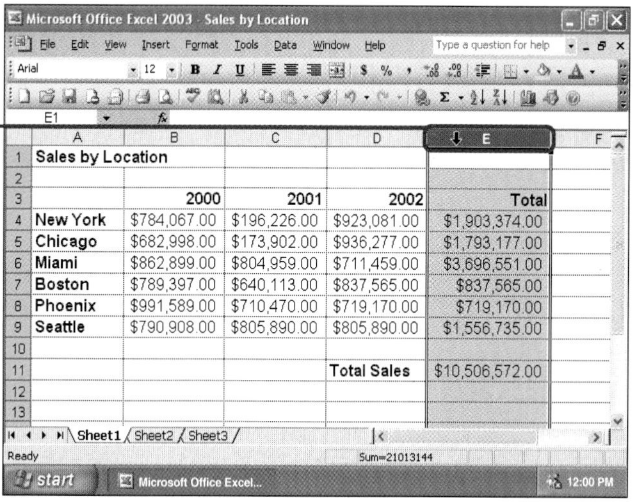

SELECT A ROW

1 Click the number of the row you want to select.

■ To select multiple rows, position the mouse ➡ over the number of the first row you want to select. Then drag the mouse ➡ until you highlight all the rows you want to select.

SELECT A COLUMN

1 Click the letter of the column you want to select.

■ To select multiple columns, position the mouse ⬇ over the letter of the first column you want to select. Then drag the mouse ⬇ until you highlight all the columns you want to select.

COMPLETE A SERIES

Excel can save you time by completing a text or number series for you. A series is a sequence of data that changes, such as a range of consecutive numbers.

You can complete a series across a row or down a column in a worksheet. Excel completes a text series based on the text you enter in one cell. Excel completes a number series based on the numbers you enter in two cells.

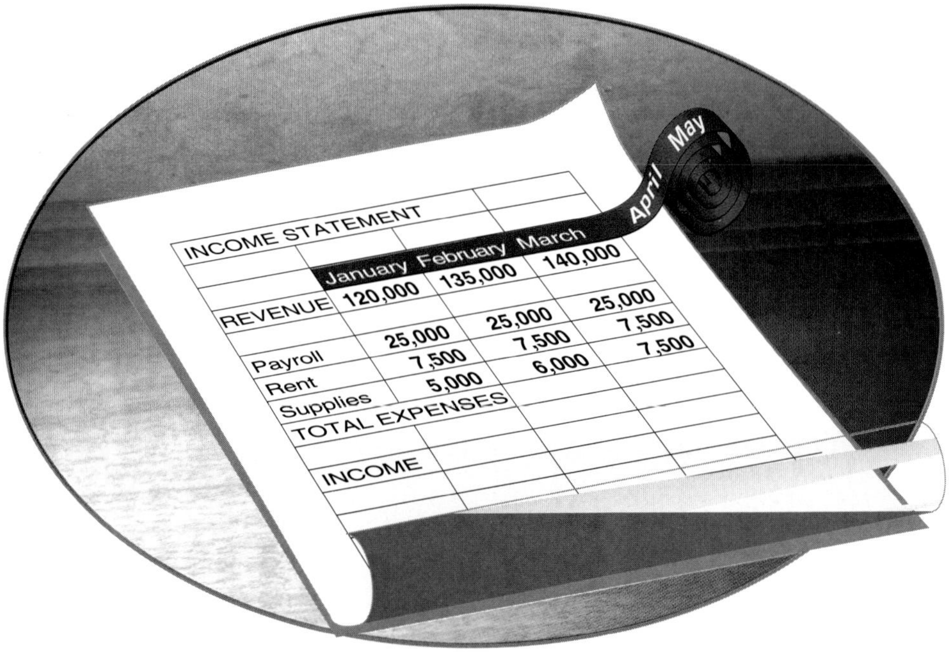

COMPLETE A TEXT SERIES

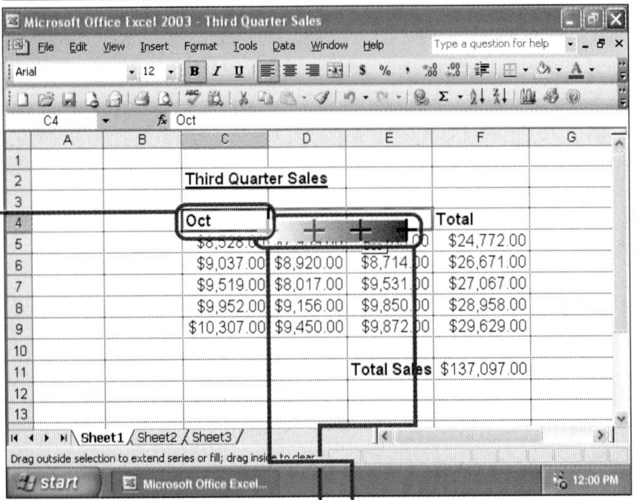

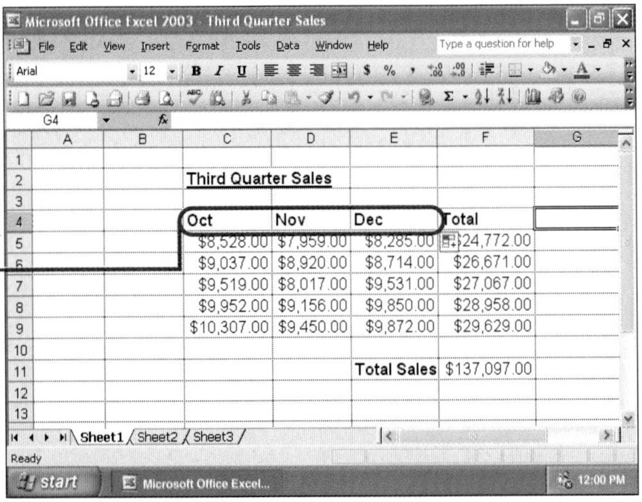

1 Enter the text you want to start the series.

2 Click the cell containing the text you entered.

3 Position the mouse ✥ over the bottom right corner of the cell (✥ changes to +).

4 Drag the mouse + over the cells you want to include in the series.

■ The cells display the text series.

Note: If Excel cannot determine the text series you want to complete, it will copy the text in the first cell to all the cells you select.

■ To deselect cells, click any cell.

Tip

Why does the Auto Fill Options button (⊞) appear when I complete a series?

You can use the Auto Fill Options button (⊞) to change the way Excel completes a series. For example, you can specify that Excel should not use the formatting from the original cell. Click the Auto Fill Options button to display a list of options and then select the option you want to use. The Auto Fill Options button is available only until you perform another task.

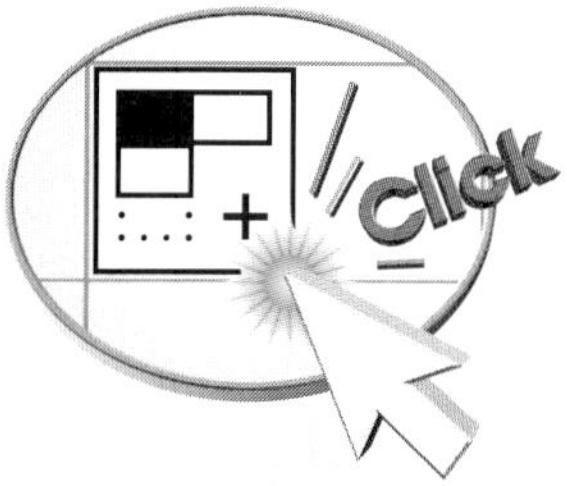

Tip

Can I complete a series that will repeat data in several cells?

Yes. Perform steps **1** to **4** on page 97, except enter the same text or data into the first two cells in step **1**. Excel will repeat the information in all the cells you select.

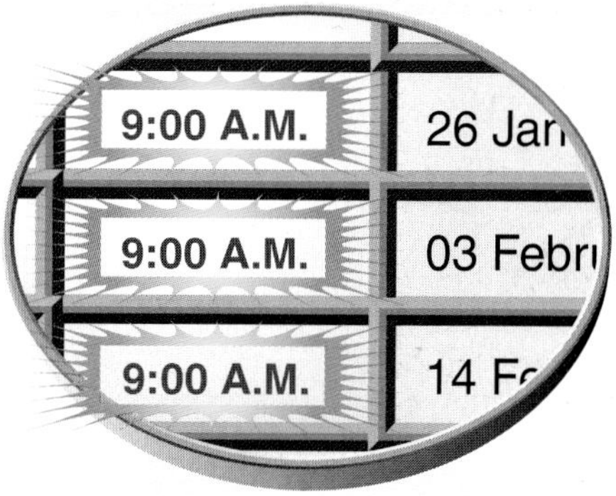

COMPLETE A NUMBER SERIES

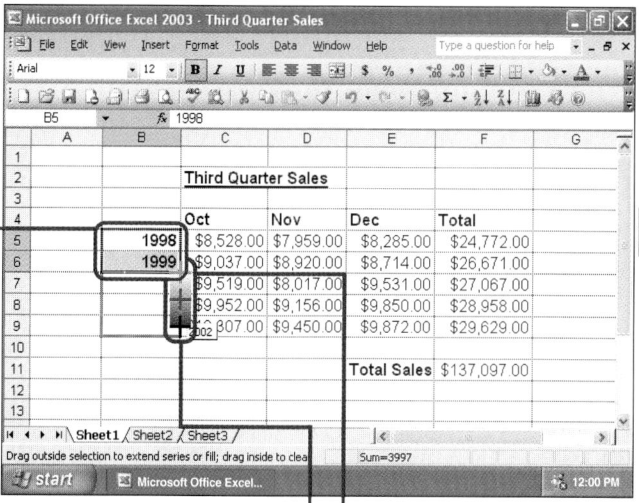

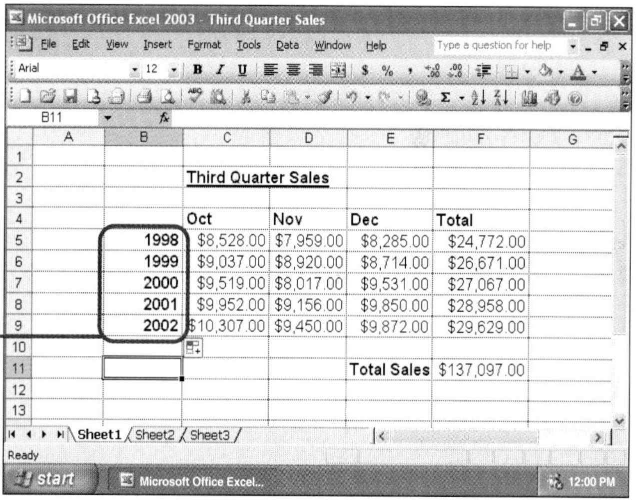

1 Enter the first two numbers you want to start the series.

2 Select the cells containing the numbers you entered. To select cells, see page 94.

3 Position the mouse ⊹ over the bottom right corner of the selected cells (⊹ changes to +).

4 Drag the mouse + over the cells you want to include in the series.

■ The cells display the number series.

■ To deselect cells, click any cell.

SWITCH BETWEEN WORKSHEETS

A workbook contains several worksheets. You can easily switch between the worksheets in your workbook to view and compare all the data.

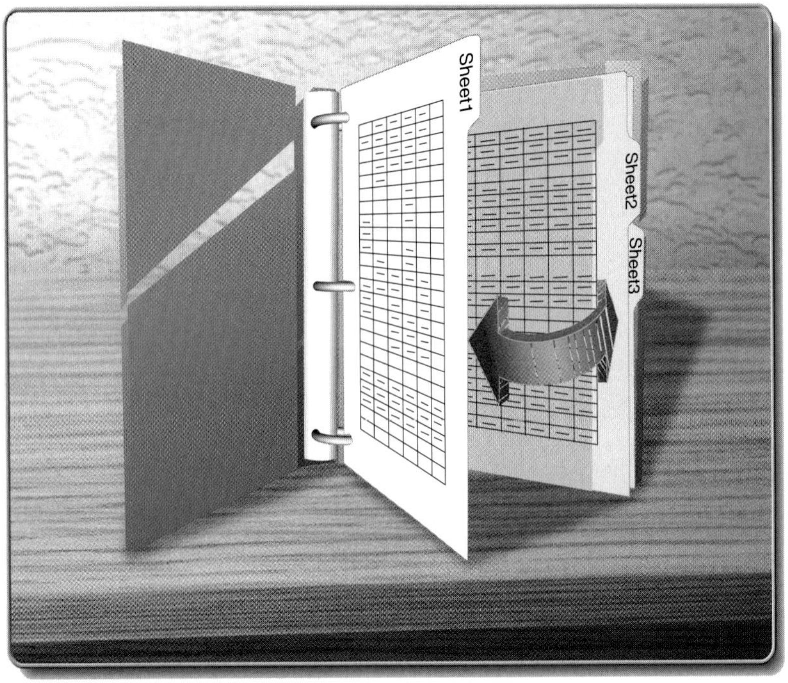

Worksheets can help you organize information in your workbook. For example, you can store information for each division of a company on a separate worksheet.

SWITCH BETWEEN WORKSHEETS

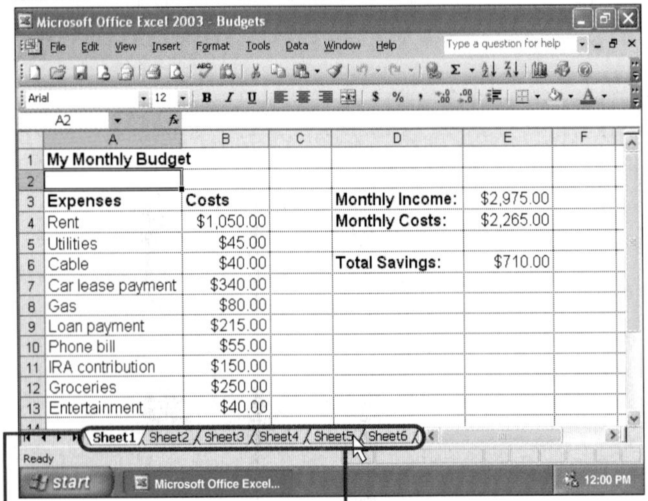

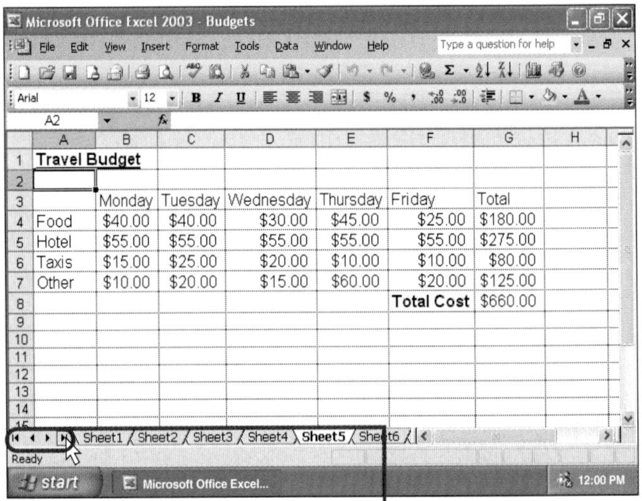

■ This area displays a tab for each worksheet in your workbook. The displayed worksheet has a white tab.

1 Click the tab for the worksheet you want to display.

■ The worksheet you selected appears.

The contents of the other worksheets in your workbook are hidden behind the displayed worksheet.

BROWSE THROUGH WORKSHEET TABS

■ If you have many worksheets in your workbook, you may not be able to see all the worksheet tabs.

Note: To insert additional worksheets, see page 100.

1 Click one of the following buttons to browse through the worksheet tabs.

- ⏮ Display first tab
- ◀ Display previous tab
- ▶ Display next tab
- ⏭ Display last tab

RENAME A WORKSHEET

You can rename a worksheet in your workbook to better describe the contents of the worksheet.

Each worksheet in a workbook must have a unique name. Short worksheet names are generally better than long names since short names allow you to display more worksheet tabs on your screen at once.

RENAME A WORKSHEET

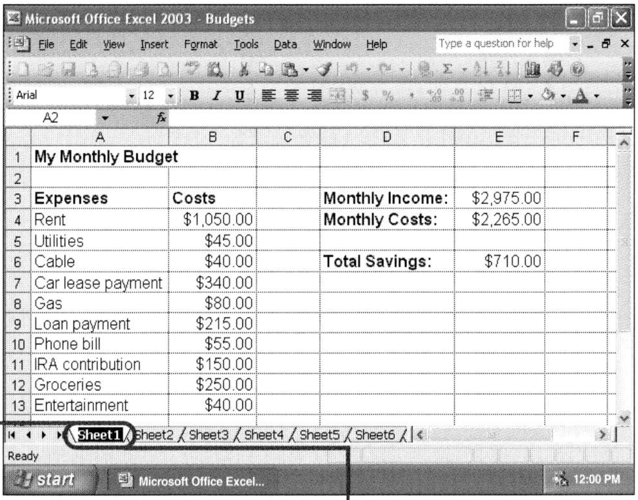

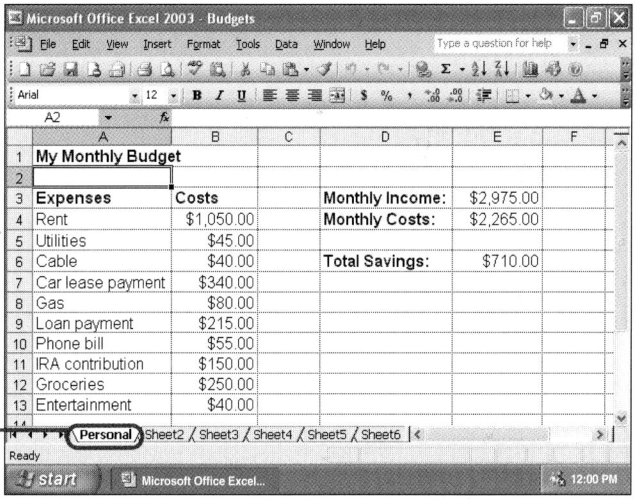

1 Double-click the tab for the worksheet you want to rename.

■ The name of the worksheet is highlighted.

2 Type a new name for the worksheet and then press the **Enter** key.

Note: A worksheet name can contain up to 31 characters, including spaces.

INSERT A WORKSHEET

You can insert a new worksheet anywhere in your workbook to include additional information.

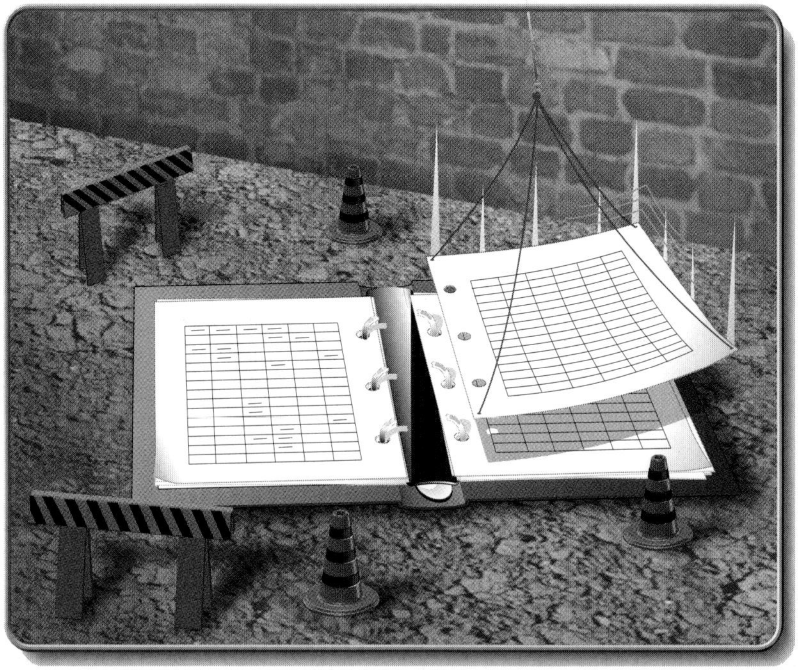

Each workbook you create automatically contains three worksheets. You can insert as many new worksheets as you need.

INSERT A WORKSHEET

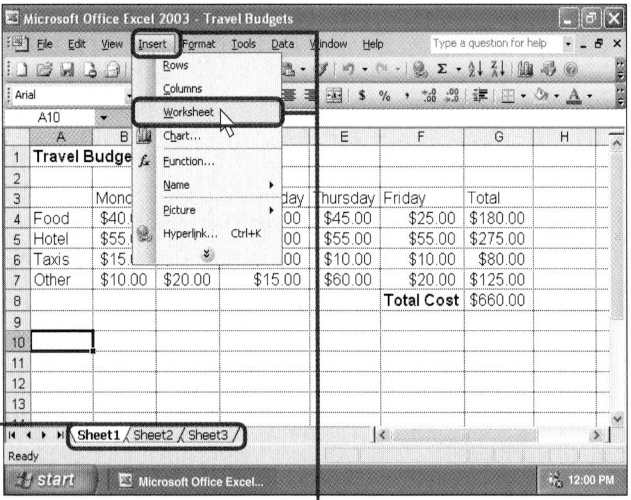

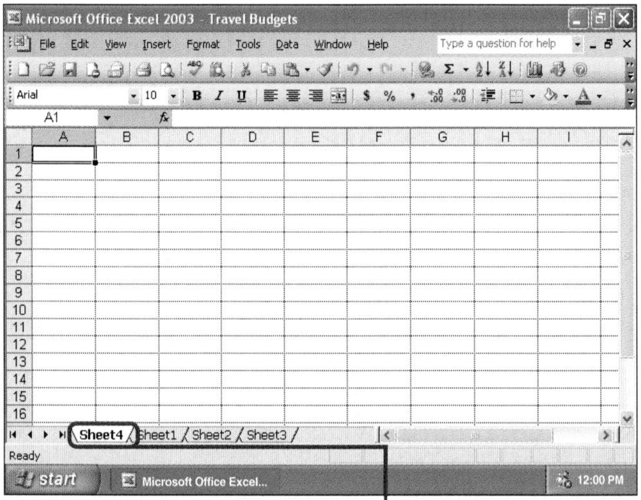

1 Click the tab for the worksheet you want to appear after the new worksheet.

2 Click **Insert**.

3 Click **Worksheet**.

■ The new worksheet appears.

■ Excel displays a tab for the new worksheet.

DELETE A WORKSHEET

You can permanently remove a worksheet you no longer need from your workbook.

You cannot restore a worksheet once it has been deleted from your workbook.

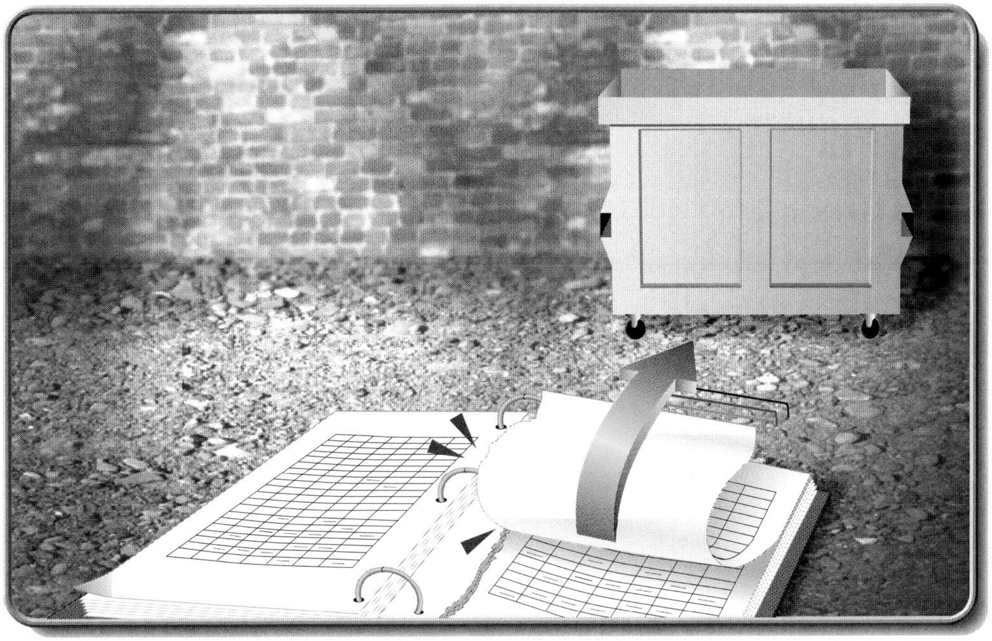

DELETE A WORKSHEET

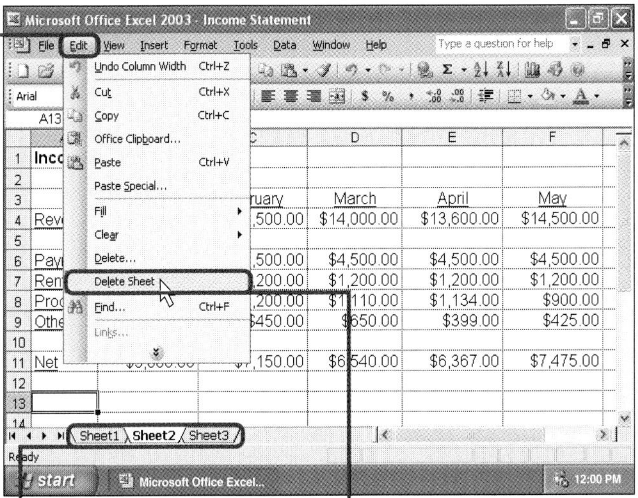

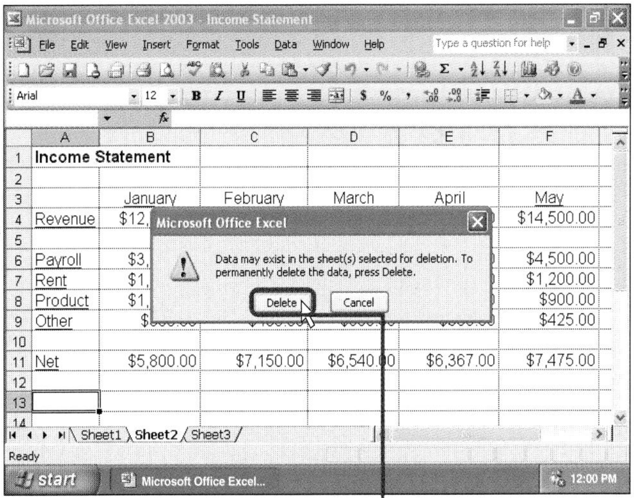

1 Click the tab for the worksheet you want to delete.

2 Click **Edit**.

3 Click **Delete Sheet**.

Note: If Delete Sheet does not appear on the menu, position the mouse over the bottom of the menu to display the menu option.

■ A warning dialog box may appear, stating that Excel will permanently delete the data in the worksheet.

4 Click **Delete** to permanently delete the worksheet.

SAVE A WORKBOOK

You can save your workbook to store it for future use. Saving a workbook allows you to later review and make changes to the workbook.

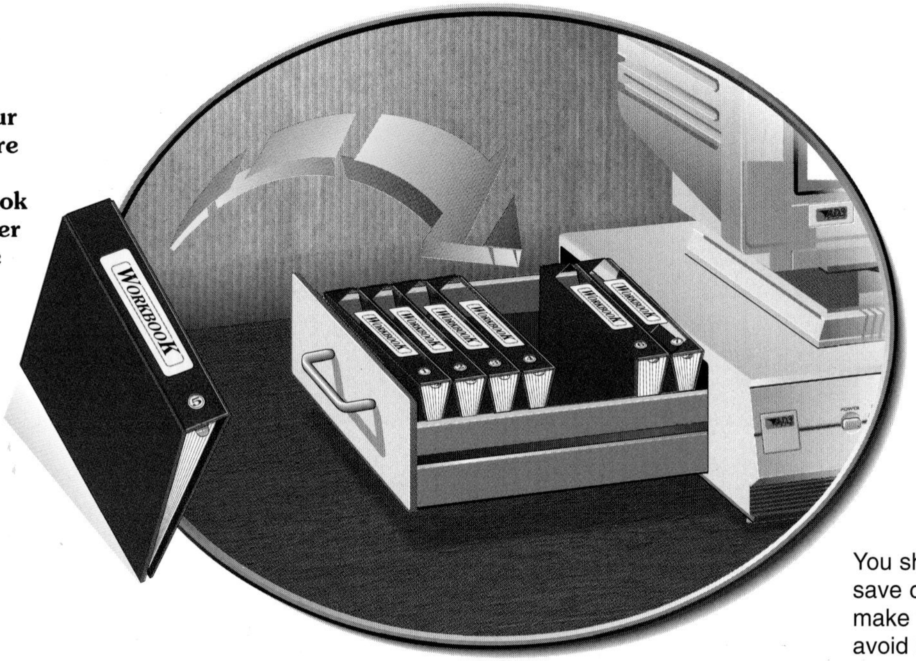

You should regularly save changes you make to a workbook to avoid losing your work.

SAVE A WORKBOOK

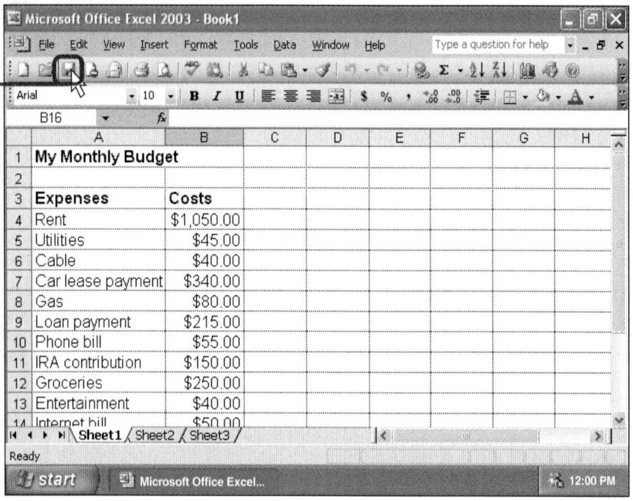

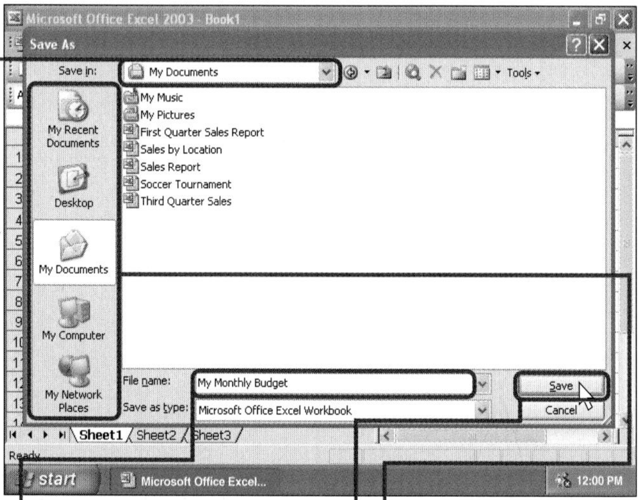

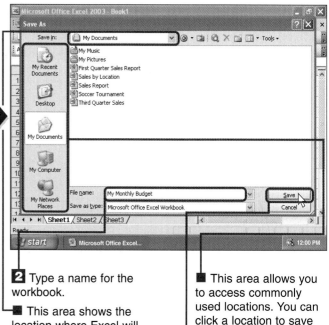

1 Click 💾 to save your workbook.

Note: If 💾 is not displayed, click ⋮ on the Standard toolbar to display the button.

■ The Save As dialog box appears.

Note: If you previously saved your workbook, the Save As dialog box will not appear since you have already named the workbook.

2 Type a name for the workbook.

■ This area shows the location where Excel will store your workbook. You can click this area to change the location.

■ This area allows you to access commonly used locations. You can click a location to save your workbook in the location.

3 Click **Save** to save your workbook.

CREATE A NEW WORKBOOK

You can easily create a new workbook to store new data, such as a budget or sales report.

When you create a new workbook, Excel displays a blank worksheet on your screen. You do not have to close the workbook currently displayed on your screen before creating a new workbook.

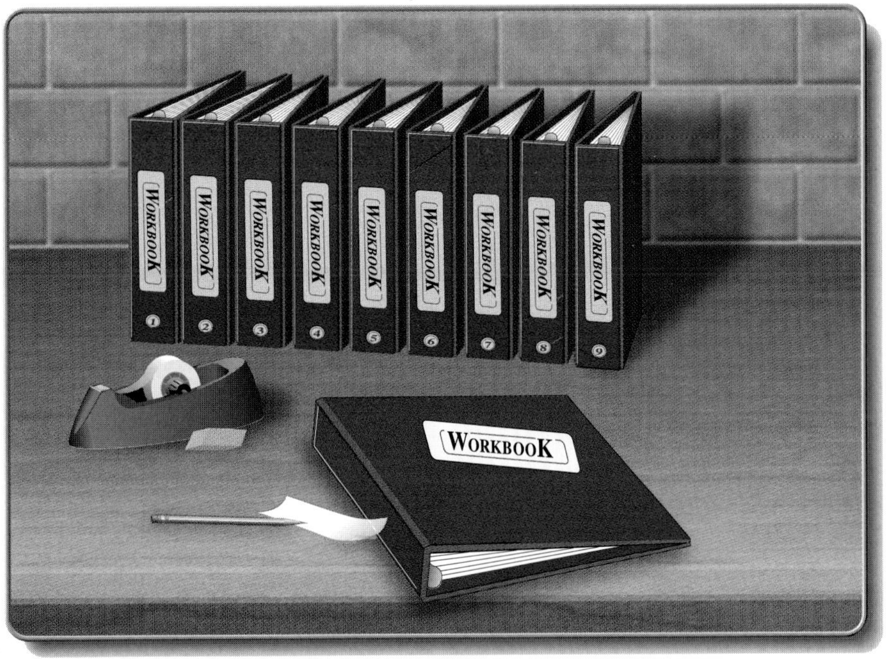

CREATE A NEW WORKBOOK

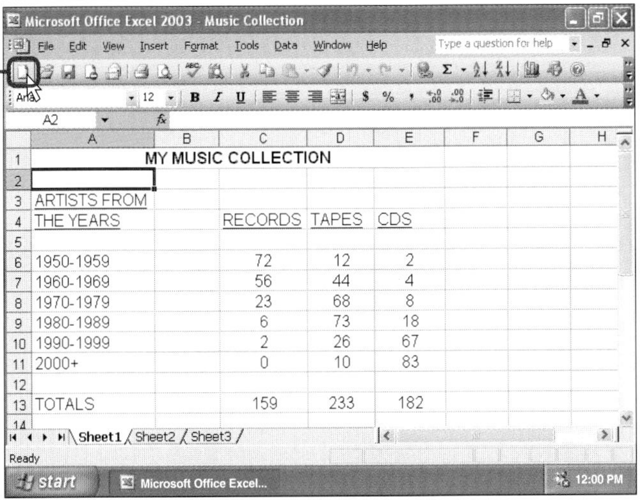

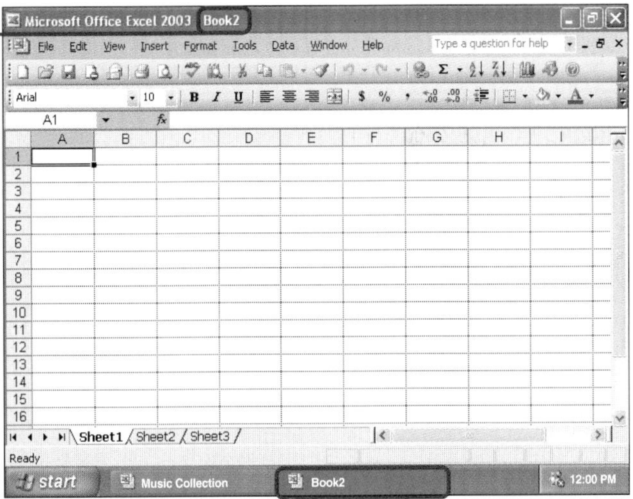

1 Click to create a new workbook.

Note: If is not displayed, click on the Standard toolbar to display the button.

■ A new workbook appears. The previous workbook is now hidden behind the new workbook.

■ Excel gives the new workbook a temporary name, such as Book2, until you save the workbook. To save a workbook, see page 102.

■ A button for the new workbook appears on the taskbar.

You can open a saved workbook to view the workbook on your screen. Opening a workbook allows you to review and make changes to the workbook.

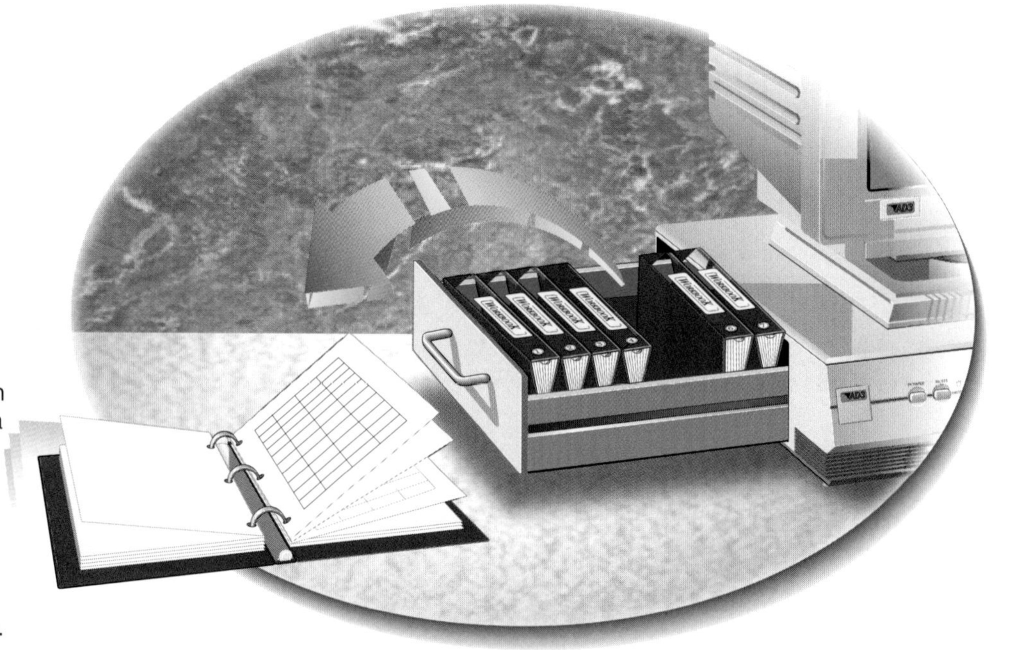

You can specify where the workbook you want to open is located. After you open a workbook, Excel displays the name of the workbook at the top of your screen.

When you finish working with your workbook, you can close the workbook to remove it from your screen.

OPEN A WORKBOOK

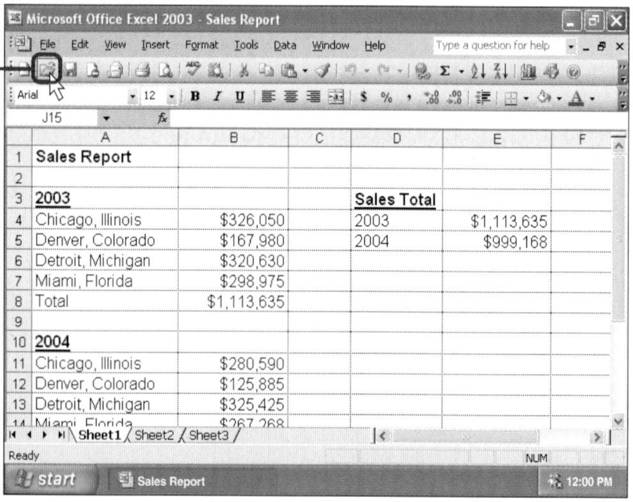

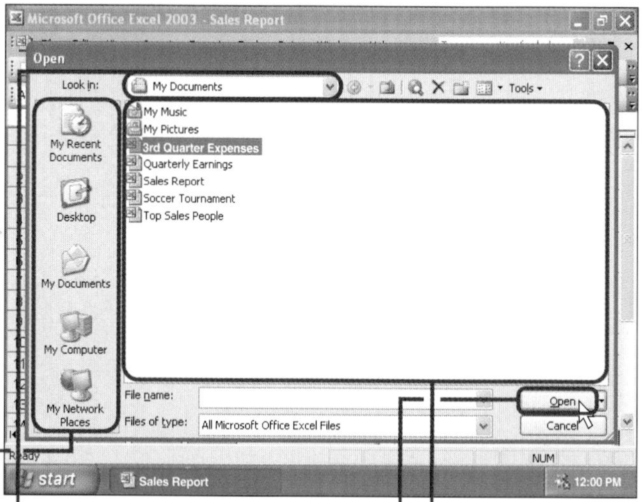

1 Click to open a workbook.

Note: If is not displayed, click on the Standard toolbar to display the button.

■ The Open dialog box appears.

■ This area shows the location of the displayed workbooks. You can click this area to change the location.

■ This area allows you to access workbooks in commonly used locations. You can click a location to display the workbooks stored in the location.

2 Click the name of the workbook you want to open.

3 Click **Open** to open the workbook.

Tip

How can I quickly open a workbook I recently worked with?

Excel remembers the names of the last four workbooks you worked with. You can use the Getting Started task pane or the File menu to quickly open one of these workbooks.

Note: The Getting Started task pane appears each time you start Excel. To display the Getting Started task pane, see page 8.

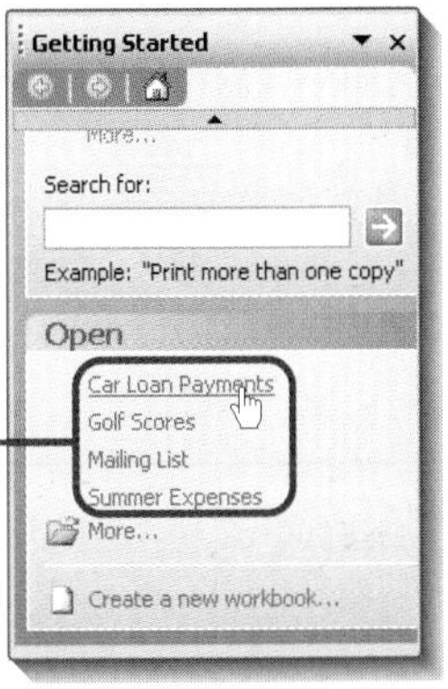

Use the Task Pane

1 Click the name of the workbook you want to open.

Note: If the name of the workbook is not displayed, position the mouse over the bottom of the task pane to display the name.

Use the File Menu

1 Click **File**.

2 Click the name of the workbook you want to open.

Note: If the name of the workbook you want is not displayed, position the mouse over the bottom of the menu to display the name.

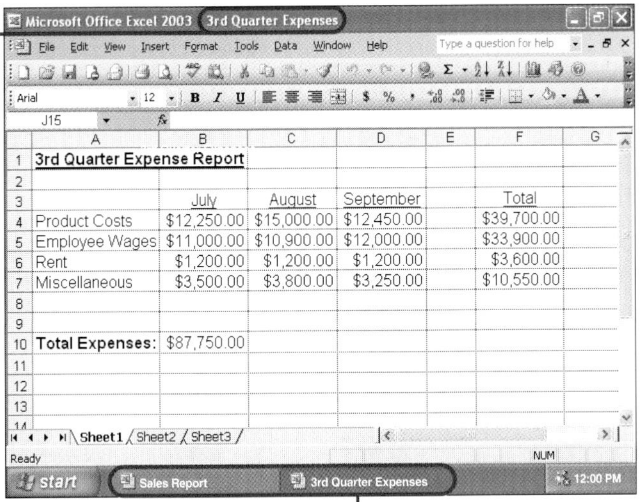

■ The workbook opens and appears on your screen. You can now review and make changes to the workbook.

■ This area displays the name of the open workbook.

■ If you already had a workbook open, the new workbook appears in a new Microsoft Office Excel window. You can click the buttons on the taskbar to switch between the open workbooks.

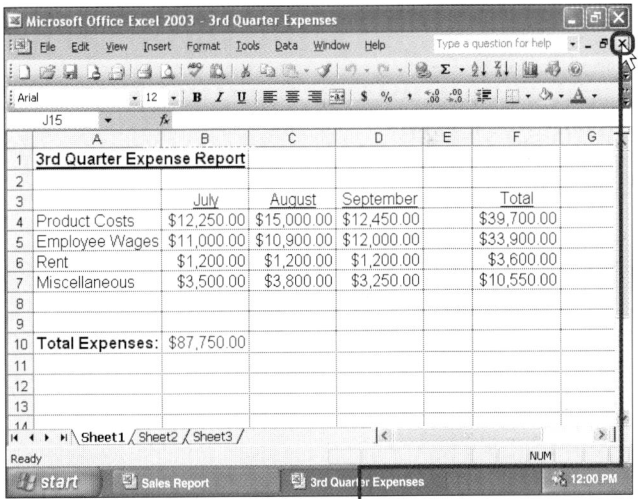

CLOSE A WORKBOOK

■ Before closing a workbook, you should save any changes you made to the workbook. To save changes to a workbook, see page 102.

1 When you finish using workbook, click ☒ to close the workbook.

■ The workbook disappears from your screen.

SWITCH BETWEEN WORKBOOKS

You can have several workbooks open at once. Excel allows you to easily switch from one open workbook to another.

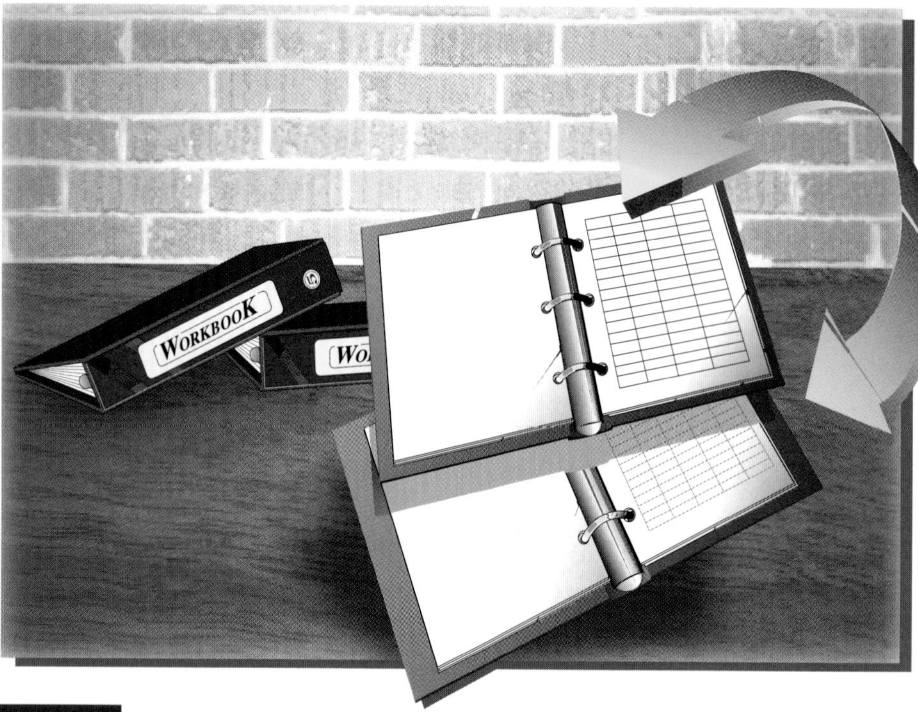

SWITCH BETWEEN WORKBOOKS

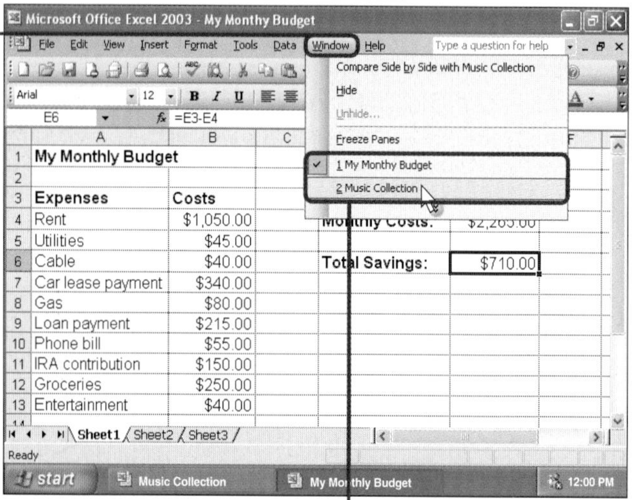

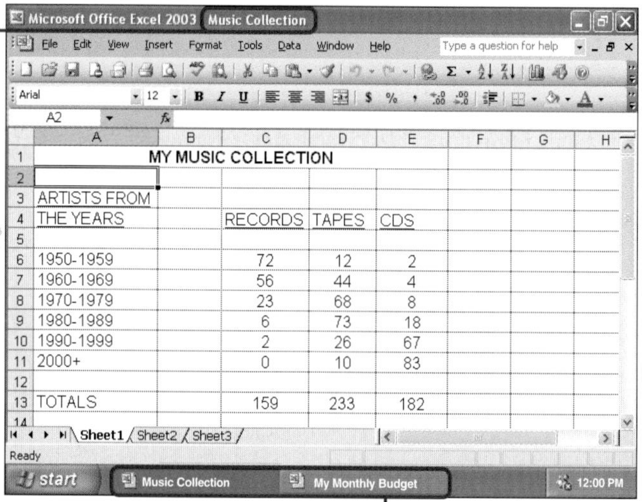

1 Click **Window** to display a list of all the workbooks you have open.

2 Click the name of the workbook you want to switch to.

■ The workbook appears.

■ This area shows the name of the displayed workbook.

■ The taskbar displays a button for each open workbook. You can also click the buttons on the taskbar to switch between the open workbooks.

COMPARE WORKBOOKS

You can display two workbooks on your screen at once. Excel displays one workbook above the other so you can easily compare data in corresponding rows. Comparing workbooks is useful if you want to compare an edited workbook to the original version of the workbook.

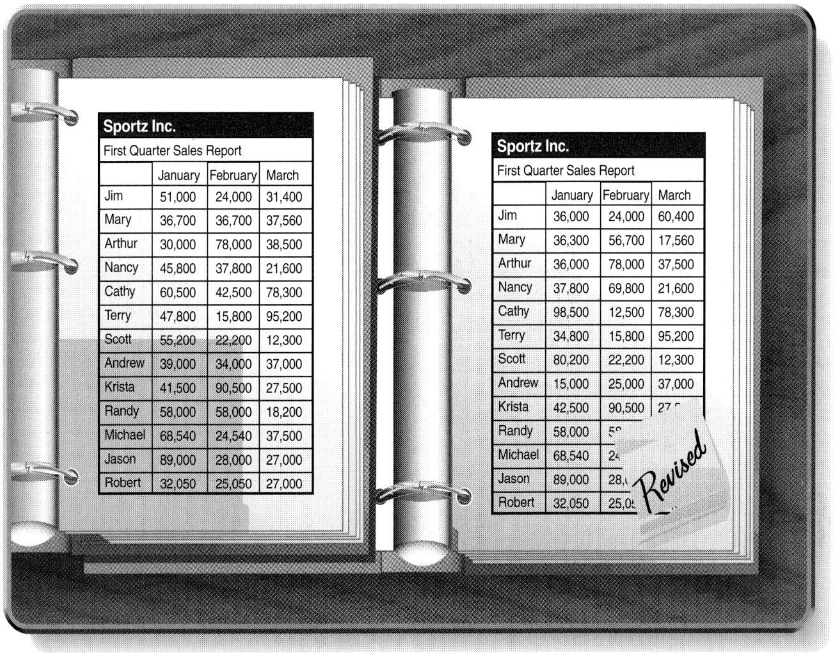

When you scroll through one workbook, Excel automatically scrolls through the other workbook for you, so you can compare the contents of the two workbooks.

COMPARE WORKBOOKS

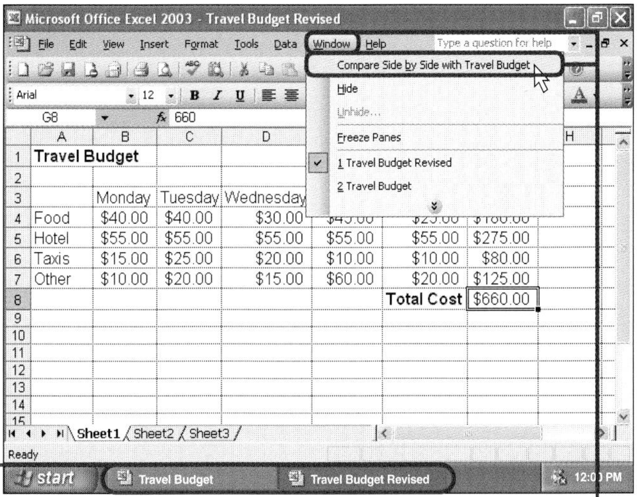

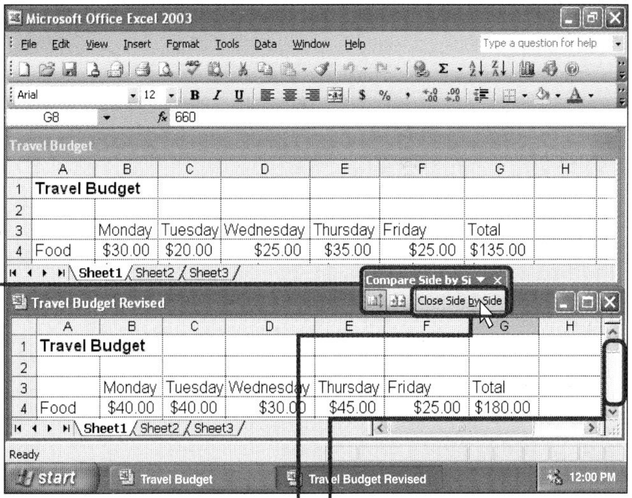

1 Open the two workbooks you want to compare.

Note: To open a workbook, see page 104.

2 Click **Window** in the current workbook.

3 Click **Compare Side by Side with** to compare the current workbook with the other open workbook.

■ Excel displays the workbooks on your screen. One workbook appears above the other workbook.

■ The Compare Side by Side toolbar also appears.

4 To scroll through the workbooks, drag the scroll box up or down in one workbook. Excel automatically scrolls the other workbook for you.

5 When you finish comparing the workbooks on your screen, click **Close Side by Side**.

E-MAIL A WORKSHEET

You can e-mail the worksheet displayed on your screen to exchange data with a friend, family member or colleague.

When you e-mail a worksheet, the worksheet appears in the body of the e-mail message.

Before you can e-mail a worksheet, Microsoft Office Outlook 2003 must be set up on your computer.

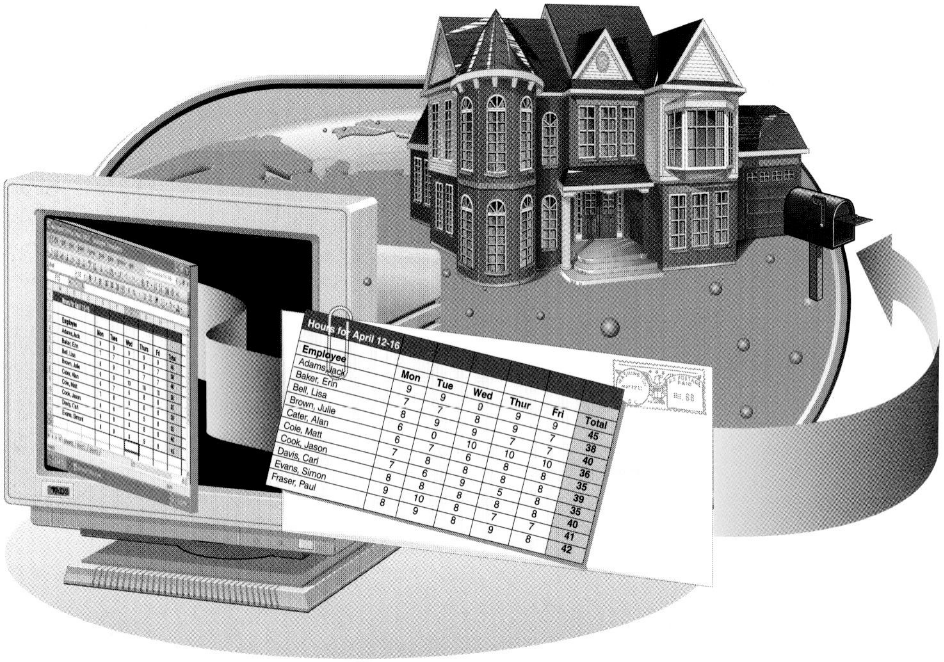

E-MAIL A WORKSHEET

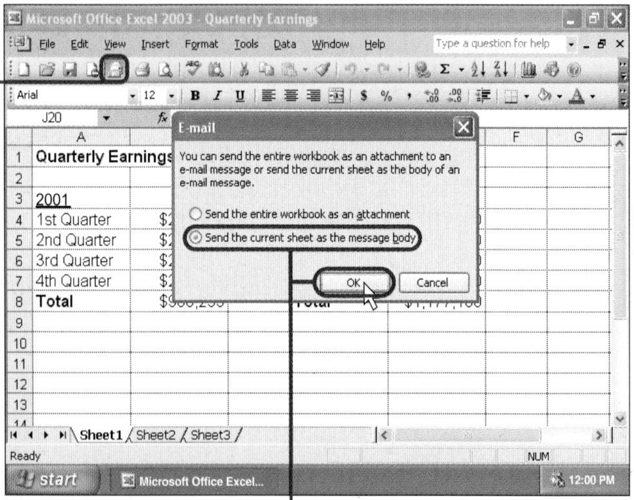

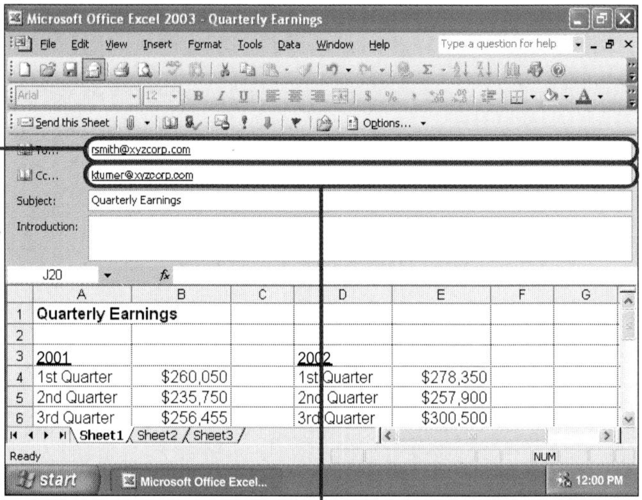

1 Click [icon] to e-mail the current worksheet.

Note: If [icon] is not displayed, click [icon] on the Standard toolbar to display the button.

■ If the workbook contains data on more than one worksheet, a dialog box appears, asking if you want to send the entire workbook or just the current worksheet.

2 Click this option to send the current worksheet.

3 Click **OK**.

■ An area appears for you to address the message.

4 Click this area and type the e-mail address of the person you want to receive the message.

5 To send a copy of the message to a person who is not directly involved but would be interested in the message, click this area and type the e-mail address.

*Note: To enter more than one e-mail address in step **4** or **5**, separate each e-mail address with a semicolon (;).*

Tip

Why would I include an introduction for a worksheet I am e-mailing?

Including an introduction allows you to provide the recipient of the message with additional information about the worksheet. For example, the recipient may require instructions or an explanation of the content of the worksheet.

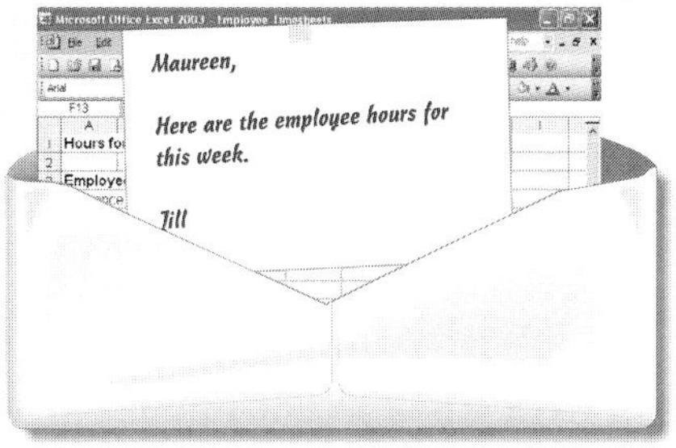

Tip

How do I e-mail an entire workbook?

To e-mail an entire workbook, perform steps **1** to **6** below, selecting **Send the entire workbook as an attachment** in step **2**. Then click **Send** to send the message. When you e-mail an entire workbook, the workbook is sent as an attached file.

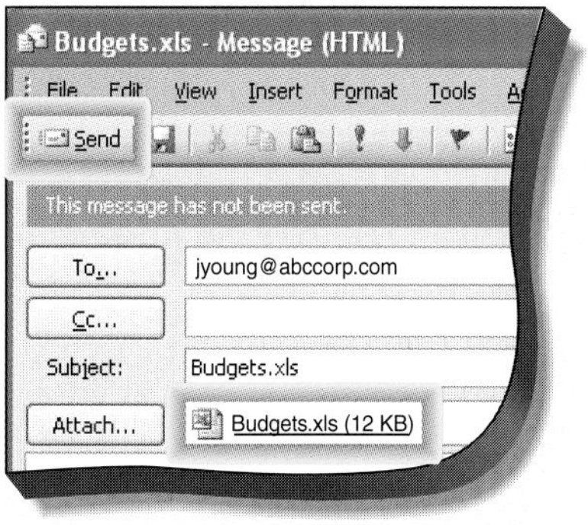

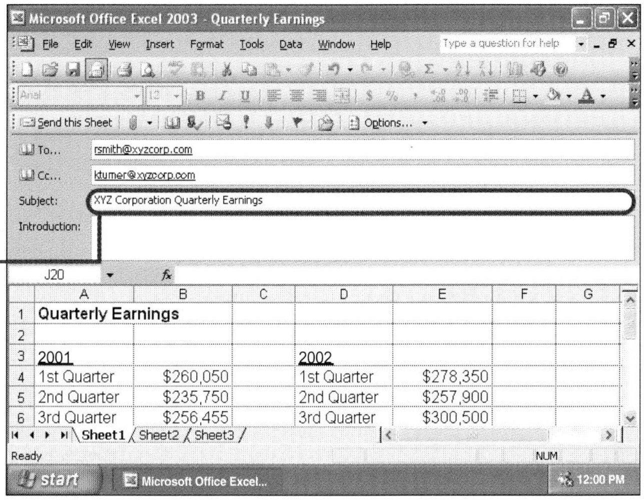

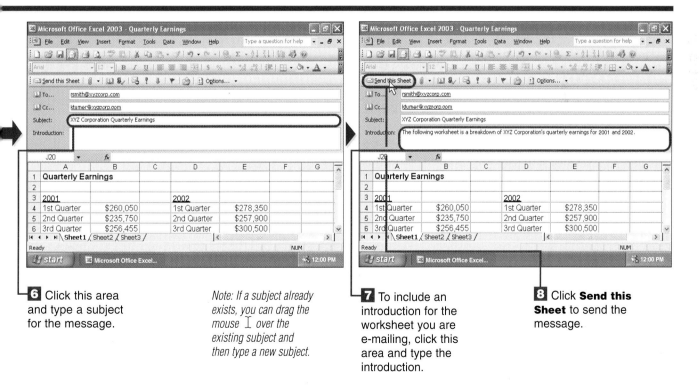

6 Click this area and type a subject for the message.

Note: If a subject already exists, you can drag the mouse I over the existing subject and then type a new subject.

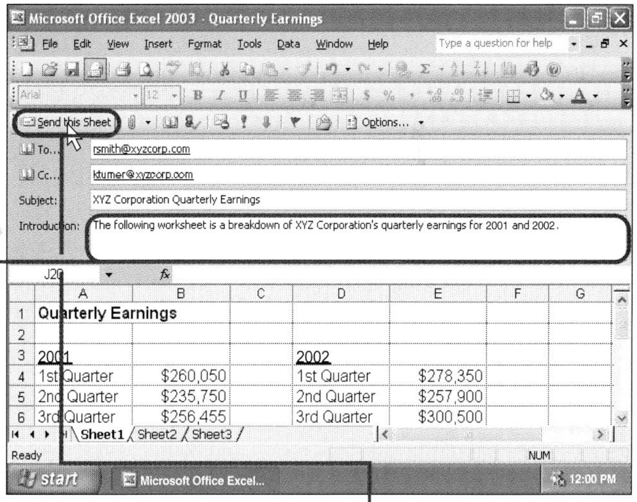

7 To include an introduction for the worksheet you are e-mailing, click this area and type the introduction.

8 Click **Send this Sheet** to send the message.

EDIT OR DELETE DATA

You can edit data in your worksheet to correct a mistake or update data. You can also remove data you no longer need.

EDIT DATA

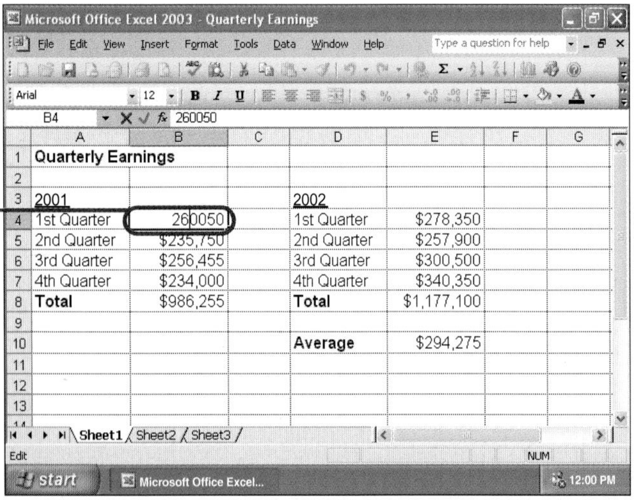

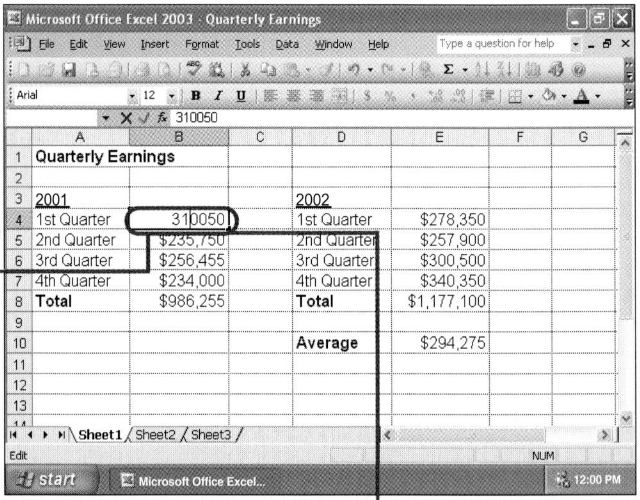

1 Double-click the cell containing the data you want to edit.

■ A flashing insertion point appears in the cell.

2 Press the ← or → key to move the insertion point to where you want to remove or add characters.

3 To remove the character to the left of the insertion point, press the Backspace key.

■ To remove the character to the right of the insertion point, press the Delete key.

4 To add data where the insertion point flashes on your screen, type the data.

5 When you finish making changes to the data, press the Enter key.

Tip

Can Excel automatically correct my typing mistakes?

Yes. Excel automatically corrects common spelling errors as you type. Here are a few examples.

adn	and
alot	a lot
comitee	committee
don;t	don't
nwe	new
occurence	occurrence
recieve	receive
seperate	separate
teh	the

Tip

When I delete the data in a cell, will Excel remove the formatting from the cell?

No. When you delete the data in a cell, Excel will not remove the formatting you applied to the cell, such as a new font or color. Any new data you enter into the cell will display the same formatting as the data you deleted.

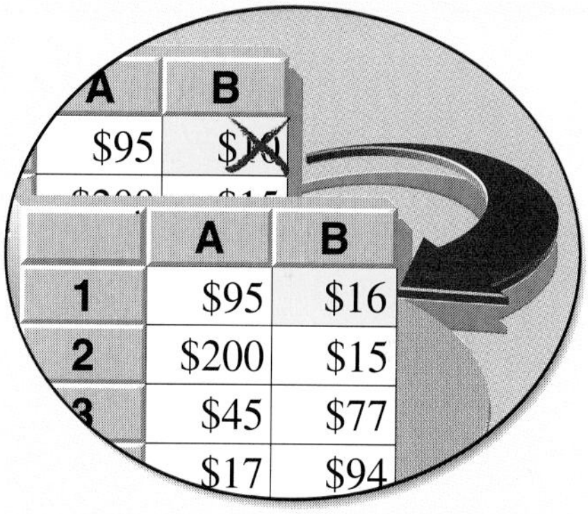

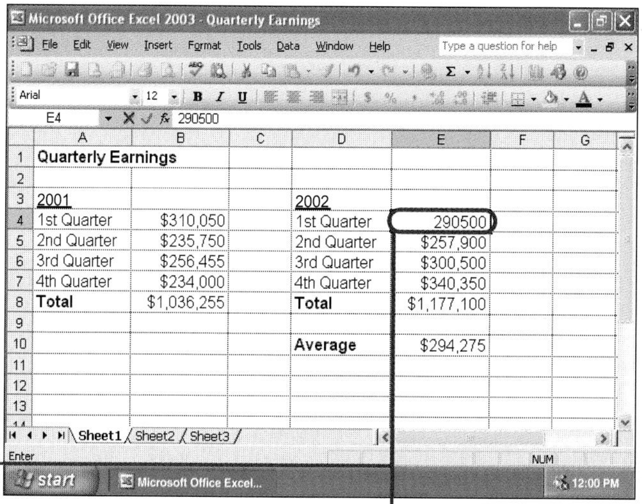

REPLACE ALL DATA IN A CELL

1. Click the cell containing the data you want to replace with new data.
2. Type the new data and then press the **Enter** key.

DELETE DATA

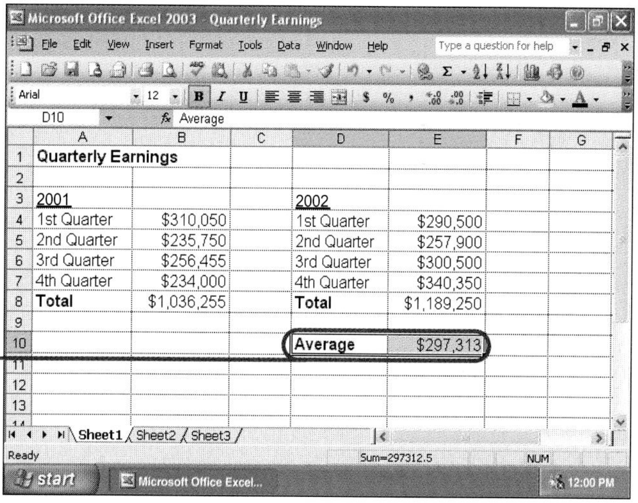

1. Select the cells containing the data you want to delete. To select cells, see page 94.
2. Press the **Delete** key.

- The data in the cells you selected disappears.
- To deselect cells, click any cell.

MOVE OR COPY DATA

You can move or copy data to a new location in your worksheet.

Moving data allows you to reorganize data in your worksheet. When you move data, the data disappears from its original location.

Copying data allows you to repeat data in your worksheet without having to retype the data. When you copy data, the data appears in both the original and new locations.

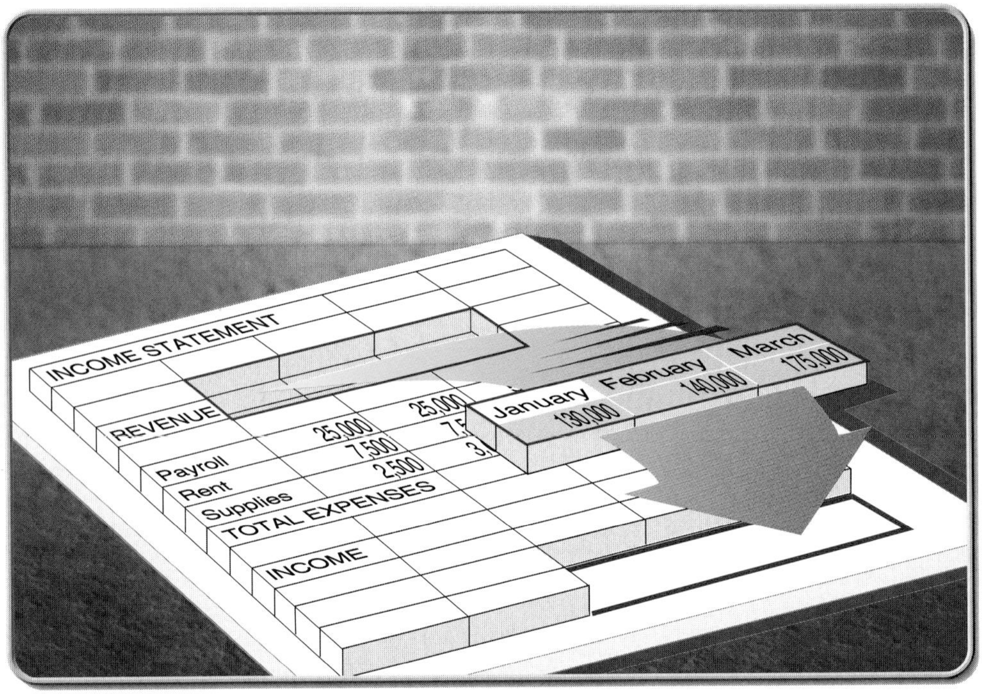

MOVE OR COPY DATA

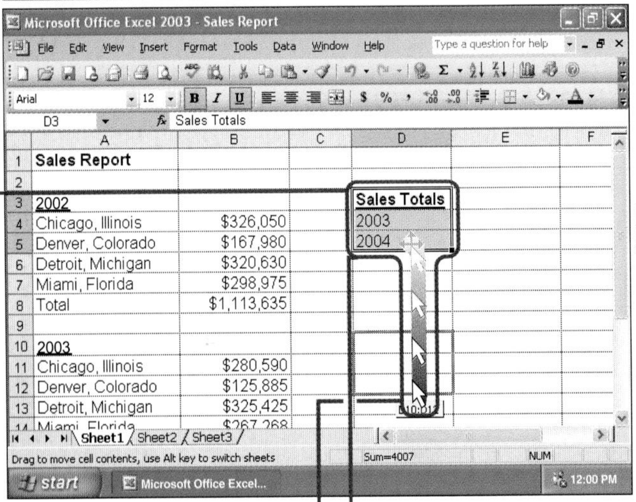

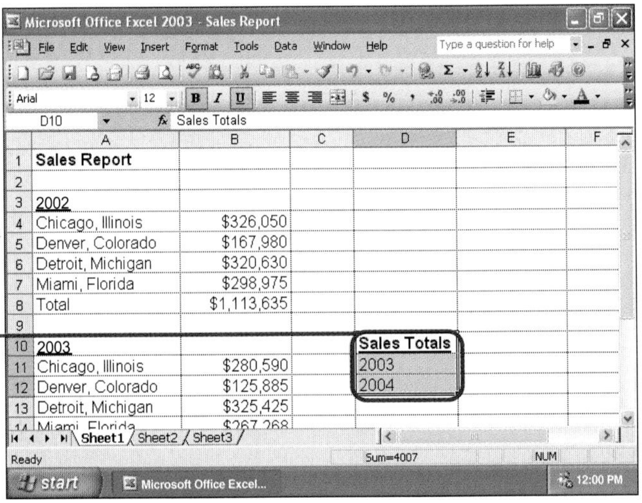

USING DRAG AND DROP

1 Select the cells containing the data you want to move. To select cells, see page 94.

2 Position the mouse over a border of the selected cells (changes to).

3 To move the data, drag the mouse to where you want to place the data.

Note: A gray box indicates where the data will appear.

■ The data moves to the new location.

■ To copy data, perform steps **1** to **3**, except press and hold down the **Ctrl** key as you perform step **3**.

Tip

How can I use the Clipboard task pane to move or copy data?

The Clipboard task pane displays the last 24 items you have selected to move or copy using the toolbar buttons. To display the Clipboard task pane, see page 8. To place a clipboard item into your worksheet, click the cell where you want to place the item and then click the item in the task pane.

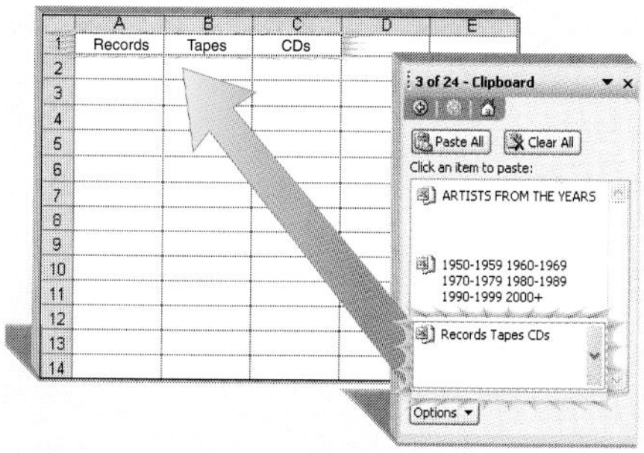

Tip

Why does the Paste Options button ( ) appear when I copy data?

You can use the Paste Options button ( ) to change the way Excel copies data when you use the Copy button ( ). For example, you can specify that you want to copy only the formatting of the original cells to the new location. Click the Paste Options button to display a list of options and then select the option you want to use. The Paste Options button is available only until you perform another task.

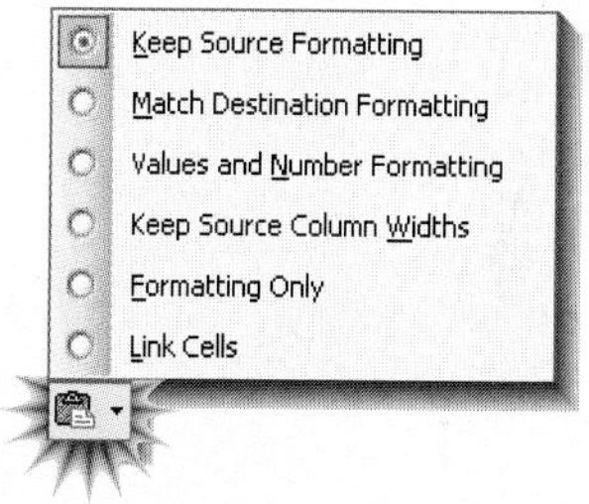

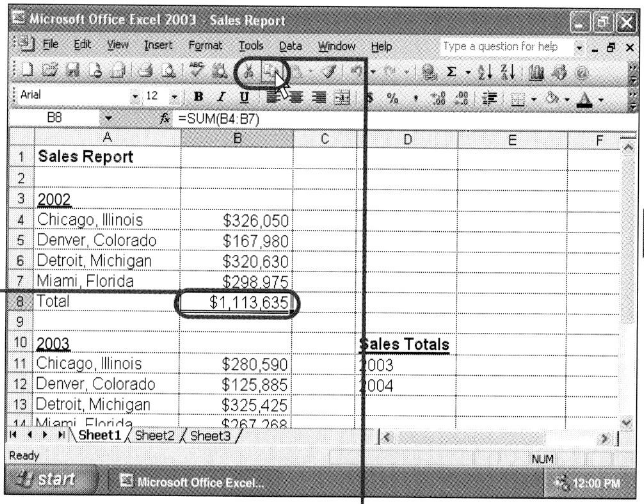

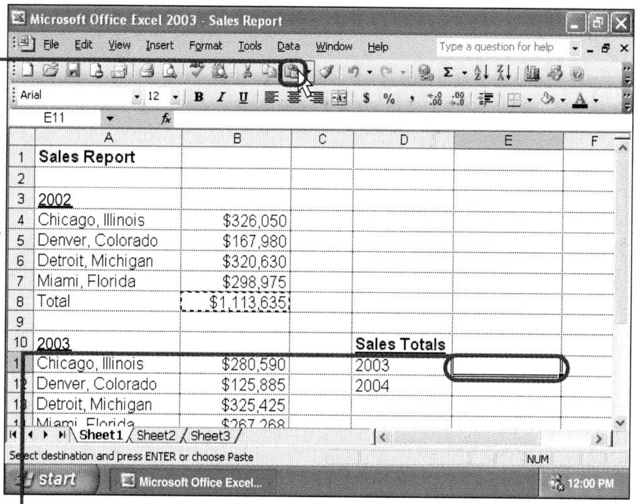

USING THE TOOLBAR BUTTONS

1 Select the cells containing the data you want to move or copy. To select cells, see page 94.

2 Click one of the following buttons.

Move data

Copy data

Note: If the button you want is not displayed, click on the Standard toolbar to display the button.

3 Click the cell where you want to place the data. This cell will become the top left cell of the new location.

4 Click to place the data in the new location.

Note: If is not displayed, click on the Standard toolbar to display the button.

■ The data appears in the new location.

INSERT A ROW OR COLUMN

You can add a row or column to your worksheet to insert additional data.

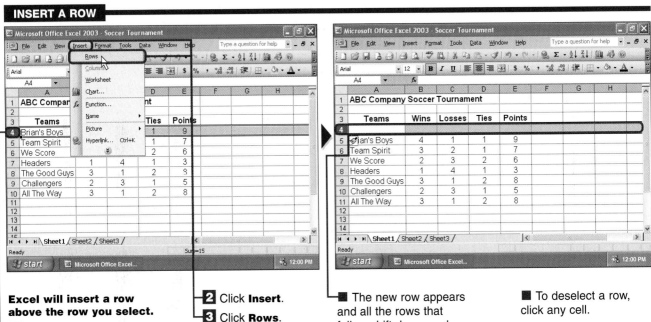

When you add a row or column, Excel automatically adjusts the row numbers and column letters in your worksheet for you.

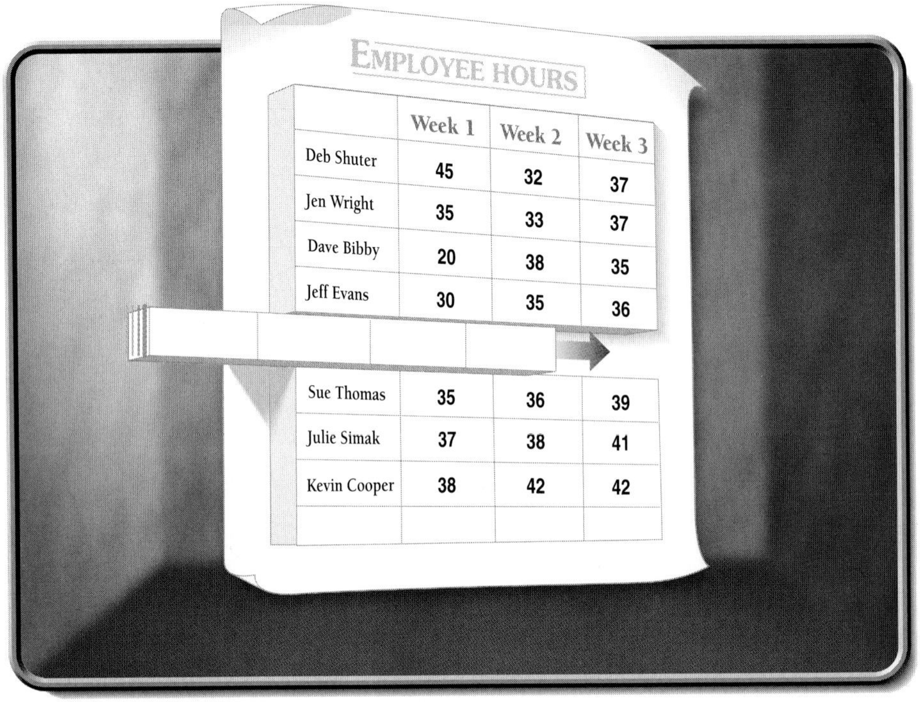

INSERT A ROW

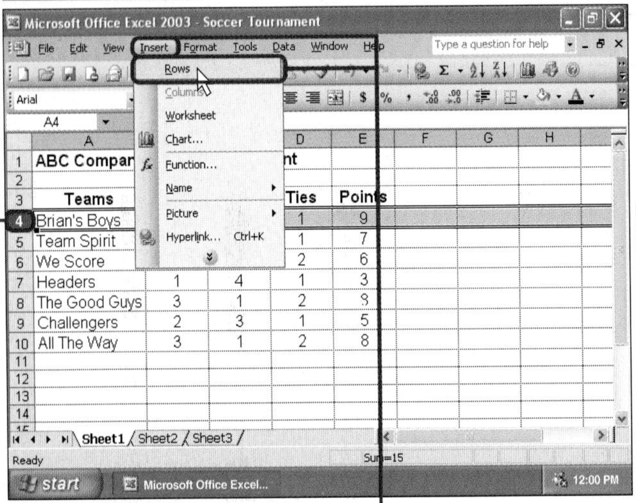

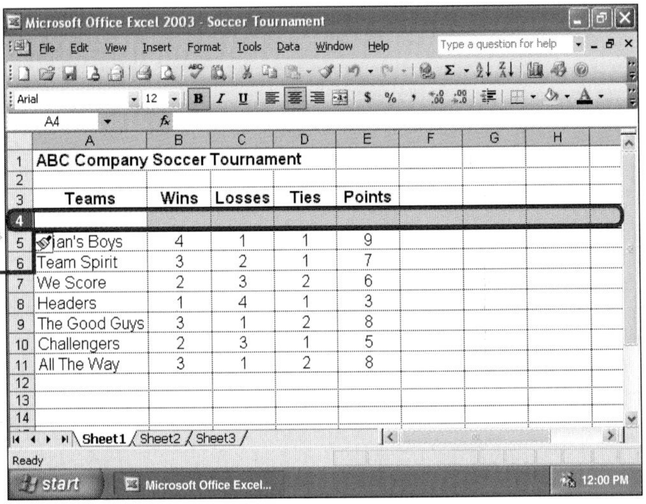

Excel will insert a row above the row you select.

1 To select a row, click the row number.

2 Click **Insert**.

3 Click **Rows**.

■ The new row appears and all the rows that follow shift downward.

■ To deselect a row, click any cell.

Tip

Do I need to adjust my formulas when I insert a row or column?

No. When you insert a row or column, Excel automatically updates any formulas affected by the insertion. For information on formulas, see pages 120 to 133.

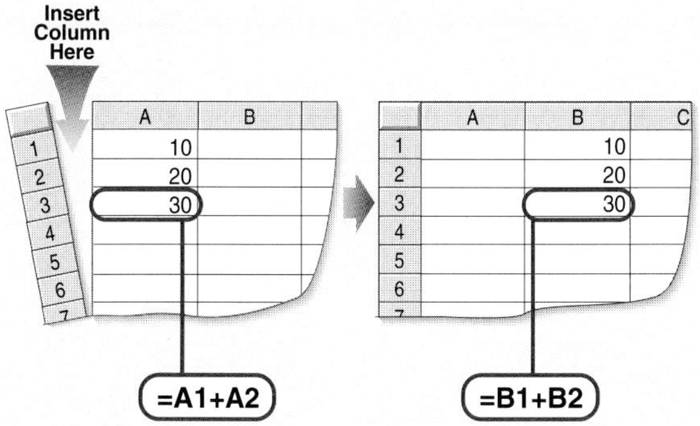

Tip

How do I insert several rows or columns at once?

You can use one of the methods shown below to insert several rows or columns at once, but you must first select the number of rows or columns you want to insert. For example, to insert two columns, select two columns and then perform steps **2** and **3** below. To select multiple rows or columns, see page 95.

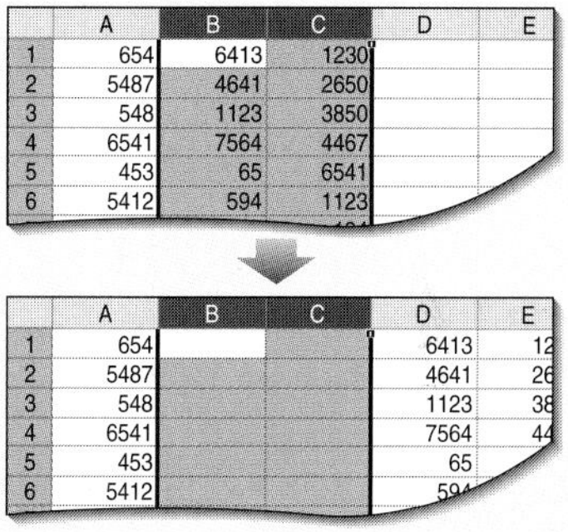

INSERT A COLUMN

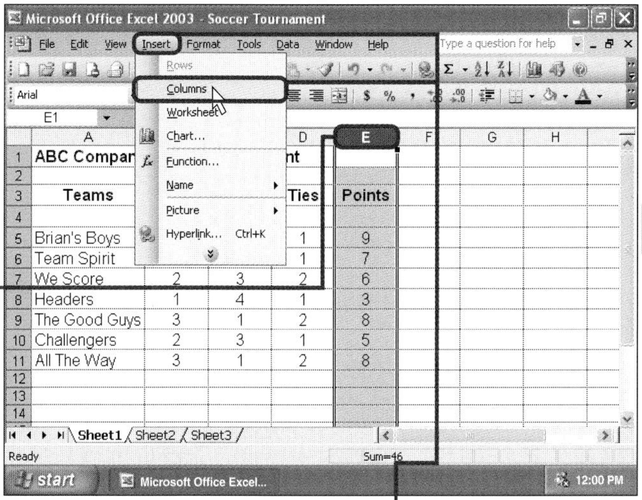

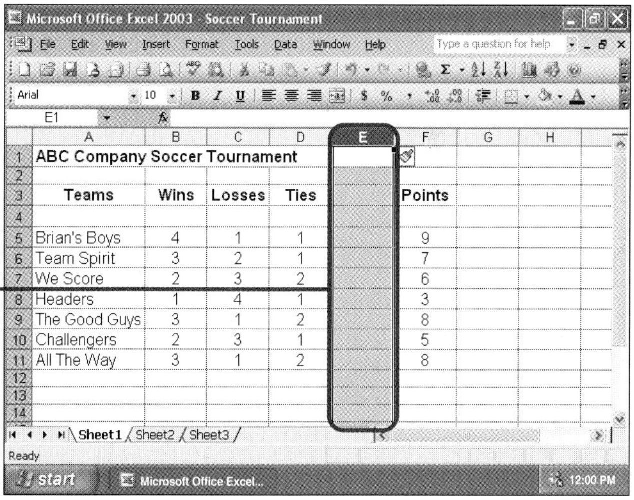

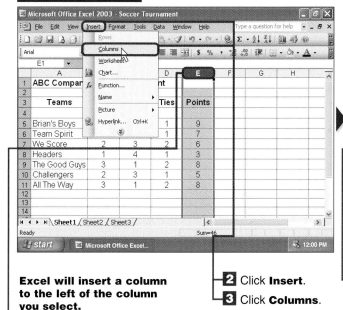

Excel will insert a column to the left of the column you select.

1 To select a column, click the column letter.

2 Click **Insert**.

3 Click **Columns**.

■ The new column appears and all the columns that follow shift to the right.

■ To deselect a column, click any cell.

DELETE A ROW OR COLUMN

You can delete a row or column to remove data you no longer want to display in your worksheet.

When you delete a row, the remaining rows in your worksheet shift upward. When you delete a column, the remaining columns shift to the left. Excel automatically adjusts the row numbers and column letters in your worksheet for you.

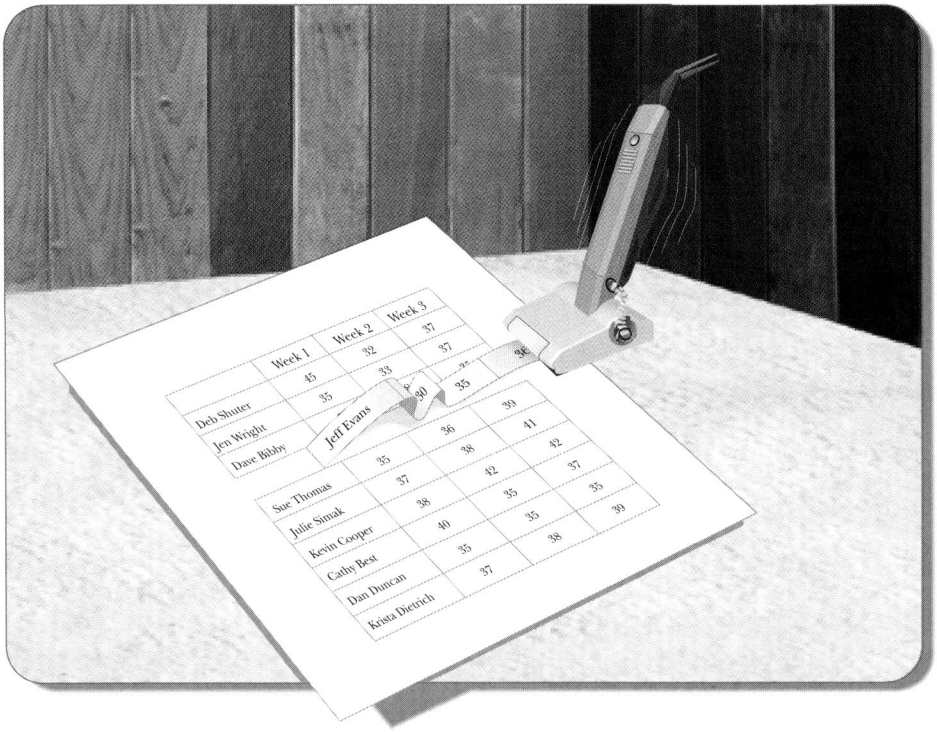

DELETE A ROW

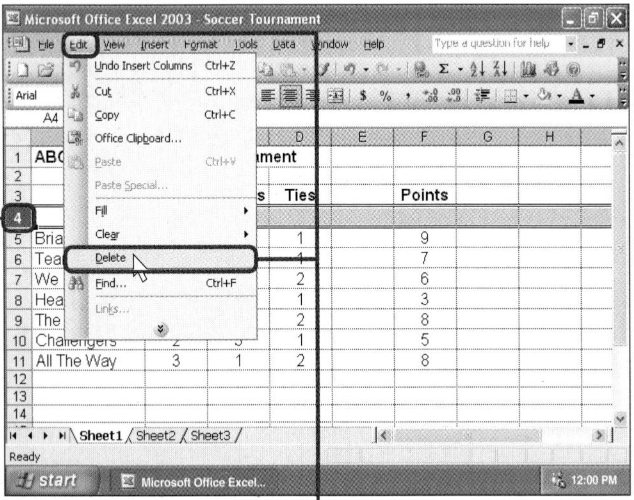

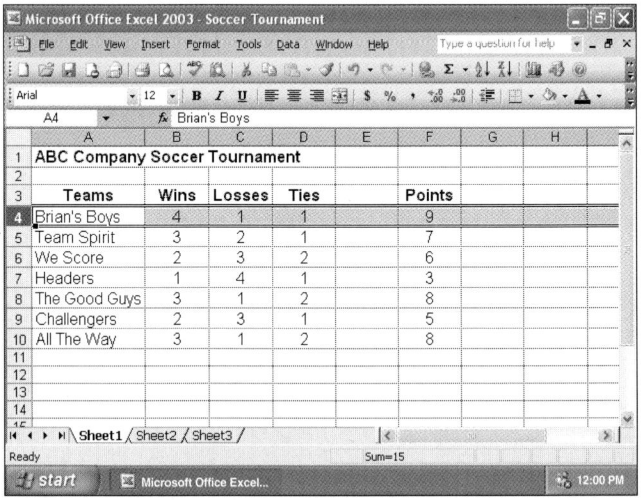

1 To select the row you want to delete, click the row number.

2 Click **Edit**.

3 Click **Delete** to delete the row.

■ The row disappears and all the rows that follow shift upward.

■ To deselect a row, click any cell.

Tip

Why did #REF! appear in a cell after I deleted a row or column?

If #REF! appears in a cell in your worksheet, you may have deleted data needed to calculate a formula. Before you delete a row or column, make sure the row or column does not contain data that is used in a formula. For information on formulas, see pages 120 to 133.

Tip

How do I delete several rows or columns at once?

You can use one of the methods shown below to delete several rows or columns at once, but you must first select the rows or columns you want to delete. For example, to delete three columns, select the columns and then perform steps **2** and **3** below. To select multiple rows or columns, see page 95.

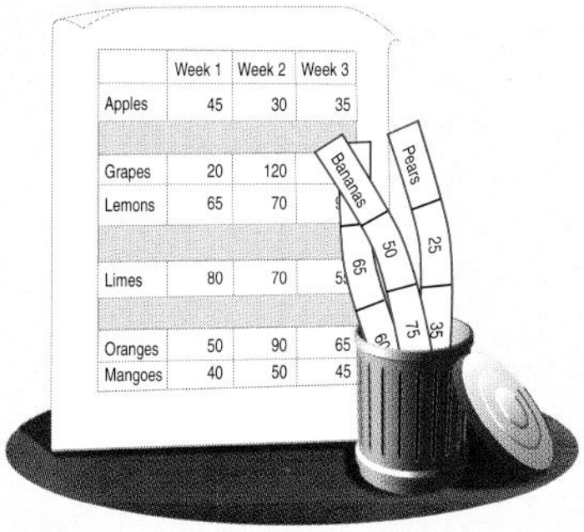

DELETE A COLUMN

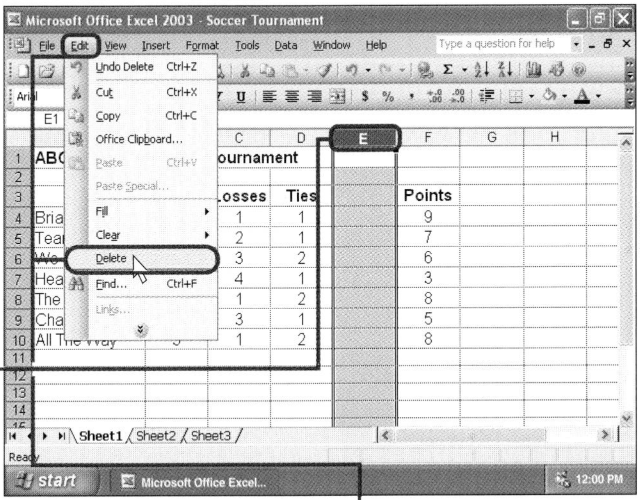

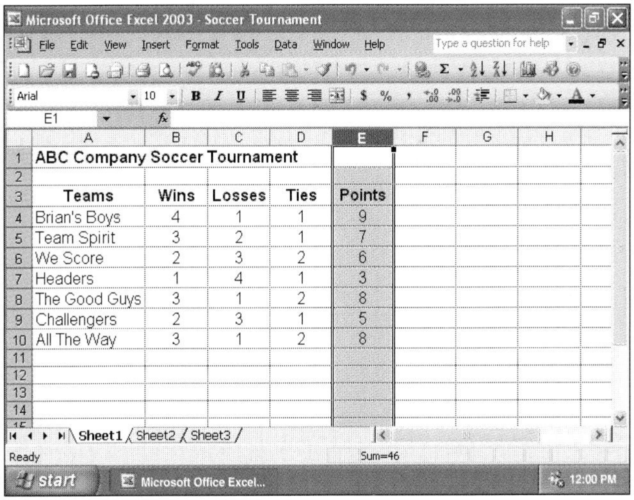

1 To select the column you want to delete, click the column letter.

2 Click **Edit**.

3 Click **Delete** to delete the column.

■ The column disappears and all the columns that follow shift to the left.

■ To deselect a column, click any cell.

UNDO CHANGES

Excel remembers the last changes you made to your worksheet. If you regret these changes, you can cancel them by using the Undo feature.

The Undo feature can cancel your last editing and formatting changes. If you do not like the results of canceling an editing or formatting change, you can easily reverse the results.

UNDO CHANGES

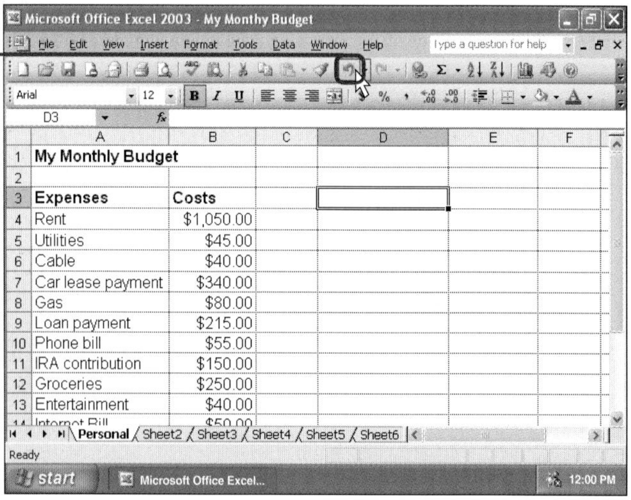

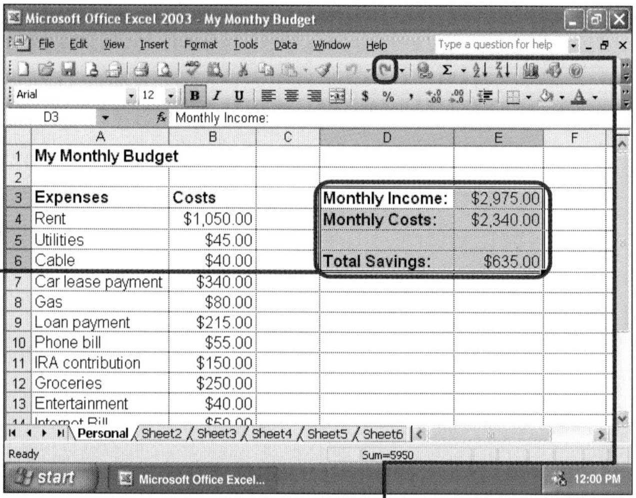

1 Click to undo the last change you made to your worksheet.

Note: If is not displayed, click on the Standard toolbar to display the button.

■ Excel cancels the last change you made to your worksheet.

■ You can repeat step **1** to cancel previous changes you made.

■ To reverse the results of using the Undo feature, click .

Note: If is not displayed, click on the Standard toolbar to display the button.

ZOOM IN OR OUT

You can enlarge or reduce the display of data on your screen.

Changing the zoom setting allows you to see data in more detail or display more data on your screen at once. Changing the zoom setting will not affect the way data appears on a printed page.

ZOOM IN OR OUT

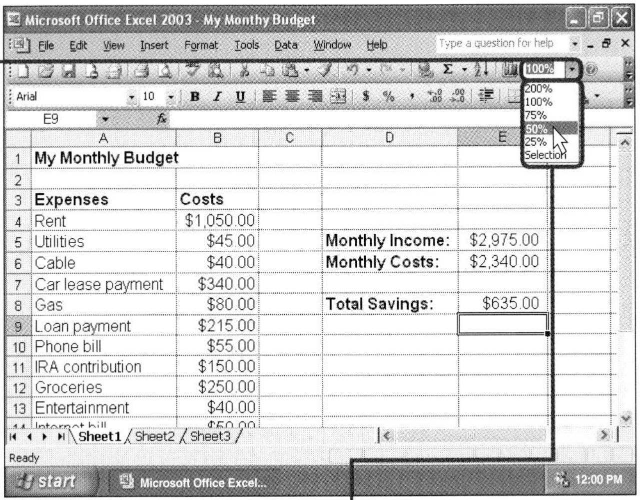

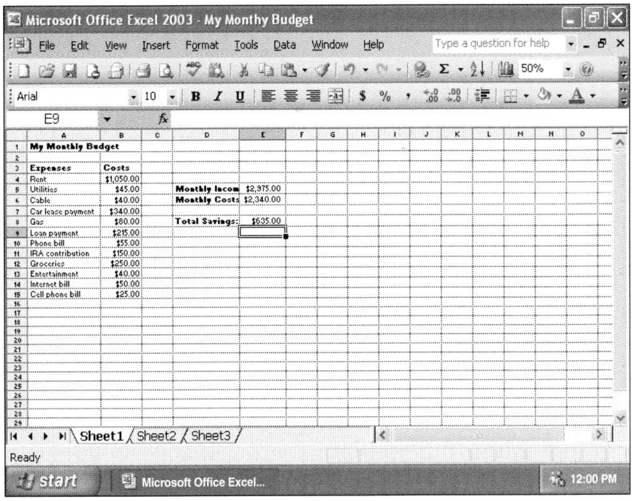

1 Click ▾ in this area to display a list of zoom settings.

Note: If the Zoom area is not displayed, click ⁝ on the Standard toolbar to display the area.

2 Click the zoom setting you want to use.

*Note: If you select cells before performing step **1**, the **Selection** setting enlarges the selected cells to fill the window. To select cells, see page 94.*

■ The worksheet appears in the new zoom setting. You can edit the worksheet as usual.

■ To return to the normal zoom setting, repeat steps **1** and **2**, selecting **100%** in step **2**.

INTRODUCTION TO FORMULAS AND FUNCTIONS

A formula allows you to calculate and analyze data in your worksheet.

A formula always begins with an equal sign (=).

OPERATORS

A formula can contain one or more operators. An operator specifies the type of calculation you want to perform.

Arithmetic Operators

You can use arithmetic operators to perform mathematical calculations.

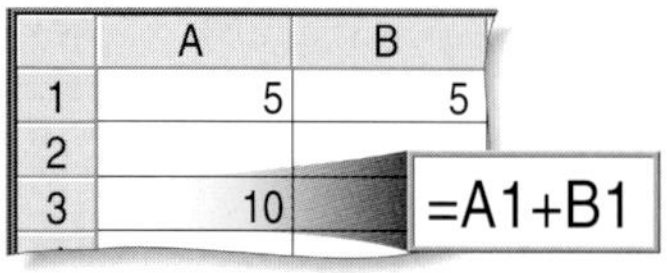

Operator	Description
+	Addition (A1+B1)
-	Subtraction (A1-B1)
*	Multiplication (A1*B1)
/	Division (A1/B1)
%	Percent (A1%)
^	Exponentiation (A1^B1)

Comparison Operators

You can use comparison operators to compare two values. Comparison operators return a value of TRUE or FALSE.

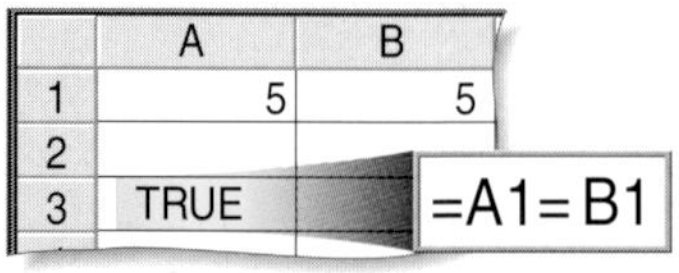

Operator	Description
=	Equal to (A1=B1)
>	Greater than (A1>B1)
<	Less than (A1<B1)
>=	Greater than or equal to (A1>=B1)
<=	Less than or equal to (A1<=B1)
<>	Not equal to (A1<>B1)

ORDER OF CALCULATIONS

Order of Calculations	
1	Percent (%)
2	Exponentiation (^)
3	Multiplication (*) and Division (/)
4	Addition (+) and Subtraction (-)
5	Comparison operators

When a formula contains more than one operator, Excel performs the calculations in a specific order.

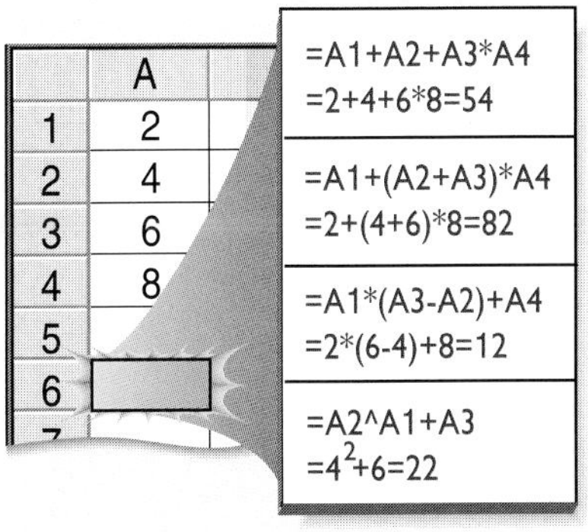

You can use parentheses ( ) to change the order in which Excel performs calculations. Excel will perform the calculations inside the parentheses first.

CELL REFERENCES

When entering formulas, use cell references instead of actual data whenever possible. For example, enter the formula =A1+A2 instead of =10+20.

When you use cell references and you change a number used in a formula, Excel will automatically redo the calculation for you.

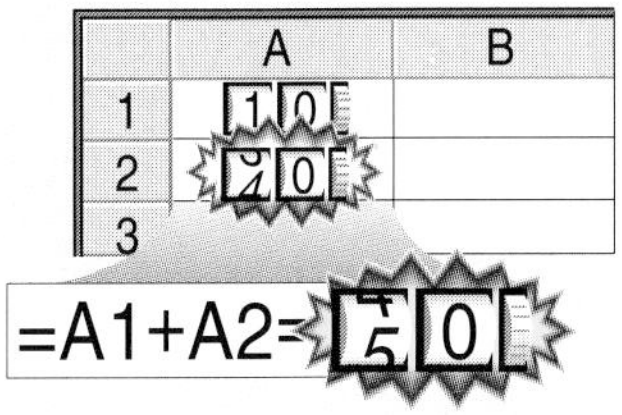

FUNCTIONS

A function is a ready-to-use formula that you can use to perform a calculation on the data in your worksheet. Examples of commonly used functions include AVERAGE, COUNT, MAX and SUM.

- A function always begins with an equal sign (=).
- The data Excel will use to calculate a function is enclosed in parentheses ( ).

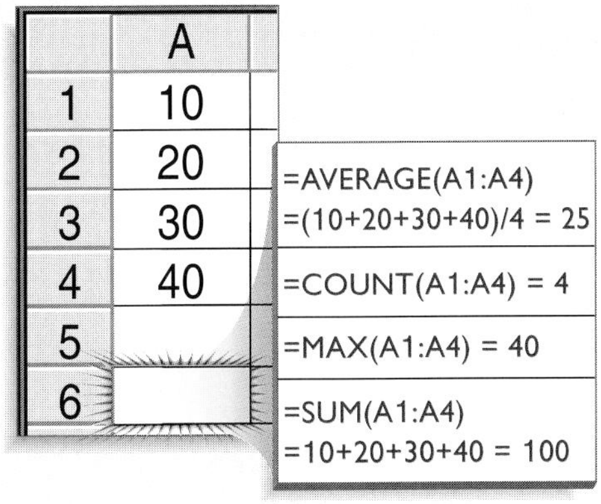

A
1 10
2 20
3 30
4 40
5
6
=AVERAGE(A1:A4)
=(10+20+30+40)/4 = 25
=COUNT(A1:A4) = 4
=MAX(A1:A4) = 40
=SUM(A1:A4)
=10+20+30+40 = 100

Specify Individual Cells

When a comma (,) separates cell references in a function, Excel uses each cell to perform the calculation. For example, =SUM(A1,A2,A3) is the same as the formula =A1+A2+A3.

Specify a Group of Cells

When a colon (:) separates cell references in a function, Excel uses the specified cells and all cells between them to perform the calculation. For example, =SUM(A1:A3) is the same as the formula =A1+A2+A3.

ENTER A FORMULA

You can enter a formula into any cell in your worksheet. A formula helps you calculate and analyze data in your worksheet.

When entering formulas, you should use cell references instead of actual data whenever possible.

A formula always begins with an equal sign (=).

ENTER A FORMULA

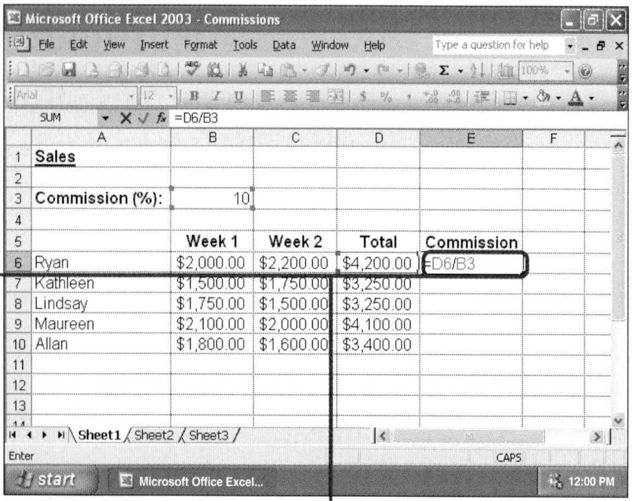

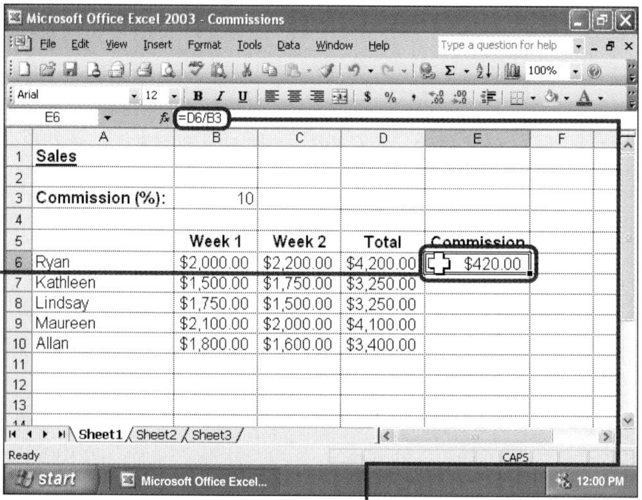

1 Click the cell where you want to enter a formula.

2 Type an equal sign (=) to begin the formula.

3 Type the formula and then press the **Enter** key.

Note: As you enter the formula, Excel adds a colored outline to each cell you refer to in the formula.

■ The result of the calculation appears in the cell.

4 To view the formula you entered, click the cell containing the formula.

■ The formula bar displays the formula for the cell.

Tip

What happens if I change a number used in a formula?

When you use cell references and you change a number used in a formula, Excel will automatically redo the calculation for you.

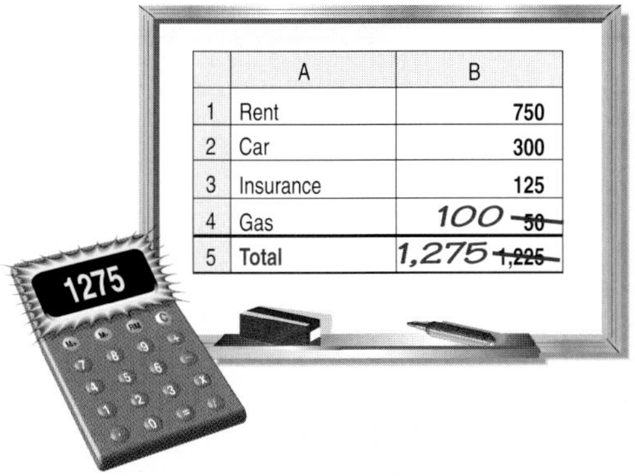

Tip

How can I quickly enter cell references into a formula?

To quickly enter cell references, perform steps **1** and **2** on page 122 and then click the first cell you want to use in the formula. Type the operator you want to use to perform the calculation and then click the next cell you want to use in the formula. When you finish entering cell references and operators, press the Enter key to perform the calculation.

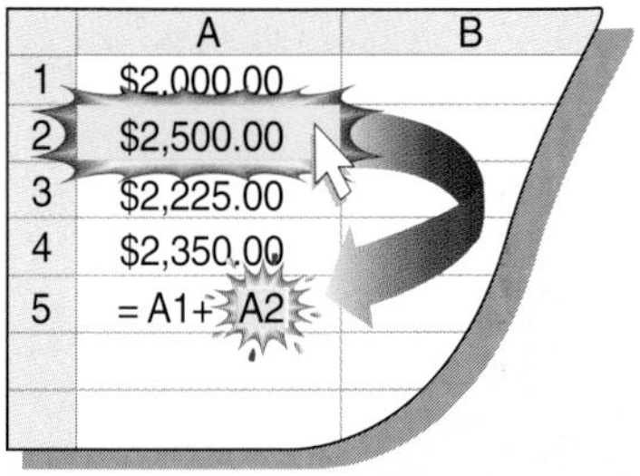

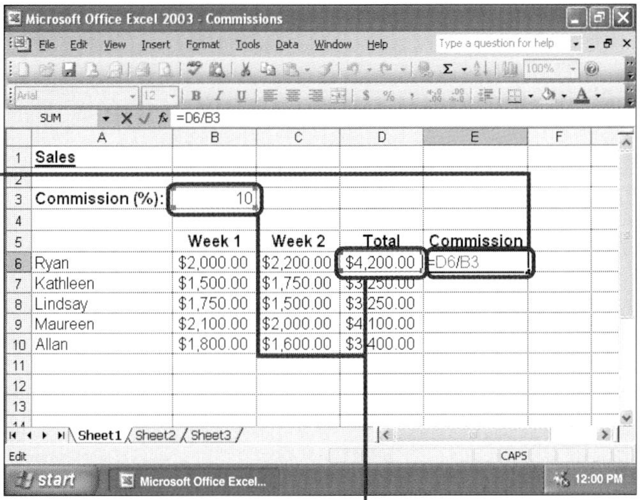

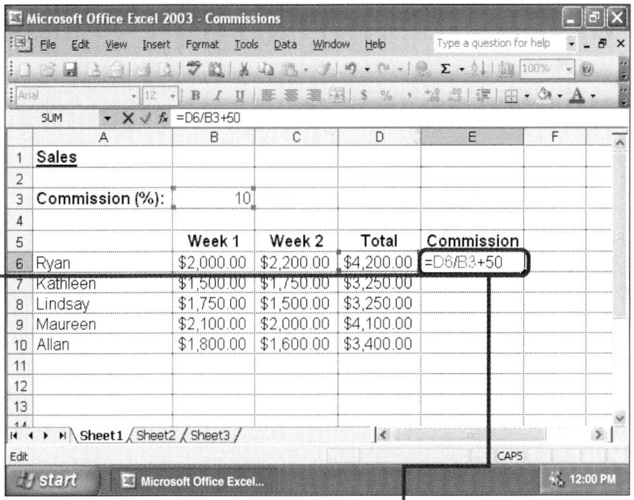

EDIT A FORMULA

1 Double-click the cell containing the formula you want to change.

■ The formula appears in the cell.

■ Excel outlines each cell used in the formula with a different color.

2 Press the ← or → key to move the flashing insertion point to where you want to remove or add characters.

■ To remove the character to the left of the insertion point, press the Backspace key.

3 To add data where the insertion point flashes on your screen, type the data.

4 When you finish making changes to the formula, press the Enter key.

ENTER A FUNCTION

Excel helps you enter functions into your worksheet. Functions allow you to perform calculations without having to type long, complex formulas.

Excel offers over 200 functions to help you analyze data in your worksheet. There are financial functions, math and trigonometry functions, date and time functions, statistical functions and many more.

ENTER A FUNCTION

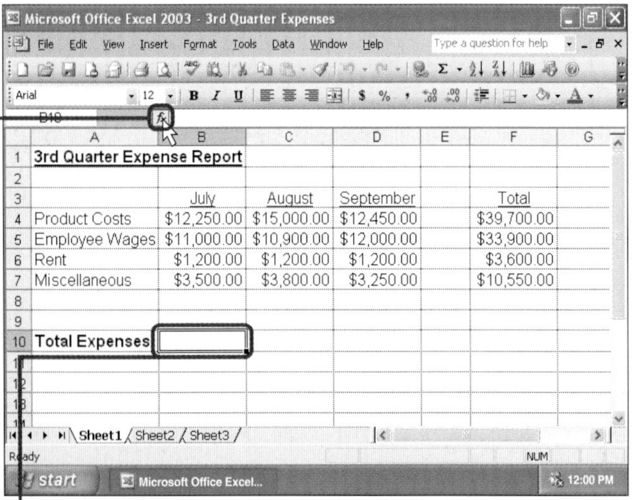

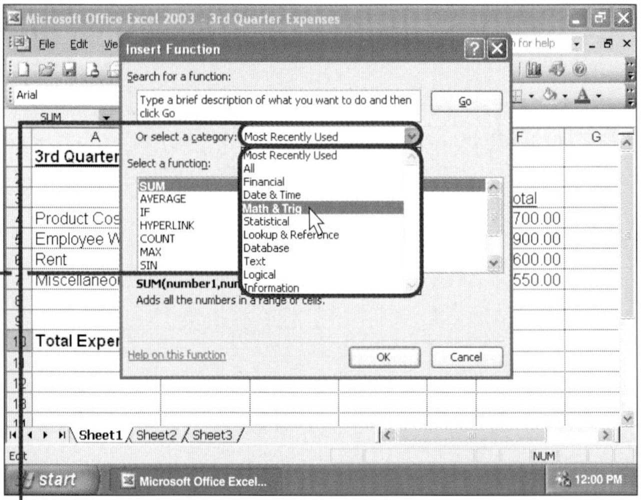

1 Click the cell where you want to enter a function.

2 Click f_x to enter a function.

■ The Insert Function dialog box appears.

3 Click this area to display the categories of available functions.

4 Click the category containing the function you want to use.

*Note: If you do not know which category contains the function you want to use, select **All** to display a list of all the functions.*

Tip

Can Excel help me find the function I should use to perform a calculation?

If you do not know which function to use to perform a calculation, you can have Excel recommend a function.

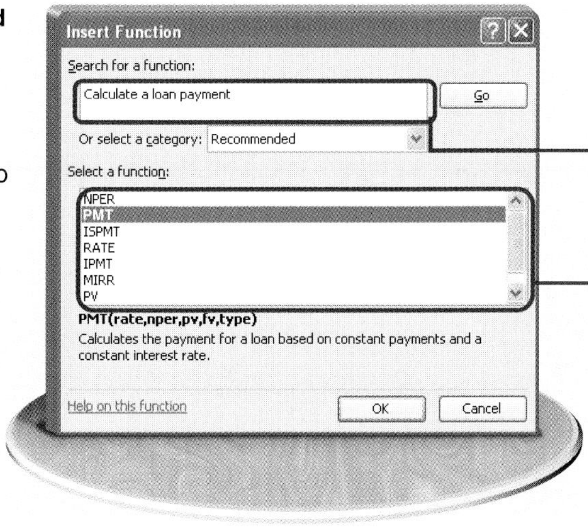

1 Perform steps **1** and **2** below to display the Insert Function dialog box.

2 Type a brief description of the calculation you want to perform and then press the Enter key.

■ This area displays a list of recommended functions you can use to perform the calculation. You can perform steps **5** to **11** below to use a function Excel recommends.

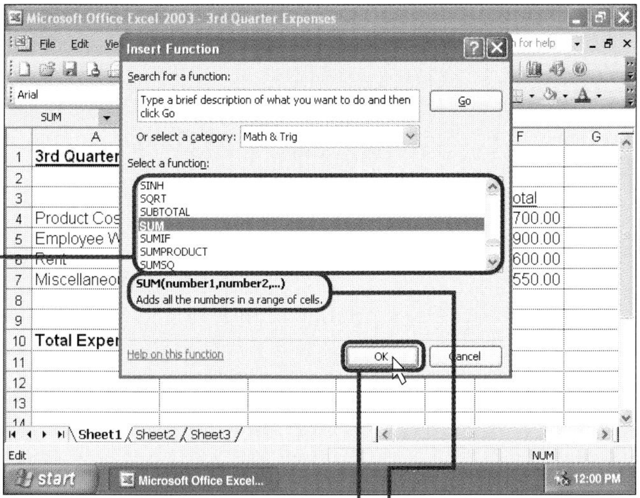

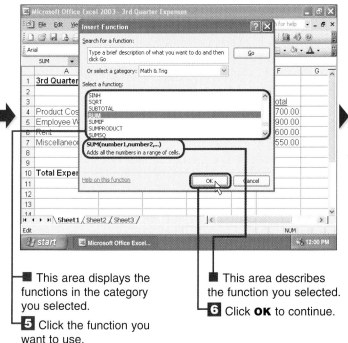

■ This area displays the functions in the category you selected.

5 Click the function you want to use.

■ This area describes the function you selected.

6 Click **OK** to continue.

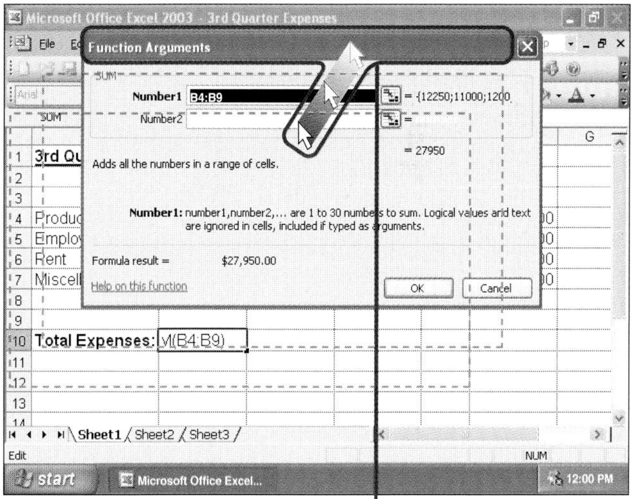

■ The Function Arguments dialog box appears. If the dialog box covers data you want to use in the function, you can move the dialog box to a new location.

7 To move the dialog box, position the mouse over the title bar and then drag the dialog box to a new location.

CONTINUED

ENTER A FUNCTION

When entering a function, you must specify which numbers you want to use in the calculation. You may need to specify several numbers or only one number, depending on the function you are using.

ENTER A FUNCTION (CONTINUED)

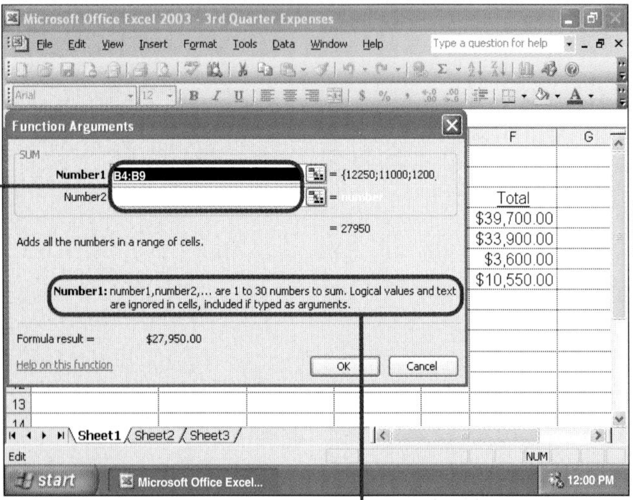

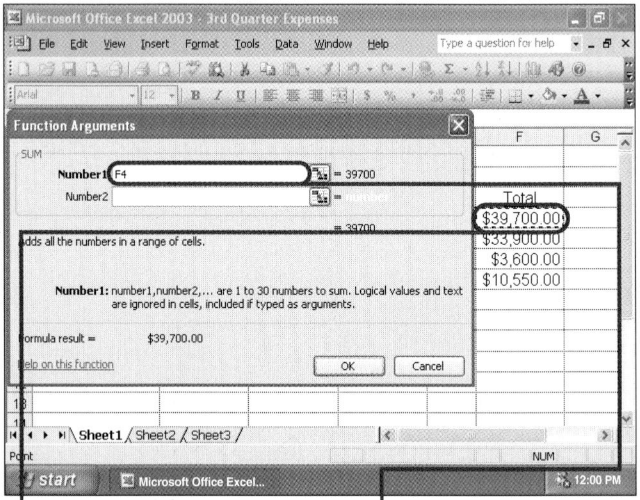

■ This area displays boxes where you enter the numbers you want to use in the function.

■ This area describes the numbers you need to enter.

8 To enter the first number for the function, click the cell that contains the number.

Note: If the number you want to use does not appear in your worksheet, type the number.

■ The cell reference for the number appears in this area.

Tip

Can I enter a function by myself?

If you know the name of the function you want to use, you can type the function and cell references directly into a cell in your worksheet. You must start the function with an equal sign (=), enclose the cell references in parentheses ( ) and separate each cell reference with a comma (,). You can also separate cell references with a colon (:) to indicate that Excel should include the specified cells and all the cells between them in the function.

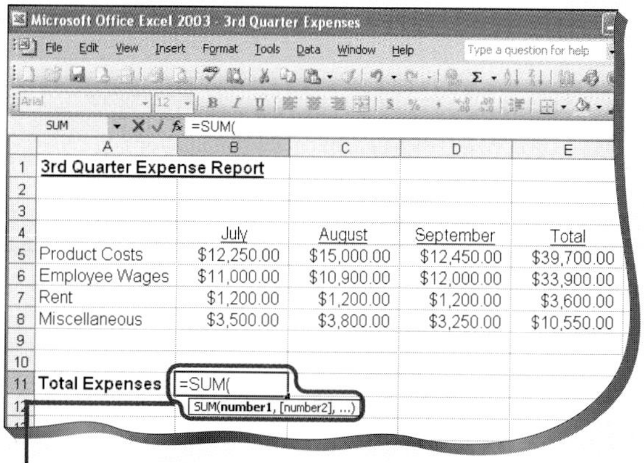

■ When you type a function directly into a cell, a yellow box appears, displaying the name of the function. You can click the name of the function to display help information about the function.

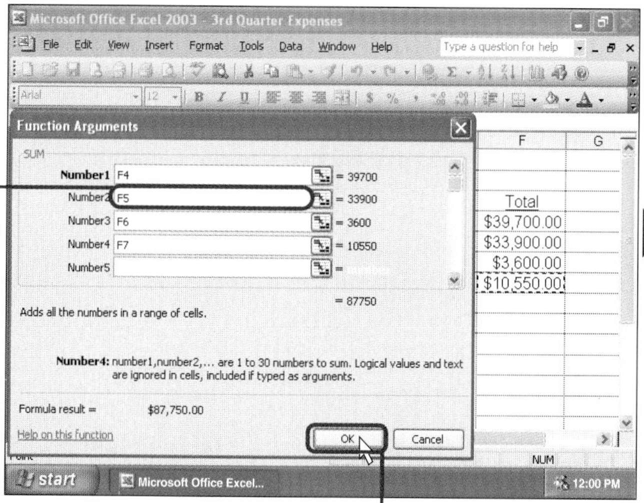

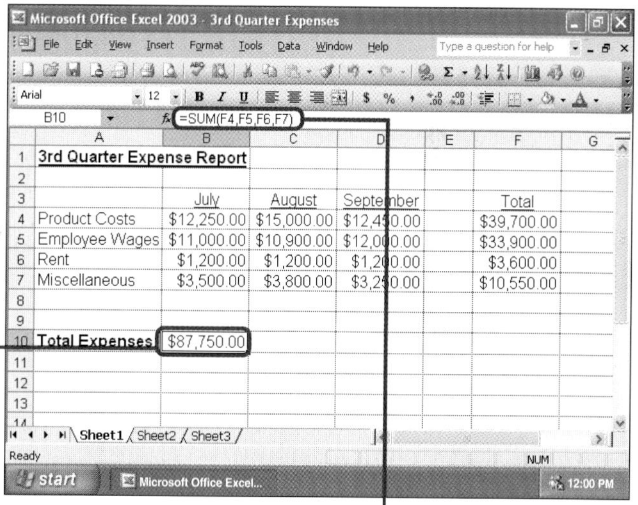

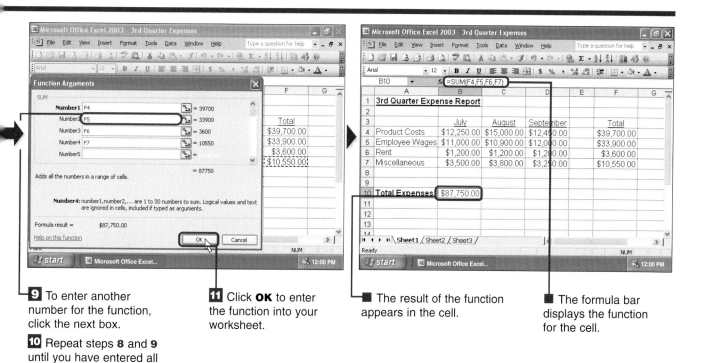

9 To enter another number for the function, click the next box.

10 Repeat steps **8** and **9** until you have entered all the numbers you want to use in the function.

11 Click **OK** to enter the function into your worksheet.

■ The result of the function appears in the cell.

■ The formula bar displays the function for the cell.

PERFORM COMMON CALCULATIONS

You can quickly perform common calculations on numbers in your worksheet. For example, you can calculate the sum of a list of numbers.

PERFORM COMMON CALCULATIONS

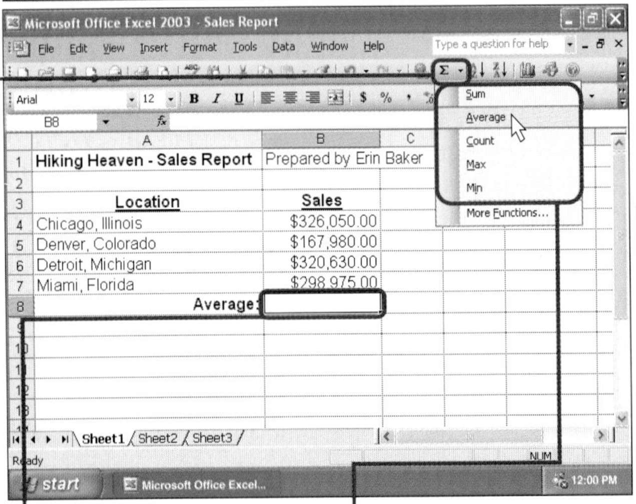

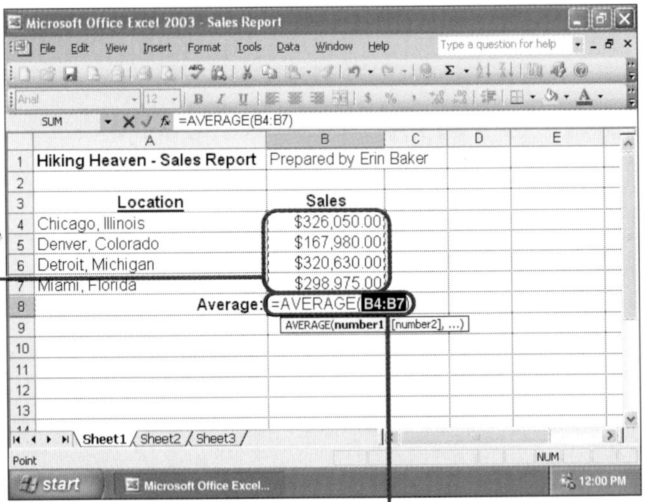

1 Click the cell below or to the right of the cells containing the numbers you want to include in the calculation.

2 Click ▾ in this area to display a list of common calculations.

Note: If Σ ▾ is not displayed, click ⁝ on the Standard toolbar to display the button.

3 Click the calculation you want to perform.

*Note: If you want to quickly add the numbers, you can click Σ instead of performing steps **2** and **3**.*

■ A moving outline appears around the cells that Excel will include in the calculation.

■ If Excel outlines the wrong cells, you can select the cells that contain the numbers you want to include in the calculation. To select cells, see page 94.

■ The cell you selected in step **1** displays the function Excel will use to perform the calculation.

Tip

What common calculations can I perform?

Sum	Adds a list of numbers.
Average	Calculates the average value of a list of numbers.
Count	Calculates the number of values in a list.
Max	Finds the largest value in a list of numbers.
Min	Finds the smallest value in a list of numbers.

Tip

Can I perform calculations on several columns or rows of data at the same time?

Yes. Select the cells below or to the right of the cells that contain the numbers you want to include in the calculation. To select cells, see page 94. Then perform steps **2** and **3** below.

	Product A	Product B	Month Totals
January	10	5	
February	20	6	
March	30	3	

	Product A	Product B	Month Totals
January	10	5	15
February	20	6	26
March	30	3	33

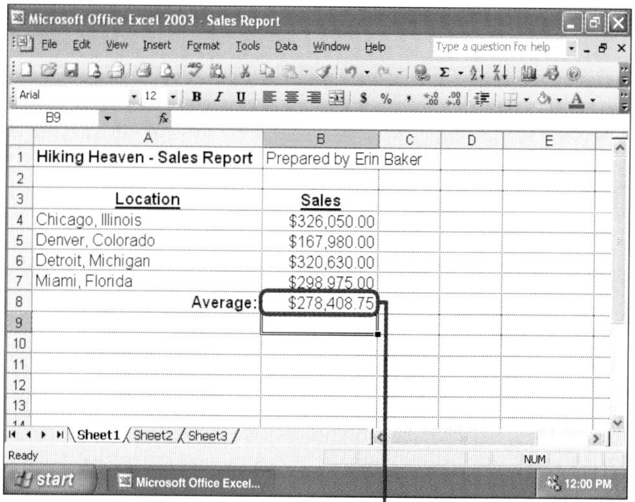

4 Press the Enter key to perform the calculation.

■ The result of the calculation appears.

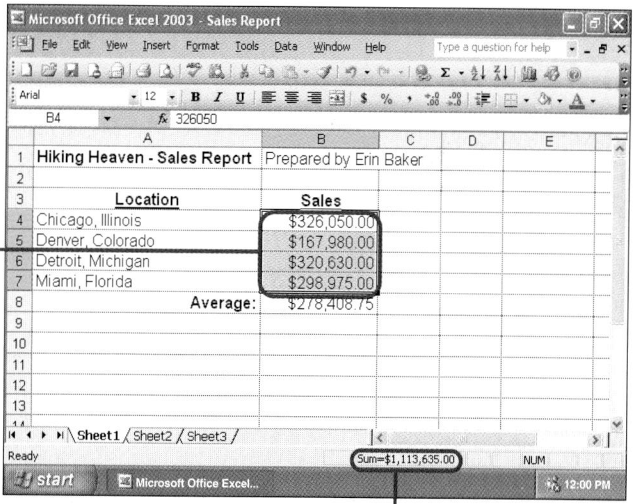

QUICKLY ADD NUMBERS

You can quickly display the sum of a list of numbers without entering a formula into your worksheet.

1 Select the cells containing the numbers you want to add. To select cells, see page 94.

■ This area displays the sum of the cells you selected.

COPY A FORMULA

If you want to use the same formula several times in your worksheet, you can save time by copying the formula.

When you copy a formula to other cells in your worksheet, Excel automatically changes the cell references in the formula to match the new location. The cell references that change are called relative references.

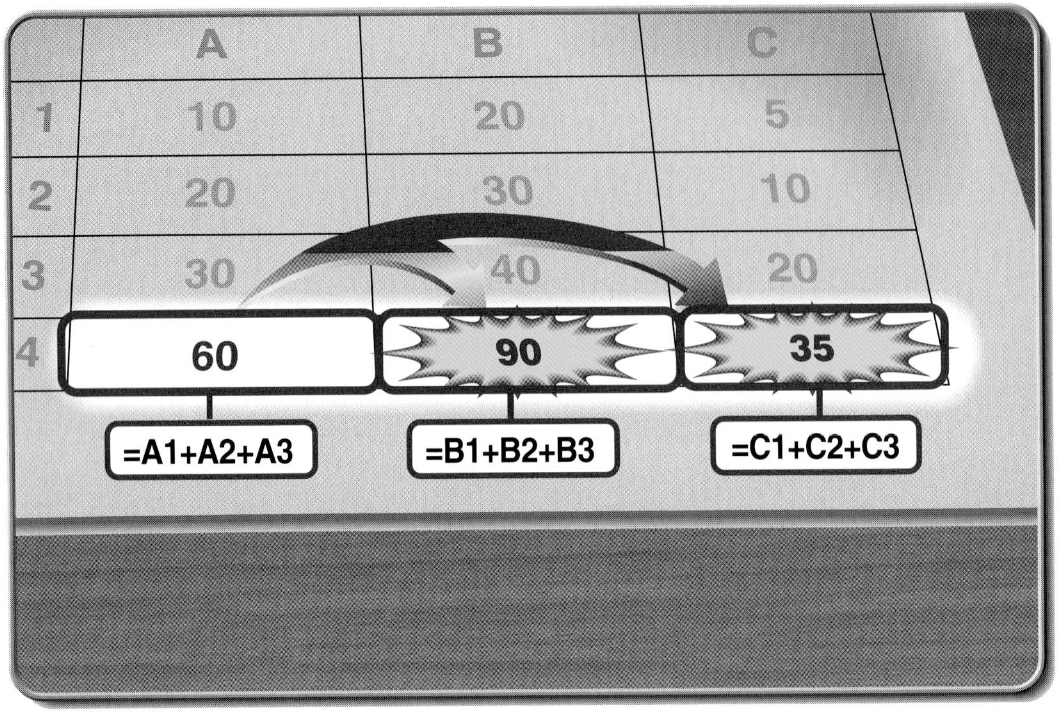

COPY A FORMULA

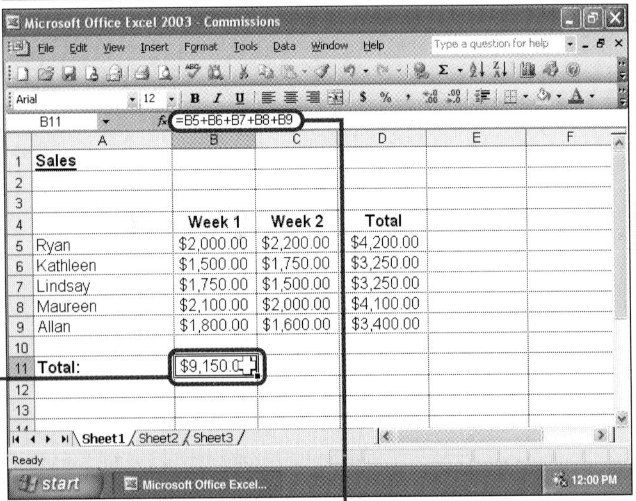

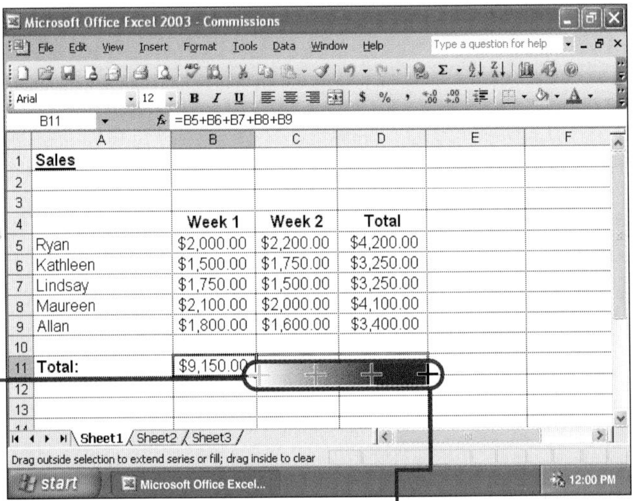

1 Enter the formula you want to copy to other cells. To enter a formula, see page 122.

2 Click the cell containing the formula you want to copy.

■ The formula bar displays the formula for the cell.

3 Position the mouse ✚ over the bottom right corner of the cell (✚ changes to +).

4 Drag the mouse + over the cells you want to receive a copy of the formula.

Tip

I do not want Excel to change a cell reference when I copy a formula. What can I do?

You can use an absolute reference in the formula. An absolute reference is a cell reference that does not change when you copy a formula. To make a cell reference absolute, type a dollar sign (**$**) before both the column letter and the row number, such as **$A$7**.

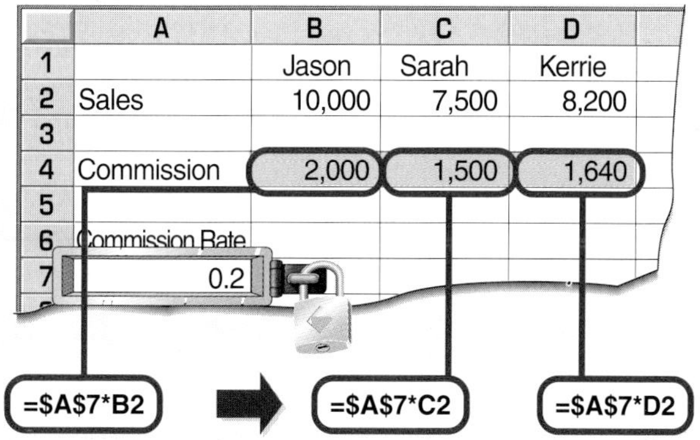
A
B
C
D
1
Jason
Sarah
Kerrie
2 Sales
10,000
7,500
8,200
3
4 Commission
2,000
1,500
1,640
5
6 Commission Rate
7
0.2
=$A$7*B2
=$A$7*C2
=$A$7*D2

This cell contains the formula =$A$7*B2.

If you copy the formula to other cells in your worksheet, Excel does not change the absolute reference in the new formulas.

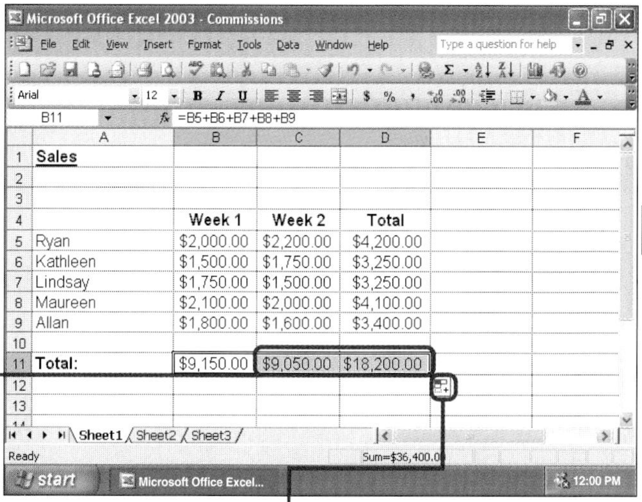

■ The results of the formulas appear.

■ The Auto Fill Options button (⊞) also appears. You can click the button and then select an option to change the way Excel copies the formula. For example, you can specify that Excel should not use the formatting from the original cell.

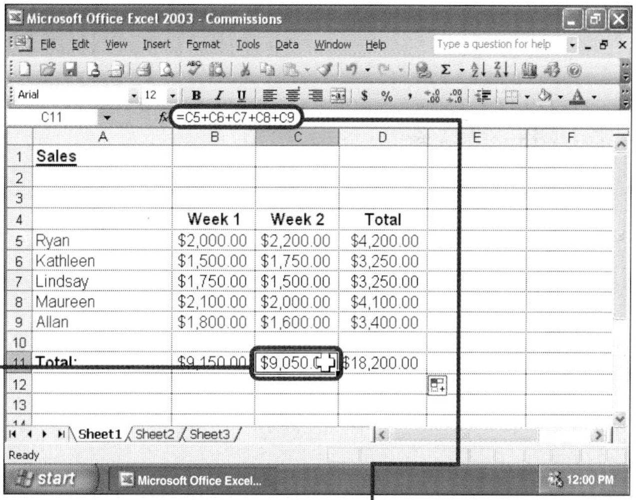

5 To view one of the new formulas, click a cell that received a copy of the formula.

■ The formula bar displays the formula with the new cell references.

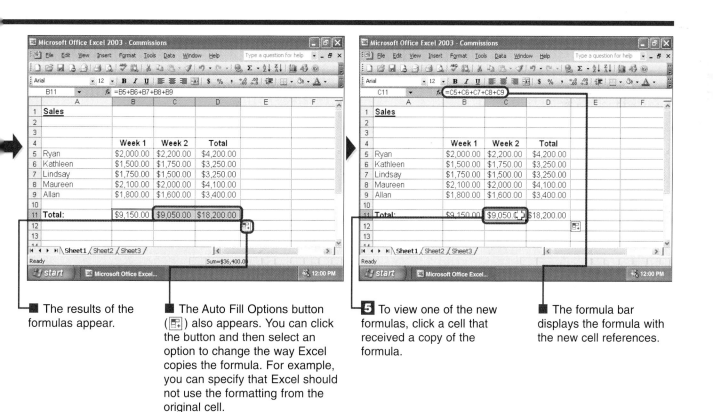

CHECK ERRORS IN FORMULAS

Excel can help you determine the cause of an error in a formula.

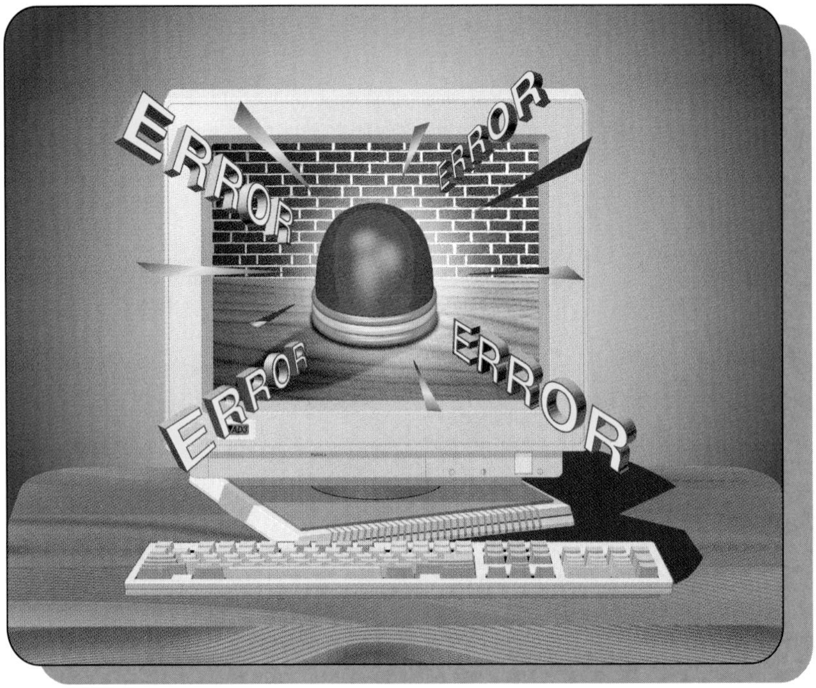

Excel checks your formulas for errors as you work and marks cells that display certain error messages. For information on common error messages, see page 133.

Errors in formulas are often the result of typing mistakes. Once you determine the cause of an error, you can edit the formula to correct the error. To edit a formula, see page 123.

CHECK ERRORS IN FORMULAS

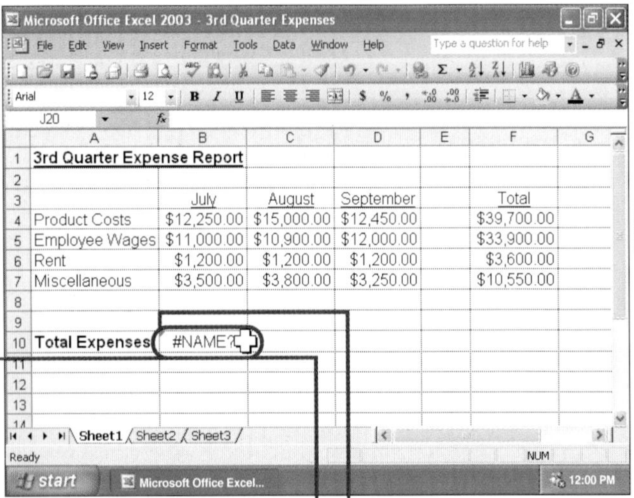

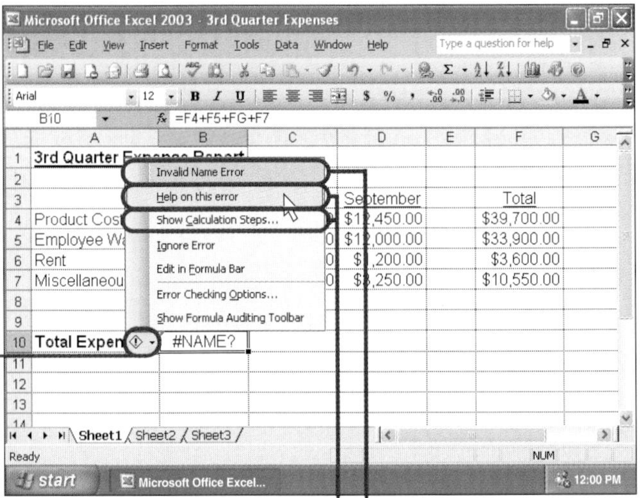

■ An error message appears in a cell when Excel cannot properly calculate the result of a formula.

■ A triangle appears in the top left corner of a cell displaying an error message when Excel can help you determine the cause of the error.

1 To determine the cause of an error, click a cell displaying a triangle.

■ The Error Checking button (⟐) appears.

2 Click the Error Checking button to display options you can use to determine the cause of the error.

■ This area displays the name of the error.

3 You can click **Help on this error** to view help information for the error.

■ You can click **Show Calculation Steps** to have Excel help you evaluate the cause of the error.

COMMON ERRORS IN FORMULAS

An error message appears when Excel cannot properly calculate or display the result of a formula.

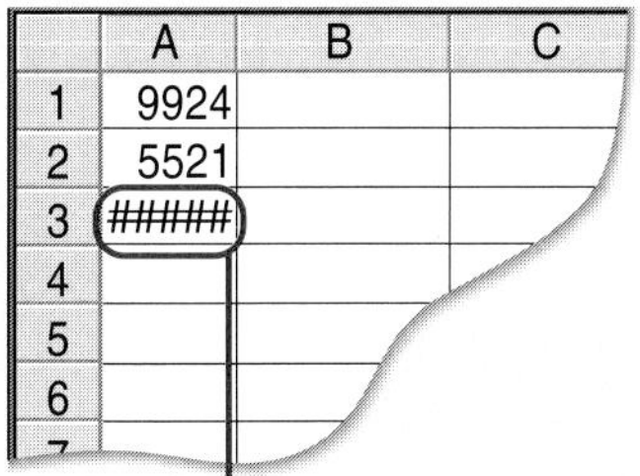

#####

The column is too narrow to display the result of the calculation. You can change the column width to display the result. To change the column width, see page 134.

■ This cell contains the formula =A1*A2

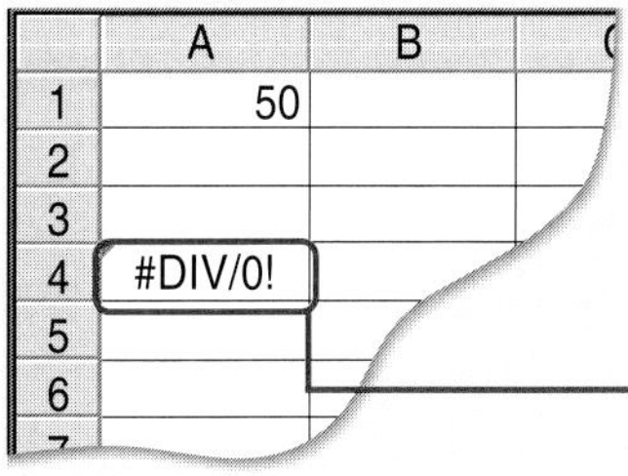

#DIV/0!

The formula divides a number by zero (0). Excel considers a blank cell to have a value of zero.

■ This cell contains the formula =A1/A2
=50/0

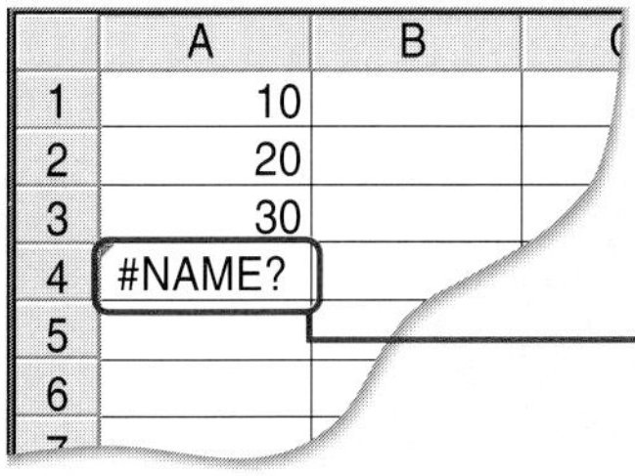

#NAME?

The formula contains a function name or cell reference Excel does not recognize.

■ This cell contains the formula =AQ+A2+A3

In this example, the cell reference A1 was typed incorrectly.

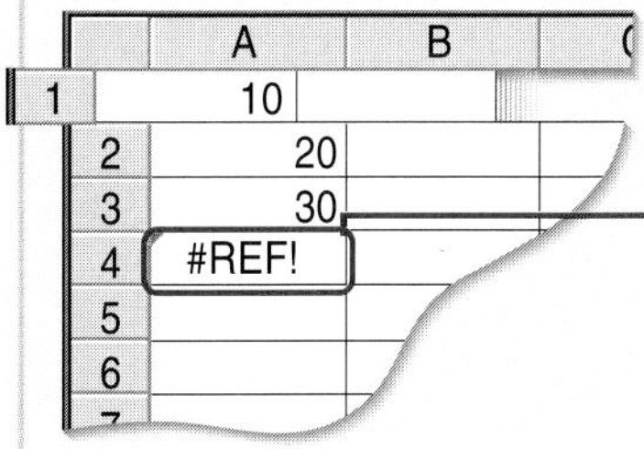

#REF!

The formula refers to a cell that is not valid.

■ This cell contains the formula =A1+A2+A3

In this example, a row containing a cell used in the formula was deleted.

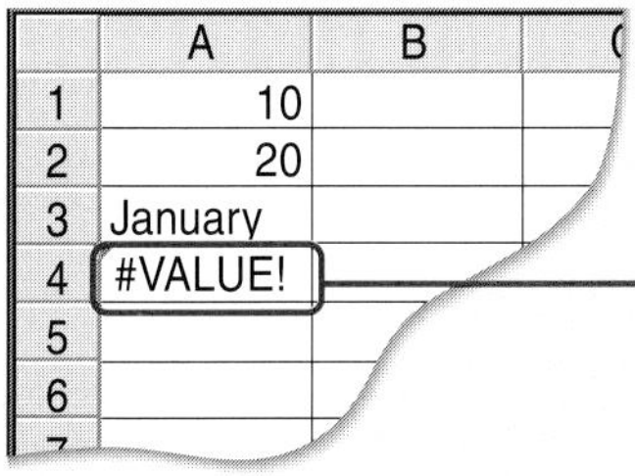

#VALUE!

The formula refers to a cell that Excel cannot use in a calculation.

■ This cell contains the formula =A1+A2+A3

In this example, a cell used in the formula contains text.

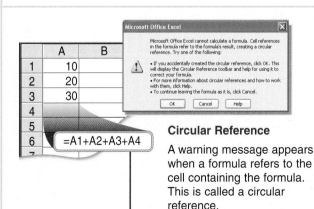

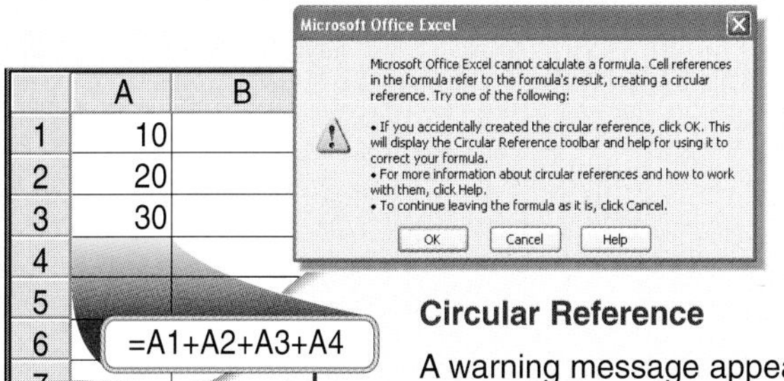

Circular Reference

A warning message appears when a formula refers to the cell containing the formula. This is called a circular reference.

■ This cell contains the formula =A1+A2+A3+A4

CHANGE COLUMN WIDTH

You can change the width of columns to improve the appearance of your worksheet and display any hidden data.

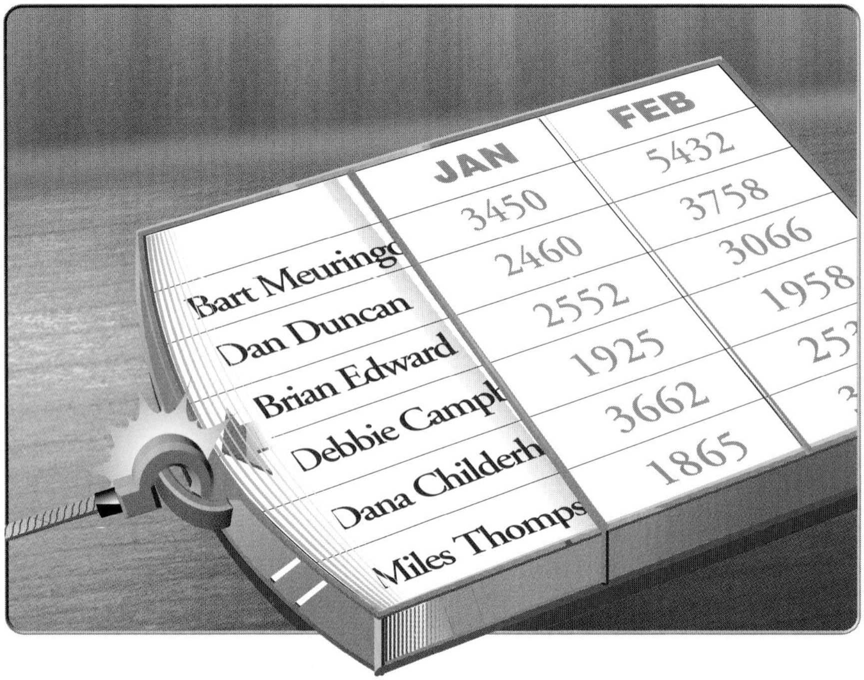

Data in a cell may be hidden if the cell is not wide enough to display the data and the neighboring cell also contains data. You can increase the column width to display all the data in the cell.

CHANGE COLUMN WIDTH

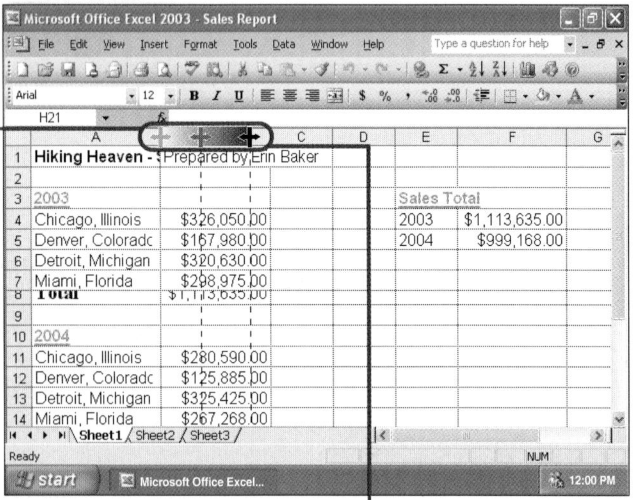

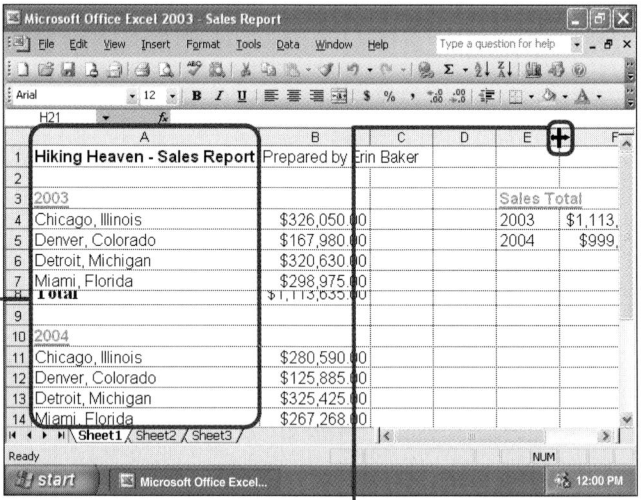

1 To change the width of a column, position the mouse ✥ over the right edge of the column heading (✥ changes to ✛).

2 Drag the column edge until the dashed line displays the column width you want.

■ The column displays the new width.

FIT LONGEST ITEM

1 To change a column width to fit the longest item in the column, double-click the right edge of the column heading.

CHANGE ROW HEIGHT

You can change the height of rows to add space between the rows of data in your worksheet.

CHANGE ROW HEIGHT

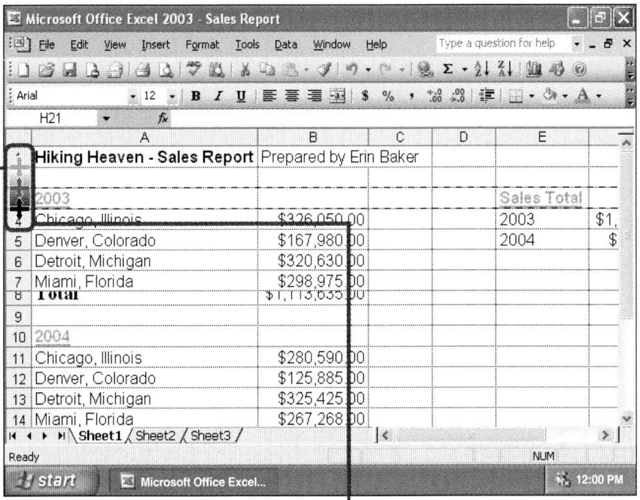

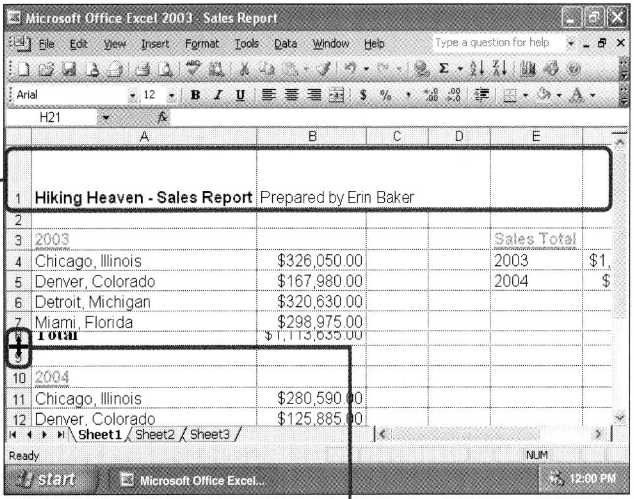

1 To change the height of a row, position the mouse ✥ over the bottom edge of the row heading (✥ changes to ┿).

2 Drag the row edge until the dashed line displays the row height you want.

■ The row displays the new height.

FIT TALLEST ITEM

1 To change a row height to fit the tallest item in the row, double-click the bottom edge of the row heading.

CHANGE FONT OF DATA

You can change the font of data to enhance the appearance of your worksheet.

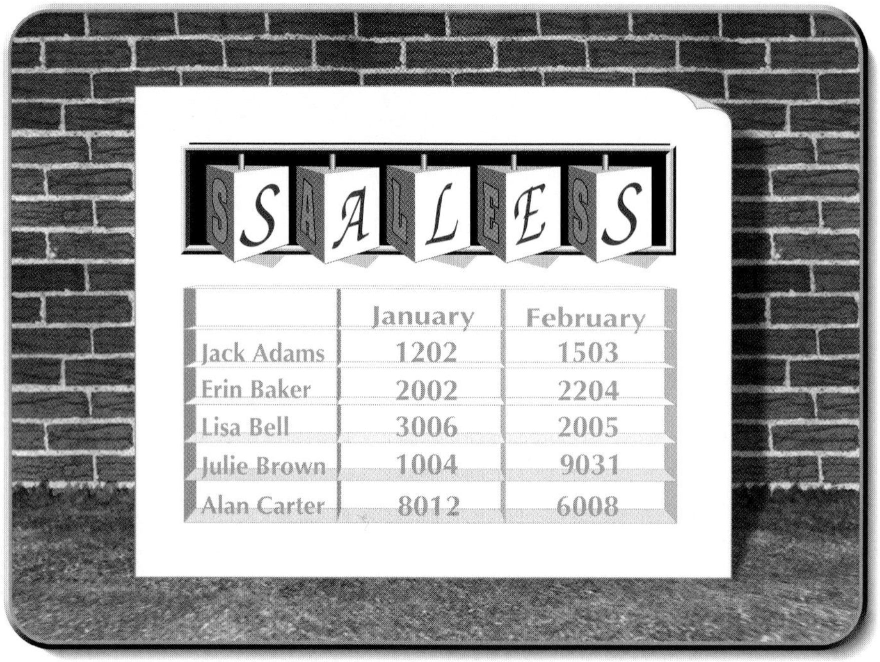

By default, Excel uses the Arial font. You can use another font to draw attention to headings or emphasize important data in your worksheet.

CHANGE FONT OF DATA

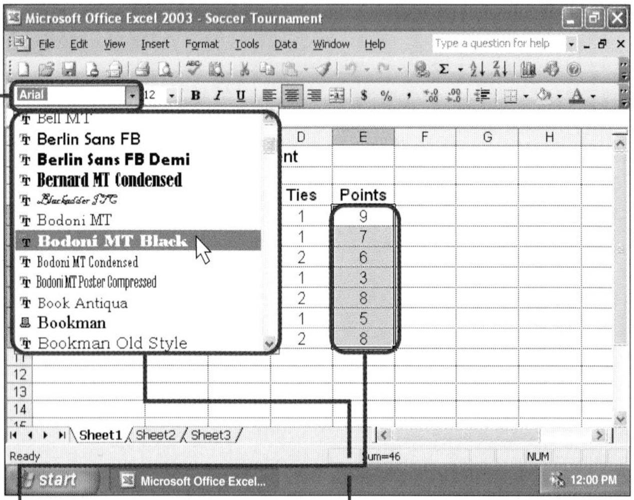

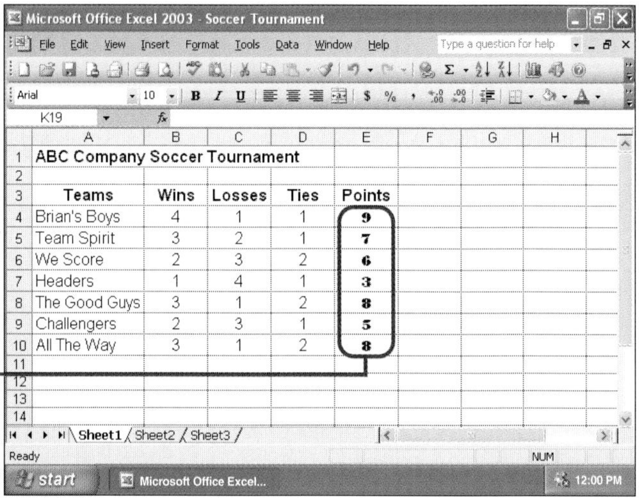

1 Select the cells containing the data you want to change to a different font. To select cells, see page 94.

2 Click ▾ in this area to display a list of the available fonts.

Note: If the Font area is not displayed, click ⁝ on the Formatting toolbar to display the area.

3 Click the font you want to use.

■ The data changes to the font you selected.

■ To deselect cells, click any cell.

CHANGE SIZE OF DATA

You can increase or decrease the size of data in your worksheet.

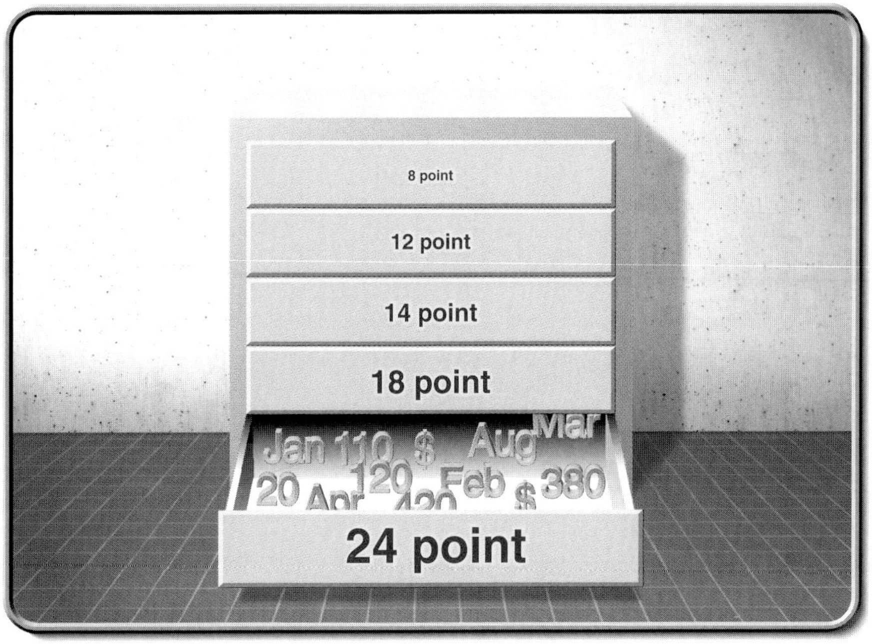

Larger data is easier to read, but smaller data allows you to fit more information on a page.

Excel measures the size of data in points. There are approximately 72 points in one inch.

CHANGE SIZE OF DATA

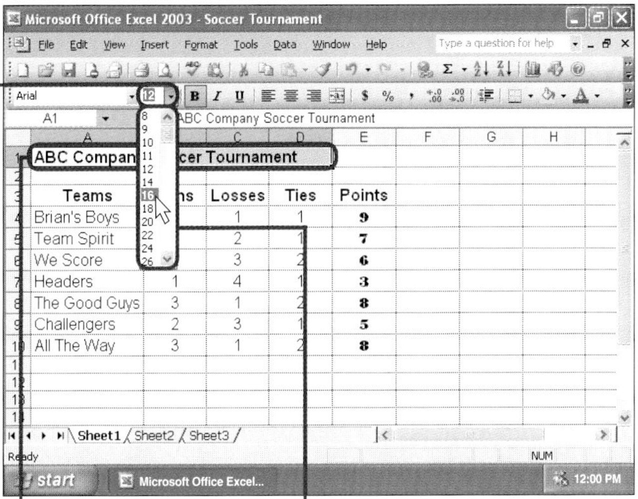

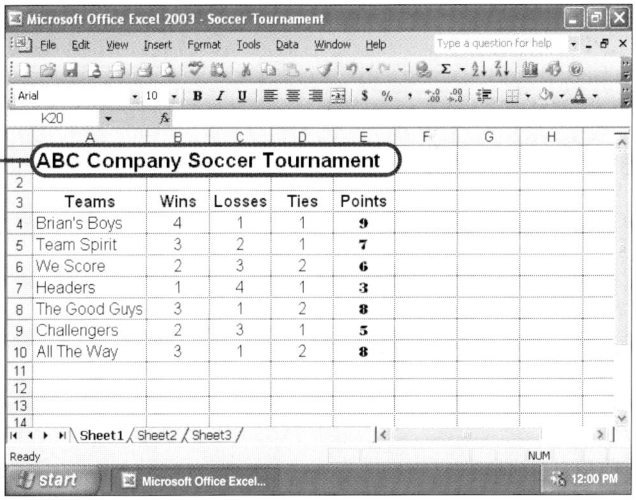

1 Select the cells containing the data you want to change to a new size. To select cells, see page 94.

2 Click in this area to display a list of the available sizes.

Note: If the Font Size area is not displayed, click on the Formatting toolbar to display the area.

3 Click the size you want to use.

■ The data changes to the size you selected.

■ To deselect cells, click any cell.

CHANGE NUMBER FORMAT

You can change the appearance of numbers in your worksheet without retyping the numbers.

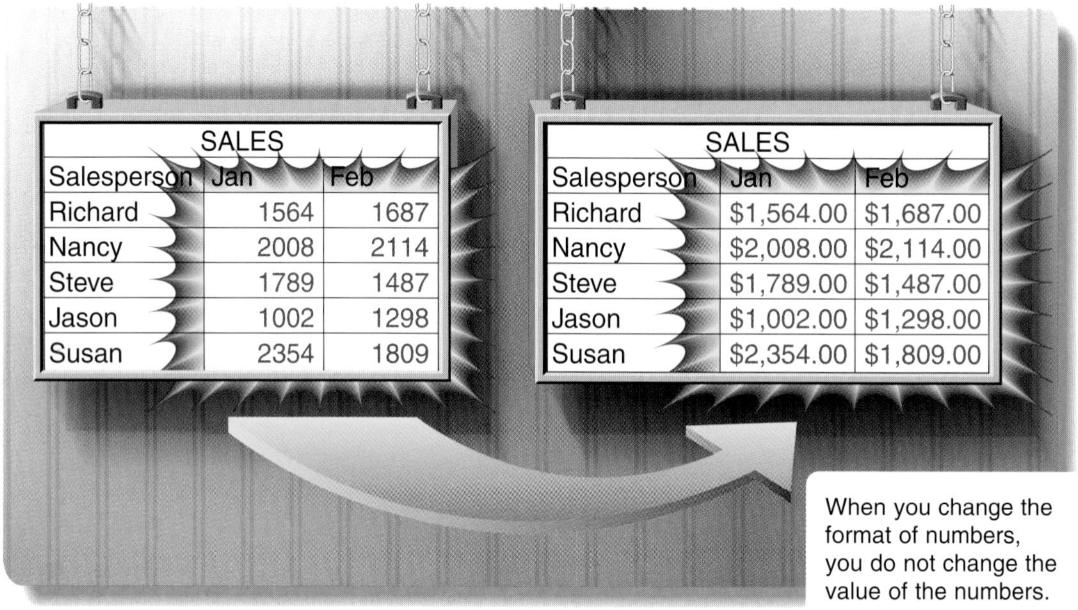

When you change the format of numbers, you do not change the value of the numbers.

CHANGE NUMBER FORMAT

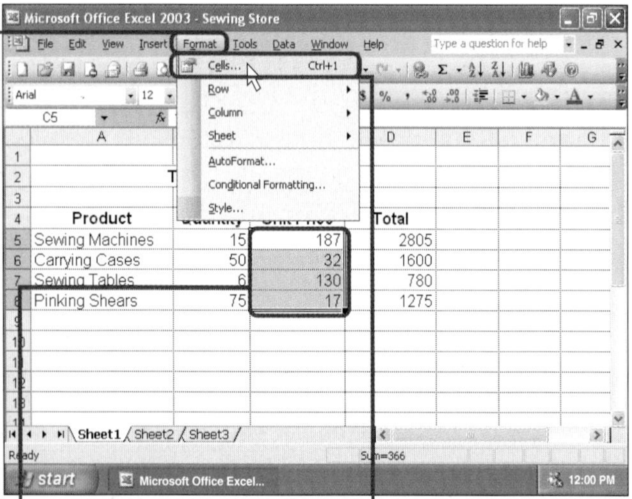

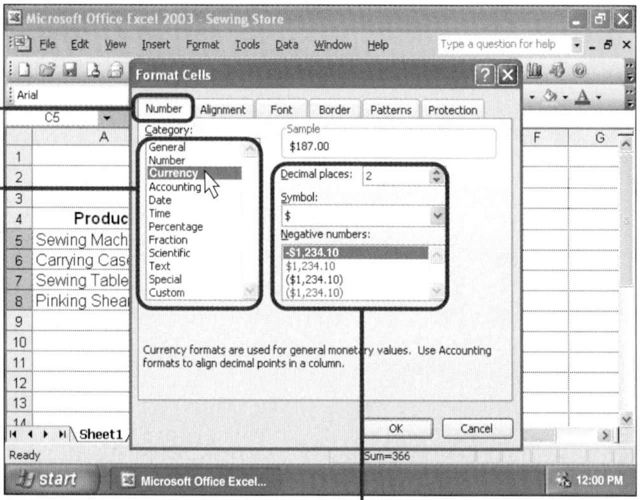

1 Select the cells containing the numbers you want to format. To select cells, see page 94.

2 Click **Format**.

3 Click **Cells**.

■ The Format Cells dialog box appears.

4 Click the **Number** tab.

5 Click the category that describes the numbers in the cells you selected.

■ This area displays the options for the category you selected. The available options depend on the category you selected.

Tip

What categories are available for formatting numbers?

Category:	Description:	Example:
General	Applies no specific number format.	100
Number	Used to format numbers for general display.	100.00
Currency	Used to format monetary values.	$100.00
Accounting	Aligns the currency symbols and decimal points in a column of monetary values.	$ 100.00 $ 1200.00
Date	Used to format dates.	23-Apr-03
Time	Used to format times.	12:00 PM
Percentage	Used to format percentages.	25.00%
Fraction	Used to format fractions.	1/4
Scientific	Used to format numbers in scientific notation.	1.00E+02
Text	Treats numbers as text.	135 Hillcrest Street
Special	Used to format special numbers, such as Zip codes.	90210
Custom	Allows you to apply your own number format.	3-45-678

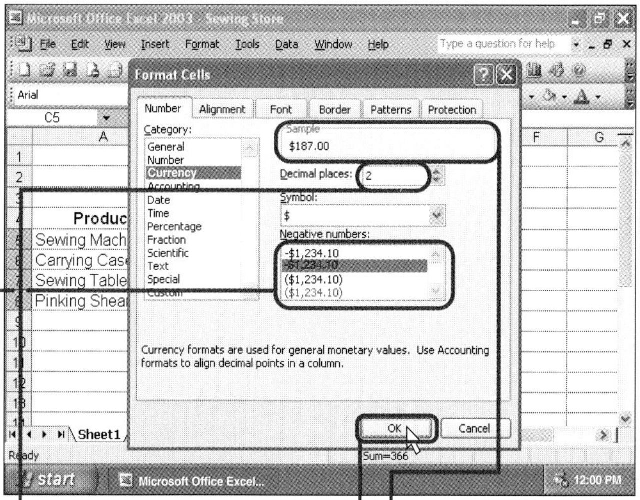

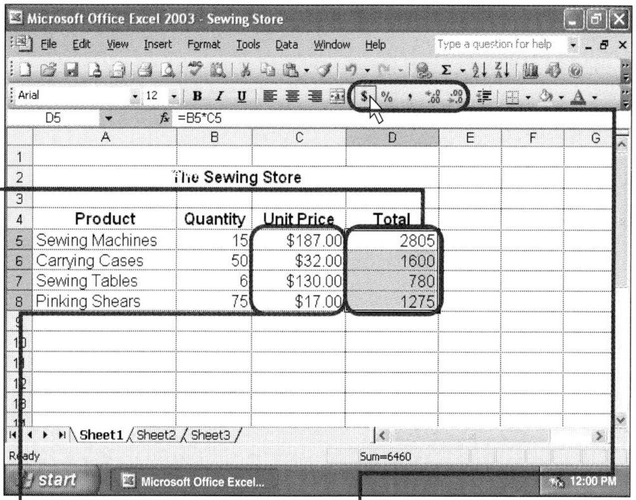

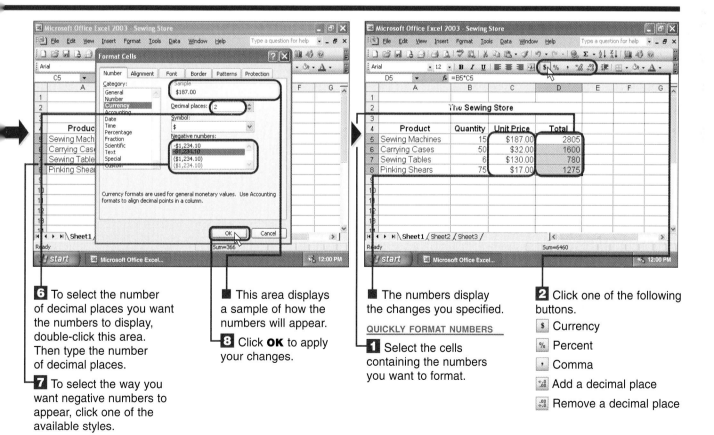

6 To select the number of decimal places you want the numbers to display, double-click this area. Then type the number of decimal places.

7 To select the way you want negative numbers to appear, click one of the available styles.

■ This area displays a sample of how the numbers will appear.

8 Click **OK** to apply your changes.

■ The numbers display the changes you specified.

QUICKLY FORMAT NUMBERS

1 Select the cells containing the numbers you want to format.

2 Click one of the following buttons.

- Currency
- Percent
- Comma
- Add a decimal place
- Remove a decimal place

CHANGE DATA COLOR

You can change the color of data in your worksheet to draw attention to headings or important information.

Adding color to data is also useful for marking data you want to review or verify later.

CHANGE DATA COLOR

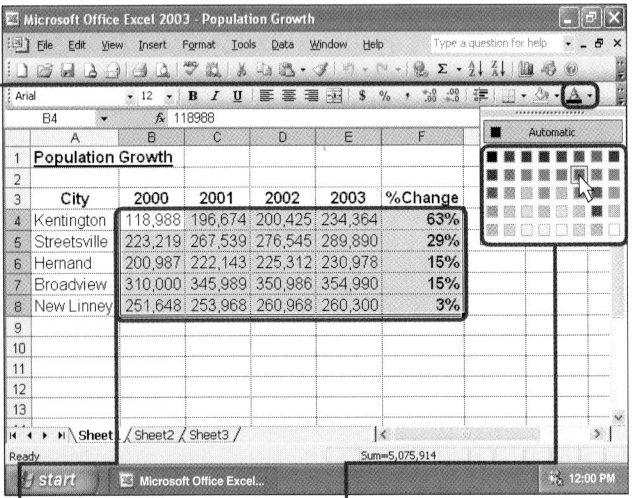

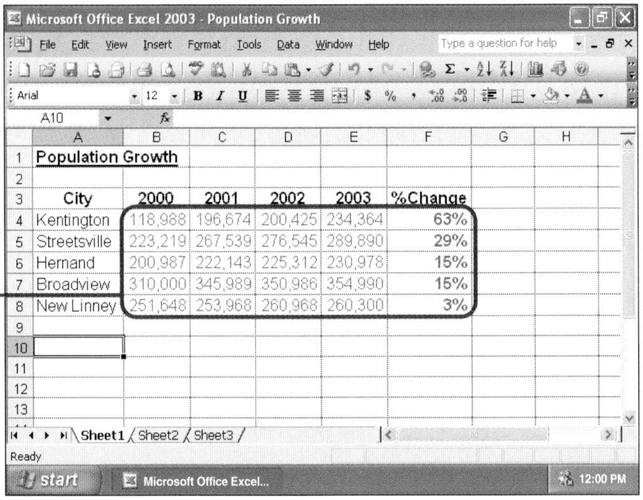

1 Select the cells containing the data you want to change to a different color. To select cells, see page 94.

2 Click in this area to display the available colors.

Note: If is not displayed, click on the Formatting toolbar to display the button.

3 Click the color you want to use.

■ The data appears in the color you selected.

■ To deselect cells, click any cell.

■ To return data to its original color, repeat steps **1** to **3**, selecting **Automatic** in step **3**.

CHANGE CELL COLOR

You can add color to cells to make the cells stand out in your worksheet.

Changing the color of cells is useful when you want to distinguish between different areas in your worksheet. For example, in a worksheet that contains monthly sales figures, you can use a different cell color for each month.

CHANGE CELL COLOR

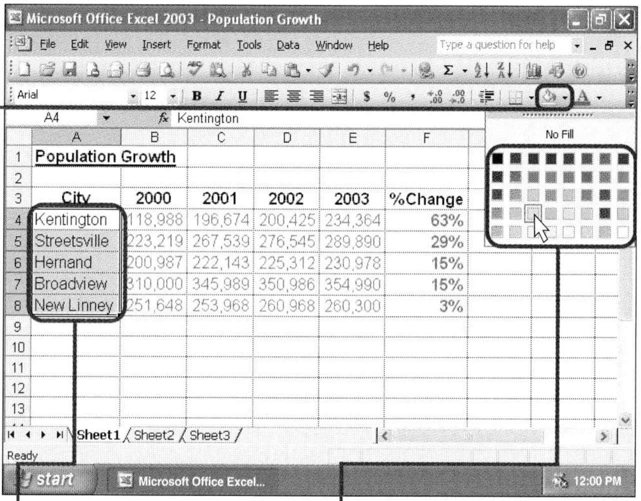

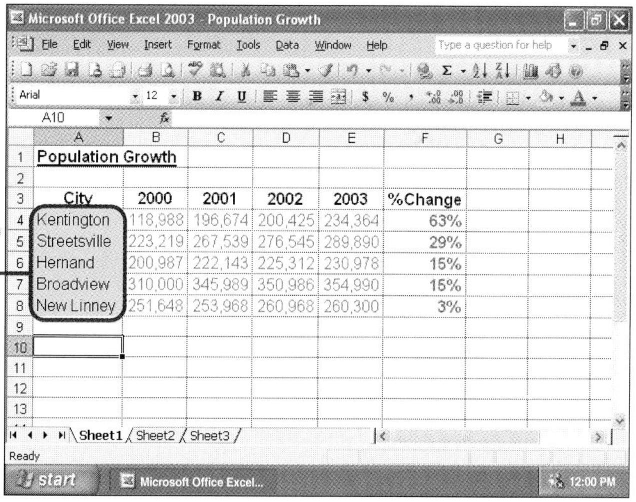

1 Select the cells you want to change to a different color. To select cells, see page 94.

2 Click ▾ in this area to display the available colors.

Note: If the Fill Color button is not displayed, click the toolbar options button on the Formatting toolbar to display the button.

3 Click the color you want to use.

■ The cells appear in the color you selected.

■ To deselect cells, click any cell.

■ To remove color from cells, repeat steps **1** to **3**, selecting **No Fill** in step **3**.

CHANGE ALIGNMENT OF DATA

You can align data in different ways to enhance the appearance of your worksheet.

When you enter data into cells, Excel automatically left aligns text and right aligns numbers and dates.

CHANGE ALIGNMENT OF DATA

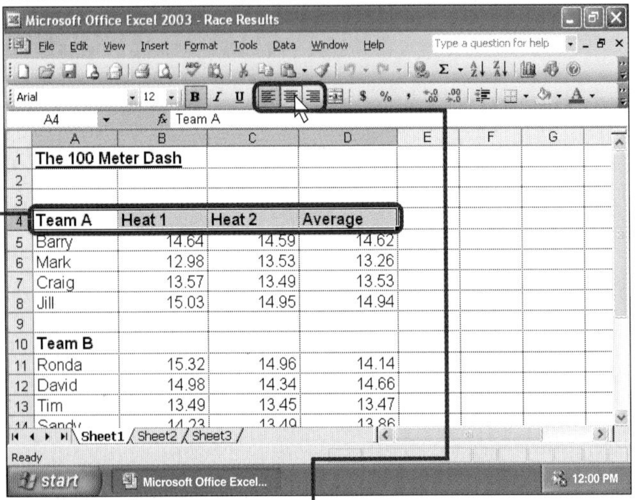

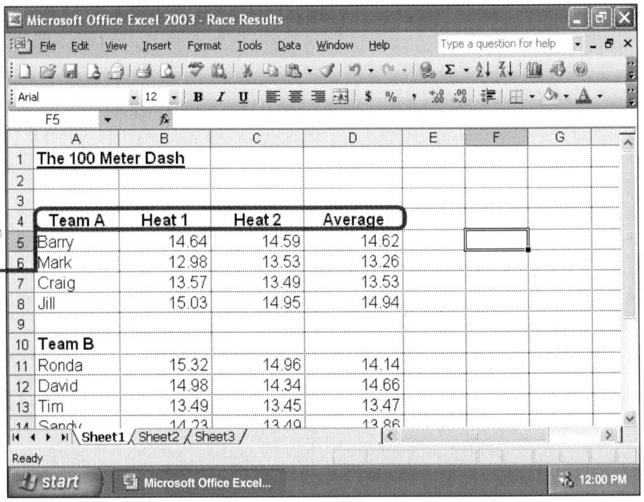

1 Select the cells containing the data you want to align differently. To select cells, see page 94.

2 Click one of the following buttons.

- Left align
- Center
- Right align

Note: If the button you want is not displayed, click on the Formatting toolbar to display the button.

■ The data appears in the new alignment.

■ To deselect cells, click any cell.

You can center data across columns in your worksheet. This is useful for centering titles over your data.

CENTER DATA ACROSS COLUMNS

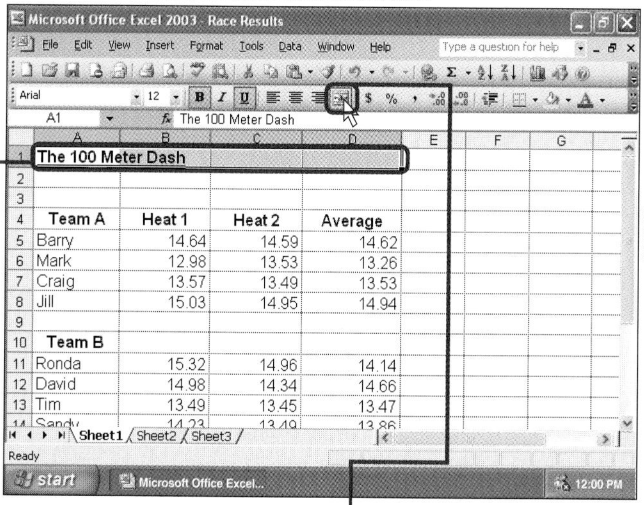

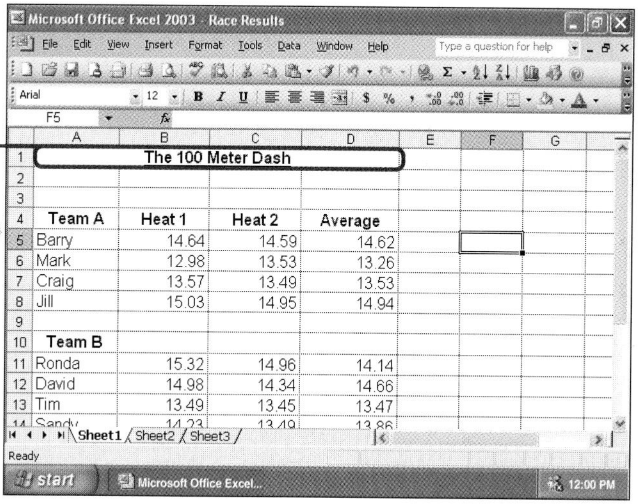

1 Select the cells you want to center the data across. To select cells, see page 94.

Note: The first cell you select should contain the data you want to center.

2 Click the Merge and Center button to center the data across the columns.

Note: If the button is not displayed, click the Toolbar Options button on the Formatting toolbar to display the button.

■ Excel centers the data across the columns.

■ If you no longer want to center the data across the columns, click the cell that contains the data and then repeat step **2**.

BOLD, ITALICIZE OR UNDERLINE DATA

You can bold, italicize or underline data to emphasize data and enhance the appearance of your worksheet.

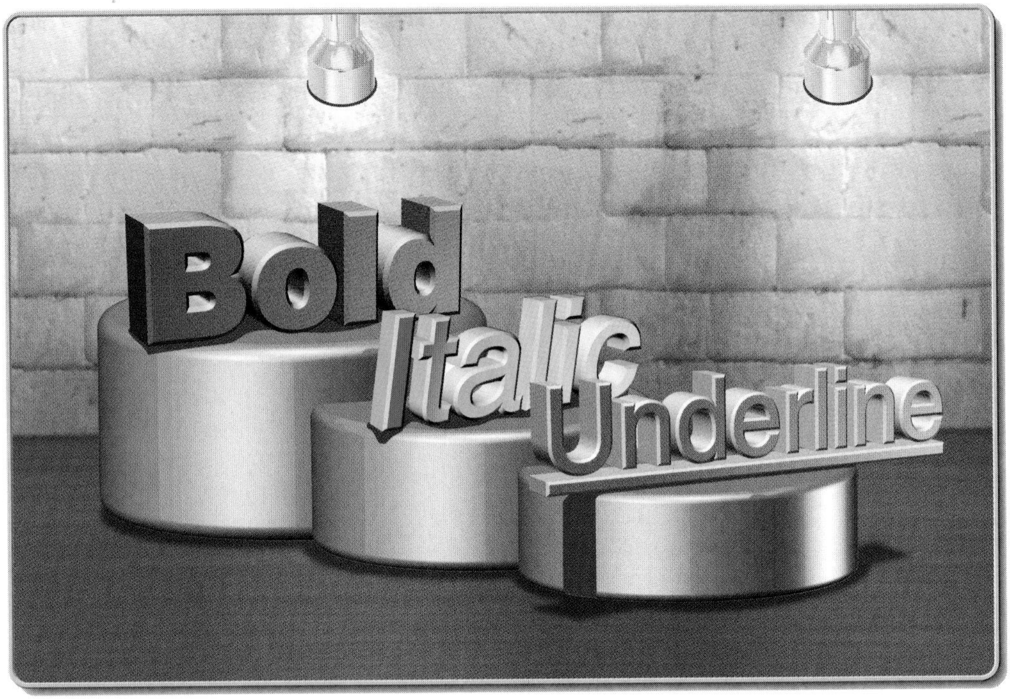

BOLD, ITALICIZE OR UNDERLINE DATA

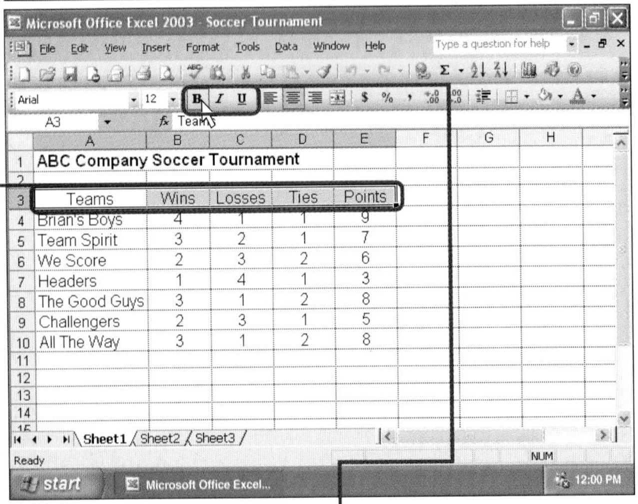

1 Select the cells containing the data you want to bold, italicize or underline. To select cells, see page 94.

2 Click one of the following buttons.

B Bold

I Italic

U Underline

Note: If the button you want is not displayed, click ⁝ on the Formatting toolbar to display the button.

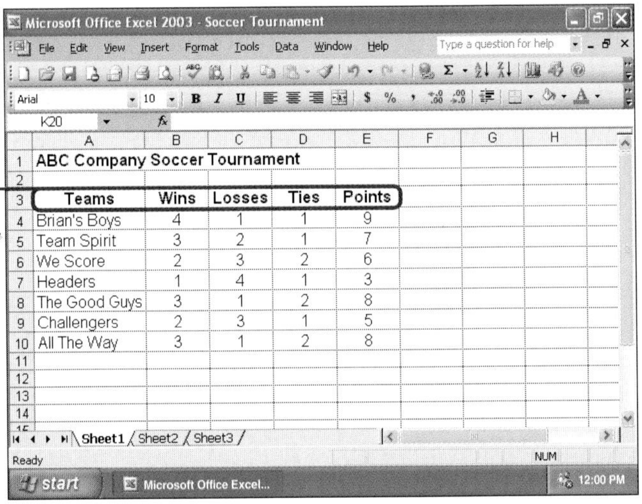

■ The data appears in the style you selected.

■ To deselect cells, click any cell.

■ To remove a bold, italic or underline style, repeat steps **1** and **2**.

COPY FORMATTING

You can copy the formatting of a cell to make other cells in your worksheet look exactly the same.

You may want to copy the formatting of cells to make all the titles in your worksheet look the same. This will give the information in your worksheet a consistent appearance.

COPY FORMATTING

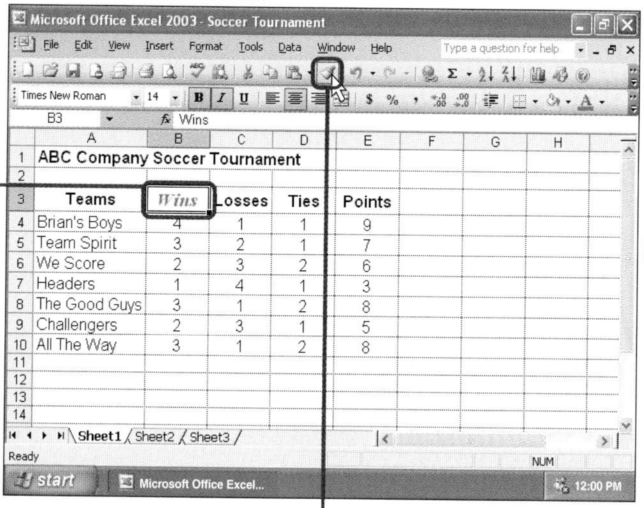

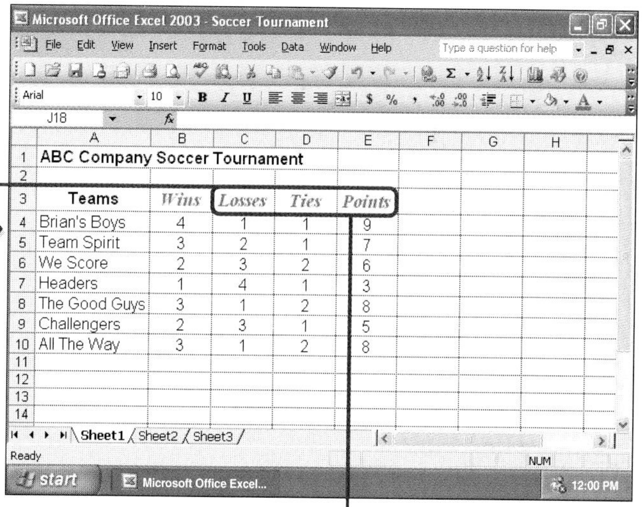

1 Click a cell that displays the formatting you want to copy to other cells.

2 Click to copy the formatting of the cell.

Note: If is not displayed, click on the Standard toolbar to display the button.

■ The mouse changes to when over your worksheet.

3 Select the cells you want to display the same formatting. To select cells, see page 94.

■ The cells you selected display the formatting.

■ To deselect cells, click any cell.

PREVIEW A WORKSHEET BEFORE PRINTING

You can use the Print Preview feature to see how your worksheet will look when printed. This allows you to confirm that the worksheet will print the way you expect.

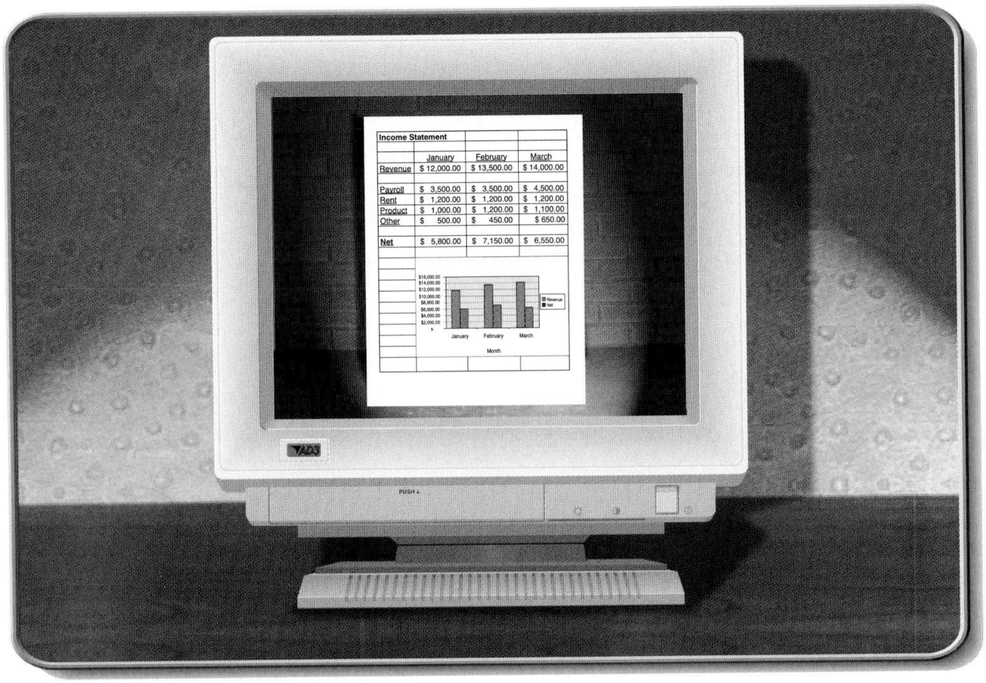

PREVIEW A WORKSHEET BEFORE PRINTING

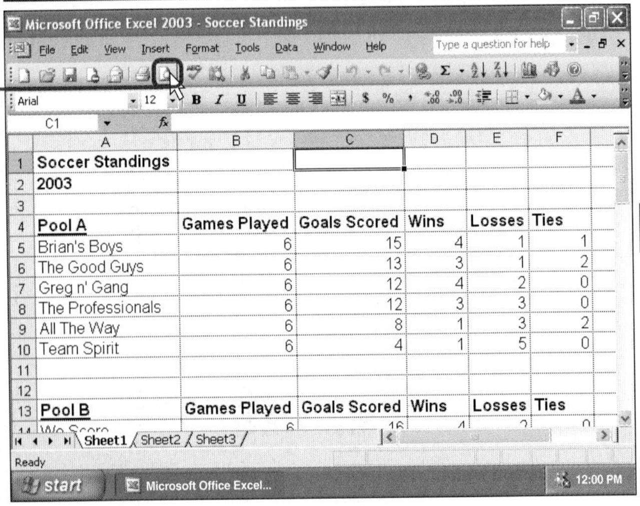

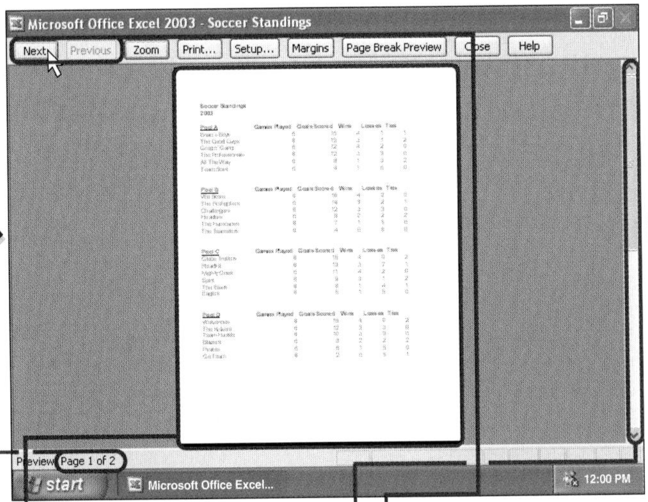

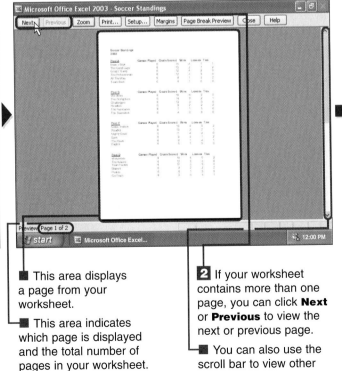

1 Click to preview your worksheet before printing.

Note: If is not displayed, click on the Standard toolbar to display the button.

■ The Print Preview window appears.

■ This area displays a page from your worksheet.

■ This area indicates which page is displayed and the total number of pages in your worksheet.

2 If your worksheet contains more than one page, you can click **Next** or **Previous** to view the next or previous page.

■ You can also use the scroll bar to view other pages.

Tip

Why does my worksheet appear in black and white in the Print Preview window?

If you are using a black-and-white printer, your worksheet appears in black and white in the Print Preview window. If you are using a color printer, your worksheet will appear in color.

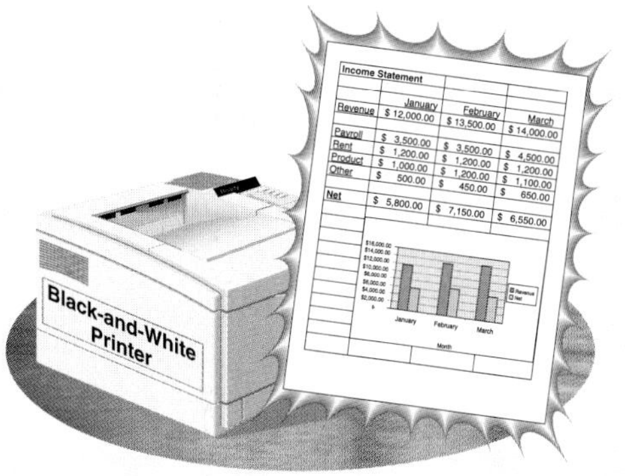

Tip

Why don't the gridlines appear on my worksheet in the Print Preview window?

By default, Excel will not print the gridlines that appear around each cell in your worksheet. To print gridlines and change other print options, see page 152.

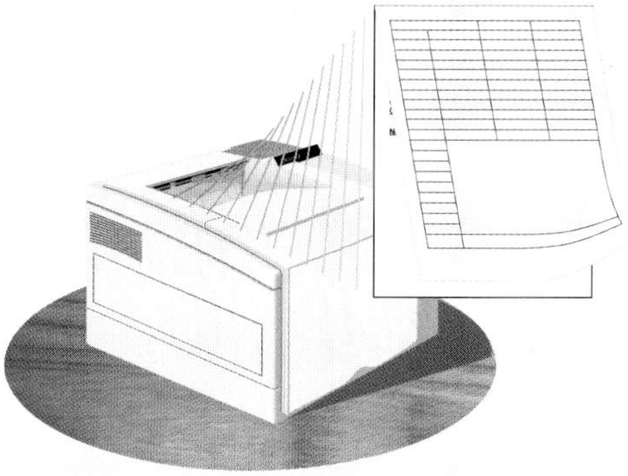

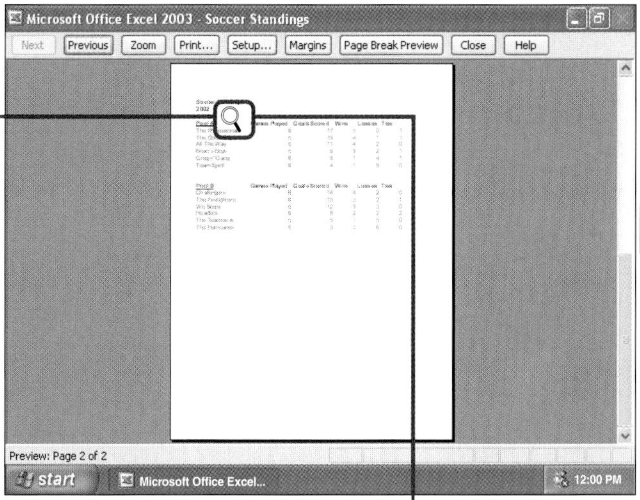

3 To magnify an area of the page, position the mouse over the area you want to magnify (changes to 🔍).

4 Click the area to magnify the area.

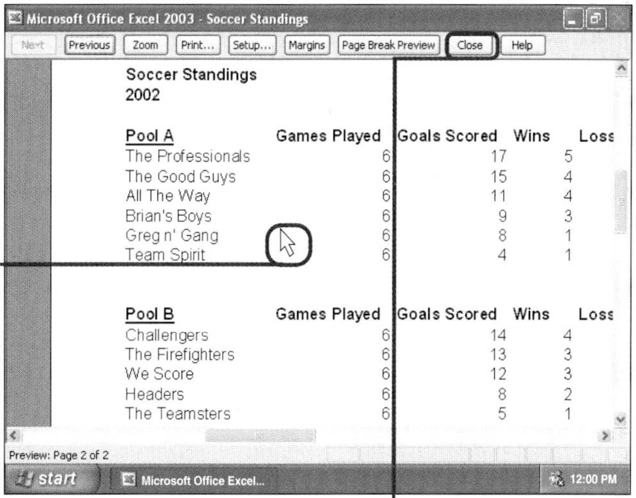

■ A magnified view of the area appears.

5 To once again display the entire page, click anywhere on the page.

6 When you finish previewing your worksheet, click **Close** to close the Print Preview window.

PRINT A WORKSHEET

You can produce a paper copy of the worksheet displayed on your screen. Printing a worksheet is useful when you want to be able to refer to the worksheet without using your computer.

Before printing your worksheet, make sure your printer is turned on and contains paper.

PRINT A WORKSHEET

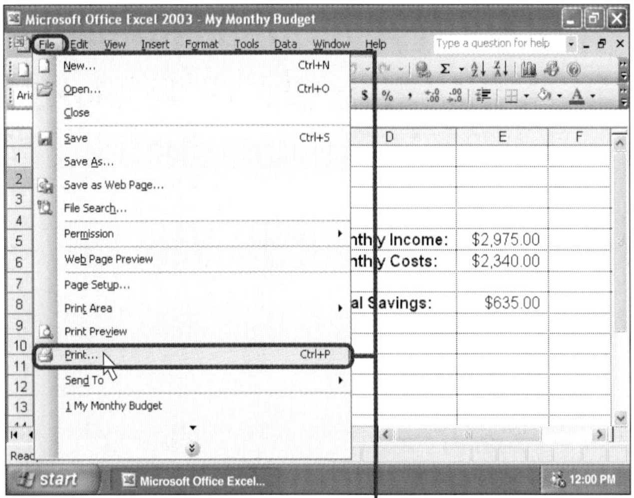

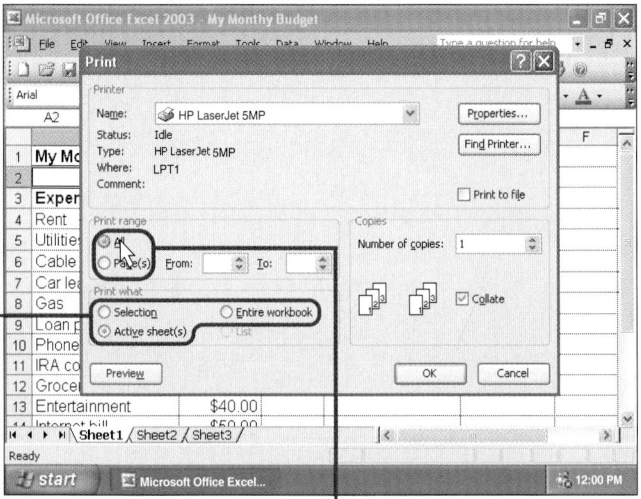

1 Click any cell in the worksheet you want to print.

■ To print only specific cells in your worksheet, select the cells you want to print. To select cells, see page 94.

2 Click **File**.

3 Click **Print**.

■ The Print dialog box appears.

4 Click the part of the workbook you want to print (○ changes to ◉).

Note: For information on the parts of the workbook that you can print, see the top of page 149.

5 If the part of the workbook you selected to print contains more than one page, click an option to specify which pages you want to print (○ changes to ◉).

All - Prints every page

Page(s) - Prints the pages you specify

Tip

What parts of a workbook can I print?

Excel allows you to specify which part of a workbook you want to print. Each workbook is divided into several worksheets.

For information on using multiple worksheets in a workbook, see pages 98 to 101.

Selection

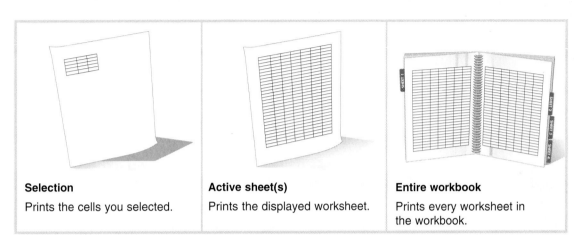

Prints the cells you selected.

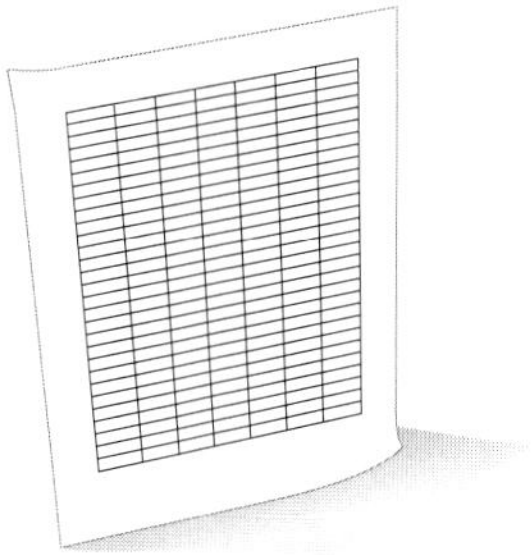

Active sheet(s)

Prints the displayed worksheet.

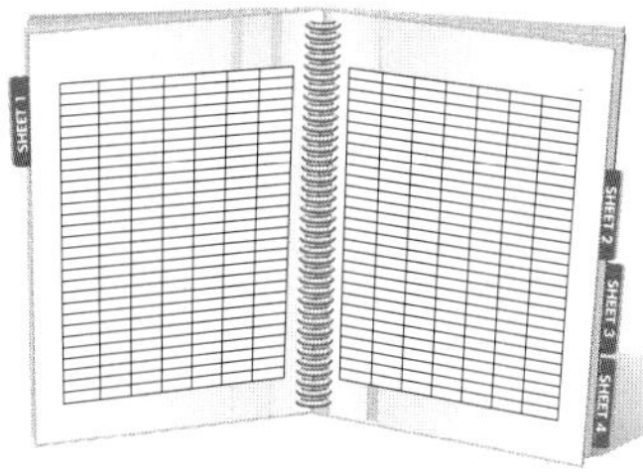

Entire workbook

Prints every worksheet in the workbook.

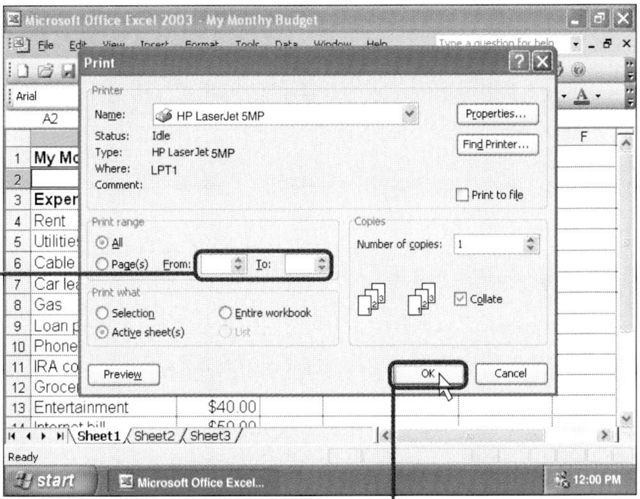

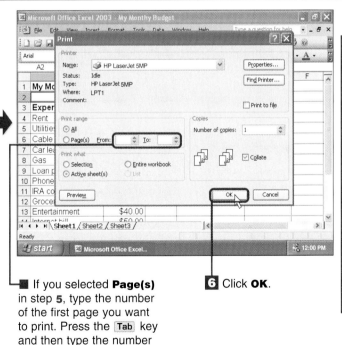

■ If you selected **Page(s)** in step **5**, type the number of the first page you want to print. Press the Tab key and then type the number of the last page you want to print.

6 Click **OK**.

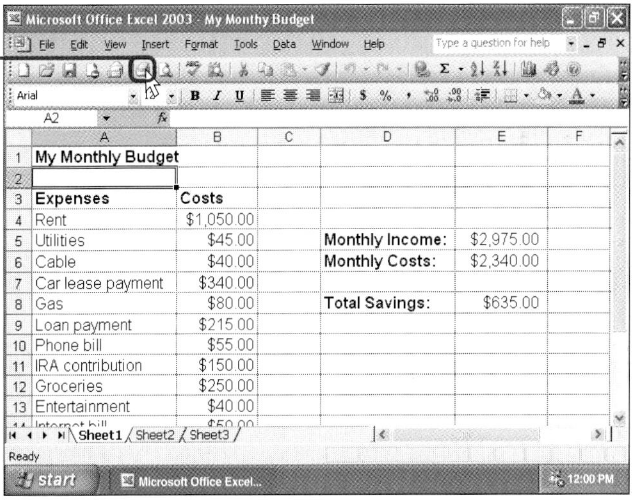

QUICKLY PRINT DISPLAYED WORKSHEET

1 Click to quickly print the worksheet displayed on your screen.

Note: If is not displayed, click on the Standard toolbar to display the button.

CHANGE PAGE ORIENTATION

You can change the page orientation to change the way your worksheet appears on a printed page.

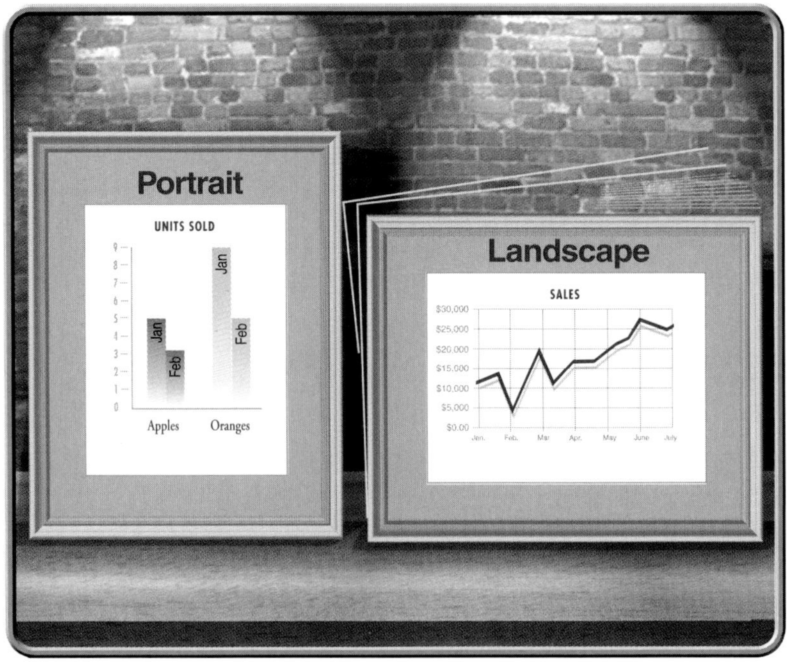

Excel automatically prints your worksheets in the portrait orientation. The landscape orientation is useful when you want a wide worksheet to fit on one printed page.

Changing the page orientation will not affect the way your worksheet appears on your screen.

CHANGE PAGE ORIENTATION

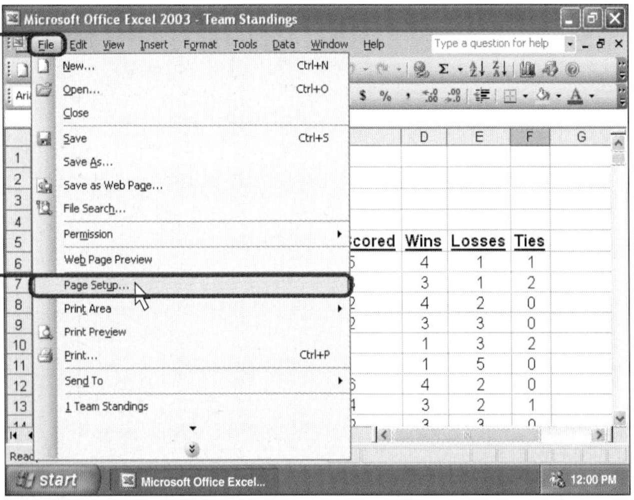

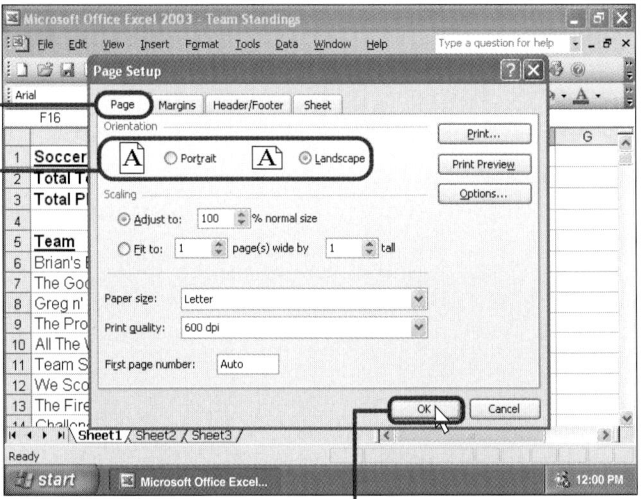

1 Click **File**.

2 Click **Page Setup**.

■ The Page Setup dialog box appears.

3 Click the **Page** tab.

4 Click the page orientation you want to use (○ changes to ◉).

5 Click **OK** to confirm your change.

Note: You can use the Print Preview feature to see how your worksheet will appear on a printed page. For information on using the Print Preview feature, see page 146.

CHANGE MARGINS

You can change the margins in your worksheet. A margin is the amount of space between the data on a page and the edge of your paper.

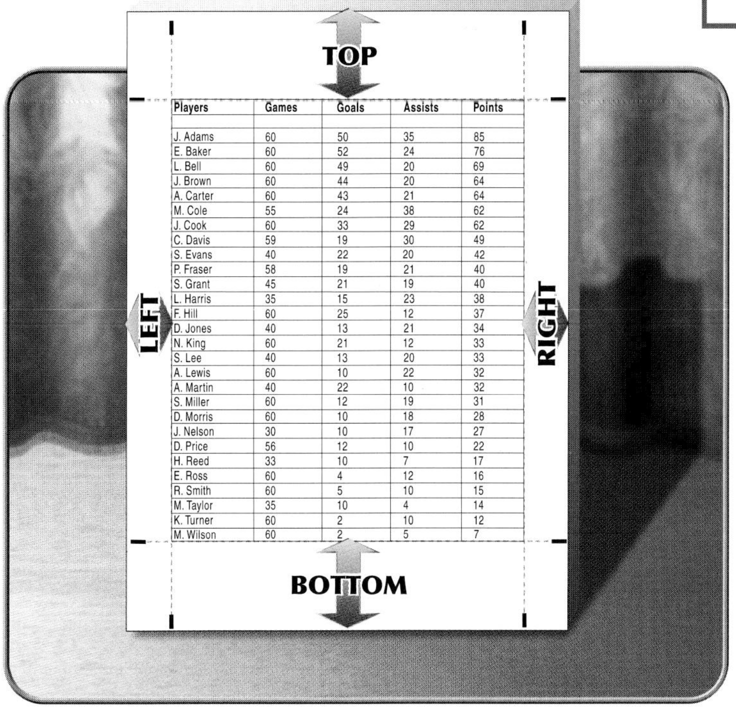

Players	Games	Goals	Assists	Points
J. Adams	60	50	35	85
E. Baker	60	52	24	76
L. Bell	60	49	20	69
J. Brown	60	44	20	64
A. Carter	60	43	21	64
M. Cole	55	24	38	62
J. Cook	60	33	29	62
C. Davis	59	19	30	49
S. Evans	40	22	20	42
P. Fraser	58	19	21	40
S. Grant	45	21	19	40
L. Harris	35	15	23	38
F. Hill	60	25	12	37
D. Jones	40	13	21	34
N. King	60	21	12	33
S. Lee	40	13	20	33
A. Lewis	60	10	22	32
A. Martin	40	22	10	32
S. Miller	60	12	19	31
D. Morris	60	10	18	28
J. Nelson	30	10	17	27
D. Price	56	12	10	22
H. Reed	33	10	7	17
E. Ross	60	4	12	16
R. Smith	60	5	10	15
M. Taylor	35	10	4	14
K. Turner	60	2	10	12
M. Wilson	60	2	5	7

Excel automatically sets the top and bottom margins to 1 inch and the left and right margins to 0.75 inches.

Changing the margins allows you to adjust the amount of information that can fit on a page. You may want to change the margins to accommodate letterhead or other specialty paper.

CHANGE MARGINS

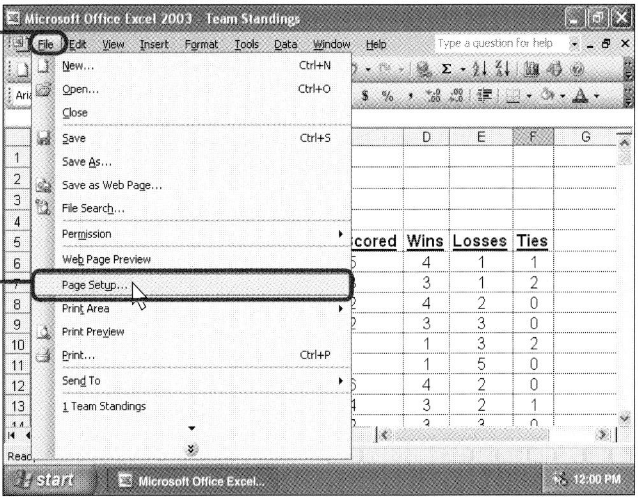

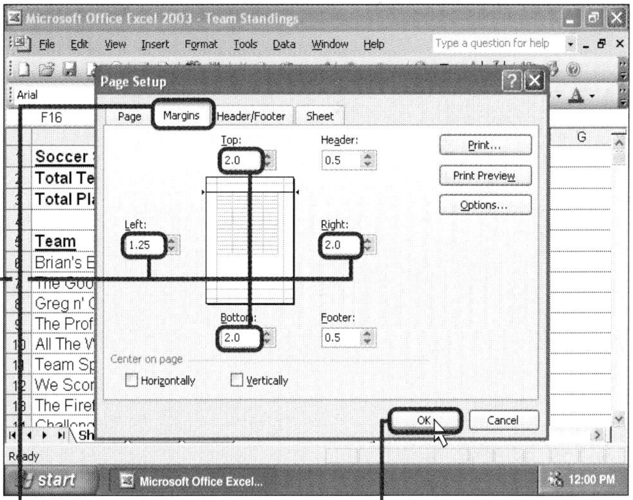

1 Click **File**.

2 Click **Page Setup**.

■ The Page Setup dialog box appears.

3 Click the **Margins** tab.

4 Double-click in the box for the margin you want to change. Then type a new margin in inches.

5 Repeat step **4** for each margin you want to change.

6 Click **OK** to confirm your changes.

Note: You can use the Print Preview feature to see how your worksheet will appear on a printed page. For information on using the Print Preview feature, *see page 146.*

CHANGE PRINT OPTIONS

You can use the print options that Excel offers to change the way your worksheet appears on a printed page.

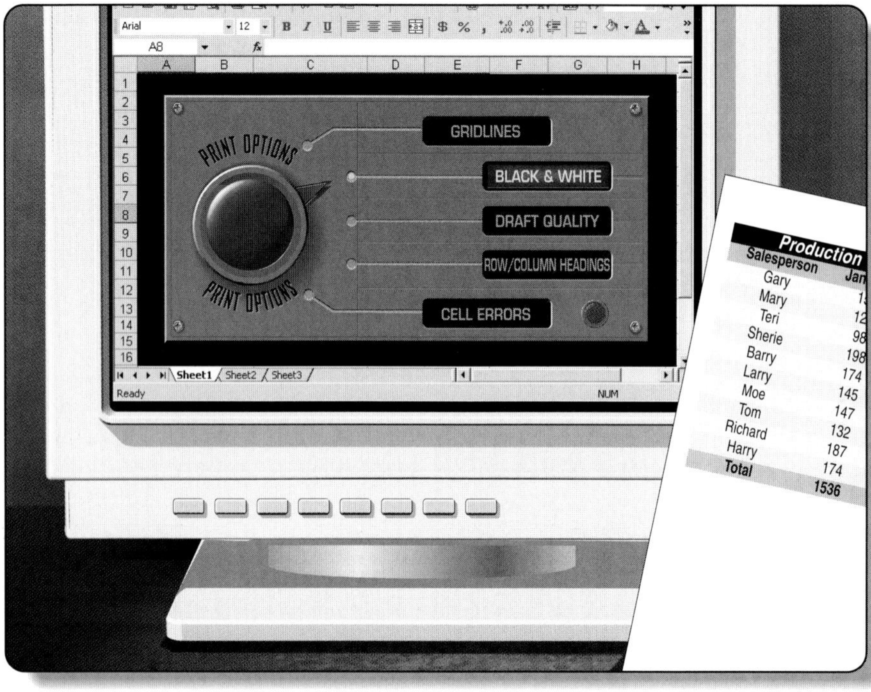

Changing the print options will not affect the way your worksheet appears on your screen.

CHANGE PRINT OPTIONS

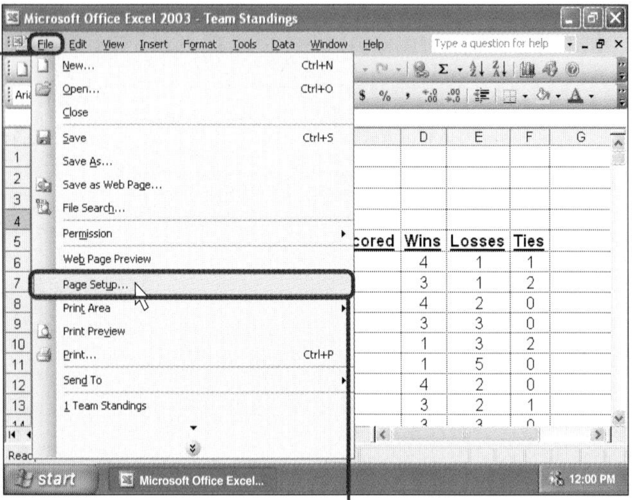

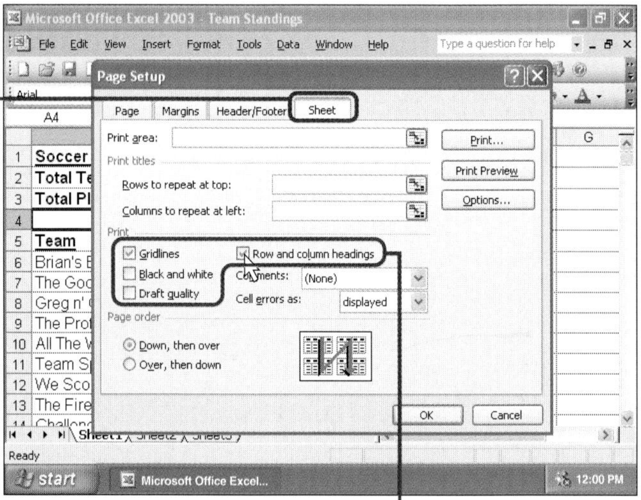

1 Click **File**.

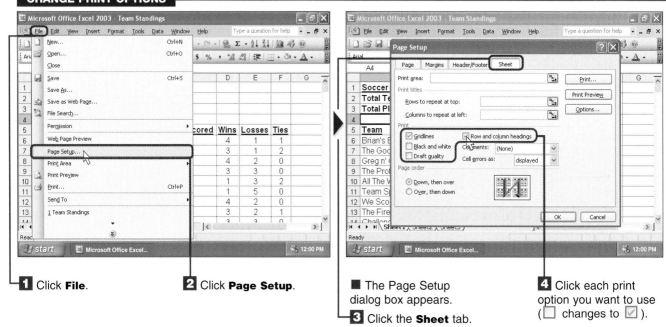

2 Click **Page Setup**.

■ The Page Setup dialog box appears.

3 Click the **Sheet** tab.

4 Click each print option you want to use (☐ changes to ☑).

Tip

What print options does Excel offer?

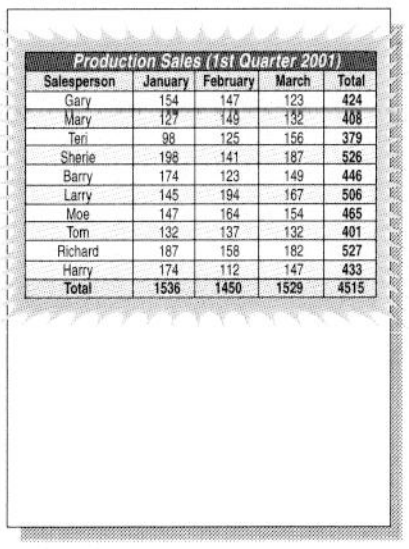

Gridlines

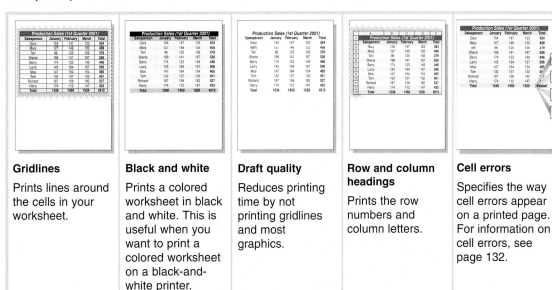

Prints lines around the cells in your worksheet.

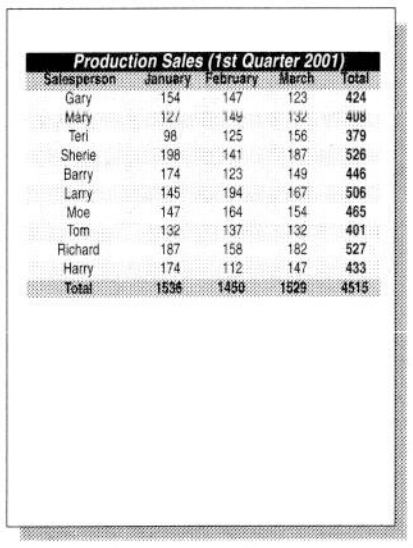

Black and white

Prints a colored worksheet in black and white. This is useful when you want to print a colored worksheet on a black-and-white printer.

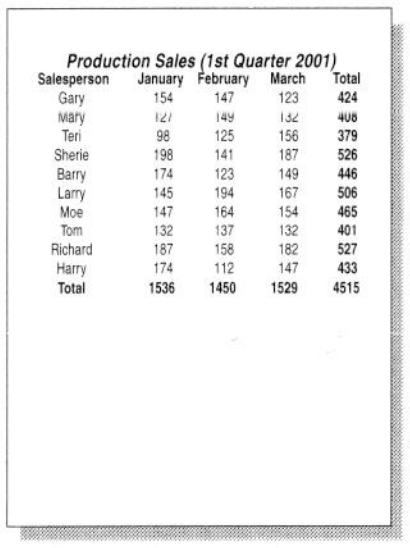

Draft quality

Reduces printing time by not printing gridlines and most graphics.

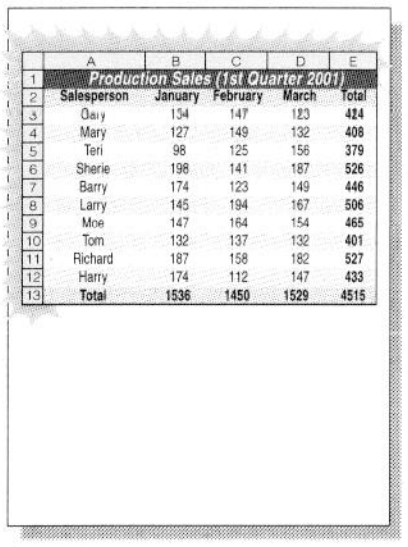

Row and column headings

Prints the row numbers and column letters.

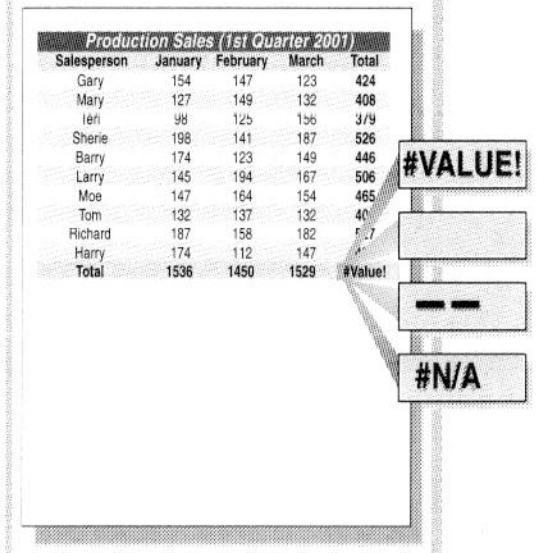

Cell errors

Specifies the way cell errors appear on a printed page. For information on cell errors, see page 132.

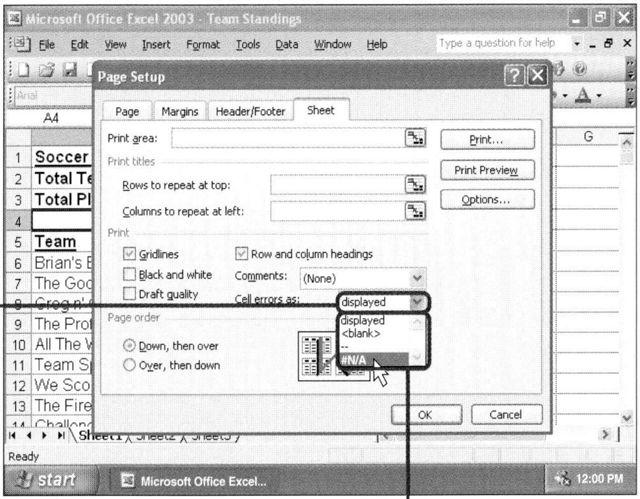

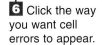

■ By default, Excel will print any cell errors that appear in your worksheet.

5 To specify how you want cell errors to appear when you print your worksheet, click this area.

6 Click the way you want cell errors to appear.

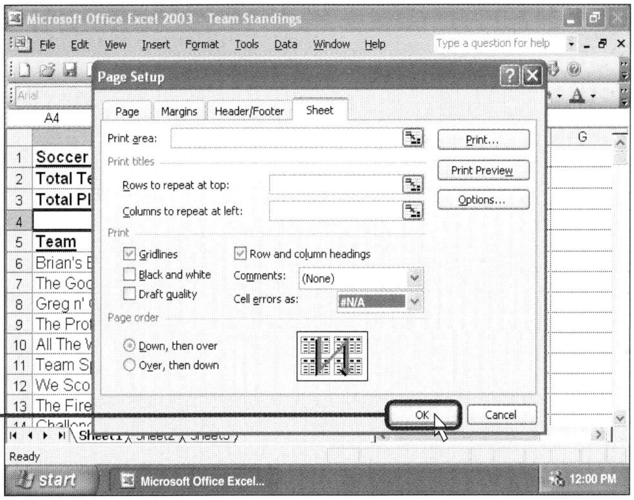

7 Click **OK** to confirm your changes.

Note: You can use the Print Preview feature to see how your worksheet will appear on a printed page. For information on using the Print Preview feature, see page 146.

CREATE A CHART

You can create a chart to graphically display your worksheet data. Charts allow you to easily compare data and view patterns and trends.

The Chart Wizard takes you step by step through the process of creating a chart.

CREATE A CHART

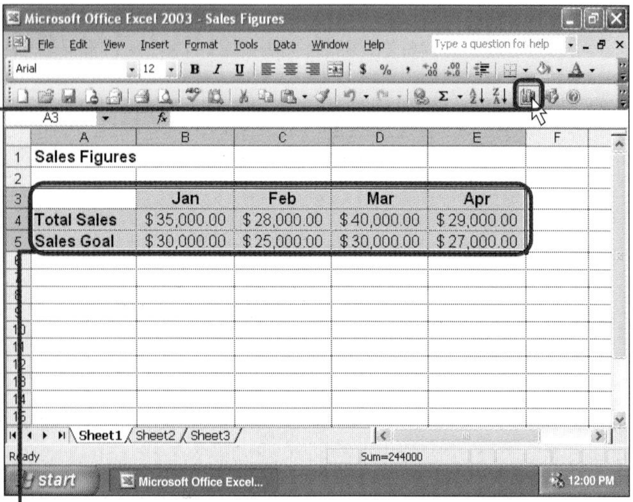

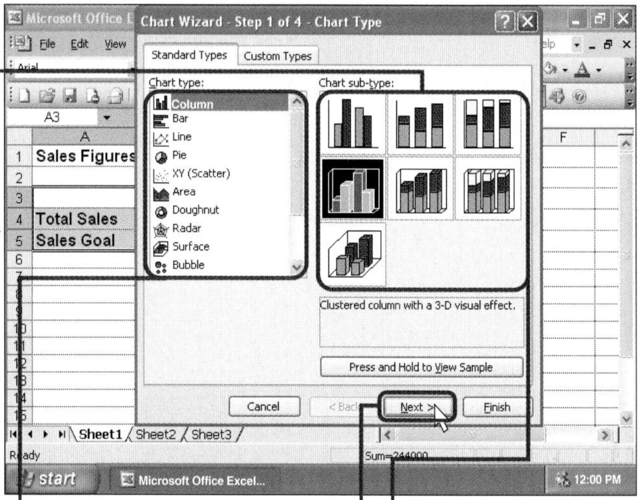

1 Select the cells containing the data you want to display in a chart, including the row and column labels. To select cells, see page 94.

2 Click to create a chart.

Note: If is not displayed, click on the Standard toolbar to display the button.

■ The Chart Wizard appears.

3 Click the type of chart you want to create.

■ This area displays the available chart designs for the type of chart you selected.

4 Click the chart design you want to use.

5 Click **Next** to continue.

Tip

Can I see a preview of my chart when I'm choosing the chart type and design?

Yes. After performing step **4** below, you can press and hold down the **Press and Hold to View Sample** button to see a preview of how your chart will appear with the chart type and design you selected.

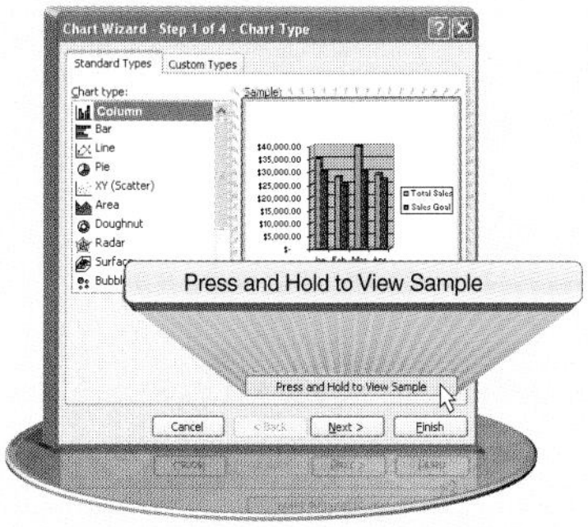

Tip

What titles can I add to my chart?

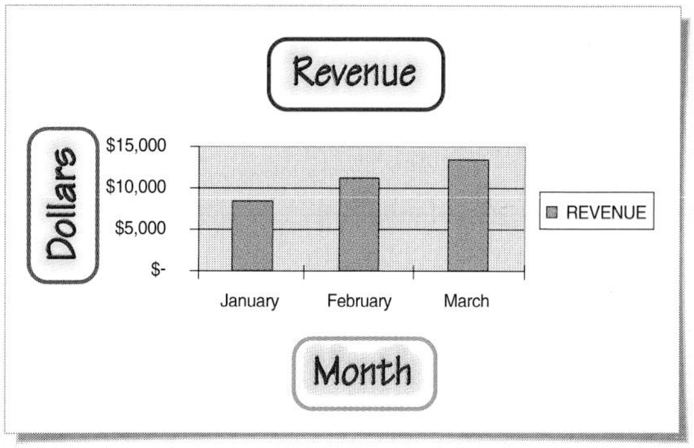

Chart title
Identifies the subject of your chart.

Value axis
Indicates the unit of measure used in your chart.

Category axis
Indicates the categories used in your chart.

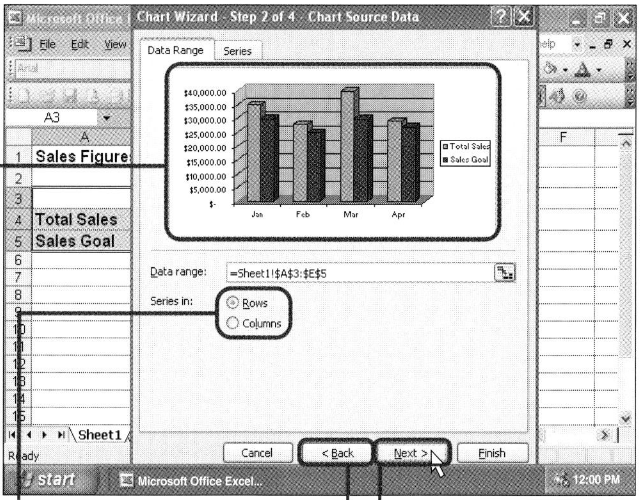

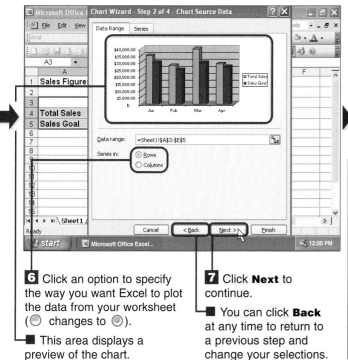

6 Click an option to specify the way you want Excel to plot the data from your worksheet (○ changes to ◉).

■ This area displays a preview of the chart.

7 Click **Next** to continue.

■ You can click **Back** at any time to return to a previous step and change your selections.

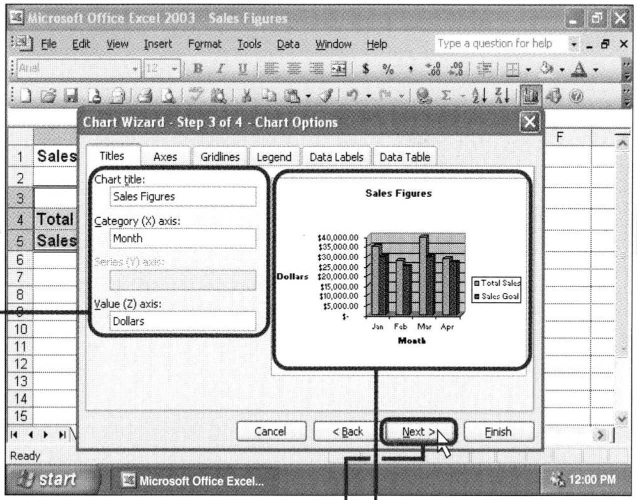

■ This area provides boxes you can use to add titles to the chart.

Note: Some boxes are not available for some chart types.

8 To add a title to the chart, click a box and type the title. Repeat this step for each title you want to add.

■ This area shows how the titles will appear in the chart.

9 Click **Next** to continue.

CONTINUED

CREATE A CHART

When creating a chart, you can choose to display the chart on the same worksheet as the data or on its own sheet, called a chart sheet.

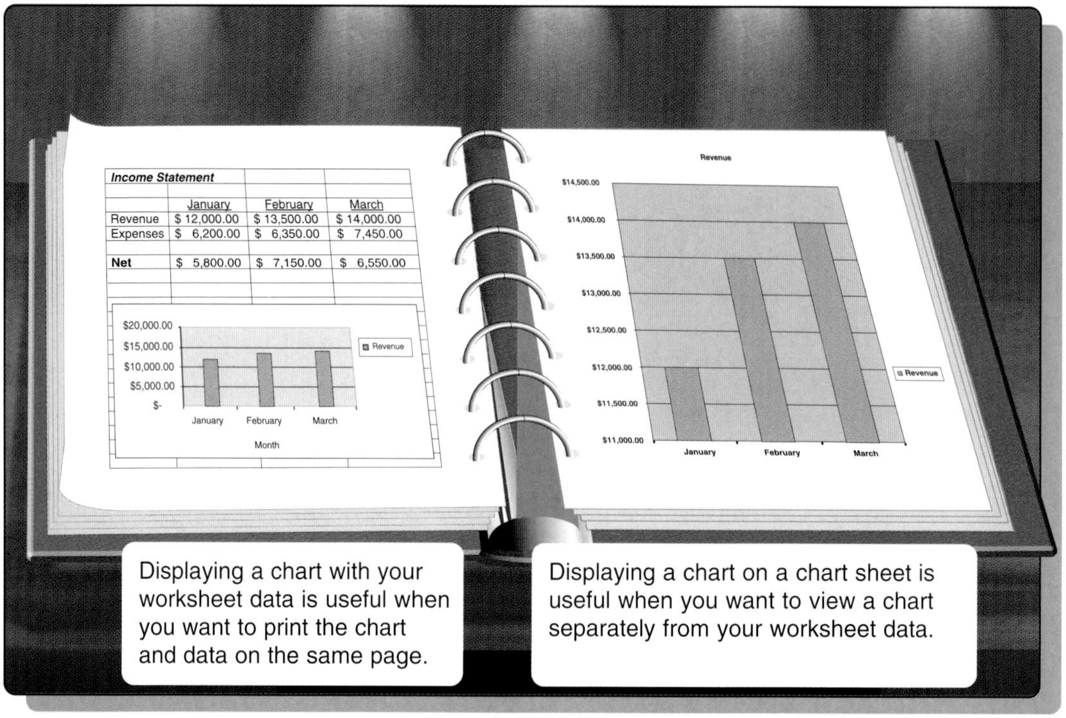

Displaying a chart with your worksheet data is useful when you want to print the chart and data on the same page.

Displaying a chart on a chart sheet is useful when you want to view a chart separately from your worksheet data.

CREATE A CHART (CONTINUED)

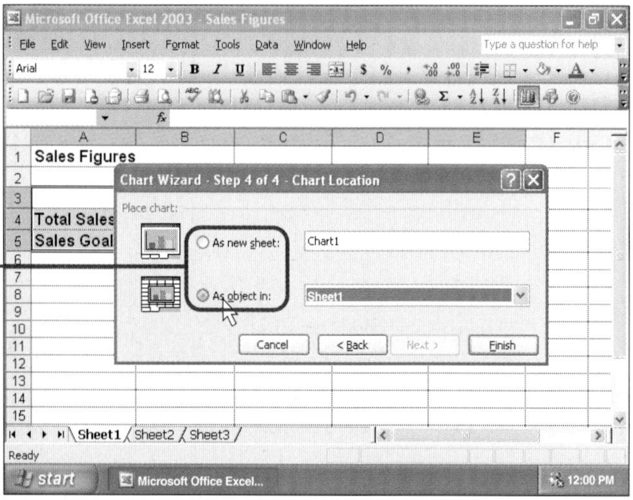

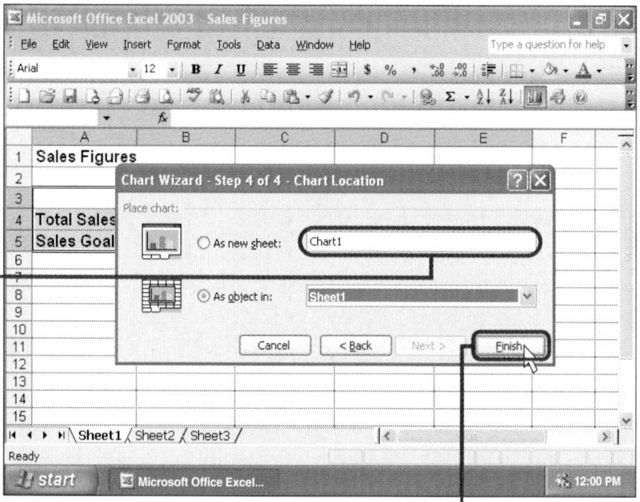

10 Click an option to specify where you want to display the chart (◯ changes to ◉).

As new sheet - Displays the chart on its own sheet, called a chart sheet.

As object in - Displays the chart on the same worksheet as the data.

■ If you selected **As new sheet** in step **10**, you can type a name for the chart sheet in this area.

11 Click **Finish** to create the chart.

Tip

What happens if I change the data I used to create a chart?

If you change the data you used to create a chart, Excel will automatically update the chart to display the changes.

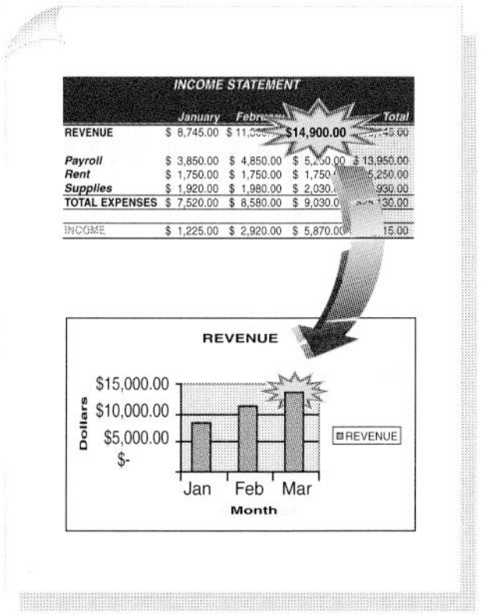

Tip

Can I change the chart titles?

Yes. After you create a chart, you can change the chart title and axis titles in the chart. Click the title you want to change. A box appears around the title. Drag the mouse I over the title until you select all the text. Type a new title and then click a blank area in the chart.

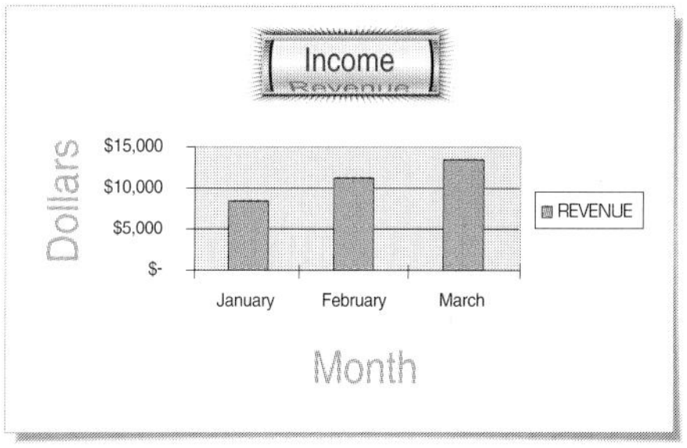

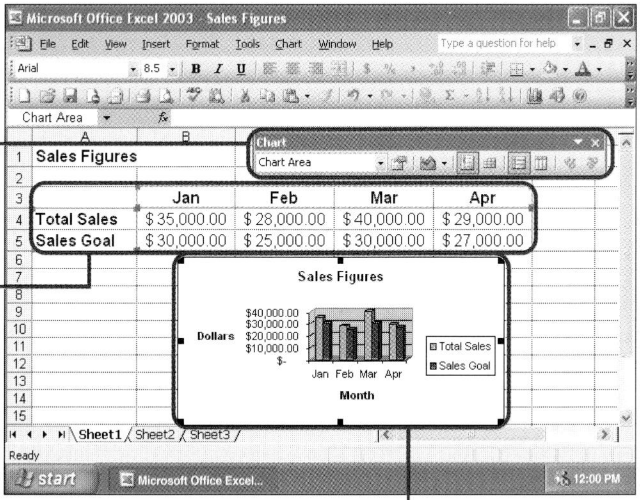

■ In this example, the chart appears on the same worksheet as the data.

■ The Chart toolbar also appears, displaying buttons that allow you to make changes to the chart.

■ Excel outlines the data you selected to create the chart.

■ The handles (■) around a chart let you change the size of the chart. To hide the handles, click outside the chart.

Note: To move or resize a chart, see page 158.

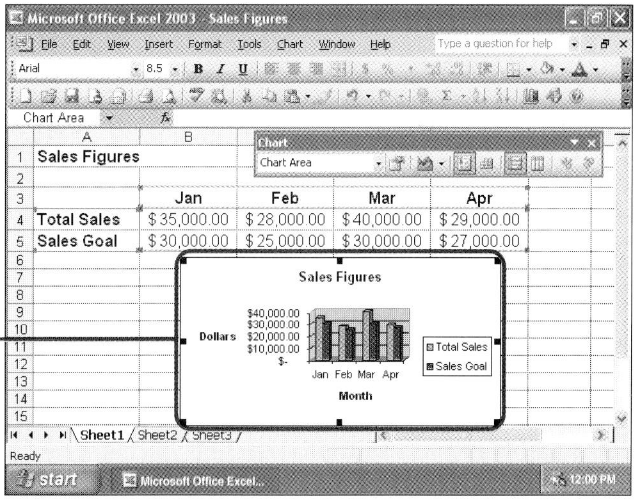

DELETE A CHART

1 Click a blank area in the chart you want to delete. Handles (■) appear around the chart.

2 Press the Delete key to delete the chart.

Note: To delete a chart displayed on a chart sheet, you must delete the sheet. To delete a worksheet, see page 101.

MOVE OR RESIZE A CHART

You can change the location and size of a chart displayed on your worksheet.

Moving a chart to another location in your worksheet is useful if the chart covers your data. Increasing the size of a chart is useful if the information in the chart is too small to read.

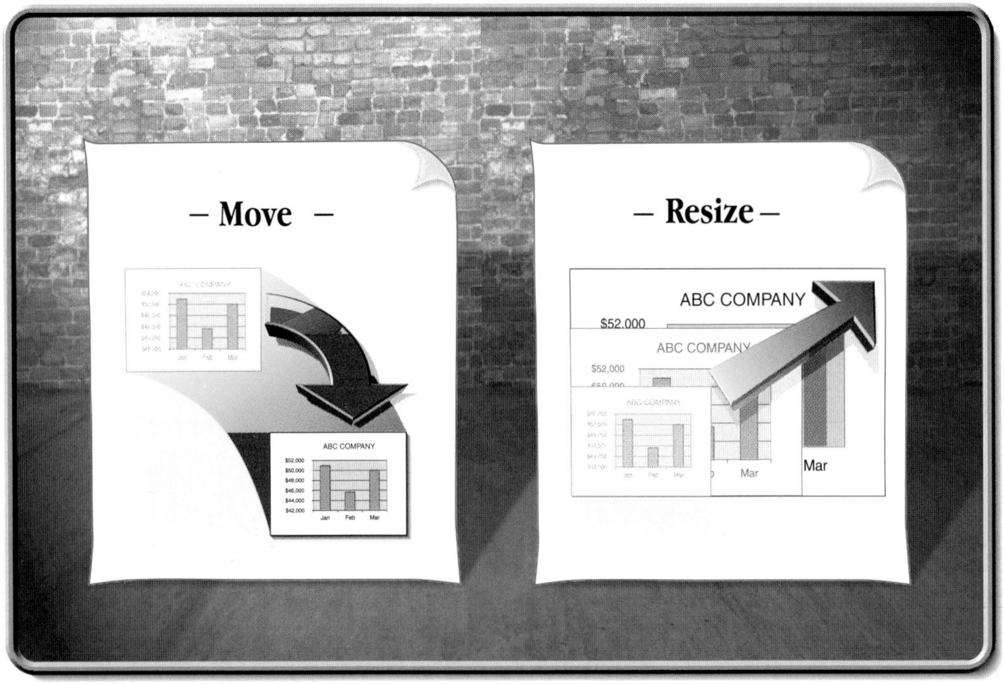

MOVE A CHART

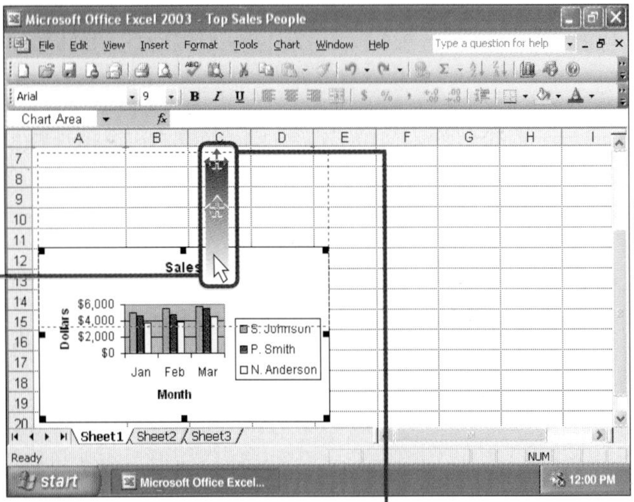

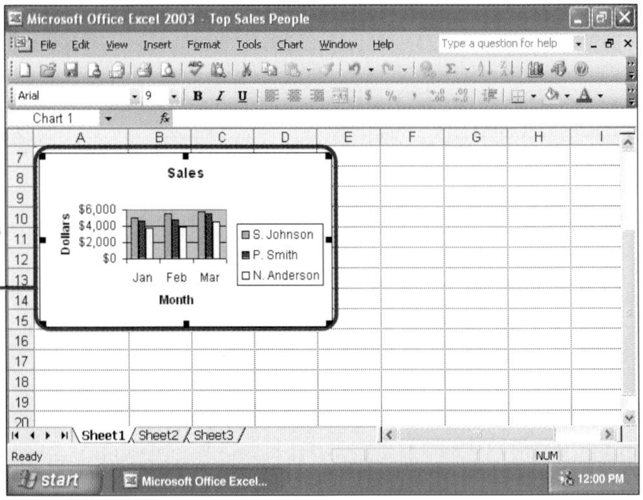

1 Position the mouse ✥ over a blank area in the chart you want to move (✥ changes to ↖).

2 Drag the chart to a new location in your worksheet.

■ A dashed line indicates where the chart will appear.

■ The chart appears in the new location.

■ To deselect the chart, click outside the chart.

Tip

What handle (■) should I use to resize a chart?

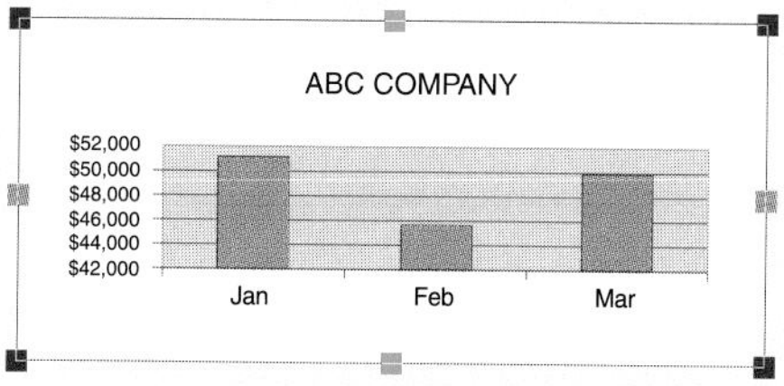

■ Changes the height of a chart

■ Changes the width of a chart

■ Changes the height and width of a chart at the same time

Tip

Can I move individual items in a chart?

Yes. To move the chart title, an axis title or the legend to a new location in a chart, position the mouse ⇖ over the item. Then drag the item to a new location. You cannot move an item outside of the chart area.

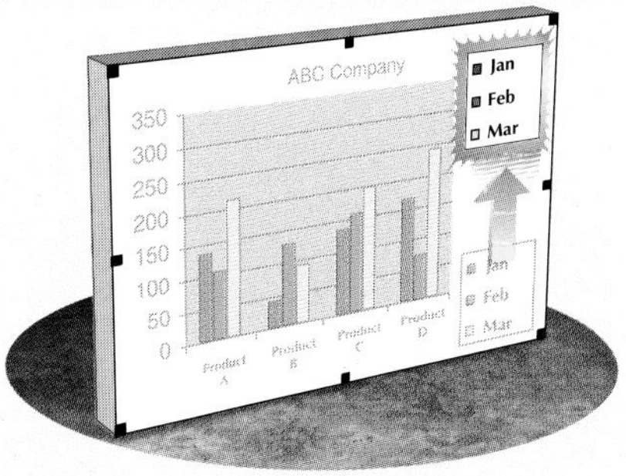

RESIZE A CHART

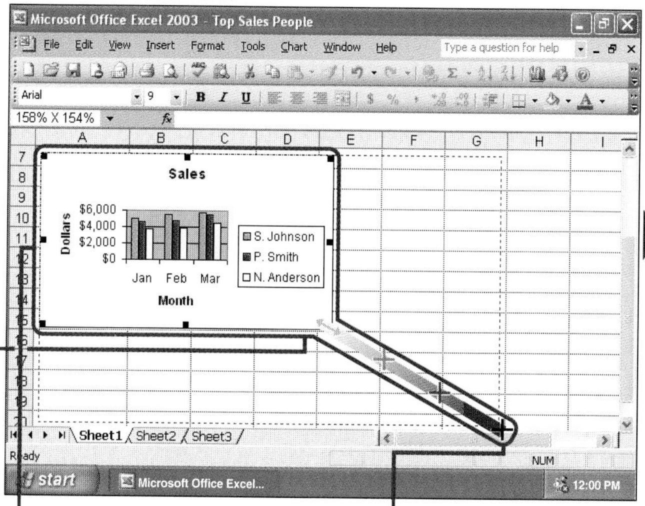

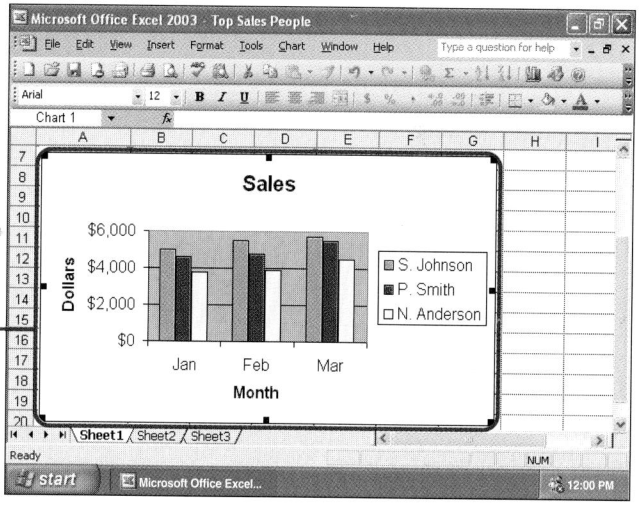

1 Click a blank area in the chart you want to resize. Handles (■) appear around the chart.

2 Position the mouse ⇖ over one of the handles (⇖ changes to ↘, ↗, ↔ or ↕).

3 Drag the handle until the chart is the size you want.

■ A dashed line shows the new size.

■ The chart appears in the new size.

■ To deselect the chart, click outside the chart.

CHANGE THE CHART TYPE

After you create a chart, you can change the chart type to present your data more effectively.

The type of chart you should use depends on your data. For example, area, column and line charts are ideal for showing changes to values over time. Pie charts are ideal for showing percentages.

CHANGE THE CHART TYPE

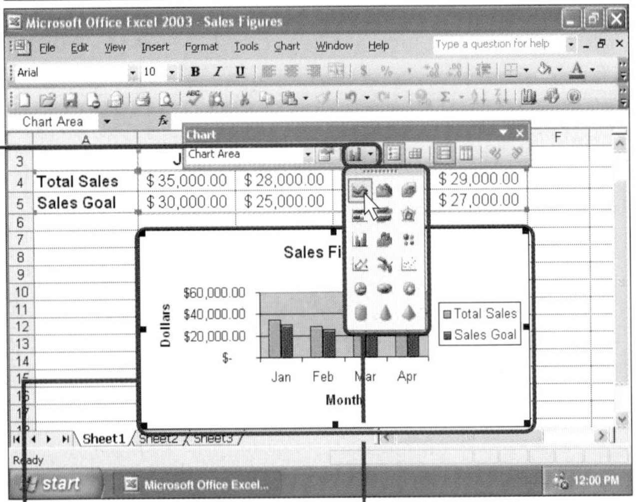

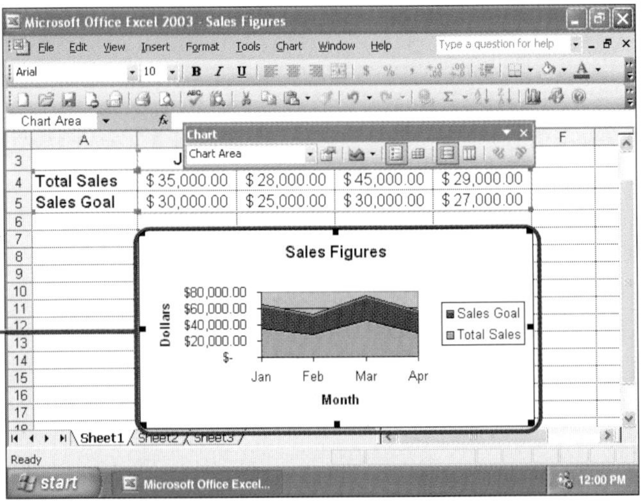

1 Click a blank area in the chart you want to change. Handles (■) appear around the chart.

2 Click ▾ in this area to display the available chart types.

Note: If the Chart toolbar is not displayed, see page 10 to display the toolbar.

3 Click the type of chart you want to use.

■ The chart displays the chart type you selected.

PRINT A CHART

You can print your chart with the worksheet data or on its own page.

When you print a chart on its own page, the chart will expand to fill the page.

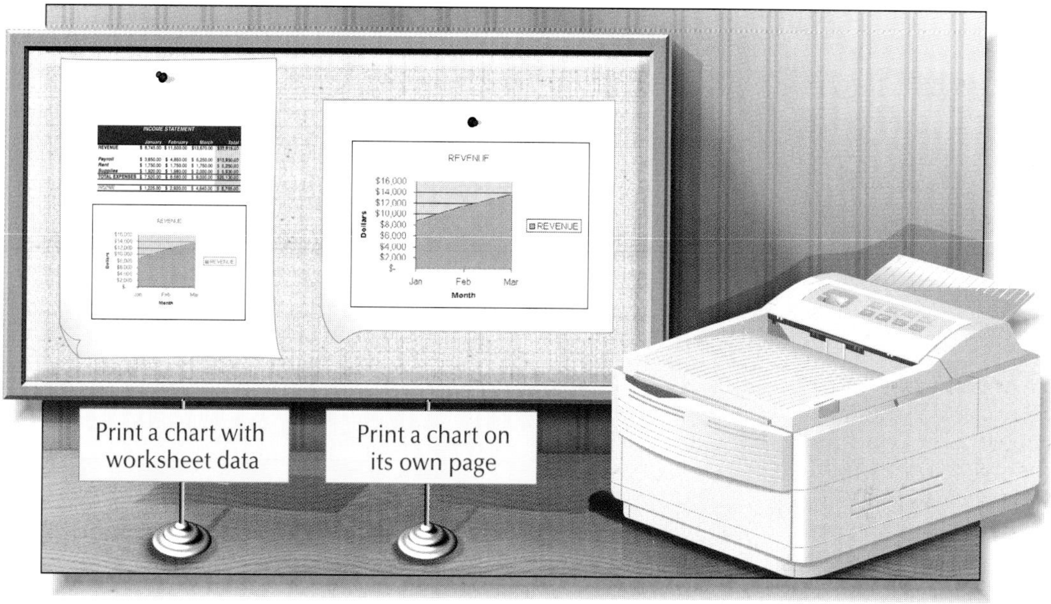

PRINT A CHART

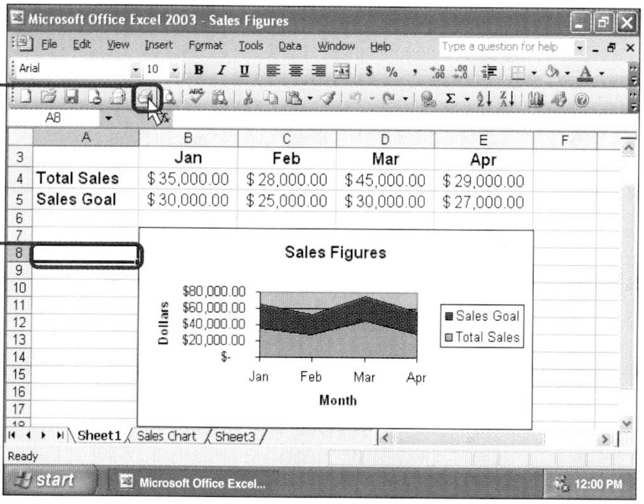

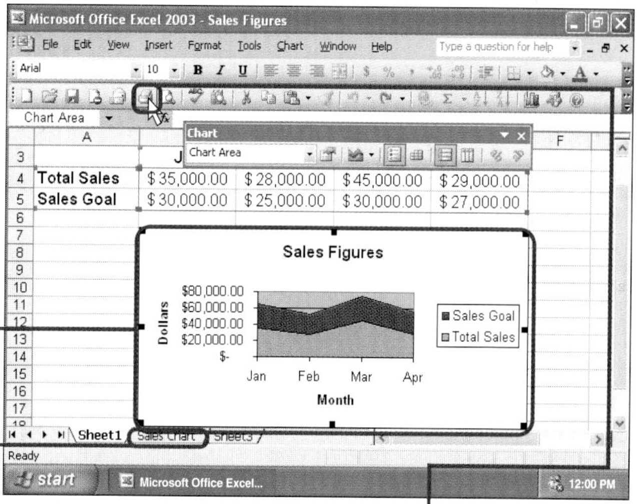

PRINT A CHART WITH WORKSHEET DATA

1 Click a cell outside the chart.

2 Click 🖨 to print the chart with your worksheet data.

Note: If 🖨 is not displayed, click on the Standard toolbar to display the button.

PRINT A CHART ON ITS OWN PAGE

1 To print a chart displayed on a worksheet, click a blank area in the chart.

■ To print a chart displayed on a chart sheet, click the tab for the chart sheet.

2 Click 🖨 to print the chart on its own page.

Note: If 🖨 is not displayed, click on the Standard toolbar to display the button.

Bill's Auto Body Shop
We perform body work on all makes and models of cars
Our fully trained mechanics will get your car up and running quickly and efficiently
Vrrrooooomm

Using PowerPoint

PowerPoint helps you plan, organize, design and deliver professional presentations.

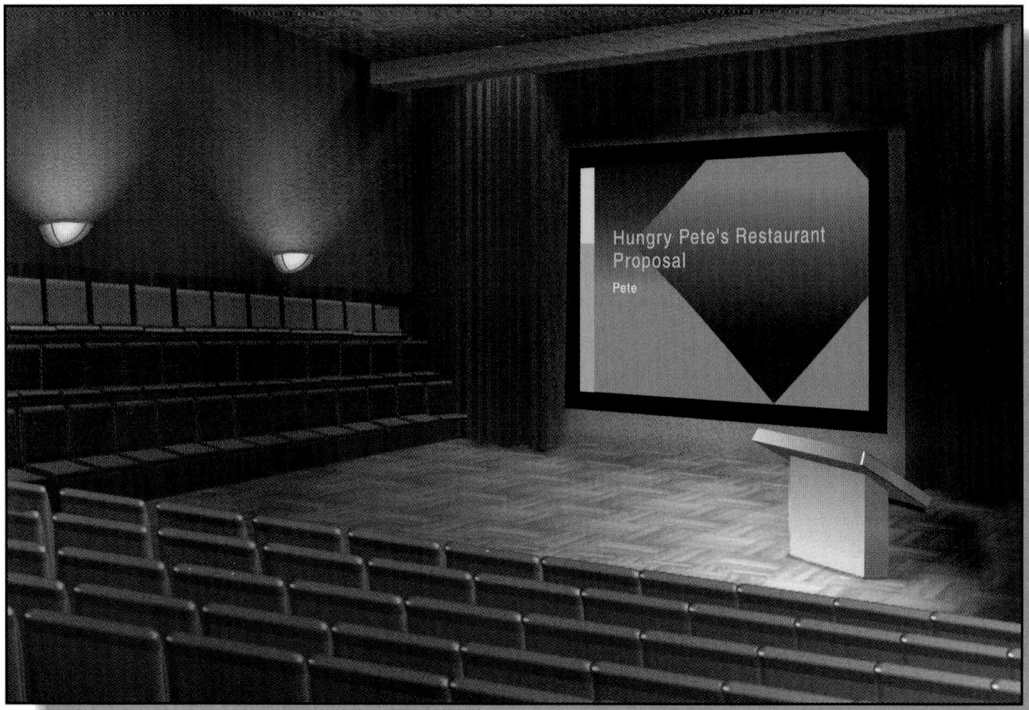

Create and Edit a Presentation

You can use PowerPoint's AutoContent Wizard to quickly create a presentation or design your own presentation one slide at a time. You can then add, delete and move text in the presentation and check the presentation for spelling errors.

Enhance a Presentation

You can emphasize the text on a slide using a bold, italic or underline style. You can also change the font, size and color of text. You can enhance your slides by adding objects such as clip art images, AutoShapes, charts and diagrams.

Fine-Tune a Presentation

If you plan to deliver a presentation on a computer screen, you can add special effects called transitions to help you move from one slide to the next. You can also reorganize the slides in your presentation and delete slides you no longer need.

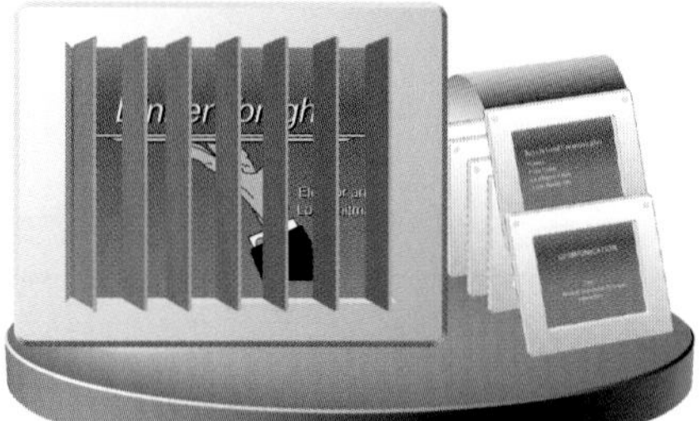

PARTS OF THE POWERPOINT WINDOW

The PowerPoint window displays several items to help you perform tasks efficiently.

Title Bar

Shows the name of the displayed presentation.

Menu Bar

Provides access to lists of commands available in PowerPoint and displays an area where you can type a question to get help information.

Standard Toolbar

Contains buttons you can use to select common commands, such as Save and Open.

Formatting Toolbar

Contains buttons you can use to select common formatting commands, such as Bold and Underline.

Outline and Slides Tabs

Provide two ways of viewing the slides in your presentation.

Slide Pane

Displays the current slide.

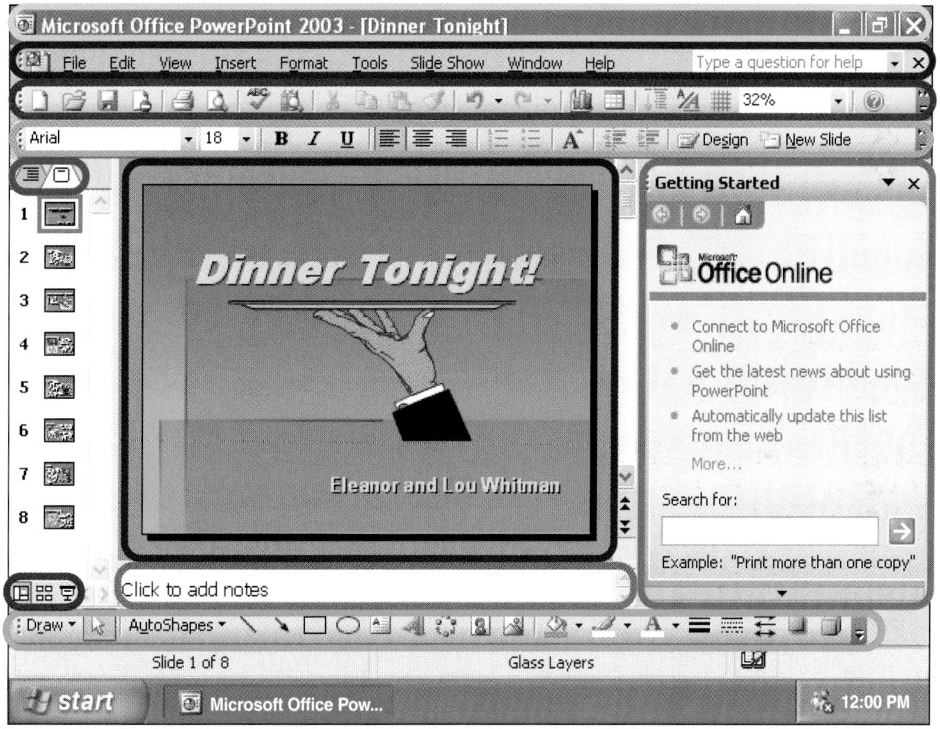

View Buttons

Allow you to quickly change the way your presentation is displayed on the screen.

Notes Pane

Displays the notes you have created for the current slide.

Drawing Toolbar

Contains buttons to help you work with objects in your presentation.

Task Pane

Contains options you can select to perform common tasks, such as creating a new presentation or searching for help information.

CREATE A PRESENTATION USING THE AUTOCONTENT WIZARD

You can use the AutoContent Wizard to create a presentation. The wizard asks you a series of questions and then sets up a presentation based on your answers.

Using the AutoContent Wizard to create a presentation is useful when you want ideas on how to compose and organize your presentation.

USING THE AUTOCONTENT WIZARD

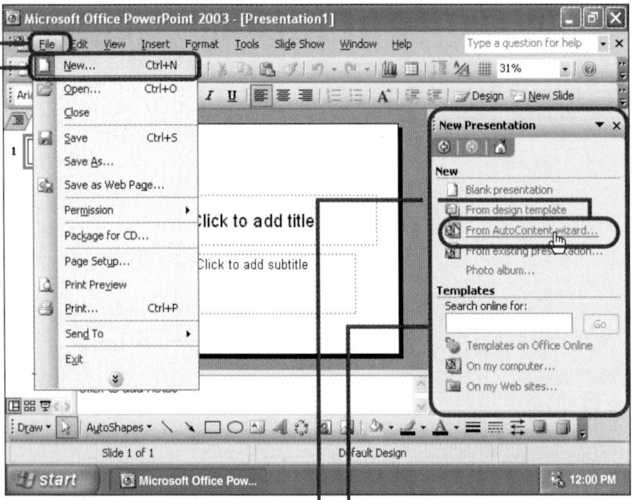

1 Click **File**.

2 Click **New**.

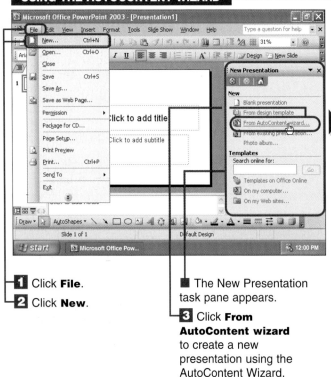

■ The New Presentation task pane appears.

3 Click **From AutoContent wizard** to create a new presentation using the AutoContent Wizard.

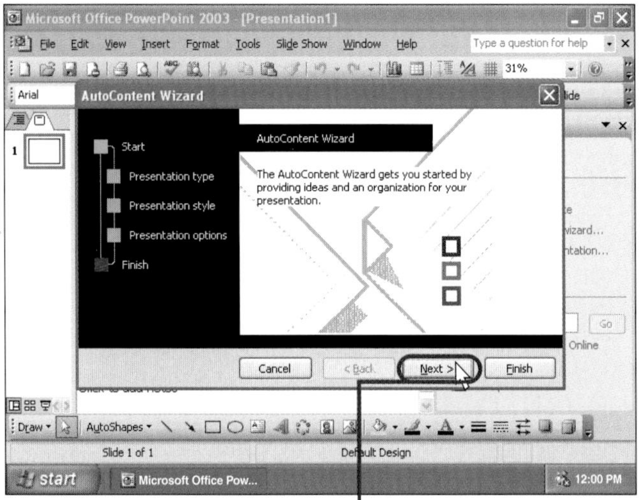

■ The AutoContent Wizard appears, displaying a brief description of the wizard.

4 Click **Next** to start creating your presentation.

Tip

Why did a dialog box appear after I selected a presentation in the AutoContent Wizard?

A dialog box appears if the presentation you selected is not installed on your computer. Insert the CD-ROM disc you used to install Office XP into your CD-ROM drive and then click **Yes** to install the presentation.

Note: A window may appear on your screen. Click ☒ in the top right corner of the window to close the window.

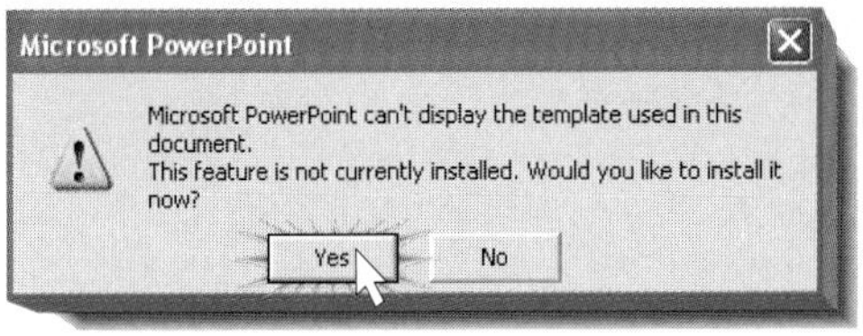

Tip

Is there another way to create a presentation?

If you want to design your own presentation without using the content and format PowerPoint suggests, you can create a blank presentation. Creating a blank presentation allows you to create and design each slide individually. To create a blank presentation, see page 170.

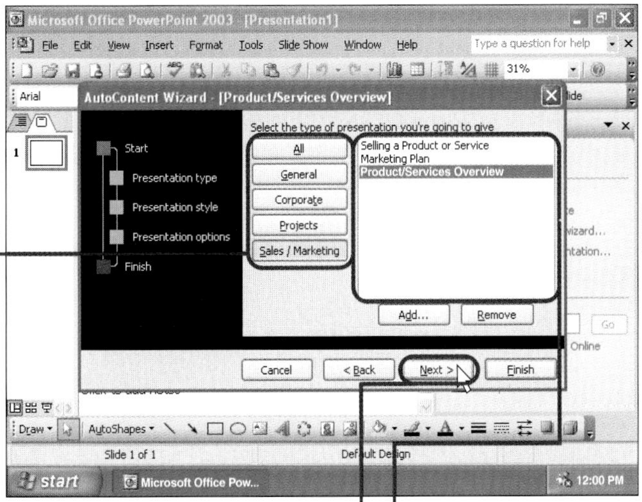

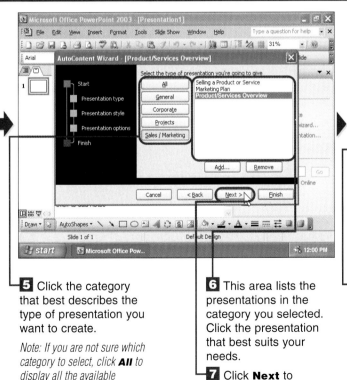

5 Click the category that best describes the type of presentation you want to create.

*Note: If you are not sure which category to select, click **All** to display all the available presentations.*

6 This area lists the presentations in the category you selected. Click the presentation that best suits your needs.

7 Click **Next** to continue.

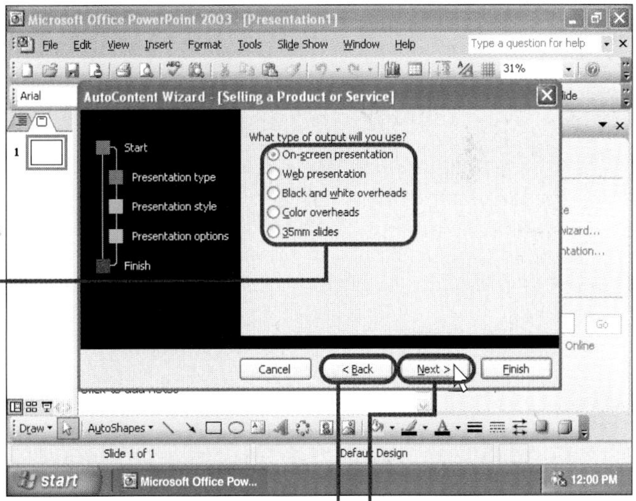

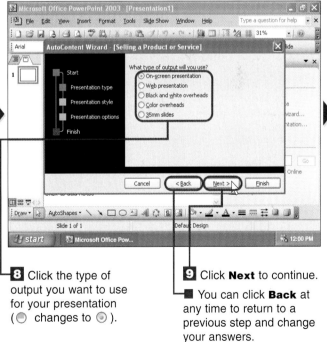

8 Click the type of output you want to use for your presentation (○ changes to ◉).

9 Click **Next** to continue.

■ You can click **Back** at any time to return to a previous step and change your answers.

CONTINUED

CREATE A PRESENTATION USING THE AUTOCONTENT WIZARD

The AutoContent Wizard allows you to specify a title for the first slide in your presentation. You can also specify information you want to appear on each slide, such as the current date and the name of your company.

USING THE AUTOCONTENT WIZARD (CONTINUED)

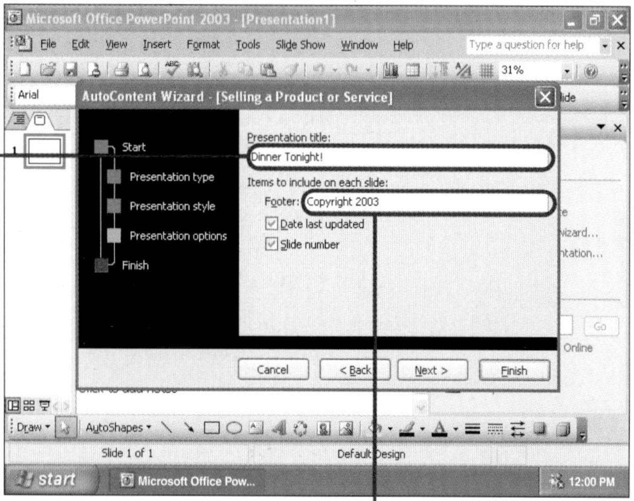

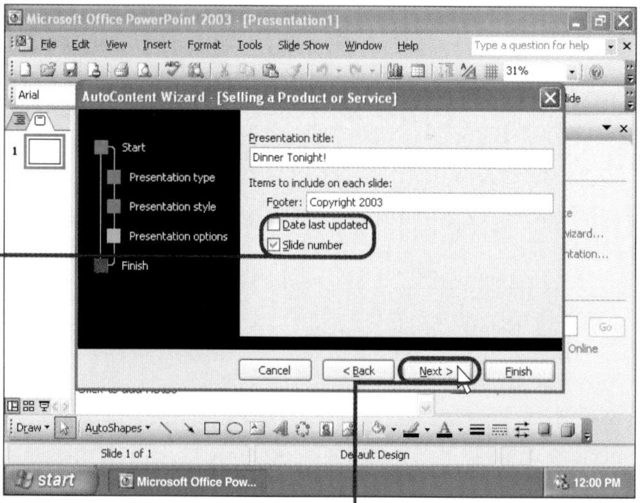

10 Click this area and type the title you want to appear on the first slide in your presentation.

11 To add footer text to each slide in your presentation, click this area and then type the text.

■ PowerPoint will add the current date and slide number to each slide in your presentation.

12 If you do not want to add the current date or slide number, click the option you do not want to add (☑ changes to ☐).

Note: If you add the current date, PowerPoint will update the date displayed on the slides every time you open the presentation.

13 Click **Next** to continue.

Tip

How do I replace the text suggestions that PowerPoint provides with my own text?

To replace the text suggestions, drag the mouse I over the text to select the text and then type the text you want to use.

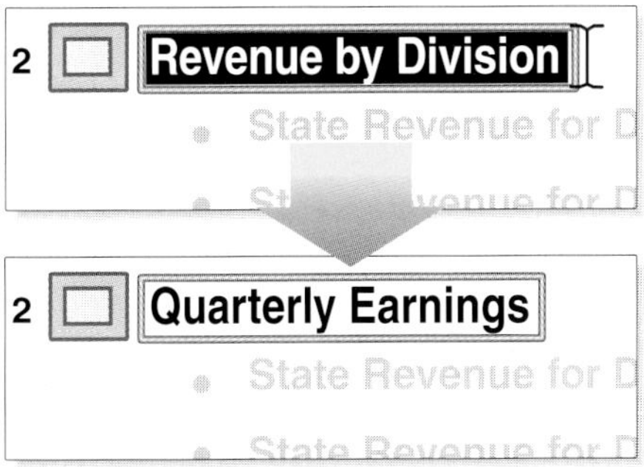

Tip

Can I change the design of the presentation I created using the AutoContent Wizard?

The design PowerPoint uses for the presentation depends on the presentation type you selected in the AutoContent Wizard. You can change the design of the presentation to better suit the content of the presentation. To change the design, see page 214.

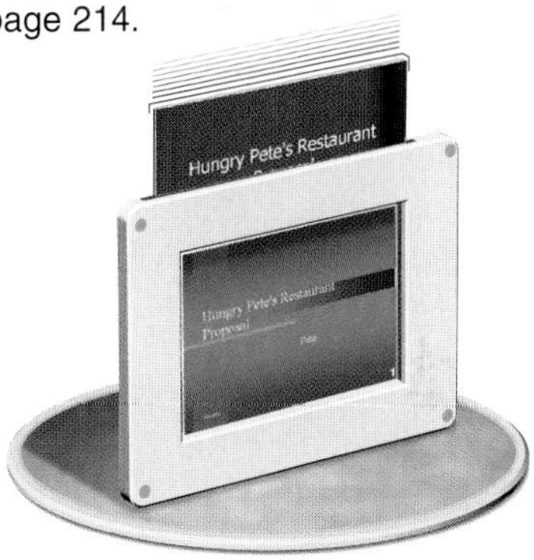

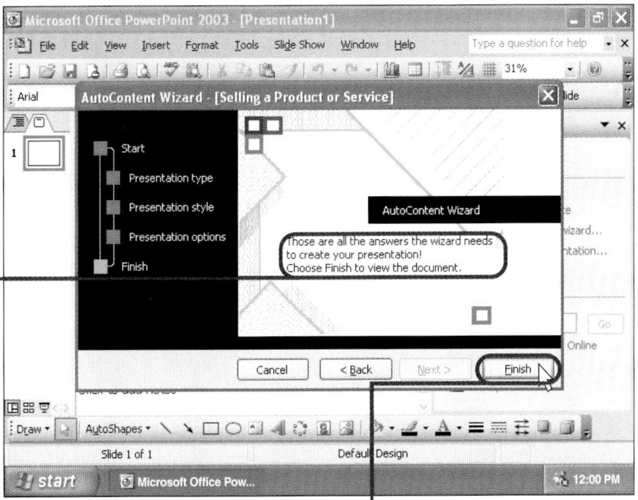

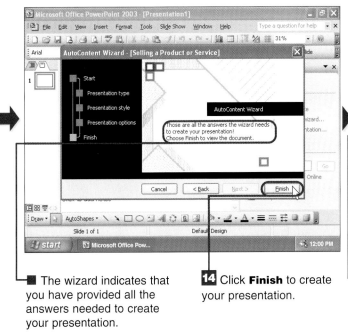

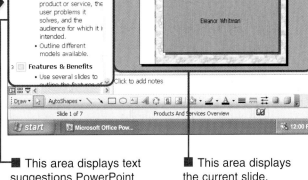

■ The wizard indicates that you have provided all the answers needed to create your presentation.

14 Click **Finish** to create your presentation.

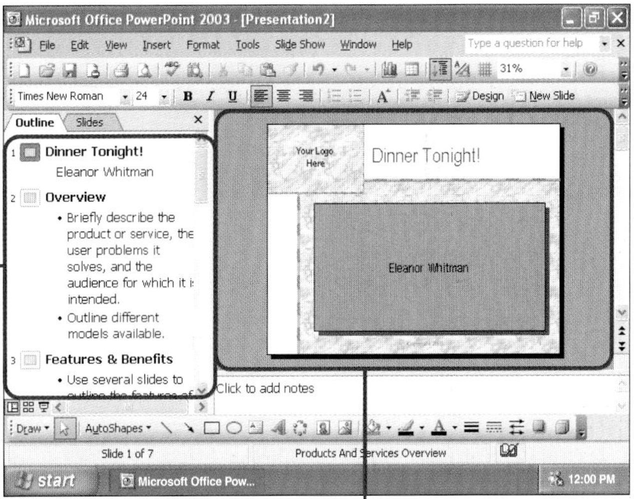

■ This area displays text suggestions PowerPoint provides for each slide in your presentation. You can replace this text with your own text. To replace the text, see the top of this page.

■ This area displays the current slide.

You can use PowerPoint to create a blank presentation. Blank presentations are useful when you want to create your own design and content for your slides.

When you create a blank presentation, PowerPoint creates only the first slide. You can add additional slides to your presentation as you need them. To add a slide to your presentation, see page 190.

CREATE A BLANK PRESENTATION

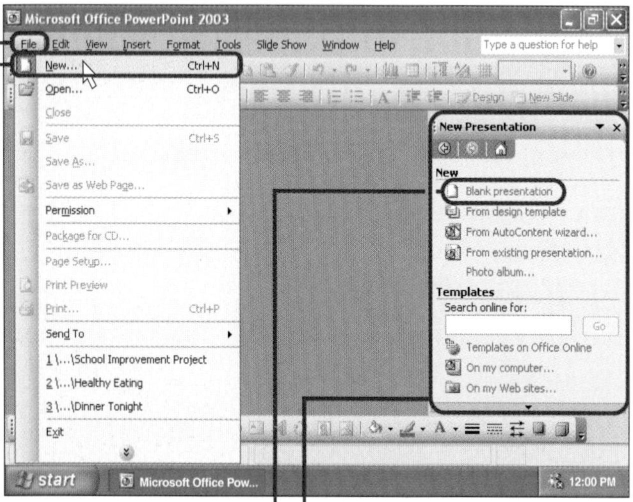

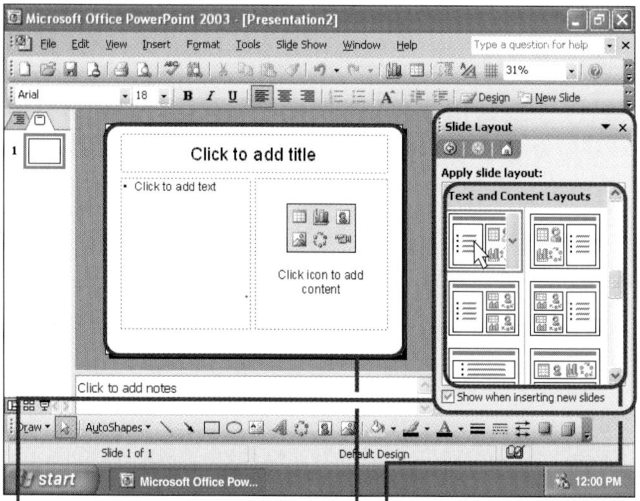

1 Click **File**.

2 Click **New**.

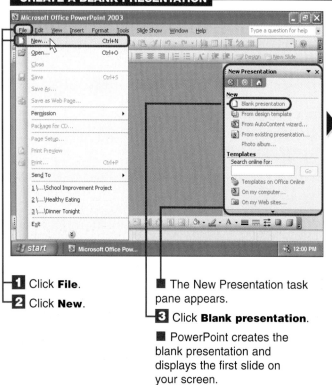

■ The New Presentation task pane appears.

3 Click **Blank presentation**.

■ PowerPoint creates the blank presentation and displays the first slide on your screen.

■ This area displays the Slide Layout task pane, which you can use to select a layout for the first slide in the presentation. For information on slide layouts, see page 192.

4 Click the layout you want to use.

■ The slide displays the layout you selected.

■ To add text to the slide, see page 182. To add objects to the slide, see pages 194 to 205.

SAVE A PRESENTATION

You can save your presentation to store it for future use. This allows you to later review and make changes to the presentation.

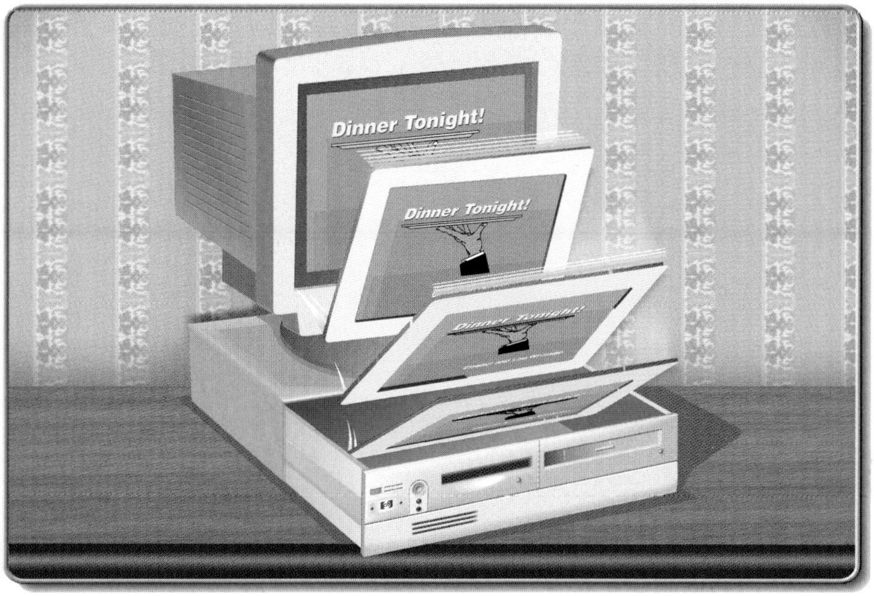

You should regularly save changes you make to a presentation to avoid losing your work.

SAVE A PRESENTATION

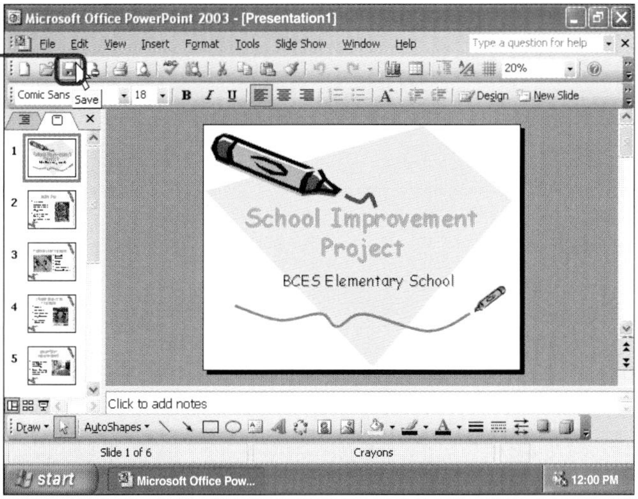

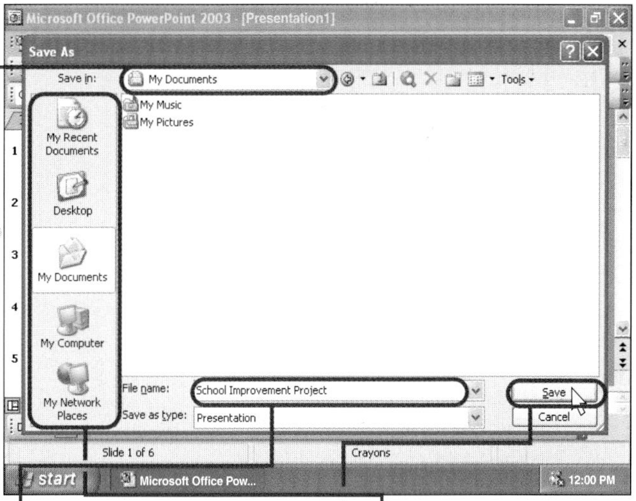

1 Click to save your presentation.

Note: If is not displayed, click on the Standard toolbar to display the button.

■ The Save As dialog box appears.

Note: If you previously saved your presentation, the Save As dialog box will not appear since you have already named the presentation.

2 Type a name for the presentation.

■ This area shows the location where PowerPoint will store your presentation. You can click this area to change the location.

■ This area allows you to access commonly used locations. You can click a location to save your presentation in the location.

3 Click **Save** to save your presentation.

OPEN A PRESENTATION

You can open a saved presentation to view the presentation on your screen. This allows you to review and make changes to the presentation.

OPEN A PRESENTATION

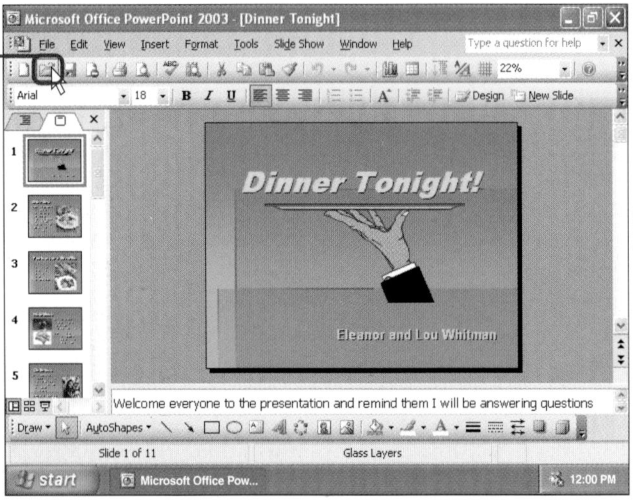

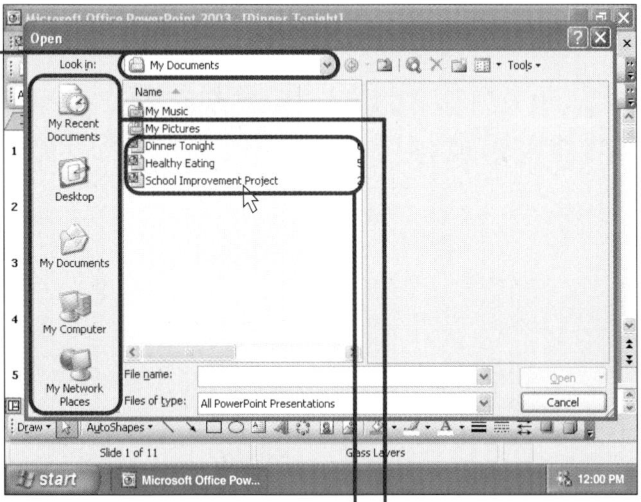

1 Click to open a presentation.

Note: If is not displayed, click on the Standard toolbar to display the button.

■ The Open dialog box appears.

■ This area shows the location of the displayed presentations. You can click this area to change the location.

■ This area allows you to access presentations in commonly used locations. You can click a location to display the presentations stored in the location.

2 Click the name of the presentation you want to open.

Tip

How can I quickly open a presentation I recently worked with?

PowerPoint remembers the names of the last four presentations you worked with. You can use the Getting Started task pane or the File menu to quickly open any of these presentations.

Note: The Getting Started task pane appears each time you start PowerPoint. To display the Getting Started task pane, see page 8.

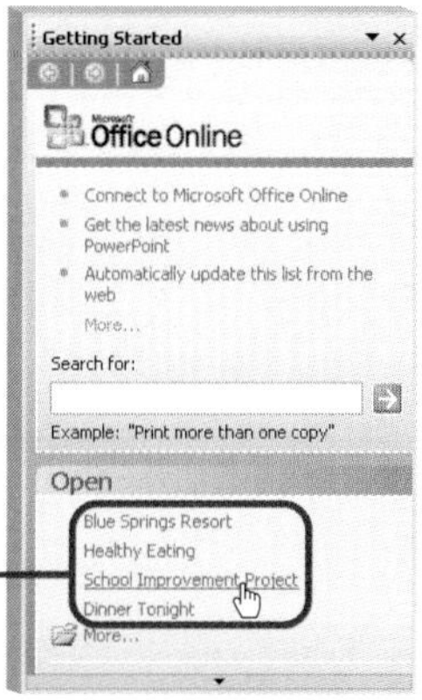

Use the Task Pane

1 Click the name of the presentation you want to open.

Note: If the name of the presentation is not displayed, position the mouse over the bottom of the task pane to display the name.

Use the File Menu

1 Click **File**.

2 Click the name of the presentation you want to open.

Note: If the name of the presentation you want is not displayed, position the mouse over the bottom of the menu to display the name.

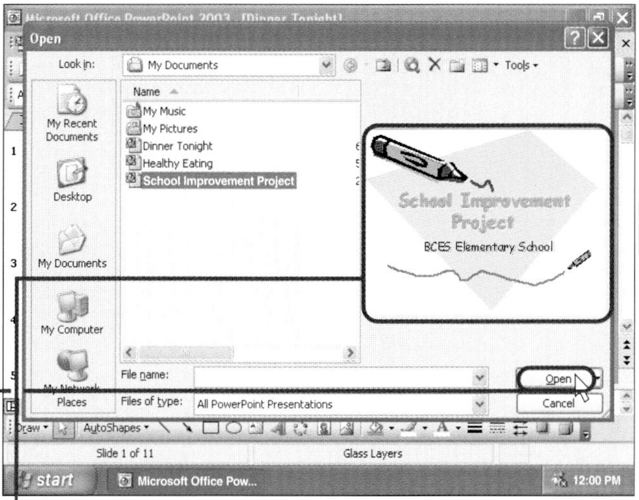

■ This area displays the first slide in the presentation you selected.

3 Click **Open** to open the presentation.

■ The presentation opens and appears on your screen. You can now review and make changes to the presentation.

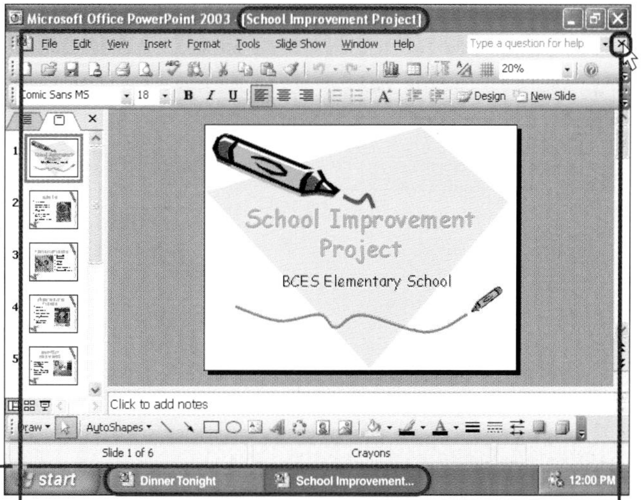

■ This area displays the name of the open presentation.

■ If you already had a presentation open, the new presentation appears in a new window. You can click the buttons on the taskbar to switch between the open presentations.

CLOSE A PRESENTATION

1 When you finish working with a presentation, click ☒ to close the presentation.

You can view your presentation in several different ways on your screen.

Each view displays the same presentation. If you make changes to your presentation in one view, the other views will also display the changes.

CHANGE THE VIEW OF A PRESENTATION

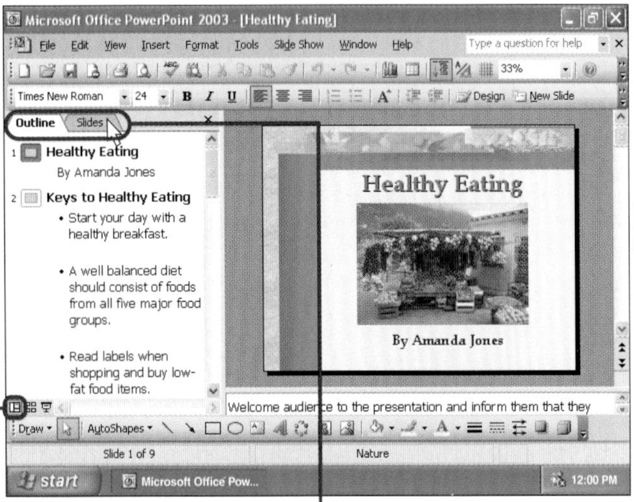

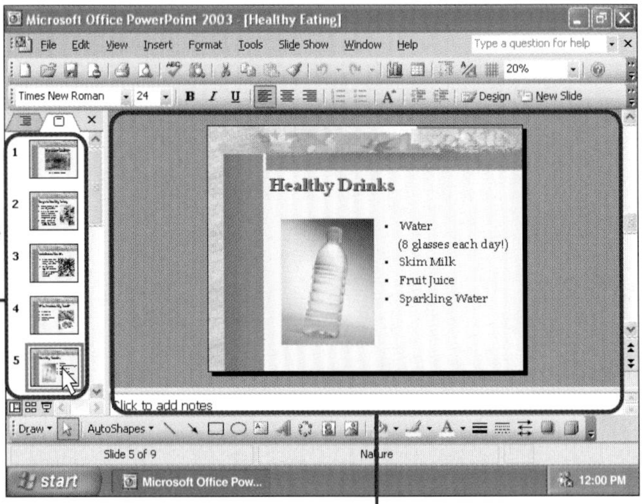

NORMAL VIEW

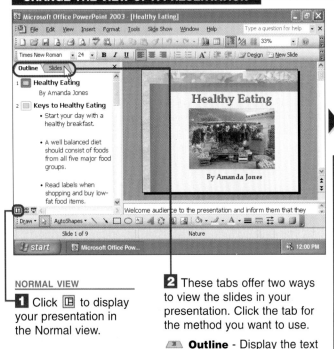

1 Click ▣ to display your presentation in the Normal view.

2 These tabs offer two ways to view the slides in your presentation. Click the tab for the method you want to use.

Outline - Display the text on each slide.

Slides - Display a miniature version of each slide.

■ This area displays a miniature version of each slide or the text on each slide, depending on the tab you selected.

3 Click a slide or the text for a slide of interest.

■ This area displays the slide you selected and any notes you have created for the slide. For information on notes, see page 226.

Tip

When would I use each view?

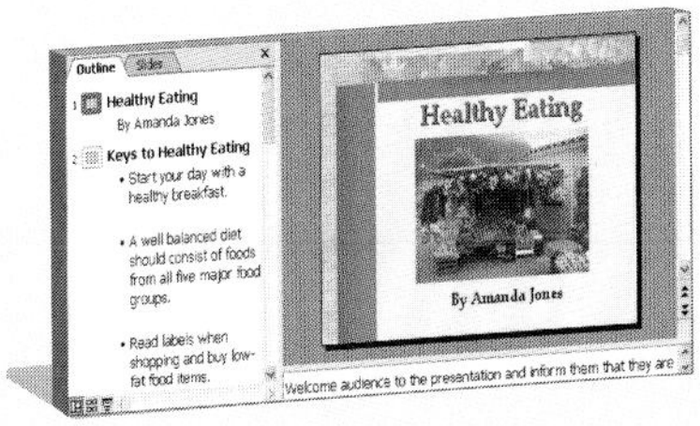

Normal view

Useful for creating and editing your presentation. The Normal view allows you to see different parts of your presentation, such as the current slide and any notes you have created for the current slide, on a single screen.

Slide Sorter view

Useful for reorganizing and deleting slides. The Slide Sorter view allows you to see the overall organization of your presentation.

Slide Show view

Useful for previewing your presentation. The Slide Show view allows you to view your presentation the way your audience will see the presentation.

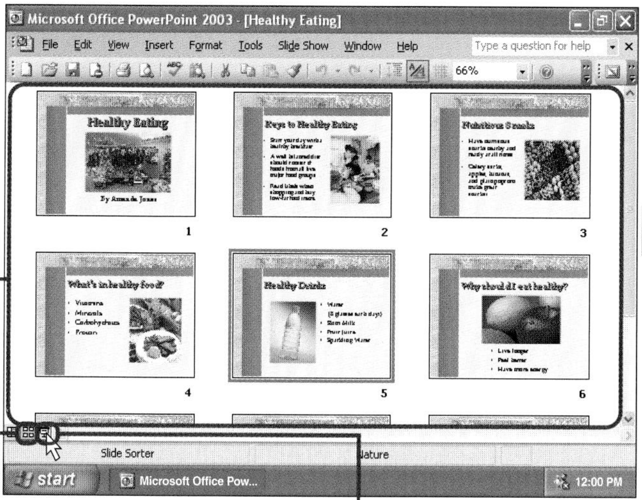

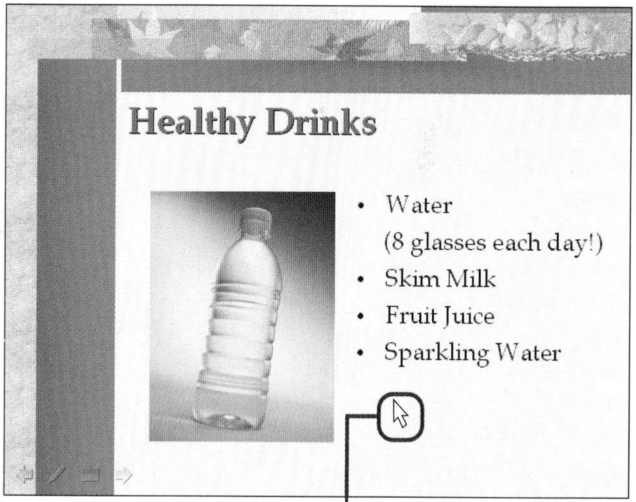

SLIDE SORTER VIEW

1 Click ⊞ to display your presentation in the Slide Sorter view.

■ This area displays a miniature version of each slide in your presentation.

SLIDE SHOW VIEW

1 Click 🖵 to display your presentation in the Slide Show view.

■ A full-screen version of the current slide appears on your screen.

■ You can click anywhere on the current slide to move through the slides in your presentation and view the entire slide show. For more information on viewing a slide show, see page 224.

BROWSE THROUGH A PRESENTATION

Since your computer screen cannot display your entire presentation at once, you must browse through your presentation to view other areas of the presentation.

BROWSE THROUGH A PRESENTATION

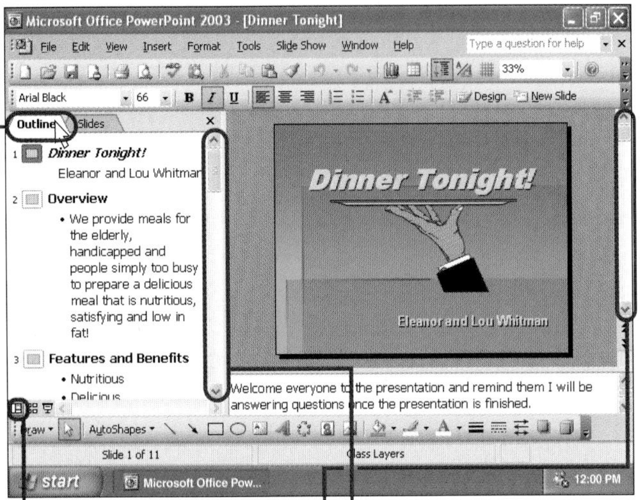

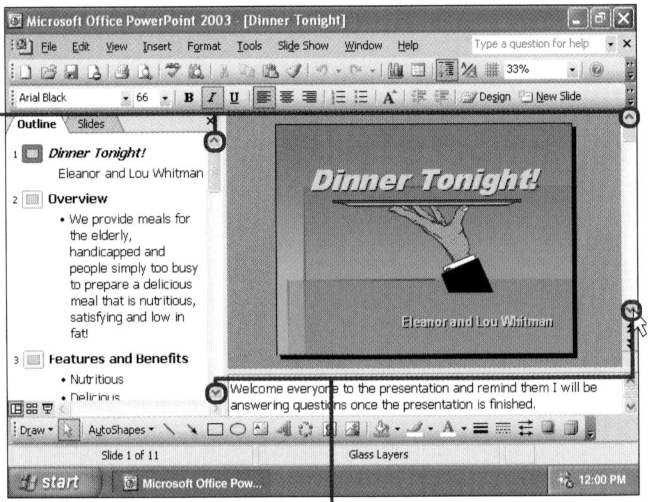

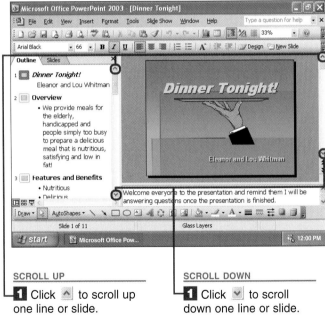

1 Click ▣ to display your presentation in the Normal view.

2 Click the **Outline** (▭) tab to display the text in your presentation.

■ You can use this scroll bar to browse through all the text in your presentation.

■ You can use this scroll bar to browse through all the slides in your presentation.

SCROLL UP

1 Click ˄ to scroll up one line or slide.

SCROLL DOWN

1 Click ˅ to scroll down one line or slide.

Tip

How can I browse through the notes in my presentation?

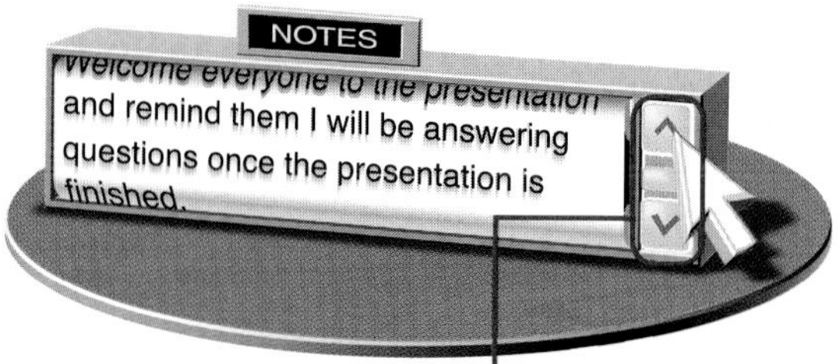

■ Any notes you have created for the current slide appear in the Notes pane.

1 To browse through the notes, click or .

Note: For information on creating notes, see page 226.

Tip

How do I use a wheeled mouse to browse through my presentation?

A wheeled mouse has a wheel between the left and right mouse buttons. Rolling this wheel forward or backward lets you quickly scroll up or down through your presentation. The Microsoft IntelliMouse is a popular example of a wheeled mouse.

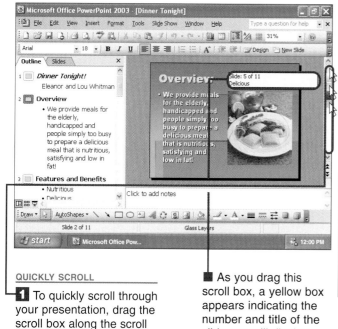

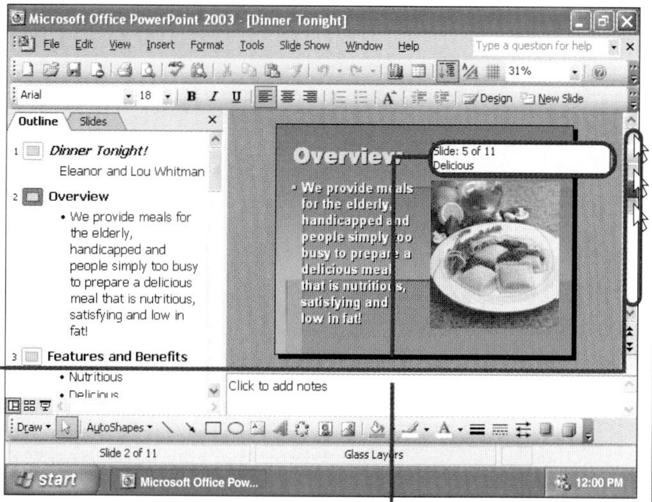

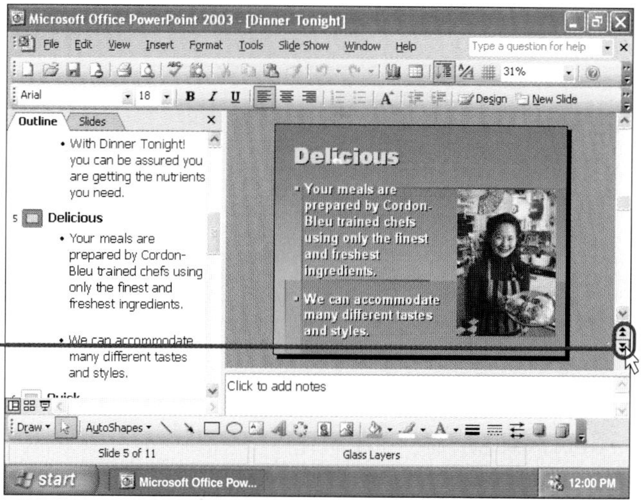

QUICKLY SCROLL

1 To quickly scroll through your presentation, drag the scroll box along the scroll bar.

■ As you drag this scroll box, a yellow box appears indicating the number and title of the slide you will display.

DISPLAY PREVIOUS OR NEXT SLIDE

1 Click one of the following buttons.

Display previous slide

Display next slide

E-MAIL A PRESENTATION

PowerPoint allows you to quickly e-mail your presentation to a friend, family member or colleague.

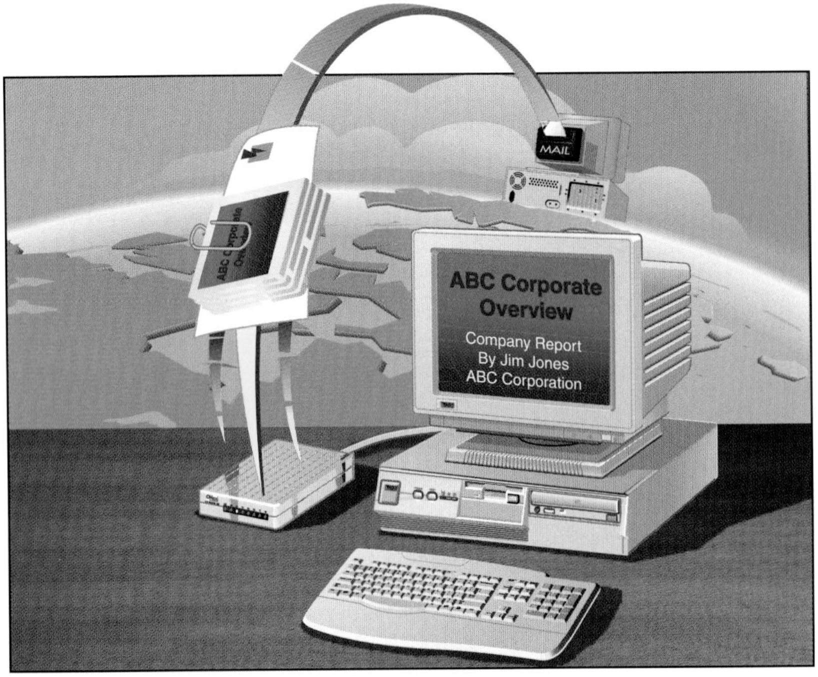

Before you can e-mail a presentation, Microsoft Office Outlook 2003 must be set up on your computer.

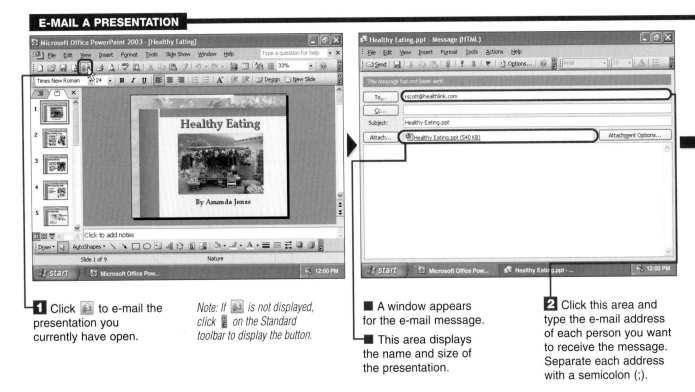

E-MAIL A PRESENTATION

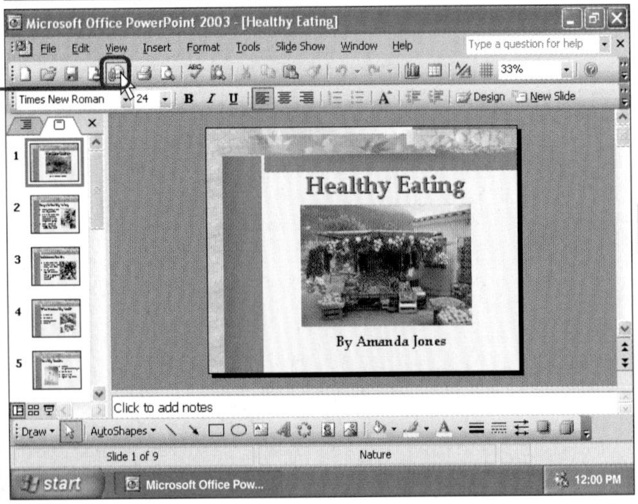

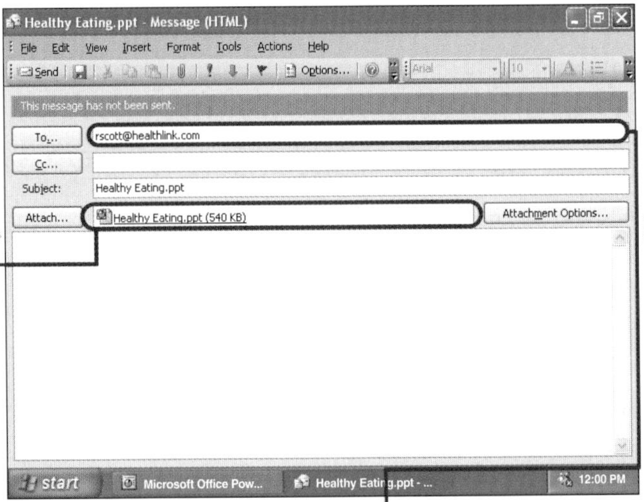

1 Click [icon] to e-mail the presentation you currently have open.

Note: If [icon] is not displayed, click [icon] on the Standard toolbar to display the button.

■ A window appears for the e-mail message.

■ This area displays the name and size of the presentation.

2 Click this area and type the e-mail address of each person you want to receive the message. Separate each address with a semicolon (;).

Tip

How can I address an e-mail message?

To

Sends the message to each person you specify.

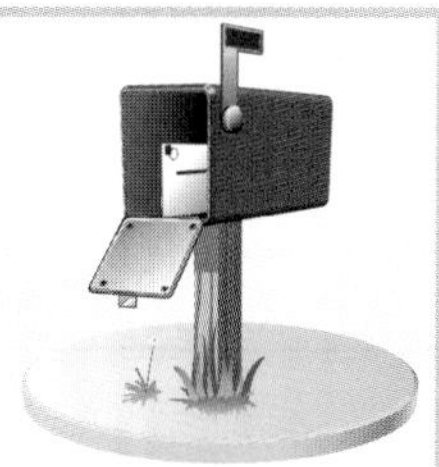

Carbon Copy (Cc)

Sends a copy of the message to people who are not directly involved, but would be interested in the message.

Tip

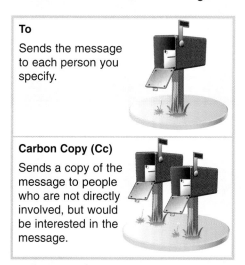

Why is the person I sent my presentation to unable to view my presentation properly?

When you e-mail a presentation, the presentation is sent as an attached file, which the recipient must open in PowerPoint on their own computer. If the recipient is using an earlier version of PowerPoint, some features of your presentation may not work properly on their computer.

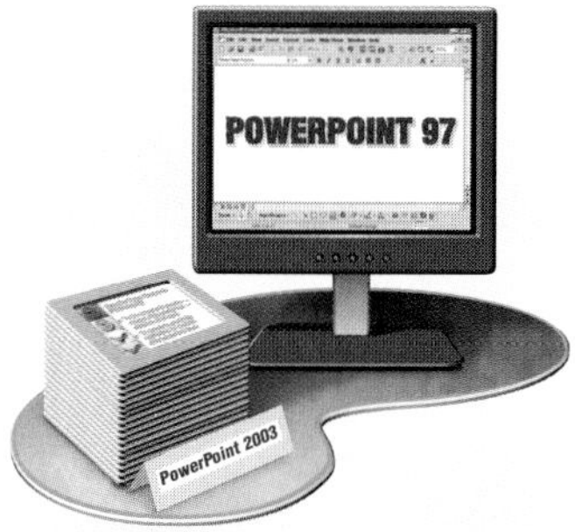

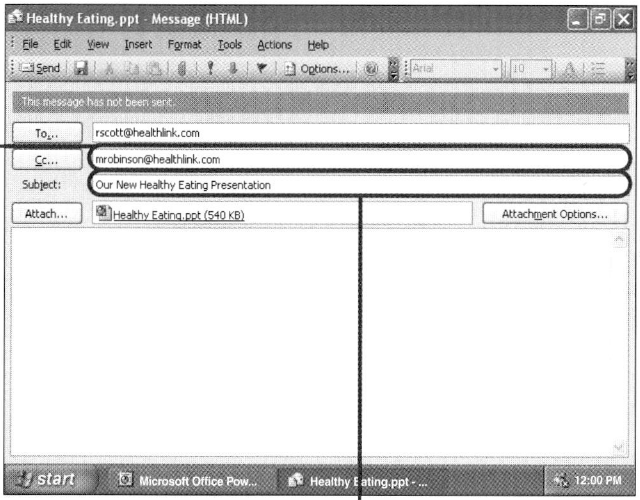

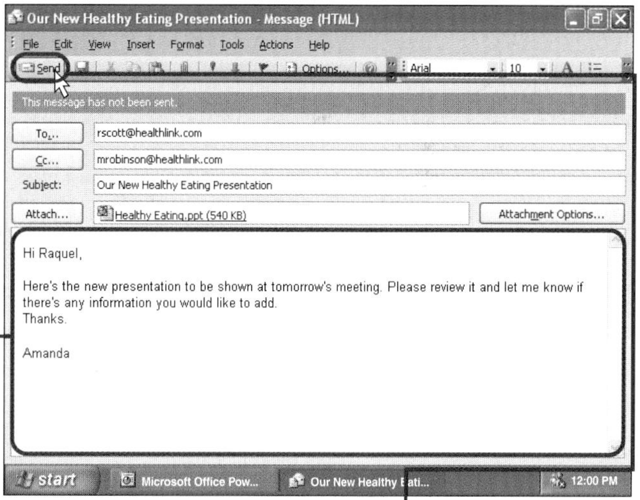

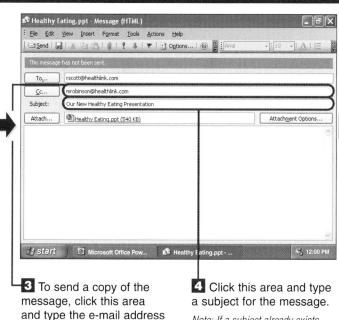

3 To send a copy of the message, click this area and type the e-mail address of each person you want to receive a copy. Separate each address with a semicolon (;).

4 Click this area and type a subject for the message.

Note: If a subject already exists, you can drag the mouse I over the existing subject and then type a new subject.

5 To include a message with the presentation you are e-mailing, click this area and type the message.

6 Click **Send** to send the message with the attached presentation.

SELECT TEXT

Before making changes to text in your presentation, you will often need to select the text you want to work with. Selected text appears highlighted on your screen.

SELECT TEXT

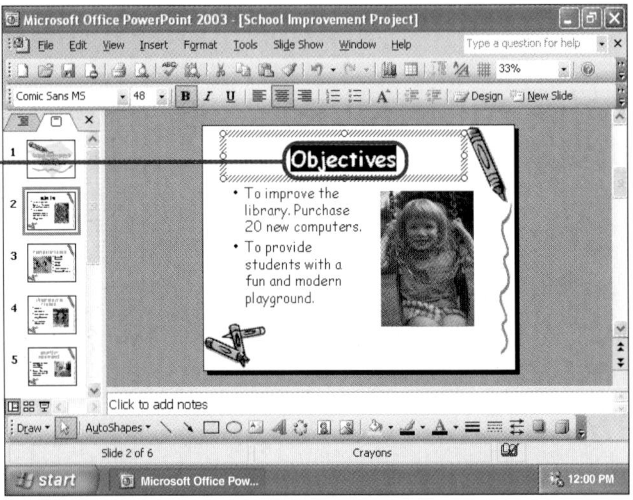

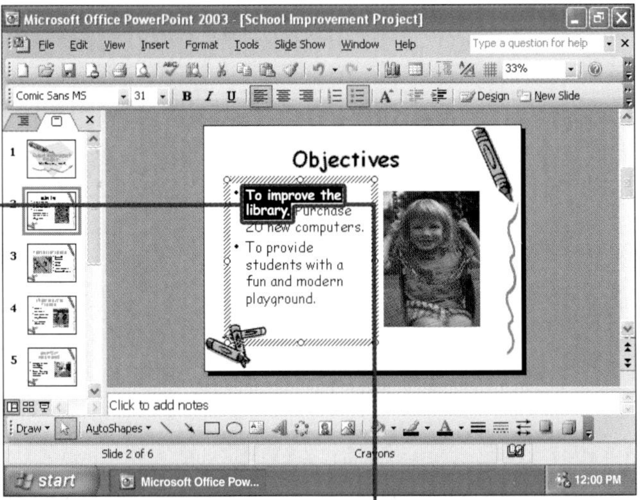

SELECT A WORD

1 Double-click the word you want to select.

■ To deselect text, click outside the selected area.

SELECT A SENTENCE

1 Click anywhere in the sentence you want to select.

2 Press and hold down the Ctrl key as you click the sentence again.

Tip

How can I quickly select all the text on a slide?

You can use the Outline tab to quickly select all the text on a slide. The Outline tab displays the text for all the slides in your presentation.

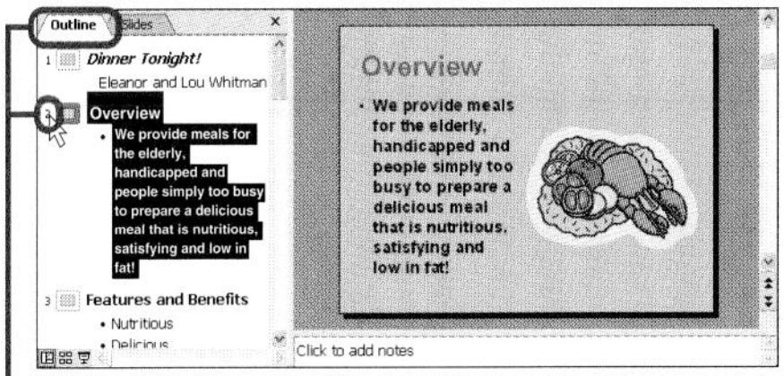

1 Click the **Outline** ( ) tab to display the text for all your slides.

2 Click the number of the slide that contains the text you want to select.

Tip

Can I quickly select all the text in my presentation?

Yes. You can use the Outline tab to quickly select all the text in your presentation.

1 Click the **Outline** ( ) tab to display the text for all your slides.

2 Click anywhere in the Outline tab.

3 Press and hold down the Ctrl key as you press the A key to select all the text.

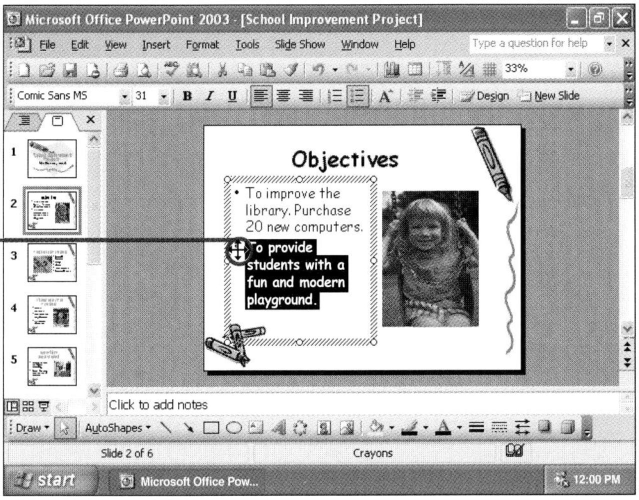

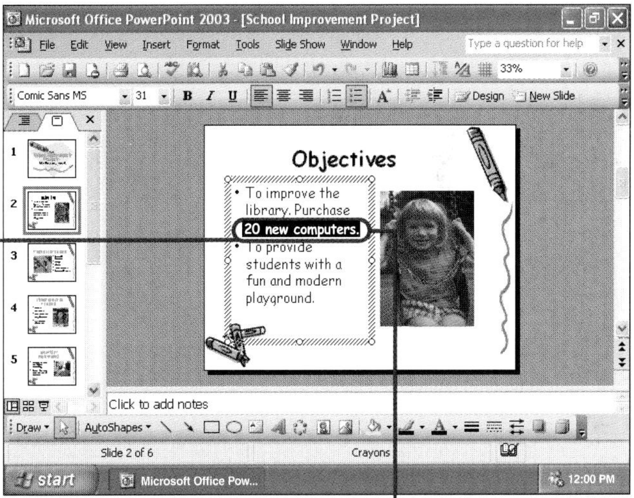

SELECT A POINT

1 Click the bullet (●) beside the point you want to select.

SELECT ANY AMOUNT OF TEXT

1 Position the mouse I over the first word you want to select.

2 Drag the mouse I over the text you want to select.

INSERT TEXT

PowerPoint allows you to type text onto a slide in your presentation quickly and easily.

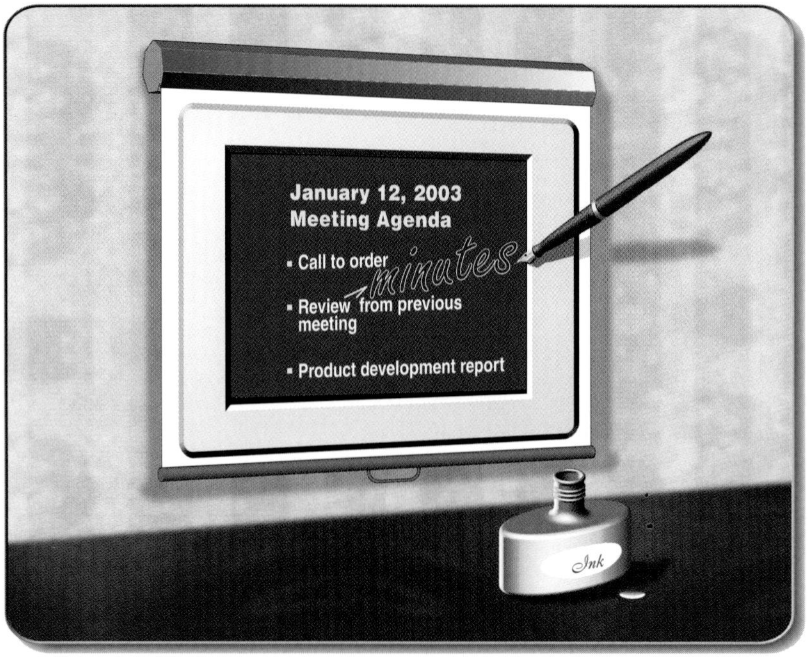

You can insert text in a text placeholder on a slide. If the slide you want to add text to does not have a text placeholder, you can change the layout of the slide. For information on changing the slide layout, see page 192.

INSERT CHARACTERS

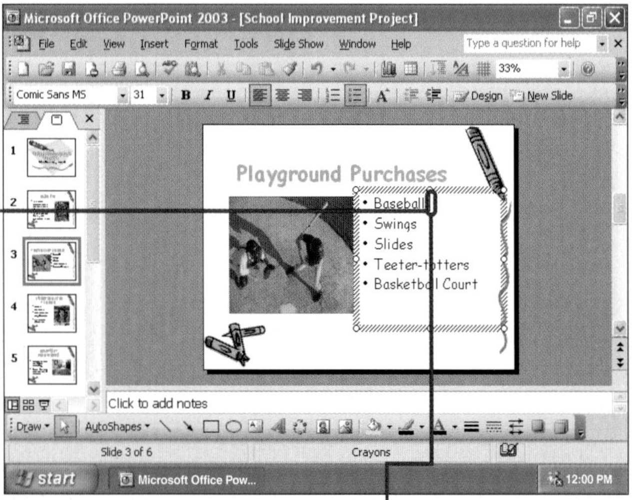

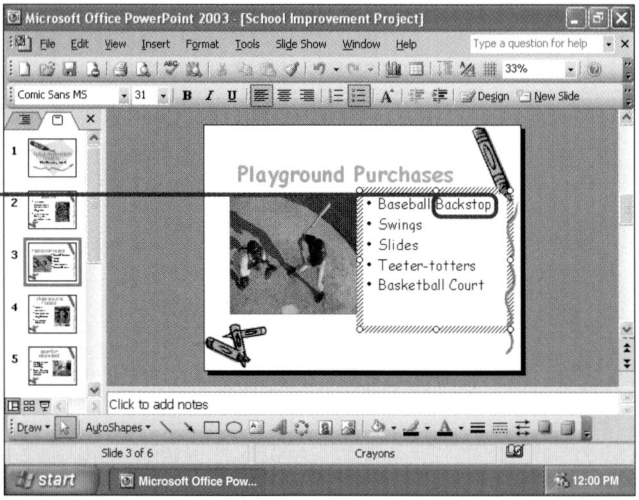

1 Click where you want to insert the new text.

■ The text you type will appear where the insertion point flashes on your screen.

Note: You can press the ←, ↓, ↑ or → key to move the insertion point.

2 Type the text you want to insert.

■ To insert a blank space, press the **Spacebar**.

Tip

Is there another way to insert text?

You can also insert text on the Outline tab in the Normal view. The Outline tab displays all the text for your presentation. Text you insert on the Outline tab will automatically appear on the slide in the Slide pane. For more information on the Outline tab, see page 174.

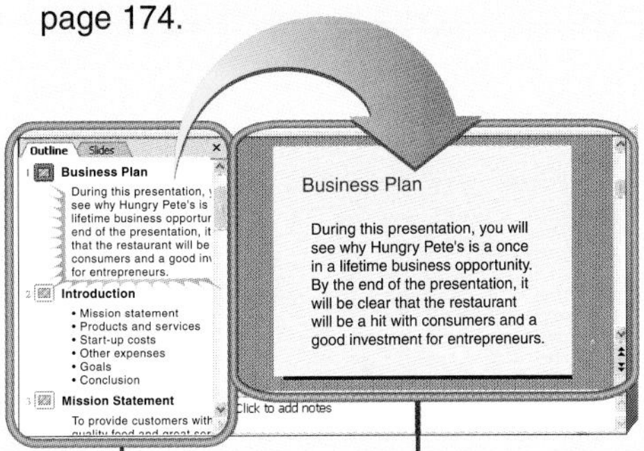

Outline tab **Slide pane**

Tip

Why does the AutoFit Options button (⊞) appear when I insert text in a placeholder on a slide?

If you insert more text than a placeholder can hold, PowerPoint automatically resizes the text to fit in the placeholder and the AutoFit Options button (⊞) appears. The AutoFit Options button allows you to change how the text fits in the placeholder. For example, you can specify you do not want PowerPoint to automatically resize the text.

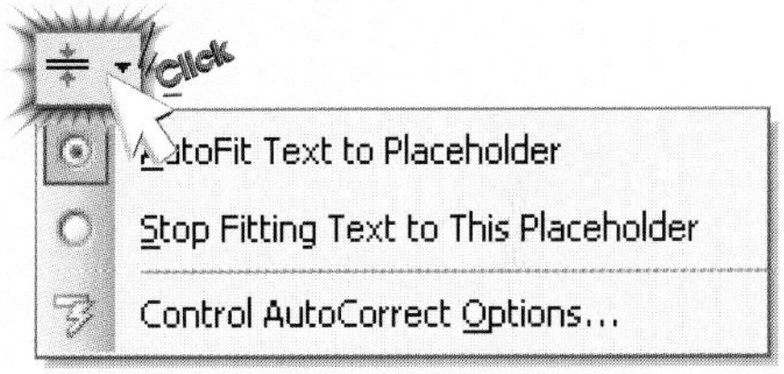

INSERT A NEW POINT

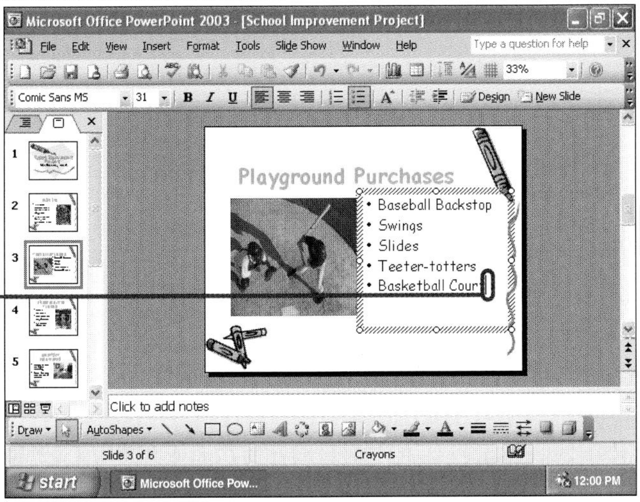

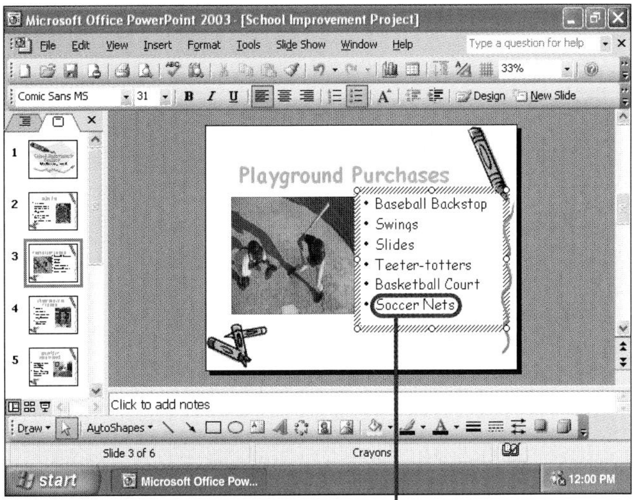

1 Click at the end of the point directly above where you want to insert a new point.

2 Press the Enter key to insert a blank line for the new point.

3 Type the text for the new point.

DELETE TEXT

You can delete text from a slide to remove information you no longer need in your presentation.

DELETE TEXT

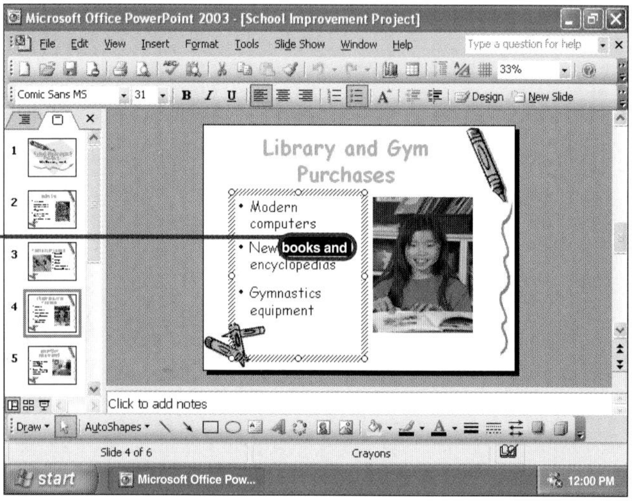

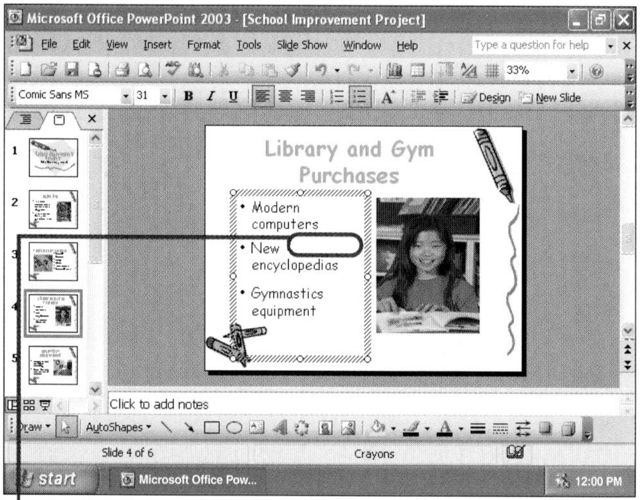

1 Select the text you want to delete. To select text, see page 180.

2 Press the **Delete** key to remove the text from your presentation.

■ The text disappears.

■ To delete a single character, click to the right of the character you want to delete and then press the **←Backspace** key. PowerPoint will delete the character to the left of the flashing insertion point.

Note: You can also perform these steps to delete text on the Outline tab in the Normal view. The Outline tab displays the text for all the slides in your presentation. For more information on the Outline tab, see page 174.

UNDO CHANGES

PowerPoint remembers the last changes you made to your presentation. If you regret these changes, you can cancel them by using the Undo feature.

When canceling changes, you must start with the change you made most recently and work backwards through your changes.

UNDO CHANGES

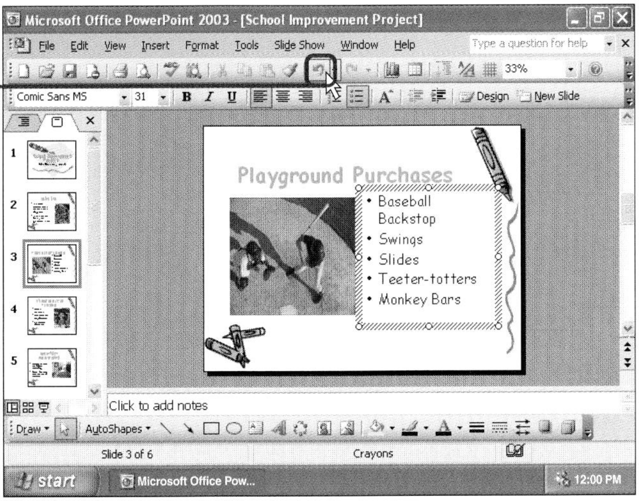

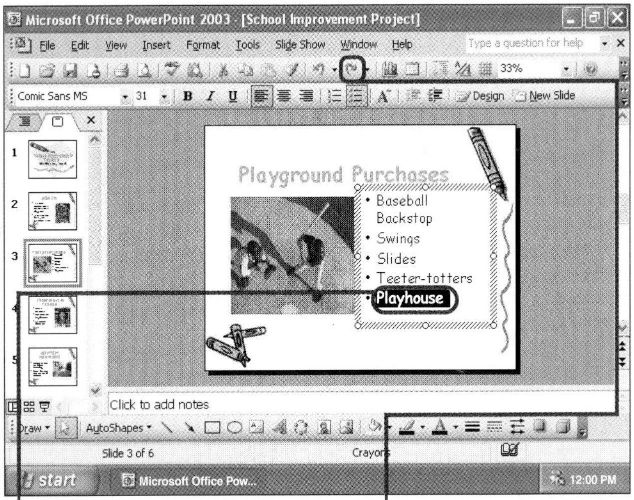

1 Click to undo the last change you made to your presentation.

Note: If the Undo button is not displayed, click on the Standard toolbar to display the button.

■ PowerPoint cancels the last change you made to your presentation.

■ You can repeat step **1** to cancel previous changes you made.

■ To reverse the results of using the Undo feature, click the Redo button.

Note: If the Redo button is not displayed, click on the Standard toolbar to display the button.

MOVE OR COPY TEXT

You can move or copy text to a new location in your presentation. You can move or copy text directly on your slides or in the outline of your presentation.

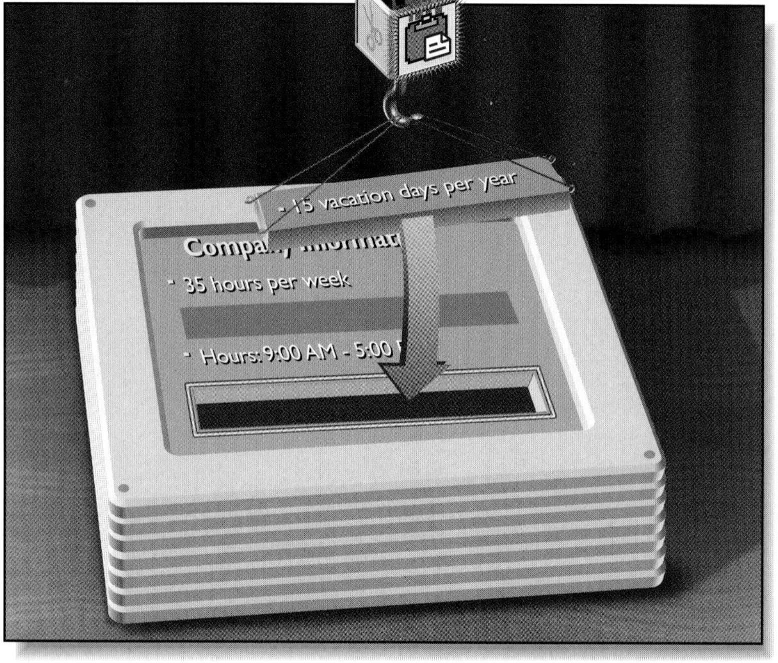

Moving text is useful when you want to reorganize the ideas in your presentation. When you move text, the text disappears from its original location.

Copying text allows you to repeat information in your presentation without having to retype the text. When you copy text, the text appears in both the original and new locations.

MOVE OR COPY TEXT

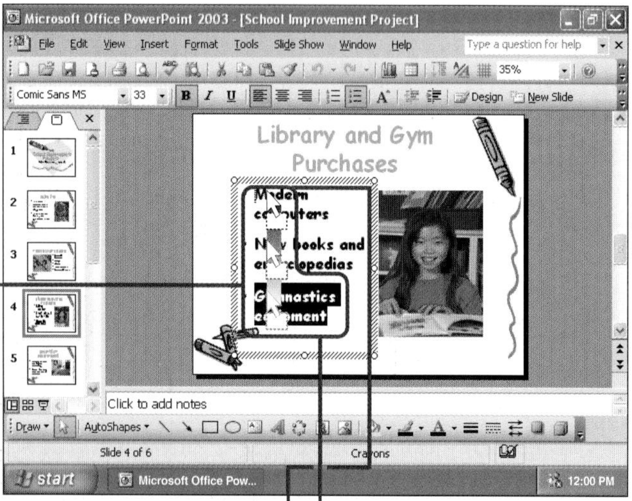

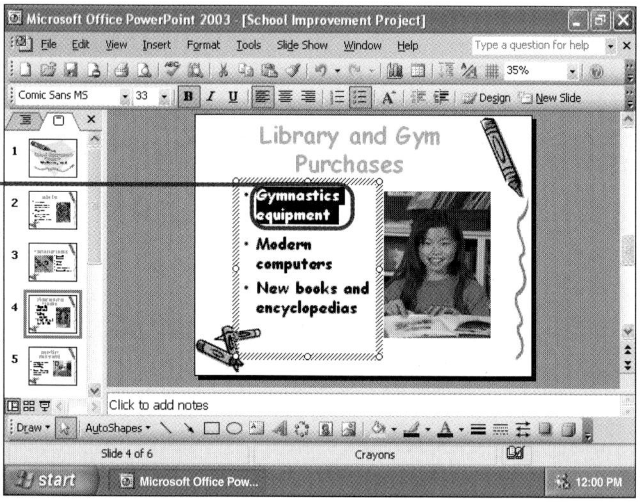

USING DRAG AND DROP

1 Select the text you want to move. To select text, see page 180.

2 Position the mouse I over the selected text (I changes to ↖).

3 To move the text, drag the mouse ↖ to where you want to place the text.

Note: The text will appear where you position the dotted insertion point on your screen.

■ The text moves to the new location.

■ To copy text, perform steps **1** to **3**, except press and hold down the **Ctrl** key as you perform step **3**.

Tip

How can I use the Clipboard task pane to move or copy text?

The Clipboard task pane displays up to the last 24 items you have selected to move or copy. To place a clipboard item in your presentation, click the location where you want the item to appear and then click the item in the task pane. For more information on task panes, see page 8.

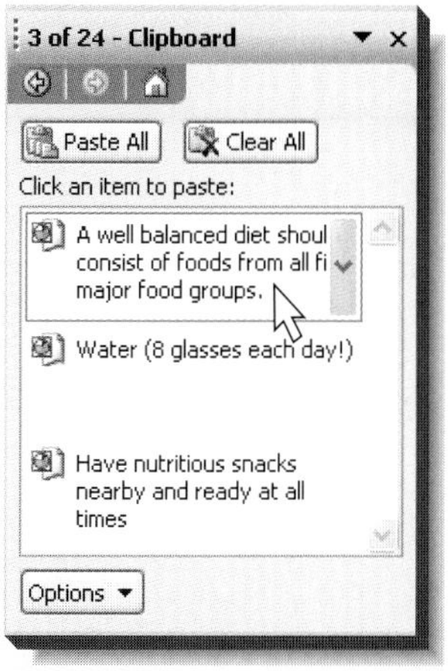

Tip

Why does the Paste Options button ( ) appear when I move or copy text?

You can use the Paste Options button ( ) to change the format of the text you have moved or copied. For example, you can choose to keep the original formatting of the text by selecting **Keep Source Formatting** or change the formatting of the text to match the text in the new location by selecting **Keep Text Only**. Click the Paste Options button to display a list of options and then select the option you want to use. The Paste Options button is available only until you perform another task.

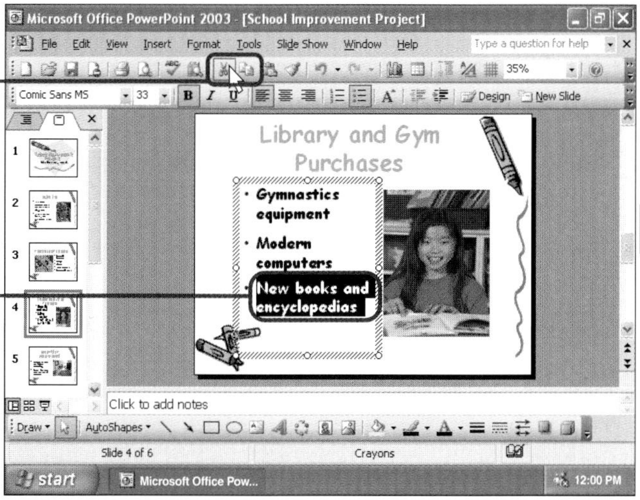

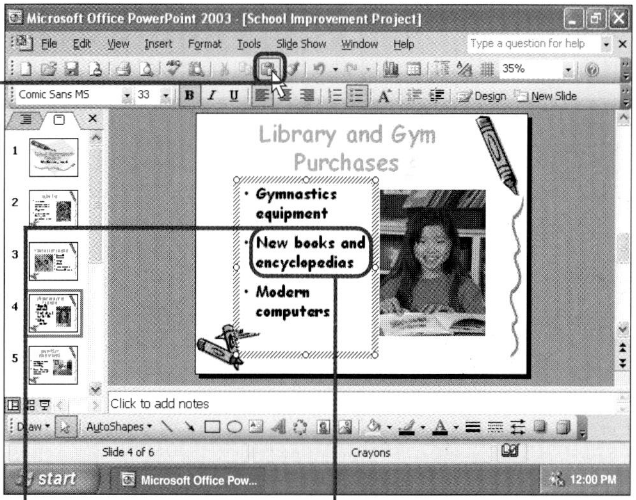

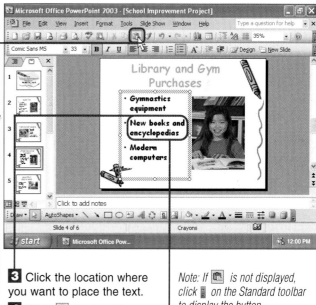

USING THE TOOLBAR BUTTONS

1 Select the text you want to move or copy. To select text, see page 180.

2 Click one of the following buttons.

- Move text
- Copy text

Note: If the button you want is not displayed, click on the Standard toolbar to display the button.

■ The Clipboard task pane may appear. To use the Clipboard task pane, see the top of this page.

3 Click the location where you want to place the text.

4 Click to place the text in the new location.

Note: If is not displayed, click on the Standard toolbar to display the button.

■ The text appears in the new location.

CHECK SPELLING

You can find and correct all the spelling errors in your presentation.

PowerPoint does not check the spelling of text in some objects, such as charts and WordArt.

PowerPoint automatically underlines misspelled words in red. The underlines will not appear when you print your presentation or view the slide show.

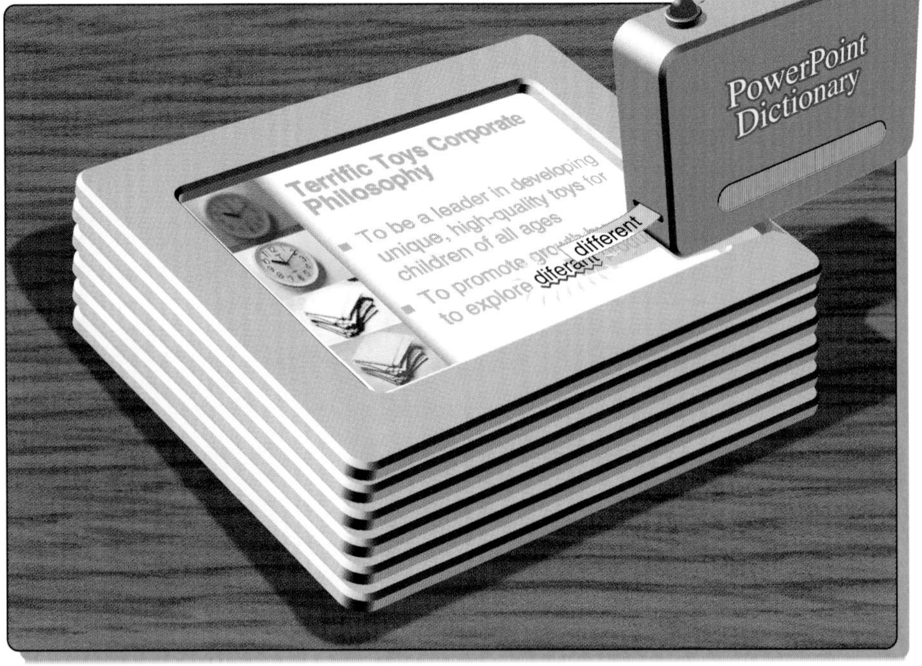

CHECK SPELLING

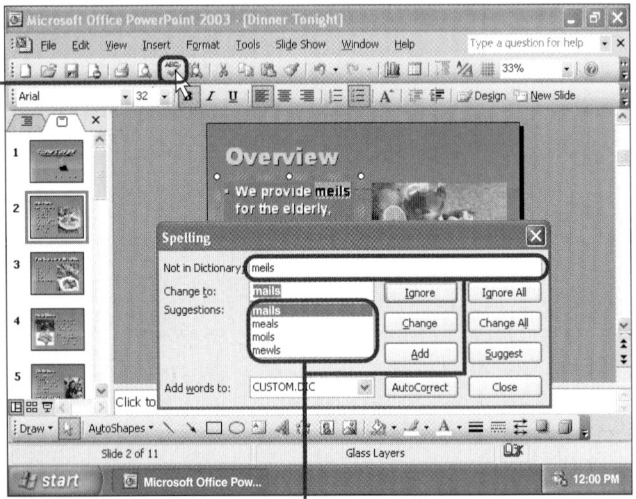

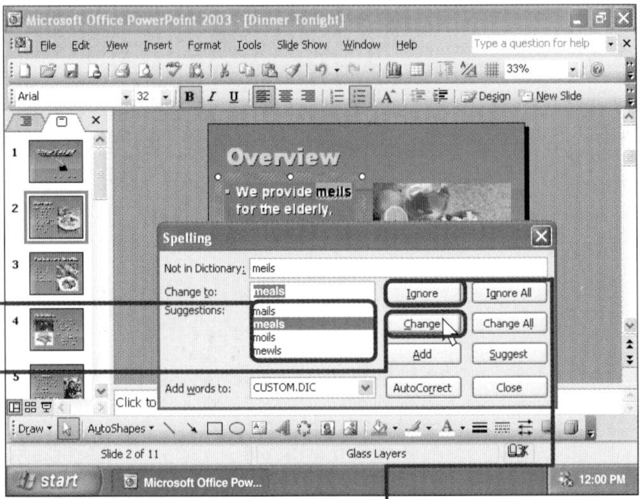

1 Click to start the spell check.

Note: If is not displayed, click on the Standard toolbar to display the button.

■ The Spelling dialog box appears if PowerPoint finds a misspelled word in your presentation.

■ This area displays the first misspelled word.

■ This area displays suggestions for correcting the word.

2 Click the word you want to use to correct the misspelled word.

3 Click **Change** to replace the misspelled word with the word you selected.

■ To skip the word and continue checking your presentation, click **Ignore**.

*Note: To skip the word and all other occurrences of the word, click **Ignore All**.*

Tip

Can PowerPoint automatically correct my typing mistakes?

PowerPoint automatically corrects common spelling errors, typos and capitalization errors as you type. Here are a few examples.

acheive → achieve
claer → clear
developement → development
foriegn → foreign
hte → the
occassion → occasion
recomend → recommend
statment → statement
wtih → with
monday → Monday
SPelling → Spelling

Tip

How does PowerPoint find spelling errors in my presentation?

PowerPoint compares every word in your presentation to words in its dictionary. If a word in your presentation does not exist in the dictionary, the word is considered misspelled. PowerPoint will not find a correctly spelled word used in the wrong context, such as, "We have been in business for **sit** years." You should review your presentation carefully to find this type of error.

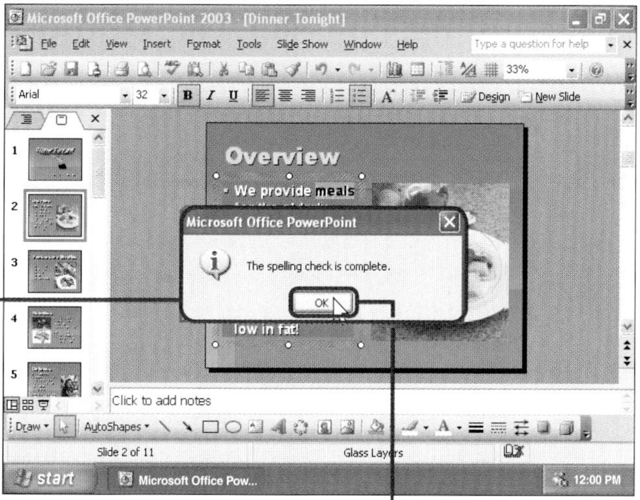

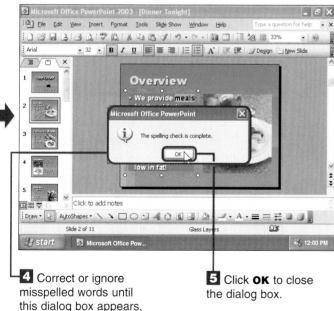

4 Correct or ignore misspelled words until this dialog box appears, telling you the spell check is complete.

5 Click **OK** to close the dialog box.

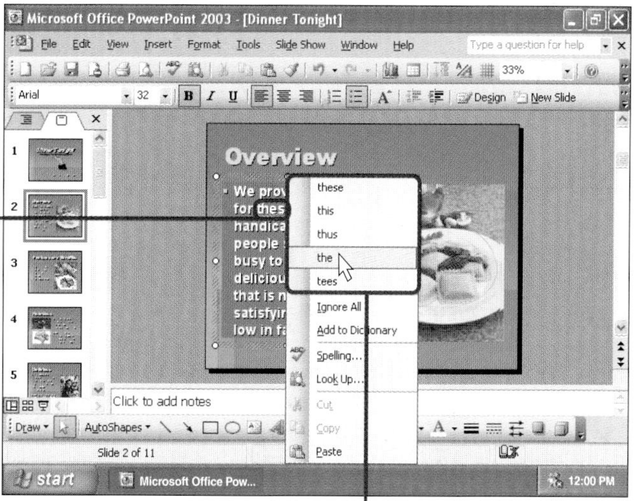

CORRECT ONE MISPELLED WORD

1 Right-click the misspelled word you want to correct.

■ A menu appears with suggestions to correct the word.

2 To replace the misspelled word with one of the suggestions, click the suggestion.

Note: If you do not want to use any of the suggestions to correct the word, click outside the menu to close the menu.

ADD A NEW SLIDE

You can insert a new slide into your presentation to add a new topic you want to discuss.

PowerPoint allows you to choose which layout you want to use for the new slide.

ADD A NEW SLIDE

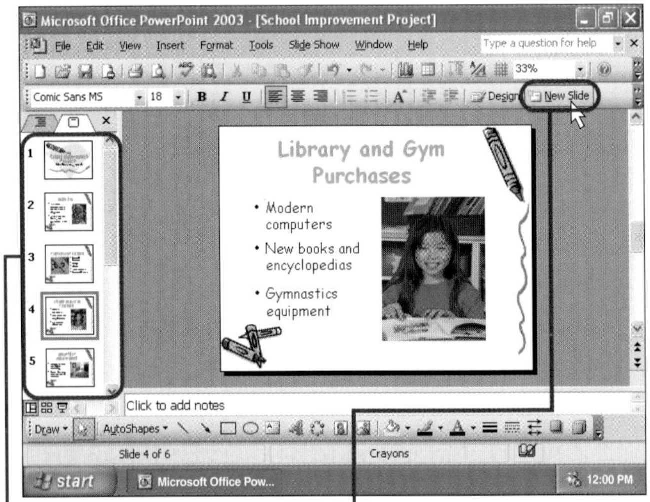

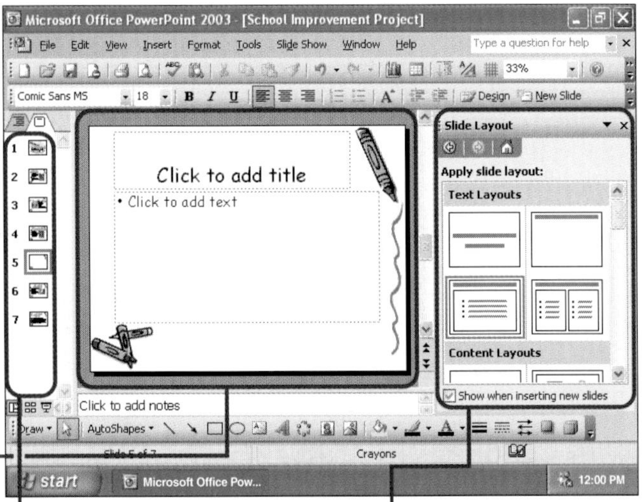

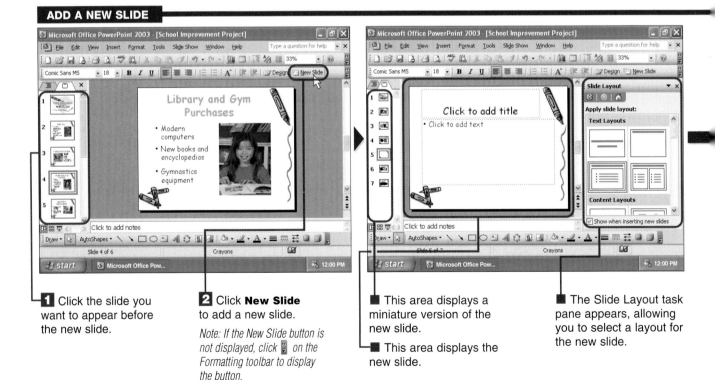

1 Click the slide you want to appear before the new slide.

2 Click **New Slide** to add a new slide.

Note: If the New Slide button is not displayed, click ▾ on the Formatting toolbar to display the button.

■ This area displays a miniature version of the new slide.

■ This area displays the new slide.

■ The Slide Layout task pane appears, allowing you to select a layout for the new slide.

Tip

How much text should I display on a slide?

You should be careful not to include too much text on a slide in your presentation. If you add too much text to a slide, the slide may be difficult to read and you will minimize the impact of important ideas. If a slide contains too much text, you should add a new slide to accommodate some of the text.

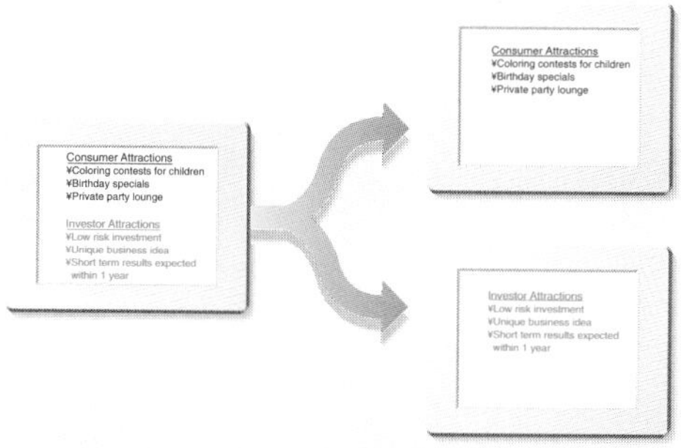

Tip

What types of layouts can I use for a new slide?

Each slide layout displays a different arrangement of placeholders, which determine the position of text and objects on a slide. The icons in the placeholders indicate the type of information you can add to the placeholder.

	A list of points
	An object such as a table, chart, clip art image or diagram
	A clip art image
	A chart

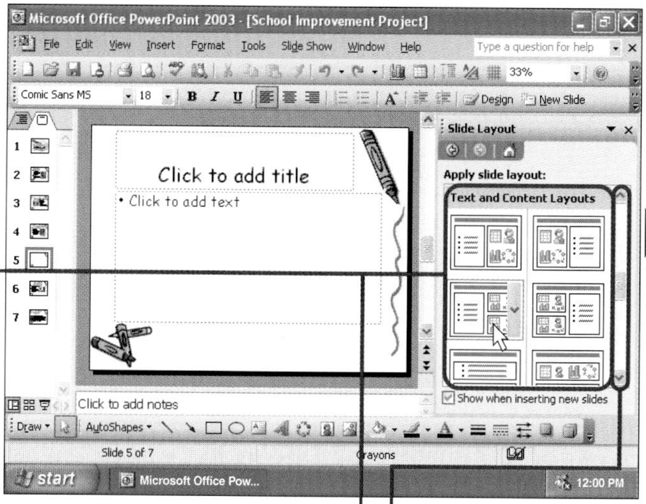

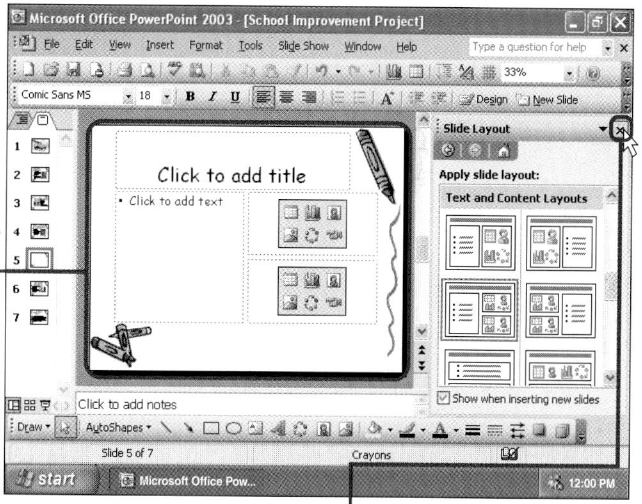

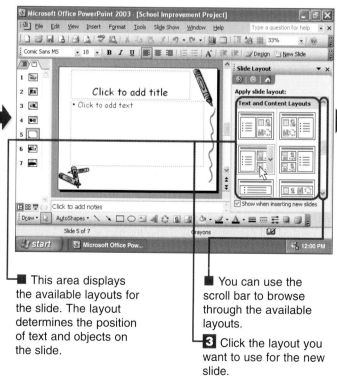

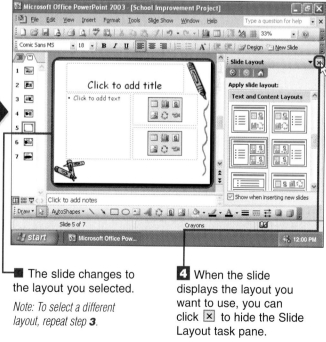

■ This area displays the available layouts for the slide. The layout determines the position of text and objects on the slide.

■ You can use the scroll bar to browse through the available layouts.

3 Click the layout you want to use for the new slide.

■ The slide changes to the layout you selected.

*Note: To select a different layout, repeat step **3**.*

4 When the slide displays the layout you want to use, you can click ☒ to hide the Slide Layout task pane.

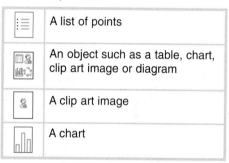

CHANGE THE SLIDE LAYOUT

You can change the layout of a slide in your presentation to accommodate text and objects you want to add.

Each slide layout displays a different arrangement of placeholders. Placeholders allow you to easily add objects you want to appear on a slide, such as a clip art image or a chart.

CHANGE THE SLIDE LAYOUT

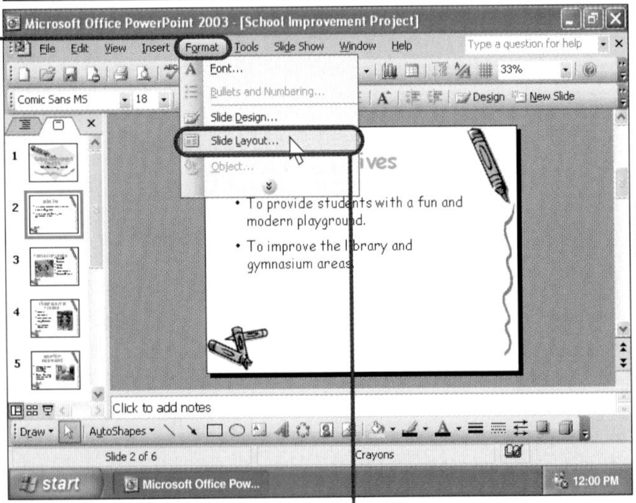

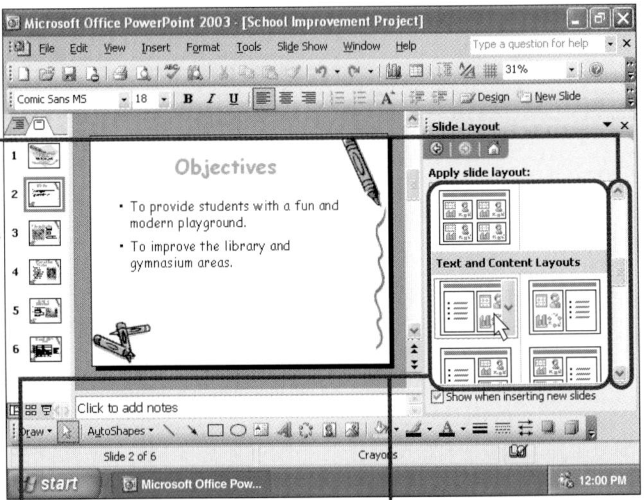

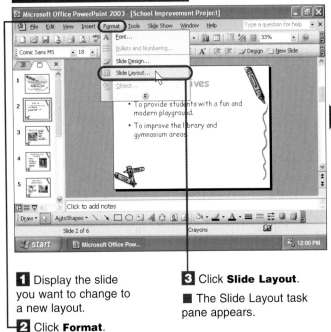

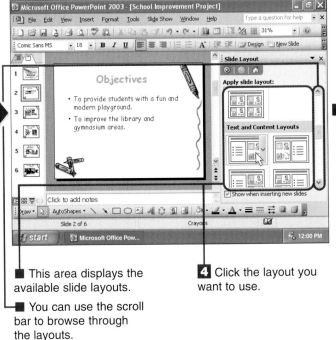

1 Display the slide you want to change to a new layout.

2 Click **Format**.

3 Click **Slide Layout**.

■ The Slide Layout task pane appears.

■ This area displays the available slide layouts.

■ You can use the scroll bar to browse through the layouts.

4 Click the layout you want to use.

Tip

How can I determine the types of placeholders a slide layout contains?

The icons displayed on each slide layout indicate the types of placeholders in the layout.

	Title
	List of points
	Object such as a table, chart, clip art image or diagram
	Clip art image
	Chart
	Media clip
	Table
	Diagram or organization chart

Tip

What should I consider when changing the slide layout?

If you have already added text or an object to a slide, you should choose a slide layout that includes a placeholder for the type of information you added. This helps to ensure that the slide will not become cluttered with overlapping objects and placeholders.

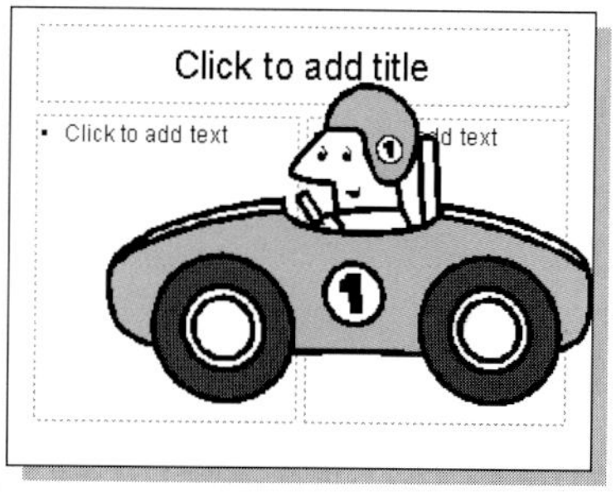

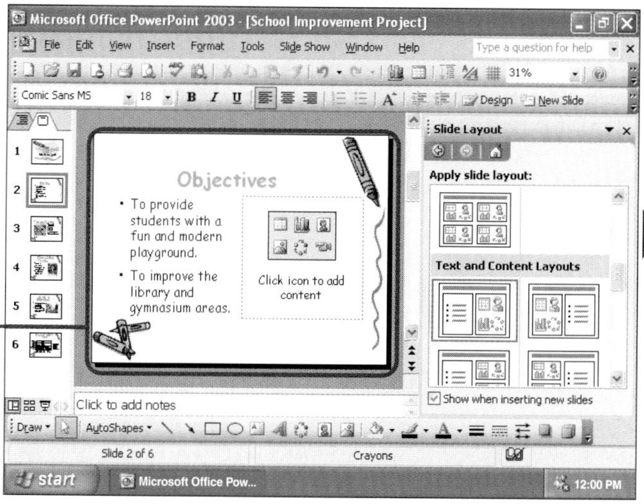

■ The slide changes to the layout you selected.

Note: To select a different layout, repeat step 4.

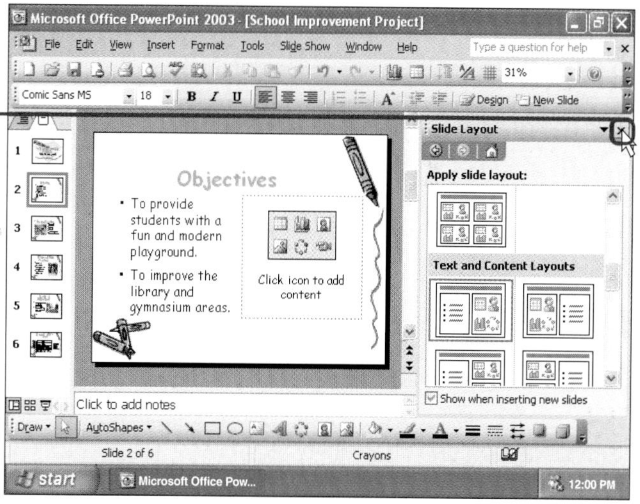

5 When you finish selecting a slide layout, you can click ☒ to hide the Slide Layout task pane.

ADD AN AUTOSHAPE

PowerPoint provides ready-made shapes, called AutoShapes, that you can add to your slides.

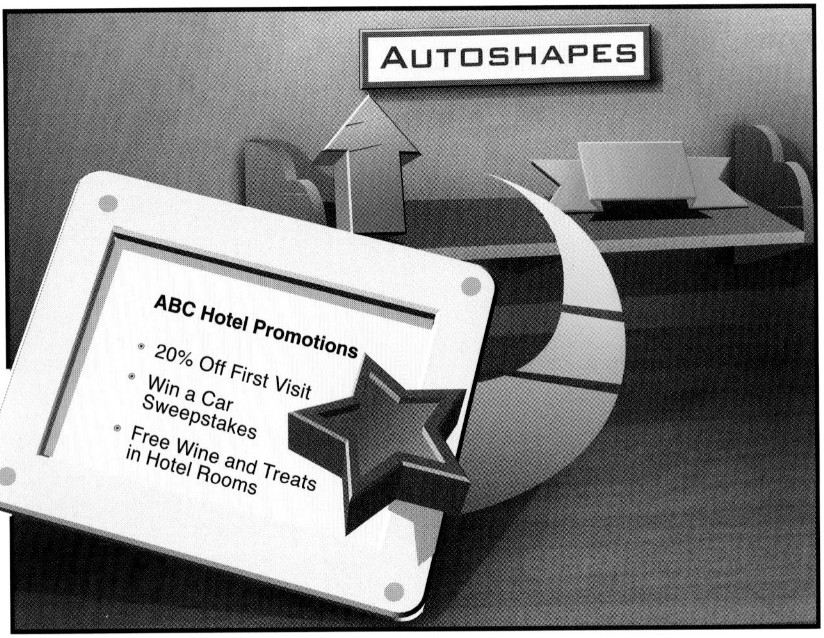

PowerPoint offers several types of AutoShapes, such as arrows, stars and banners.

ADD AN AUTOSHAPE

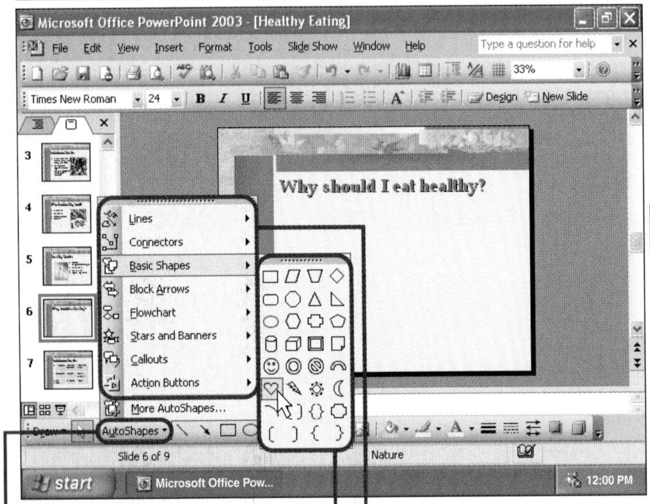

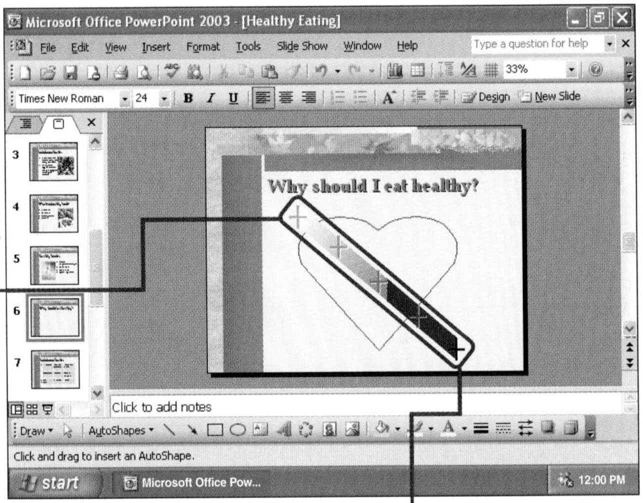

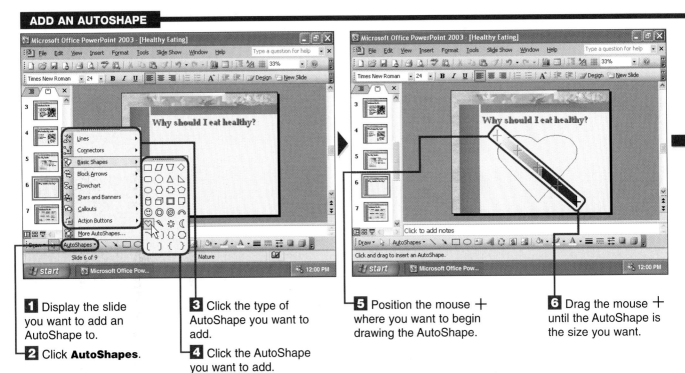

1 Display the slide you want to add an AutoShape to.

2 Click **AutoShapes**.

3 Click the type of AutoShape you want to add.

4 Click the AutoShape you want to add.

5 Position the mouse + where you want to begin drawing the AutoShape.

6 Drag the mouse + until the AutoShape is the size you want.

Tip

Can I add text to an AutoShape?

You can add text to most AutoShapes. This is particularly useful when creating banner and callout AutoShapes. To add text to an AutoShape, click the AutoShape and then type the text you want the AutoShape to display. To change the size of the text, see page 209.

Tip

Why do green and yellow dots appear on some AutoShapes?

You can use the green and yellow dots to change the appearance of an AutoShape.

To rotate an AutoShape, position the mouse over the green dot (●) and then drag the mouse to a new position.

To change the design of an AutoShape, position the mouse over the yellow dot (◇) and then drag the mouse ▷ until the shape displays the design you want.

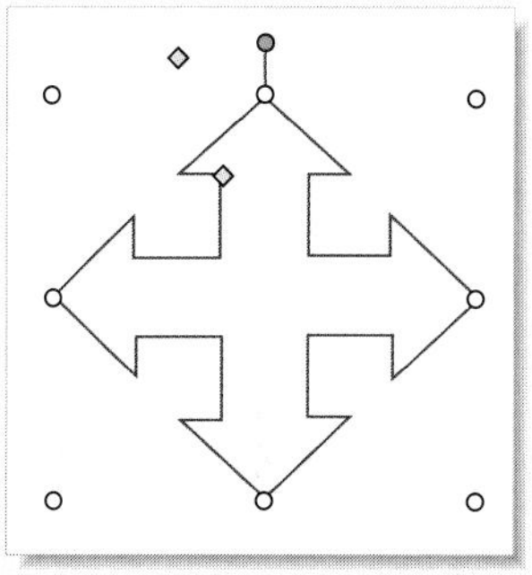

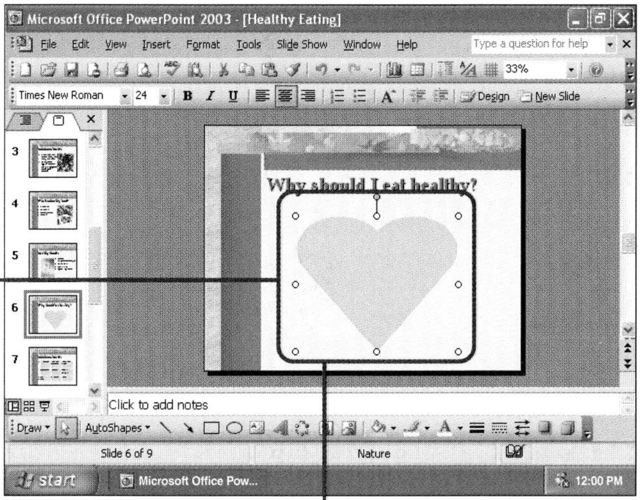

■ The AutoShape appears on the slide.

Note: To change the color of an AutoShape, see page 213.

■ The handles (○) around the AutoShape allow you to change the size of the AutoShape. To move or resize an AutoShape, see page 206.

■ To deselect an AutoShape, click outside the AutoShape.

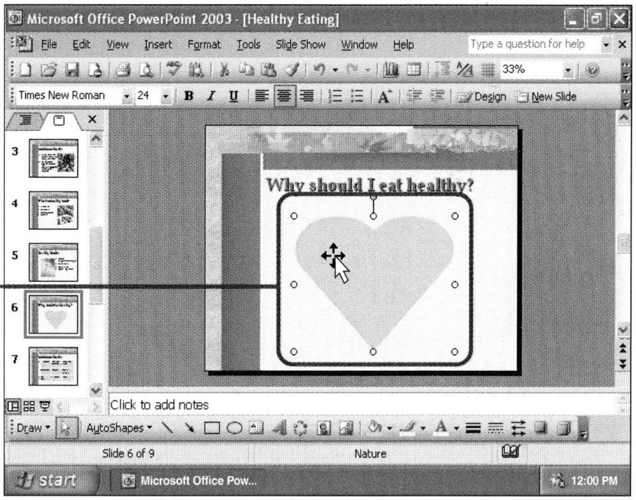

DELETE AN AUTOSHAPE

1 Click the AutoShape you want to delete.

2 Press the Delete key to remove the AutoShape from the slide.

ADD WORDART

You can add WordArt to a slide in your presentation to display a decorative title or draw attention to important information.

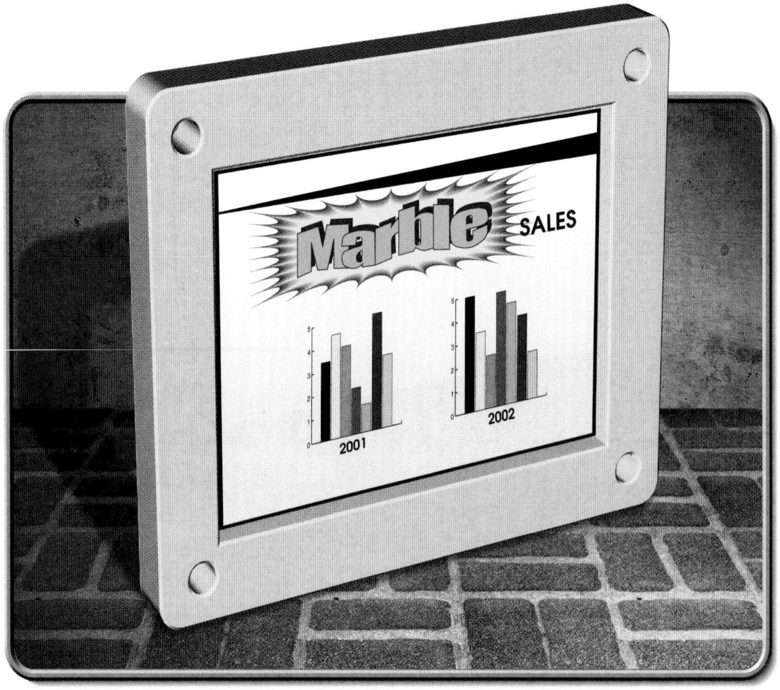

WordArt allows you to create eye-catching text that is skewed, curved, rotated, stretched, three-dimensional or even vertical.

ADD WORDART

1 Display the slide you want to add WordArt to.

2 Click [icon] to add WordArt.

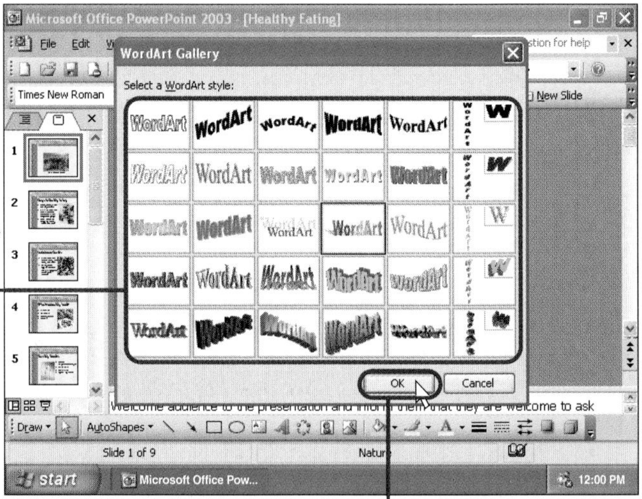

■ The WordArt Gallery dialog box appears.

3 Click the WordArt style you want to use.

4 Click **OK** to confirm your selection.

Tip

How do I edit WordArt?

To edit WordArt text, double-click the WordArt to display the Edit WordArt Text dialog box. Then perform steps **5** and **6** below to specify the new text you want the WordArt to display.

Tip

When I add WordArt to a slide, why does the WordArt toolbar appear?

The WordArt toolbar contains buttons that allow you to change the appearance of WordArt. For example, you can click [Aa] to display all the letters in WordArt at the same height.

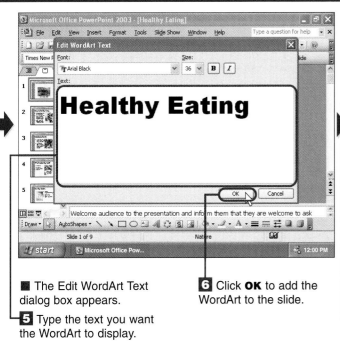

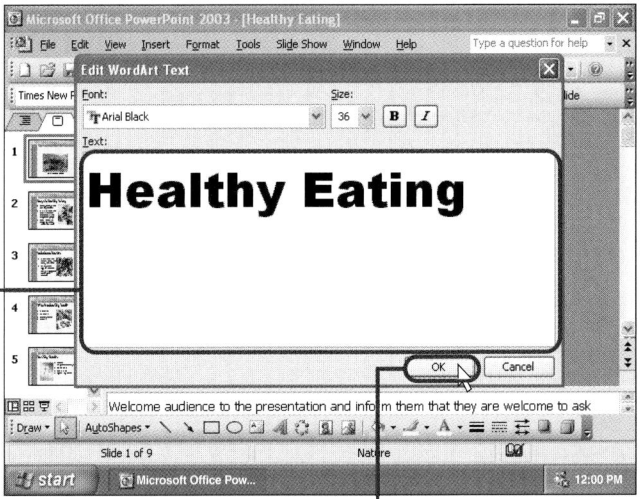

■ The Edit WordArt Text dialog box appears.

5 Type the text you want the WordArt to display.

6 Click **OK** to add the WordArt to the slide.

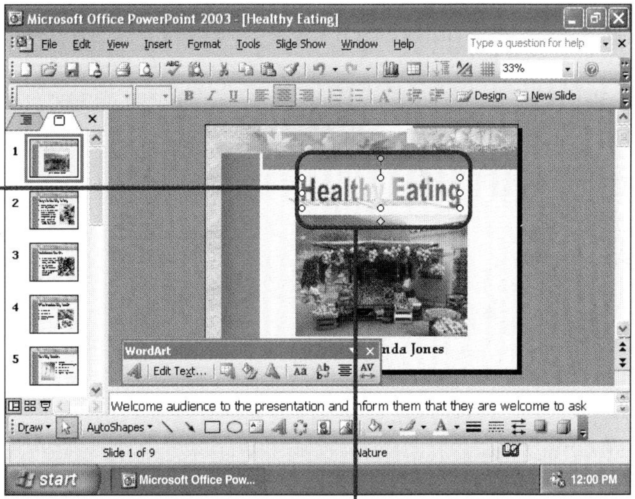

■ The WordArt appears on the slide.

■ The handles (○) around the WordArt allow you to change the size of the WordArt. To move or resize WordArt, see page 206.

■ To deselect WordArt, click outside the WordArt.

DELETE WORDART

1 Click the WordArt you want to delete and then press the Delete key.

ADD A PICTURE

You can add a picture stored on your computer to a slide in your presentation.

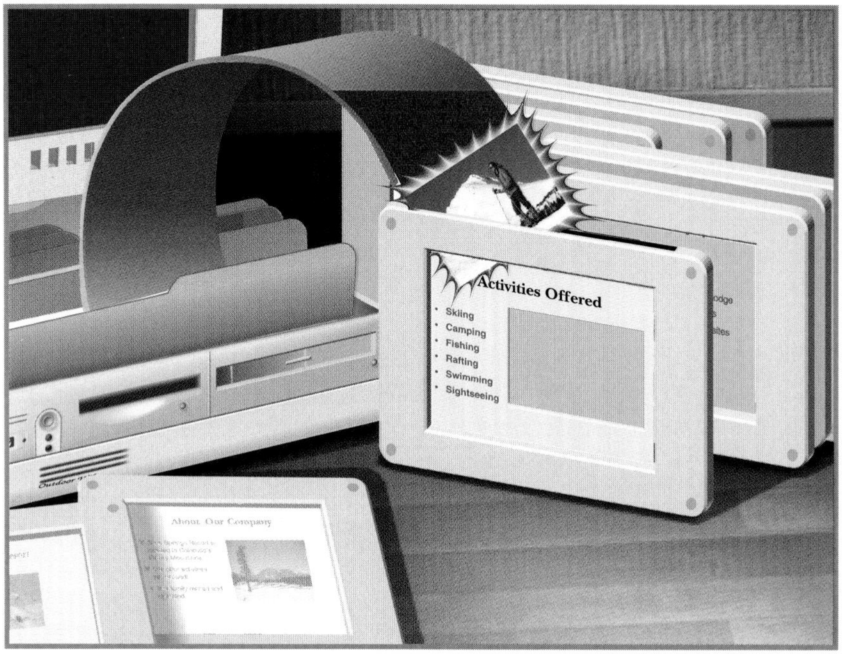

Adding a picture is useful when you want to display your company logo or a picture of your products on a slide.

ADD A PICTURE

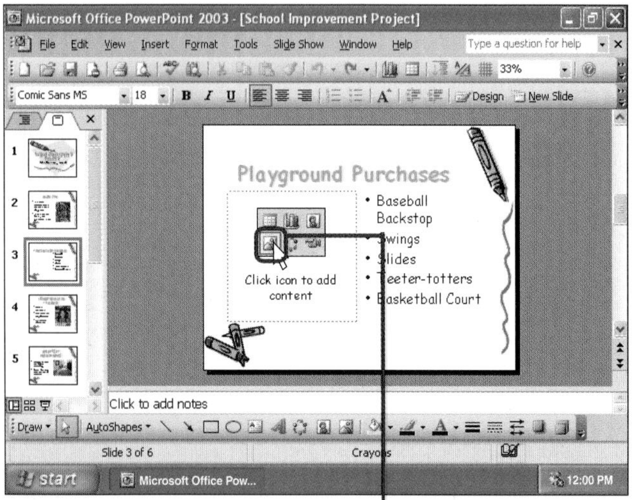

1 Display the slide you want to add a picture to.

2 Change the layout of the slide to one that includes a placeholder for a picture. To change the slide layout, see page 192.

3 Click the picture icon ( ) to add a picture to the slide.

■ The Insert Picture dialog box appears.

■ This area shows the location of the displayed pictures. You can click this area to change the location.

■ This area allows you to access pictures in commonly used locations. You can click a location to display the pictures stored in the location.

Tip

Where can I obtain pictures?

There are many places, such as Web sites and computer stores, that offer images you can use on your slides. You can also use a scanner to scan pictures into your computer or create your own pictures using an image editing program, such as Jasc Paint Shop Pro.

Tip

Why did the Picture toolbar appear when I added a picture to a slide?

The Picture toolbar contains buttons that allow you to change the appearance of a picture. For example, you can click or to increase or decrease the brightness of a picture. If the Picture toolbar does not appear, see page 10 to display the toolbar.

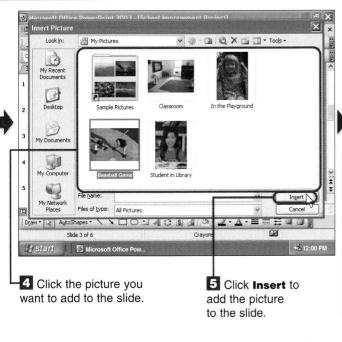

4 Click the picture you want to add to the slide.

5 Click **Insert** to add the picture to the slide.

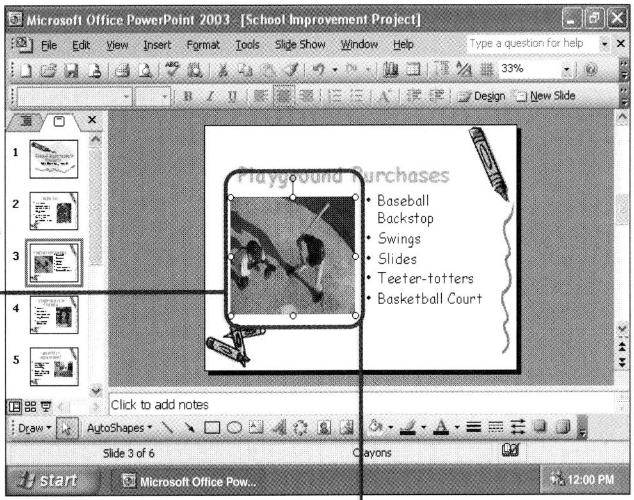

■ The picture appears on the slide.

■ The handles (○) around the picture allow you to change the size of the picture. To move or resize a picture, see page 206.

■ To deselect the picture, click outside the picture.

DELETE A PICTURE

1 Click the picture you want to delete and then press the Delete key.

ADD A CLIP ART IMAGE

You can add a professionally designed clip art image to a slide. Clip art images can help illustrate concepts and make your presentation more interesting and entertaining.

ADD A CLIP ART IMAGE

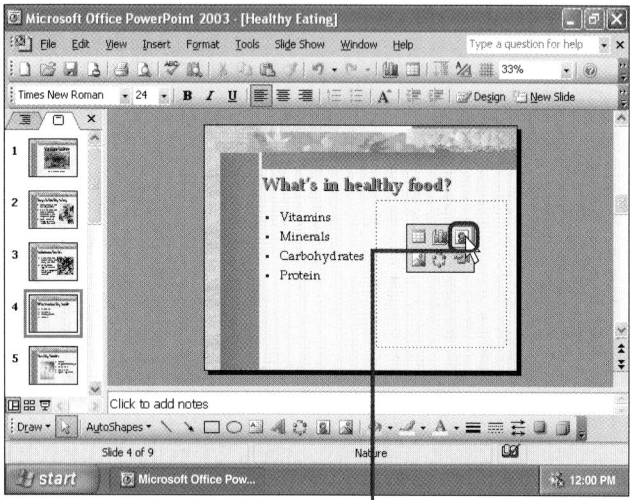

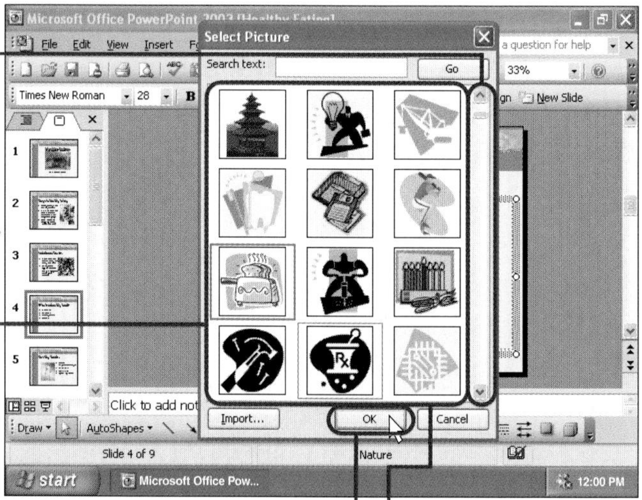

1 Display the slide you want to add a clip art image to.

2 Change the layout of the slide to one that includes a placeholder for a clip art image. To change the layout of a slide, see page 192.

3 Click the clip art icon ( ) to add a clip art image.

Note: Depending on the layout you chose in step **2**, *you may need to double-click the placeholder to add a clip art image.*

■ The Select Picture dialog box appears.

■ This area displays the clip art images you can add to your slide.

■ You can use the scroll bar to browse through the clip art images.

4 Click the clip art image you want to add to your slide.

5 Click **OK** to add the clip art image to your slide.

Tip

Can I search for clip art images?

You can search for clip art images by specifying one or more words of interest in the Select Picture dialog box.

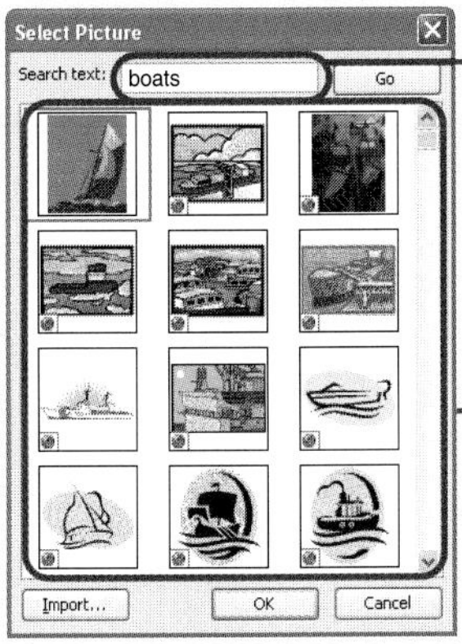

1 In the Select Picture dialog box, click this area and type a word that describes the clip art image you want to search for. Then press the Enter key.

■ The dialog box will display the clip art images that match the words you specify.

Tip

Where can I obtain more clip art images?

You can buy collections of clip art images at computer stores. Many Web sites, such as www.clipartconnection.com and www.noeticart.com, also offer clip art images you can use on your slides.

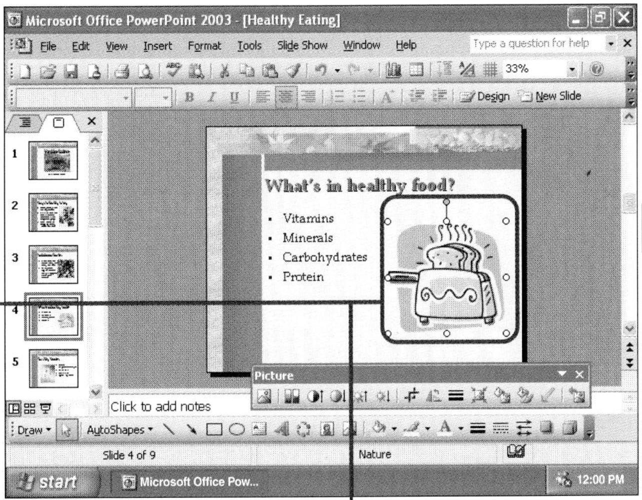

■ The clip art image appears on the slide.

■ The handles (○) around the clip art image allow you to change the size of the image. To move or resize a clip art image, see page 206.

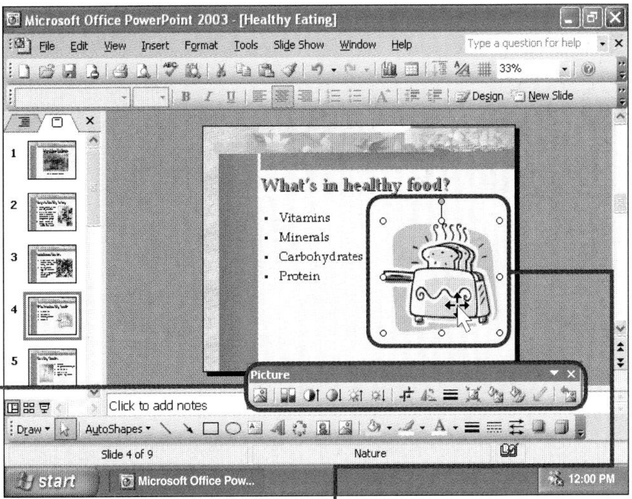

■ The Picture toolbar may also appear, displaying buttons that allow you to change the clip art image.

Note: If the Picture toolbar does not appear, see page 10 to display the toolbar.

■ To deselect a clip art image, click outside the image.

DELETE A CLIP ART IMAGE

1 Click the clip art image you want to delete and then press the Delete key.

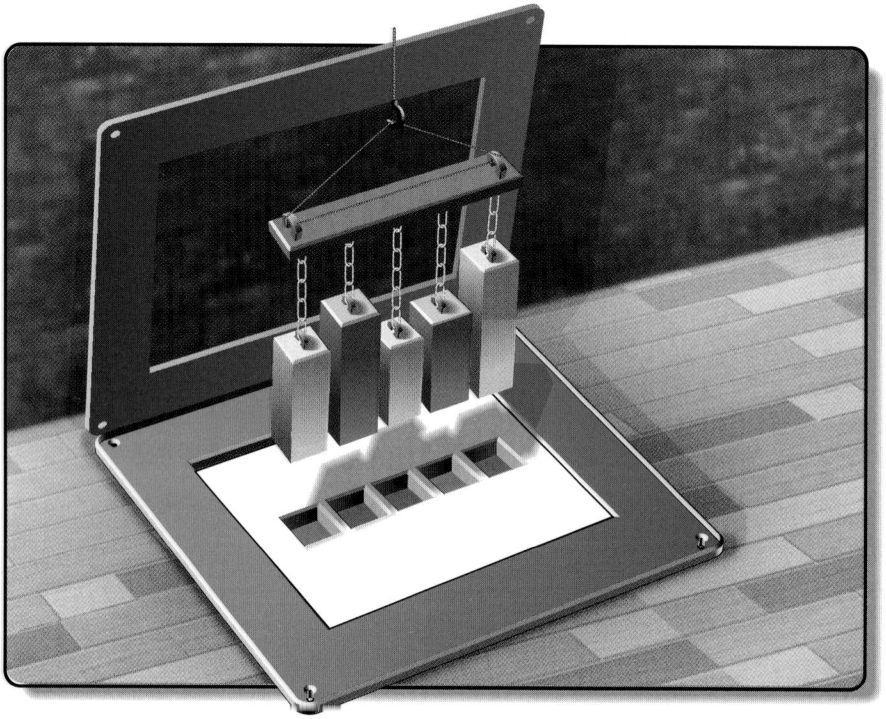

You can add a chart to a slide to show trends and compare data.

A chart is more visually appealing and often easier to understand than a list of numbers.

ADD A CHART

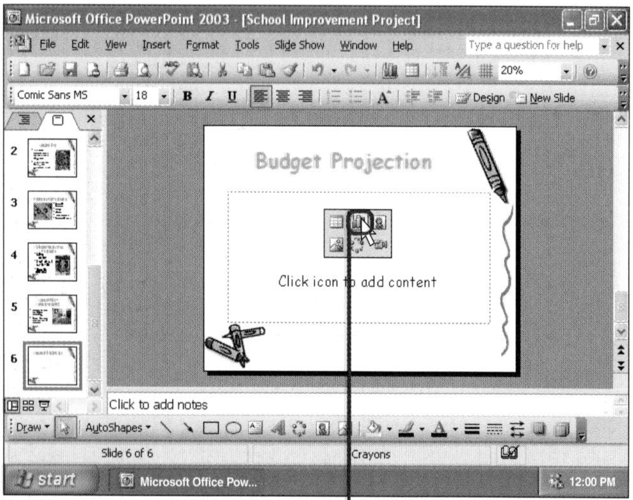

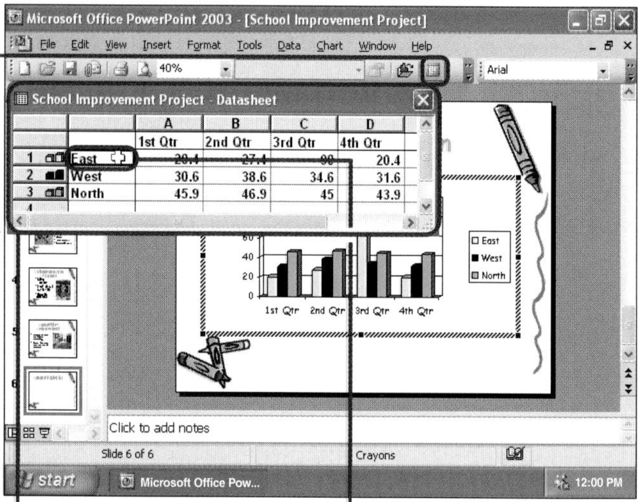

1 Display the slide you want to add a chart to.

2 Change the layout of the slide to one that includes a placeholder for a chart. To change the slide layout, see page 192.

3 Click the chart icon ( ) to add a chart.

Note: Depending on the layout you chose, you may need to double-click the placeholder to add a chart.

■ A datasheet appears, displaying sample data to show you where to enter information.

■ If the datasheet does not appear, click to display the datasheet.

Note: If is not displayed, click on the Standard toolbar to display the button.

4 To replace the data in a cell, click the cell. A thick border appears around the cell.

Tip

How do I change the data displayed in a chart?

Double-click the chart to activate the chart and display the datasheet. You can then perform steps **4** to **7** below to change the data displayed in the chart.

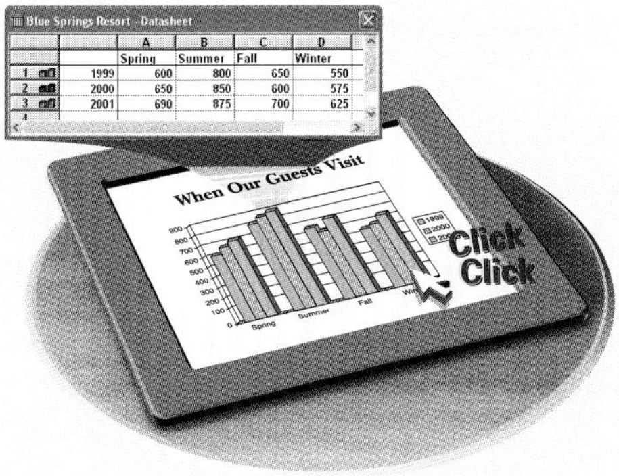

Tip

How can I add a chart without changing the slide layout?

You can click the Insert Chart button ( ) and then perform steps **4** to **7** below to add a chart to a slide without first changing the layout of the slide.

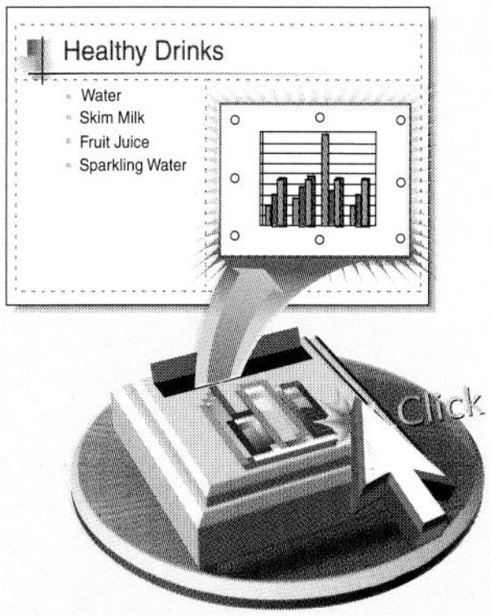

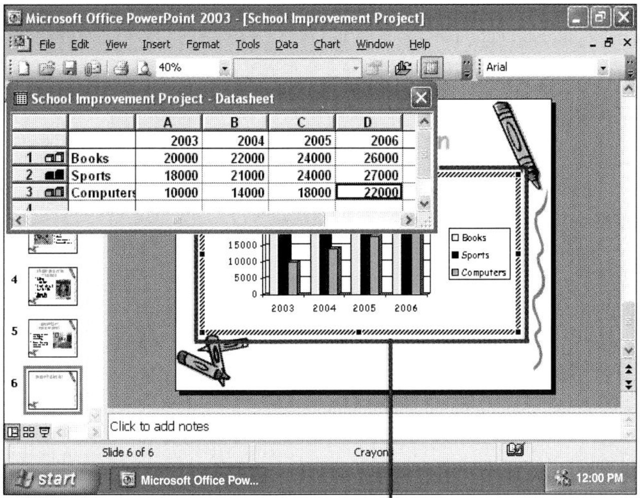

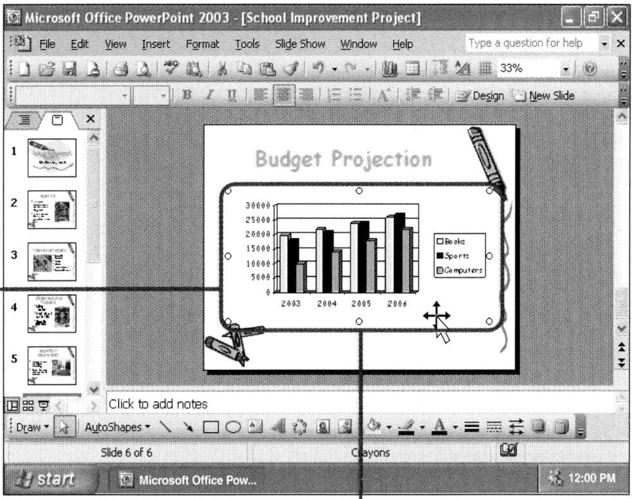

5 Type your data and then press the **Enter** key.

Note: To remove data from a cell and leave the cell empty, click the cell and then press the **Delete** *key.*

6 Repeat steps **4** and **5** until you finish entering all your data.

■ As you enter data, PowerPoint updates the chart on the slide.

7 When you finish entering data for the chart, click a blank area on your screen.

■ The datasheet disappears and you can clearly view the chart on the slide.

■ The handles (○) around the chart allow you to change the size of the chart. To move or resize a chart, see page 206.

DELETE A CHART

1 Click the chart you want to delete and then press the **Delete** key.

ADD A DIAGRAM

You can add a diagram to a slide to illustrate a concept or idea.

PowerPoint offers several types of diagrams you can choose from, including Pyramid, Radial, Venn and Target diagrams.

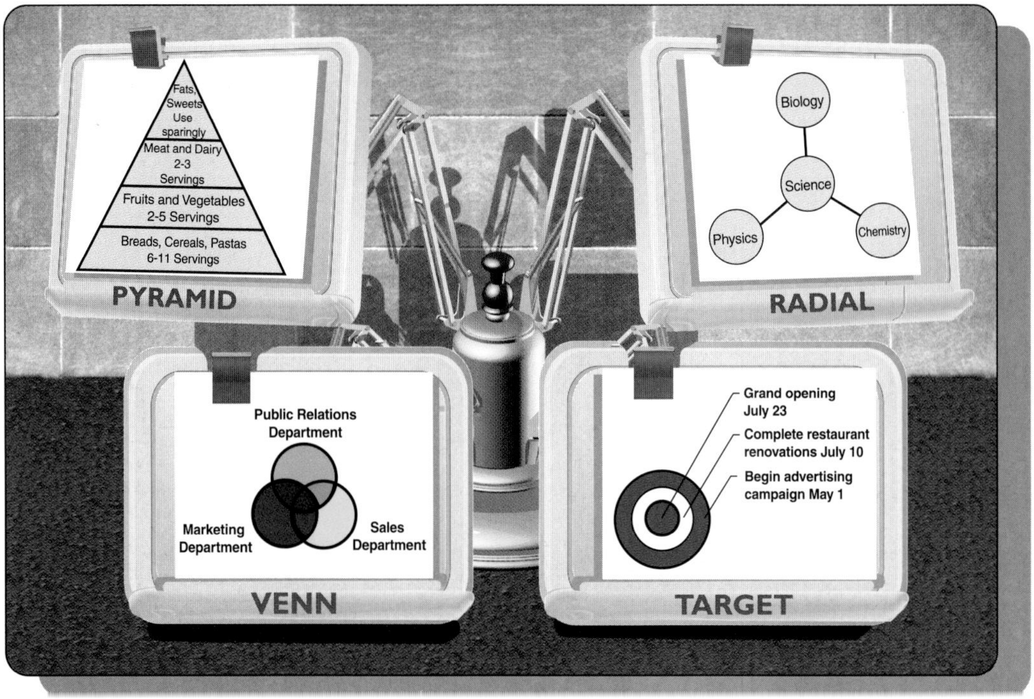

ADD A DIAGRAM

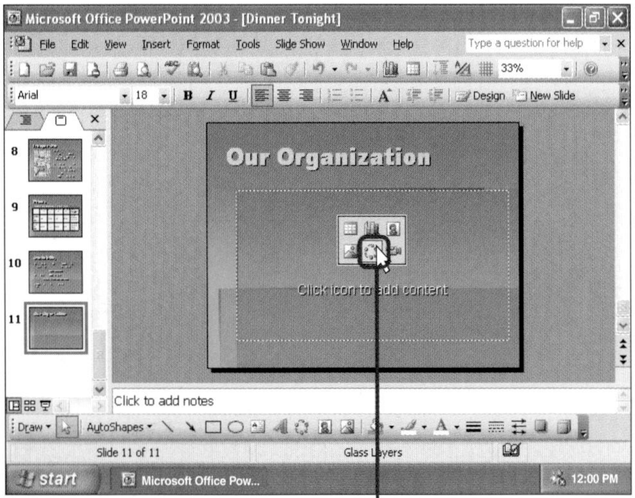

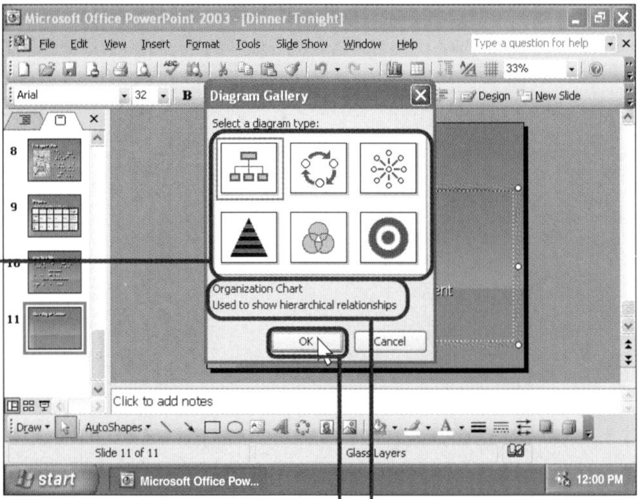

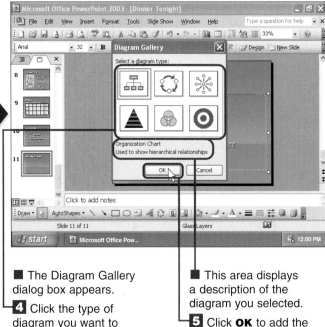

1 Display the slide you want to add a diagram to.

2 Change the layout of the slide to one that includes a placeholder for a diagram. To change the slide layout, see page 192.

3 Click the diagram icon ( ) to add a diagram to the slide.

Note: Depending on the layout you chose, you may need to double-click the placeholder to add a diagram.

■ The Diagram Gallery dialog box appears.

4 Click the type of diagram you want to add to the slide.

■ This area displays a description of the diagram you selected.

5 Click **OK** to add the diagram to the slide.

Tip

When adding a shape to an organization chart, what options are available?

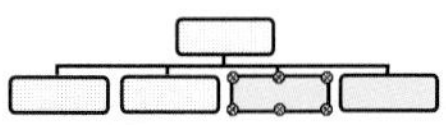

Coworker

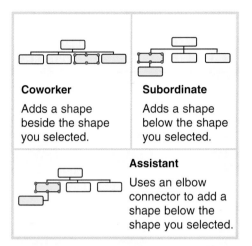

Adds a shape beside the shape you selected.

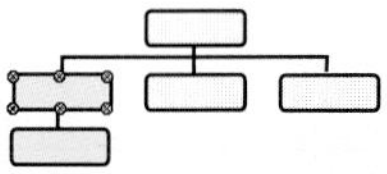

Subordinate

Adds a shape below the shape you selected.

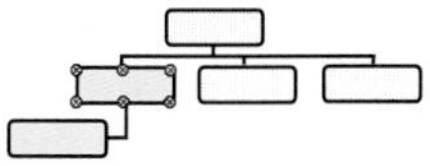

Assistant

Uses an elbow connector to add a shape below the shape you selected.

Tip

How do I delete a diagram?

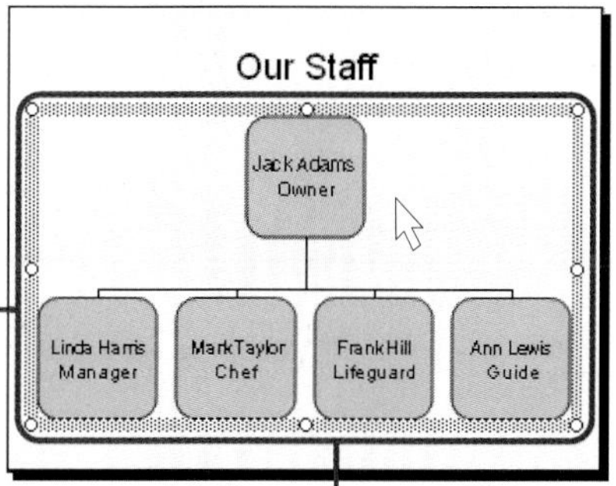

1 To delete a diagram, click a blank area in the diagram you want to delete.

■ A border appears around the diagram.

2 Press the **Delete** key.

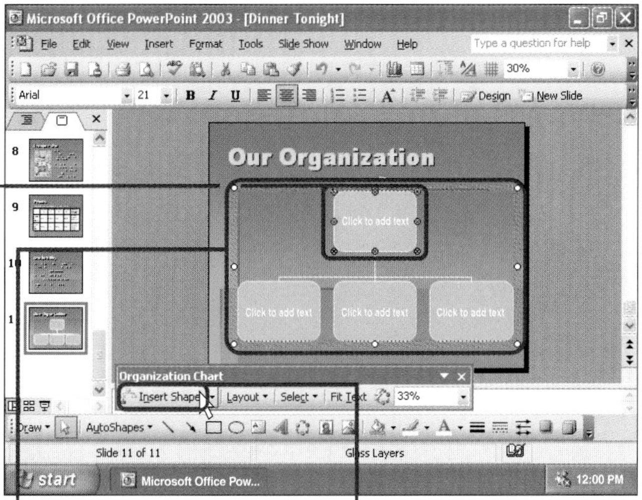

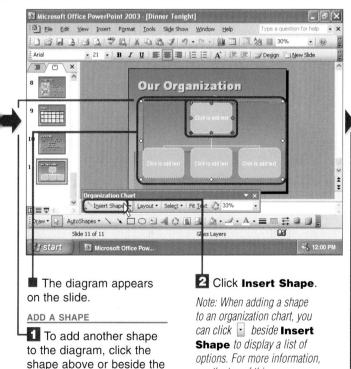

■ The diagram appears on the slide.

ADD A SHAPE

1 To add another shape to the diagram, click the shape above or beside the area where you want the new shape to appear.

2 Click **Insert Shape**.

Note: When adding a shape to an organization chart, you can click ▾ beside **Insert Shape** *to display a list of options. For more information, see the top of this page.*

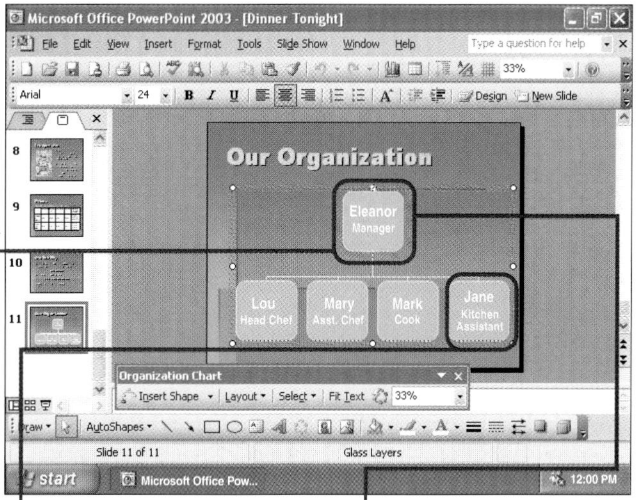

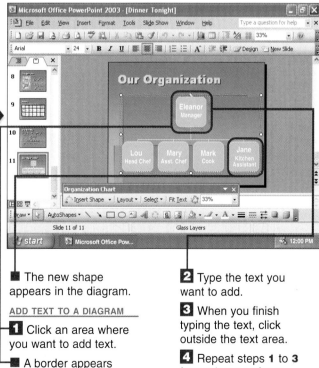

■ The new shape appears in the diagram.

ADD TEXT TO A DIAGRAM

1 Click an area where you want to add text.

■ A border appears around the area if you can add text to the area.

2 Type the text you want to add.

3 When you finish typing the text, click outside the text area.

4 Repeat steps **1** to **3** for each area of text you want to add.

MOVE OR RESIZE AN OBJECT

You can change the location and size of an object on a slide.

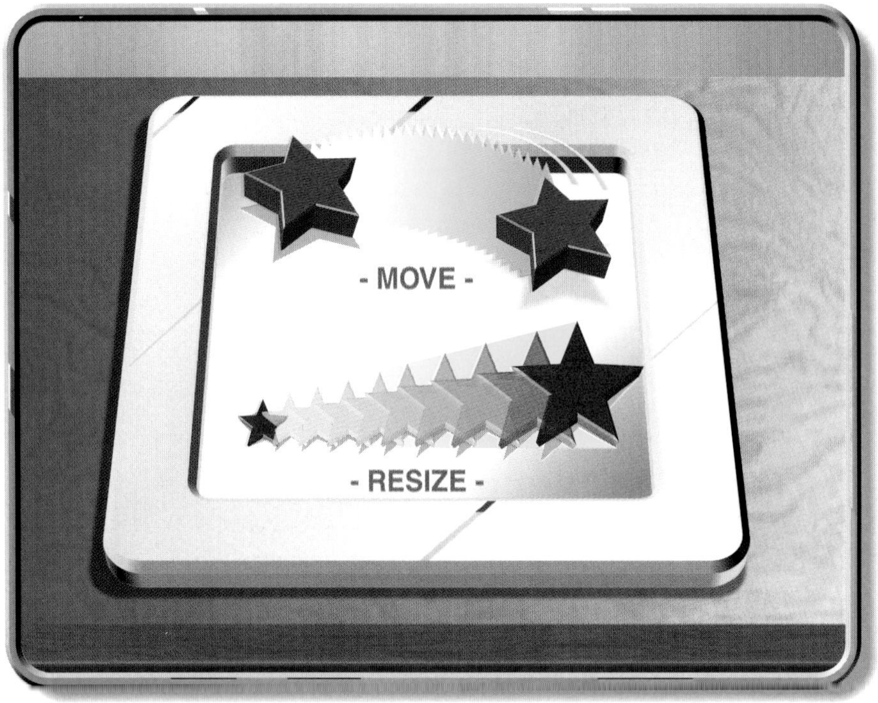

PowerPoint allows you to move and resize objects such as AutoShapes, WordArt, pictures, clip art images and charts.

MOVE AN OBJECT

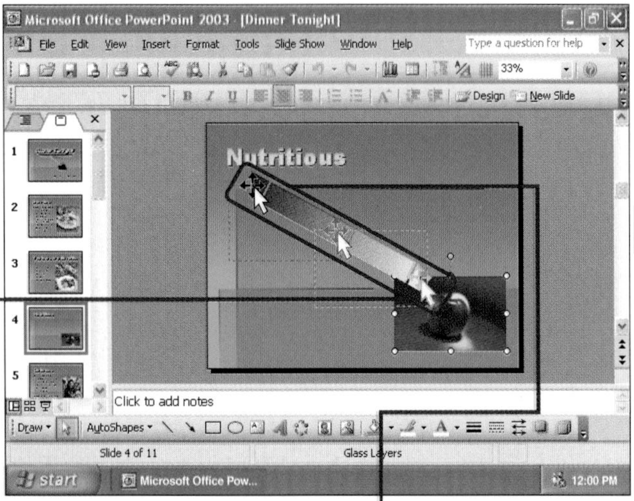

1 Click the object you want to move. Handles (○) appear around the object.

2 Position the mouse ↖ over an edge of the object (↖ changes to ✥).

3 Drag the object to a new location on the slide.

■ A dashed line indicates where the object will appear.

■ The object appears in the new location.

■ To deselect the object, click outside the object.

Tip

How can I change the way an object is moved or resized?

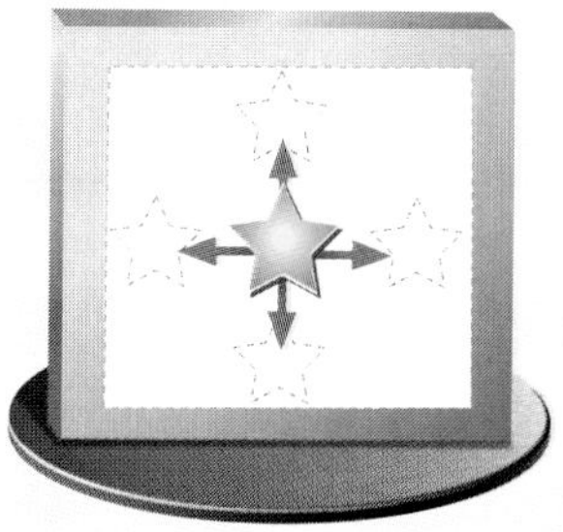

Move Only Horizontally or Vertically

To move an object only horizontally or vertically on a slide, press and hold down the Shift key as you move the object.

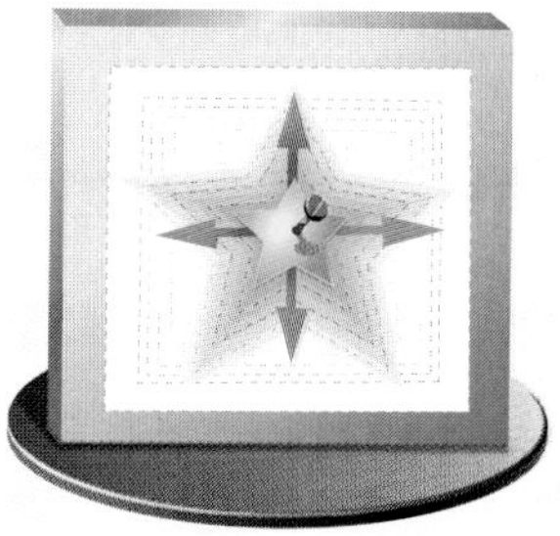

Maintain Object's Center When Resizing

To keep the center of an object in the same place while resizing the object, press and hold down the Ctrl key as you resize the object.

RESIZE AN OBJECT

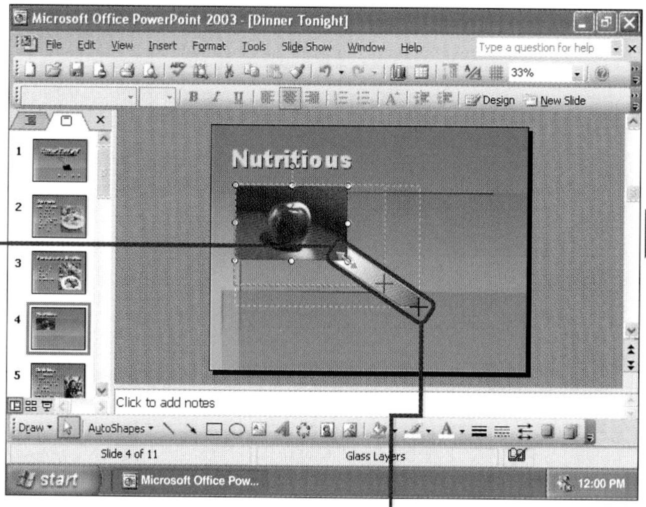

1 Click the object you want to resize. Handles (○) appear around the object.

2 Position the mouse over one of the handles (changes to ↘, ↗, ↔ or ↕).

3 Drag the handle until the object is the size you want.

■ A dashed line shows the new size.

■ The object appears in the new size.

■ To deselect the object, click outside the object.

CHANGE FONT OF TEXT

You can change the font of text to enhance the appearance of a slide.

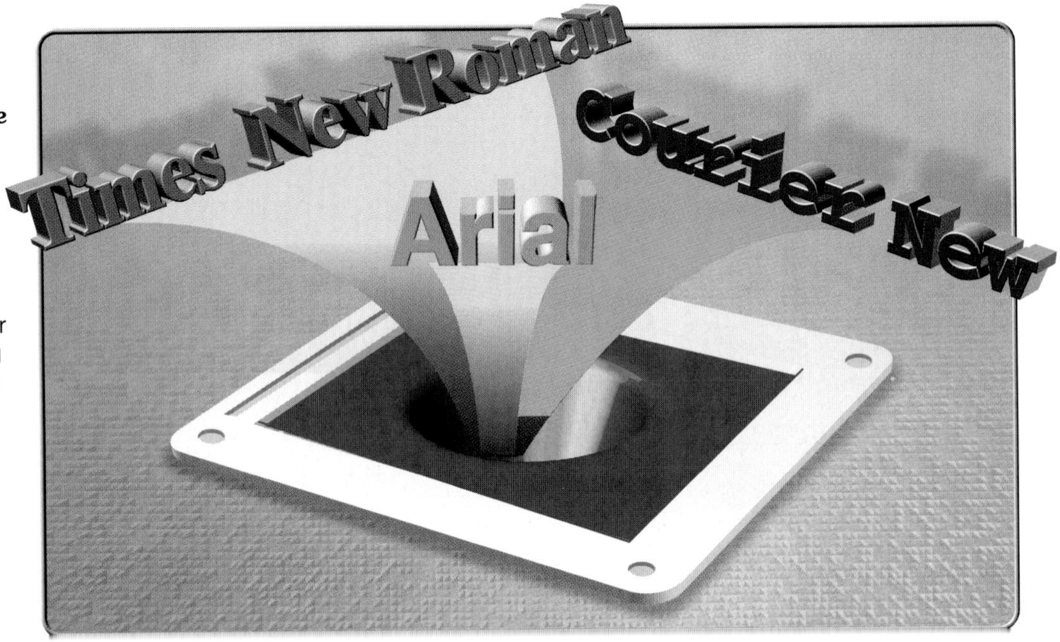

You should consider your audience when choosing a font. For example, you may want to choose an informal font, such as Comic Sans MS, for a presentation to your co-workers and a conservative font, such as Times New Roman, for a presentation to your clients.

CHANGE FONT OF TEXT

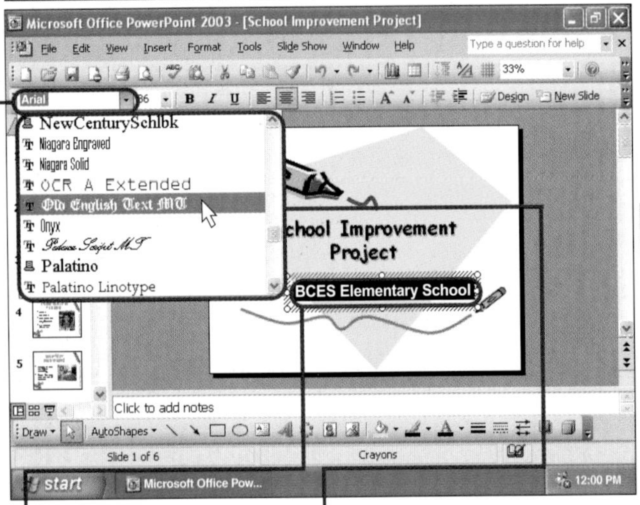

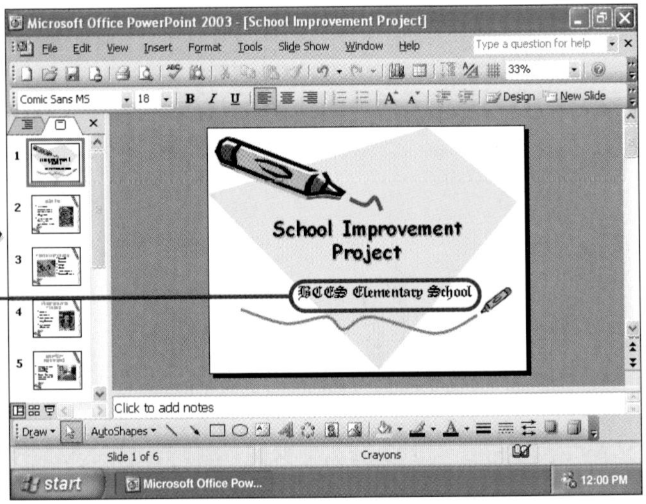

1 Select the text you want to change to a different font. To select text, see page 180.

2 Click ▾ in this area to display a list of the available fonts.

Note: If the Font area is not displayed, click ⁝ on the Formatting toolbar to display the area.

3 Click the font you want to use.

Note: PowerPoint displays the fonts you have most recently used at the top of the list.

■ The text you selected changes to the new font.

■ To deselect text, click outside the selected area.

CHANGE SIZE OF TEXT

You can increase or decrease the size of text on a slide.

Larger text is easier to read, but smaller text allows you to fit more information on a slide.

PowerPoint measures the size of text in points. There are 72 points in an inch.

CHANGE SIZE OF TEXT

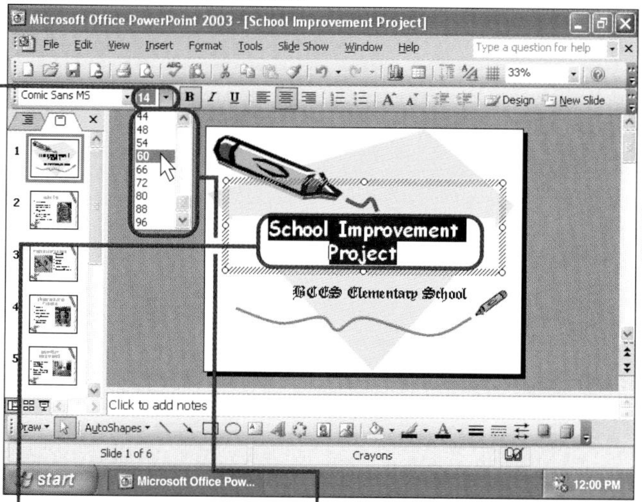

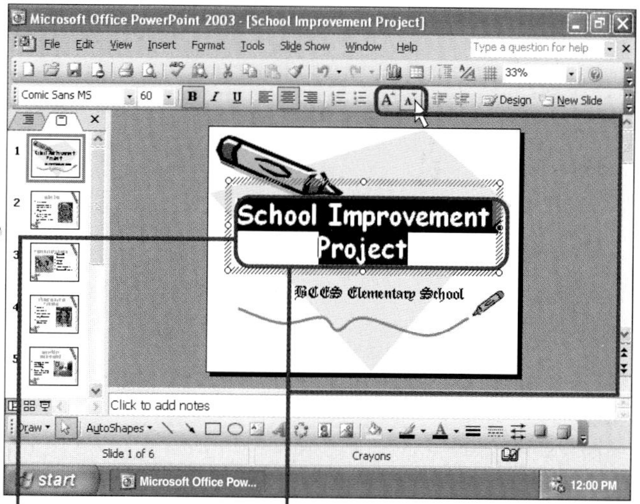

1 Select the text you want to change to a new size. To select text, see page 180.

2 Click in this area to display a list of the available sizes.

Note: If the Font Size area is not displayed, click on the Formatting toolbar to display the area.

3 Click the size you want to use.

■ The text you selected changes to the new size.

■ To deselect text, click outside the selected area.

QUICKLY CHANGE SIZE OF TEXT

1 Select the text you want to change to a new size.

2 Click or to increase or decrease the size of the text.

Note: If the button you want is not displayed, click on the Formatting toolbar to display the button.

CHANGE STYLE OF TEXT

You can bold, italicize, underline or add a shadow to text to emphasize information on a slide.

You can add one style or a combination of styles to text. However, keep in mind that adding too many styles to text can be distracting and make the text difficult to read

CHANGE STYLE OF TEXT

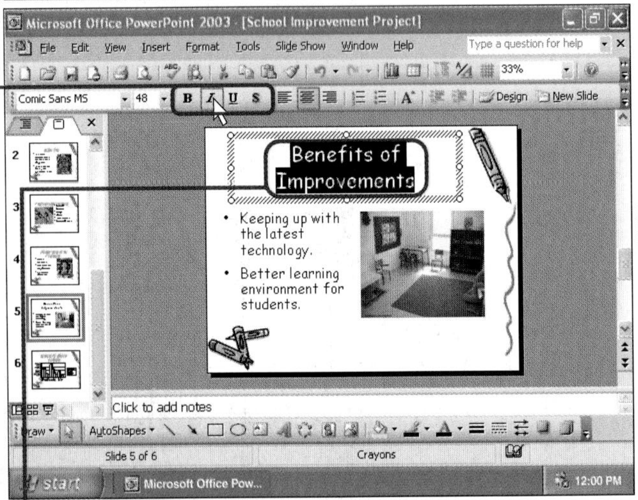

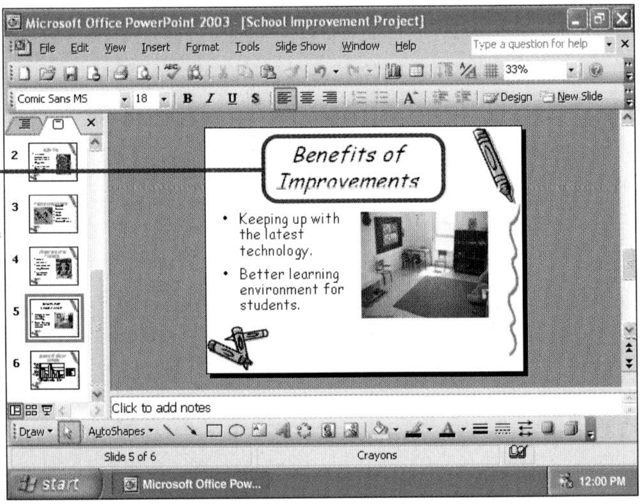

1 Select the text you want to bold, italicize, underline or add a shadow to. To select text, see page 180.

2 Click one of the following buttons.

- **B** Bold
- *I* Italic
- U Underline
- S Shadow

Note: If the button you want is not displayed, click on the Formatting toolbar to display the button.

■ The text you selected appears in the new style.

■ To deselect text, click outside the selected area.

■ To remove a bold, italic, underline or shadow style, repeat steps **1** and **2**.

CHANGE ALIGNMENT OF TEXT

You can change the alignment of text on a slide to enhance the appearance of the slide.

CHANGE ALIGNMENT OF TEXT

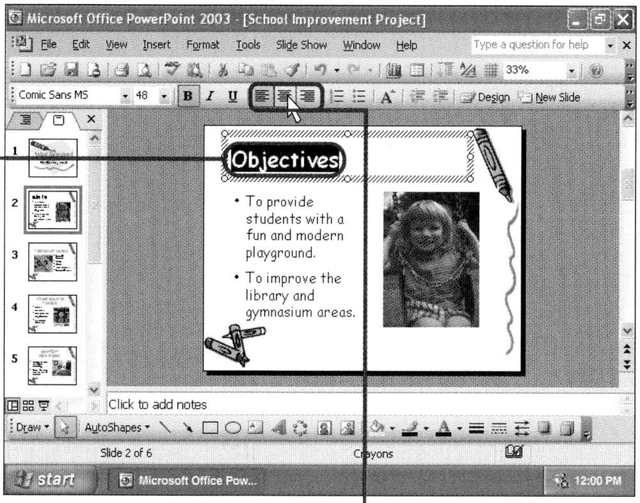

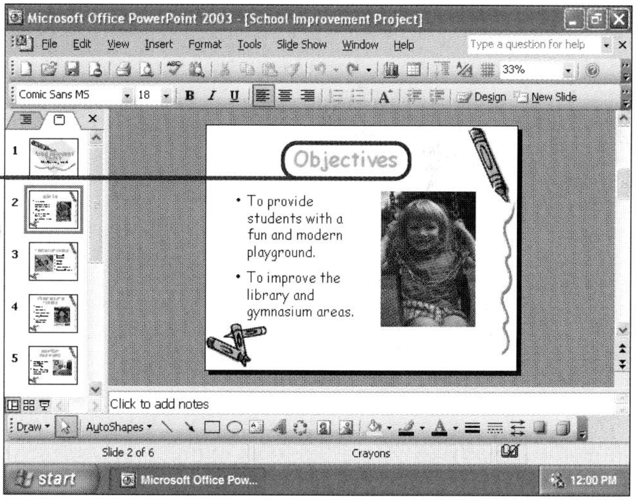

1 Select the text you want to align differently. To select text, see page 180.

2 Click one of the following buttons.

- Left align
- Center
- Right align

Note: If the button you want is not displayed, click on the Formatting toolbar to display the button.

■ The text appears in the new alignment.

■ To deselect text, click outside the selected area.

CHANGE TEXT COLOR

You can change the color of text on a slide to enhance the appearance of the slide and draw attention to important information.

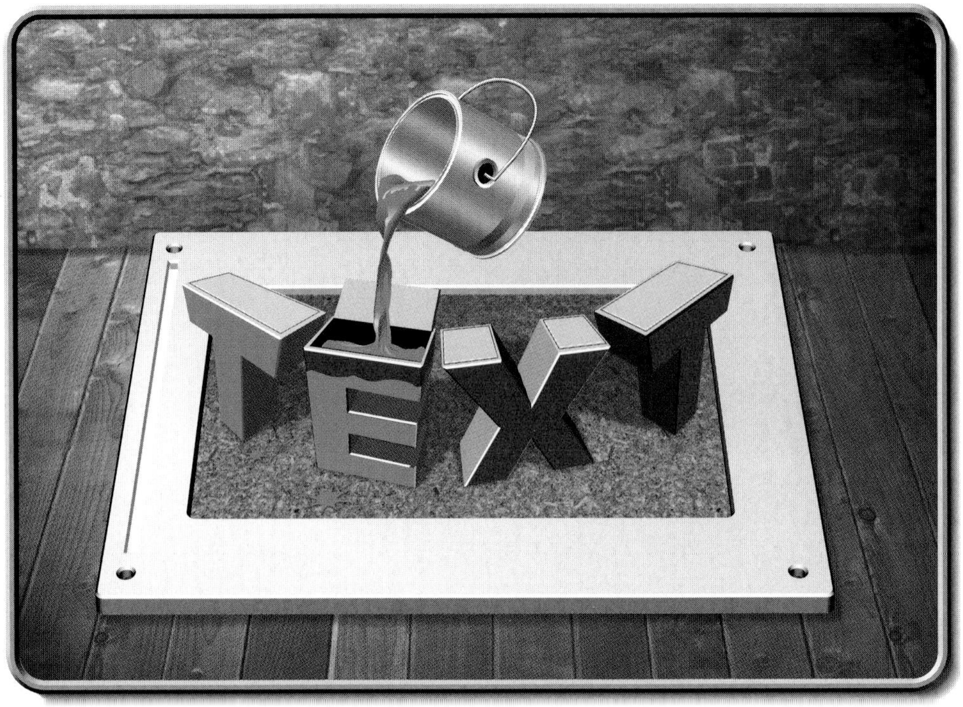

CHANGE TEXT COLOR

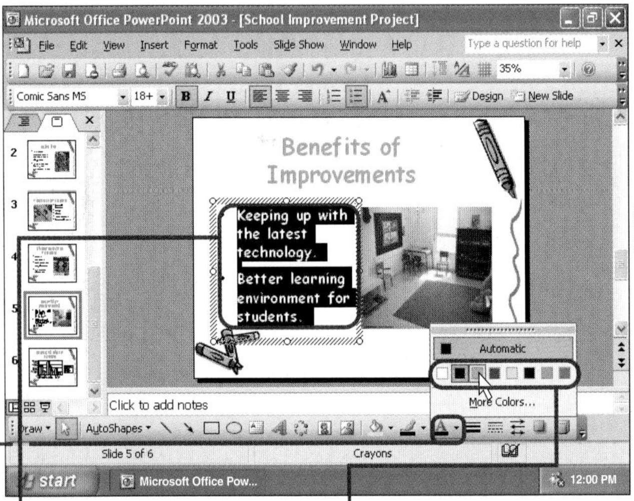

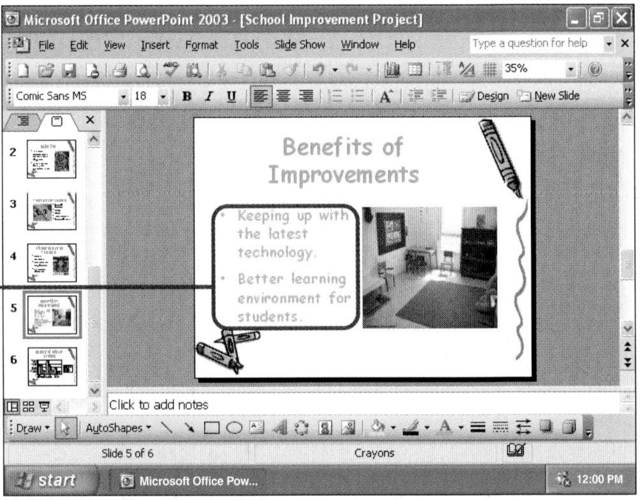

1 Select the text you want to change to a different color. To select text, see page 180.

2 Click ▾ in this area to display the available colors.

3 Click the color you want to use.

Note: The available colors depend on the color scheme of the slide. For information on color schemes, see page 216.

■ The text appears in the color you selected.

■ To deselect text, click outside the selected area.

■ To once again display the text in the default color, repeat steps **1** to **3**, selecting **Automatic** in step **3**.

CHANGE OBJECT COLOR

You can change the color of an object on a slide to better suit the design of the slide.

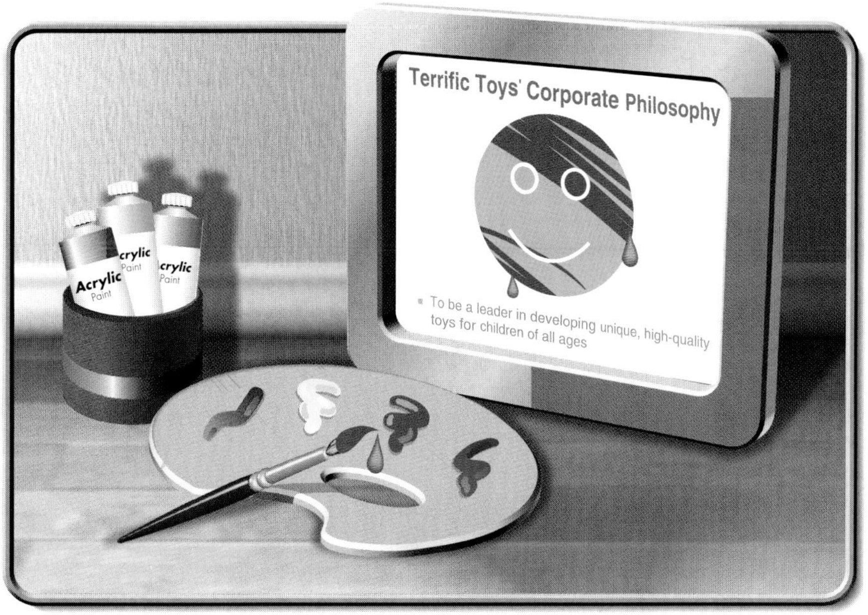

PowerPoint allows you to change the color of objects such as WordArt and charts. You can also change the color of most AutoShapes and some clip art images.

CHANGE OBJECT COLOR

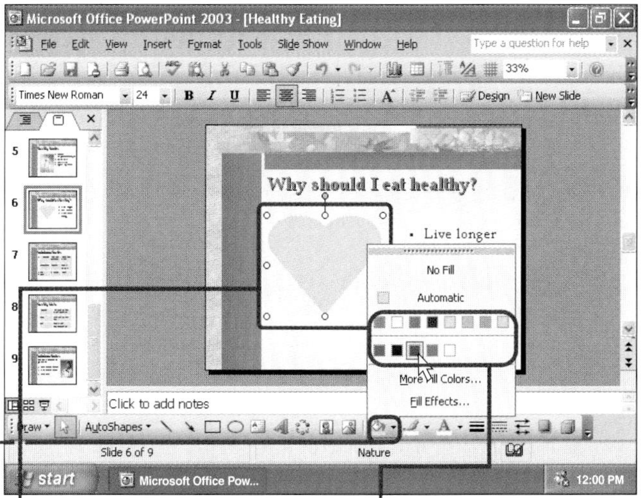

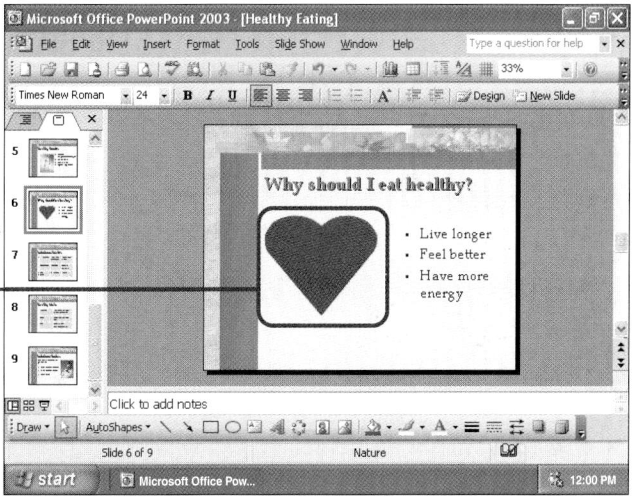

1 Click the object you want to change to a different color. Handles (○) appear around the object.

2 Click ▾ in this area to display the available colors.

3 Click the color you want to use.

Note: The available colors depend on the color scheme of the slide. For information on color schemes, see page 216.

■ The object appears in the color you selected.

■ To deselect the object, click outside the object.

■ To once again display the object in the default color, repeat steps **1** to **3**, selecting **Automatic** in step **3**.

CHANGE THE DESIGN TEMPLATE

PowerPoint offers many design templates that you can choose from to give the slides in your presentation a professional look.

You can change the design template for your entire presentation or for a single slide. Changing the design template for a single slide can make the slide stand out from the rest of your presentation.

CHANGE THE DESIGN TEMPLATE

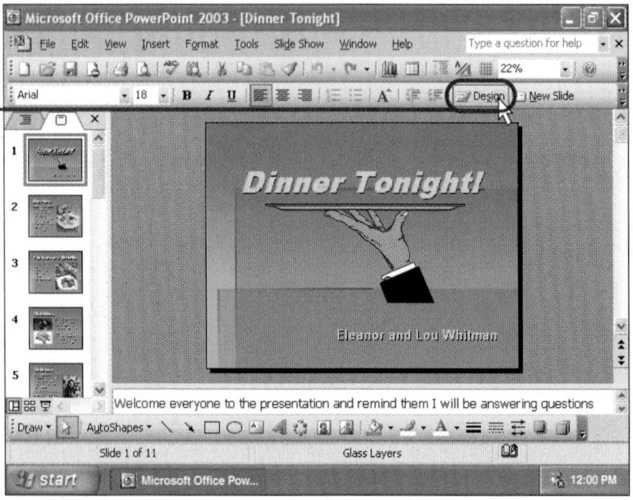

1 Click **Design** to display the Slide Design task pane.

Note: If the Design button is not displayed, click on the Formatting toolbar to display the button.

■ The Slide Design task pane appears.

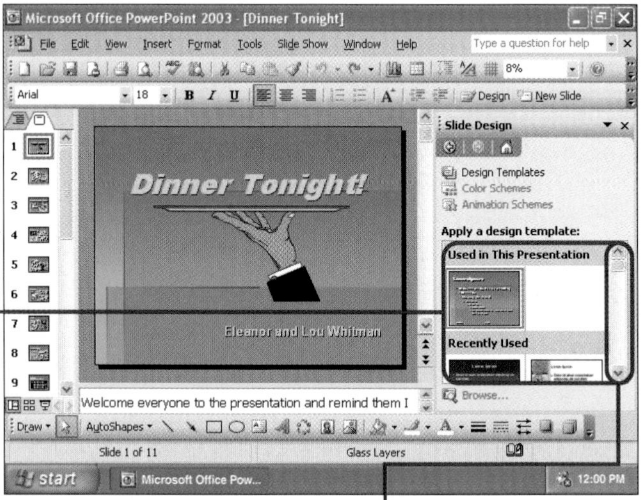

■ This area displays the available design templates.

Note: The design templates are organized into three sections—Used in This Presentation, Recently Used and Available For Use.

■ You can use the scroll bar to browse through the design templates.

Tip

When I changed the design template for my presentation, why did some parts of my slides not change?

The new design template may not affect parts of a slide you have previously formatted. For example, if you changed the color of text on a slide before changing the design template, the new design template will not affect the text you changed.

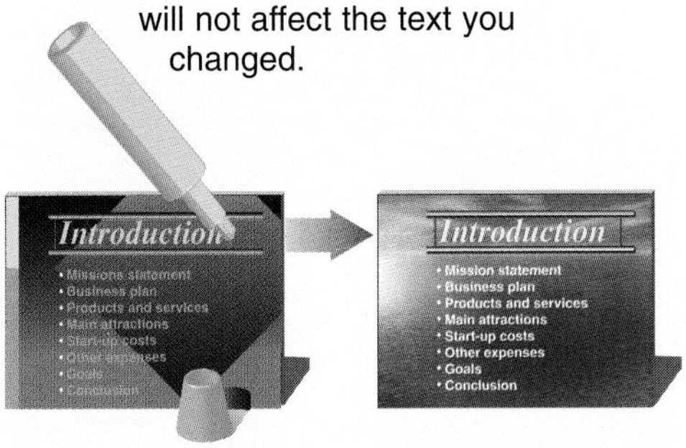

Tip

Are there other design templates that I can use?

Yes. You can install additional design templates on your computer. Click **Additional Design Templates** at the end of the list of templates. PowerPoint will begin installing additional design templates on your computer.

You can also click **Design Templates on Microsoft Office Online** at the end of the list of templates. A Web page appears, allowing you to download additional design templates.

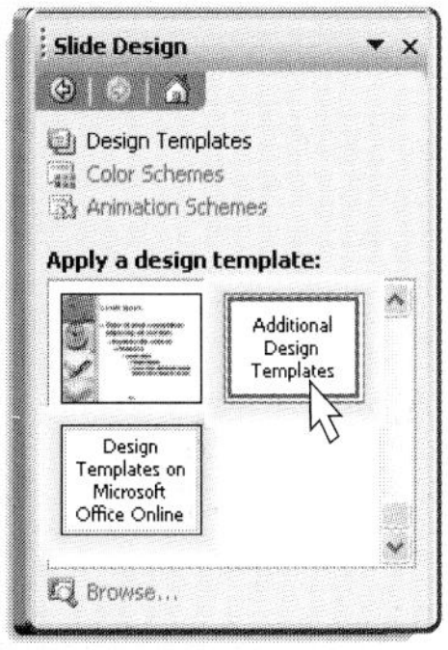

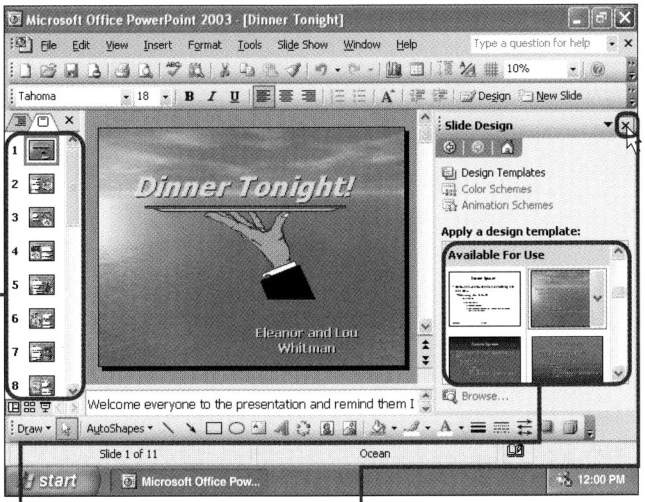

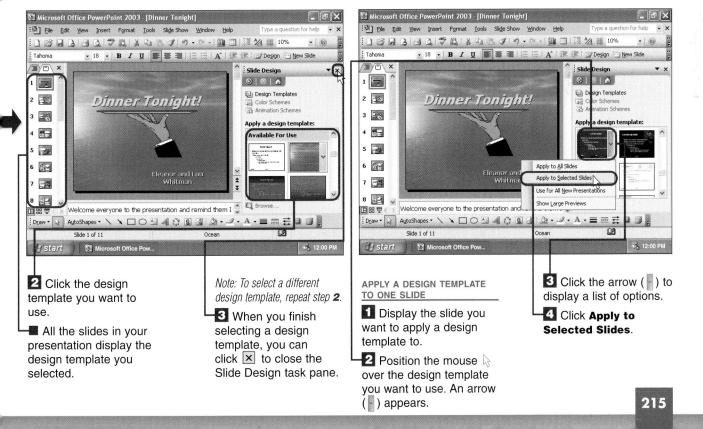

2 Click the design template you want to use.

■ All the slides in your presentation display the design template you selected.

*Note: To select a different design template, repeat step **2**.*

3 When you finish selecting a design template, you can click ☒ to close the Slide Design task pane.

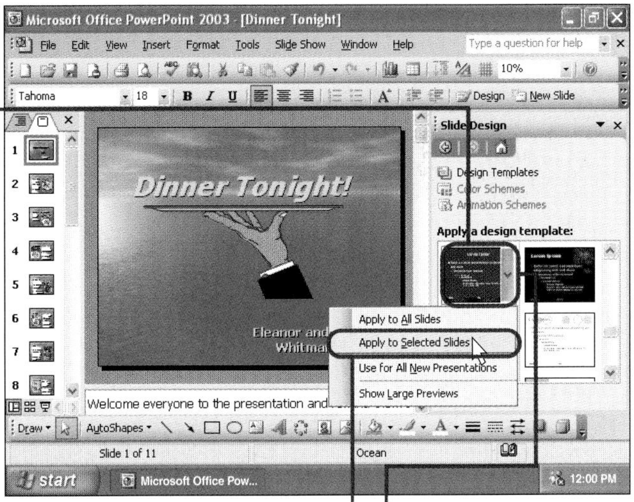

APPLY A DESIGN TEMPLATE TO ONE SLIDE

1 Display the slide you want to apply a design template to.

2 Position the mouse over the design template you want to use. An arrow ( ) appears.

3 Click the arrow ( ) to display a list of options.

4 Click **Apply to Selected Slides**.

CHANGE THE COLOR SCHEME

You can change the color scheme of all the slides in your presentation.

You can also change the color scheme of a single slide. Changing the color scheme for a single slide can make the slide stand out from the rest of your presentation.

Each color scheme contains a set of eight coordinated colors, including colors for the background, text, lines, shadows, titles and accents.

CHANGE THE COLOR SCHEME

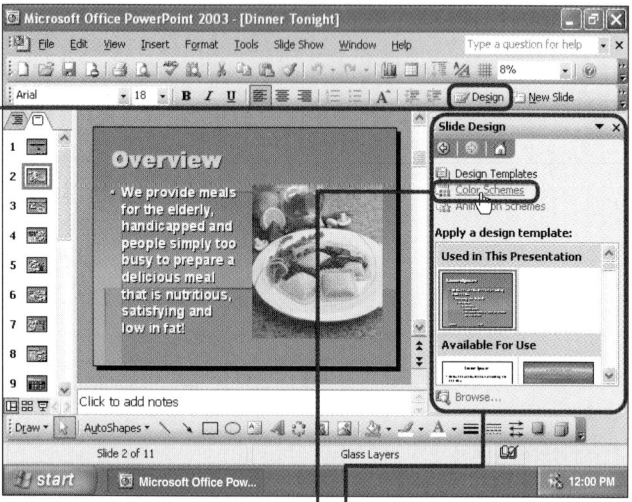

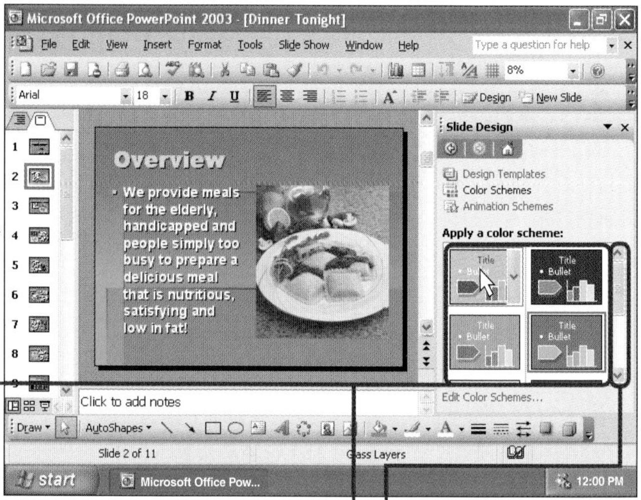

1 Click **Design** to display the Slide Design task pane.

Note: If the Design button is not displayed, click ▮ on the Formatting toolbar to display the button.

■ The Slide Design task pane appears.

2 Click **Color Schemes** to display the available color schemes.

■ This area displays the available color schemes.

Note: The available color schemes depend on the current design template. For information on design templates, see page 214.

■ You can use the scroll bar to browse through the color schemes.

3 Click the color scheme you want to use.

Tip

What should I consider when changing the color scheme of slides?

When selecting a color scheme, you should consider how you will deliver the presentation. If you will be using overheads, you should choose a color scheme with a light background and dark text. If you will be using 35mm slides or delivering your presentation on a computer screen, you should choose a color scheme with a dark background and light text.

Tip

Some of the slides in my presentation did not change to the new color scheme. What is wrong?

You may have used more than one design template in your presentation. By default, PowerPoint only applies the new color scheme to slides with the same design template as the current slide. To apply the color scheme to all the slides in your presentation, perform steps **2** to **4** on page 217, selecting **Apply to All Slides** in step **4**. For more information on design templates, see page 214.

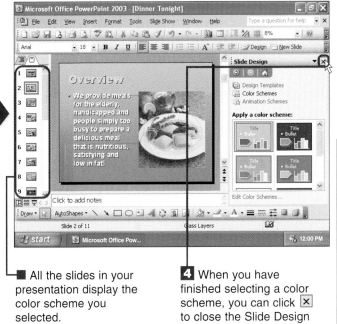

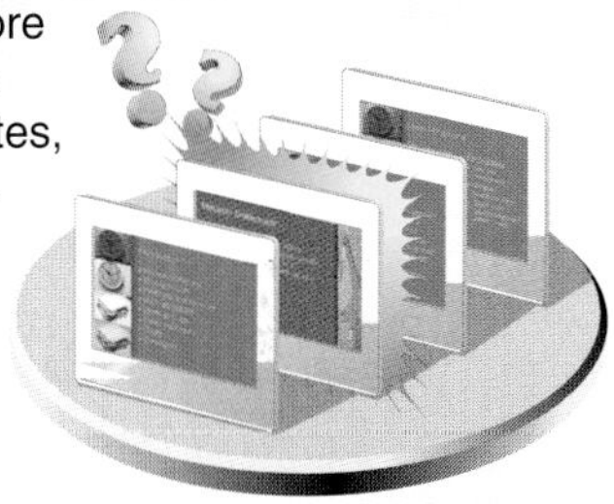

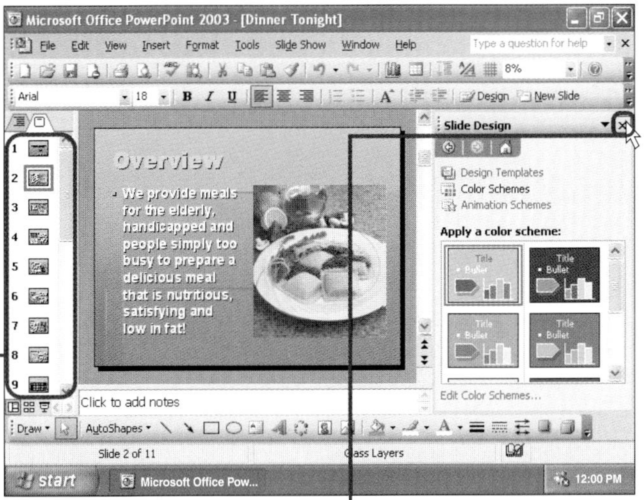

■ All the slides in your presentation display the color scheme you selected.

Note: To select a different color scheme, repeat step ***3****.*

4 When you have finished selecting a color scheme, you can click ☒ to close the Slide Design task pane.

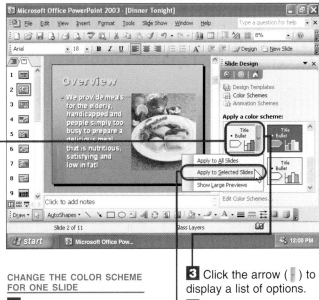

CHANGE THE COLOR SCHEME FOR ONE SLIDE

1 Display the slide you want to use a different color scheme.

2 Position the mouse over the color scheme you want to use. An arrow ( ) appears.

3 Click the arrow ( ) to display a list of options.

4 Click **Apply to Selected Slides**.

ANIMATE SLIDES

You can animate slides in your presentation to help keep your audience's attention throughout the presentation. PowerPoint provides many preset animation schemes that you can use to add animation and movement to titles, bulleted text and paragraphs on your slides.

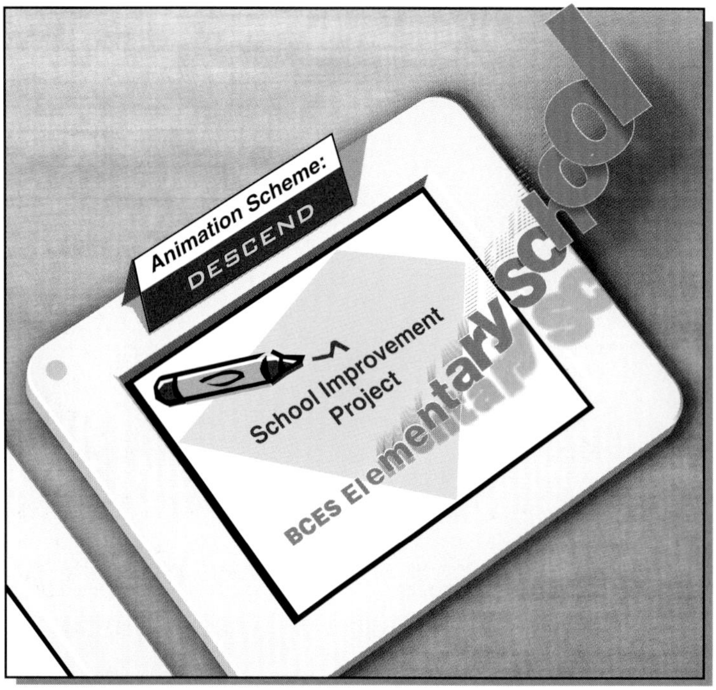

Although PowerPoint allows you to add a different animation scheme to each slide in your presentation, using too many different animation schemes may take the audience's attention away from the information you present.

ANIMATE SLIDES

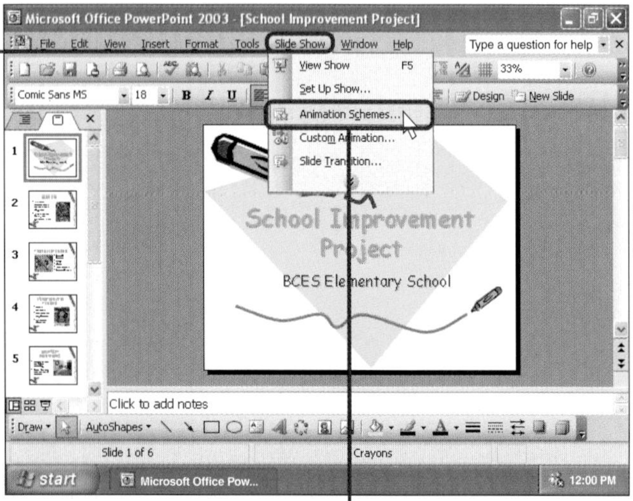

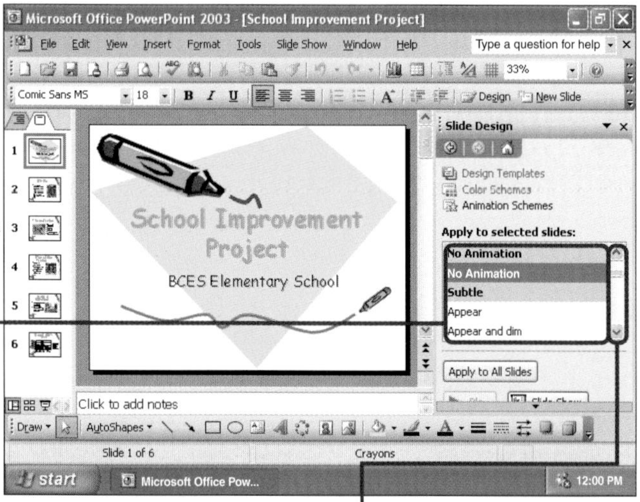

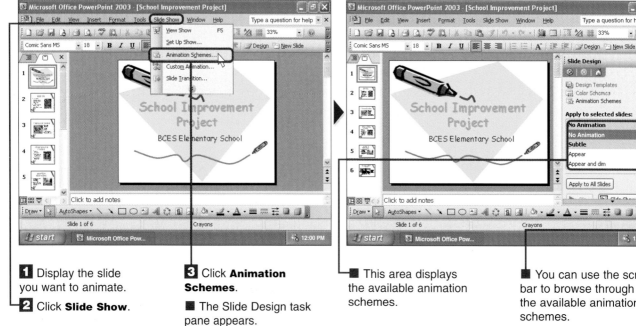

1 Display the slide you want to animate.

2 Click **Slide Show**.

3 Click **Animation Schemes**.

■ The Slide Design task pane appears.

■ This area displays the available animation schemes.

■ You can use the scroll bar to browse through the available animation schemes.

Tip

How do I preview the animation in a slide show?

You can click the **Slide Show** button in the Slide Design task pane to preview the animation in a slide show. You may need to click the current slide to display each animated item on the slide during the slide show. For more information on viewing a slide show, see page 224.

Tip

How do I remove an animation scheme from a slide?

To remove an animation scheme from a slide, repeat steps **1** to **4** below, except select **No Animation** in step **4**.

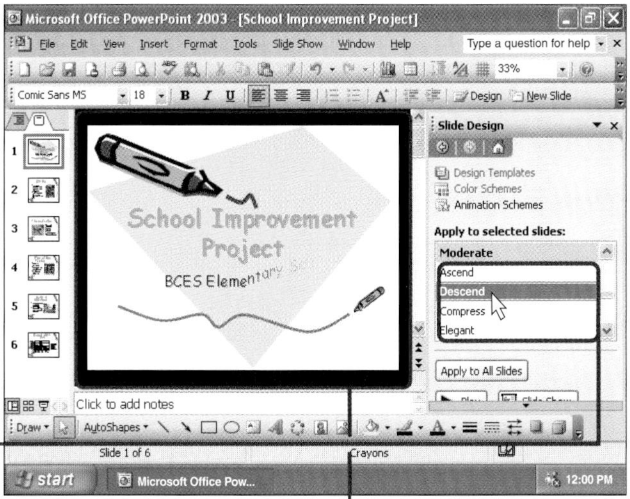

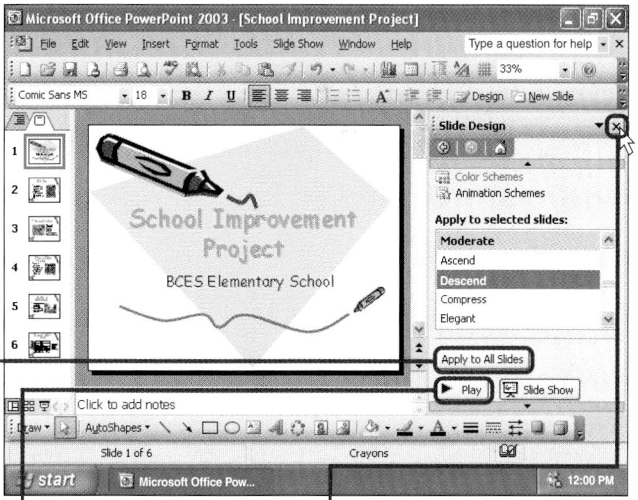

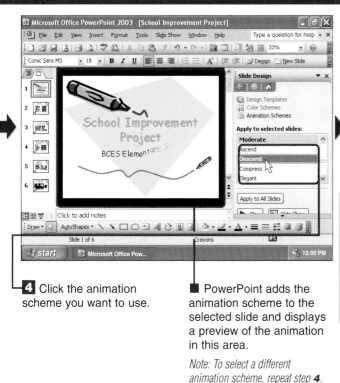

4 Click the animation scheme you want to use.

■ PowerPoint adds the animation scheme to the selected slide and displays a preview of the animation in this area.

*Note: To select a different animation scheme, repeat step **4**.*

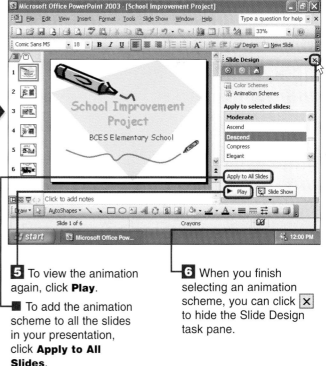

5 To view the animation again, click **Play**.

■ To add the animation scheme to all the slides in your presentation, click **Apply to All Slides**.

6 When you finish selecting an animation scheme, you can click ☒ to hide the Slide Design task pane.

REORDER SLIDES

You can change the order of the slides in your presentation. Reordering slides is useful when you want to reorganize the ideas in your presentation.

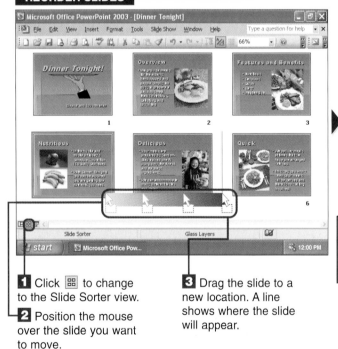

REORDER SLIDES

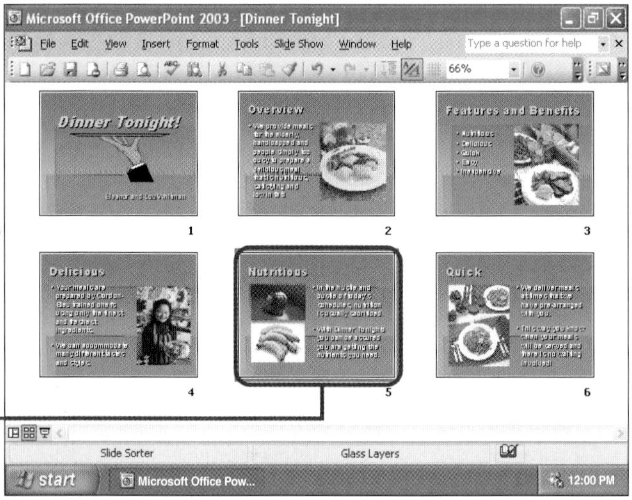

1 Click the Slide Sorter button to change to the Slide Sorter view.

2 Position the mouse over the slide you want to move.

3 Drag the slide to a new location. A line shows where the slide will appear.

■ The slide appears in the new location.

■ PowerPoint automatically renumbers the slides in your presentation.

DELETE A SLIDE

You can remove a slide you no longer need from your presentation. Deleting a slide is useful if the slide contains outdated or incorrect information.

DELETE A SLIDE

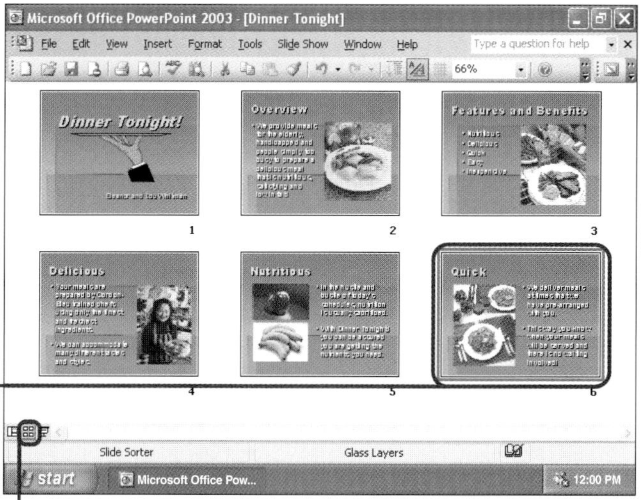

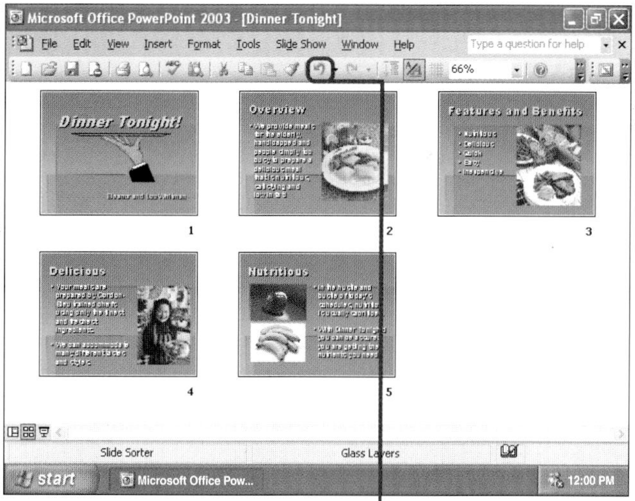

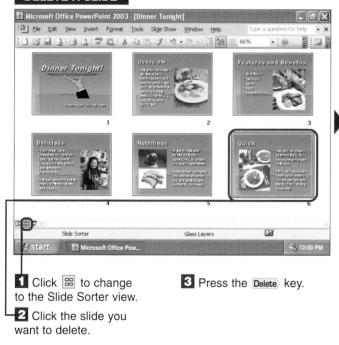

1 Click ⊞ to change to the Slide Sorter view.

2 Click the slide you want to delete.

3 Press the Delete key.

■ The slide disappears.

■ PowerPoint automatically renumbers the remaining slides in your presentation.

■ To immediately return the slide to the presentation, click ↶.

ADD SLIDE TRANSITIONS

You can add transitions to slides in your presentation. A transition is a visual effect that appears when you move from one slide to the next.

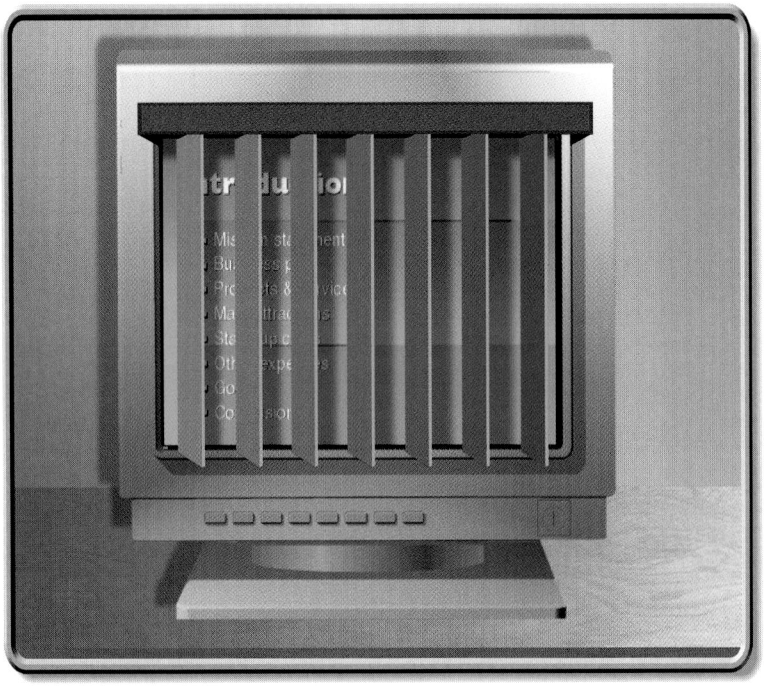

Using transitions can help you introduce each slide during an on-screen slide show and signal your audience that new information is appearing.

ADD SLIDE TRANSITIONS

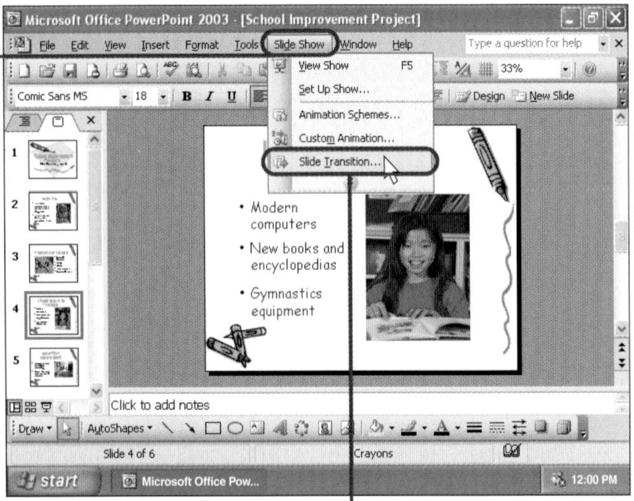

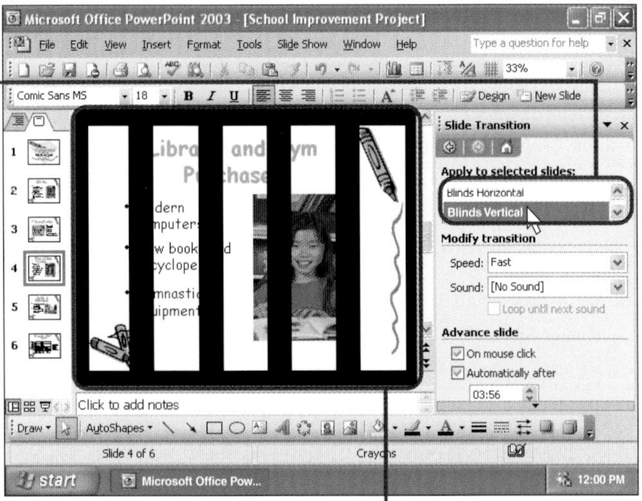

1 Display the slide you want to add a transition to.

2 Click **Slide Show**.

3 Click **Slide Transition**.

■ The Slide Transition task pane appears.

■ This area displays the available transitions. You can use the scroll bar to browse through the transitions.

4 Click the transition you want to use.

■ PowerPoint adds the transition to the displayed slide and displays a preview of the transition.

*Note: To view the transition again, repeat step **4**.*

Tip

What should I consider when adding transitions to slides?

Although PowerPoint allows you to add a different transition to each slide in your presentation, using too many different transitions may distract the audience. The audience may focus on how each slide is introduced, rather than the information you are presenting.

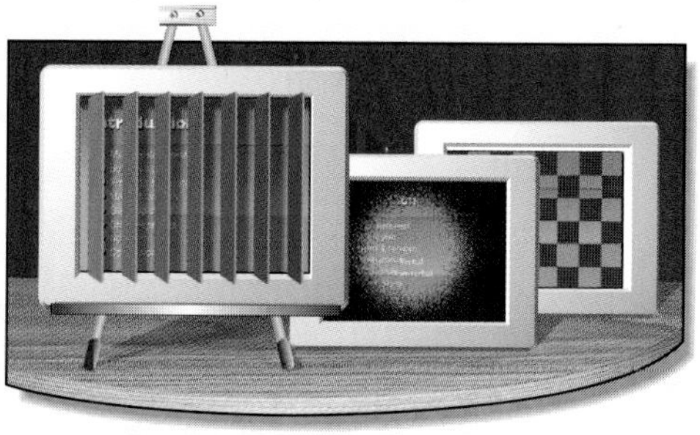

Tip

How do I remove a transition from a slide?

Display the slide you want to remove a transition from and then perform steps **2** to **4** below, selecting **No Transition** in step **4**.

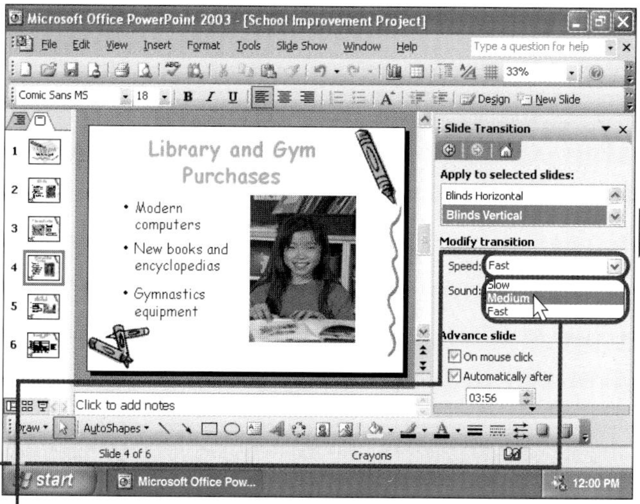

5 To change the speed of the transition, click this area to display a list of speed options.

6 Click the speed you want to use.

■ PowerPoint displays a preview of the transition with the speed you selected.

*Note: To view the transition with the speed again, repeat steps **5** and **6**.*

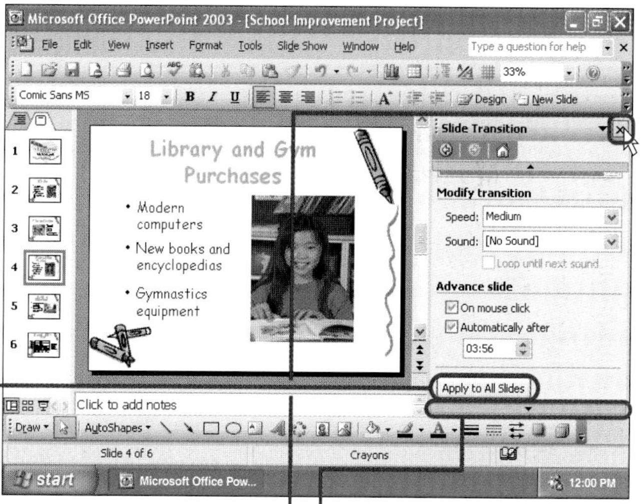

7 To add the transition to all the slides in your presentation, click **Apply to All Slides**.

*Note: To apply the transition to only the slide you displayed in step **1**, skip to step **8**.*

■ If you cannot see the Apply to All Slides button, click ▼ to browse through the information in the task pane.

8 When you finish selecting a transition, you can click ☒ to close the Slide Transition task pane.

VIEW A SLIDE SHOW

You can view a slide show of your presentation on a computer screen. A slide show displays one slide at a time using the entire screen.

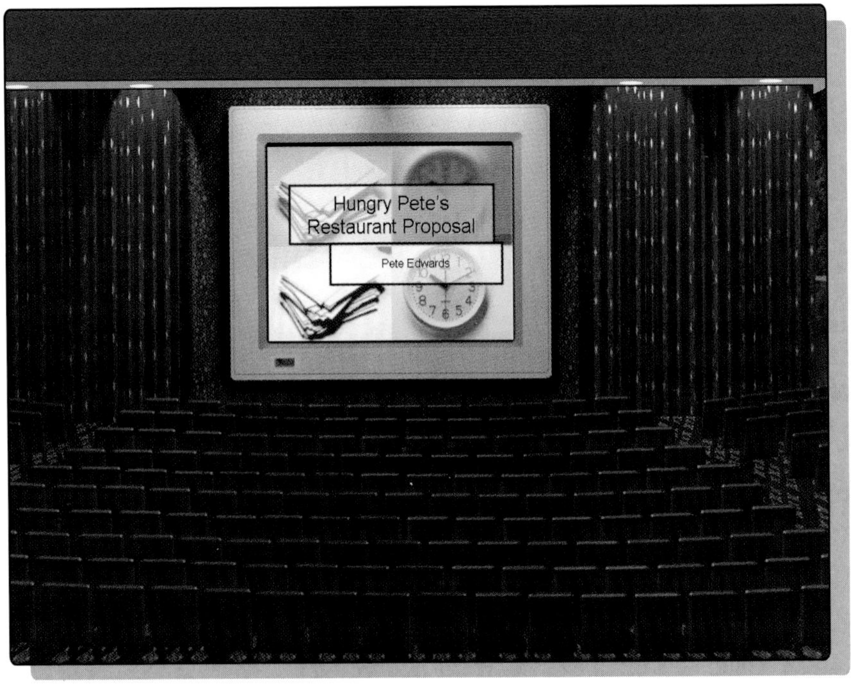

Before presenting a slide show to an audience, you can view the slide show to rehearse your presentation.

VIEW A SLIDE SHOW

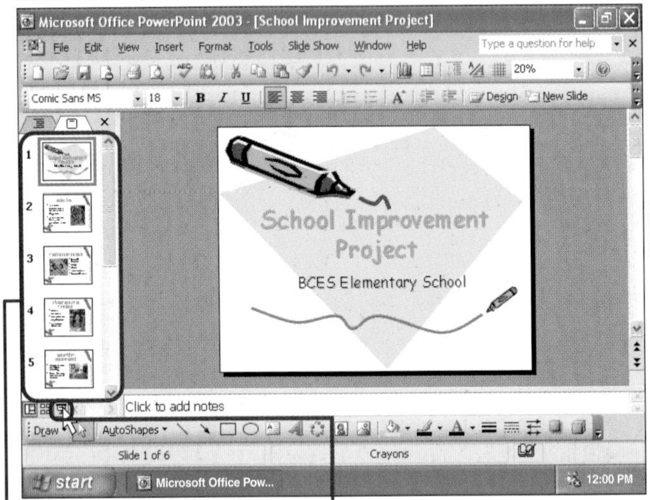

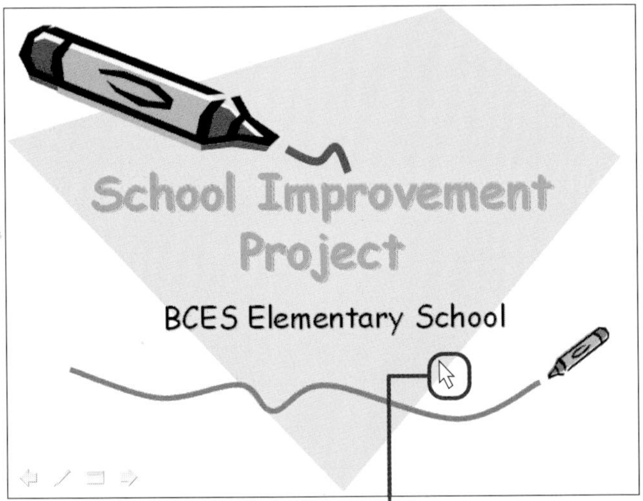

1 Click the first slide you want to view in the slide show.

2 Click the slide show button to start the slide show.

■ The slide you selected fills your screen.

Note: You can press the **Esc** *key to end the slide show at any time.*

3 To display the next slide, click anywhere on the current slide.

Tip

How can I use my keyboard to move through a slide show?

Task:	**Press this key:**
Display the next slide	Spacebar
Display the previous slide	Backspace
Display any slide	Type the number of the slide and then press Enter
End the slide show	Esc
Pause the slide show and turn the screen black	B (Press B again to return to the slide show)
Pause the slide show and turn the screen white	W (Press W again to return to the slide show)

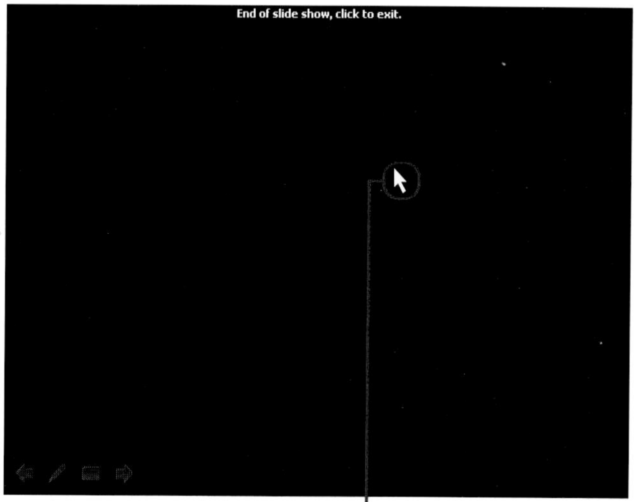

■ The next slide appears.

■ To return to the previous slide, press the Backspace key.

4 Repeat step **3** until this screen appears, indicating you have reached the end of the slide show.

5 Click the screen to exit the slide show.

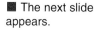

CREATE NOTES

You can create notes that include the ideas you want to discuss for each slide in your presentation. You can use your notes as a guide when delivering your presentation.

Notes can include statistics and information that you may need to refer to when answering questions from the audience.

CREATE NOTES

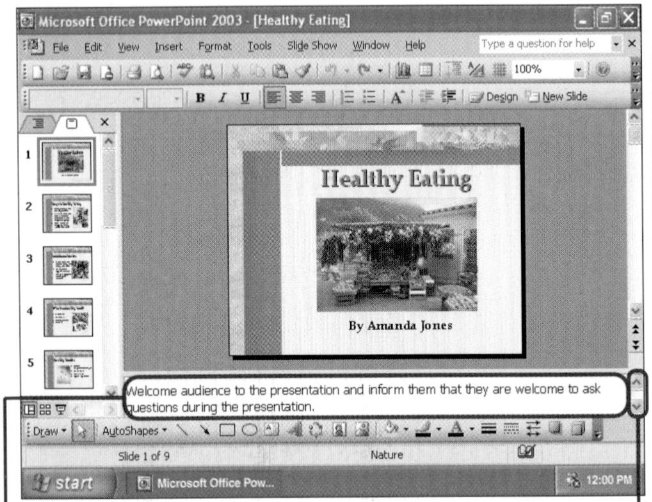

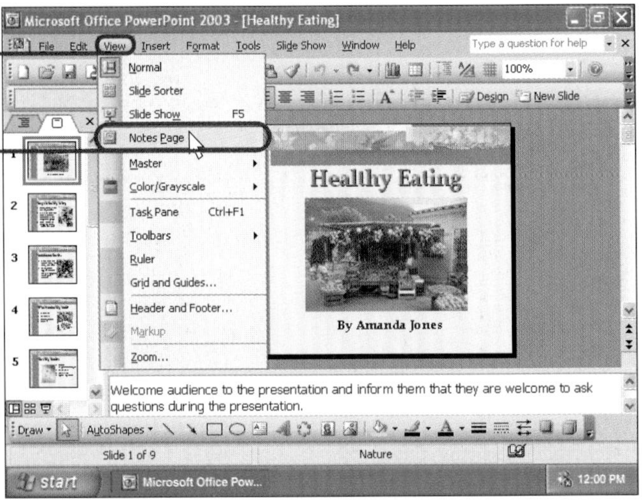

USING THE NORMAL VIEW

1 Display the slide you want to create notes for.

2 Click this area and then type the notes for the slide.

■ If you type more than one line of text, you can use the scroll bar to browse through the text.

USING NOTES PAGES

1 Click **View**.

2 Click **Notes Page** to display your notes pages.

Note: If Notes Page does not appear on the menu, position the mouse over the bottom of the menu to display the menu option.

Tip

When using the Normal view to create notes, how do I increase the size of the notes area?

To increase the size of the notes area in the Normal view, position the mouse I over the top border of the area (I changes to ÷) and then drag the border up to a new location.

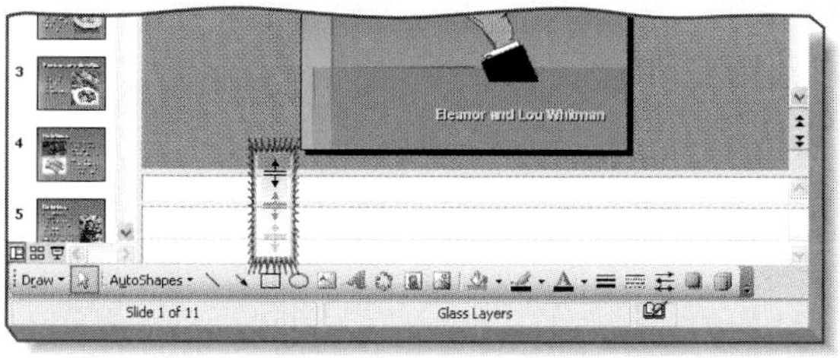

Tip

Can I print my notes pages?

You can print your notes pages so you will have a paper copy of the notes to refer to while delivering your presentation. Printing notes pages is also useful if you want to use the pages as handouts to help your audience follow your presentation. For information on printing notes pages, see page 230.

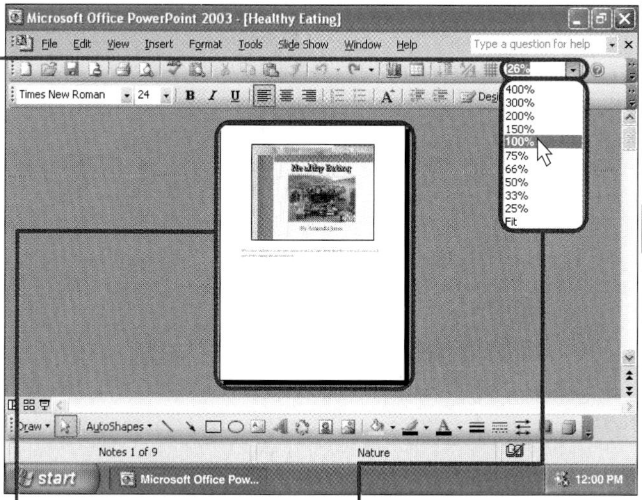

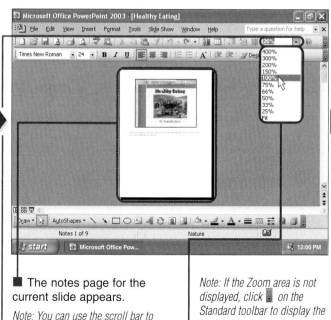

■ The notes page for the current slide appears.

Note: You can use the scroll bar to view the notes pages for other slides.

3 To magnify the notes page so you can clearly view the notes, click ▾ in this area.

Note: If the Zoom area is not displayed, click ▾ on the Standard toolbar to display the area.

4 Click the magnification you want to use.

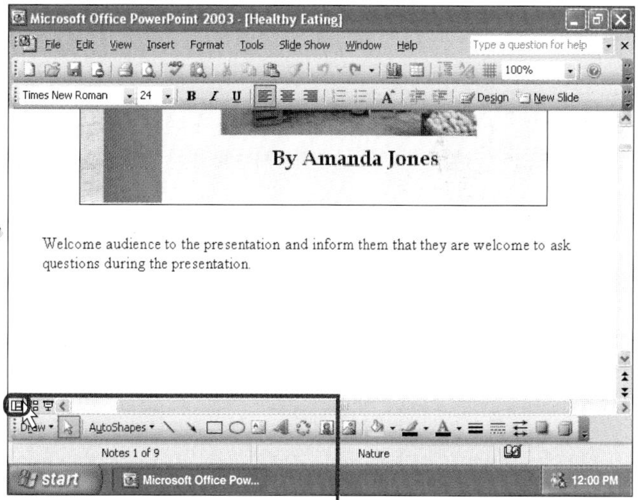

■ The notes page appears in the new magnification.

■ You can edit and format the notes page as you would any text in your presentation.

*Note: To once again display the entire notes page, repeat steps **3** and **4**, selecting **Fit** in step **4**.*

5 When you finish reviewing your notes pages, click ▣ to return to the Normal view.

PREVIEW A PRESENTATION BEFORE PRINTING

You can use the Print Preview feature to see how your presentation will look when printed. Using this feature allows you to confirm your presentation will print the way you want.

You can choose the part of your presentation you want to preview, such as the slides, handouts, notes pages or outline.

PREVIEW A PRESENTATION BEFORE PRINTING

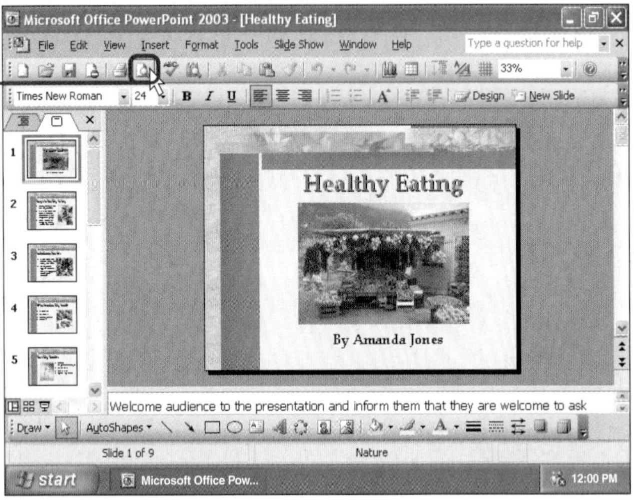

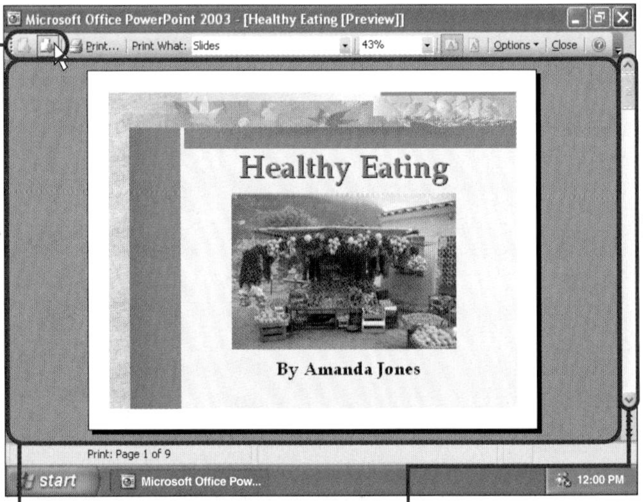

1 Click to preview your presentation before printing.

Note: If is not displayed, click on the Standard toolbar to display the button.

■ The Print Preview window appears.

■ This area displays a preview of the slide that will appear on the first printed page.

2 To view the slides that will appear on the other printed pages, click one of the following buttons.

Display previous page

Display next page

■ You can also use the scroll bar to view the slides that will appear on other printed pages.

Tip

How do I magnify an area of a page I am previewing?

Position the mouse over the area you want to magnify (changes to) and then click the area to display a magnified view of the area. To once again display the entire page, you can click anywhere on the page.

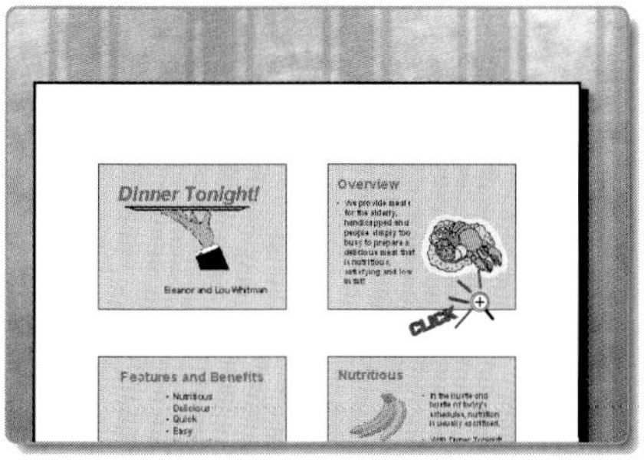

Tip

How do I quickly print my presentation while working in the Print Preview window?

You can click the Print button (Print...) to quickly print the presentation you are previewing.

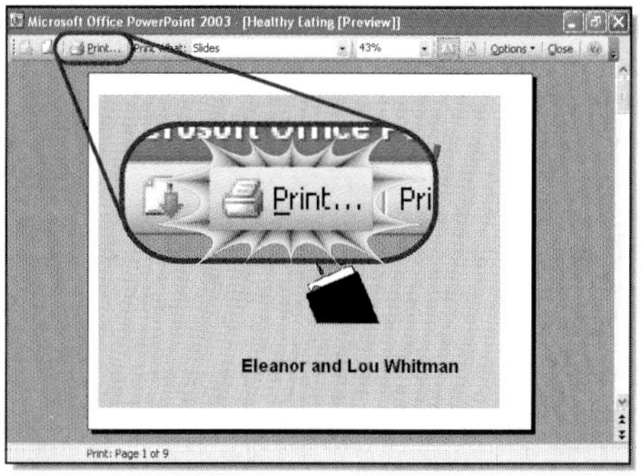

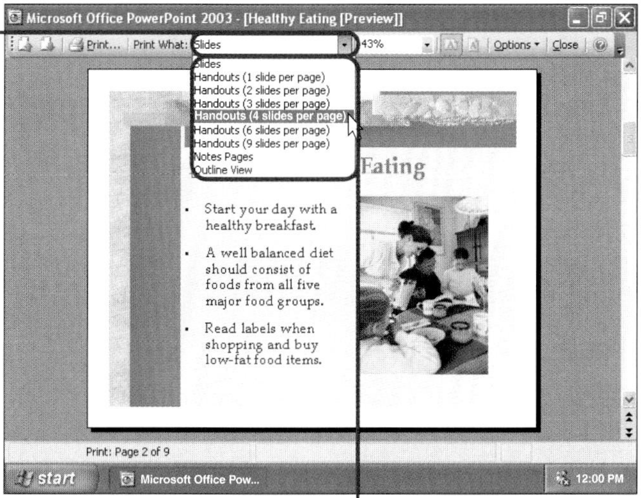

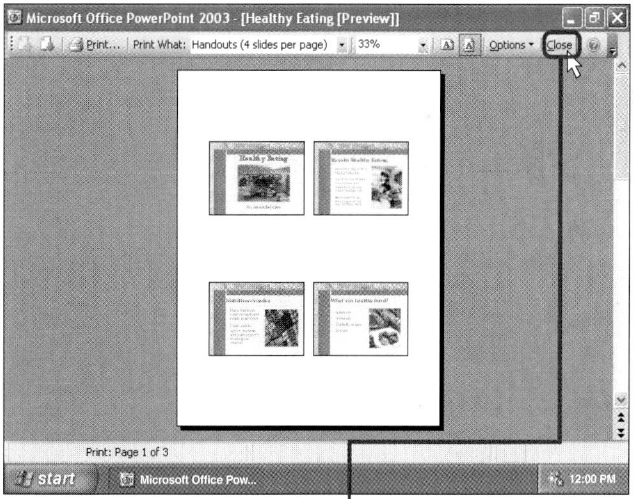

3 To preview a different part of your presentation before printing, click this area.

4 Click the part of the presentation you want to preview. For information on the parts of your presentation that you can print, see the top of page 231.

■ A preview of the part of the presentation you selected appears.

5 When you finish previewing your presentation, click **Close** to close the Print Preview window.

PRINT A PRESENTATION

You can produce a paper copy of a presentation for your own use or to hand out to your audience.

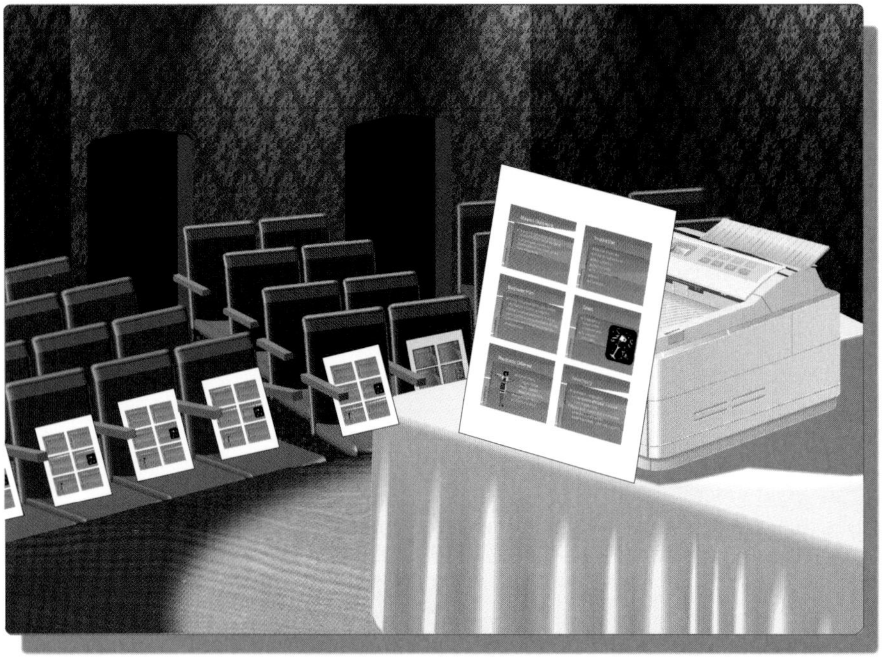

Before printing your presentation, make sure your printer is turned on and contains paper.

PRINT A PRESENTATION

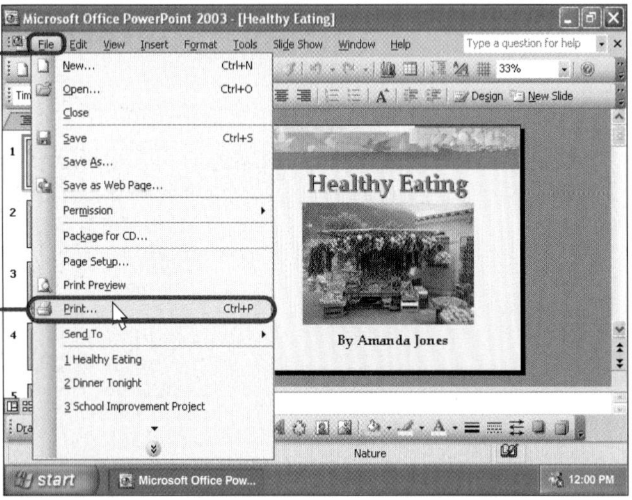

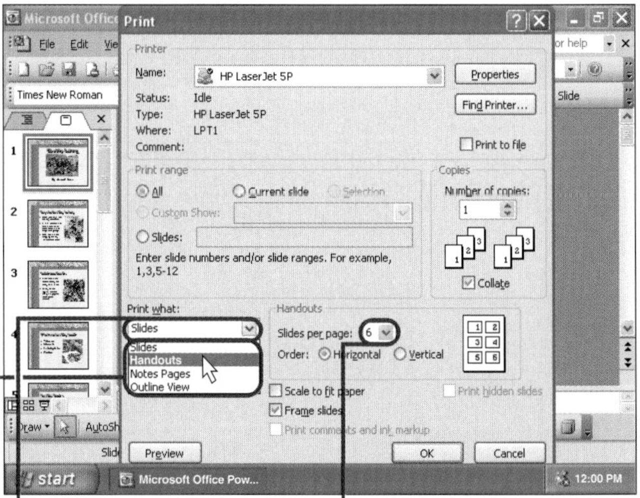

1 Click **File**.

2 Click **Print**.

■ The Print dialog box appears.

3 Click this area to select the part of the presentation you want to print.

4 Click the part of the presentation you want to print.

Note: For information on the available options, see the top of page 231.

■ If you selected **Handouts** in step **4**, you can click this area to change the number of slides that will print on each page.

Tip

What parts of my presentation can I print?

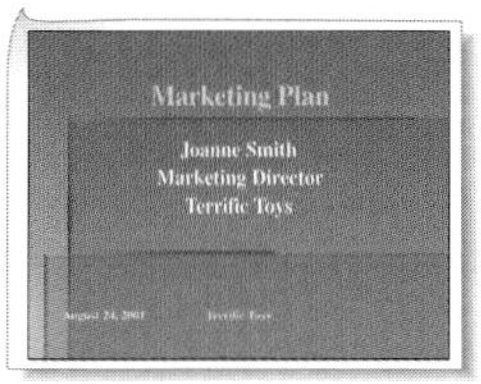

Slides

Prints one slide on each page. This is useful when you are printing transparencies for an overhead projector.

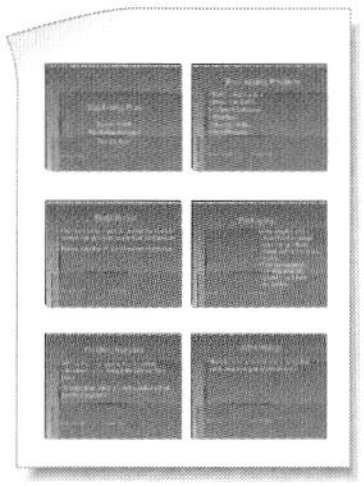

Handouts

Prints one or more slides on each page. You can give handouts to your audience to help them follow your presentation.

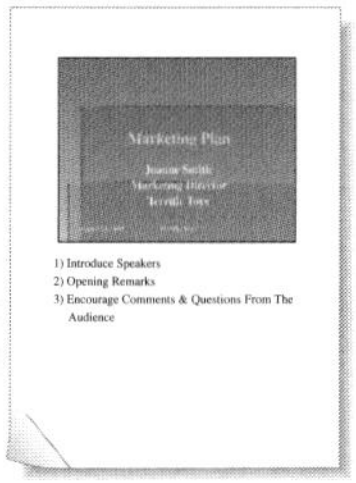

Notes Pages

Prints one slide and any notes you added to the slide on each page. You can use notes pages as a guide when delivering your presentation. To add notes to your slides, see page 226.

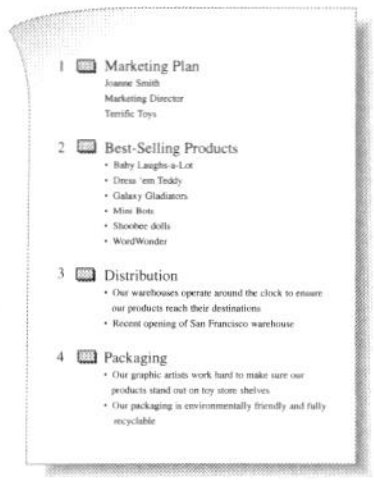

Outline View

Prints the text displayed in the Outline view of your presentation. For information on the Outline view, see page 174.

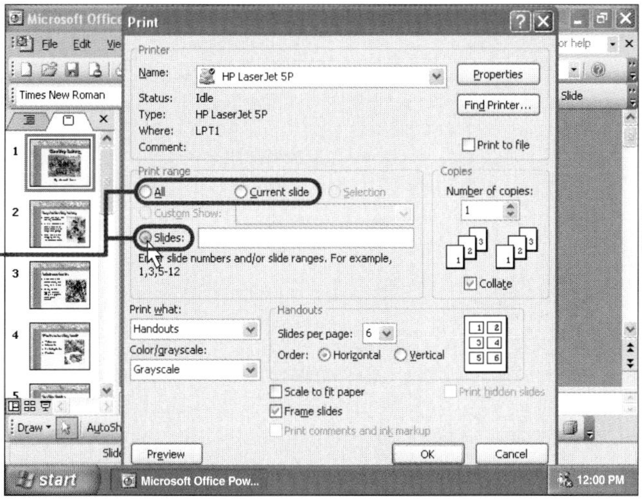

5 Click an option to specify which slides you want to print (◯ changes to ◉).

All - Print every slide in your presentation.

Current slide - Print the slide displayed on your screen.

Slides - Print the slides you specify.

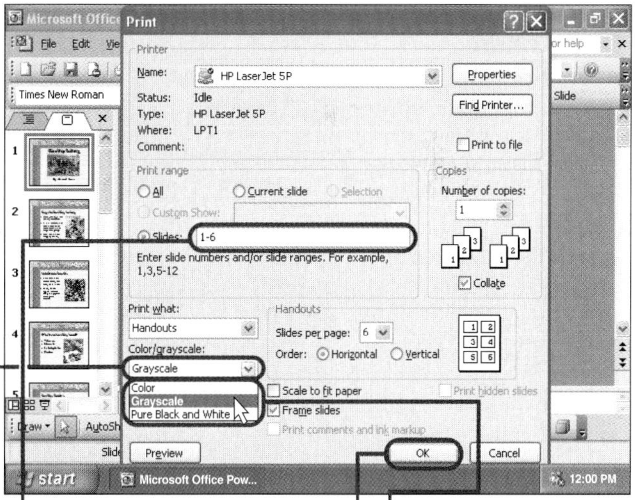

6 If you selected **Slides** in step **5**, type the numbers of the slides you want to print in this area (example: 1,2,4 or 1-4).

7 Click this area to specify if you want to print your slides in color, grayscale or pure black and white.

8 Click the way you want to print the slides.

9 Click **OK** to print your presentation.

PACKAGE YOUR PRESENTATION ONTO A CD

You can package your presentation onto a CD and transport it to another computer.

PowerPoint packages your presentation and all the files associated with the presentation, such as picture files. PowerPoint then compresses, or squeezes, the entire presentation to make the presentation easier to transport.

When the CD containing the presentation is inserted into a drive on another computer, the presentation will automatically play as a fullscreen slide show.

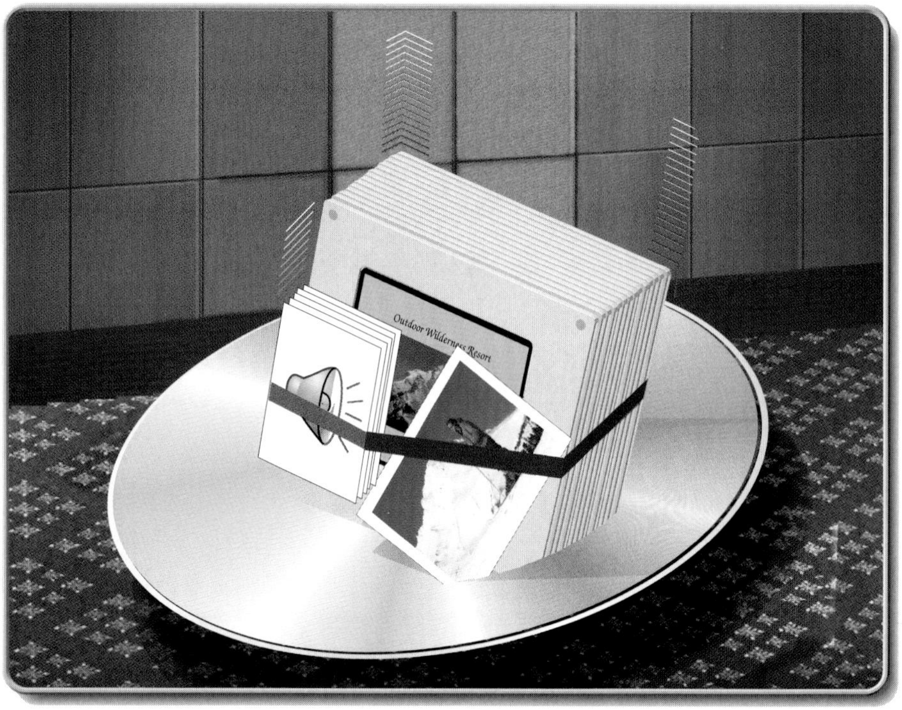

PACKAGE YOUR PRESENTATION ONTO A CD

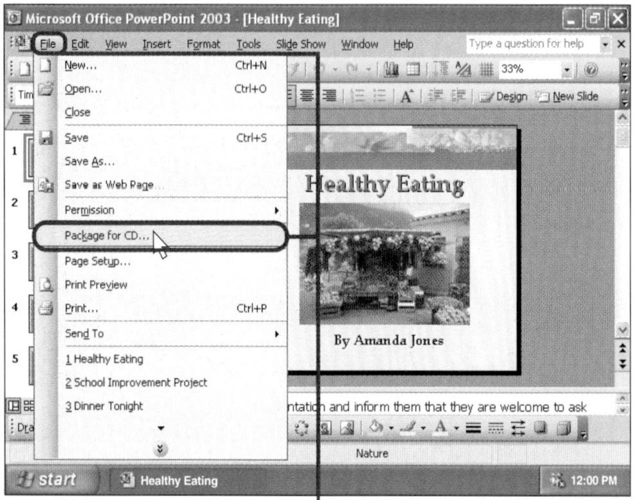

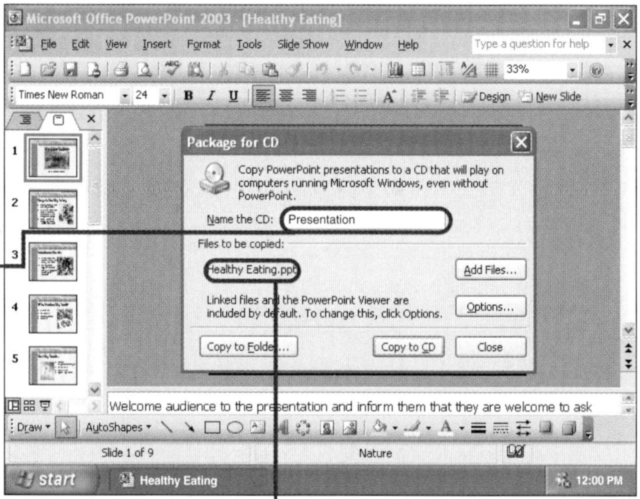

1 Insert a CD-R or CD-RW disc into your recordable CD drive.

*Note: When you insert a CD, a dialog box appears, asking what you want Windows to do. Click **Cancel** to close the dialog box.*

2 Open the presentation you want to package and transport to another computer. To open a presentation, see page 172.

3 Click **File**.

4 Click **Package for CD**.

■ The Package for CD dialog box appears.

5 Type a name for the CD you will store the presentation on.

■ This area displays the name of the presentation you will copy to the CD.

Note: Files associated with the presentation, such as picture files, are automatically included with the presentation. The PowerPoint Viewer is also included, so you can display the presentation on a computer that does not have PowerPoint installed.

Tip

What type of CD can I use?

You can package your presentation onto a recordable CD, such as a blank CD-R (Compact Disc-Recordable), a blank CD-RW (Compact Disc-ReWritable) or a CD-RW disc with existing data on the disc. You can copy a presentation onto a CD-R disc only once. A CD-RW disc allows you to copy a presentation onto the disc many times. However, if you use a CD-RW disc with existing data, PowerPoint will ask you to erase the existing data before you package your presentation onto the disc.

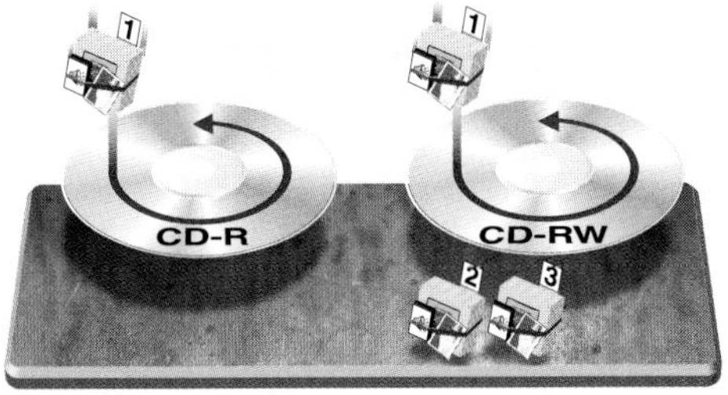

Tip

Why can't I copy my presentation directly onto a CD?

If you are not using Windows XP, you may need to package your presentation to a specific location on your computer and then use the software that came with your recordable CD drive to copy the presentation onto a CD.

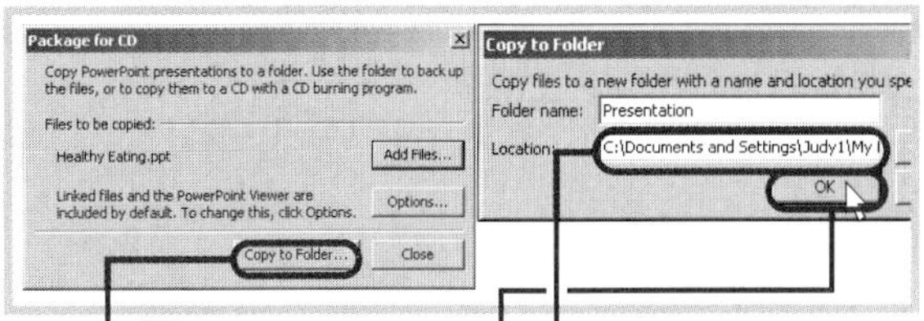

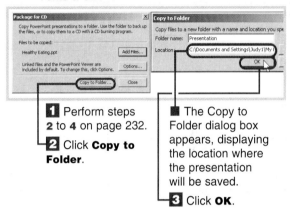

1 Perform steps **2** to **4** on page 232.

2 Click **Copy to Folder**.

■ The Copy to Folder dialog box appears, displaying the location where the presentation will be saved.

3 Click **OK**.

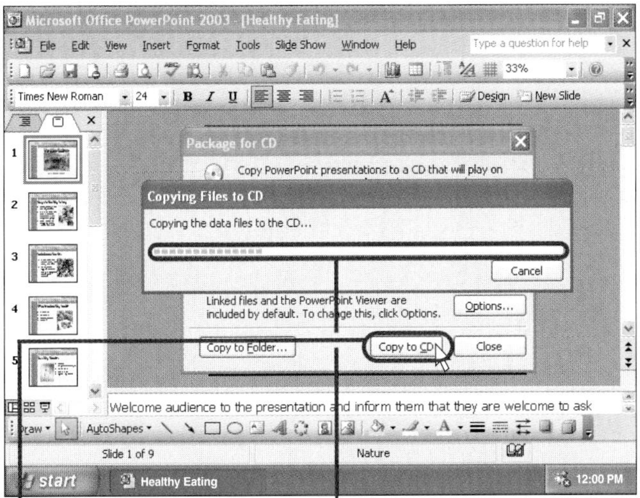

6 Click **Copy to CD** to package the presentation onto the CD.

■ The Copying Files to CD dialog box appears.

■ This area displays the progress of copying the files.

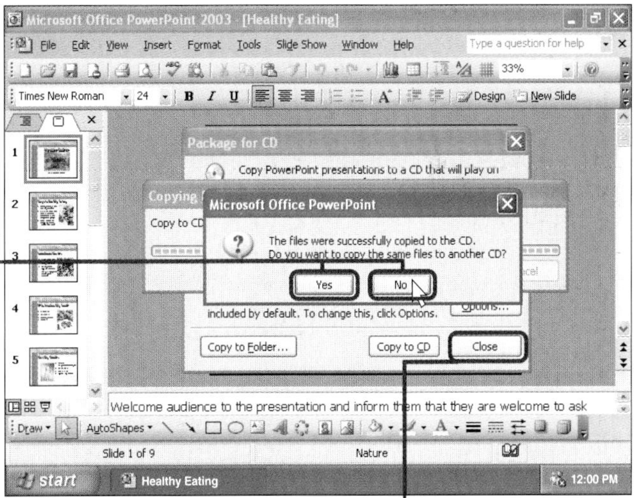

■ A dialog box appears when PowerPoint has successfully copied the files to the CD.

7 Click **No** to close the dialog box.

■ If you want to copy the same files to another CD, click **Yes** and then insert a CD into the drive.

8 Click **Close** to close the Package for CD dialog box.

Note: When you insert the CD into a CD drive on another computer, the presentation will automatically begin playing.

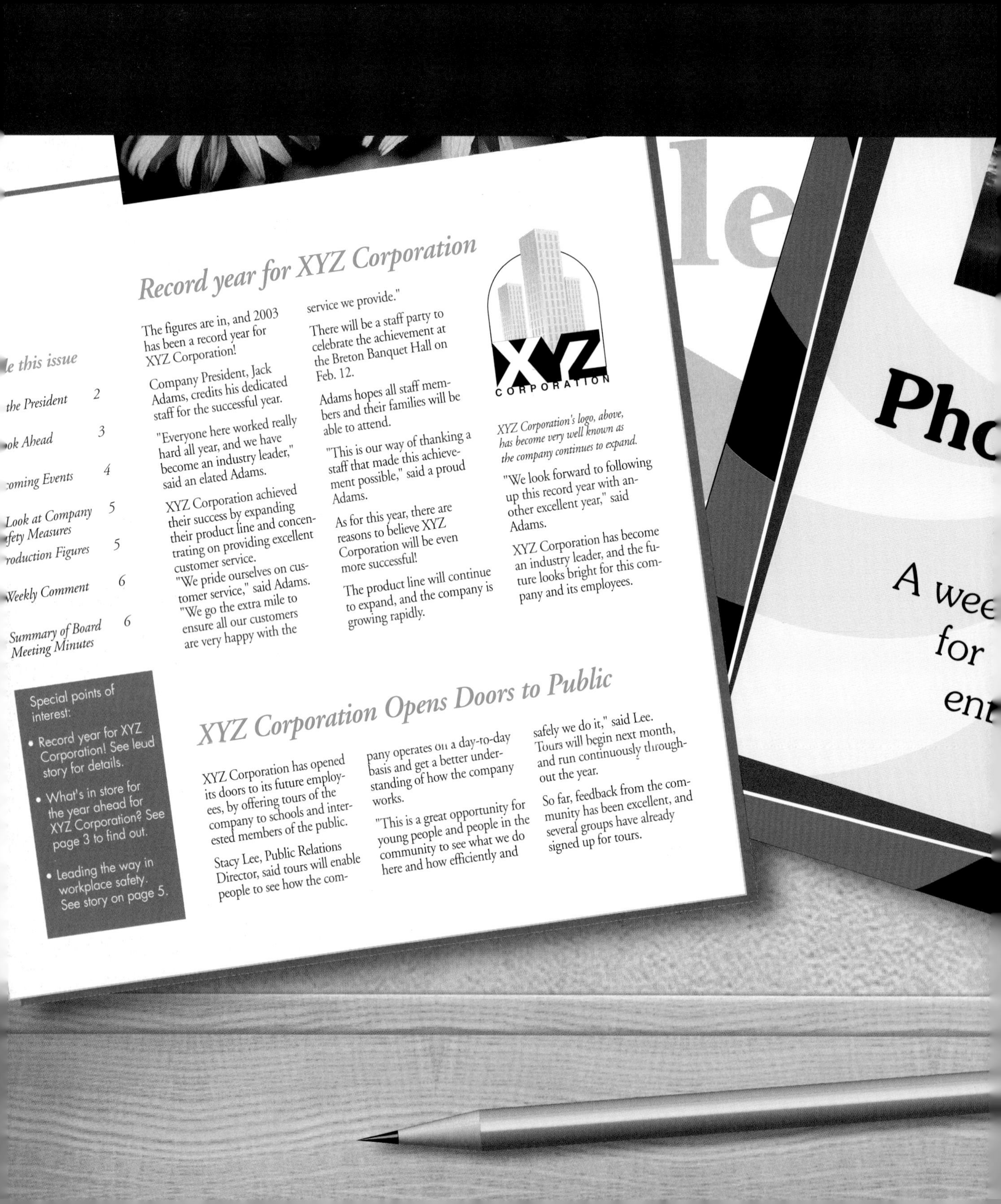

Record year for XYZ Corporation

The figures are in, and 2003 has been a record year for XYZ Corporation!

Company President, Jack Adams, credits his dedicated staff for the successful year.

"Everyone here worked really hard all year, and we have become an industry leader," said an elated Adams.

XYZ Corporation achieved their success by expanding their product line and concentrating on providing excellent customer service.
"We pride ourselves on customer service," said Adams.
"We go the extra mile to ensure all our customers are very happy with the service we provide."

There will be a staff party to celebrate the achievement at the Breton Banquet Hall on Feb. 12.

Adams hopes all staff members and their families will be able to attend.

"This is our way of thanking a staff that made this achievement possible," said a proud Adams.

As for this year, there are reasons to believe XYZ Corporation will be even more successful!

The product line will continue to expand, and the company is growing rapidly.

XYZ CORPORATION

XYZ Corporation's logo, above, has become very well known as the company continues to expand.

"We look forward to following up this record year with another excellent year," said Adams.

XYZ Corporation has become an industry leader, and the future looks bright for this company and its employees.

le this issue

Special points of interest:

- Record year for XYZ Corporation! See lead story for details.
- What's in store for the year ahead for XYZ Corporation? See page 3 to find out.
- Leading the way in workplace safety. See story on page 5.

XYZ Corporation Opens Doors to Public

XYZ Corporation has opened its doors to its future employees, by offering tours of the company to schools and interested members of the public.

Stacy Lee, Public Relations Director, said tours will enable people to see how the company operates on a day-to-day basis and get a better understanding of how the company works.

"This is a great opportunity for young people and people in the community to see what we do here and how efficiently and safely we do it," said Lee.
Tours will begin next month, and run continuously throughout the year.

So far, feedback from the community has been excellent, and several groups have already signed up for tours.

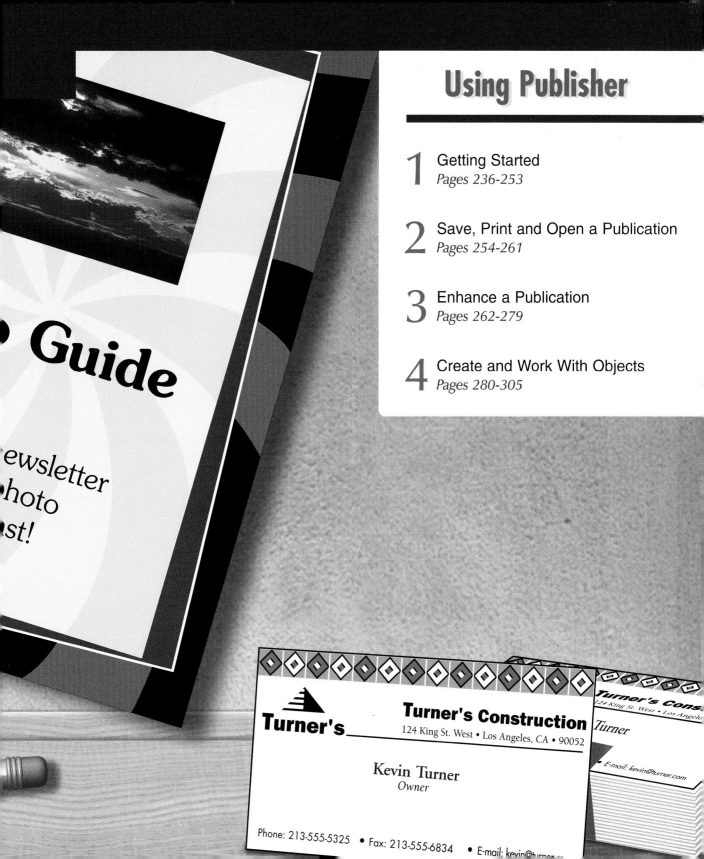

Using Publisher

Publisher is a desktop publishing program you can use to create professionally designed publications that combine text and graphics.

A document created in Publisher is called a publication.

Creating Publications

You can use Publisher to create a wide variety of publications, such as advertisements, business cards, calendars, invitation cards, labels, newsletters and resumes. You can even create publications you can display on the Web or send in e-mail messages. Publisher provides the layout and formatting for publications so you can concentrate on the content of your publications.

Enhance Publications

Publisher offers many ways to improve the appearance of your publications. You can change the font, size, alignment and color of text in a publication. You can also add a background color or pattern to a page. Publisher can also find design problems that you may not have noticed in a publication.

Adding Objects to Publications

Publisher allows you to add many types of objects to enhance your publications. You can add pictures stored on your computer, professionally designed clip art images, AutoShapes, WordArt and tables. You can also add special design gallery objects, such as borders, calendars and coupons, to your publications.

PARTS OF THE PUBLISHER WINDOW

The Publisher window displays many items that allow you to create and work with your publications.

Title Bar
Shows the name of the displayed publication.

Menu Bar
Provides access to lists of commands available in Publisher and displays an area where you can type a question to get help information.

Standard Toolbar
Contains buttons that allow you to select common commands, such as Save and Print.

Formatting Toolbar
Contains buttons that allow you to select common formatting commands, such as Bold and Italic.

Connect Text Boxes Toolbar
Contains buttons that allow you to create and work with connected text boxes. When text boxes are connected, text that will not fit in the first text box will flow into the next connected text box.

Objects Toolbar
Contains buttons that allow you to add objects, such as tables and pictures, to a publication.

Task Pane
Contains options you can select to perform common tasks, such as creating a new publication.

Rulers
Help you align objects in a publication.

Workspace
Displays the publication you are currently working with.

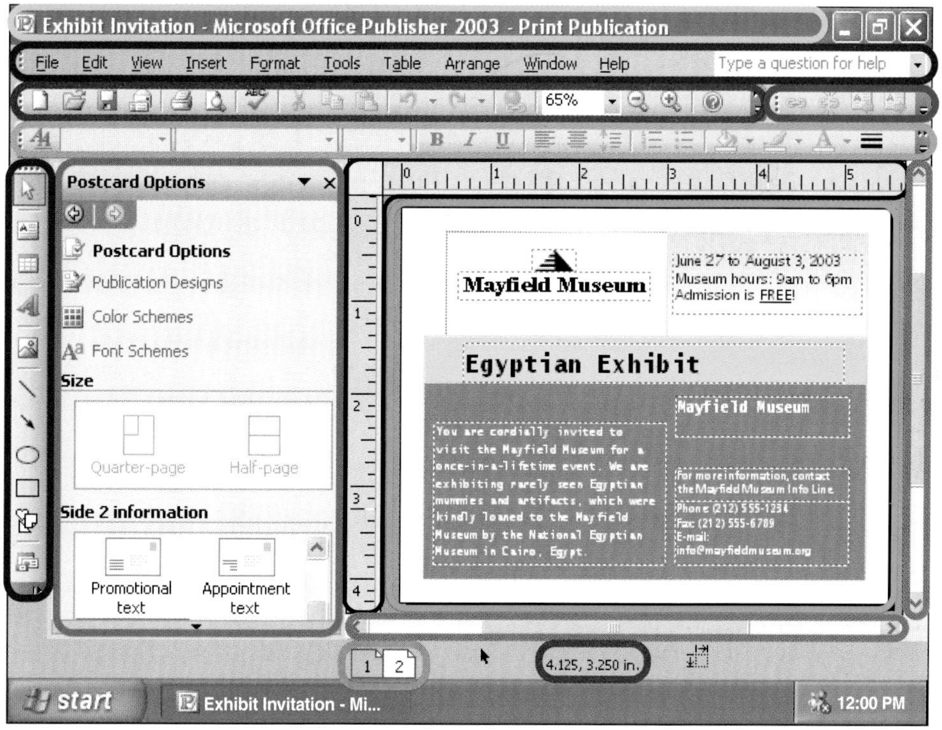

Scroll Bars
Allow you to move through the current page in a publication.

Page Icons
Allow you to switch between the pages in a publication.

Object Position
Displays the position of a selected object or the mouse pointer from the left and top edges of the current page, in inches.

CREATE A PUBLICATION

You can quickly and easily create a professionally designed publication.

Publisher provides the layout and formatting for most types of publications so you can concentrate on the content of your publications.

CREATE A PUBLICATION

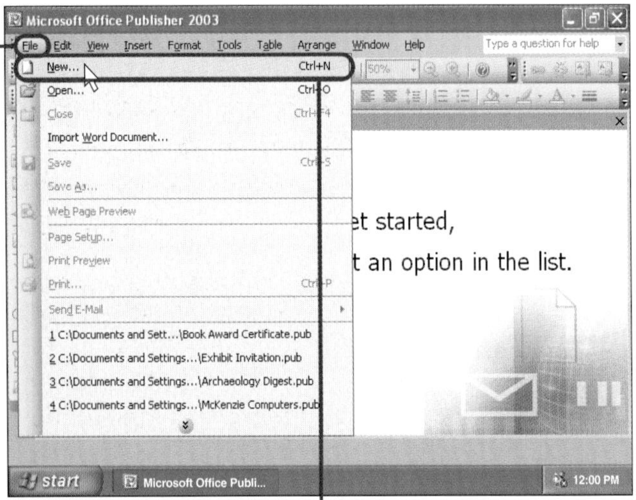

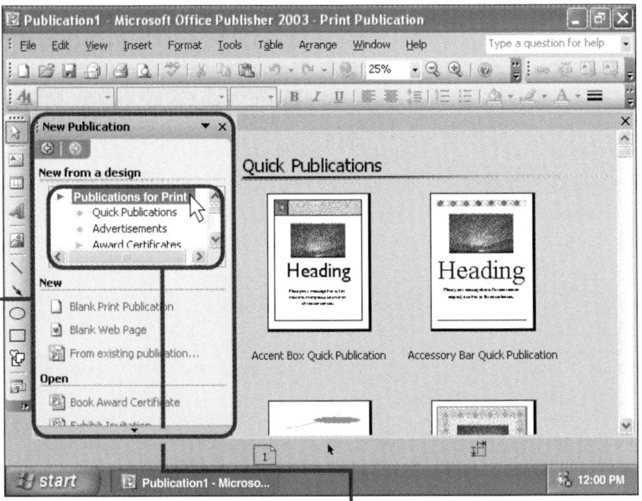

1 Click **File**.

2 Click **New**.

■ The New Publication task pane appears.

Note: The New Publication task pane also appears each time you start Publisher.

3 Click the category that best describes the type of publication you want to create.

Tip

What types of publications can I create?

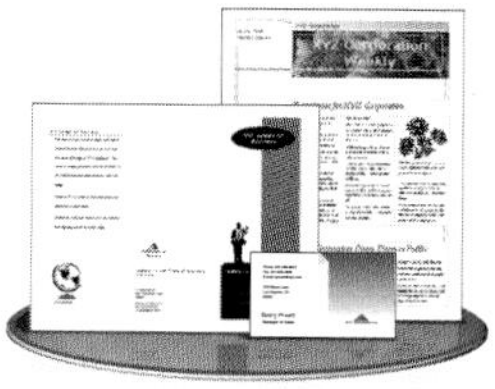

Publications for Print

Creates publications you can print, such as advertisements, brochures, business cards, calendars, invitation cards, labels, newsletters and resumes.

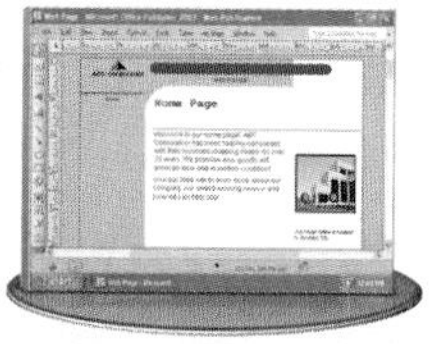

Web Sites and E-mail

Creates publications you can display on the Web or send in e-mail messages.

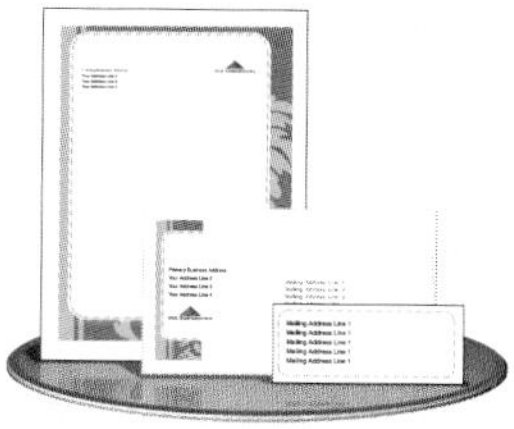

Design Sets

Creates publications that have a similar design. For example, the Personal Stationery Sets allows you to create an address label, envelope and letterhead that display the same design.

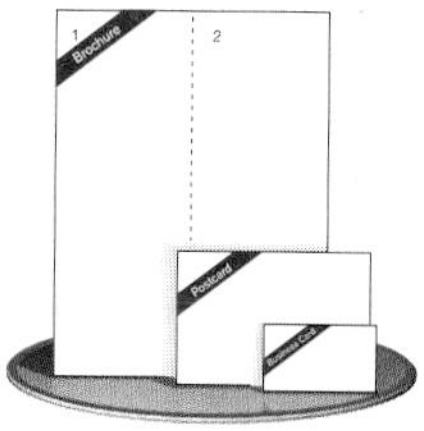

Blank Publications

Creates blank publications so you can produce and design the publication yourself.

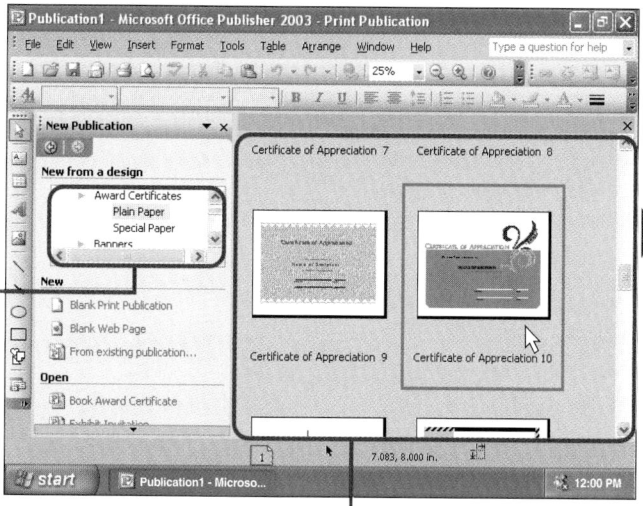

■ A list of the types of publications in the category appears.

4 Click the type of publication you want to create.

5 If another list of publication types appears, click a type of publication in the list.

■ This area displays the available designs for the type of publication you selected. You can use the scroll bar to browse through the designs.

6 Click the design you want to use.

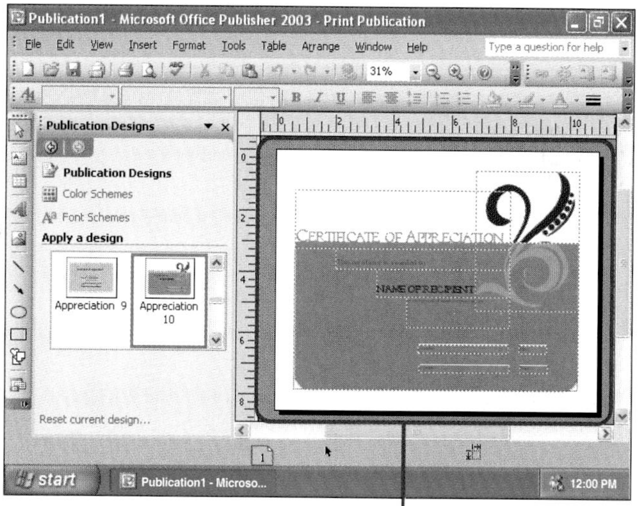

■ Publisher creates the publication.

Note: The first time you create a publication, the Personal Information dialog box appears, asking you to provide personal information. Publisher automatically adds this information to your publications. Enter the information and then click ***OK*** *to close the dialog box.*

■ This area displays a page in the publication.

■ You can replace the sample text and pictures in the publication with your own text and pictures.

ZOOM IN OR OUT

You can enlarge or reduce the display of a publication on your screen.

You can increase the zoom setting to view an area of your publication in more detail or decrease the zoom setting to view more of your publication at once.

ZOOM IN OR OUT

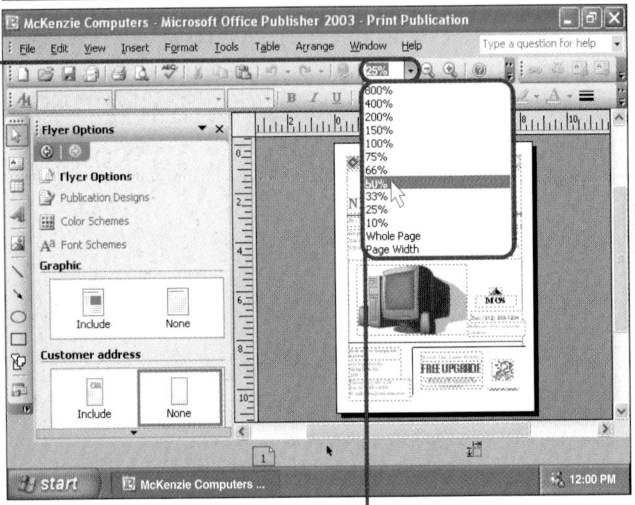

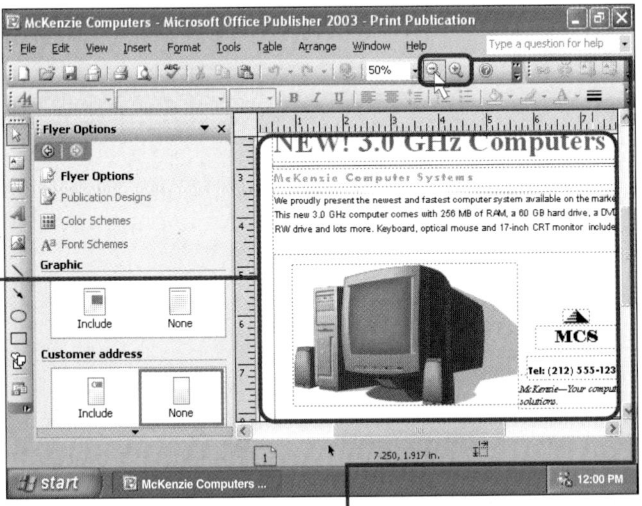

1 Click in this area to display a list of zoom settings.

2 Click the zoom setting you want to use.

*Note: You can also select an object before performing steps **1** and **2** to enlarge the selected object to fill the workspace. To select an object, click the object.*

■ The publication appears in the new zoom setting. You can edit the publication as usual.

■ To once again display the entire page, repeat steps **1** and **2**, selecting **Whole Page** in step **2**.

QUICKLY ZOOM IN OR OUT

1 You can click these buttons to quickly zoom out ( ) or zoom in ( ).

MOVE THROUGH PAGES

If your publication contains more than one page, you can easily display the contents of another page.

MOVE THROUGH PAGES

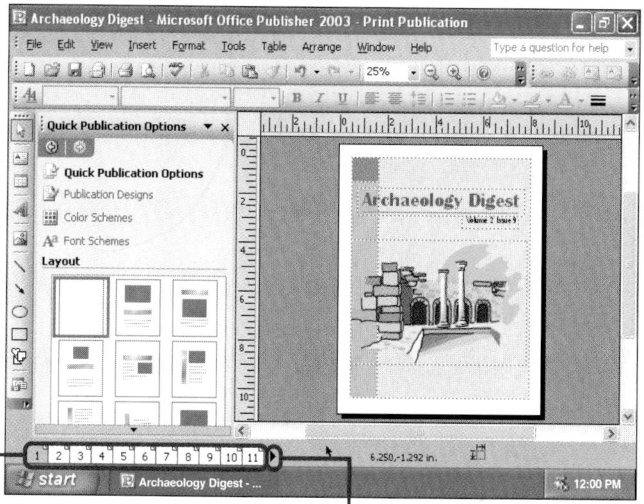

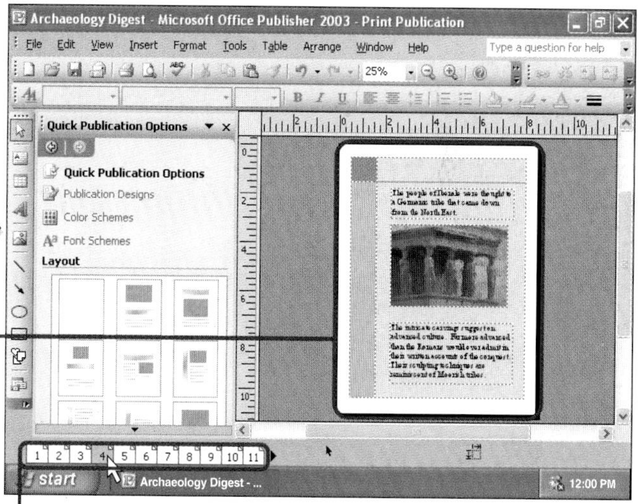

■ This area displays an icon for each page in your publication. The icon for the current page is highlighted.

■ One or two arrows (◀, ▶) appear if Publisher cannot show all the page icons. You can click an arrow to display the hidden page icons.

1 Click the icon for the page you want to view.

■ The page you selected appears.

Note: Two pages may appear on your screen if your publication has facing pages like those found in a book. Publications such as newsletters and catalogs often have facing pages.

ADD A NEW PAGE

You can add a new page to your publication to include additional information.

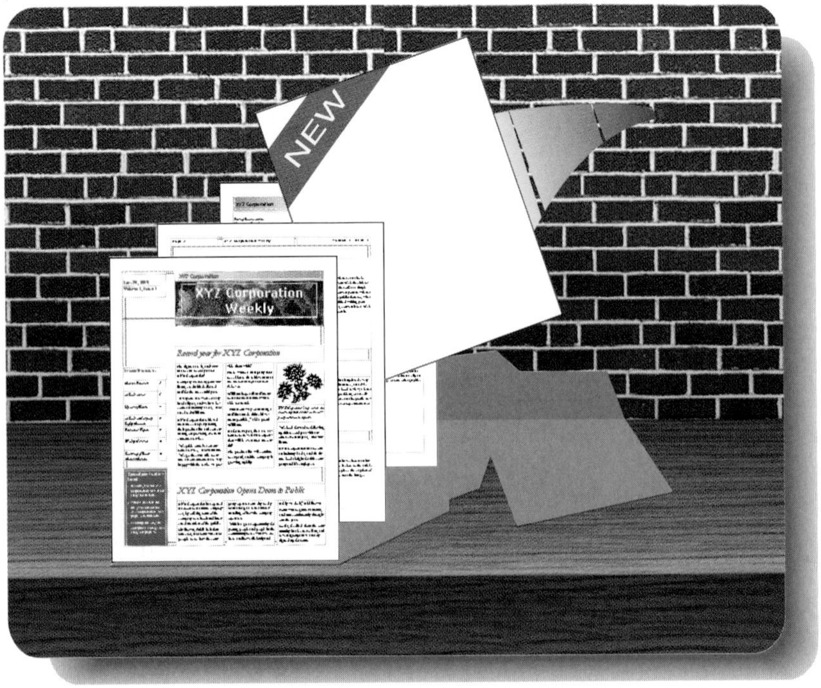

ADD A NEW PAGE

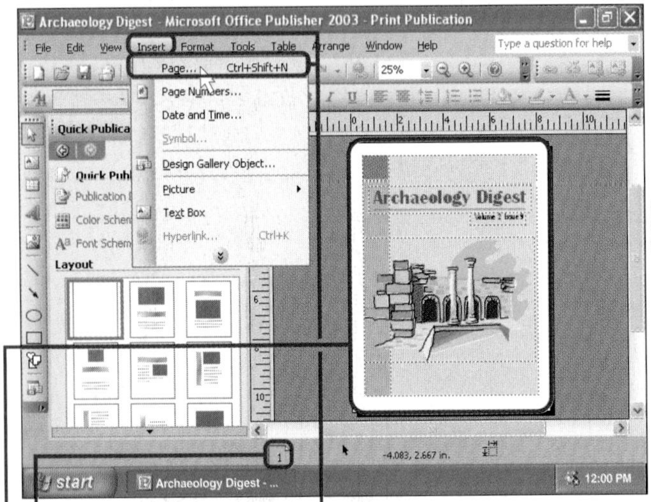

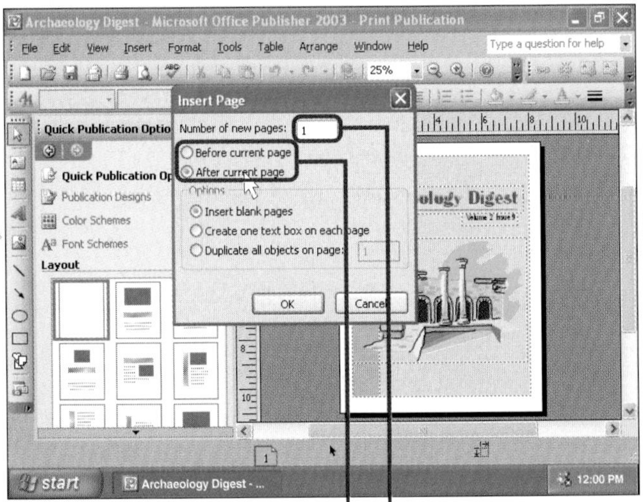

1 Click the icon for the page you want to appear before or after the new page.

■ This area displays the page you selected.

2 Click **Insert**.

3 Click **Page**.

■ The Insert Page dialog box appears.

Note: The dialog box may be different, depending on the type of publication you are working with. Publications such as catalogs, newsletters and Web sites display a different dialog box.

4 Double-click the number in this area and type the number of new pages you want to add.

5 Click an option to specify if you want to add the new page before or after the current page (○ changes to ◉).

Tip

Which option should I select when adding a new page?

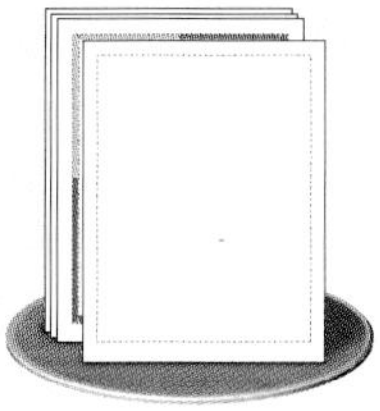

Insert blank pages

Adds a blank page to your publication so you can create all the content for the page yourself.

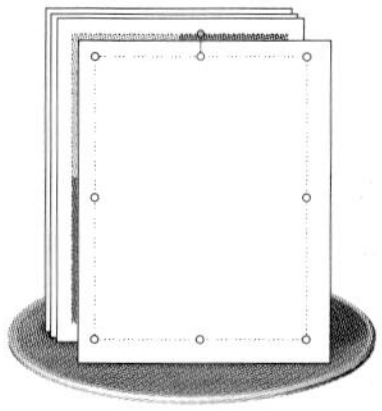

Create one text box on each page

Adds a page that contains a large text box so you can immediately start adding text to the page.

Duplicate all objects on page

Adds a page that displays all the objects shown on another page so you can quickly create a new page based on the content and appearance of an existing page.

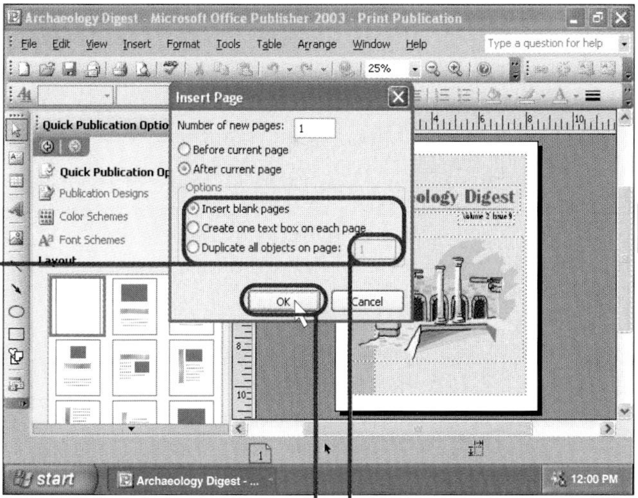

6 Click an option to add a blank page, add a page that contains one text box or add a page that displays all the objects shown on another page (○ changes to ◉).

7 If you selected **Duplicate all objects on page** in step **6**, double-click the number in this area and type the number of the page that contains the objects you want to duplicate.

8 Click **OK** to add the new page.

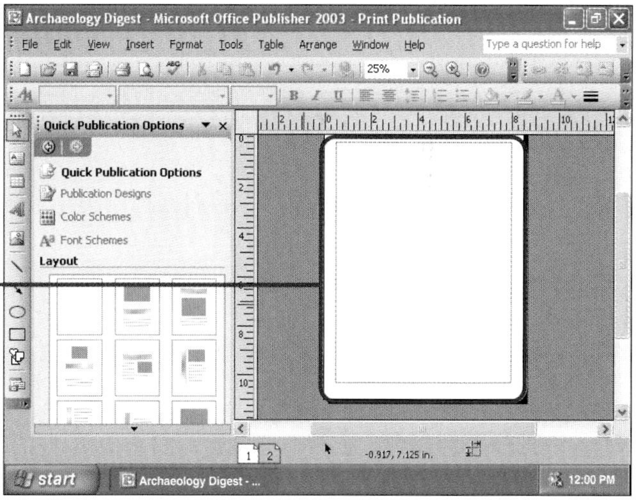

■ The new page appears in your publication.

MOVE A PAGE

You can change the order of the pages in your publication. Moving pages in a publication is useful when you want to reorganize information.

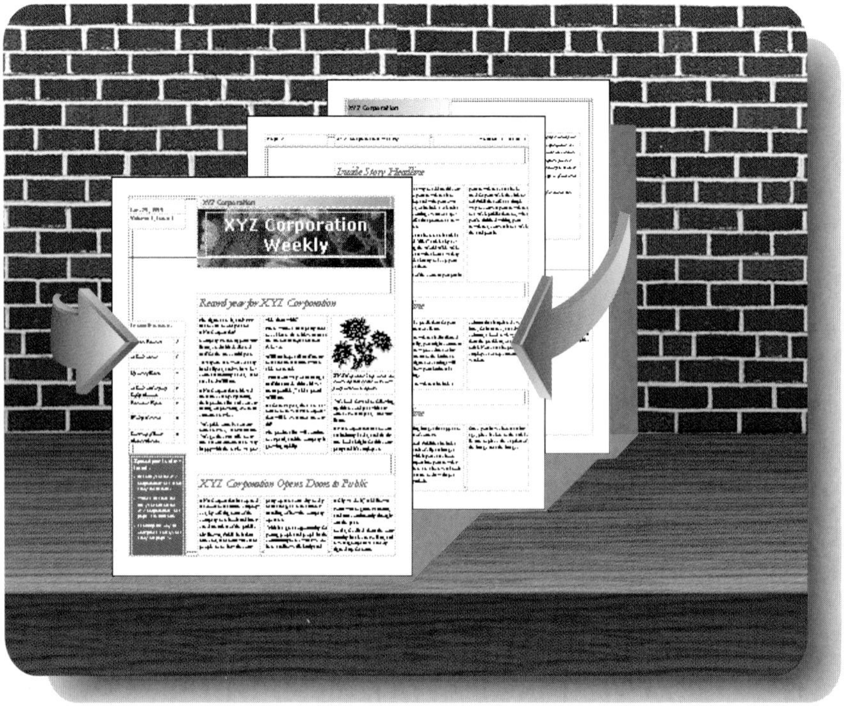

MOVE A PAGE

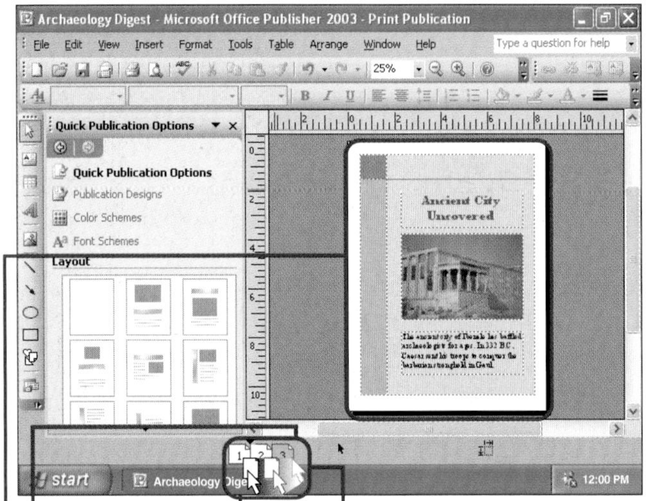

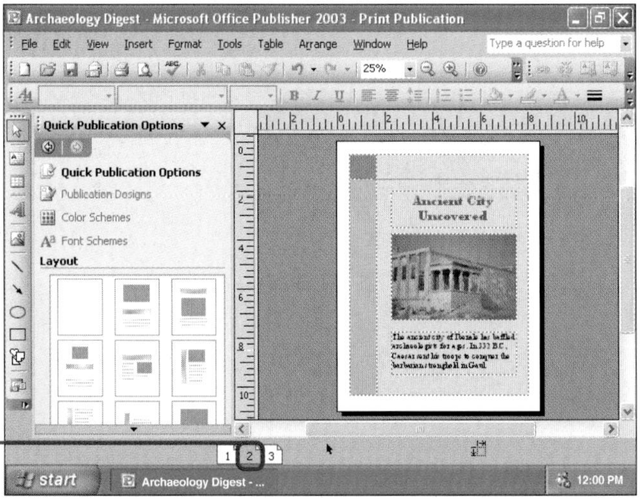

1 Click the icon for the page you want to move.

■ This area displays the page you selected.

2 To move the page, position the mouse ⇖ over the icon for the page.

3 Drag the icon for the page to a new location.

■ An arrow (▼) shows where the page will appear.

■ The page appears in the new location.

Note: If your publication has facing pages like those found in a book, you should move both pages of a two-page spread together.

DELETE A PAGE

You can delete a page you no longer want to include in your publication.

If your publication has facing pages like those found in a book, you should delete only an even number of pages. If you delete an odd number of pages, some pages which are right-hand pages will become left-hand pages and vice versa.

In publications that print pages in multiples of four, such as catalogs, you should delete pages in multiples of four.

DELETE A PAGE

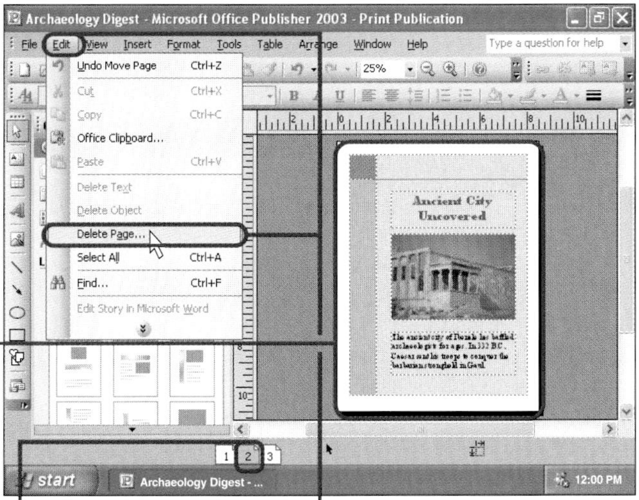

1 Click the icon for the page you want to delete.

■ This area displays the page you selected.

2 To delete the page, click **Edit**.

3 Click **Delete Page**.

Note: If Delete Page is not displayed, position the mouse over the bottom of the menu to display the option.

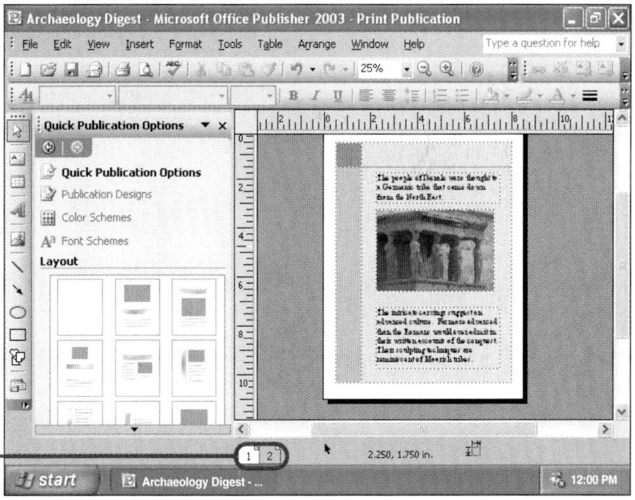

■ The page disappears from your publication.

■ Publisher renumbers the pages in your publication.

*Note: If your publication has facing pages like those found in a book, the Delete Page dialog box may appear. Click an option to delete both pages, only the left page or only the right page. Then click **OK**. If other dialog boxes appear, click **OK** to close the dialog boxes.*

UNDO CHANGES

Publisher remembers the last changes you made to your publication. If you regret these changes, you can cancel them by using the Undo feature.

The Undo feature cancels your changes in the order you made the changes, starting with the last change.

UNDO CHANGES

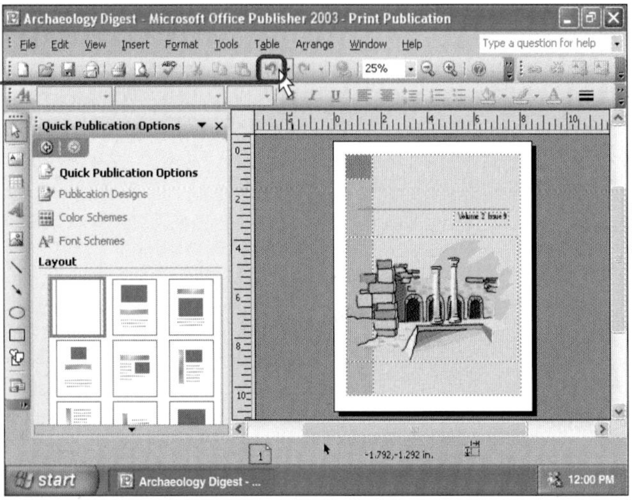

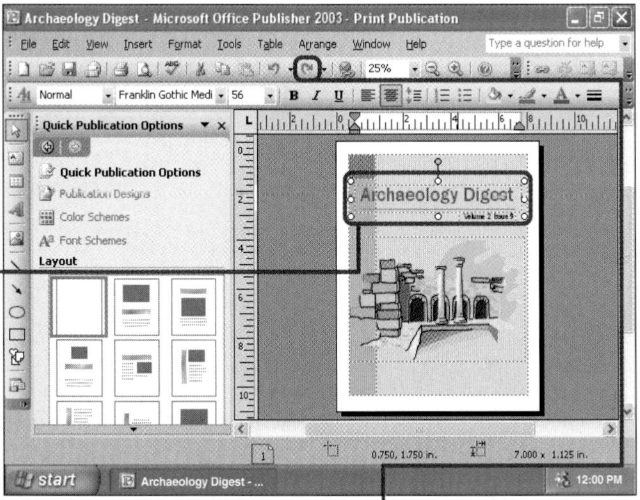

1 Click to undo the last change you made to your publication.

■ Publisher cancels the last change you made to your publication.

■ You can repeat step **1** to cancel previous changes you made.

■ To reverse the results of using the Undo feature, click .

SELECT TEXT

Before making changes to text in your publication, you must first select the text you want to work with. Selected text appears highlighted on your screen.

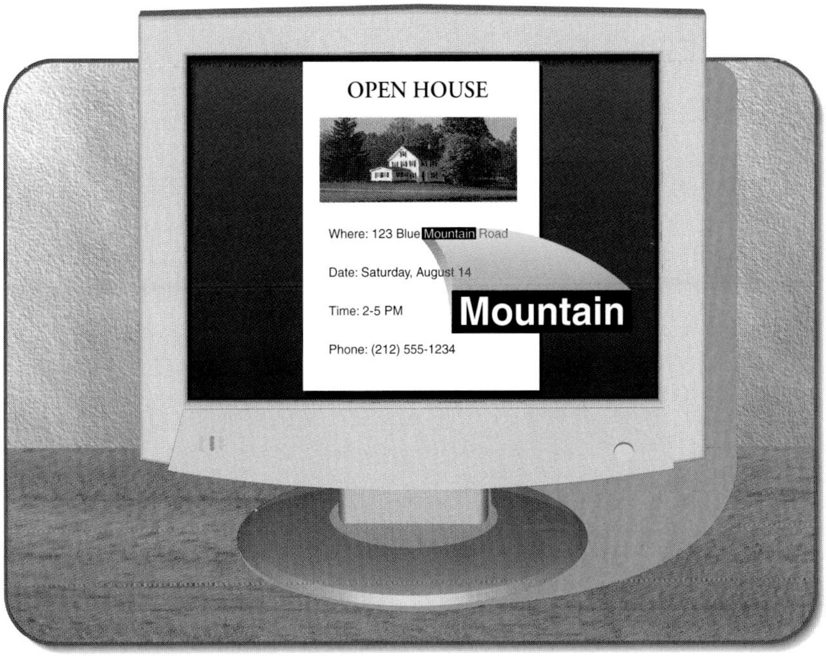

SELECT TEXT

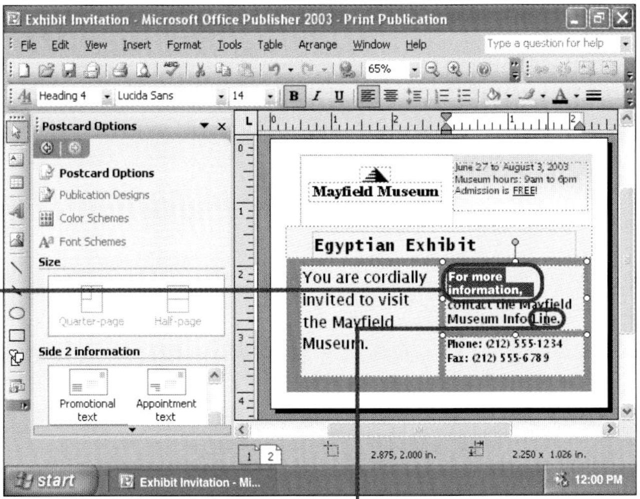

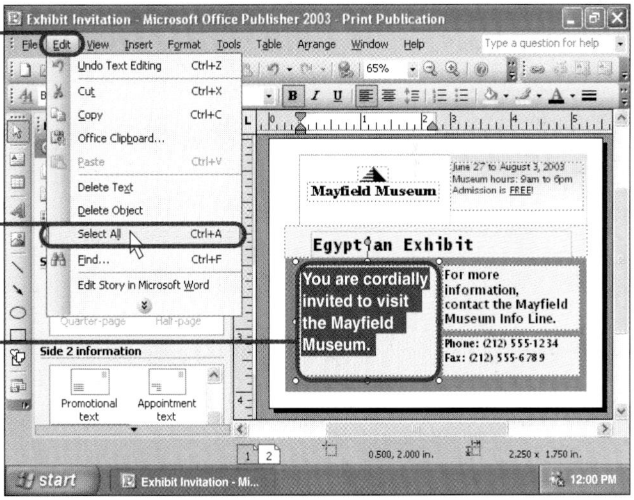

SELECT ANY AMOUNT OF TEXT

1 Position the mouse over the first word you want to select.

2 Drag the mouse over the text you want to select.

SELECT A WORD

1 Double-click the word you want to select.

SELECT ALL THE TEXT IN A TEXT BOX

1 Click anywhere in the text box that contains the text you want to select.

2 Click **Edit**.

3 Click **Select All**.

DESELECT TEXT

1 To deselect text, click outside the selected area.

CHECK SPELLING

You can find and correct all the spelling errors in your publication.

Publisher compares words in your publication to words in its dictionary. If a word does not exist in Publisher's dictionary, the word is considered misspelled.

Publisher will not find a correctly spelled word used in the wrong context, such as "We have been in business for **sit** years." You should carefully review your publication to find this type of error.

Publisher will not spell check words typed in UPPERCASE letters.

CHECK SPELLING

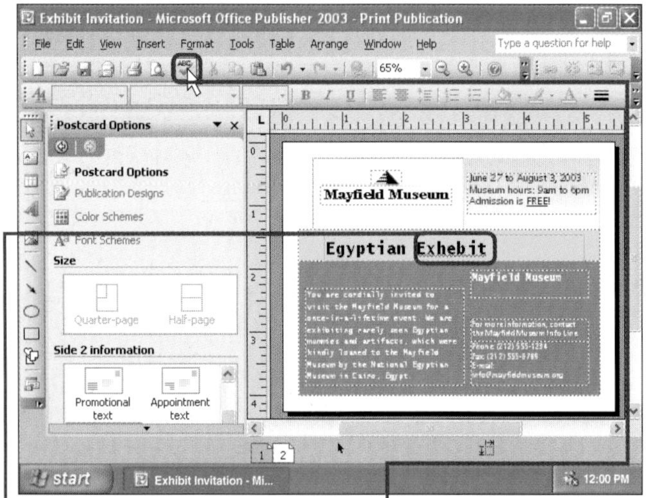

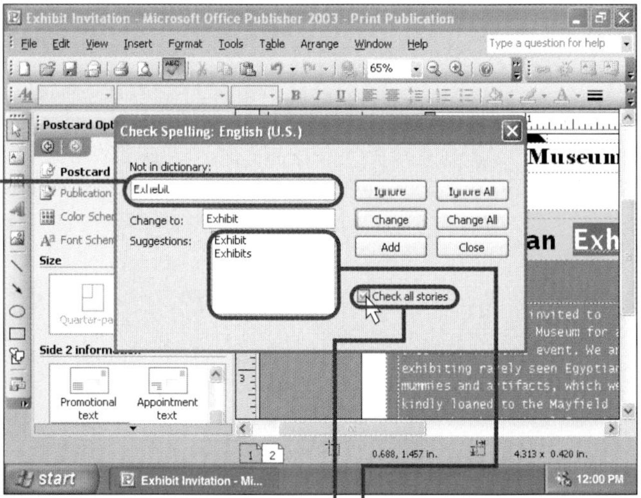

■ Publisher automatically underlines misspelled words in red. The underlines will not appear when you print your publication.

1 Click to spell check your publication.

■ To spell check only one text box in your publication, click inside the text box before performing step **1**.

■ The Check Spelling dialog box appears if Publisher finds a misspelled word in your publication.

■ This area displays the first misspelled word.

■ This area displays suggestions for correcting the word.

2 The **Check all stories** option spell checks your entire publication. You can click this option to turn the option on ( ) or off ( ).

Tip: Can Publisher automatically correct my typing mistakes?

Yes. Publisher automatically corrects common spelling and capitalization errors as you type. Here are a few examples.

adn	and
alot	a lot
comittee	committee
don;t	don't
nwe	new
occurence	occurrence
recieve	receive
seperate	separate
teh	the
THe	The
friday	Friday

Tip: How can I quickly correct a misspelled word in my publication?

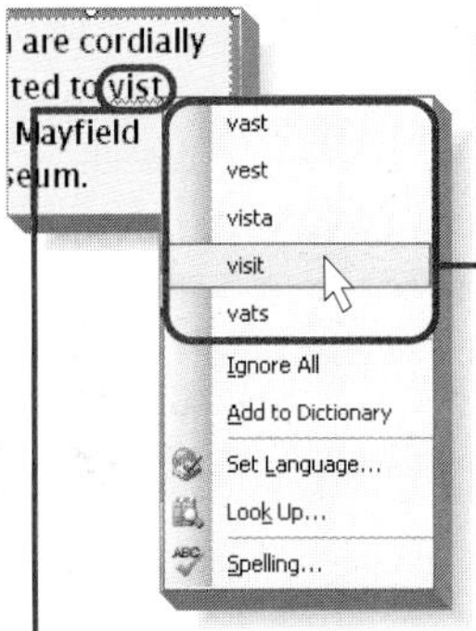

1 Right-click the misspelled word.

■ A menu appears with suggestions to correct the word.

2 Click the suggestion you want to use to correct the word.

Note: If you do not want to use any of the suggestions, click outside the menu to close the menu.

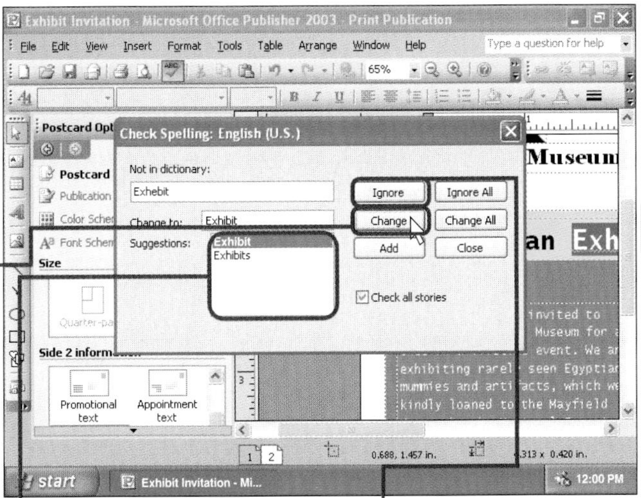

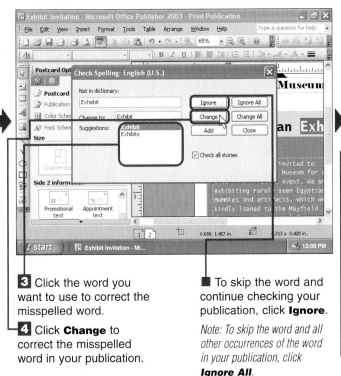

3 Click the word you want to use to correct the misspelled word.

4 Click **Change** to correct the misspelled word in your publication.

■ To skip the word and continue checking your publication, click **Ignore**.

*Note: To skip the word and all other occurrences of the word in your publication, click **Ignore All**.*

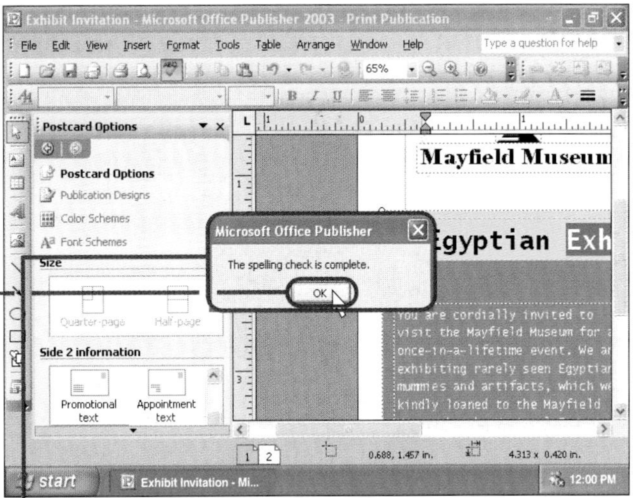

5 Correct or ignore misspelled words until this dialog box appears, telling you the spell check is complete.

6 Click **OK** to close the dialog box.

*Note: If you did not choose to spell check your entire publication in step **2**, a dialog box appears after Publisher finishes checking the current text box. You can click **Yes** or **No** to specify if you want to spell check the rest of your publication.*

FIND AND REPLACE TEXT

You can find and replace every occurrence of a word or phrase in your publication. This is useful if you have frequently misspelled a name or typed an incorrect product price.

FIND AND REPLACE TEXT

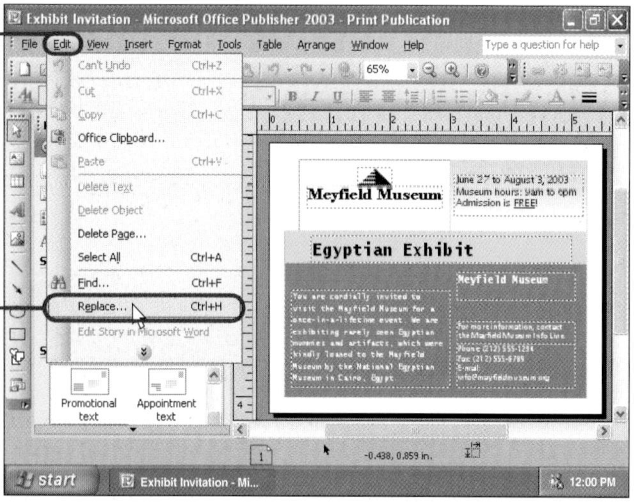

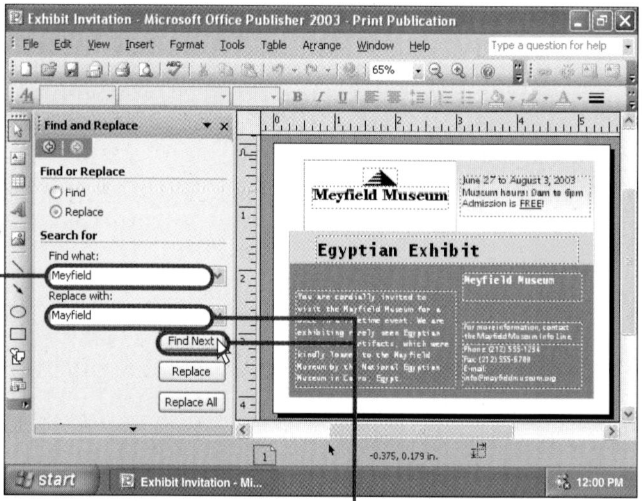

1 Click **Edit**.

2 Click **Replace**.

Note: If Replace is not displayed, position the mouse over the bottom of the menu to display the option.

■ The Find and Replace task pane appears.

3 Click this area and type the text you want to find.

4 Click this area and type the text you want to replace the text you typed in step **3**.

5 Click **Find Next** to start the search.

Tip

How can the Find and Replace feature help me quickly enter text?

You can type a short form of a word or phrase, such as UM, throughout a publication. You can then use the Find and Replace feature to replace the short form with the full word or phrase, such as University of Massachusetts.

Tip

Can I find text in my publication if I do not want to replace the text?

Yes. You can use the Find feature to locate a word or phrase in your publication. To find text in your publication, perform steps **1** to **3** below, except select **Find** in step **2**. Then perform step **5** until you find the text of interest.

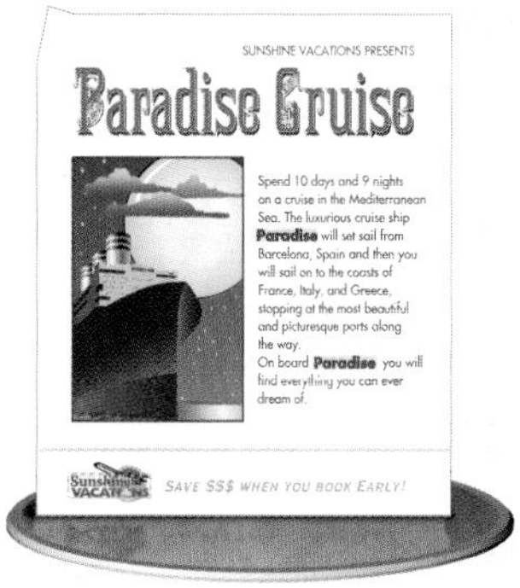

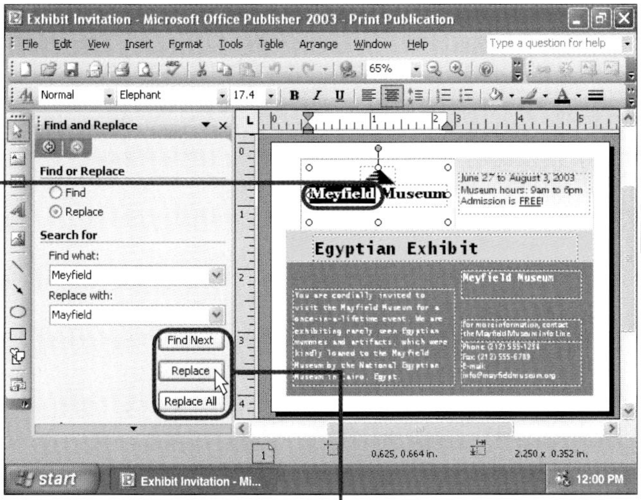

■ Publisher highlights the first matching text it finds.

Note: To zoom in on your publication so you can more clearly view the highlighted text, see page 240.

6 Click one of the following options.

Find Next to ignore the text.

Replace to replace the text with the text you specified.

Replace All to replace the text everywhere in your publication.

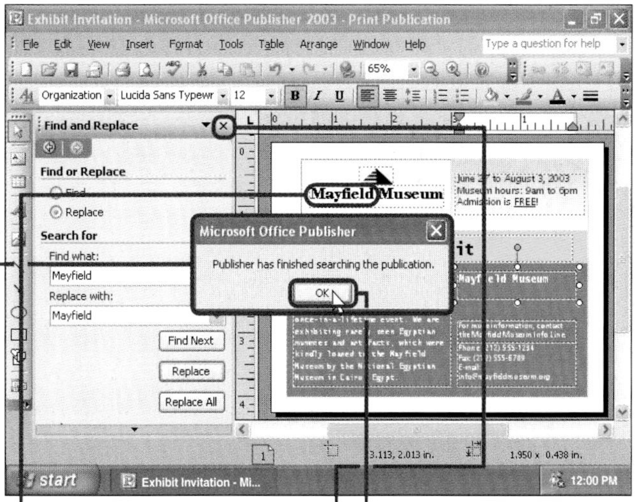

■ In this example, Publisher replaces the text and searches for the next matching text.

7 Ignore or replace matching text until a dialog box appears, telling you that Publisher has finished searching.

8 Click **OK** to close the dialog box.

9 When you finish finding and replacing text in your publication, click ☒ to close the Find and Replace task pane.

IMPORT TEXT FROM ANOTHER DOCUMENT

You can add text to your publication from a document you previously created.

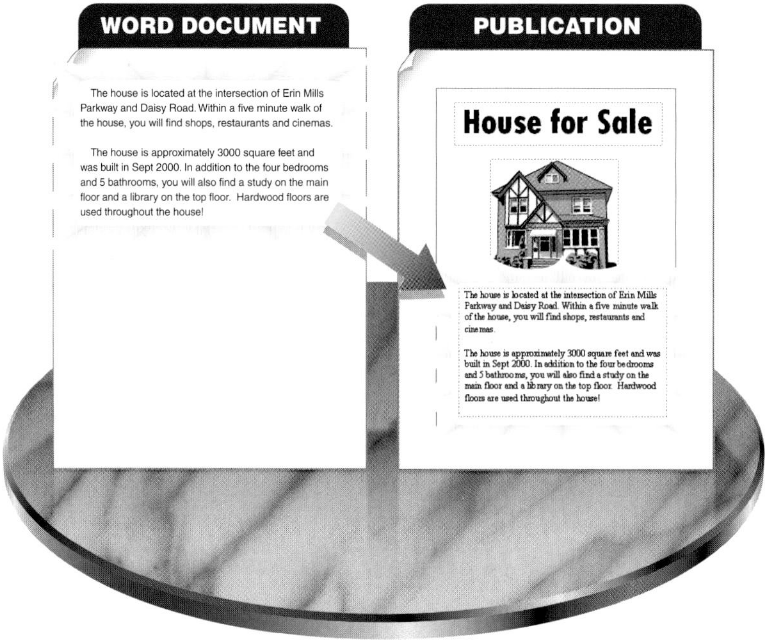

WORD DOCUMENT
PUBLICATION
The house is located at the intersection of Erin Mills Parkway and Daisy Road. Within a five minute walk of the house, you will find shops, restaurants and cinemas.
The house is approximately 3000 square feet and was built in Sept 2000. In addition to the four bedrooms and 5 bathrooms, you will also find a study on the main floor and a library on the top floor. Hardwood floors are used throughout the house!
House for Sale

Importing text from another document allows you to first create the text for your publication in a word processing program, such as Word. This lets you take advantage of a word processor's powerful editing features to create the text for your publication.

IMPORT TEXT FROM ANOTHER DOCUMENT

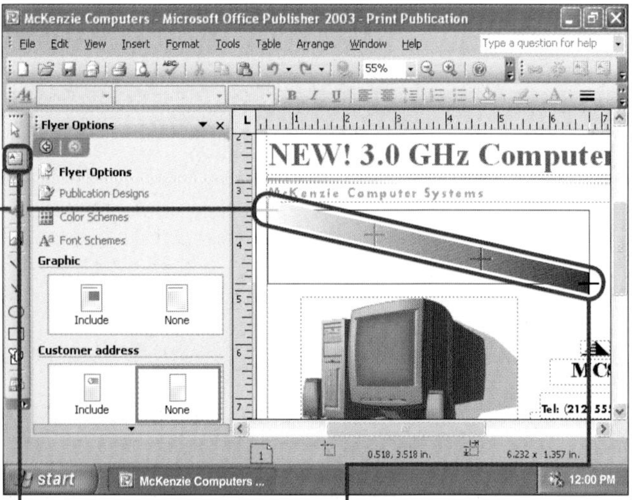

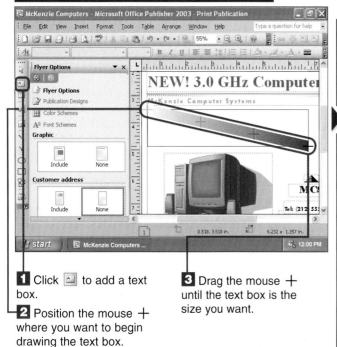

1 Click to add a text box.

2 Position the mouse + where you want to begin drawing the text box.

3 Drag the mouse + until the text box is the size you want.

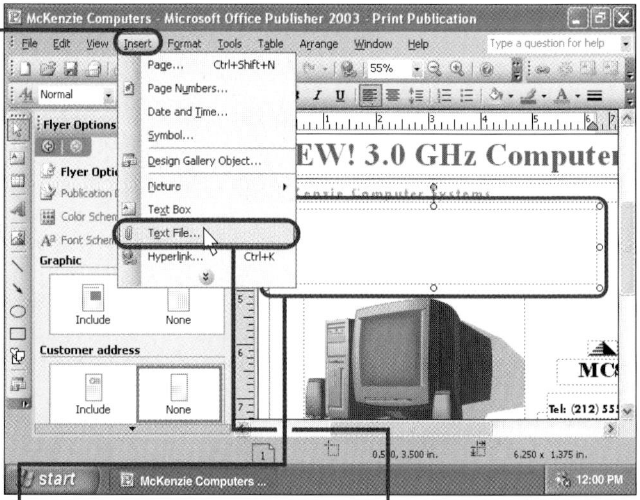

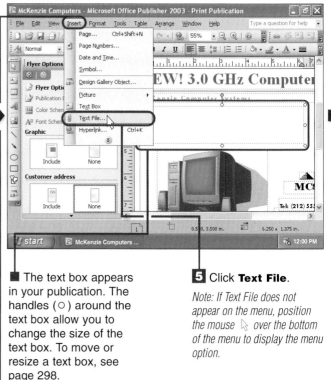

■ The text box appears in your publication. The handles (○) around the text box allow you to change the size of the text box. To move or resize a text box, see page 298.

4 Click **Insert**.

5 Click **Text File**.

Note: If Text File does not appear on the menu, position the mouse over the bottom of the menu to display the menu option.

Tip

What types of documents can I import text from?

You can import text from any text document on your computer, such as a document created in Word, WordPad or Notepad.

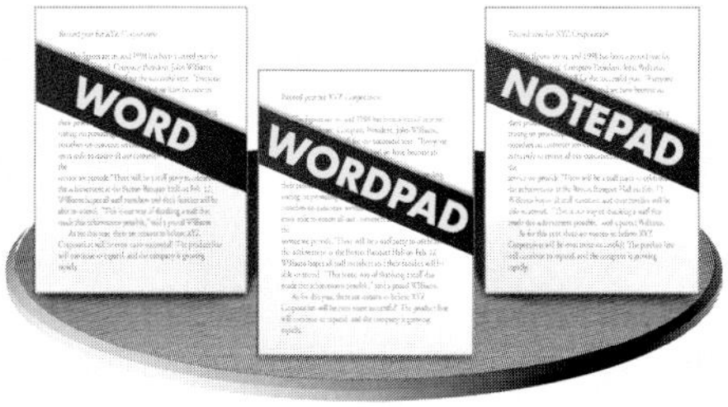

Tip

Why does a dialog box appear, asking if I want to use autoflow?

If the text you are importing from another document does not fit within the text box you created in your publication, Publisher asks if you want to use autoflow.

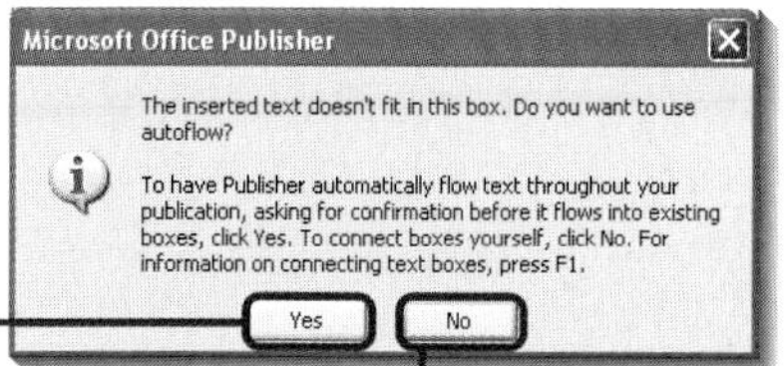

■ Click **Yes** to have Publisher create a new text box on a new page to display the extra text. Then follow the instructions on your screen.

■ Click **No** to close the dialog box without using autoflow. You can then create another text box to display the extra text and connect the text boxes. To connect text boxes, see page 292.

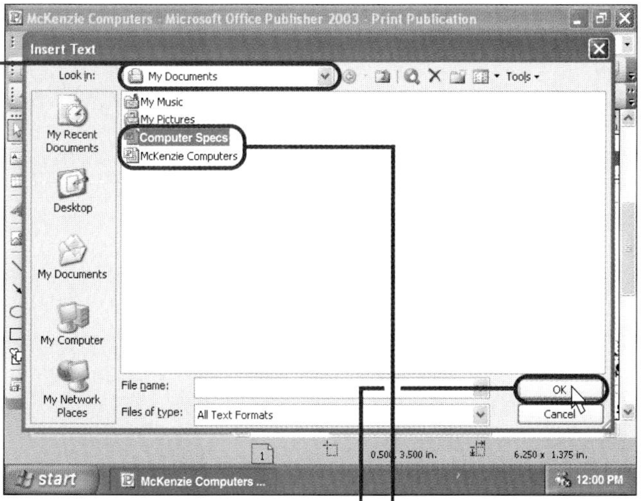

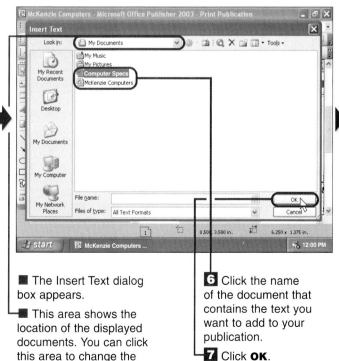

■ The Insert Text dialog box appears.

■ This area shows the location of the displayed documents. You can click this area to change the location.

6 Click the name of the document that contains the text you want to add to your publication.

7 Click **OK**.

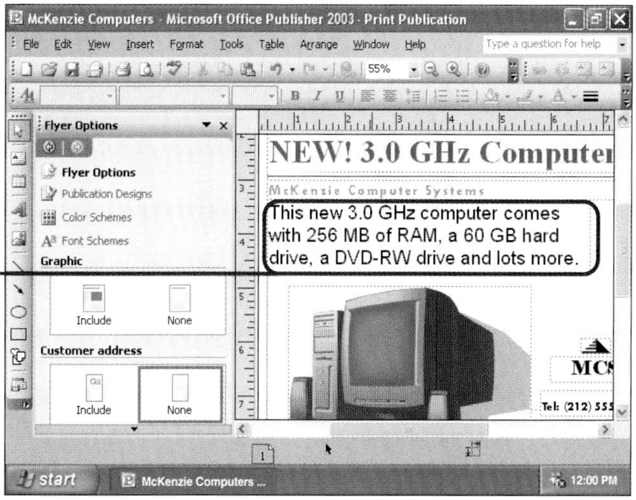

■ The text from the document you selected appears in the text box you created.

■ Formatting that was applied to the text in the original document may appear in the text box.

■ To deselect the text box, click outside the selected area.

SAVE A PUBLICATION

You can save your publication to store it for future use. Saving a publication allows you to later review and make changes to the publication.

You should regularly save changes you make to a publication to avoid losing your work.

SAVE A PUBLICATION

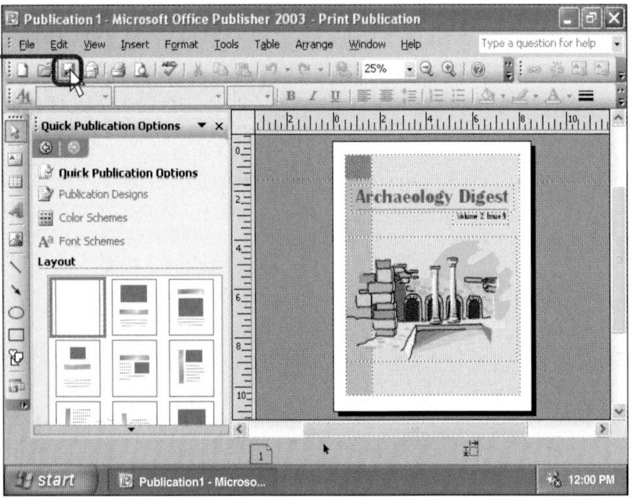

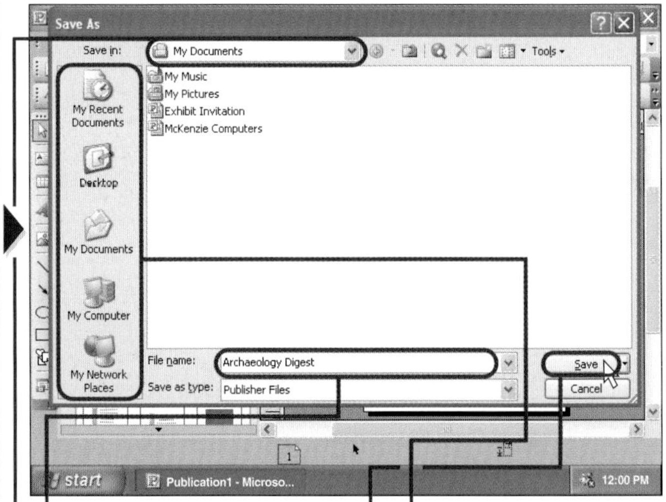

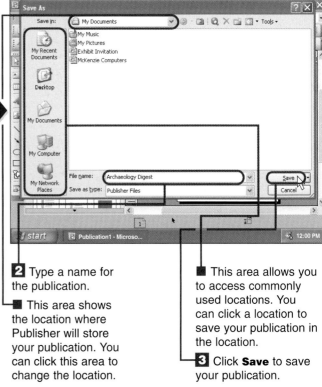

1 Click ▪ to save your publication.

■ The Save As dialog box appears.

Note: If you previously saved your publication, the Save As dialog box will not appear since you have already named the publication.

2 Type a name for the publication.

■ This area shows the location where Publisher will store your publication. You can click this area to change the location.

■ This area allows you to access commonly used locations. You can click a location to save your publication in the location.

3 Click **Save** to save your publication.

PRINT A PUBLICATION

You can produce a paper copy of the publication displayed on your screen.

Before printing, make sure your printer is turned on and contains an adequate supply of paper. You should also make sure your printer contains the type and size of paper your publication requires. The type and size of paper you can use depends on the printer.

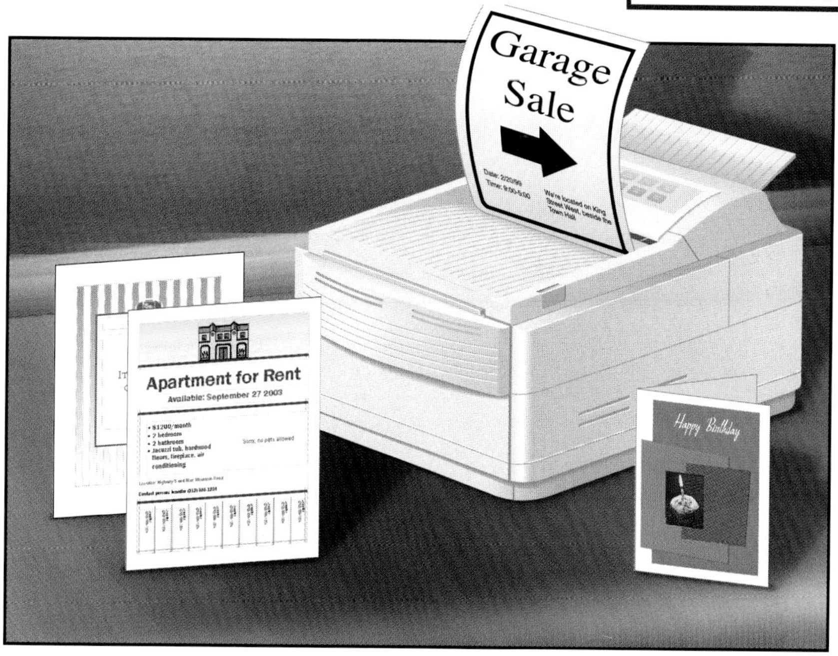

PRINT A PUBLICATION

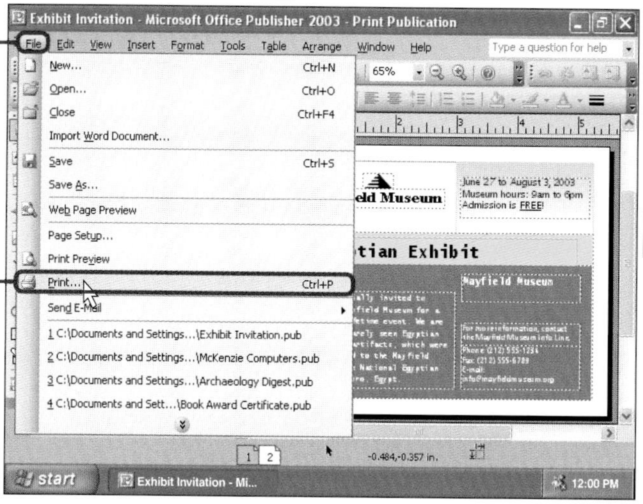

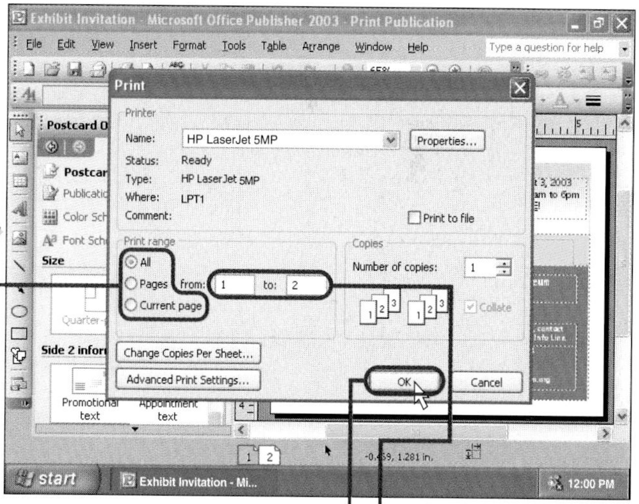

1 Click **File**.

2 Click **Print**.

■ The Print dialog box appears.

3 Click an option to specify if you want to print all the pages, specific pages or the currently displayed page (○ changes to ◉).

■ If you selected **Pages** in step **3**, type the number of the first page you want to print. Press the Tab key and then type the number of the last page you want to print.

4 Click **OK**.

PREVIEW A PUBLICATION BEFORE PRINTING

You can use the Print Preview feature to see how your publication will look when printed. The Print Preview feature allows you to confirm that your publication will print the way you expect.

You cannot make changes to your publication in the Preview window.

PREVIEW A PUBLICATION BEFORE PRINTING

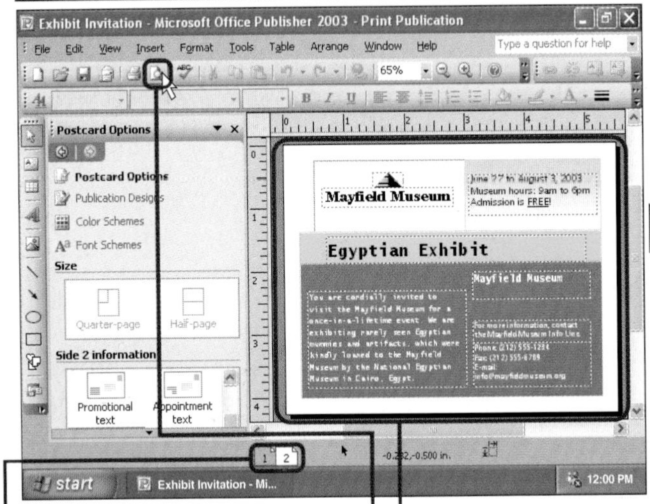

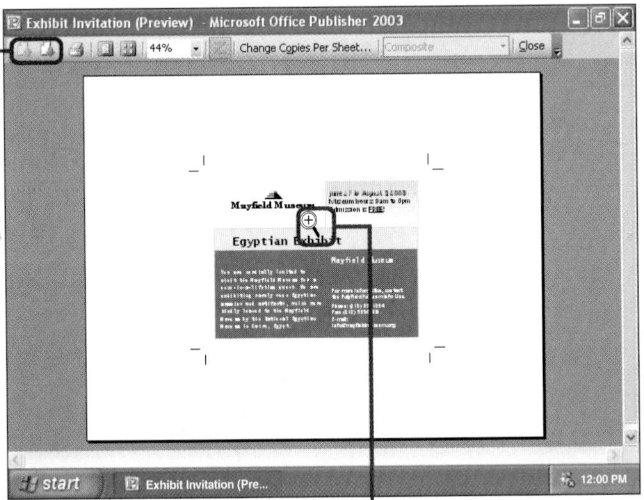

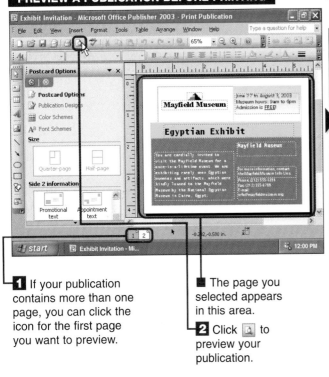

1 If your publication contains more than one page, you can click the icon for the first page you want to preview.

■ The page you selected appears in this area.

2 Click (icon) to preview your publication.

■ The Preview window appears, displaying the page you selected from your publication.

3 If your publication contains more than one page, you can click these buttons to display the previous page (icon) or the next page (icon).

4 To magnify an area of a page, position the mouse (icon) over the area of the page you want to magnify.

5 Click the area to magnify the area of the page.

Tip

Can I print directly from the Preview window?

Yes. In the Preview window, you can click the Print button ( ) to quickly print all the pages in your publication.

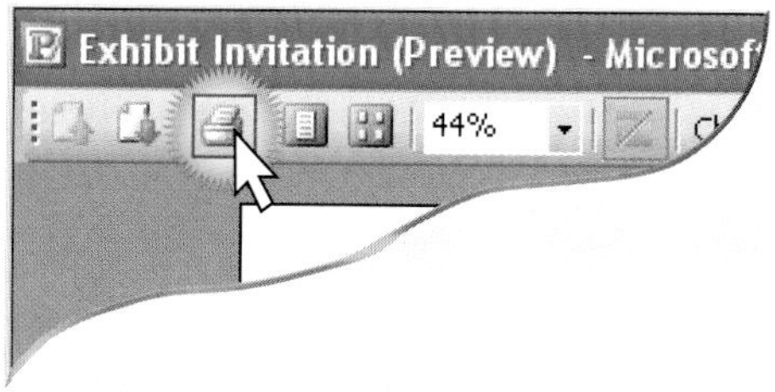

Tip

Why does my publication appear in black and white in the Preview window?

If you are using a black-and-white printer, your publication appears in black and white in the Preview window. If you are using a color printer, your publication will appear in color.

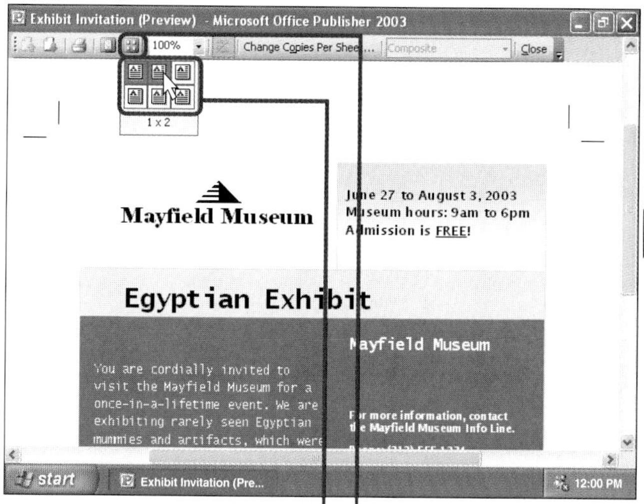

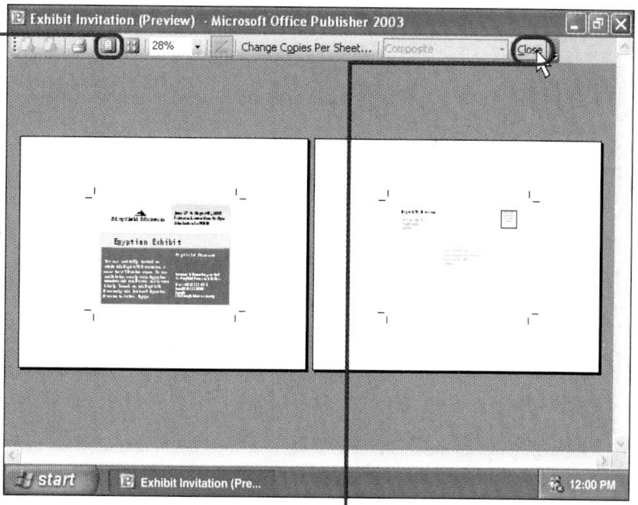

■ A magnified view of the area appears.

■ To once again display the entire page, click anywhere on the page.

6 To display more than one page at once so you can see the overall style of your publication, click .

7 Drag the mouse down and to the right until you select the number of pages you want to display.

■ The number of pages you specified appears.

■ To once again display a single page, click .

8 When you finish previewing your publication, click **Close** to close the Preview window.

OPEN A PUBLICATION

You can open a saved publication to view the publication on your screen. Opening a saved publication allows you to review and make changes to the publication.

OPEN A PUBLICATION

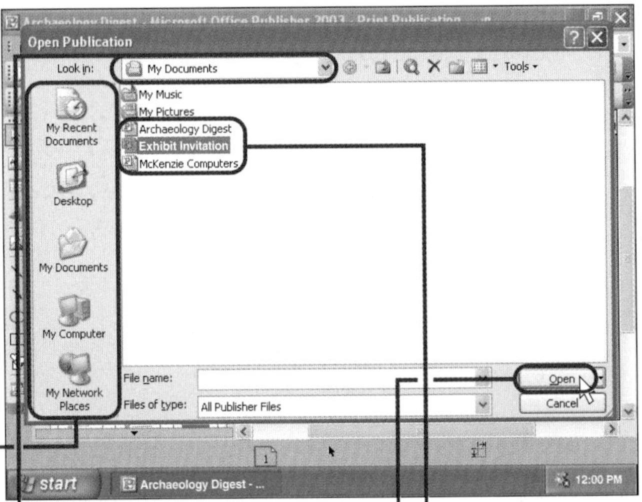

1 Click to open a publication.

■ The Open Publication dialog box appears.

■ This area shows the location of the displayed publications. You can click this area to change the location.

■ This area allows you to access publications stored in commonly used locations. You can click a location to display the publications stored in the location.

2 Click the name of the publication you want to open.

3 Click **Open** to open the publication.

Tip

How can I quickly open a publication I recently worked with?

Publisher remembers the names of the last few publications you worked with. You can use one of the following methods to quickly open one of these publications.

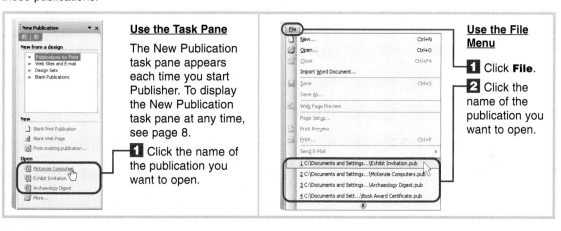

Use the Task Pane

The New Publication task pane appears each time you start Publisher. To display the New Publication task pane at any time, see page 8.

1 Click the name of the publication you want to open.

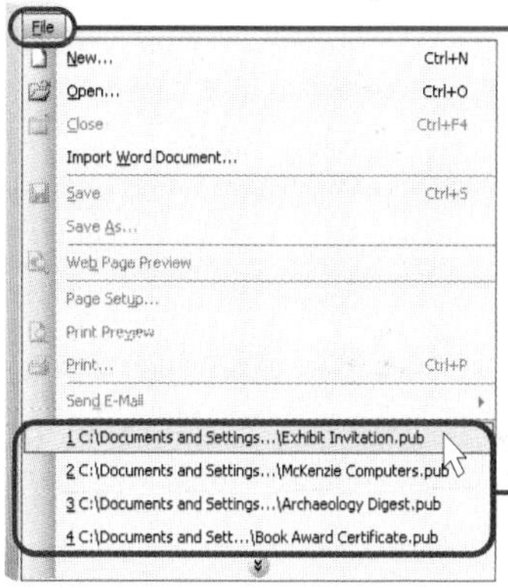

Use the File Menu

1 Click **File**.

2 Click the name of the publication you want to open.

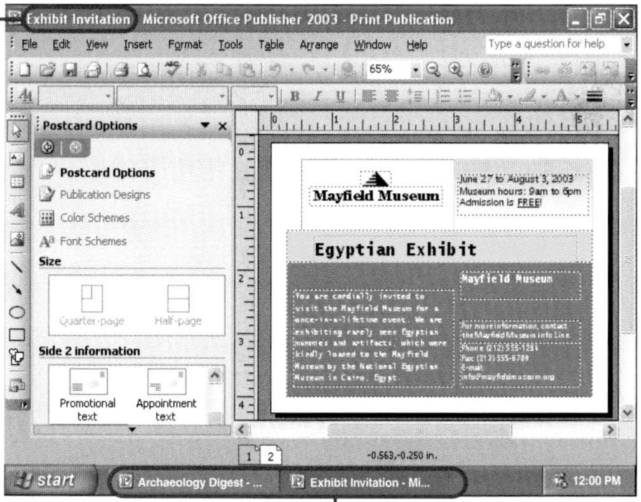

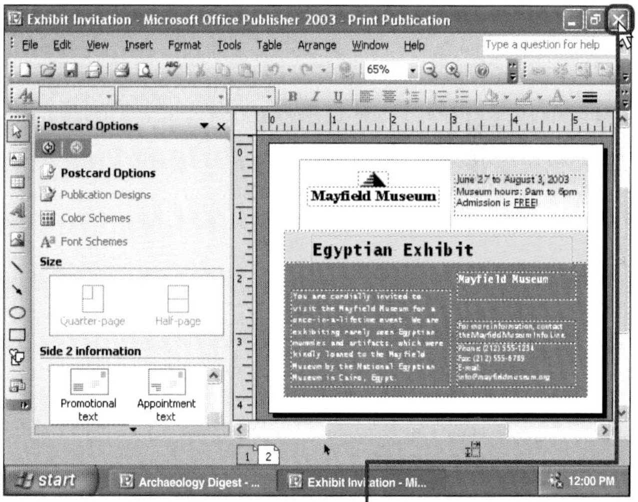

■ The publication opens and appears on your screen. You can now review and make changes to the publication.

■ This area displays the name of the publication.

■ If you already had a publication open, the publication you selected appears in a new Microsoft Office Publisher window. You can click the buttons on the taskbar to switch between the open publications.

CLOSE A PUBLICATION

■ Before closing a publication, you should save any changes you made to the publication. To save changes to a publication, see page 254.

1 When you finish working with a publication, click ☒ to close the publication.

■ The publication disappears from your screen.

E-MAIL A PUBLICATION

You can e-mail your publication to a friend, colleague or family member. Publisher allows you to send just one page of a publication or send an entire publication as an attached file in an e-mail message.

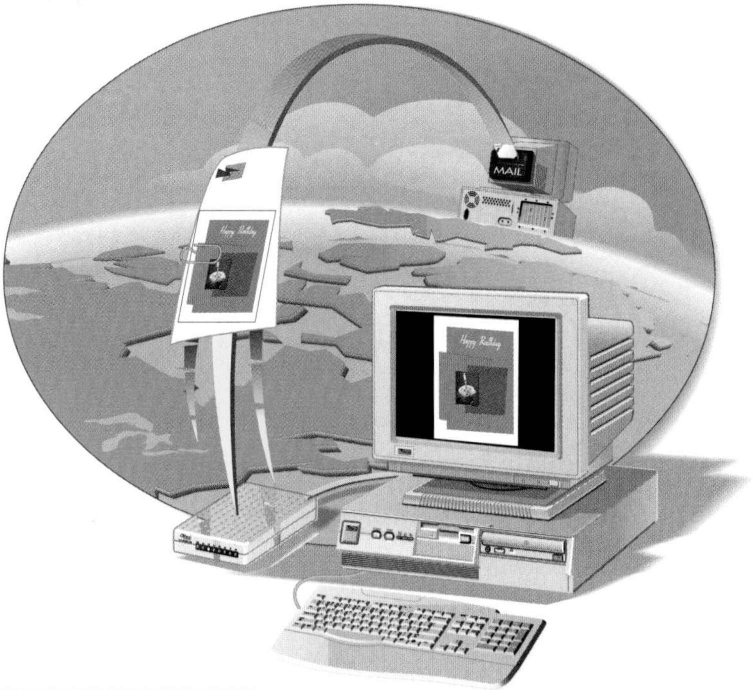

To e-mail a publication, you must have the Outlook 2003 or Outlook Express (version 5.0 or later) e-mail program set up on your computer.

E-MAIL ONE PAGE IN YOUR PUBLICATION

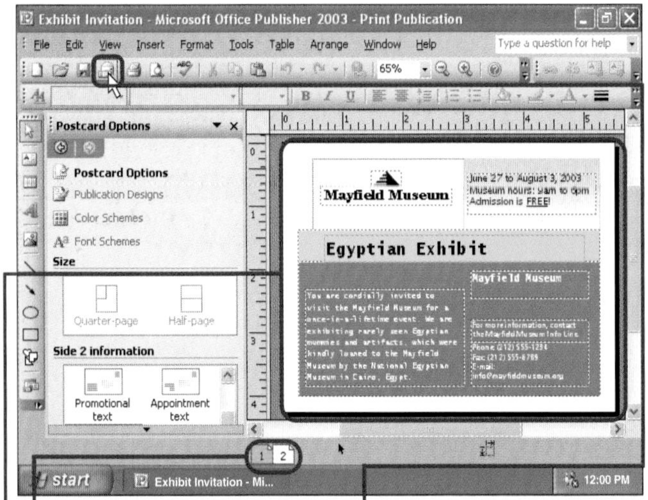

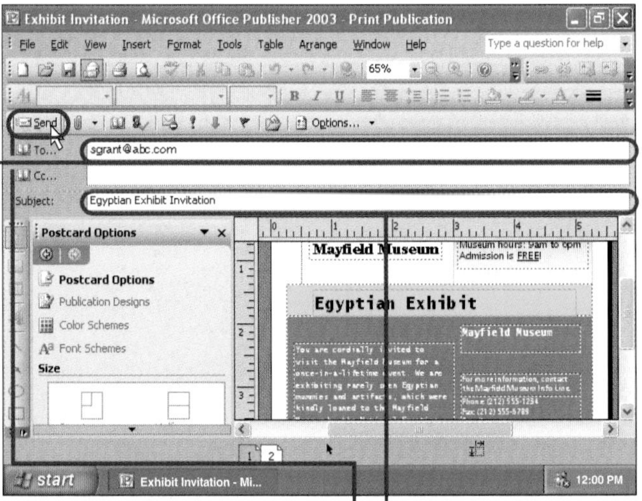

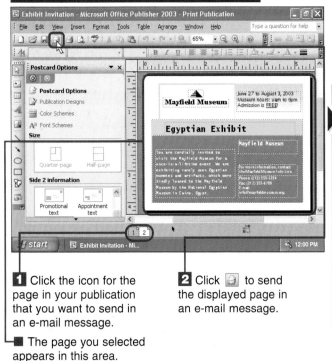

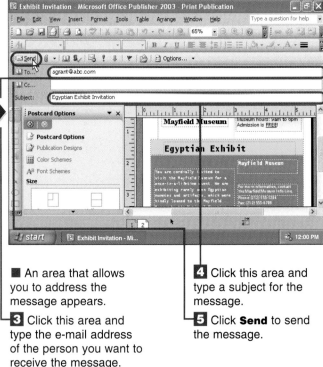

1 Click the icon for the page in your publication that you want to send in an e-mail message.

■ The page you selected appears in this area.

2 Click to send the displayed page in an e-mail message.

■ An area that allows you to address the message appears.

3 Click this area and type the e-mail address of the person you want to receive the message.

4 Click this area and type a subject for the message.

5 Click **Send** to send the message.

Tip

Will the person receiving the e-mail message need Publisher installed to view the publication?

When sending just one page of a publication in an e-mail message, the person receiving the message does not need to have Publisher installed to view the page. When sending your entire publication as an attached file, the person receiving the message must have Publisher 2002 or later installed to view the publication.

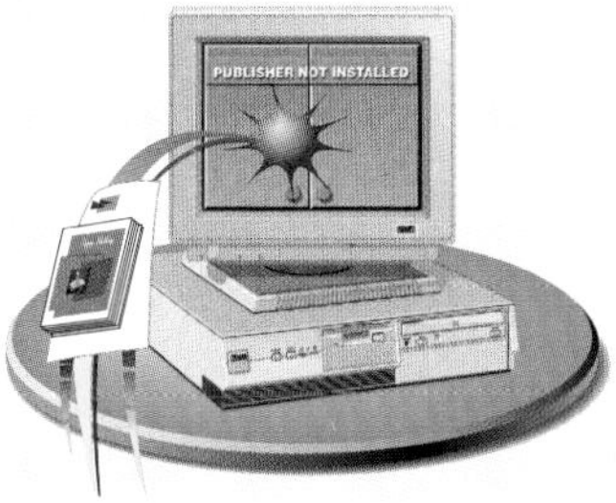

Tip

Can I send the e-mail message to more than one person?

Yes. To send the e-mail message to more than one person, use a semicolon (;) to separate each e-mail address you type. To send a carbon copy of the message to a person who is not directly involved but would be interested in the message, click inside the **Cc** area and type the e-mail address of the person.

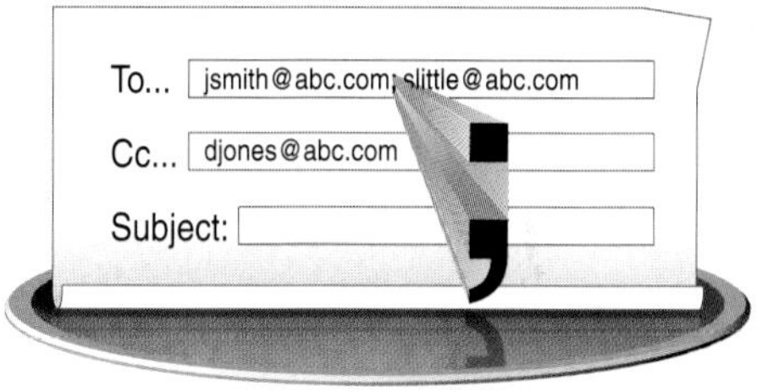

E-MAIL YOUR ENTIRE PUBLICATION

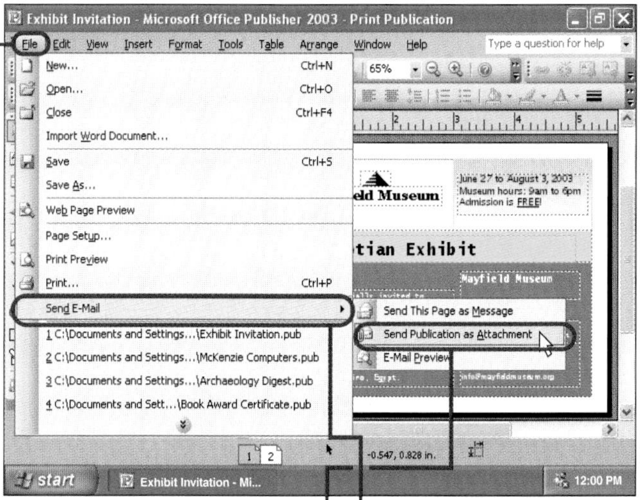

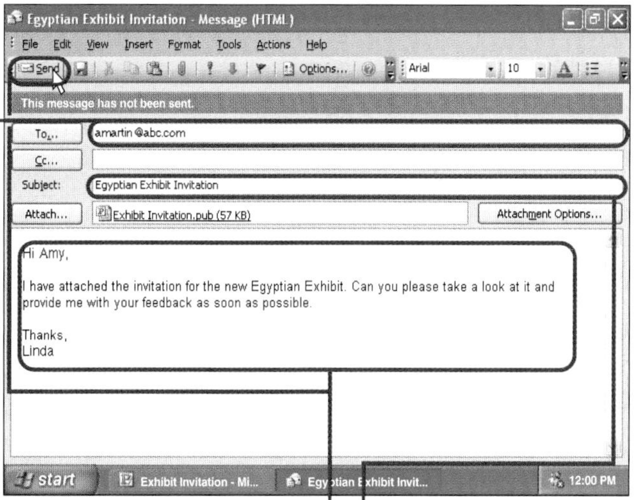

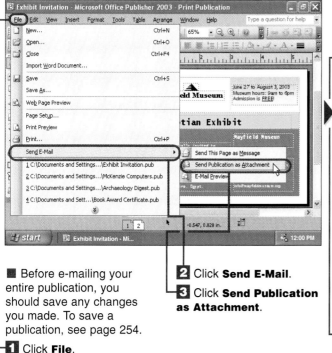

■ Before e-mailing your entire publication, you should save any changes you made. To save a publication, see page 254.

1 Click **File**.

2 Click **Send E-Mail**.

3 Click **Send Publication as Attachment**.

■ A window that allows you to send the entire publication in an e-mail message appears.

4 Click this area and type the e-mail address of the person you want to receive the message.

5 Click this area and type a subject for the message.

6 Click this area and type the message you want to include with the publication.

7 Click **Send** to send the message.

CHANGE FONT OF TEXT

You can change the font of text to enhance the appearance of your publication.

CHANGE FONT OF TEXT

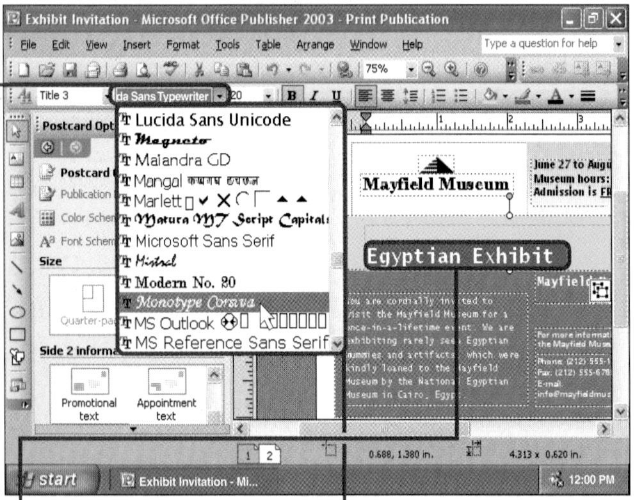

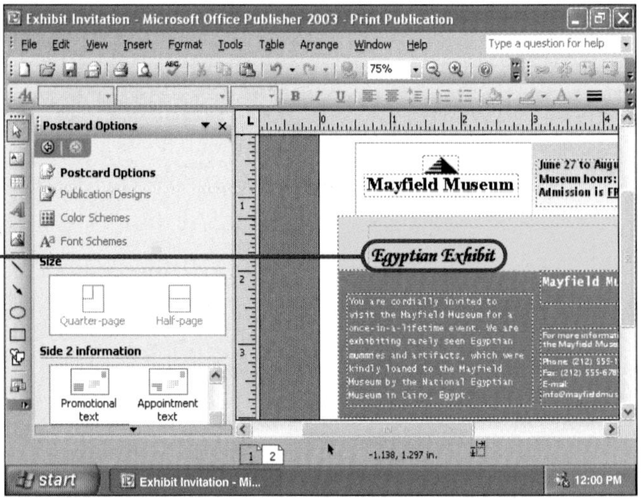

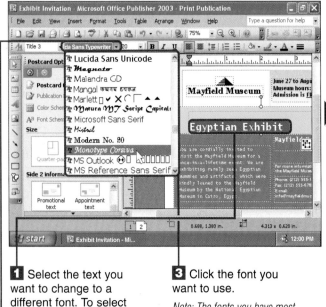

1 Select the text you want to change to a different font. To select text, see page 247.

2 Click ▾ in this area to display a list of the available fonts.

3 Click the font you want to use.

Note: The fonts you have most recently used appear at the top of the list.

■ The text you selected changes to the new font.

■ To deselect text, click outside the selected area.

CHANGE SIZE OF TEXT

You can increase or decrease the size of text in your publication.

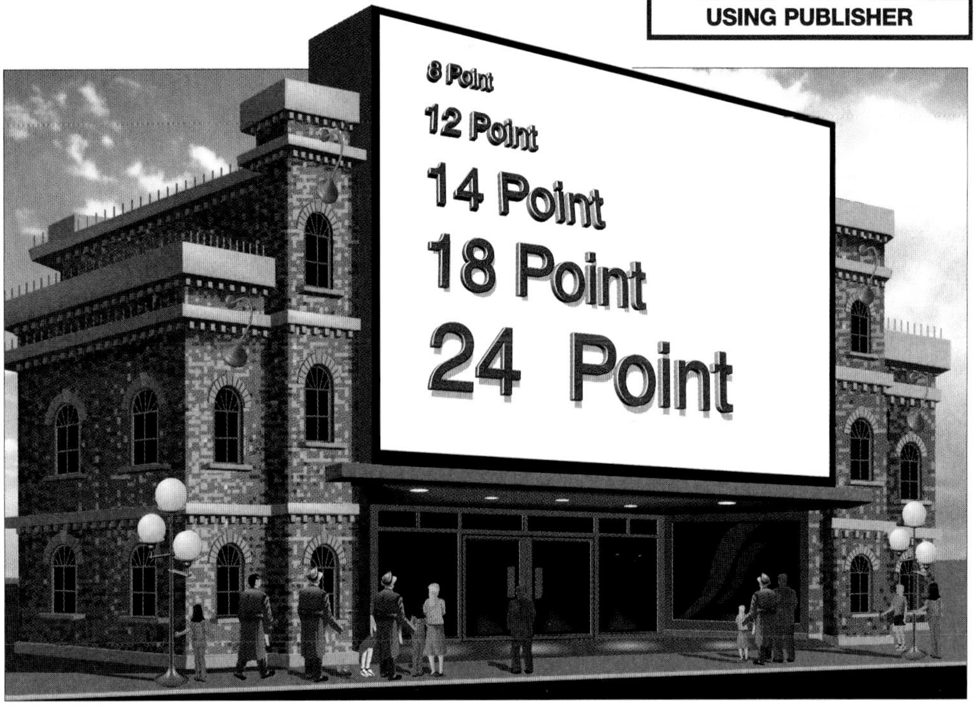

Larger text is easier to read, but smaller text allows you to fit more information on a page.

Publisher measures the size of text in points. There are 72 points in an inch.

CHANGE SIZE OF TEXT

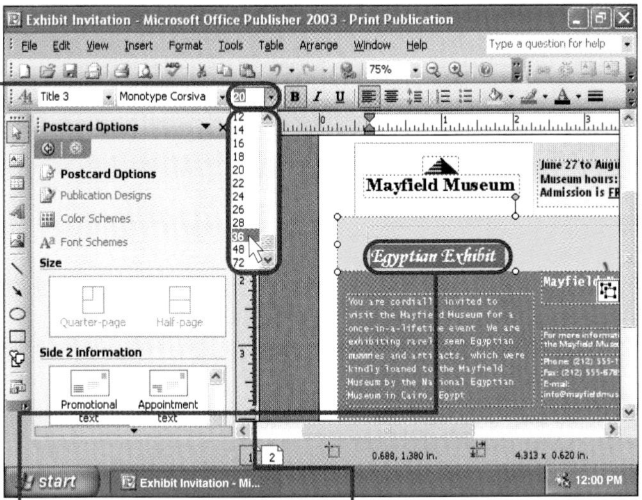

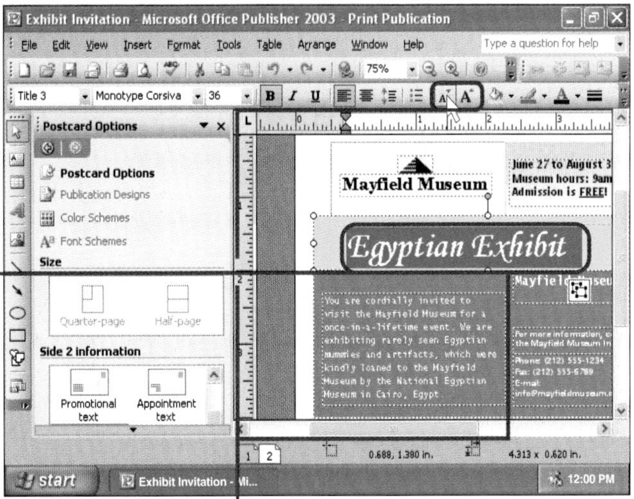

1 Select the text you want to change to a new size. To select text, see page 247.

2 Click ▾ in this area to display a list of the available sizes.

3 Click the size you want to use.

■ The text you selected changes to the new size.

■ To deselect text, click outside the selected area.

QUICKLY CHANGE THE SIZE OF TEXT

1 Select the text you want to change to a new size.

2 Click a button to decrease (A) or increase (A) the size of the text.

Note: If the button you want is not displayed, click ▾ on the Formatting toolbar to display the button.

BOLD, ITALICIZE OR UNDERLINE TEXT

You can bold, italicize or underline text to emphasize information in your publication.

BOLD, ITALICIZE OR UNDERLINE TEXT

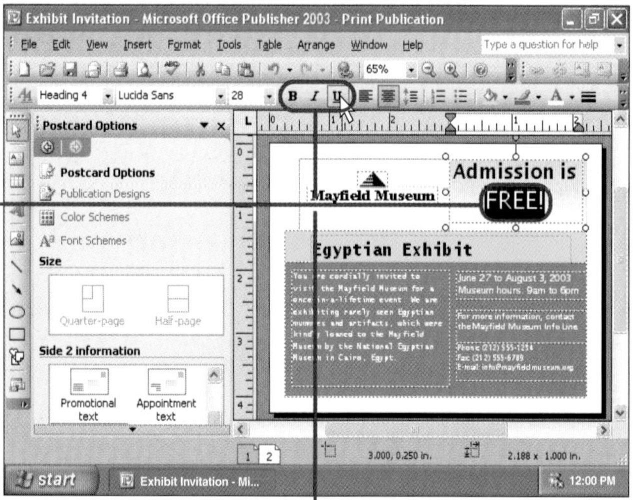

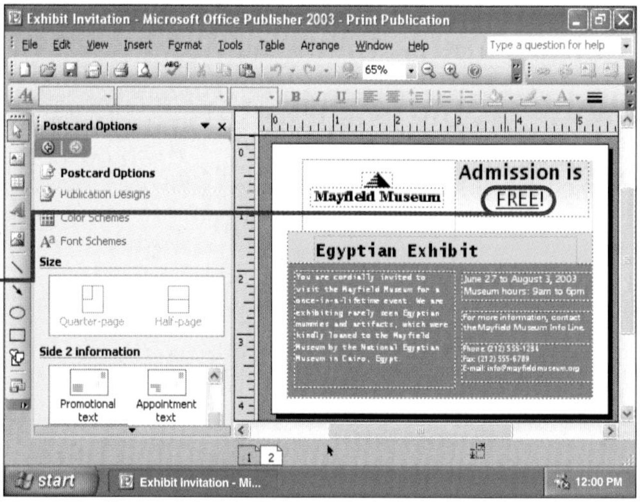

1 Select the text you want to bold, italicize or underline. To select text, see page 247.

2 Click one of the following buttons.

B Bold

I Italic

U Underline

Note: If the button you want to use is not displayed, click on the Formatting toolbar to display the button.

■ The text you selected appears in the new style.

■ To deselect text, click outside the selected area.

■ To remove a bold, italic or underline style from text, repeat steps **1** and **2**.

CHANGE ALIGNMENT OF TEXT

You can enhance the appearance of your publication by aligning text in different ways.

Changing the alignment of text affects how the left and right edges of text appear within a text box.

CHANGE ALIGNMENT OF TEXT

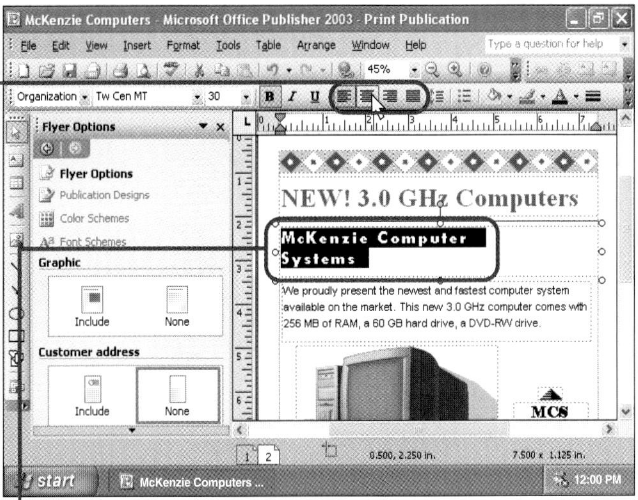

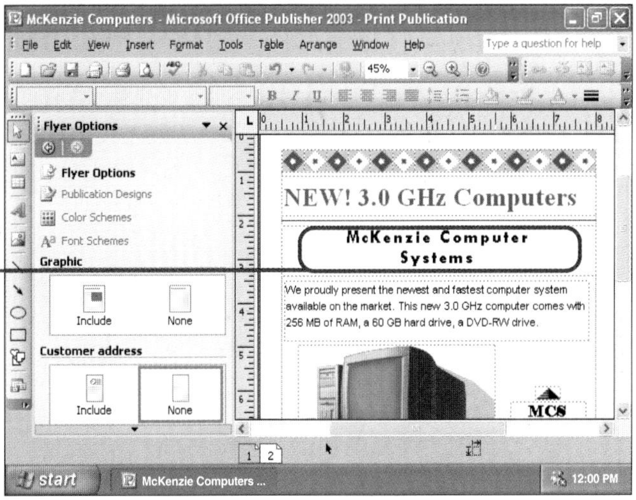

1 Select the text you want to align differently. To select text, see page 247.

2 Click one of the following buttons.

- Left align
- Center
- Right align
- Justify

Note: If the button you want to use is not displayed, click ▾ on the Formatting toolbar to display the button.

■ The text appears in the new alignment.

■ To deselect text, click outside the selected area.

CHANGE TEXT COLOR

You can change the color of text in your publication to draw attention to a heading or to enhance a section of information.

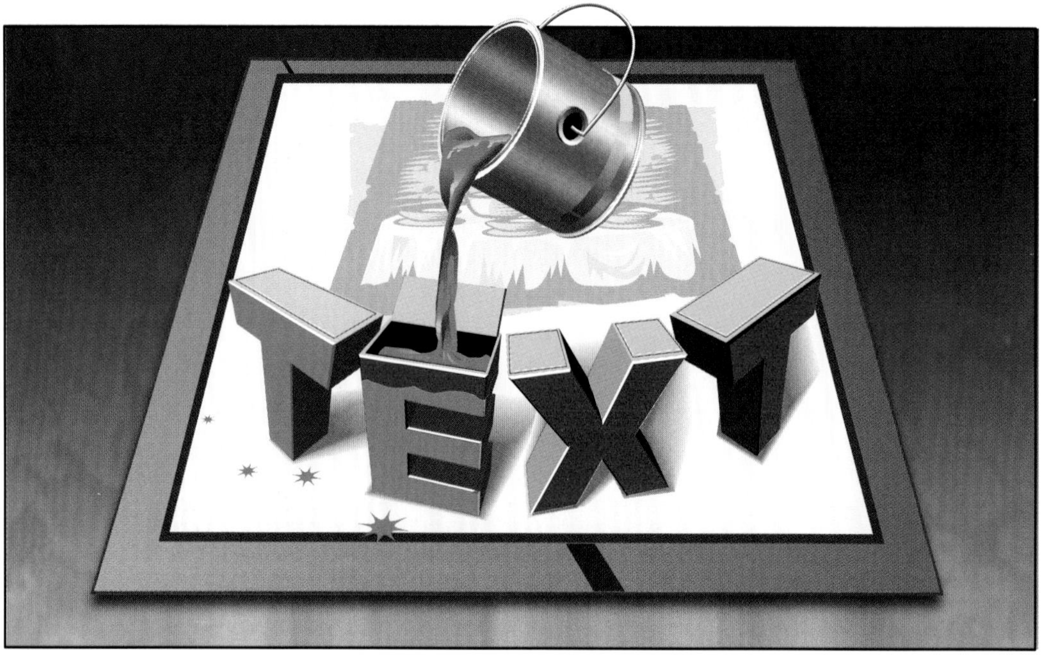

CHANGE TEXT COLOR

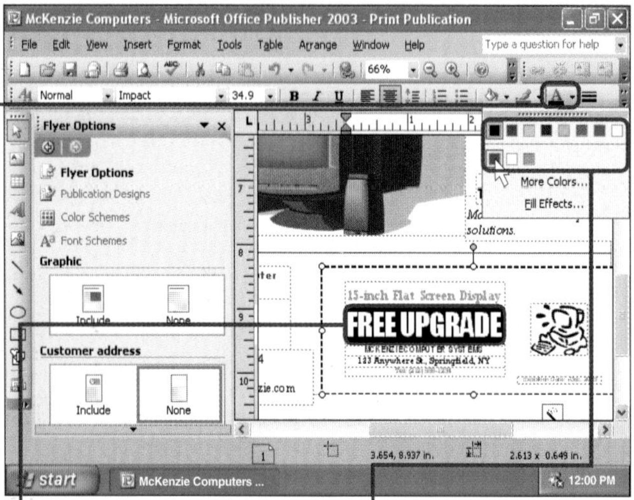

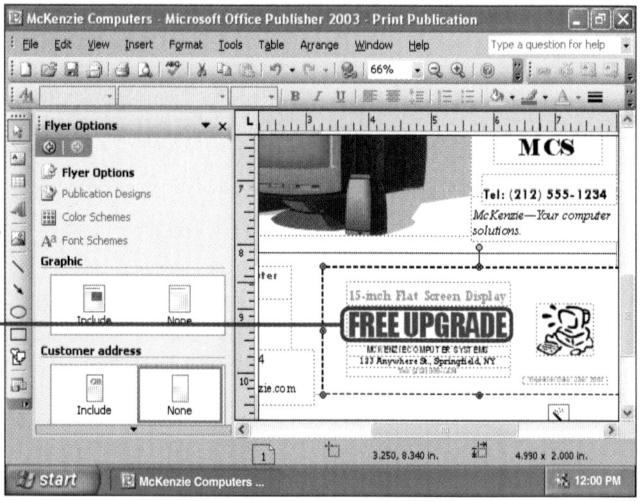

1 Select the text you want to change to a different color. To select text, see page 247.

2 Click ▾ in this area to display the available colors.

3 Click the color you want to use.

Note: The available colors depend on the color scheme used in your publication. To change the color scheme, see page 277.

■ The text appears in the color you selected.

■ To deselect text, click outside the selected area.

ADD A BACKGROUND COLOR OR PATTERN TO A PAGE

You can add a background color or pattern to a page in your publication to help add visual interest to the page.

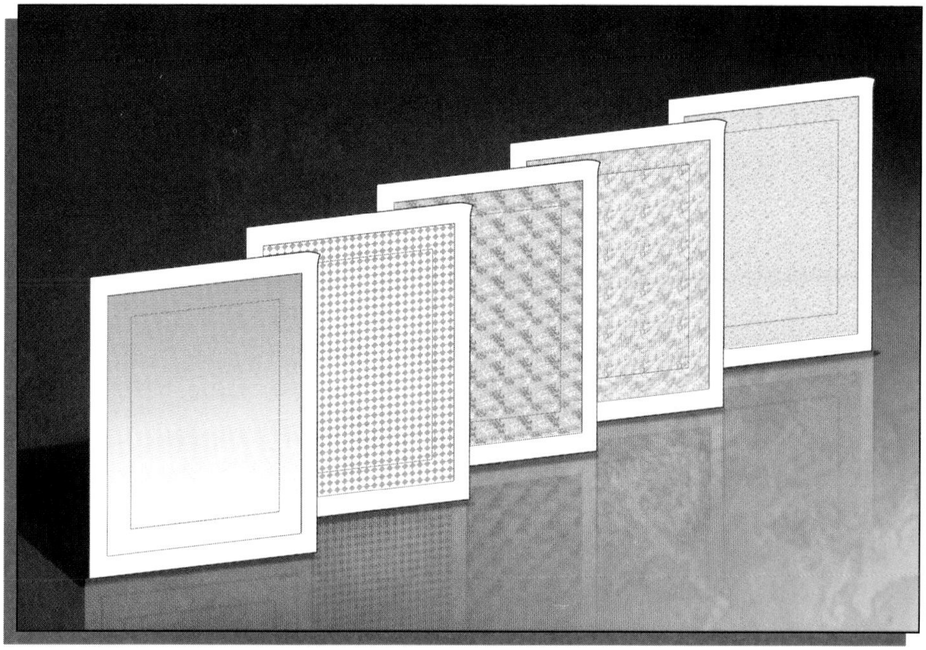

ADD A BACKGROUND COLOR OR PATTERN TO A PAGE

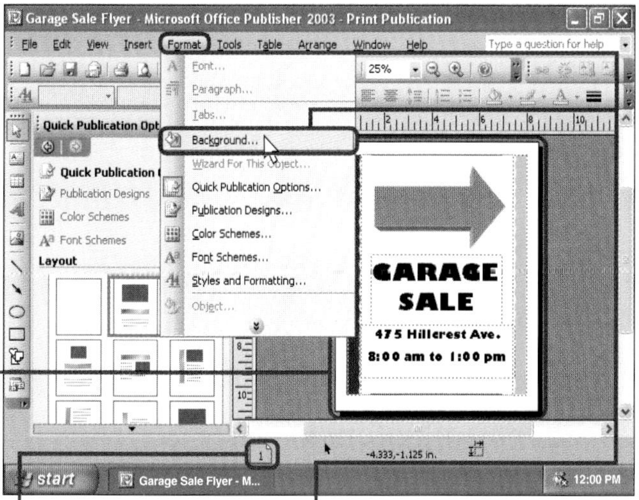

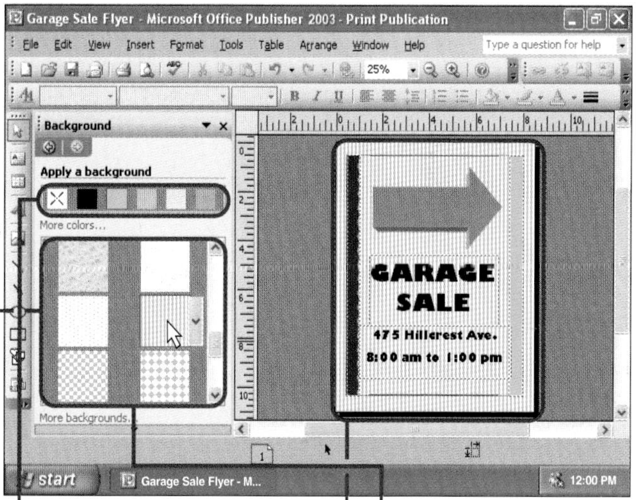

1 Click the icon for the page you want to add a background color or pattern to.

■ This area displays the page you selected.

2 Click **Format**.

3 Click **Background**.

Note: If Background is not displayed, position the mouse over the bottom of the menu to display the menu option.

■ The Background task pane appears.

4 Click the background color you want to use.

■ This area displays the available colors and patterns for the background color you selected. You can use the scroll bar to browse through the available colors and patterns.

5 Click the color or pattern you want to use.

Note: If you do not want the page to display a color or pattern, click ☒.

■ The page instantly displays the color or pattern you selected.

CREATE A DROP CAP

You can create a large capital letter at the beginning of a paragraph to enhance the appearance of the paragraph.

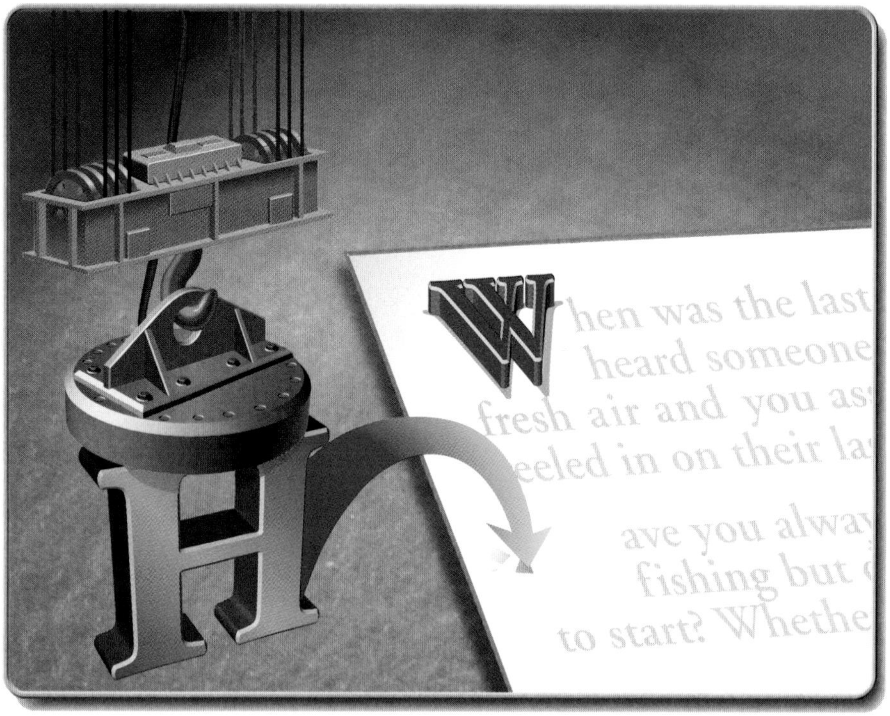

Drop caps are frequently used in the first paragraph of a publication to catch the reader's eye.

CREATE A DROP CAP

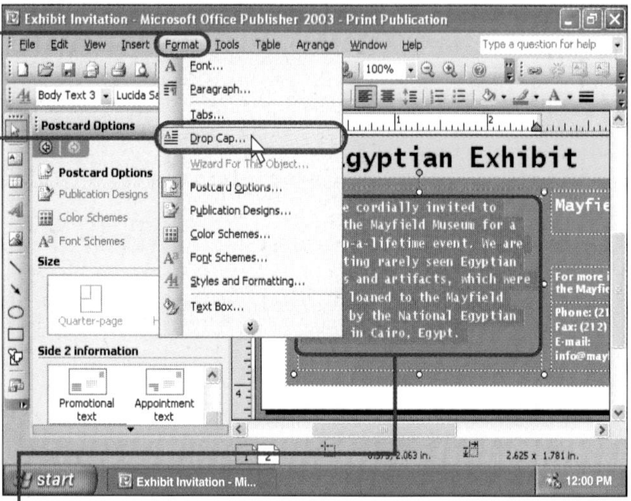

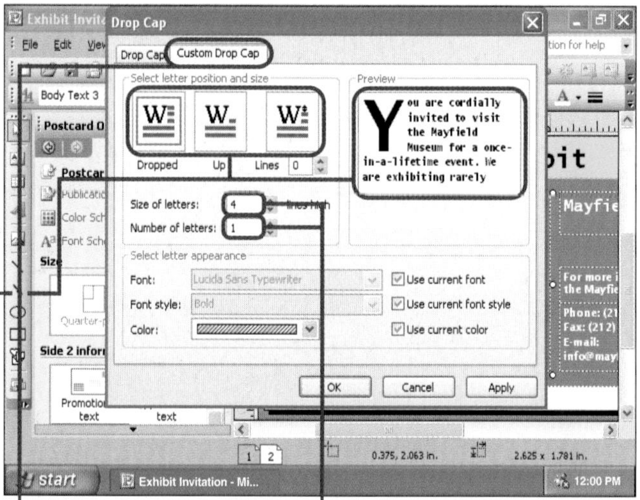

1 Click the paragraph you want to display a drop cap.

2 Click **Format**.

3 Click **Drop Cap**.

Note: If Drop Cap does not appear on the menu, position the mouse over the bottom of the menu to display the menu option.

■ The Drop Cap dialog box appears.

4 Click the **Custom Drop Cap** tab.

5 Click the position and size you want to use for the drop cap.

■ This area displays a preview of the drop cap.

6 Double-click the number in this area and type the number of lines high you want the drop cap to be.

7 Double-click the number in this area and type the number of letters you want to use for the drop cap.

Tip

Does Publisher offer any other drop cap styles?

Yes. Publisher offers several pre-made drop cap styles that you can quickly apply to a paragraph in your publication.

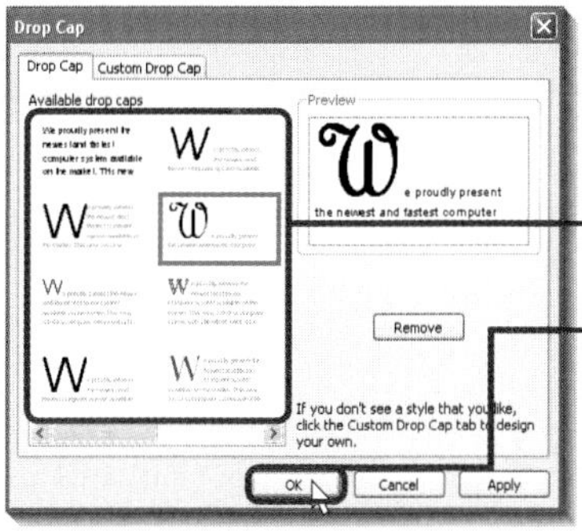

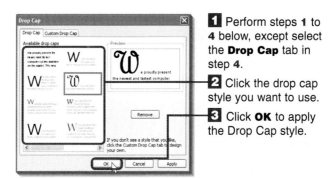

1 Perform steps **1** to **4** below, except select the **Drop Cap** tab in step **4**.

2 Click the drop cap style you want to use.

3 Click **OK** to apply the Drop Cap style.

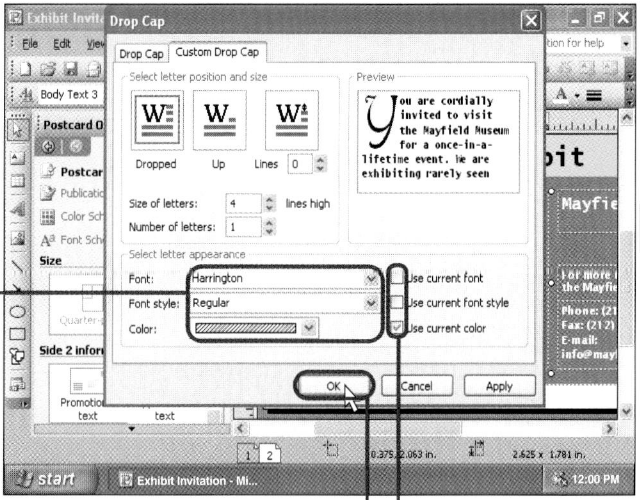

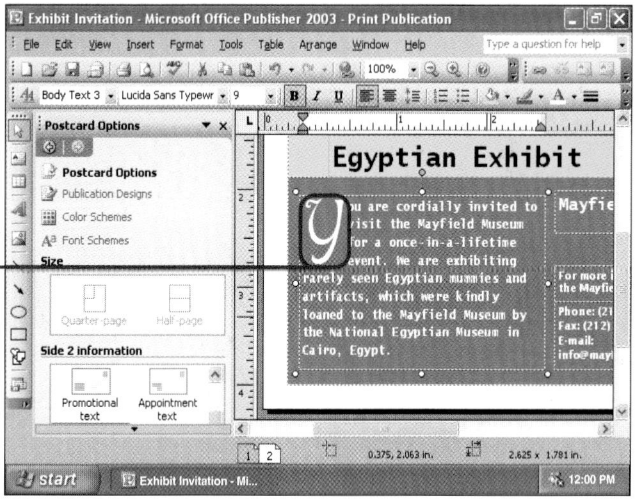

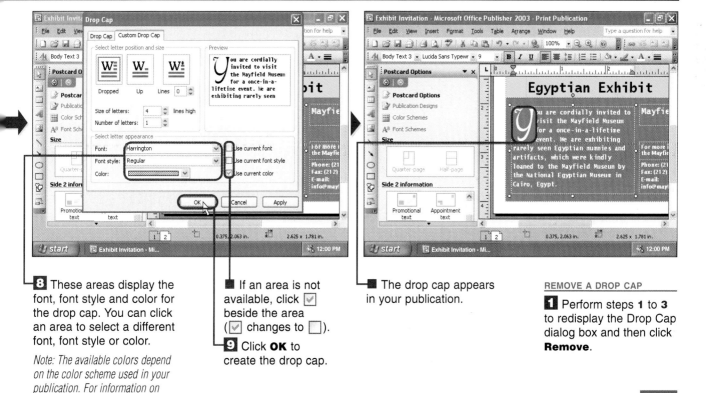

8 These areas display the font, font style and color for the drop cap. You can click an area to select a different font, font style or color.

Note: The available colors depend on the color scheme used in your publication. For information on color schemes, see page 277.

■ If an area is not available, click ☑ beside the area (☑ changes to ☐).

9 Click **OK** to create the drop cap.

■ The drop cap appears in your publication.

REMOVE A DROP CAP

1 Perform steps **1** to **3** to redisplay the Drop Cap dialog box and then click **Remove**.

CHANGE LINE SPACING

You can change the amount of space between the lines of text in your publication.

By default, Publisher uses the size of text to determine the size of line spacing. The larger the text in your publication, the larger the space between lines.

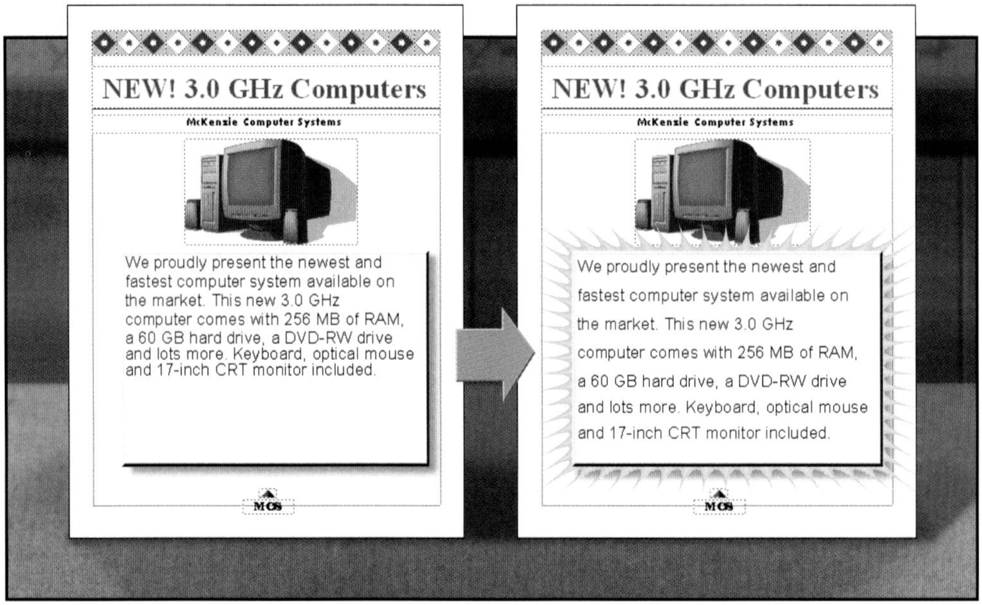

CHANGE LINE SPACING

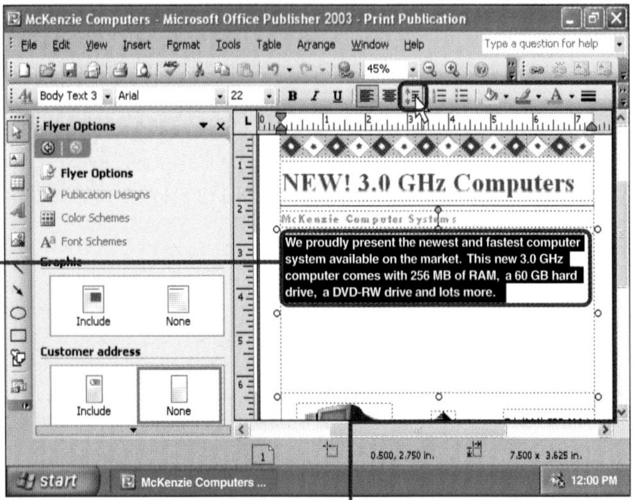

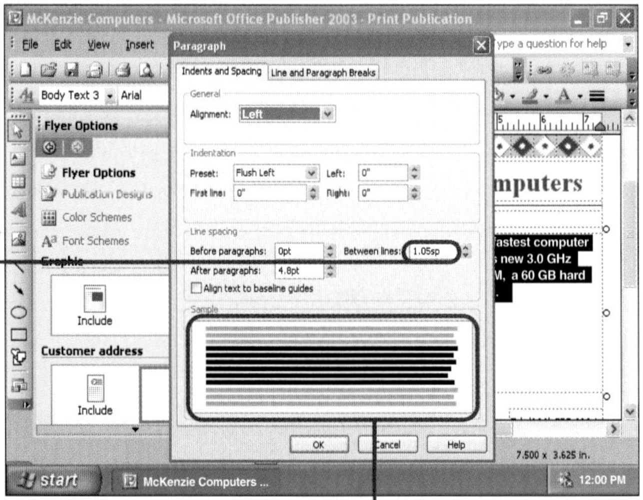

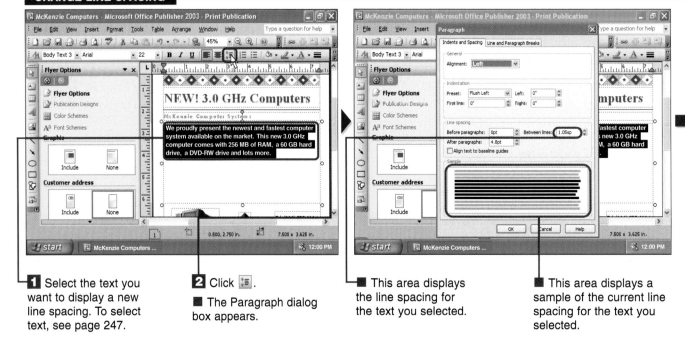

1 Select the text you want to display a new line spacing. To select text, see page 247.

2 Click .

■ The Paragraph dialog box appears.

■ This area displays the line spacing for the text you selected.

■ This area displays a sample of the current line spacing for the text you selected.

Tip

Why would I want to change the line spacing in my publication?

Line spacing prevents letters in a line of text from touching letters in the line above or the line below. Proper line spacing can help make your publication easier to read.

Tip

Can I change the line spacing between paragraphs?

Yes. You can change the amount of space that appears before or after a paragraph.

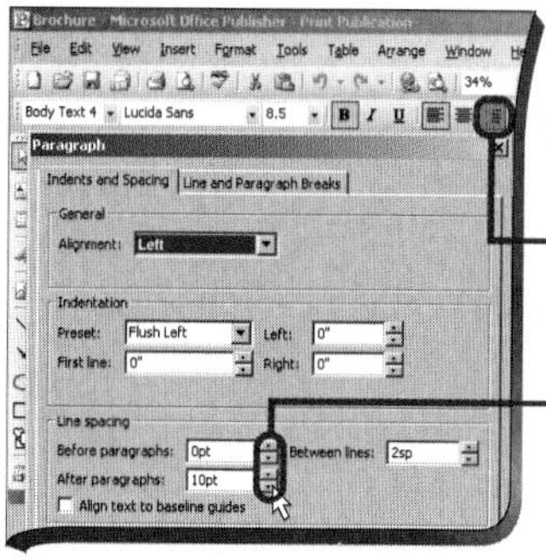

1 To change the line spacing before or after a paragraph, select the paragraph.

2 Click to display the Paragraph dialog box.

3 Click or in one of these areas to increase or decrease the amount of space before or after the paragraph.

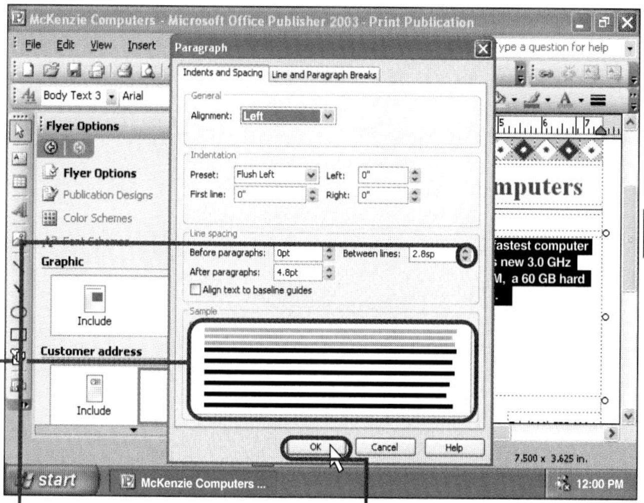

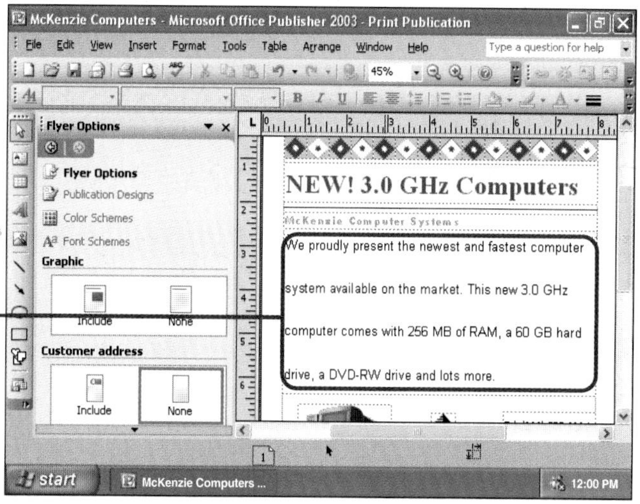

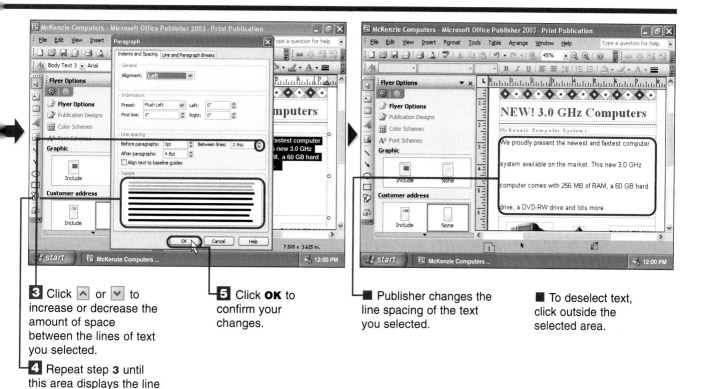

3 Click or to increase or decrease the amount of space between the lines of text you selected.

4 Repeat step **3** until this area displays the line spacing you want to use in your publication.

5 Click **OK** to confirm your changes.

■ Publisher changes the line spacing of the text you selected.

■ To deselect text, click outside the selected area.

CREATE A BULLETED OR NUMBERED LIST

You can separate items in a list by beginning each item with a bullet or number.

Bulleted lists are useful for items in no particular order, such as items in a shopping list. Numbered lists are useful for items in a specific order, such as instructions.

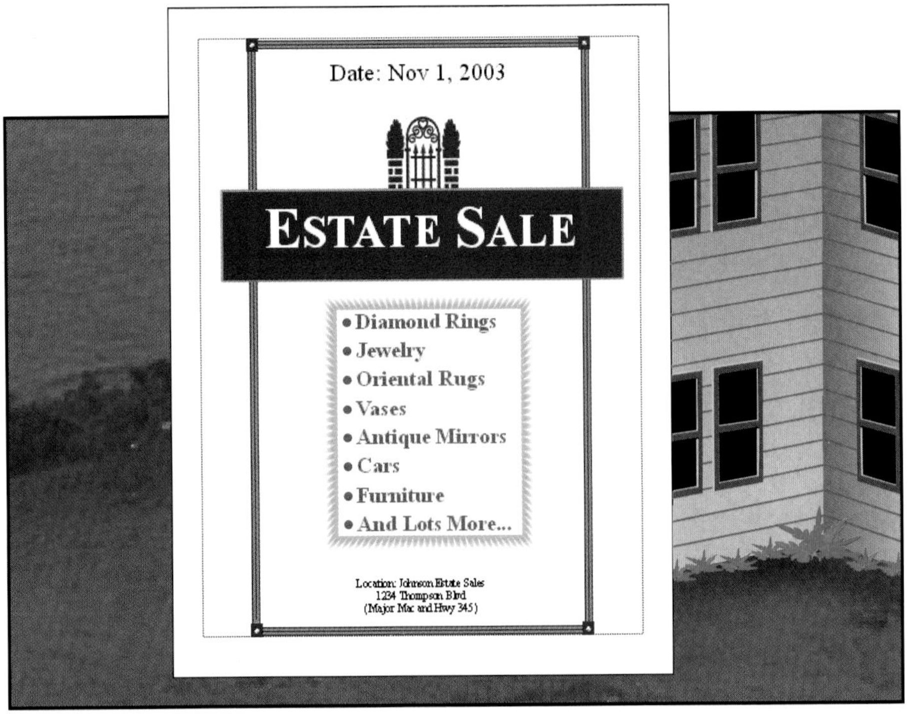

CREATE A BULLETED OR NUMBERED LIST

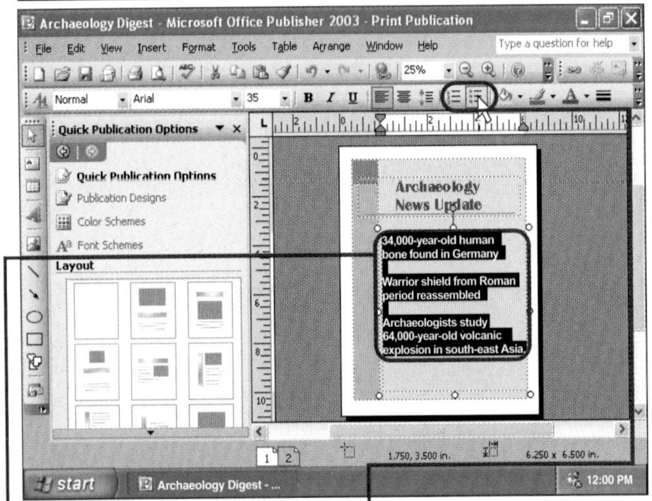

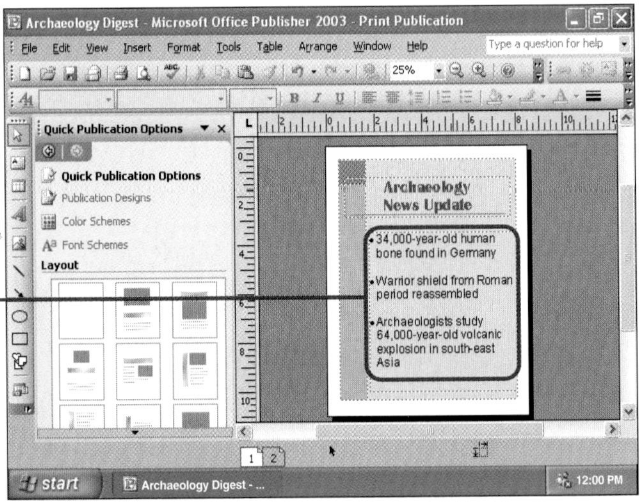

1 Select the text you want to display as a bulleted or numbered list. To select text, see page 247.

2 Click one of the following buttons.

☰ Add numbers

☰ Add bullets

Note: If the button you want is not displayed, click ⁝ on the Formatting toolbar to display the button.

■ A bullet or number appears in front of each item in the list.

■ To deselect text, click outside the selected area.

■ To remove bullets or numbers from a list, repeat steps **1** and **2**.

COPY FORMATTING

You can copy the formatting of text to make one area of text in your publication look exactly like another.

You may want to copy the formatting of text to make all the important words in your publication look the same. This will give the text in your publication a consistent appearance.

COPY FORMATTING

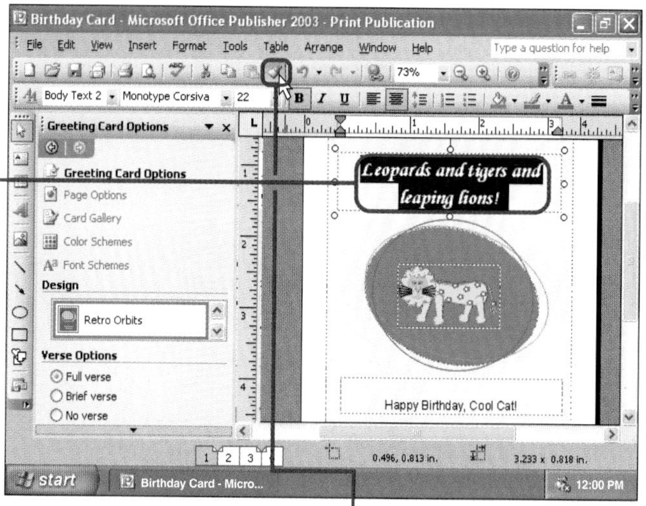

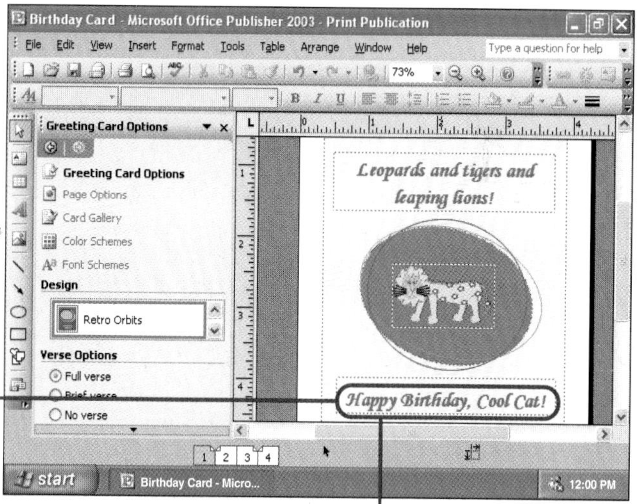

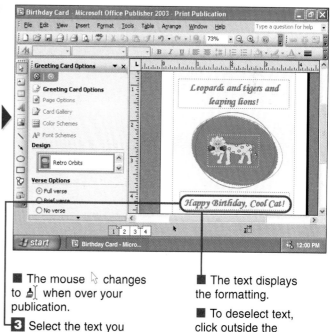

1 Select the text that displays the formatting you want to copy. To select text, see page 247.

2 Click to copy the formatting of the text.

Note: If is not displayed, click on the Standard toolbar to display the button.

■ The mouse changes to when over your publication.

3 Select the text you want to display the same formatting.

■ The text displays the formatting.

■ To deselect text, click outside the selected area.

CREATE COLUMNS

You can display text in columns like those found in a newspaper to make the text easier to read and improve the layout of your publication.

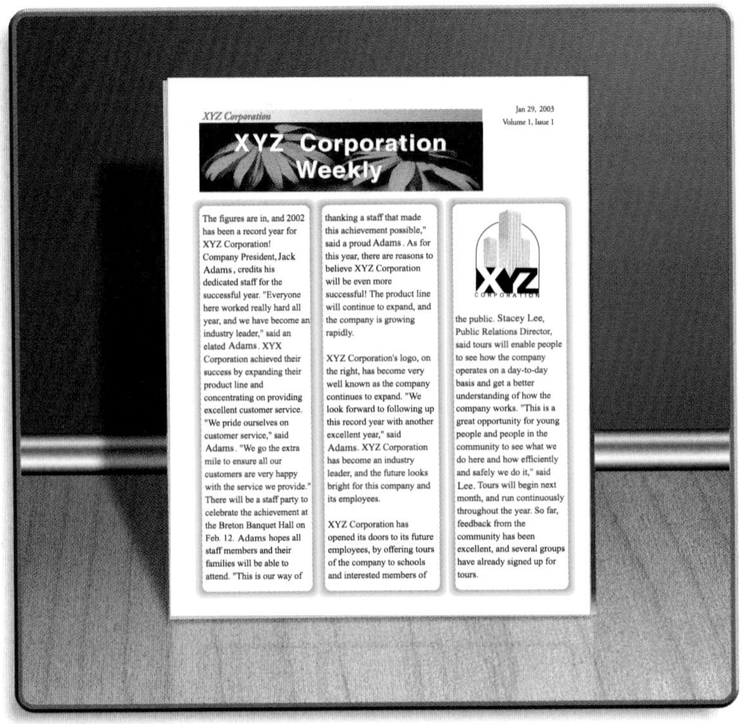
XYZ Corporation

Jan 29, 2003
Volume 1, Issue 1

XYZ Corporation Weekly

The figures are in, and 2002 has been a record year for XYZ Corporation! Company President, Jack Adams, credits his dedicated staff for the successful year. "Everyone here worked really hard all year, and we have become an industry leader," said an elated Adams. XYX Corporation achieved their success by expanding their product line and concentrating on providing excellent customer service. "We pride ourselves on customer service," said Adams. "We go the extra mile to ensure all our customers are very happy with the service we provide." There will be a staff party to celebrate the achievement at the Breton Banquet Hall on Feb. 12. Adams hopes all staff members and their families will be able to attend. "This is our way of thanking a staff that made this achievement possible," said a proud Adams. As for this year, there are reasons to believe XYZ Corporation will be even more successful! The product line will continue to expand, and the company is growing rapidly.

XYZ Corporation's logo, on the right, has become very well known as the company continues to expand. "We look forward to following up this record year with another excellent year," said Adams. XYZ Corporation has become an industry leader, and the future looks bright for this company and its employees.

XYZ Corporation has opened its doors to its future employees, by offering tours of the company to schools and interested members of the public. Stacey Lee, Public Relations Director, said tours will enable people to see how the company operates on a day-to-day basis and get a better understanding of how the company works. "This is a great opportunity for young people and people in the community to see what we do here and how efficiently and safely we do it," said Lee. Tours will begin next month, and run continuously throughout the year. So far, feedback from the community has been excellent, and several groups have already signed up for tours.

CREATE COLUMNS

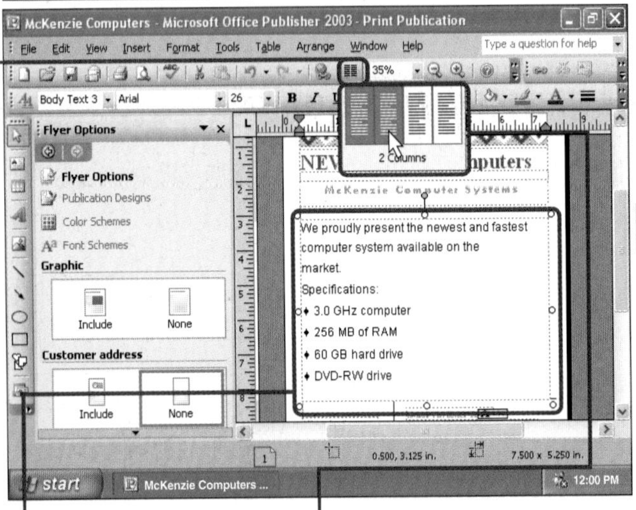

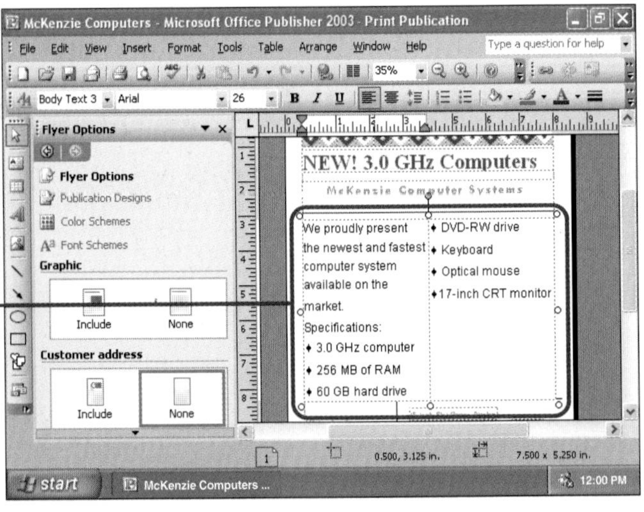

1 Click the text box that contains the text you want to display in columns. Handles (○) appear around the text box.

2 Click ▥ to create columns.

Note: If the ▥ button is not displayed, click ⁝ on the Standard toolbar to display the button.

3 Drag the mouse until you highlight the number of columns you want to create.

■ The text in the text box appears in the number of columns you specified.

■ To remove columns, repeat steps **1** to **3**, selecting one column in step **3**.

CHANGE THE PUBLICATION DESIGN

You can instantly change the overall design of your publication to suit your preferences.

CHANGE THE PUBLICATION DESIGN

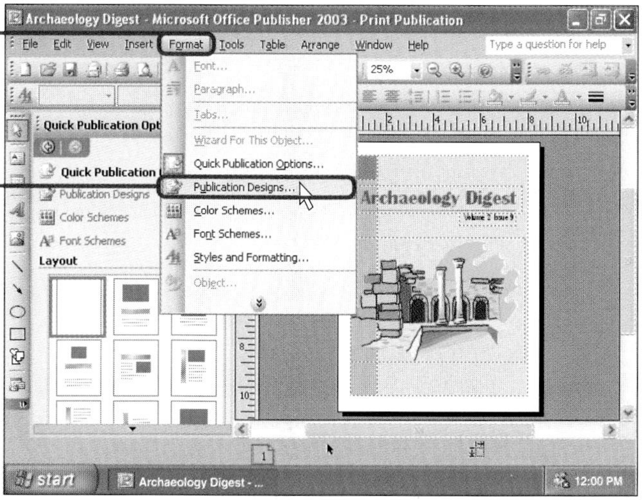

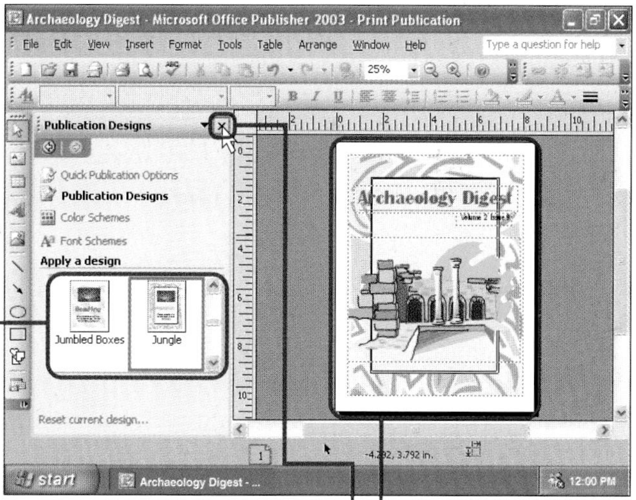

1 Click **Format**.

2 Click **Publication Designs**.

■ The Publication Designs task pane appears.

■ This area displays the available designs. You can use the scroll bar to browse through the available designs.

3 Click the design you want to use.

■ The publication instantly displays the new design.

4 When you finish selecting a design, you can click ☒ to close the Publication Designs task pane.

CHANGE THE FONT SCHEME

You can change the font scheme used in your publication. Each font scheme gives your entire publication a consistent, professional appearance.

Each font scheme contains both a major font and a minor font. A major font is usually used for titles and headings and a minor font is usually used for body text.

When you select a new font scheme, Publisher will change all the text in your publication to match the new font scheme, including text you previously changed to another font.

CHANGE THE FONT SCHEME

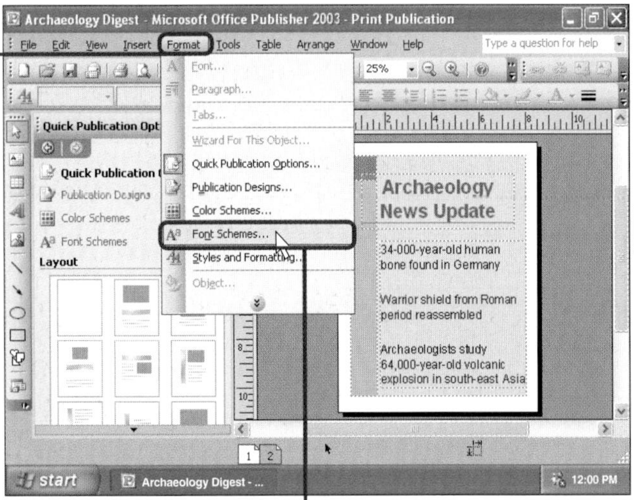

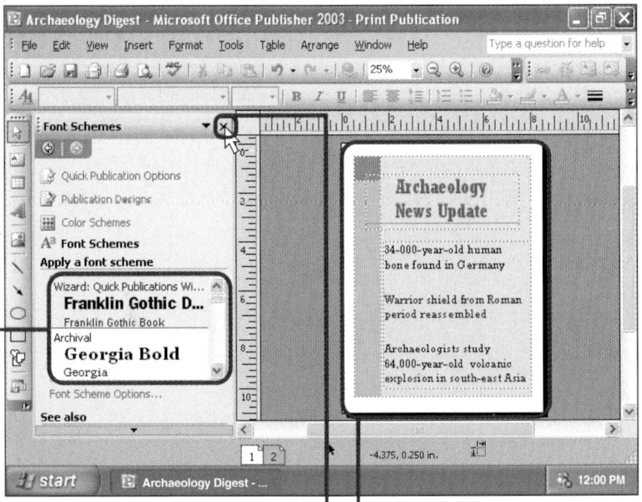

1 Click **Format**.

2 Click **Font Schemes**.

■ The Font Schemes task pane appears.

■ This area displays the available font schemes. You can use the scroll bar to browse through the available font schemes.

3 Click the font scheme you want to use.

■ The text in your publication instantly displays the font scheme you selected.

4 When you finish selecting a font scheme, you can click ☒ to close the Font Schemes task pane.

CHANGE THE COLOR SCHEME

You can change the color scheme used in your publication. Each color scheme contains a set of coordinated colors to enhance your publication.

CHANGE THE COLOR SCHEME

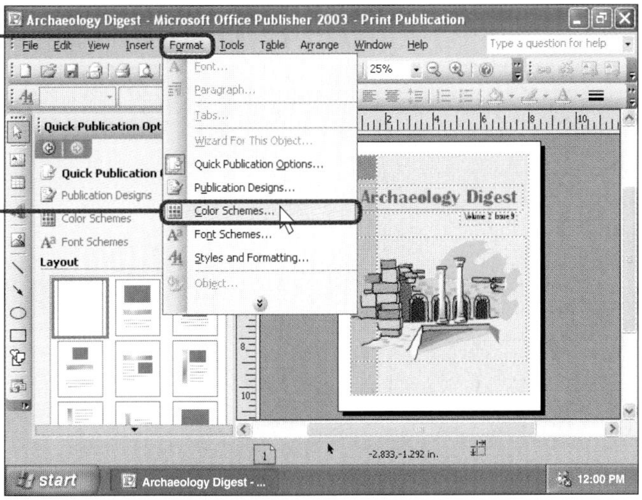

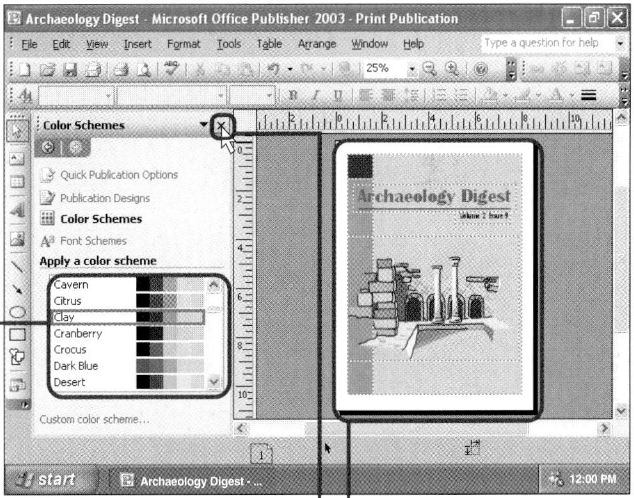

1 Click **Format**.

2 Click **Color Schemes**.

■ The Color Schemes task pane appears.

■ This area displays the available color schemes. You can use the scroll bar to browse through the available color schemes.

3 Click the color scheme you want to use.

■ The publication instantly displays the color scheme you selected.

4 When you finish selecting a color scheme, you can click ☒ to close the Color Schemes task pane.

CHANGE THE PUBLICATION OPTIONS

Most publications offer a set of options you can select to change different aspects of the publication, such as the layout.

For example, when working with a calendar, you can choose a different page orientation, display a monthly or yearly calendar and specify if you want to include a schedule of events.

Some types of publications, such as award certificates, labels and resumes, do not offer publication options.

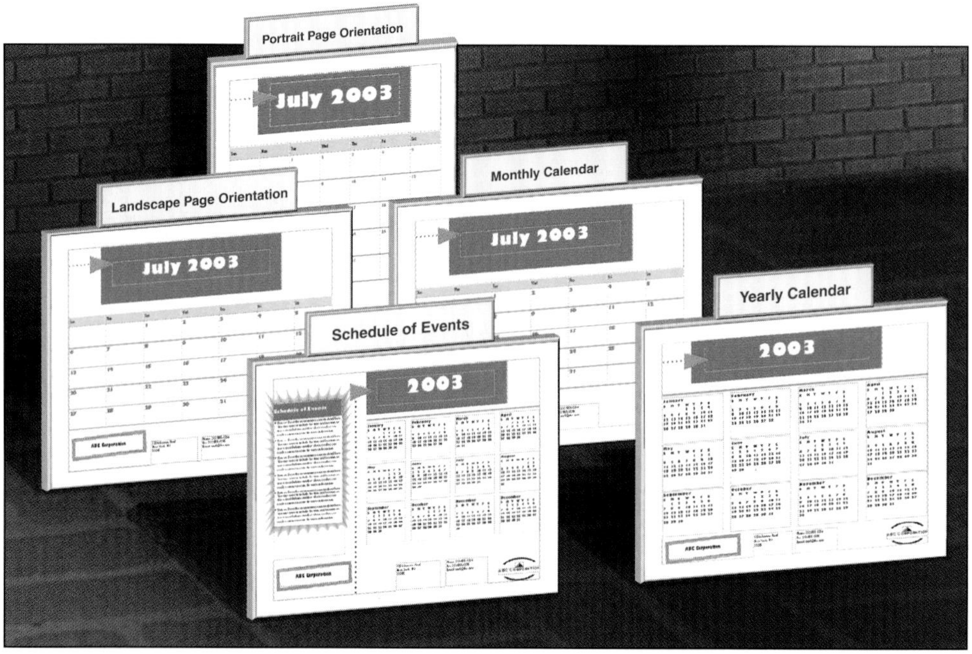

CHANGE THE PUBLICATION OPTIONS

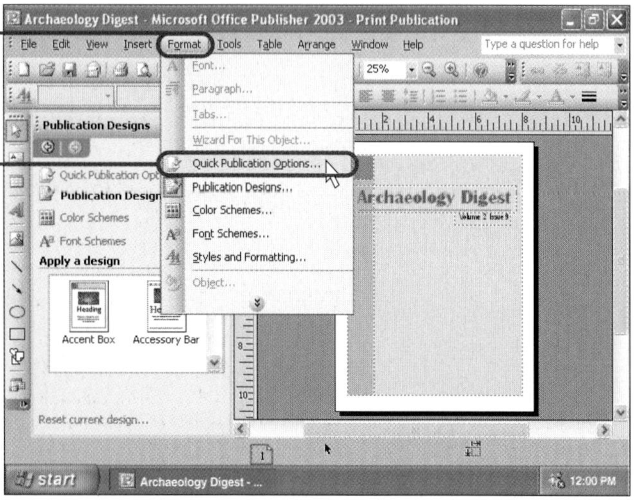

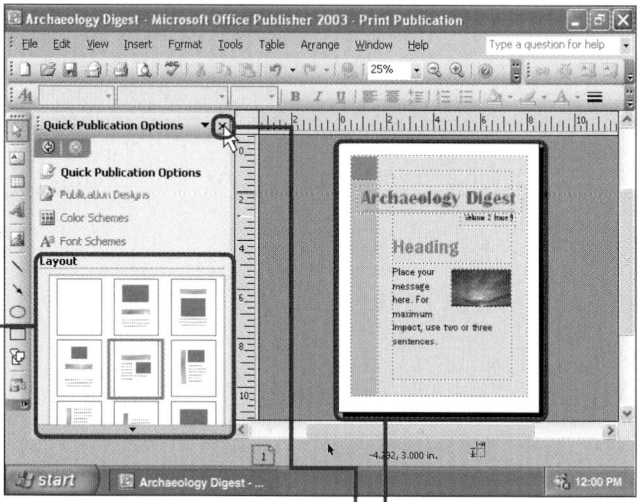

1 Click **Format**.

2 Click **Quick Publication Options**.

Note: The name of the command depends on the type of publication you are working with. For example, look for Newsletter Options when working with a newsletter and Calendar Options when working with a calendar.

■ The Options task pane appears.

■ This area displays the available options for the current publication. In this example, you can change the layout of the publication.

3 Click the layout you want to use.

■ The publication instantly displays the new layout.

4 When you finish changing the options for the publication, you can click ☒ to close the Options task pane.

CHECK YOUR PUBLICATION FOR DESIGN PROBLEMS

You can use Design Checker to find design problems that you might not have noticed in your publication.

Design Checker will find design problems such as an object that is partially off a page, an empty text box, text that does not fit in a text box and a picture that is not sized proportionally.

Design Checker will not find every design problem in your publication. You should still carefully review your publication for design flaws.

CHECK YOUR PUBLICATION FOR DESIGN PROBLEMS

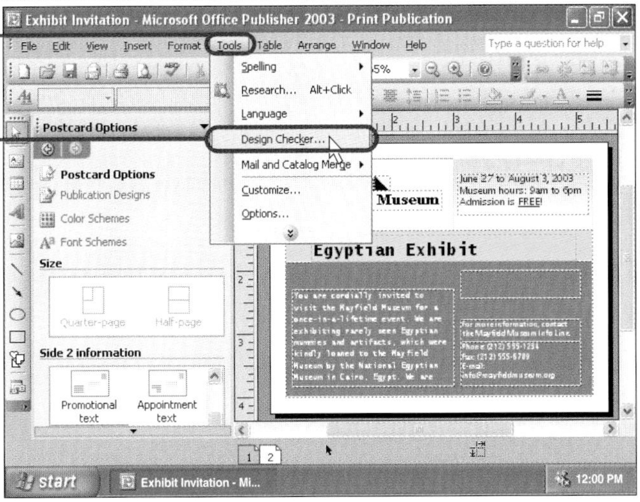

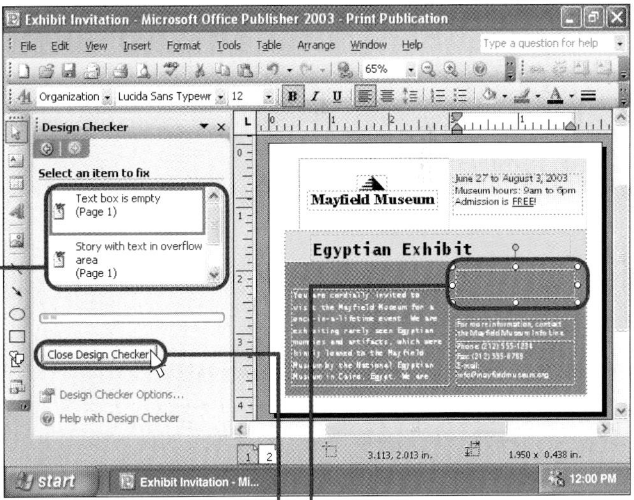

1 Click **Tools**.

2 Click **Design Checker**.

■ The Design Checker task pane appears and Publisher checks your publication for design problems.

■ This area displays each design problem that Design Checker finds in your publication.

3 Click a problem of interest.

■ Publisher selects the object that is causing the problem. You can correct the problem by making the necessary changes.

4 When you finish reviewing the design problems in your publication, click **Close Design Checker**.

ADD AN AUTOSHAPE

Publisher provides a group of ready-made shapes, called AutoShapes, that you can add to your publication.

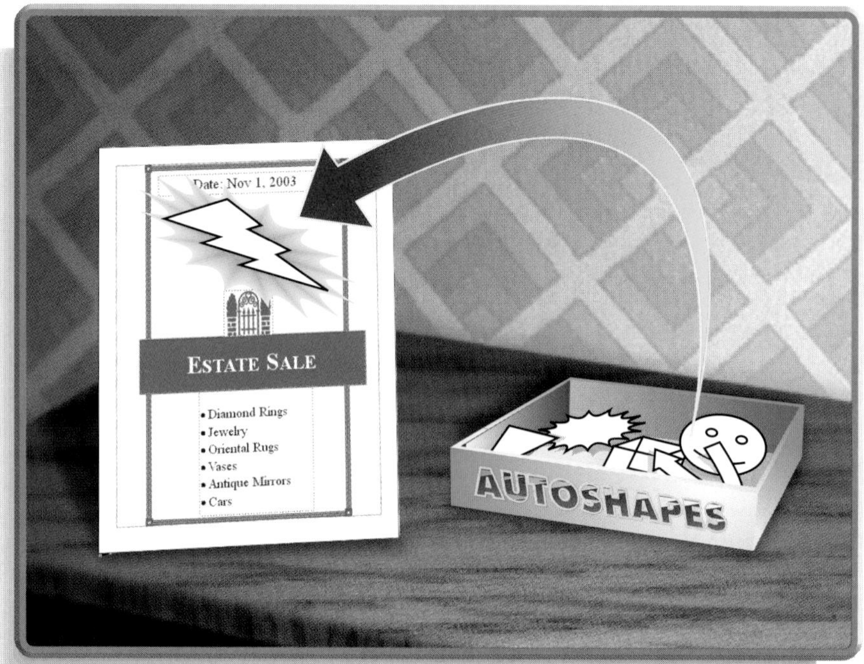

Publisher offers several types of AutoShapes, including lines, arrows, stars and banners.

ADD AN AUTOSHAPE

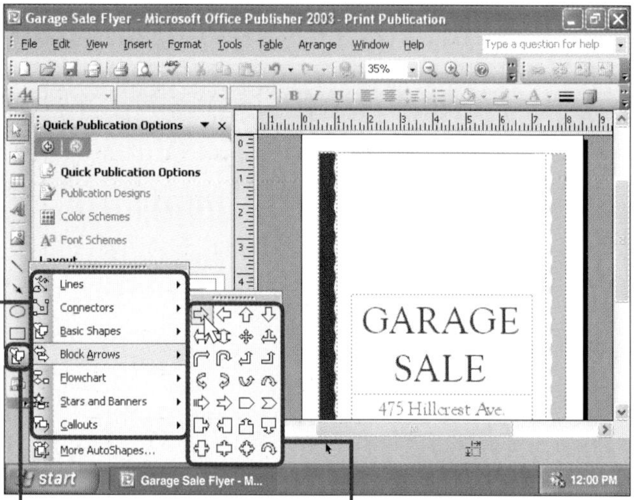

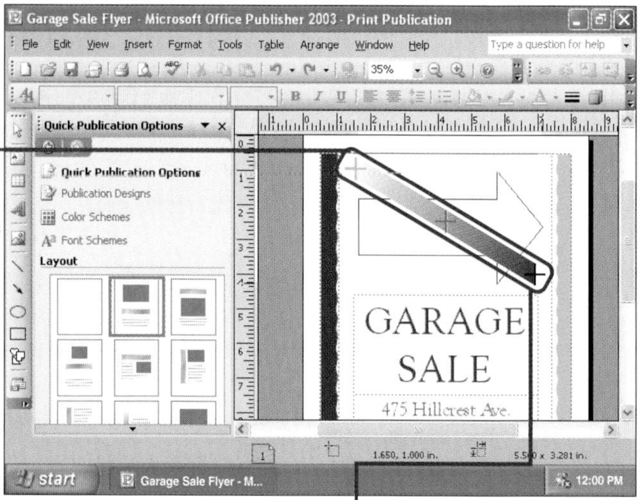

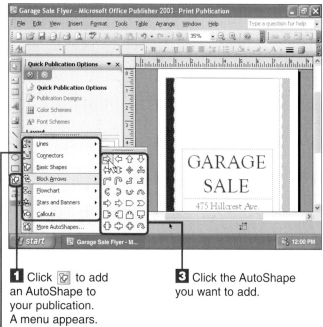

1 Click 🗗 to add an AutoShape to your publication.

A menu appears.

2 Click the type of AutoShape you want to add.

3 Click the AutoShape you want to add.

4 Position the mouse + where you want to begin drawing the AutoShape.

5 Drag the mouse + until the AutoShape appears the way you want.

Tip

Can I add text to an AutoShape?

You can add text to most AutoShapes. Adding text is particularly useful for AutoShapes such as banners and callouts. To add text to an AutoShape, click the AutoShape and then type the text you want to add. When you finish typing the text, click outside the AutoShape.

Tip

How can I change the design of an AutoShape?

You can change the design of any AutoShape that displays a yellow handle (◇). To redesign an AutoShape, click the AutoShape and position the mouse ⇖ over the yellow handle (⇖ changes to ▷). Then drag the mouse until the AutoShape appears the way you want.

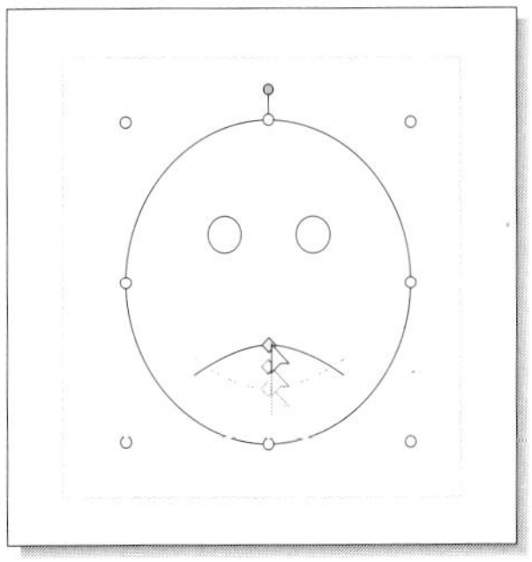

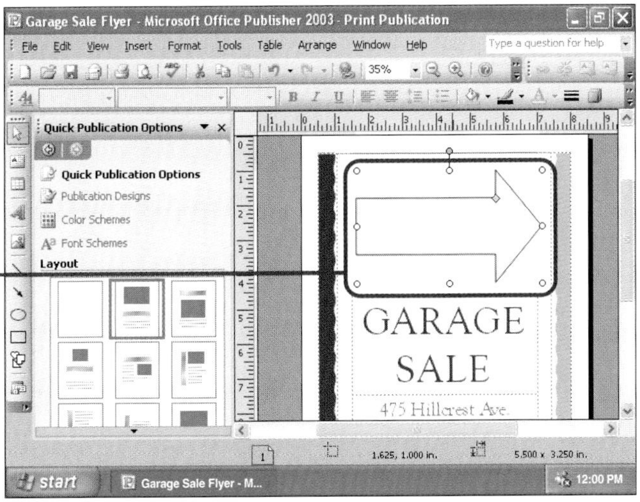

■ The AutoShape appears in your publication. The handles (○) around the AutoShape allow you to change the size of the AutoShape. To move or resize an AutoShape, see page 298.

■ To hide the handles (○) around the AutoShape, click outside the AutoShape.

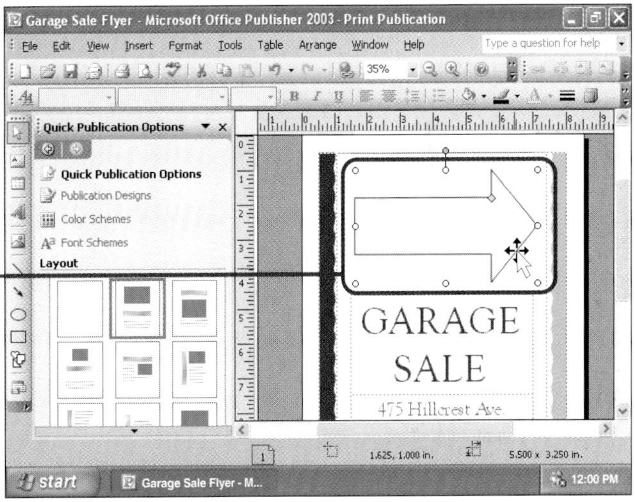

DELETE AN AUTOSHAPE

1 Click the edge of the AutoShape you want to delete. Handles (○) appear around the AutoShape.

2 Press the Delete key to delete the AutoShape.

ADD A PICTURE

You can add a picture stored on your computer to your publication.

Adding a picture is useful if you want to display your company logo, a picture of your products or a favorite family photograph in your publication.

ADD A PICTURE

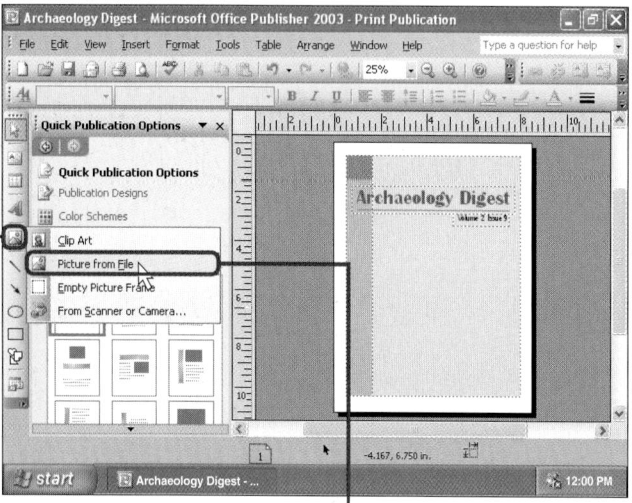

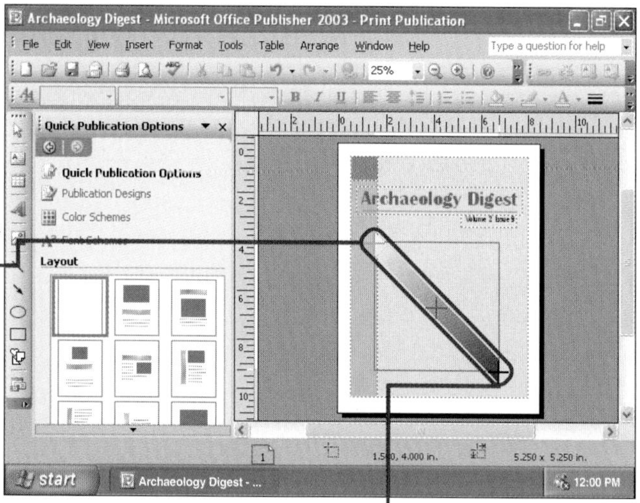

1 Click to add a picture. A menu appears.

2 Click **Picture from File**.

3 Position the mouse + where you want to begin drawing the frame for the picture.

4 Drag the mouse + until the frame for the picture is the size you want.

■ The Insert Picture dialog box appears.

Tip

Where can I get pictures that I can add to my publication?

You can purchase collections of pictures at computer stores or obtain pictures on the Internet. You can also use a scanner to scan pictures into your computer or create your own pictures using a drawing program.

Tip

How do I delete a picture I no longer want to appear in my publication?

Click the picture you want to delete. Handles (○) appear around the picture. Press the Delete key to delete the picture.

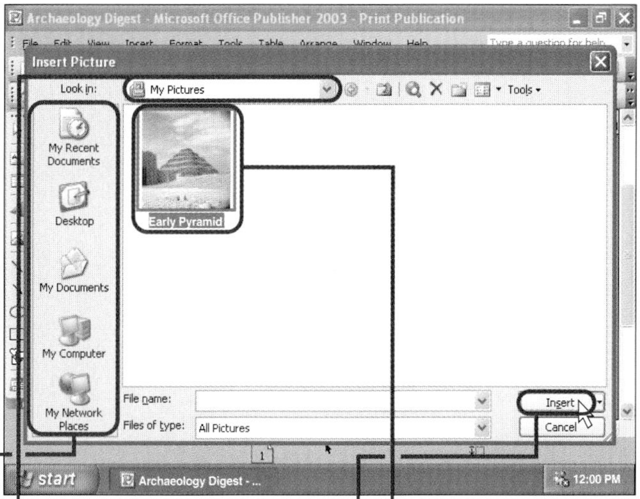

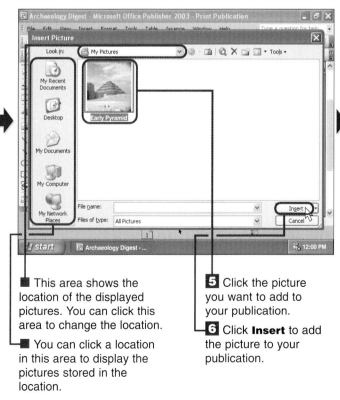

■ This area shows the location of the displayed pictures. You can click this area to change the location.

■ You can click a location in this area to display the pictures stored in the location.

5 Click the picture you want to add to your publication.

6 Click **Insert** to add the picture to your publication.

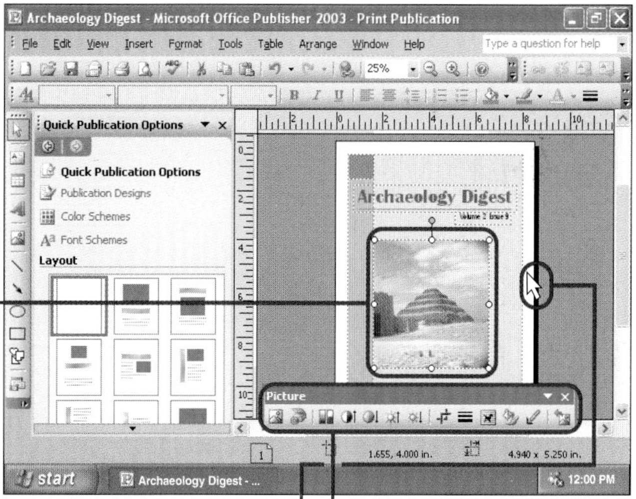

■ The picture appears in your publication. The handles (○) around the picture allow you to change the size of the picture. To move or resize a picture, see page 298.

■ When a picture is selected, the Picture toolbar appears, displaying buttons that allow you to change the appearance of the picture.

7 To hide the Picture toolbar and the handles (○) around the picture, click outside the picture.

ADD CLIP ART

You can add professionally designed clip art images to your publication. Clip art images can help illustrate ideas and make your publication more visually appealing.

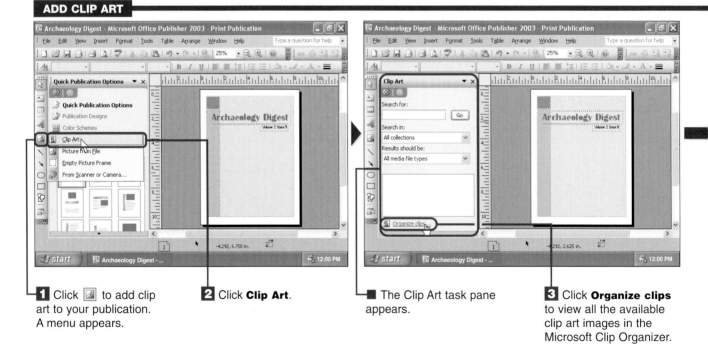

ADD CLIP ART

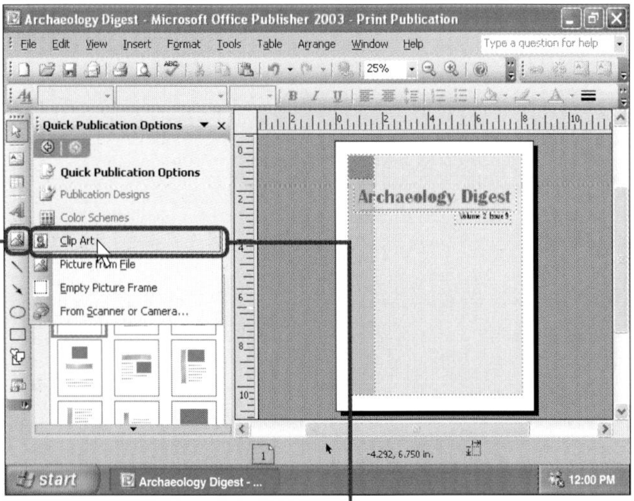

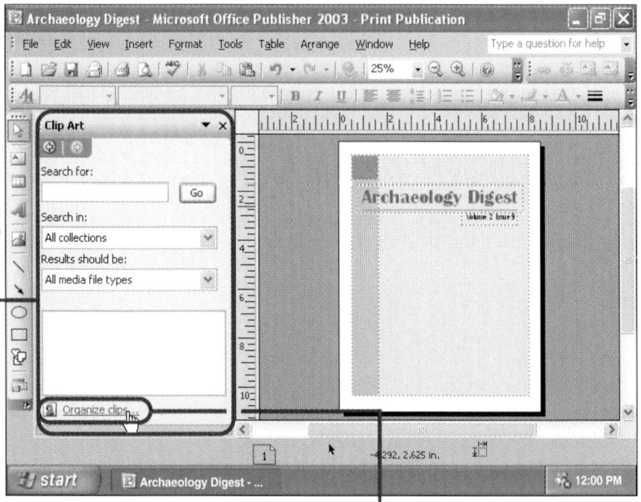

1 Click [icon] to add clip art to your publication. A menu appears.

2 Click **Clip Art**.

■ The Clip Art task pane appears.

3 Click **Organize clips** to view all the available clip art images in the Microsoft Clip Organizer.

Tip

In the Microsoft Clip Organizer, what type of clip art images will I find in each collection?

My Collections

Displays the pictures that came with Microsoft Windows and pictures you created or obtained on your own.

Office Collections

Displays the pictures that came with Microsoft Office.

Web Collections

Displays the pictures that are available at Microsoft's Web site and at Web sites in partnership with Microsoft.

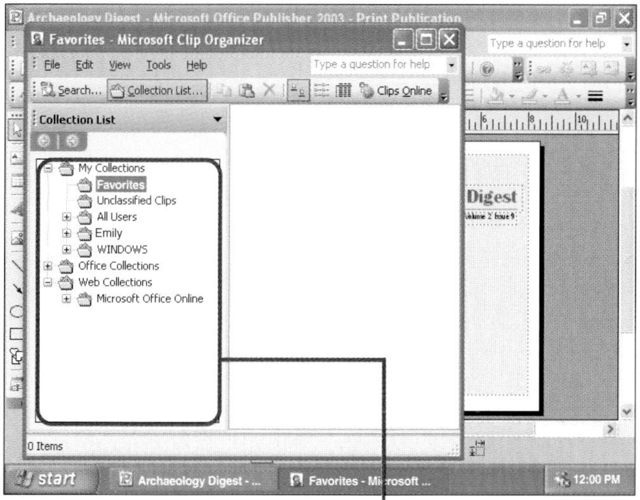

■ The Microsoft Clip Organizer window appears.

*Note: The first time you add clip art to a publication, the Add Clips to Organizer dialog box appears. To catalog the clip art images and other media files on your computer, click **Now** in the dialog box.*

■ This area displays the folders that contain the clip art images you can add to your publication. A folder displaying a plus sign (+) contains hidden folders.

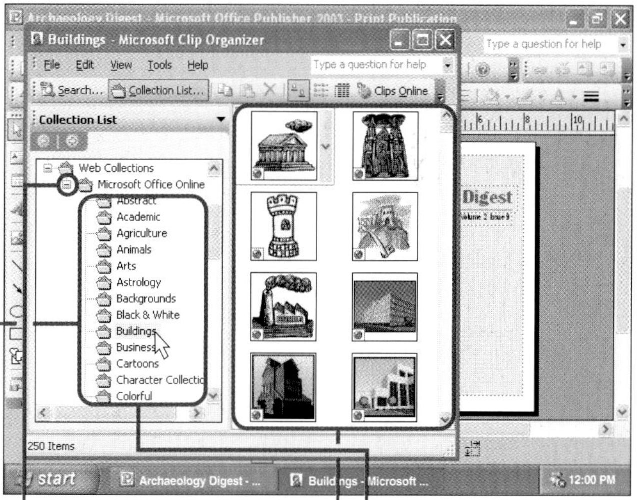

4 To display the hidden folders within a folder, click the plus sign (+) beside a folder (+ changes to −).

■ The hidden folders appear.

Note: You must be connected to the Internet to view the contents of the Web Collections folder.

5 Click a folder of interest.

■ This area displays the clip art images in the folder you selected.

CONTINUED

ADD CLIP ART

After you locate a clip art image you want to use, you can easily place the image in your publication.

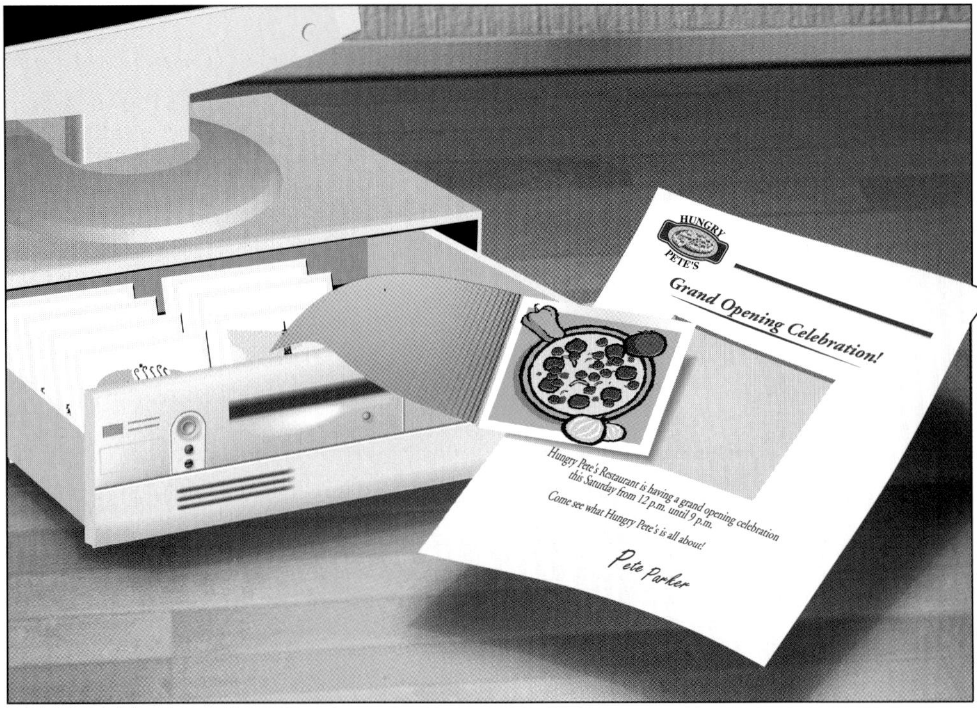

ADD CLIP ART (CONTINUED)

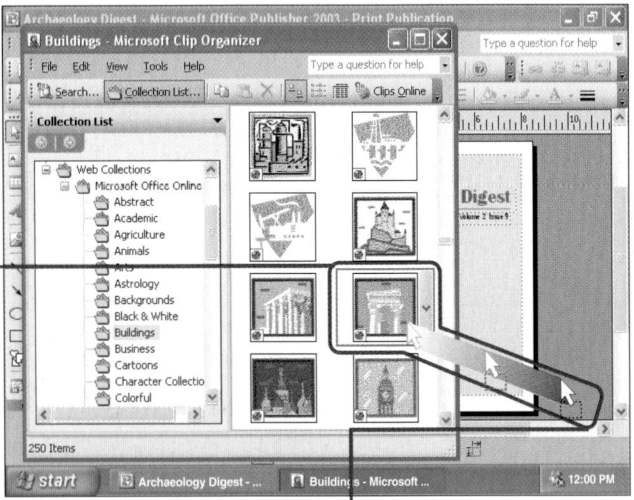

6 To add a clip art image to your publication, position the mouse over the image.

7 Drag the clip art image to the workspace in your publication.

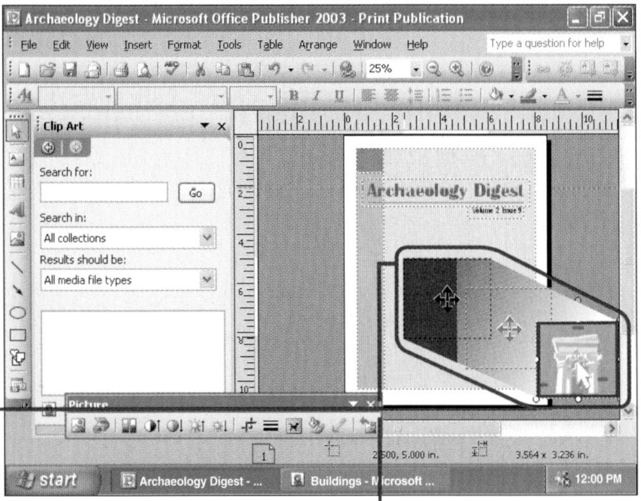

■ The clip art image appears in the workspace of your publication.

8 To place the clip art image on a page in your publication, position the mouse over the image.

9 Drag the clip art image to the location where you want the image to appear.

Tip

After I add a clip art image, why does the button for the Microsoft Clip Organizer window remain on the taskbar?

The button for the Microsoft Clip Organizer window remains on the taskbar so you can easily redisplay the window and add another clip art image to your publication. If you do not want to add another clip art image, click the button on the taskbar to redisplay the window. Then click ☒ to close the window.

Tip

How do I delete a clip art image I no longer want to appear in my publication?

Click the image you want to delete. Handles (○) appear around the image. Press the Delete key to delete the clip art image.

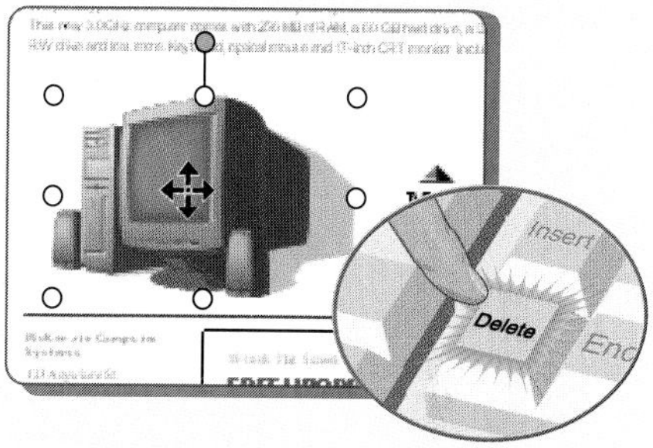

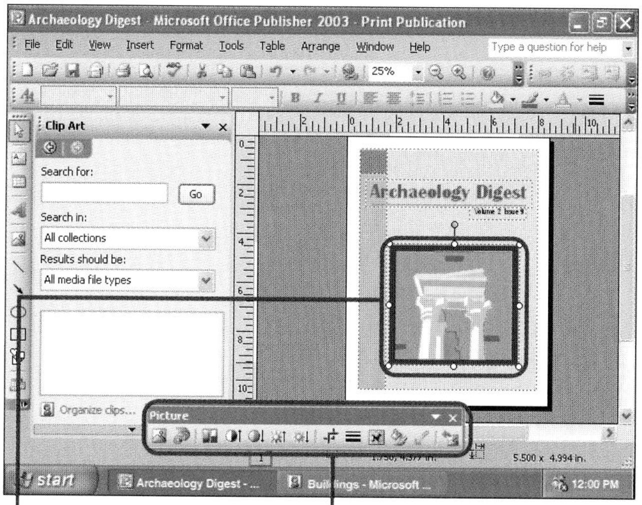

■ The clip art image appears on the page. The handles (○) around the image allow you to change the size of the image. To move or resize an image, see page 298.

■ When a clip art image is selected, the Picture toolbar appears, displaying buttons that allow you to change the appearance of the image.

■ To hide the Picture toolbar and the handles (○) around the clip art image, click outside the image.

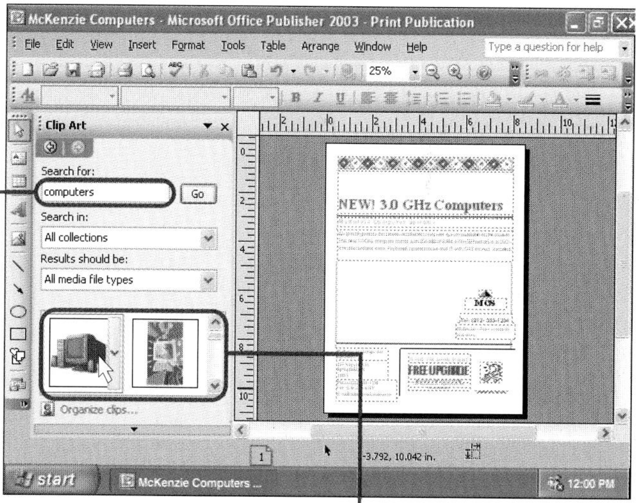

SEARCH FOR CLIP ART IMAGES

■ You can search for clip art images by specifying a word in the Clip Art task pane.

1 Double-click this area and type a word that describes the clip art image you want to search for. Then press the Enter key.

■ A list of matching clip art images appears.

2 To add a clip art image to your publication, click the image.

ADD WORDART

You can add WordArt to your publication to enhance a title or draw attention to important information.

ADD WORDART

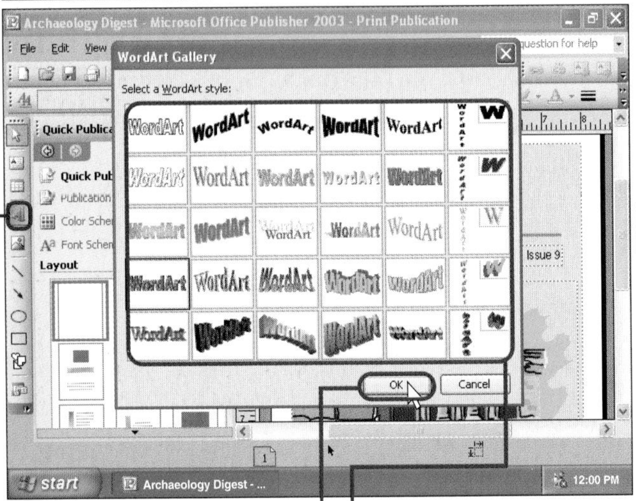

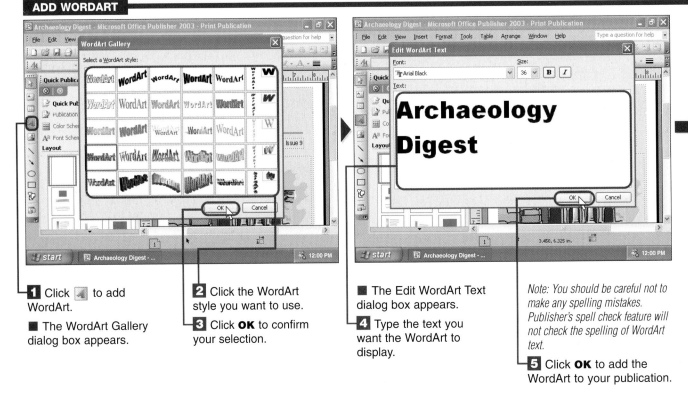

1 Click to add WordArt.

■ The WordArt Gallery dialog box appears.

2 Click the WordArt style you want to use.

3 Click **OK** to confirm your selection.

■ The Edit WordArt Text dialog box appears.

4 Type the text you want the WordArt to display.

Note: You should be careful not to make any spelling mistakes. Publisher's spell check feature will not check the spelling of WordArt text.

5 Click **OK** to add the WordArt to your publication.

Tip

How do I edit WordArt text?

To edit WordArt text, double-click the WordArt to redisplay the Edit WordArt Text dialog box. Then perform steps **4** and **5** below to specify the new text you want the WordArt to display.

Tip

How can I change the shape of WordArt?

To change the shape of WordArt, click the WordArt you want to change. In the WordArt toolbar that appears, click the WordArt Shape ( ) button. Then select the shape you want to use for the WordArt.

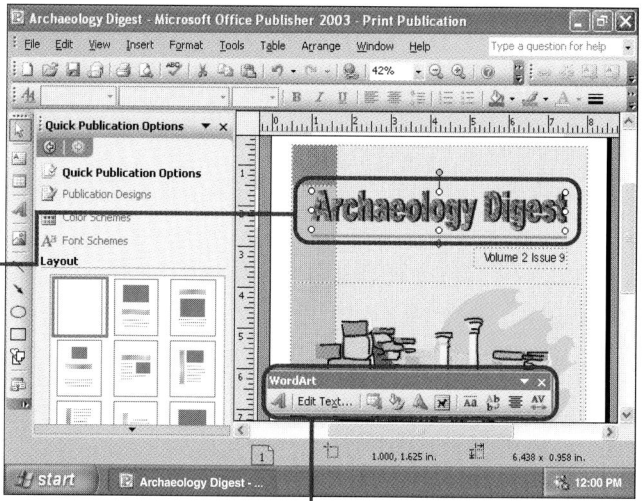

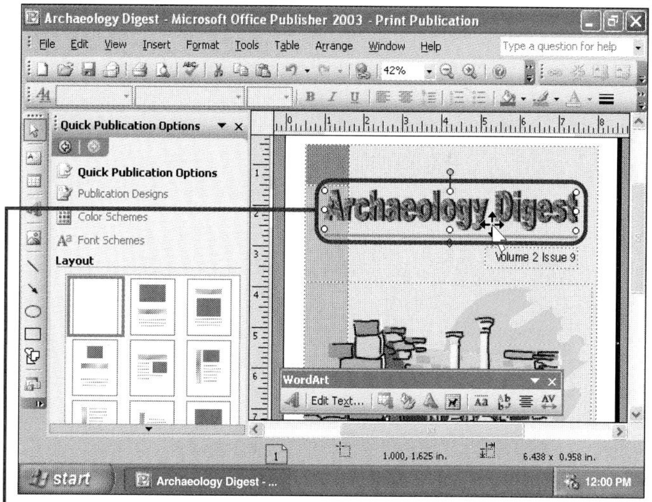

■ The WordArt appears in your publication. The handles (○) around the WordArt allow you to change the size of the WordArt. To move or resize WordArt, see page 298.

■ When WordArt is selected, the WordArt toolbar appears, displaying buttons that allow you to change the appearance of the WordArt.

■ To hide the WordArt toolbar and the handles (○) around the WordArt, click outside the WordArt.

DELETE WORDART

1 Click the WordArt you want to delete. Handles (○) appear around the WordArt.

2 Press the Delete key to delete the WordArt.

ADD A TEXT BOX

When you want to add text to your publication, you need to add a text box to hold the text. Text boxes control the placement of text in a publication.

ADD A TEXT BOX

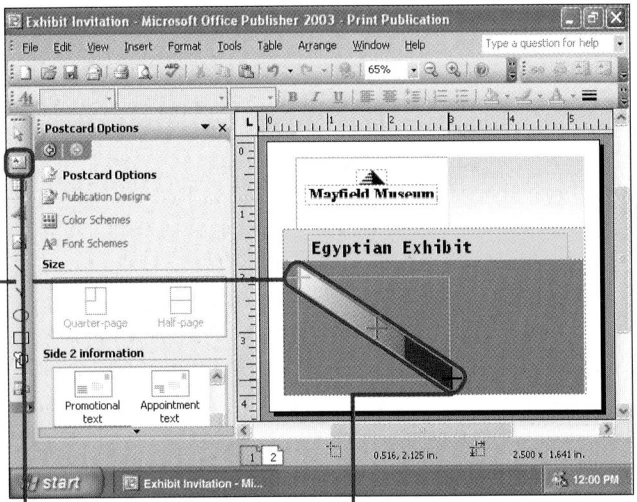

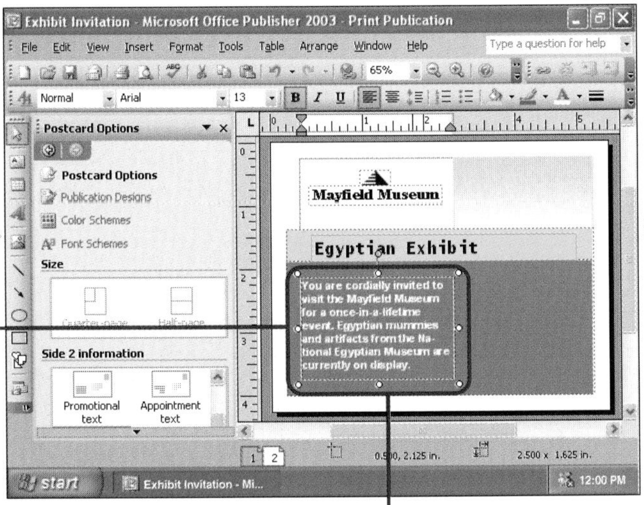

1 Click to add a text box.

2 Position the mouse + where you want to begin drawing the text box.

3 Drag the mouse + until the text box is the size you want.

■ The text box appears in your publication. The handles (○) around the text box allow you to change the size of the text box. To move or resize a text box, see page 298.

4 Type the text you want to appear in the text box.

Tip

The text I entered in a text box does not fit in the text box. What can I do?

When you type more text than a text box can hold, Publisher displays the overflow indicator (A ▪▪▪) below the text box. To display the extra text, you can increase the size of the text box (see page 298), decrease the size of the text (see page 263) or connect the text box to another text box (see page 292).

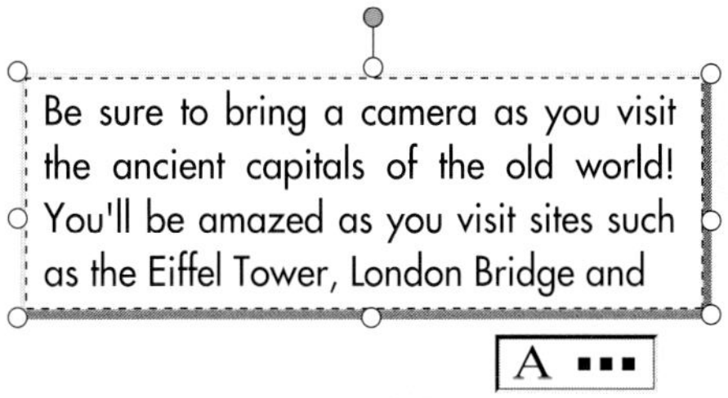

Be sure to bring a camera as you visit the ancient capitals of the old world! You'll be amazed as you visit sites such as the Eiffel Tower, London Bridge and
A ▪▪▪

Tip

When I type text in a text box, why do some words display a wavy, red underline?

Publisher automatically underlines possible misspelled words in red. The red underlines will not appear when you print your publication. To correct misspelled words, see page 248.

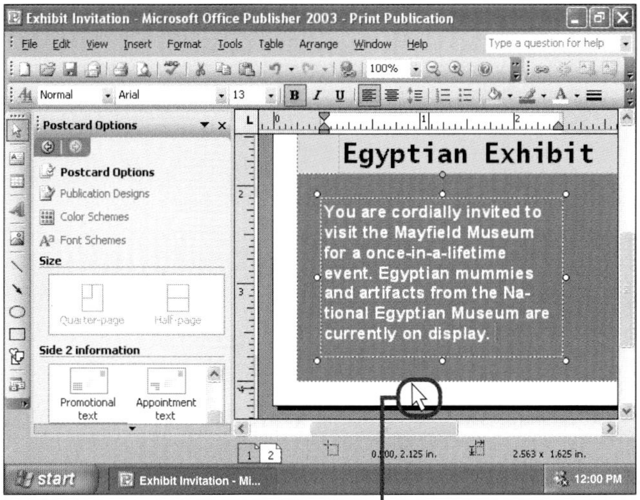

5 If the text you are typing is too small to read, press the F9 key to zoom in so you can clearly view the text.

Note: For more information on zooming in and out of your publication, see page 240.

6 When you finish typing the text, click outside the text box to hide the handles (○) around the text box.

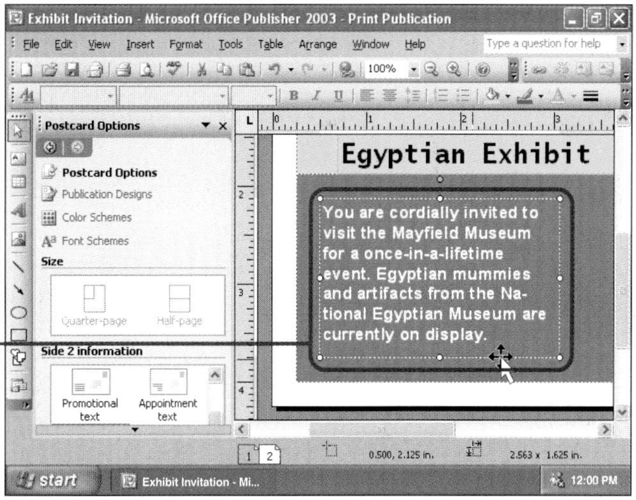

DELETE A TEXT BOX

1 Click an edge of the text box you want to delete. Handles (○) appear around the text box.

2 Press the Delete key to delete the text box.

CONNECT TEXT BOXES

You can connect text boxes so you can continue information in another location in your publication. Text that will not fit in one text box will flow into the next connected text box.

A series of connected text boxes is referred to as a story. Connected text boxes can appear on the same page or across many pages.

CONNECT TEXT BOXES

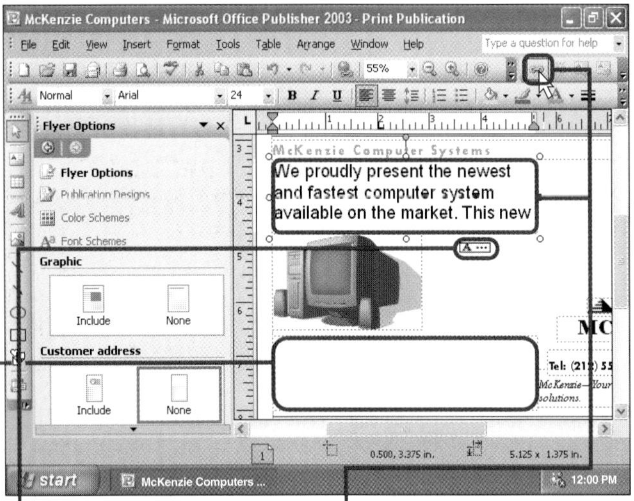

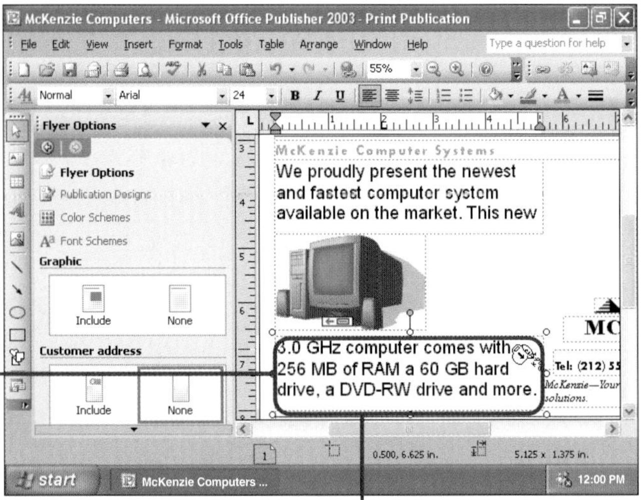

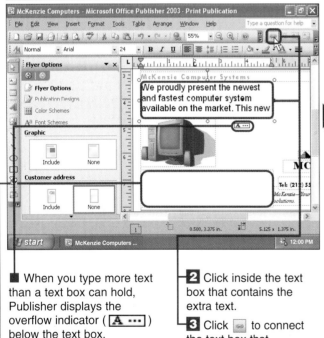

■ When you type more text than a text box can hold, Publisher displays the overflow indicator (A ···) below the text box.

1 Create a new text box. To create a text box, see page 290.

2 Click inside the text box that contains the extra text.

3 Click to connect the text box that contains the extra text to the new text box (changes to).

4 Click inside the new text box to connect the text boxes.

■ Publisher connects the text boxes. Any text that did not fit in the first text box appears in the connected text box.

Tip

How can I quickly determine which text boxes are connected?

Click anywhere inside a text box that connects to another text box. Press and hold down the Ctrl key as you press the A key. Publisher highlights all the text in the connected text boxes. To deselect the text, click a blank area in your publication.

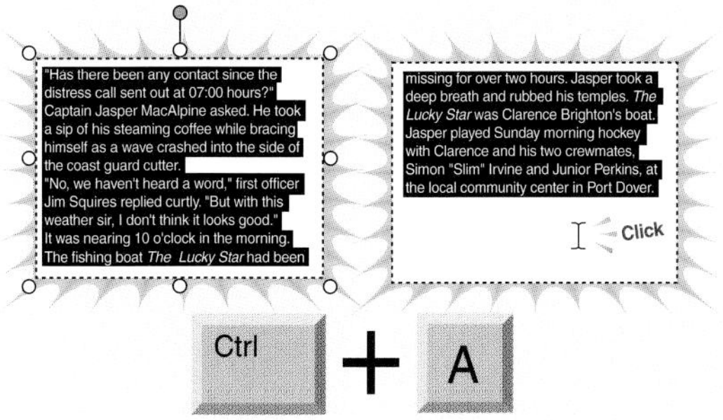

Tip

How can I move text from the bottom of one connected text box to the top of another?

You can insert a section break. Click to the left of the text you want to move to the next text box. Then press and hold down the Ctrl key as you press the Enter key. To remove a section break, click to the left of the text you moved to the second text box and then press the ←Backspace key.

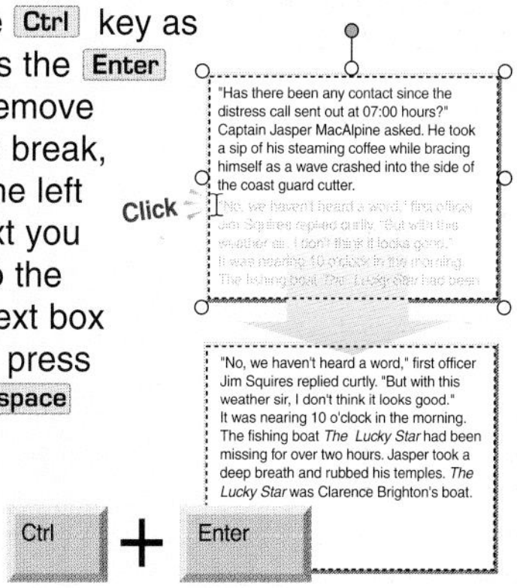

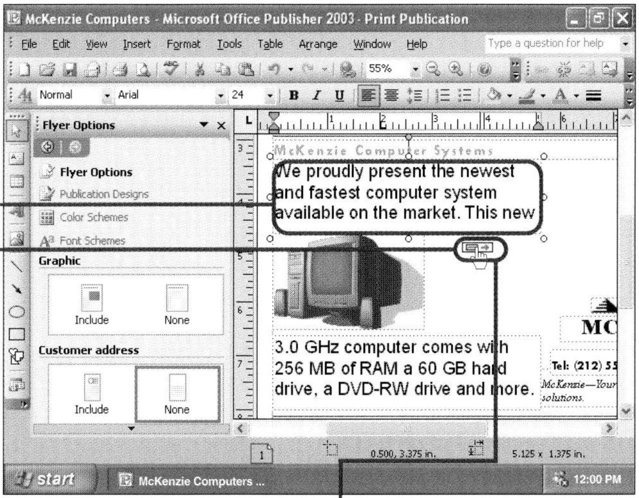

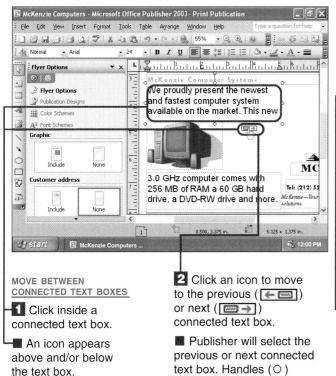

MOVE BETWEEN CONNECTED TEXT BOXES

1 Click inside a connected text box.

■ An icon appears above and/or below the text box.

2 Click an icon to move to the previous ( ) or next ( ) connected text box.

■ Publisher will select the previous or next connected text box. Handles (○) appear around the selected text box.

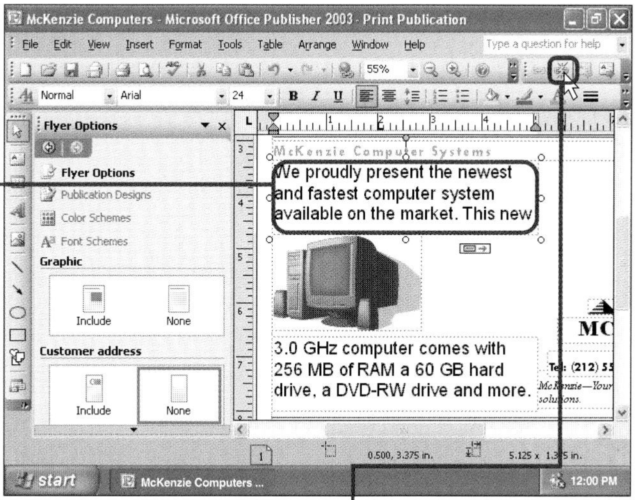

BREAK THE CONNECTION BETWEEN TWO TEXT BOXES

1 Click inside the first text box you no longer want to connect to another text box.

2 Click ( ) to break the connection between the text boxes.

■ Publisher will remove the text from the second text box and add the text back to the first text box.

ADD A TABLE

You can add a table to neatly display information in your publication. Tables can help you organize lists of information, such as product details or sales figures.

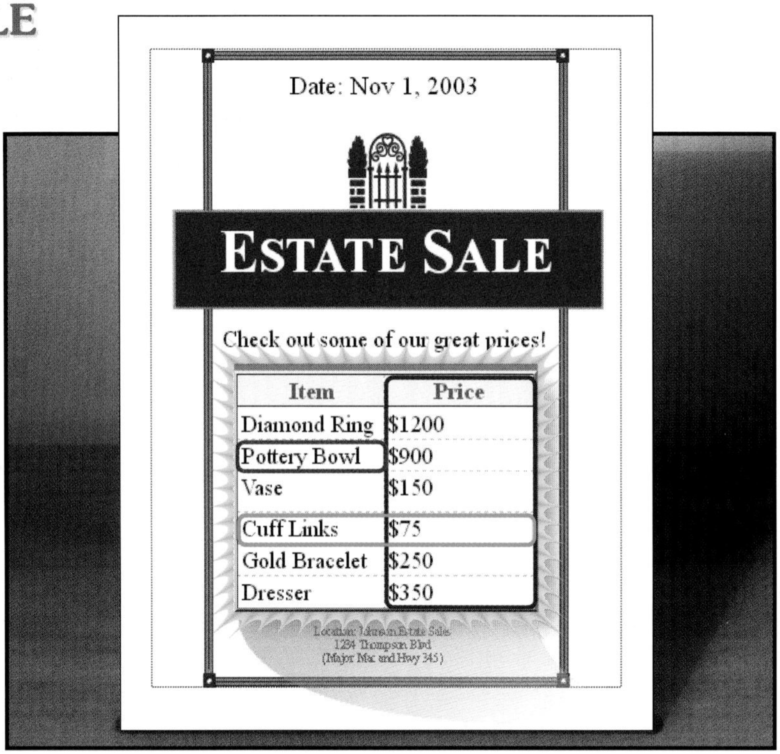

A table consists of rows, columns and cells.

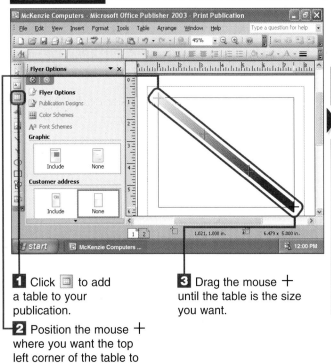

Row

Column

Cell

ADD A TABLE

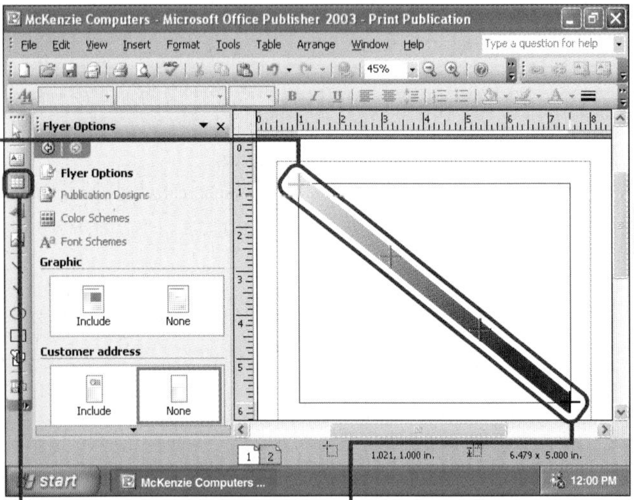

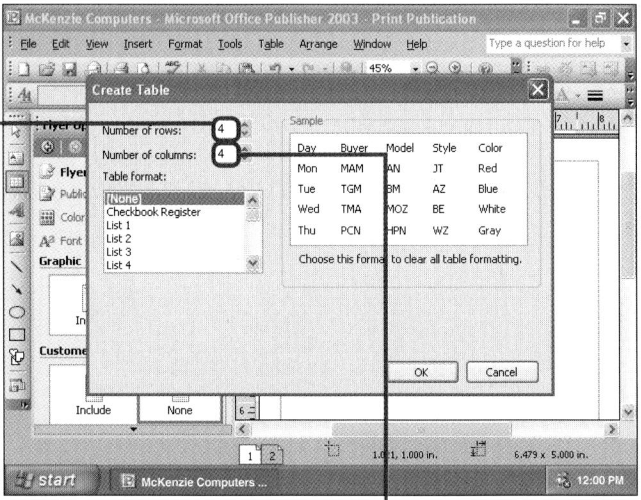

1 Click ▦ to add a table to your publication.

2 Position the mouse + where you want the top left corner of the table to appear.

3 Drag the mouse + until the table is the size you want.

■ The Create Table dialog box appears.

4 Double-click the number in this area and type the number of rows you want to include in your table.

5 Double-click the number in this area and type the number of columns you want to include in your table.

Tip

How can I quickly add a row to the bottom of a table?

To quickly add a row to the bottom of a table, click the bottom right cell in the table and then press the Tab key.

Item
Price
Diamond Ring
$1200
Pottery Bowl
$900
Vase
$150
Cuff Links
$75
Gold Bracelet
$250
Dresser
$350
"Click"

Tip

How do I delete a table I no longer want to appear in my publication?

Click the edge of the table you want to delete. Handles (○) appear around the table. Press the Delete key to delete the table.

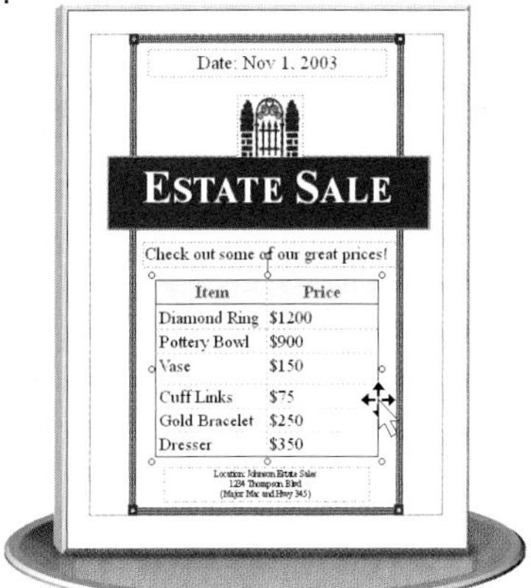

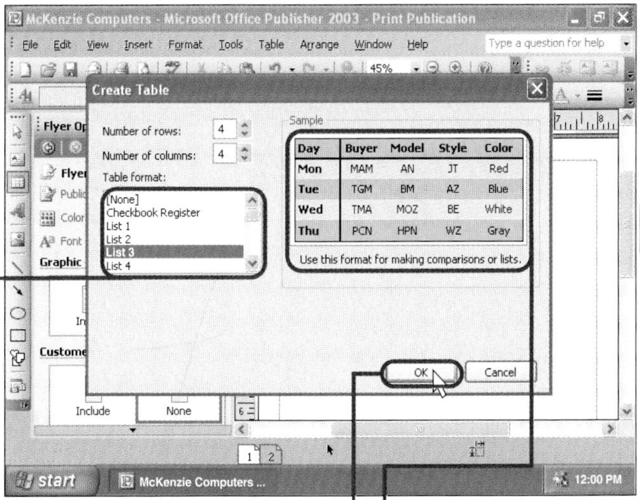

6 Click the style you want to use for your table.

■ This area displays a sample of the table style you selected and information about the type of data this style of table usually stores.

7 Click **OK** to add the table to your publication.

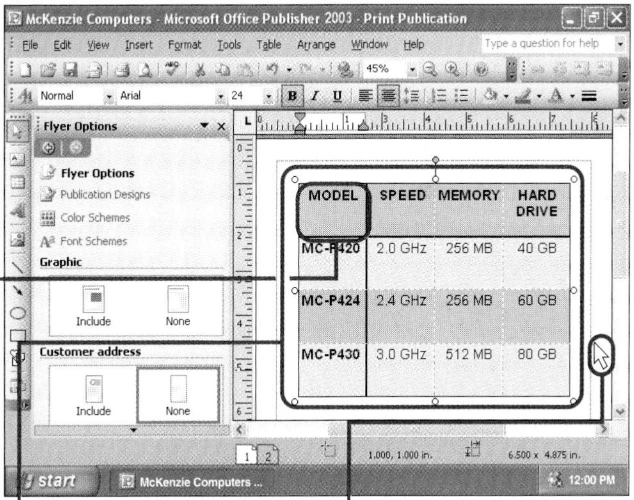

■ The table appears in your publication. The handles (○) around the table allow you to change the size of the table. To move or resize a table, see page 298.

8 To add text to the table, click inside a cell and then type the text.

Note: To zoom in so you can clearly view the text you type, see page 240.

9 When you finish adding text to the table, click outside the table.

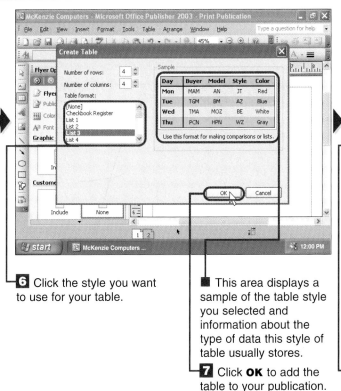

ADD A DESIGN GALLERY OBJECT

You can add attractive design gallery objects, such as reply forms, calendars, logos, coupons and borders, to your publication.

Many of the objects available in the design gallery contain sample text that you can replace with your own text.

ADD A DESIGN GALLERY OBJECT

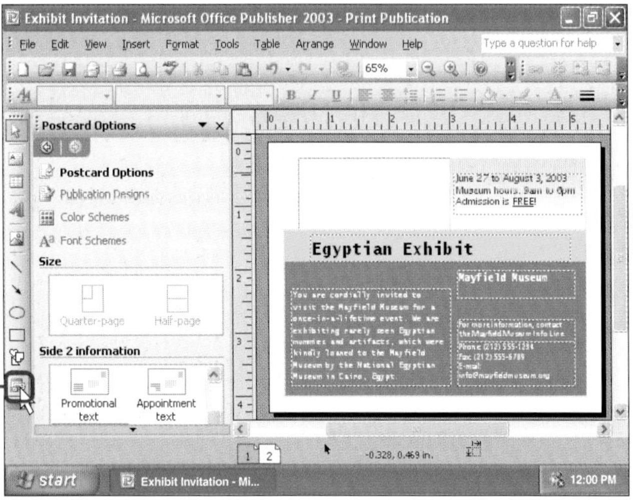

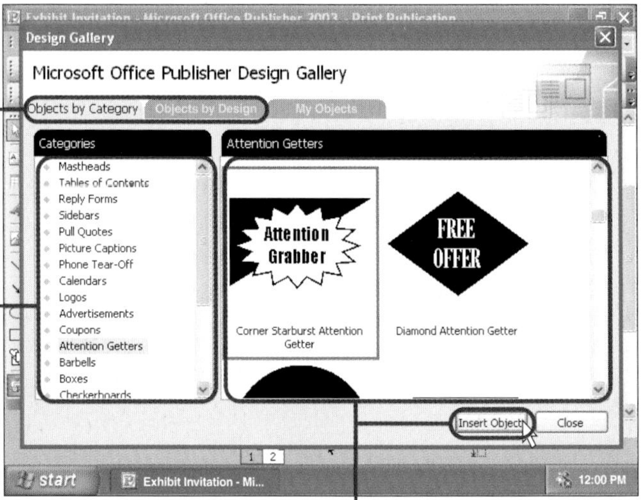

1 Click to add a design gallery object to your publication.

■ The Design Gallery dialog box appears.

2 Click a tab to display the available design gallery objects by category or by design.

3 Click the category or design set of interest.

■ This area displays the objects in the category or design set you selected.

4 Click the object you want to add to your publication.

5 Click **Insert Object** to add the object.

Tip

How can I change the appearance of a design gallery object I added to my publication?

To change the appearance of a design gallery object, click the design gallery object, click the object and then click the icon ( ) that appears below the object. A task pane appears that allows you to choose a new design for the object. In the task pane, click the design you want to use.

Note: If the icon ( ) does not appear below the design gallery object, you cannot change the appearance of the object.

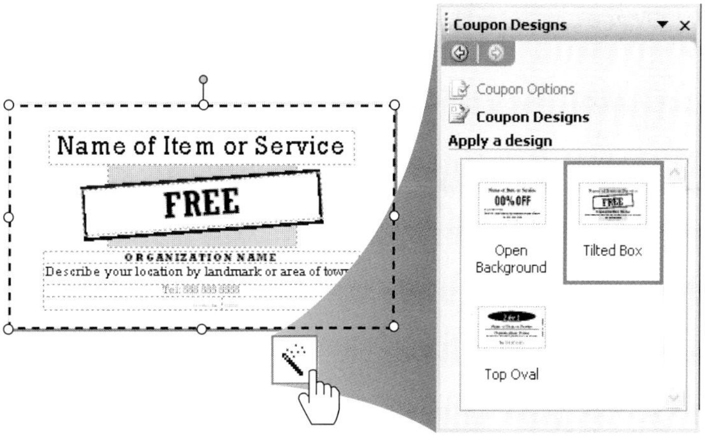

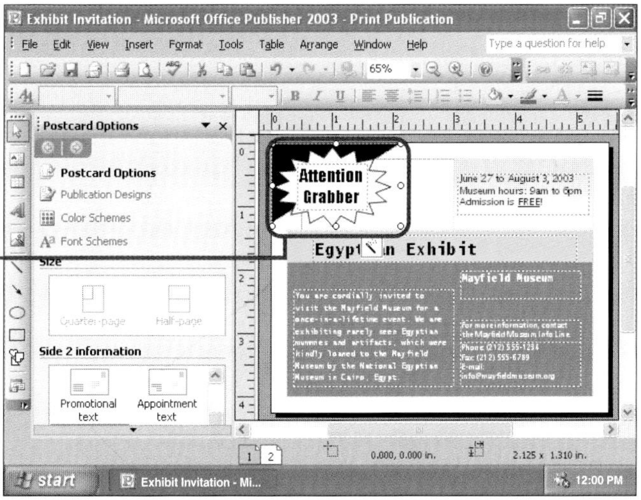

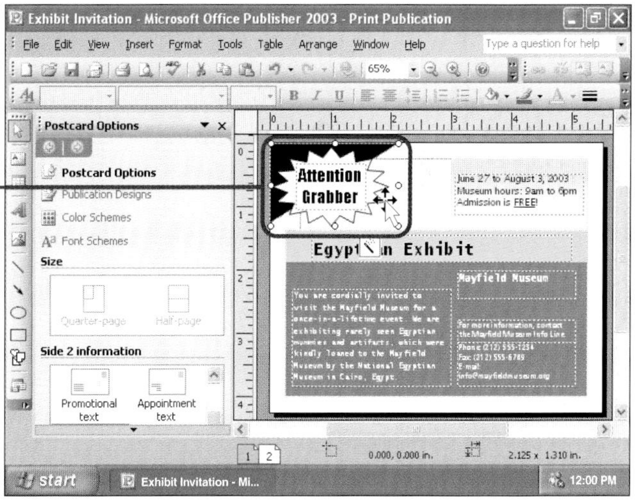

■ The design gallery object appears in your publication. The handles (○) around the object allow you to change the size of the object. To move or resize an object, see page 298.

■ To hide the handles (○) around the object, click outside the object.

DELETE A DESIGN GALLERY OBJECT

1 Click the edge of the object you want to delete. Handles (○) appear around the object.

2 Press the Delete key to delete the object.

MOVE OR RESIZE AN OBJECT

You can change the location and size of an object in your publication.

For example, you may want to move a picture to a more suitable location or increase the size of a text box to display more text.

MOVE AN OBJECT

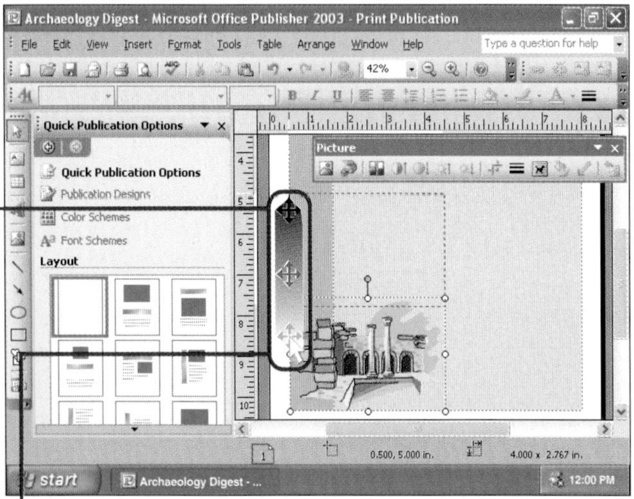

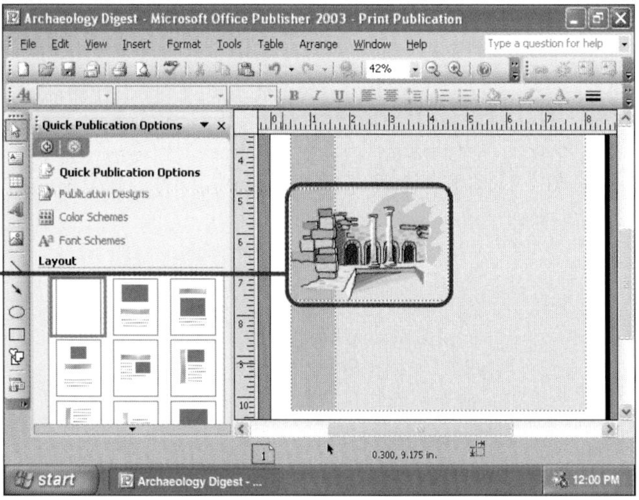

1 Position the mouse over an edge of the object you want to move (changes to).

2 Drag the object to a new location.

Note: To drag the object in a straight line, press and hold down the **Shift** *key as you drag the object.*

■ A dashed line indicates where the object will appear.

■ The object appears in the new location.

■ To deselect the object, click outside the object.

Tip

Which handle (○) should I use to resize an object?

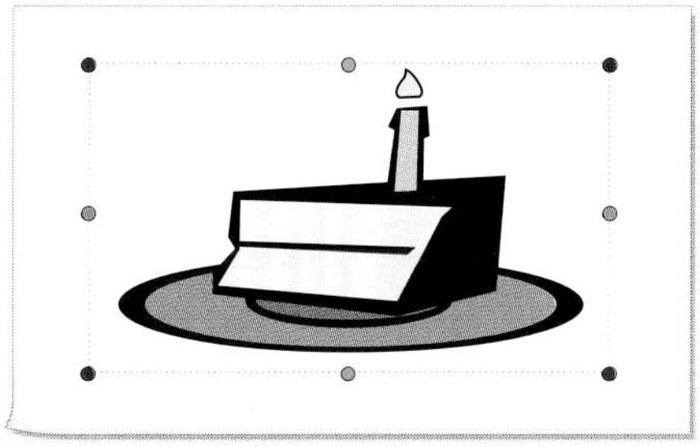

- Changes the height of an object
- Changes the width of an object
- Changes the height and width of an object at the same time

Tip

When I select an object, why does a green handle (○) appear?

You can use the green handle (○) to rotate the object. To rotate an object, position the mouse ↖ over the green handle (↖ changes to ↻). Then drag the mouse in the direction you want to rotate the object.

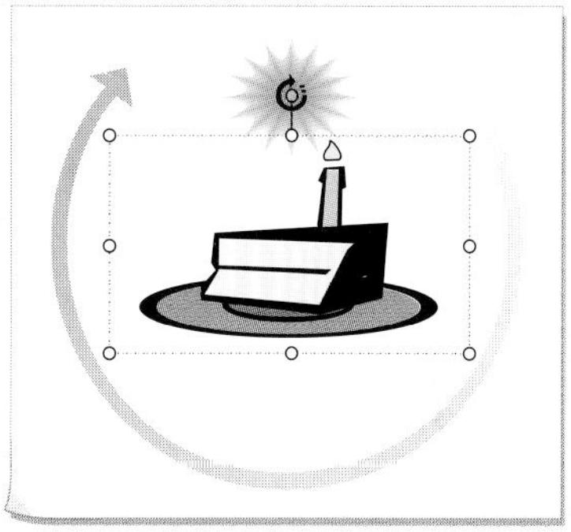

RESIZE AN OBJECT

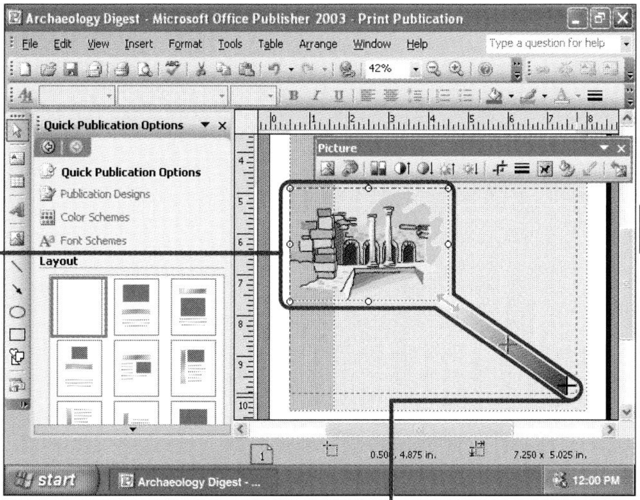

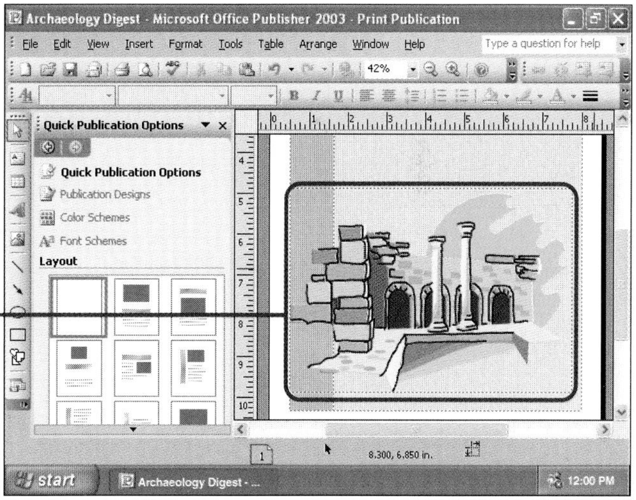

1 Click the object you want to resize. Handles (○) appear around the object.

2 Position the mouse ↖ over one of the handles (↖ changes to ↘, ↗, ↕ or ↔).

3 Drag the handle until the object is the size you want.

Note: To maintain the object's proportions, press and hold down the **Shift** *key as you drag a corner handle.*

■ A dashed line indicates the new size.

■ The object appears in the new size.

■ To deselect the object, click outside the object.

CHANGE THE COLOR OF AN OBJECT

You can change the color of an object to draw attention to the object or to improve the appearance of the object.

Publisher allows you to change the color of objects such as text boxes, AutoShapes and WordArt.

CHANGE THE COLOR OF AN OBJECT

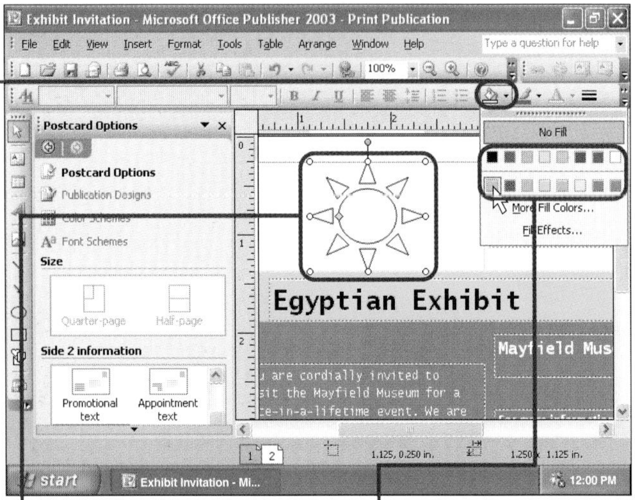

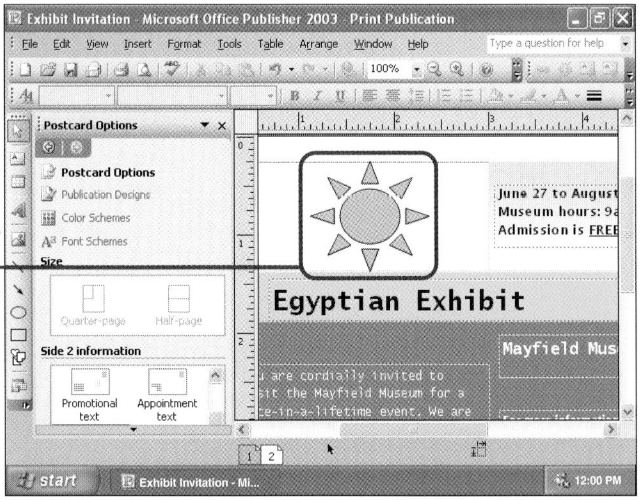

1 Click the object you want to display in a different color. Handles (○) appear around the object.

2 Click ▾ in this area to display the available colors.

3 Click the color you want to use.

Note: The available colors depend on the color scheme used in your publication. For information on color schemes, *see page 277.*

■ The object displays the color you selected.

■ To deselect the object, click outside the object.

*Note: If you do not want the object to display a color, perform steps **1** to **3**, selecting **No Fill** in step **3**.*

CHANGE THE COLOR OF THE LINE AROUND AN OBJECT

You can enhance an object by changing the color of the line surrounding the object.

Publisher allows you to change the line color for objects such as text boxes, pictures, clip art images and WordArt.

By default, many types of objects are surrounded by a dashed line, which will not appear when you print your publication. When you change the line color, Publisher will print the line in the color you selected.

CHANGE THE COLOR OF THE LINE AROUND AN OBJECT

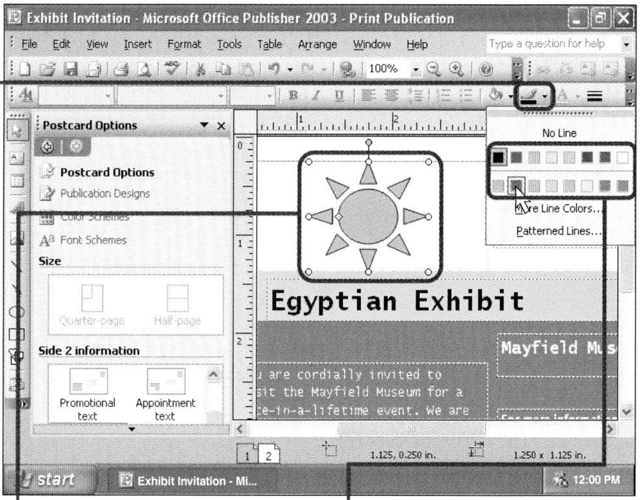

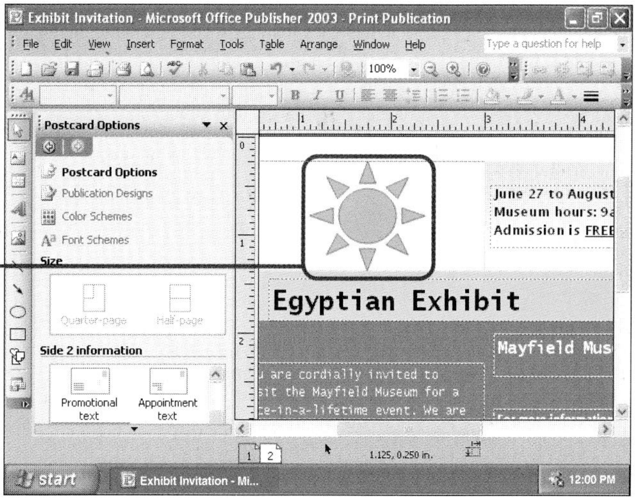

1 Click the object you want to display a different line color. Handles (○) appear around the object.

2 Click ▾ in this area to display the available line colors.

3 Click the line color you want to use.

Note: The available line colors depend on the color scheme used in your publication. For information on color schemes, see page 277.

■ The line surrounding the object displays the new color.

■ To deselect the object, click outside the object.

*Note: If you do not want the object to display a line, perform steps **1** to **3**, selecting **No Line** in step **3**.*

CHANGE THE STYLE OF THE LINE AROUND AN OBJECT

You can enhance an object by changing the style of the line surrounding the object.

Publisher allows you to change the line style for objects such as text boxes, pictures, clip art images and AutoShapes.

By default, many types of objects are surrounded by a dashed line, which will not appear when you print your publication. When you change the line style, Publisher will print the line in the style you selected.

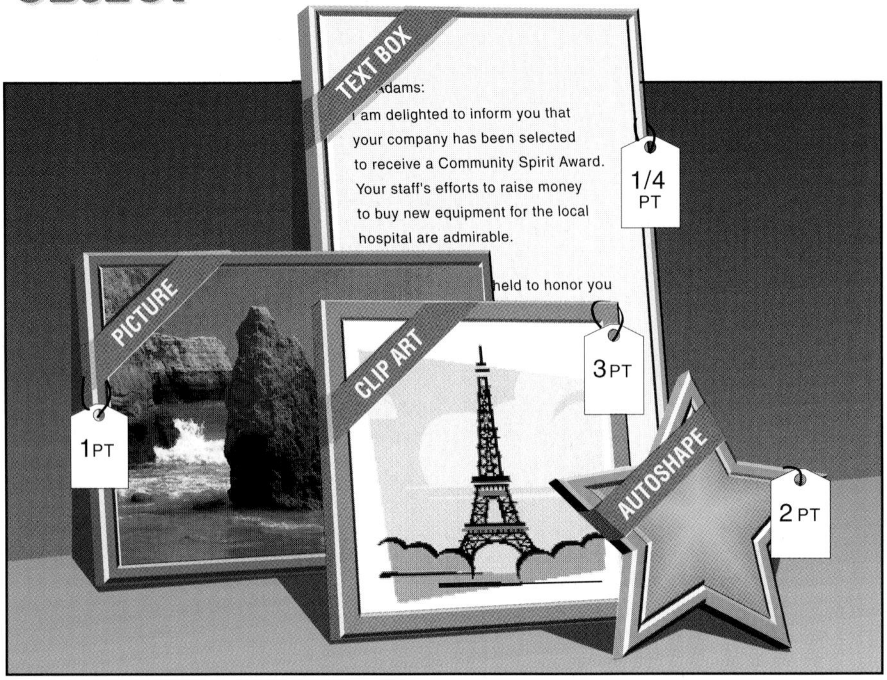

CHANGE THE STYLE OF THE LINE AROUND AN OBJECT

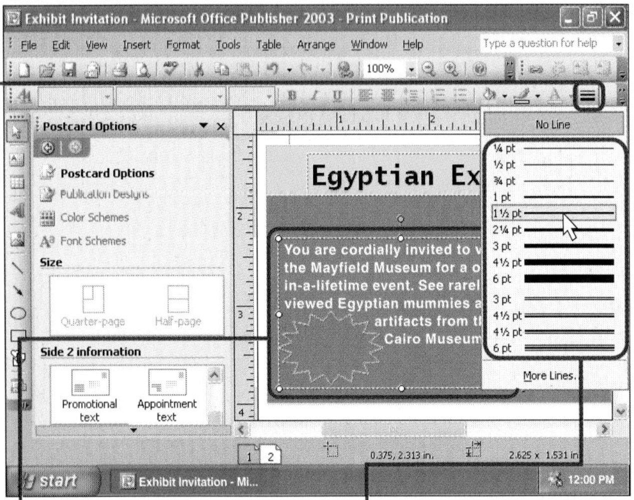

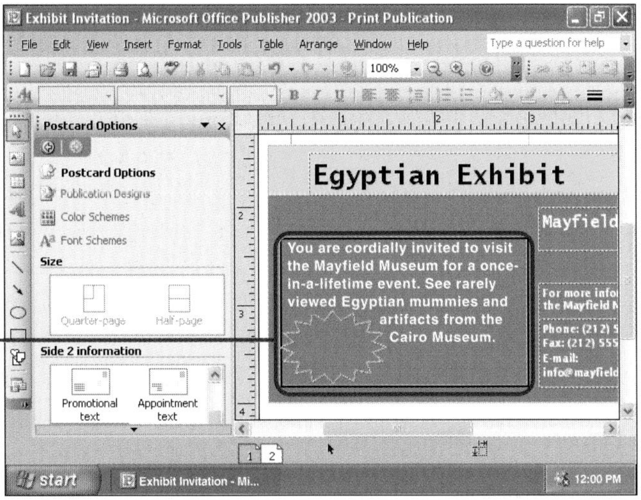

1 Click the object you want to display a different line style. Handles (○) appear around the object.

2 Click ≡ to display the available line styles.

3 Click the line style you want to use.

■ The line surrounding the object displays the new style.

■ To deselect the object, click outside the object.

*Note: If you do not want the object to display a line, perform steps **1** to **3**, selecting **No Line** in step **3**.*

CHANGE THE WAY TEXT WRAPS AROUND AN OBJECT

After you add an object to your publication, you can change the way the text wraps around the object.

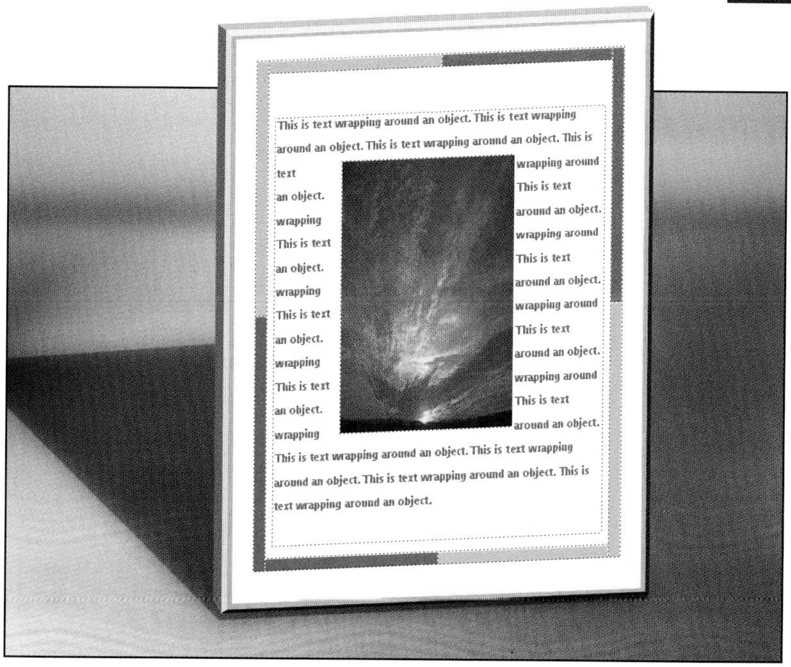

You can have Publisher wrap text to form a square around an object or fit tightly around an object. Publisher can also wrap text around the top and bottom of an object.

CHANGE THE WAY TEXT WRAPS AROUND AN OBJECT

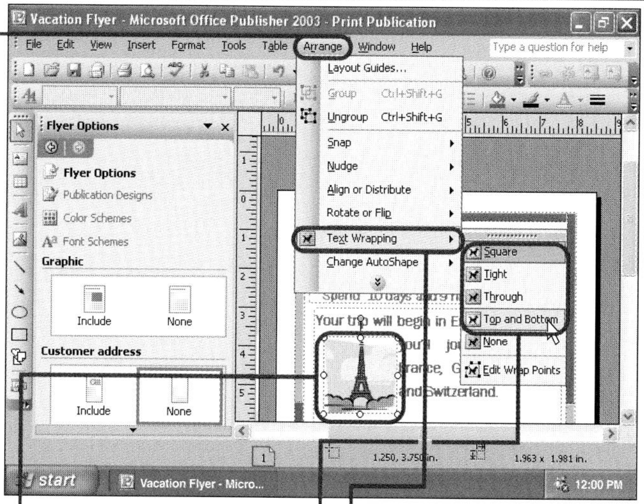

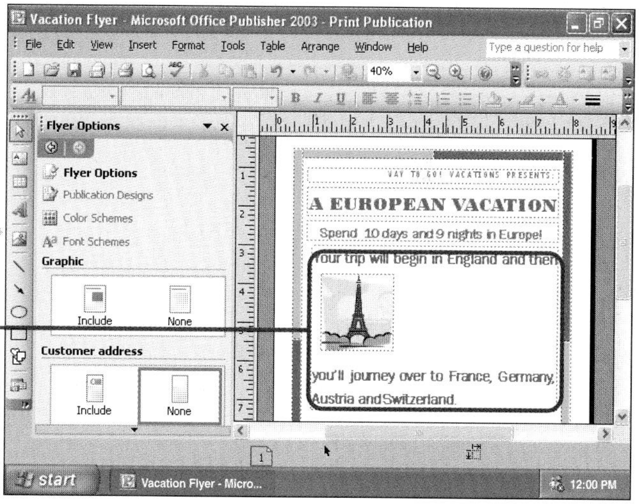

1 Click the object you want to wrap text around. Handles (○) appear around the object.

2 Click **Arrange**.

3 Click **Text Wrapping**.

4 Click the way you want the text to wrap around the object.

■ The text wraps around the object in the way you selected.

■ To deselect the object, click outside the object.

■ If you do not want Publisher to wrap the text around the object, perform steps **1** to **4**, selecting **None** in step **4**.

ADD A SHADOW TO AN OBJECT

You can add a shadow to an object to make the object appear as if it is raised off the page.

Publisher allows you to add a shadow to objects such as text boxes, clip art images and AutoShapes.

ADD A SHADOW TO AN OBJECT

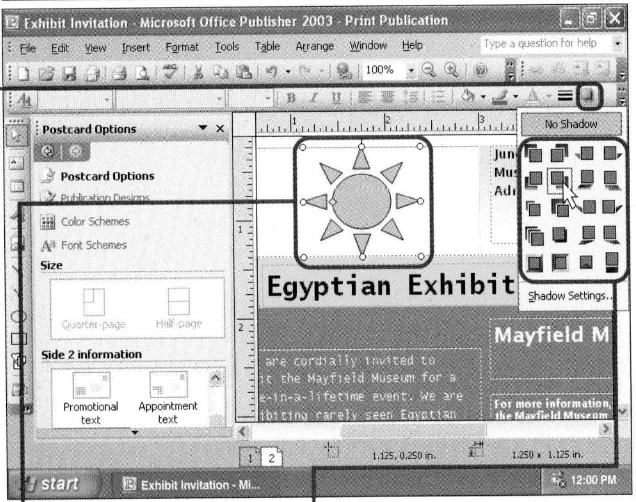

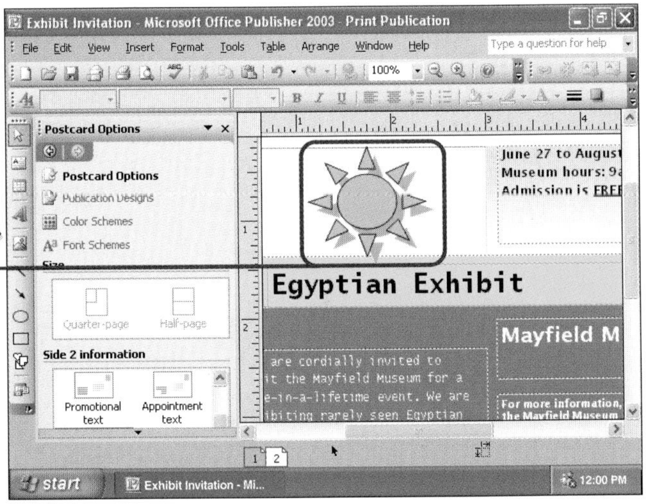

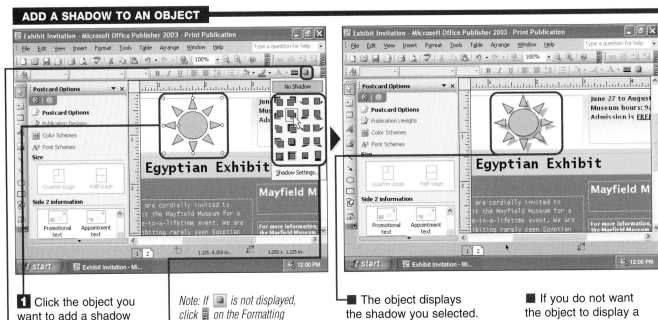

1 Click the object you want to add a shadow to. Handles (○) appear around the object.

2 Click to select a shadow style.

Note: If is not displayed, click on the Formatting toolbar to display the button.

3 Click the shadow style you want to use.

■ The object displays the shadow you selected.

■ To deselect the object, click outside the object.

■ If you do not want the object to display a shadow, perform steps **1** to **3**, selecting **No Shadow** in step **3**.

ADD A 3-D EFFECT TO AN OBJECT

You can add a three-dimensional effect to an object to give the object depth in your publication.

Publisher allows you to add a 3-D effect to many AutoShapes, WordArt and design gallery objects.

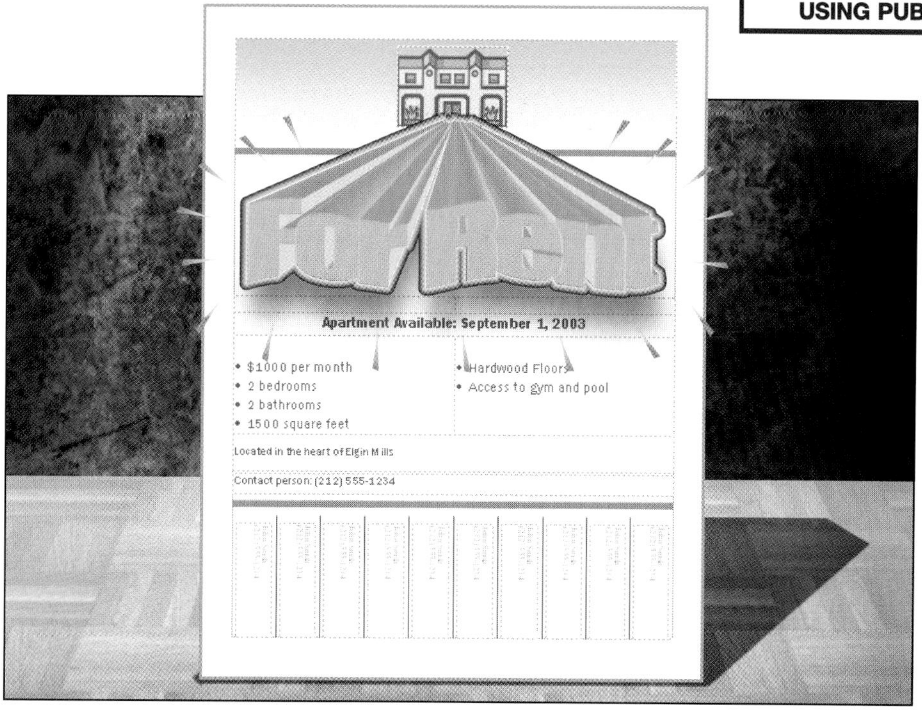

ADD A 3-D EFFECT TO AN OBJECT

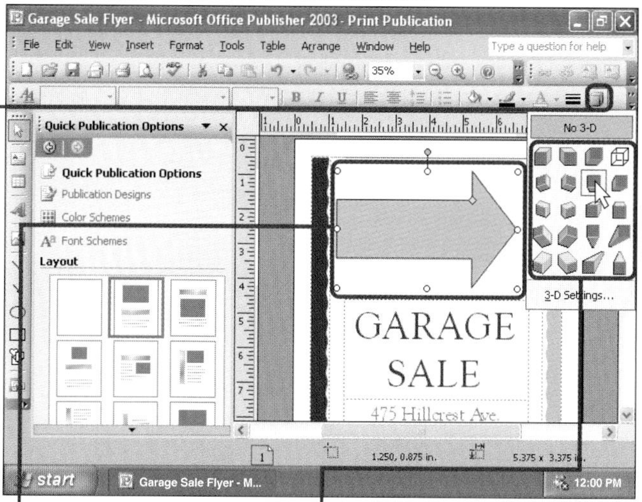

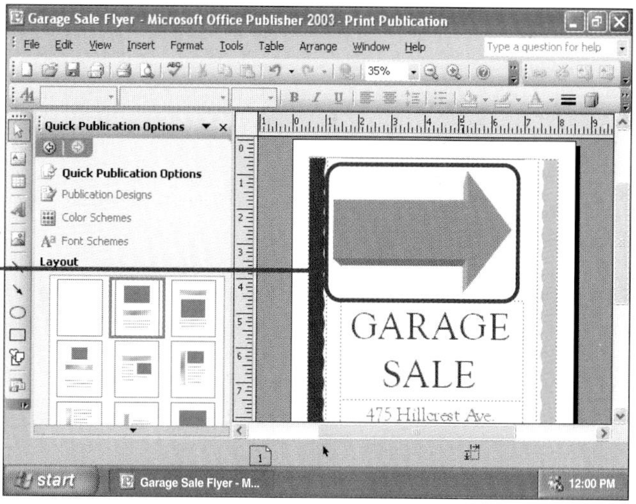

1 Click the object you want to add a 3-D effect to. Handles (○) appear around the object.

2 Click to select a 3-D effect.

Note: If is not displayed, click on the Formatting toolbar to display the button.

3 Click the 3-D effect you want to use.

Note: If the 3-D effects are dimmed, you cannot add a 3-D effect to the object you selected.

- The object displays the 3-D effect you selected.
- To deselect the object, click outside the object.
- If you do not want the object to display a 3-D effect, perform steps **1** to **3**, selecting **No 3-D** in step **3**.

Octobe
1
2
3
6
7
8
9
10
13
16
22
Doctor's Appointment
2pm
Time
12:30
2:00
3:50

Using Outlook

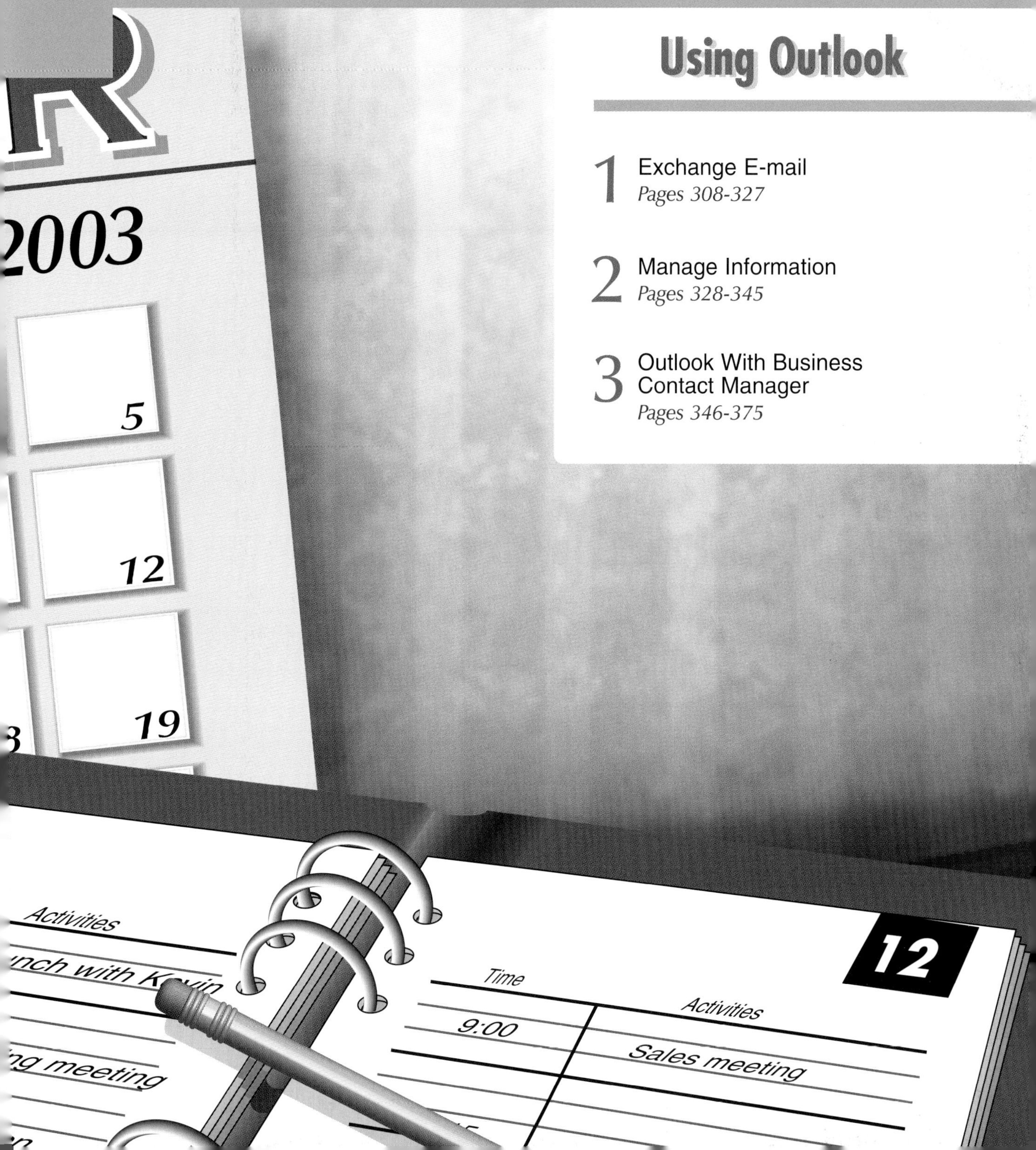

INTRODUCTION TO OUTLOOK

Outlook can help you manage your e-mail messages, appointments, contacts, tasks and notes.

Some editions of Microsoft Office 2003 include Outlook with Business Contact Manager to help you keep track of your business contacts and activities. For information on Outlook with Business Contact Manager, see page 346.

Exchange E-mail

You can use Outlook to exchange e-mail messages with friends, family members and colleagues. You can create and send a new message or reply to a message you have received. Outlook provides several mail folders to help you organize your e-mail messages and reduce the number of junk mail messages that arrive in your Inbox.

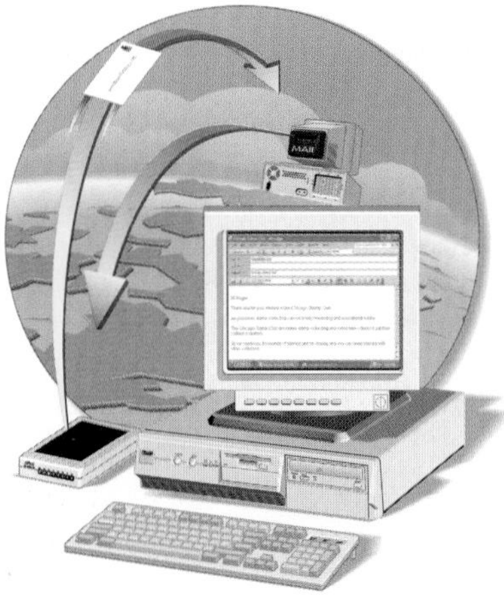

Manage Information

Outlook offers many features that allow you to manage information. You can keep track of your appointments, store information about your contacts and create a list of things to do. You can also create notes to store small pieces of information, such as reminders or ideas. Outlook also provides a Journal that you can use to keep track of your daily activities.

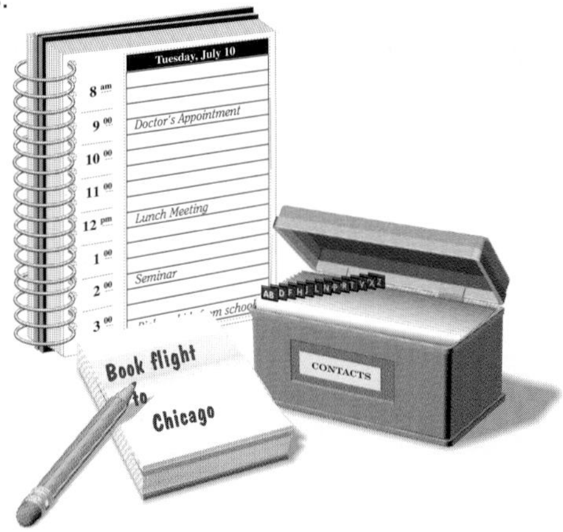

PARTS OF THE OUTLOOK WINDOW

The Outlook window displays several items to help you perform tasks efficiently.

Title Bar

Shows the name of the Outlook feature or folder you are currently working with.

Menu Bar

Provides access to lists of commands available in Outlook and displays an area where you can type a question to get help information.

Toolbar

Contains buttons that allow you to create new items and select common commands, such as Print.

Navigation Pane

Provides an easy way to access all the Outlook features and folders.

Reading Pane

Displays the contents of the Outlook feature or folder you are currently working with.

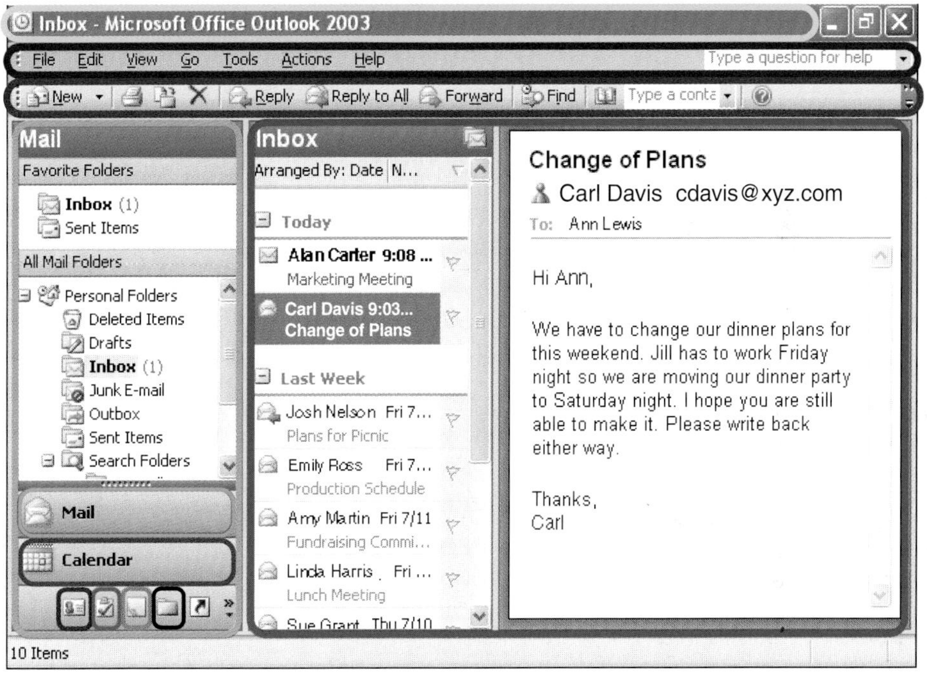

OUTLOOK FEATURES

Mail

Allows you to compose, store and work with e-mail messages.

Calendar

Allows you to keep track of appointments.

Contacts

Contains an address book where you can store contact information.

Tasks

Allows you to create a list of things to do.

Notes

Allows you to create and store brief reminder notes.

Folder List

Allows you to quickly access all your personal folders in Outlook.

READ MESSAGES

You can easily open and read the contents of your e-mail messages.

When you receive a new message, your computer plays a sound, an envelope icon appears at the bottom right corner of your screen and a desktop alert briefly appears. The desktop alert displays the person's name, a subject and a short preview of the message so you can determine if you want to read the message right away.

READ MESSAGES

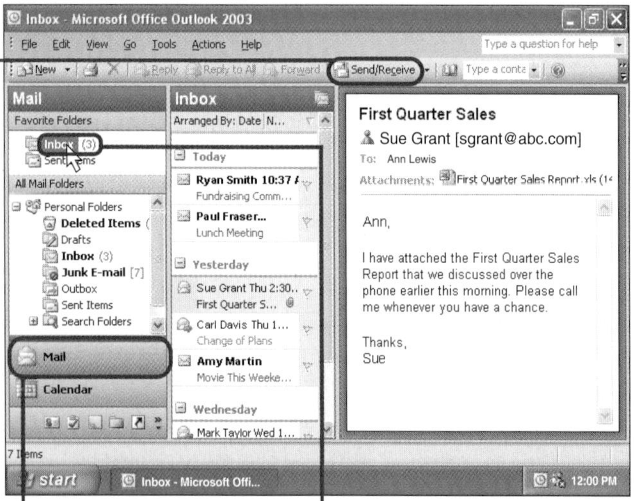

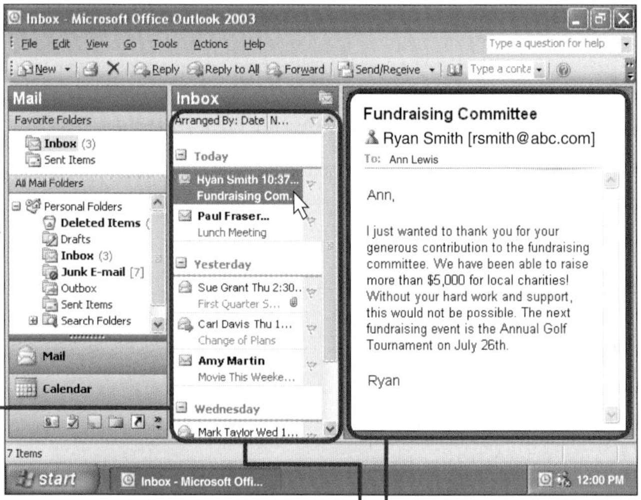

1 Click **Mail** to be able to read and work with your e-mail messages.

2 To immediately check for new messages, click **Send/Receive** or press the F9 key.

3 Click **Inbox** to view the messages you have received.

■ The number in brackets beside the Inbox folder indicates the number of messages you have not yet read.

■ This area displays your messages. Unread messages display a closed envelope ( ) and appear in **bold** type.

4 Click a message you want to read.

■ This area displays the contents of the message you selected.

■ To view the contents of another message, click the message.

Tip

What mail folders does Outlook use to store my messages?

Deleted Items	Stores messages you have deleted.
Drafts	Stores messages you have not yet completed.
Inbox	Stores messages sent to you.
Junk E-mail	Stores messages Outlook considers to be junk mail.
Outbox	Temporarily stores messages that have not yet been sent.
Sent Items	Stores copies of messages you have sent.
Search Folders	Contains folders that display messages that meet certain conditions, such as messages you have flagged (🏴), messages larger than 100 KB and messages you have not yet read.

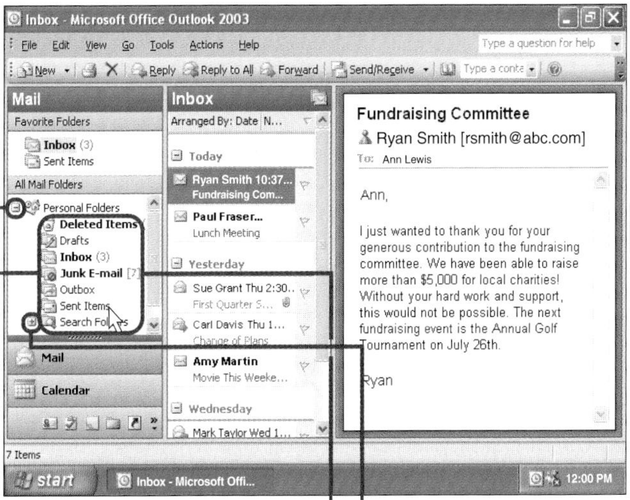

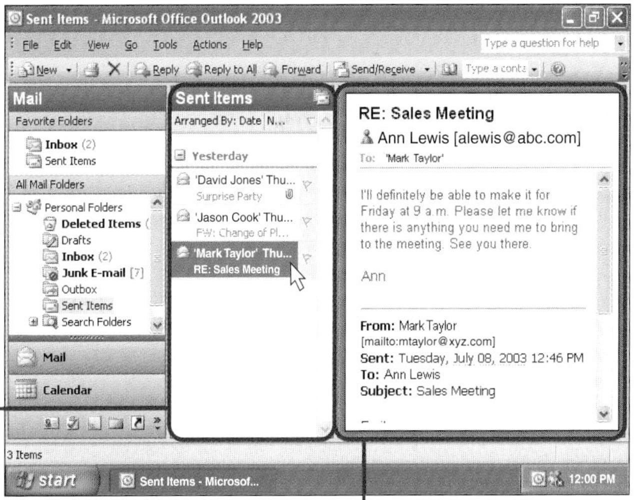

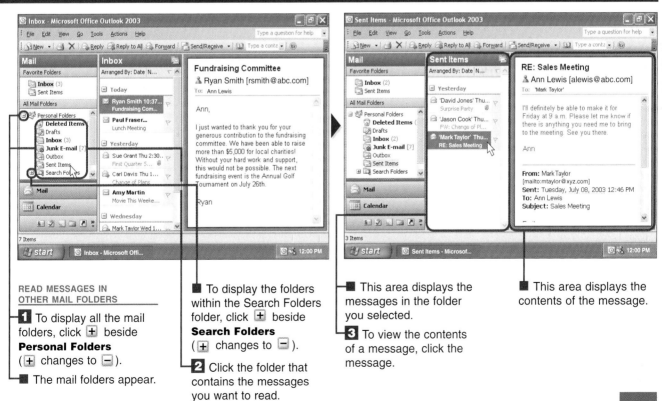

READ MESSAGES IN OTHER MAIL FOLDERS

1 To display all the mail folders, click + beside **Personal Folders** (+ changes to −).

■ The mail folders appear.

■ To display the folders within the Search Folders folder, click + beside **Search Folders** (+ changes to −).

2 Click the folder that contains the messages you want to read.

■ This area displays the messages in the folder you selected.

3 To view the contents of a message, click the message.

■ This area displays the contents of the message.

You can send an e-mail message to express an idea or request information.

To practice sending a message, you can send a message to yourself.

SEND A MESSAGE

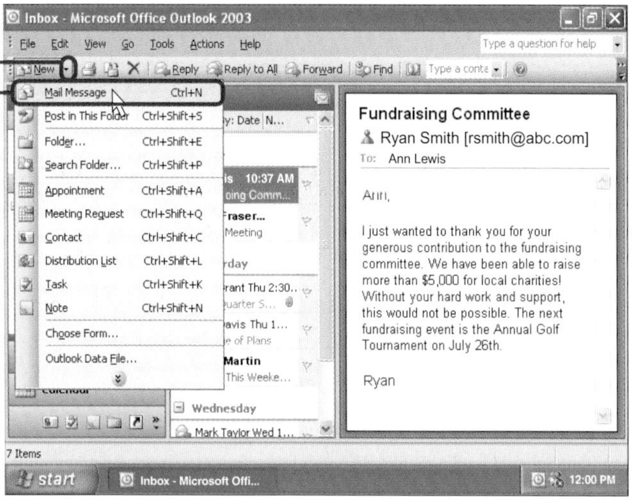

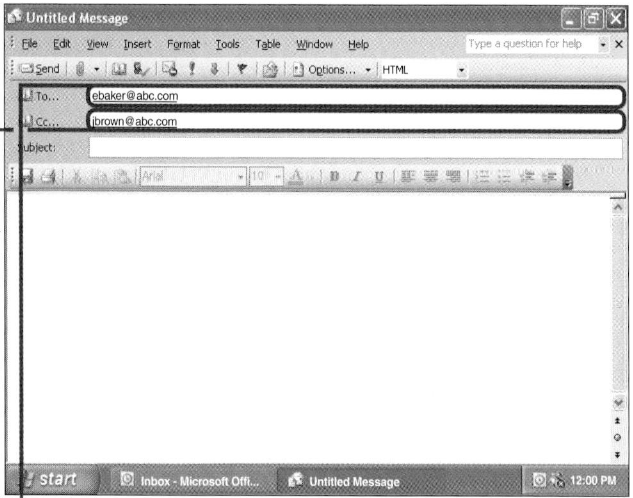

1 Click ▾ beside **New**.

2 Click **Mail Message** to send a new message.

■ A window that allows you to compose a message appears.

3 Type the e-mail address of the person you want to receive the message.

4 To send a copy of the message to a person who is not directly involved but would be interested in the message, click this area and then type the e-mail address of the person.

*Note: To send the message or a copy of the message to more than one person in step **3** or **4**, separate each e-mail address you type with a semicolon (;).*

Tip

How can I express emotions in my messages?

You can type sets of characters to express emotions in your messages. These characters resemble human faces if you turn them sideways. When you type certain sets of characters to express a happy, sad or indifferent emotion, Outlook will automatically replace the characters with an image.

Emotion:	Type:
Cry	:'-(
Laugh	:-D
Surprise	:-O
Happy	:) changes to ☺
Sad	:(changes to ☹
Indifferent	:I changes to 😐

Tip

How can I save time when typing messages?

You can use abbreviations for commonly used words and phrases to save time when typing messages.

	Meaning
BTW	by the way
FAQ	frequently asked questions
FWIW	for what it's worth
IMO	in my opinion
JK	just kidding
L8R	later
LOL	laugh out loud
ROTFL	rolling on the floor laughing
SO	significant other
WRT	with respect to

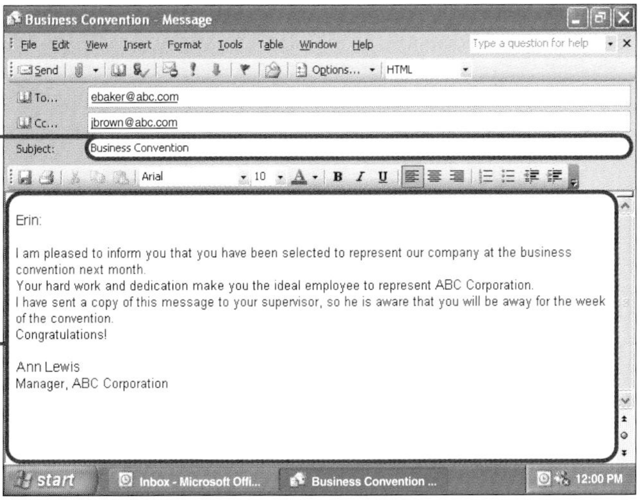

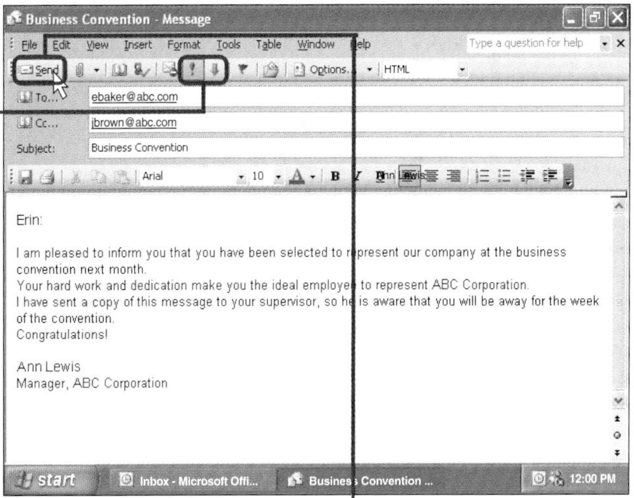

5 Click this area and then type a subject for the message.

6 Click this area and then type the message.

■ Outlook automatically underlines misspelled words in red and grammar errors in green as you type. To correct spelling and grammar errors, see page 318.

Note: You should use upper and lower case letters when typing the message. A message written in all CAPITAL LETTERS is annoying and difficult to read.

7 If you want to indicate the importance of the message, click a button to mark the message as very important (!) or not very important (↓).

Note: You can click the button again if you no longer want to indicate the importance of the message.

8 Click **Send** to send the message.

■ Outlook sends the message and stores a copy of the message in the Sent Items folder. To display the messages in the Sent Items folder, see page 311.

SELECT A NAME FROM THE ADDRESS BOOK

When sending a message, you can use the Address Book to quickly select the name of the person you want to receive the message.

Selecting names from the Address Book saves you from having to remember the e-mail addresses of people you often send messages to.

SELECT A NAME FROM THE ADDRESS BOOK

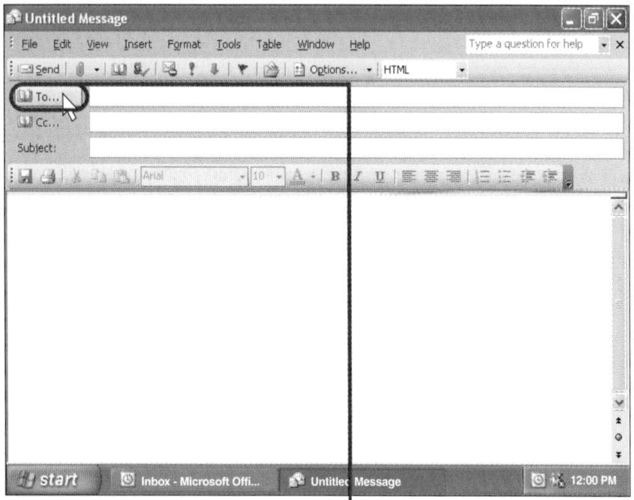

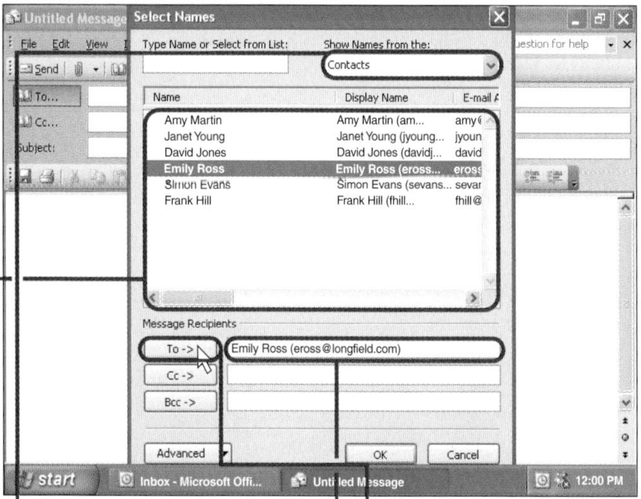

1 To create a new message, perform steps **1** and **2** on page 312.

■ A window that allows you to compose a message appears.

2 To select a name from the Address Book, click **To**.

■ The Select Names dialog box appears.

■ This area shows the name of the address list that contains the displayed names. You can click this area to display the names in another list.

3 Click the name of the person you want to receive the message.

4 Click **To**.

■ This area displays the name of the person you selected.

■ You can repeat steps **3** and **4** for each person you want to receive the message.

Tip

When selecting a name from the Address Book, what address lists are available to select names from?

You can select names from the Contacts list, which displays the name of every person you have entered an e-mail address for in your contact list. To add a person to your list of contacts, see page 332. If you have Outlook with Business Contact Manager installed on your computer, you can also select names from the Accounts and Business Contacts lists. To add an account or business contact, see page 348 or 352.

Tip

What is the difference between a carbon copy and a blind carbon copy?

A carbon copy (Cc) sends an exact copy of a message to a person. A blind carbon copy (Bcc) sends an exact copy of a message to a person, without anyone else knowing that the person received the message.

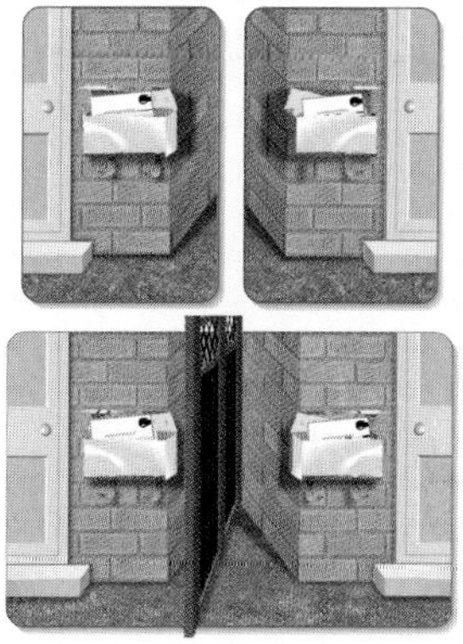

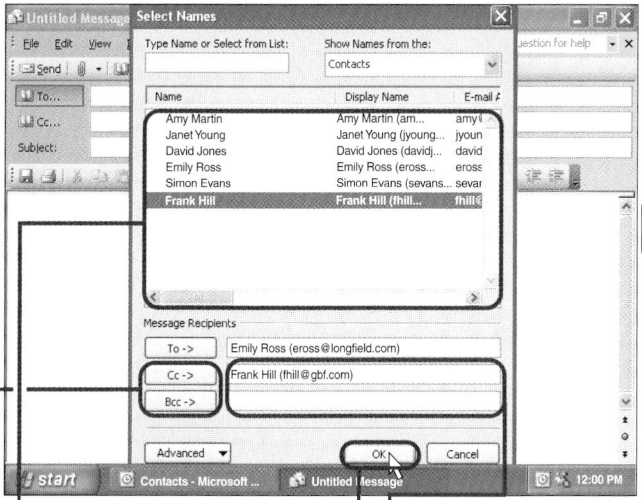

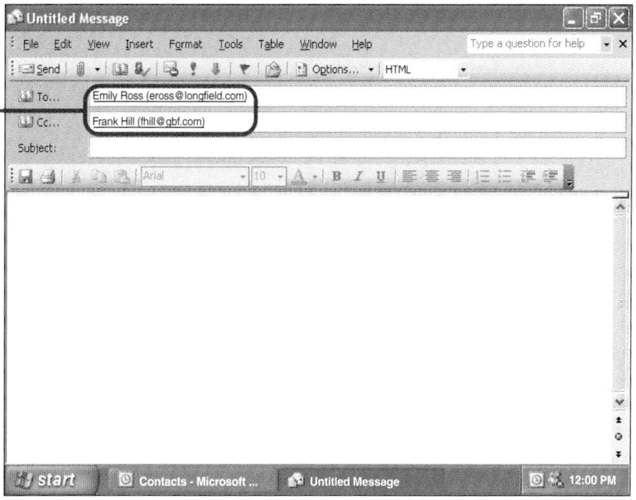

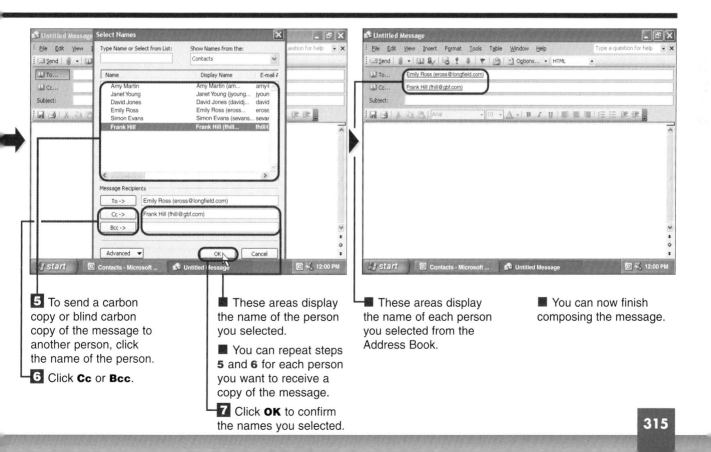

5 To send a carbon copy or blind carbon copy of the message to another person, click the name of the person.

6 Click **Cc** or **Bcc**.

■ These areas display the name of the person you selected.

■ You can repeat steps **5** and **6** for each person you want to receive a copy of the message.

7 Click **OK** to confirm the names you selected.

■ These areas display the name of each person you selected from the Address Book.

■ You can now finish composing the message.

ATTACH A FILE TO A MESSAGE

You can attach a file to a message you are sending. Attaching a file is useful when you want to include additional information with a message.

You can attach many types of files to a message, including documents, pictures, videos and sounds. The computer receiving the message must have the necessary hardware and software installed to display or play the file you attach.

When you attach a picture to a message, you can change the size of the picture. Changing the size of a picture is useful for reducing the file size of the picture so it will transfer faster over the Internet.

ATTACH A FILE TO A MESSAGE

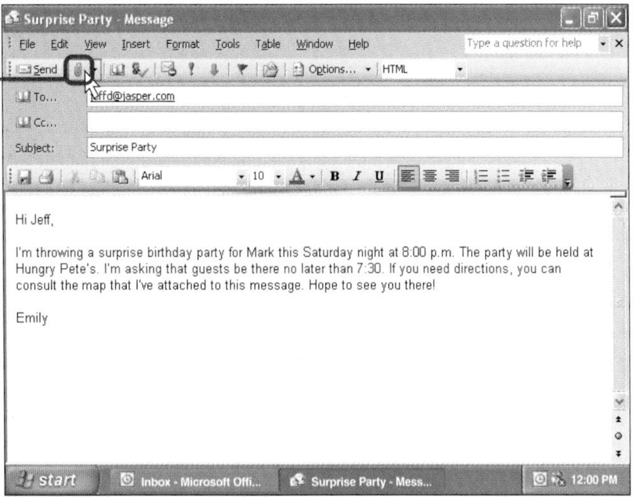

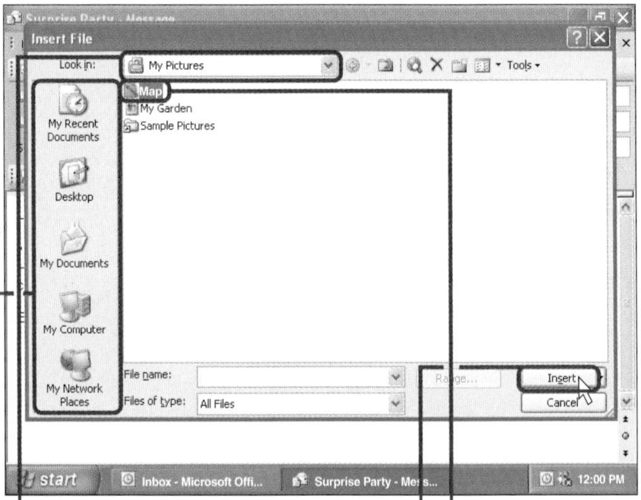

1 To create a message, perform steps **1** to **6** starting on page 312.

2 Click 📎 to attach a file to the message.

■ The Insert File dialog box appears.

■ This area shows the location of the displayed files. You can click this area to change the location.

■ This area allows you to access files stored in commonly used locations. You can click a location to display the files stored in the location.

3 Click the name of the file you want to attach to the message.

4 Click **Insert** to attach the file to the message.

Tip

Why did a dialog box appear, stating that the file I attached is potentially unsafe?

Some types of files, such as program files, may contain viruses, which can damage the information on a computer. If the recipient of your message uses Outlook, the person may not be able to open the file you attached. To specify if you want to send the file, click **Yes** or **No** in the dialog box.

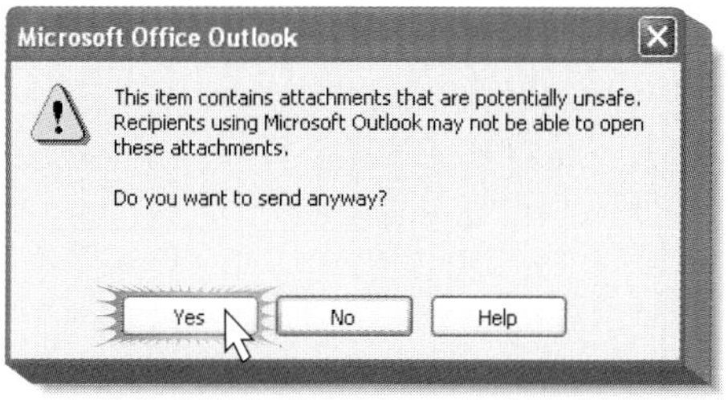

Tip

What should I consider before opening an attached file?

You will not be able to open attached files that Outlook believes may contain viruses. If Outlook allows you to open an attached file, you should still check the file for viruses with an anti-virus program before opening the file. Anti-virus programs, such as McAfee VirusScan and Norton AntiVirus, are available in computer stores and on the Internet.

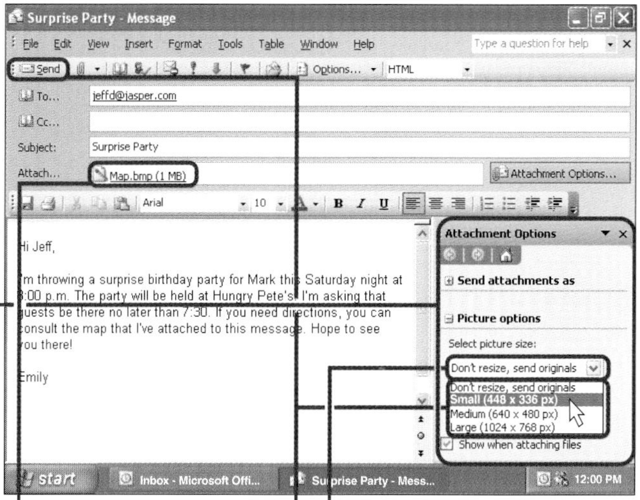

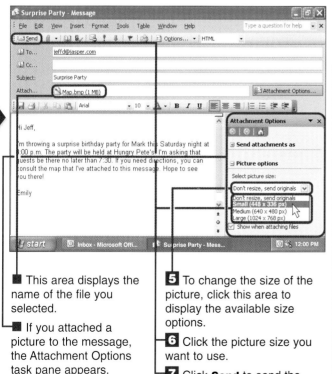

■ This area displays the name of the file you selected.

■ If you attached a picture to the message, the Attachment Options task pane appears.

5 To change the size of the picture, click this area to display the available size options.

6 Click the picture size you want to use.

7 Click **Send** to send the message.

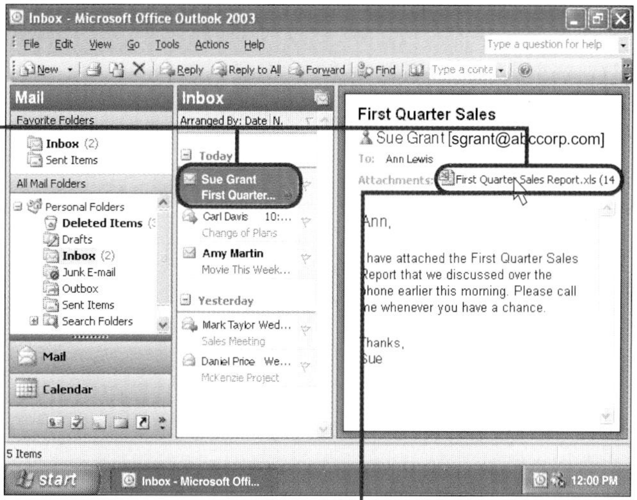

OPEN AN ATTACHED FILE

1 Click a message with an attached file. A message with an attached file displays a paper clip icon (📎).

■ This area displays the name(s) of the file(s) attached to the message.

2 To open an attached file, double-click the name of the file.

■ A dialog box may appear, asking if you want to open or save the file. Click **Open** or **Save** in the dialog box to open or save the file.

CHECK SPELLING AND GRAMMAR

Before you send a message, you can find and correct all the spelling and grammar errors in the message.

Outlook compares every word in your message to words in its dictionary. If a word does not exist in the dictionary, the word is considered misspelled.

Outlook will not find a correctly spelled word used in the wrong context, such as "We have been in business for **sit** years." You should carefully review your message to find this type of error.

By default, Outlook will not spell check words typed in all UPPERCASE letters.

CHECK SPELLING AND GRAMMAR

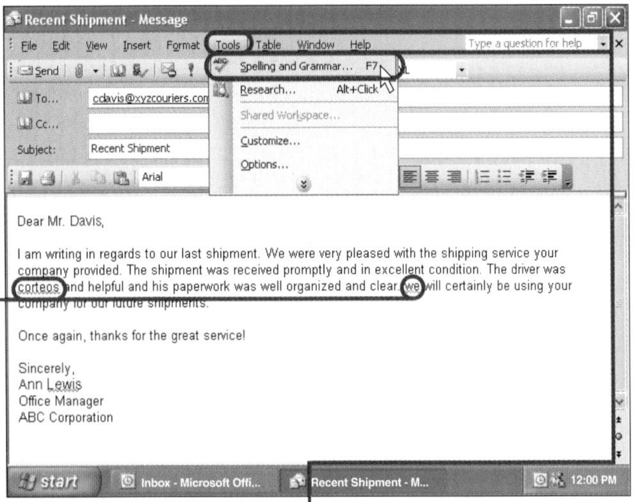

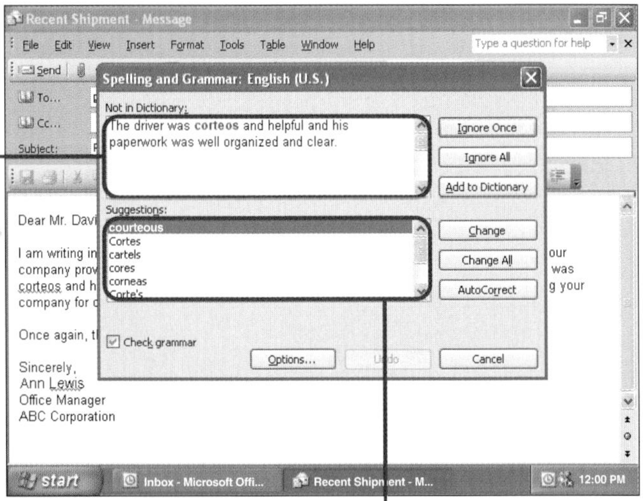

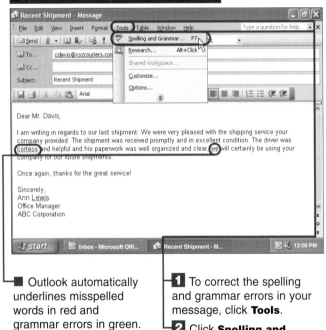

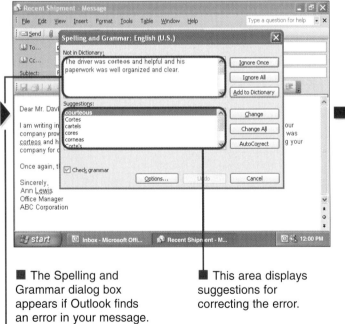

■ Outlook automatically underlines misspelled words in red and grammar errors in green. The underlines will not appear when the person receives your message.

1 To correct the spelling and grammar errors in your message, click **Tools**.

2 Click **Spelling and Grammar**.

■ The Spelling and Grammar dialog box appears if Outlook finds an error in your message.

■ This area displays the first misspelled word or grammar error.

■ This area displays suggestions for correcting the error.

Tip

Can Outlook automatically correct my spelling mistakes?

Yes. Outlook automatically corrects common spelling and capitalization errors as you type. Here are a few examples.

adn	and
alot	a lot
comittee	committee
don;t	don't
nwe	new
occurence	occurrence
recieve	receive
seperate	separate
teh	the
friday	Friday
DOg	Dog

Tip

How can I quickly correct a misspelled word or grammar error in a message?

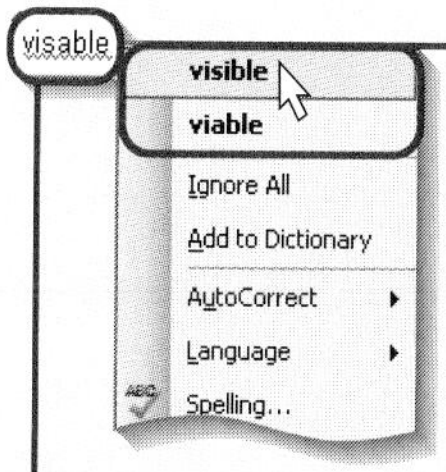

1 Right-click the misspelled word or grammar error.

■ A menu appears with suggestions to correct the error.

2 Click the suggestion you want to use to correct the error.

Note: If you do not want to use any of the suggestions, click outside the menu to close the menu.

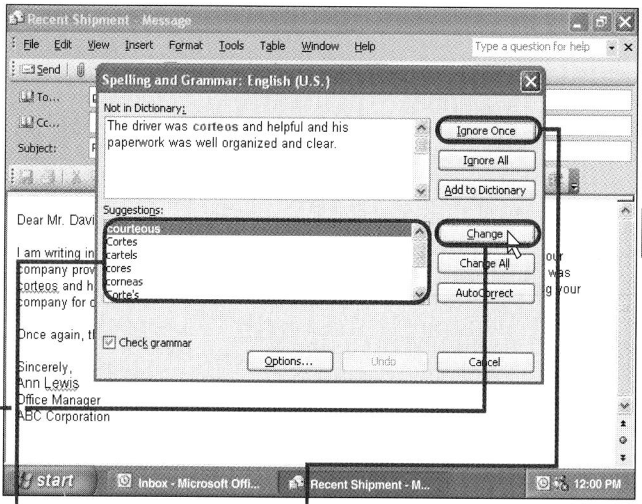

3 Click the suggestion you want to use to correct the error.

4 Click **Change** to correct the error in your message.

■ To skip the error and continue checking your message, click **Ignore Once**.

Note: To skip the error and all other occurrences of the error in your message, click ***Ignore All*** *or* ***Ignore Rule****. The name of the button depends on whether the error is a misspelled word or a grammar error.*

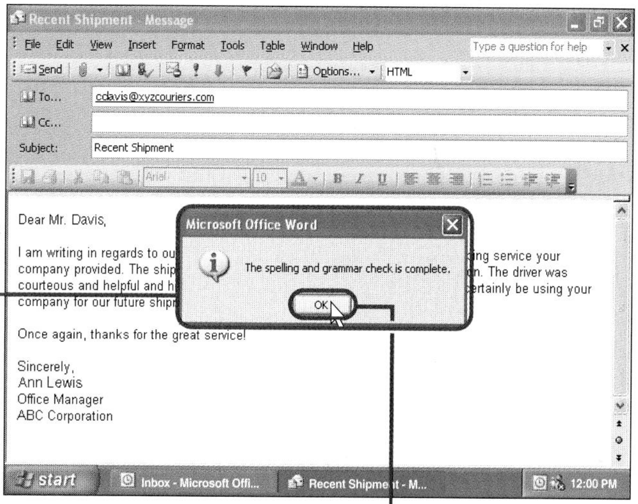

5 Correct or ignore misspelled words and grammar errors until this dialog box appears, telling you the spelling and grammar check is complete.

6 Click **OK** to close the dialog box.

REPLY TO A MESSAGE

You can reply to a message to answer a question, express an opinion or supply additional information.

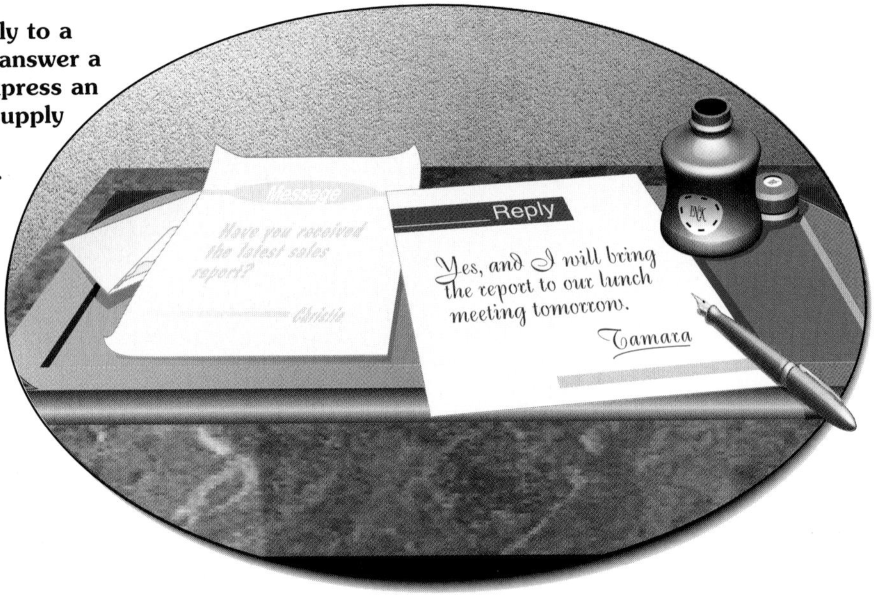

When you reply to a message, Outlook includes a copy of the original message to help the reader identify which message you are replying to. To save the reader time, you can delete all parts of the original message that do not directly relate to your reply.

After you reply to a message, an arrow ( ) appears in the icon beside the message.

REPLY TO A MESSAGE

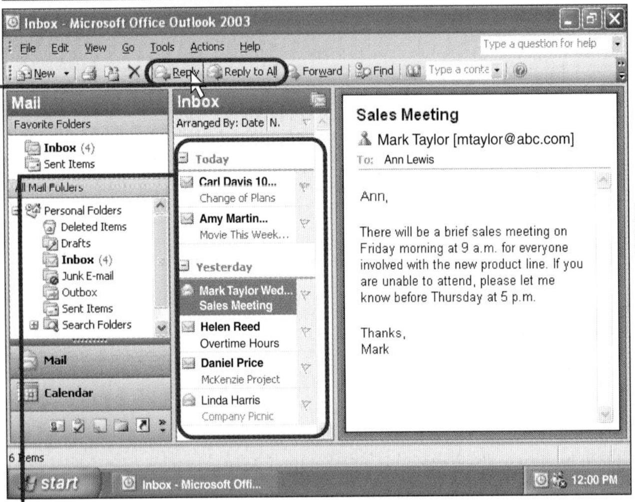

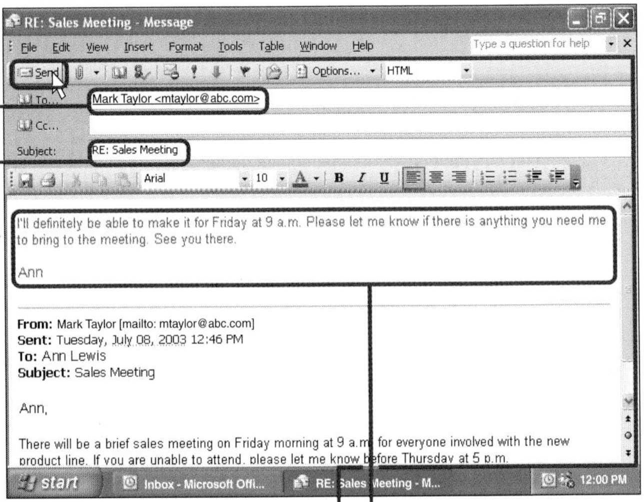

1 Click the message you want to reply to.

2 Click the reply option you want to use.

Reply - Sends a reply to the author only.

Reply to All - Sends a reply to the author and everyone who received the original message.

■ A window that allows you to compose your reply appears.

■ Outlook fills in the e-mail address(es) for you.

■ Outlook also fills in the subject, starting the subject with **RE**:. To use a different subject, drag the mouse I over the text to highlight the text and then type a new subject.

3 Click this area and then type your reply.

4 Click **Send** to send the reply.

■ Outlook sends the reply and stores a copy in the Sent Items folder. To view the messages in the Sent Items folder, see page 311.

FORWARD A MESSAGE

After reading a message, you can add comments and then forward the message to a friend, colleague or family member.

Forwarding a message is useful when another person would be interested in the message.

After you forward a message, an arrow (➡) appears in the icon beside the message.

FORWARD A MESSAGE

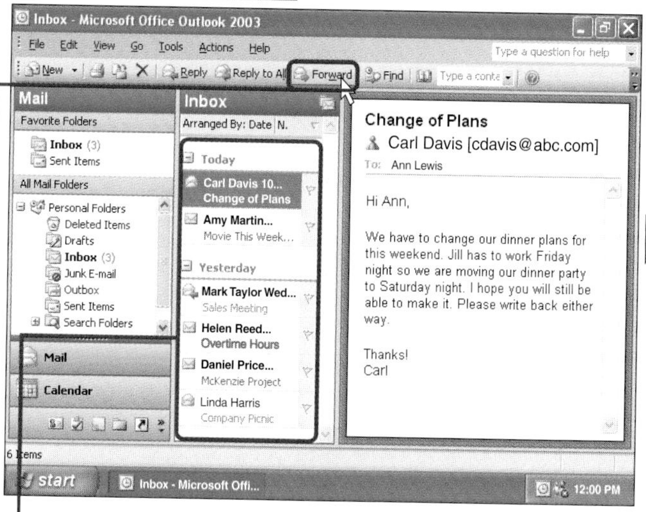

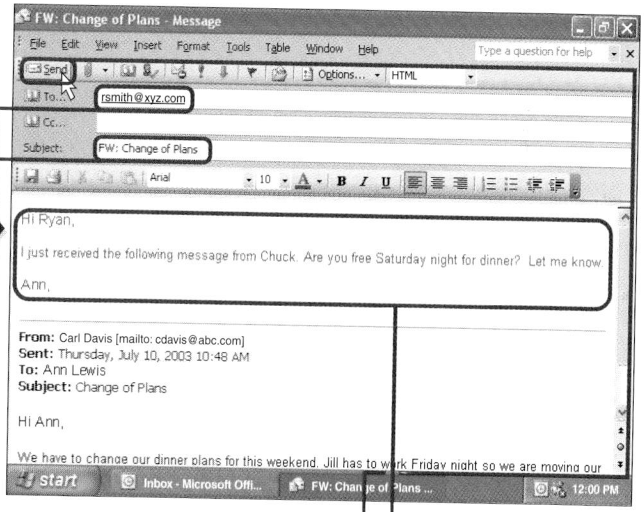

1 Click the message you want to forward to another person.

2 Click **Forward**.

■ A window that displays the contents of the message you are forwarding appears.

3 Type the e-mail address of the person you want to receive the message.

■ Outlook fills in the subject for you, starting the subject with **FW**:. To use a different subject, drag the mouse I over the text to highlight the text and then type a new subject.

4 Click this area and then type any comments about the message.

5 Click **Send** to forward the message.

FLAG A MESSAGE

You can have Outlook display a flag beside a message to make the message stand out. Flagging a message can help remind you to follow up on the message at a later time.

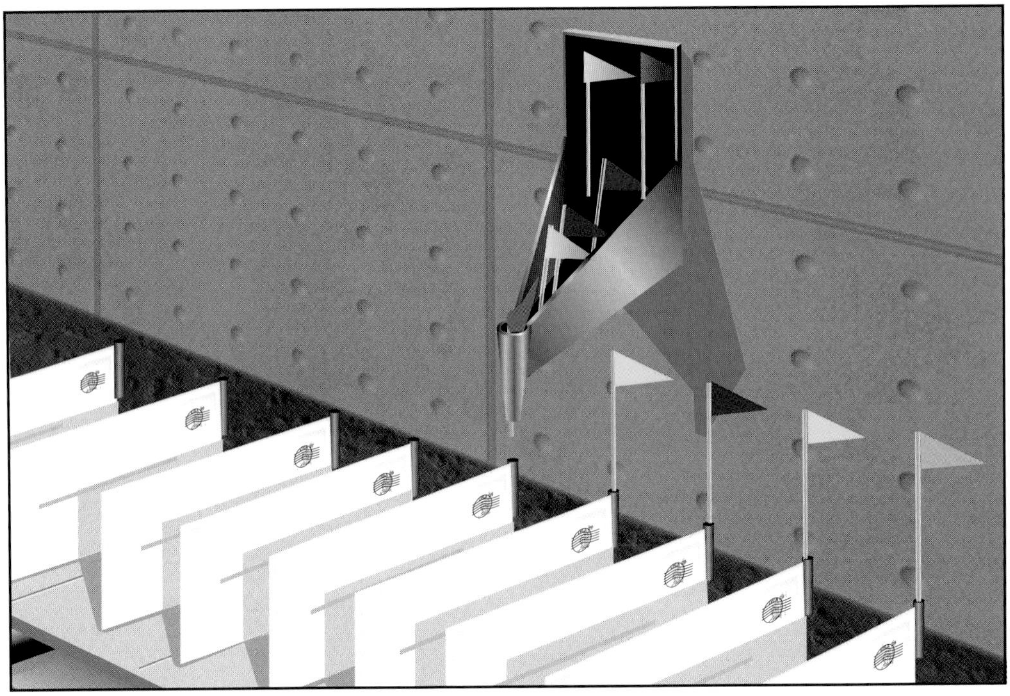

FLAG A MESSAGE

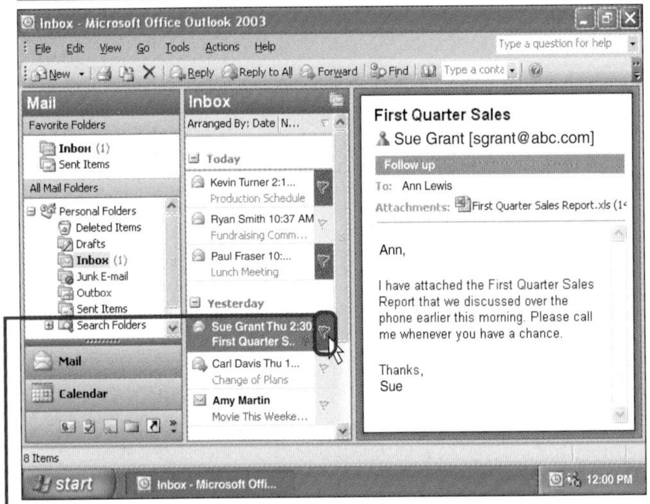

1 Click beside the message you want to flag (changes to).

■ You can repeat step **1** for each message you want to flag.

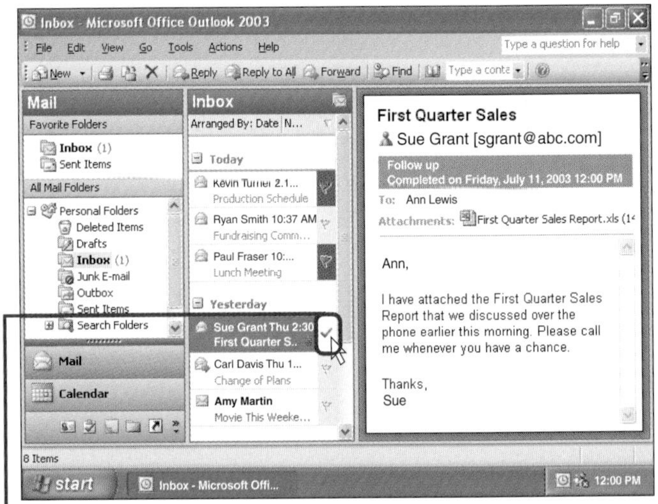

MARK A FLAGGED MESSAGE AS COMPLETE

1 Click beside the flagged message you want to mark as complete (changes to ✓).

Note: If you accidentally marked a flagged message as complete, you can click ✓ beside the message to once again flag the message (✓ changes to).

Tip

How do I change the color of a flag?

Changing the color of flags allows you to categorize your flagged messages. For example, you can use red flags to mark messages you need to deal with right away and yellow flags to mark messages you can deal with at a later time. To change the color of a flag, right-click the flag and then click the flag color you want to use from the menu that appears.

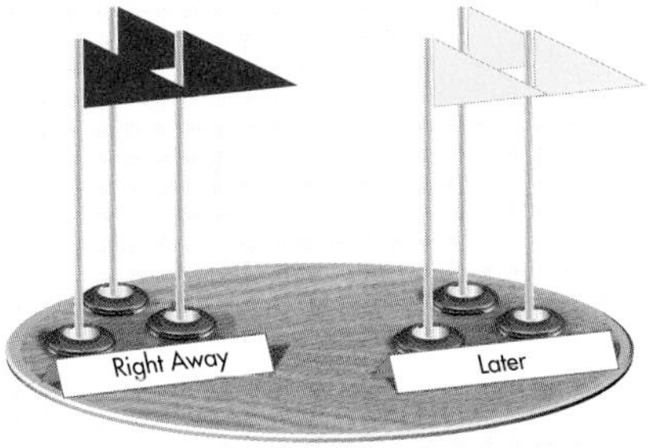

Tip

How do I remove a flag from a message?

If you accidentally flagged a message, you can remove the flag from the message. To remove a flag, right-click the flag and then select **Clear Flag** from the menu that appears (⚑ changes to ⚐).

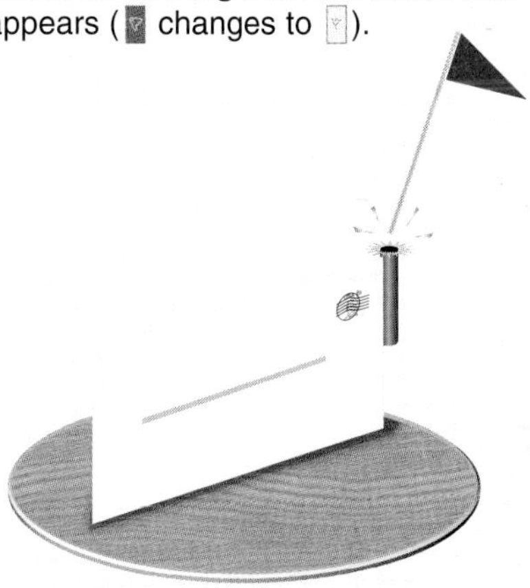

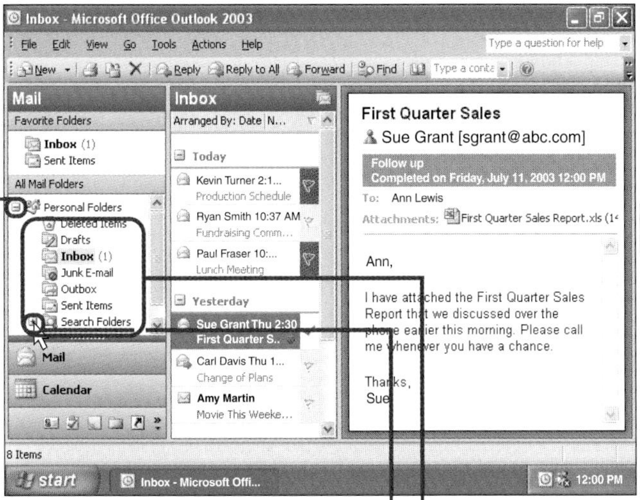

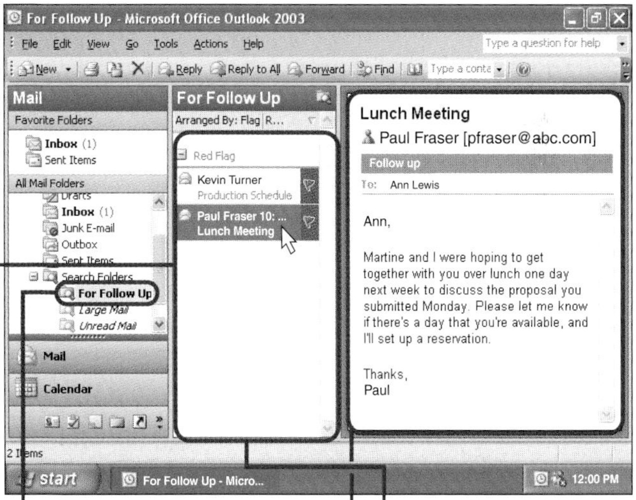

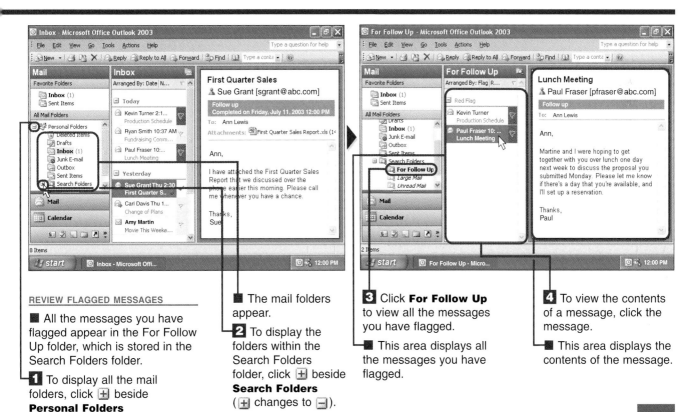

REVIEW FLAGGED MESSAGES

■ All the messages you have flagged appear in the For Follow Up folder, which is stored in the Search Folders folder.

1 To display all the mail folders, click ⊞ beside **Personal Folders** (⊞ changes to ⊟).

■ The mail folders appear.

2 To display the folders within the Search Folders folder, click ⊞ beside **Search Folders** (⊞ changes to ⊟).

3 Click **For Follow Up** to view all the messages you have flagged.

■ This area displays all the messages you have flagged.

4 To view the contents of a message, click the message.

■ This area displays the contents of the message.

ARRANGE MESSAGES

You can change the way Outlook arranges your messages to help you more easily locate messages of interest.

You can arrange messages in many ways, including by date, by conversation, by subject or by messages you have flagged (🚩).

ARRANGE MESSAGES

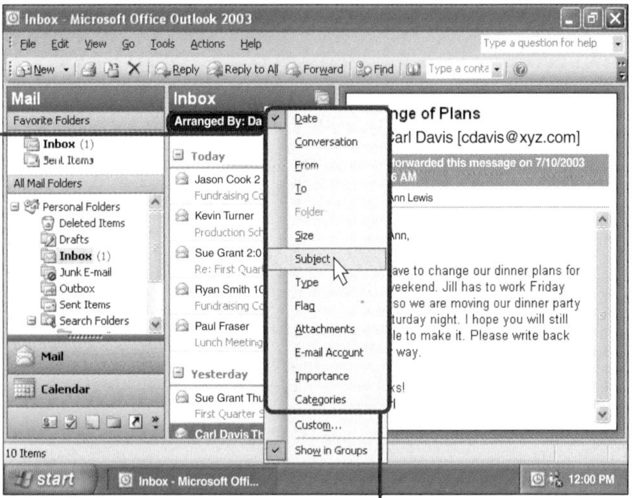

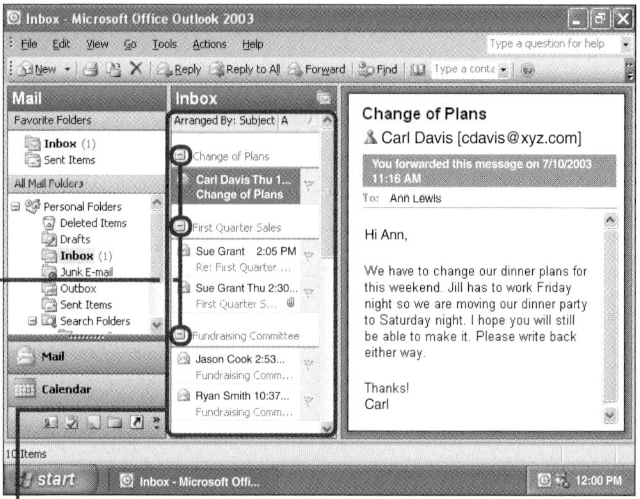

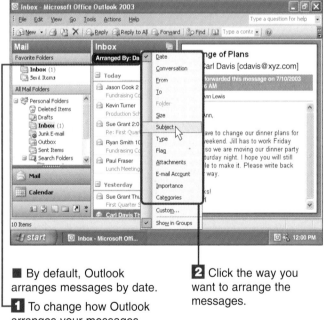

■ By default, Outlook arranges messages by date.

1 To change how Outlook arranges your messages, click the **Arranged By** column heading. A menu appears.

2 Click the way you want to arrange the messages.

■ The messages are arranged in the way you specified.

■ To hide the messages displayed in a group to make your screen less cluttered, click the minus sign (⊟) beside the group heading (⊟ changes to ⊞).

Note: To once again display the messages in a group, click the plus sign (⊞) beside the group heading (⊞ changes to ⊟).

DELETE A MESSAGE

You can delete a message you no longer need. Deleting messages prevents your mail folders from becoming cluttered with messages.

DELETE A MESSAGE

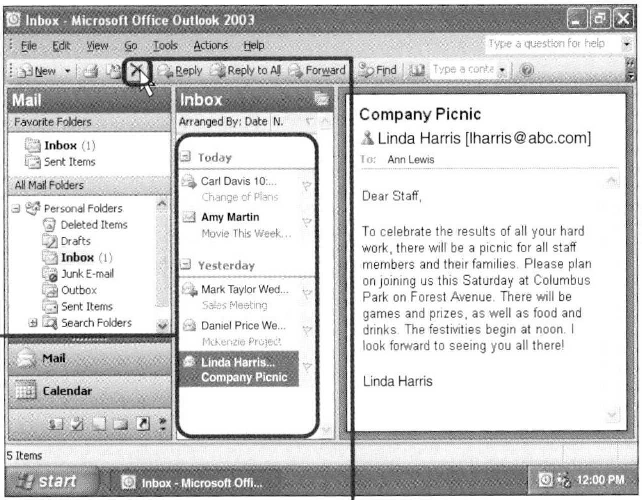

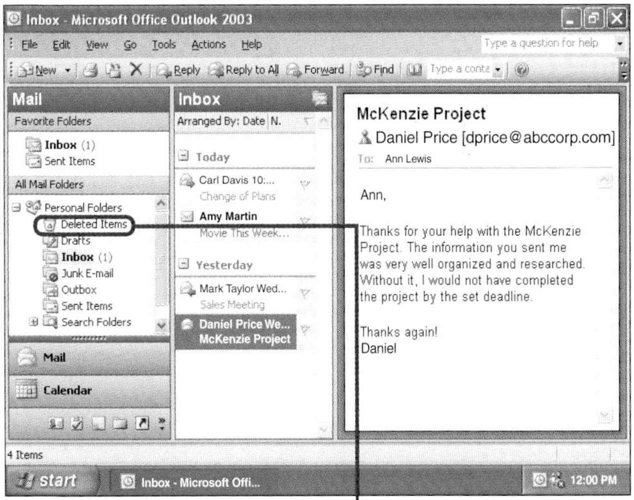

1 Click the message you want to delete.

2 Click ☒ to delete the message.

■ The message disappears.

■ Outlook places the message in the Deleted Items folder. To view the contents of the Deleted Items folder, see page 311.

WORK WITH JUNK MAIL

Outlook examines messages you receive to determine which messages are junk mail. Messages that Outlook considers to be junk mail are automatically placed in the Junk E-mail folder.

When Outlook receives a message that appears to be junk mail, a dialog box will appear, indicating that the message was automatically moved to the Junk E-mail folder.

You should check the Junk E-mail folder regularly to make sure the folder does not contain messages you wish to read.

WORK WITH JUNK MAIL

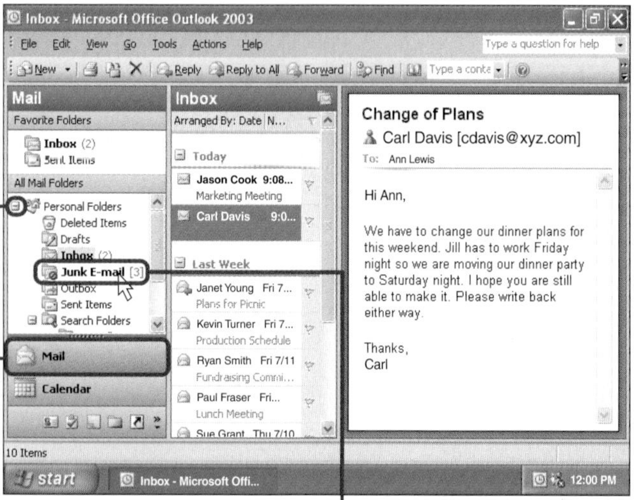

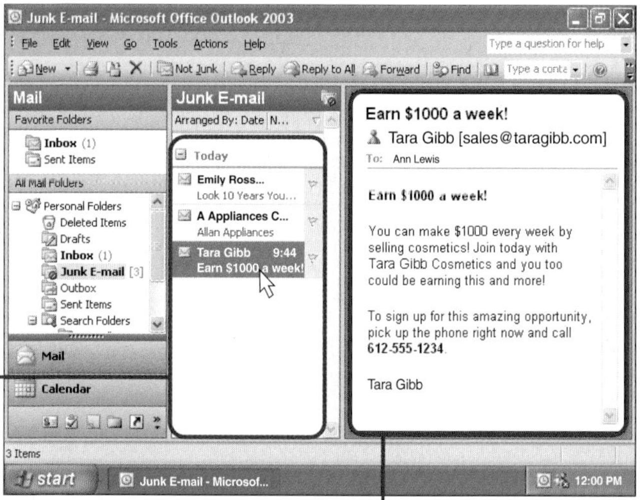

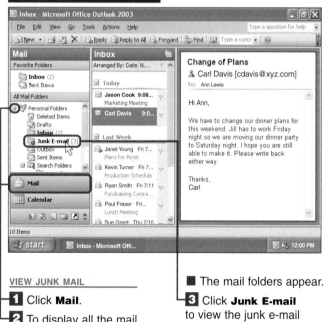

VIEW JUNK MAIL

1 Click **Mail**.

2 To display all the mail folders, click ⊞ beside **Personal Folders** (⊞ changes to ⊟).

■ The mail folders appear.

3 Click **Junk E-mail** to view the junk e-mail messages you have received.

Note: The number in brackets beside the Junk E-mail folder indicates the number of messages in the folder.

■ This area displays the junk e-mail messages you have received. Unread junk e-mail messages display a closed envelope (✉) and appear in **bold** type.

4 To view the contents of a message, click the message.

■ This area displays the contents of the message you selected.

Tip

How do I mark a message I received as junk mail?

If Outlook did not correctly identify a message as junk mail, you can instruct Outlook to identify the message (and all future messages sent by the same person) as junk mail. Right-click the message you want to identify as junk mail. On the menu that appears, click **Junk E-mail** and then click **Add Sender to Blocked Senders List**. In the confirmation dialog box that appears, click **OK**.

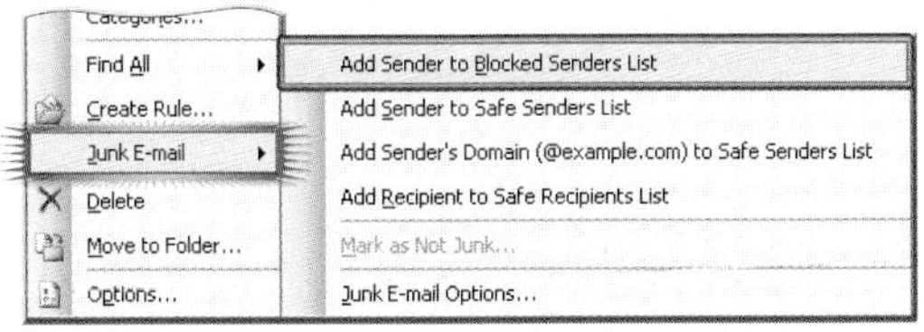

Tip

How do I empty the Junk E-mail folder?

To empty the Junk E-mail folder, right-click the folder and then click **Empty "Junk E-mail" Folder** on the menu that appears. In the confirmation dialog box that appears, click **Yes** to permanently delete the messages in the folder.

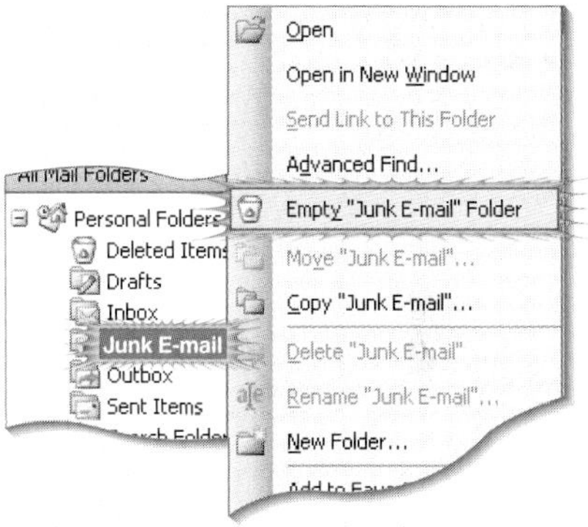

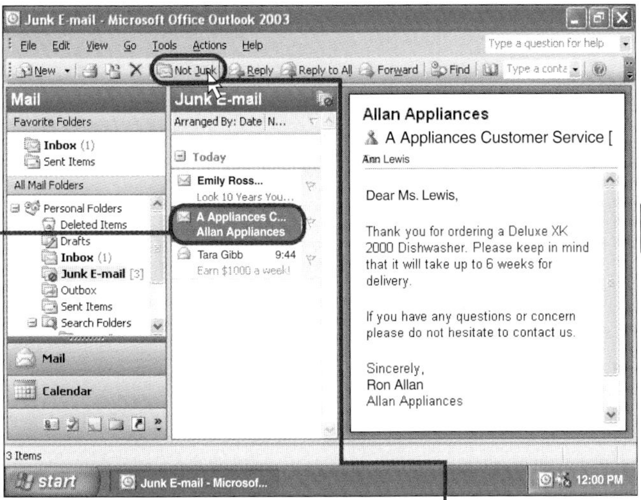

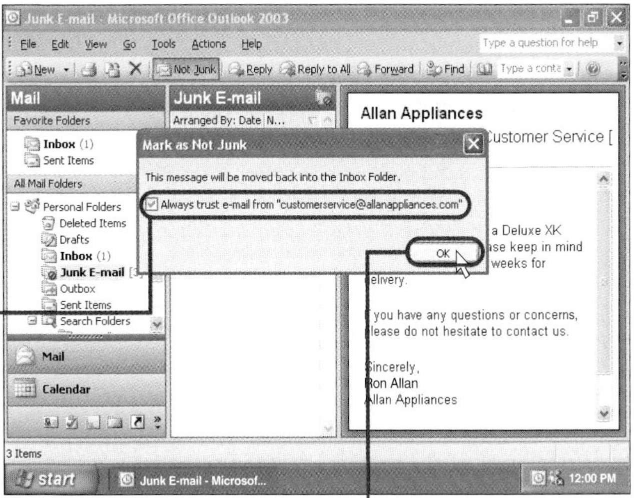

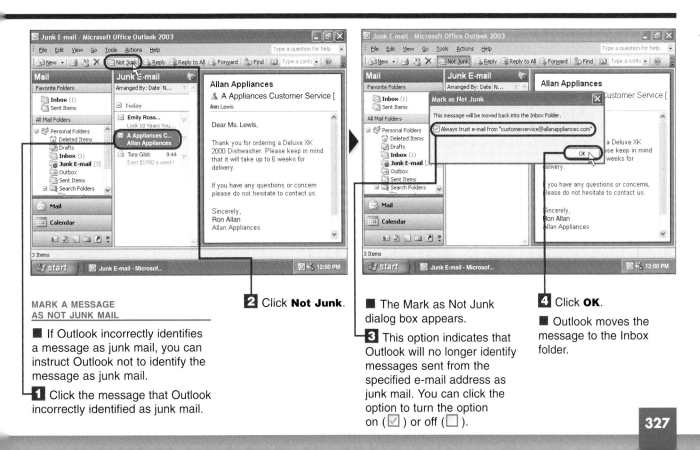

MARK A MESSAGE AS NOT JUNK MAIL

■ If Outlook incorrectly identifies a message as junk mail, you can instruct Outlook not to identify the message as junk mail.

1 Click the message that Outlook incorrectly identified as junk mail.

2 Click **Not Junk**.

■ The Mark as Not Junk dialog box appears.

3 This option indicates that Outlook will no longer identify messages sent from the specified e-mail address as junk mail. You can click the option to turn the option on (☑) or off (☐).

4 Click **OK**.

■ Outlook moves the message to the Inbox folder.

USING THE CALENDAR

You can use the Calendar to keep track of your appointments, such as business meetings and lunch dates.

Outlook uses the date and time set in your computer to determine today's date. To change the date and time set in your computer, refer to your Windows manual.

DISPLAY THE CALENDAR

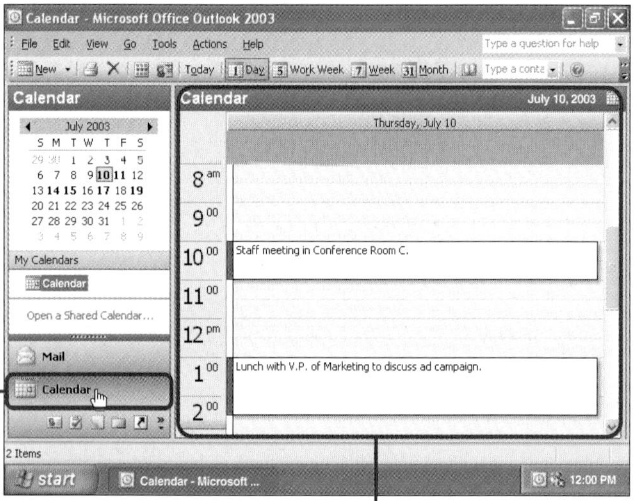

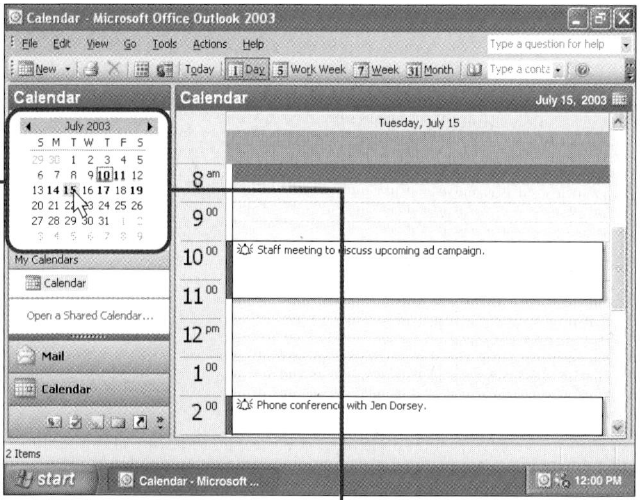

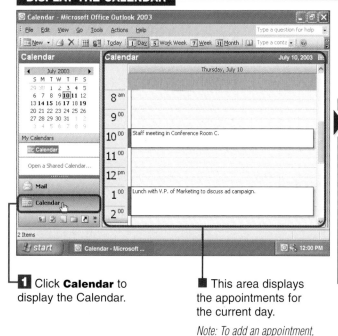

1 Click **Calendar** to display the Calendar.

■ This area displays the appointments for the current day.

Note: To add an appointment, see page 330.

■ This area displays the days in the current month. Days with appointments are shown in **bold**.

2 To display the appointments for another day, click the day. The day you select is highlighted.

■ The current day displays a red outline.

Tip

What ways can I view the Calendar?

You can change the view of the Calendar to display your appointments in one of the following views.

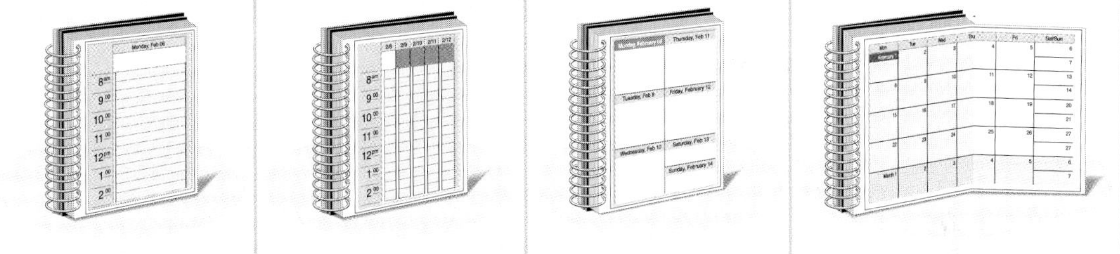

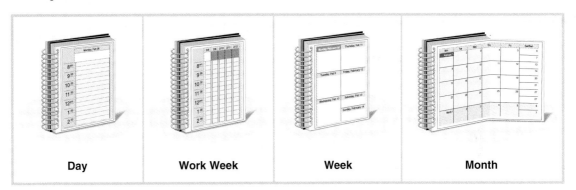

Day	Work Week	Week	Month

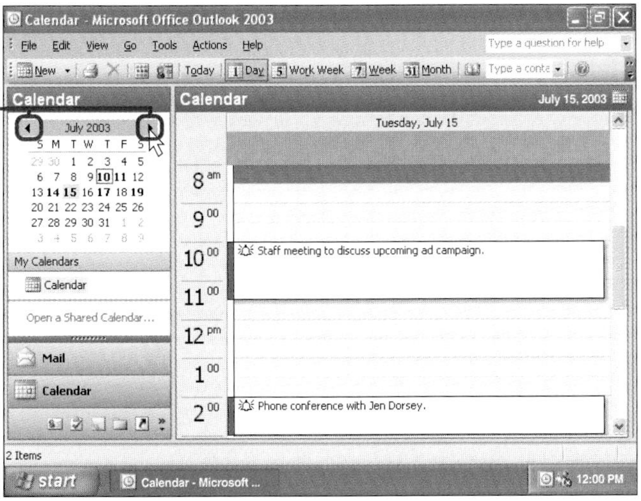

3 To display the days in another month, click one of the following options.

◀ Display previous month

▶ Display next month

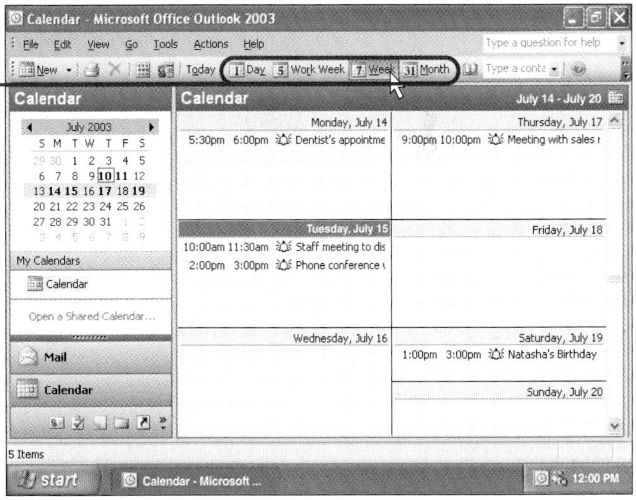

CHANGE VIEW OF CALENDAR

1 Click the way you want to view the Calendar.

Day

Work Week

Week

Month

Note: If the button you want is not displayed, click on the toolbar to display the button.

CONTINUED

USING THE CALENDAR

You can add an appointment to the Calendar to remind you of an activity, such as a seminar or doctor's appointment.

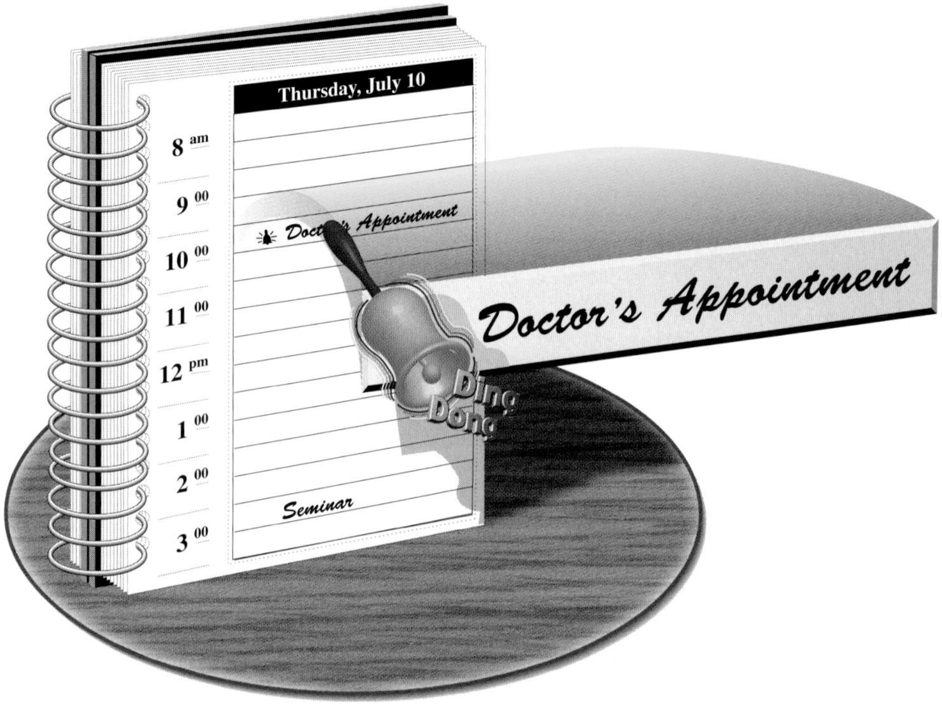

SCHEDULE AN APPOINTMENT

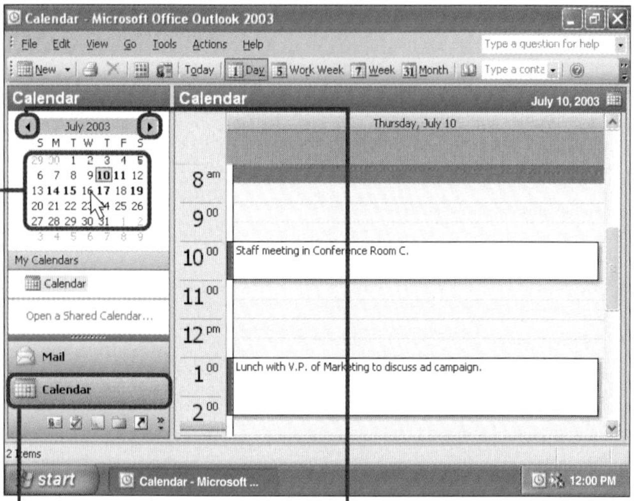

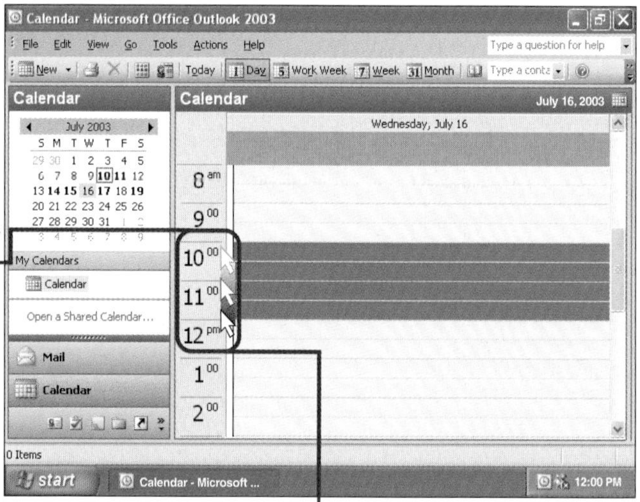

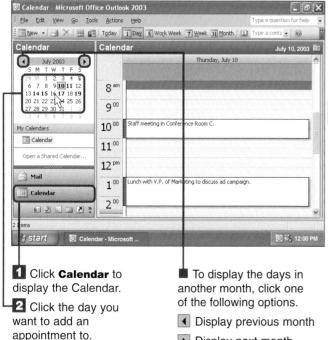

1 Click **Calendar** to display the Calendar.

2 Click the day you want to add an appointment to.

■ To display the days in another month, click one of the following options.

◀ Display previous month

▶ Display next month

3 Position the mouse ⇖ over the starting time for the appointment.

4 Drag the mouse ⇖ to select the amount of time you want to set aside for the appointment.

Tip

Will Outlook remind me of an appointment I have scheduled?

Outlook will play a brief sound and display the Reminder dialog box 15 minutes before a scheduled appointment.

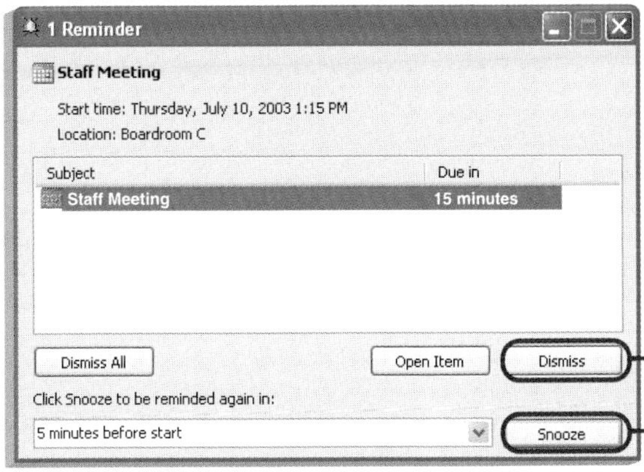

■ To close the Reminder dialog box, click one of the following options.

Dismiss - Close the reminder

Snooze - Remind again five minutes before the appointment

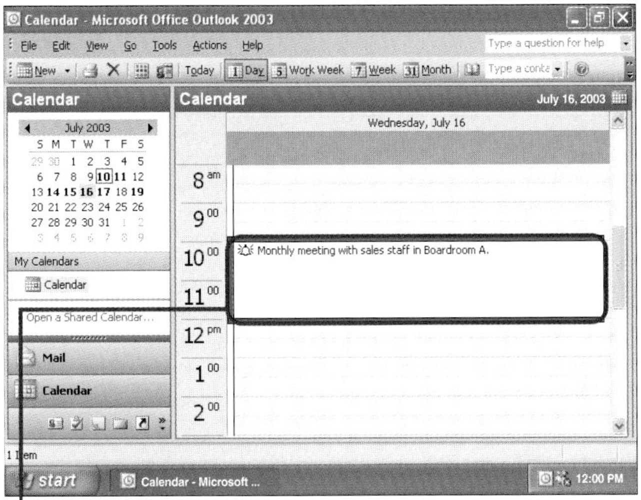

5 Type a subject for the appointment and then press the Enter key.

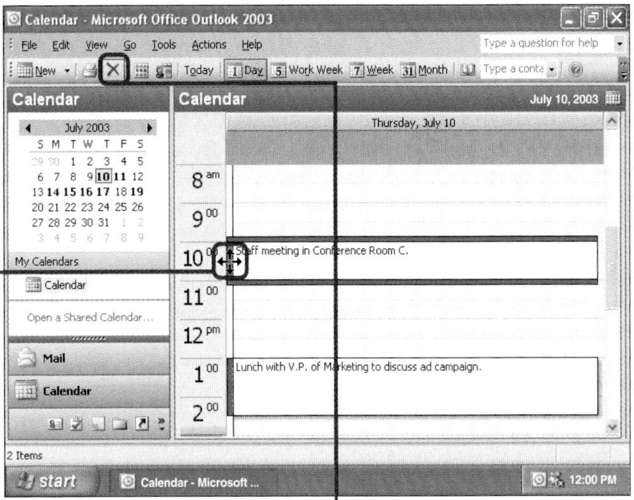

DELETE AN APPOINTMENT

1 Position the mouse over the left edge of the appointment you want to delete (↖ changes to ✥). Then click the edge of the appointment.

2 Click ✕ to delete the appointment.

■ Outlook places the appointment in the Deleted Items folder. To view the contents of the Deleted Items folder, see page 311.

USING CONTACTS

Outlook allows you to keep detailed information about your colleagues, friends and family members.

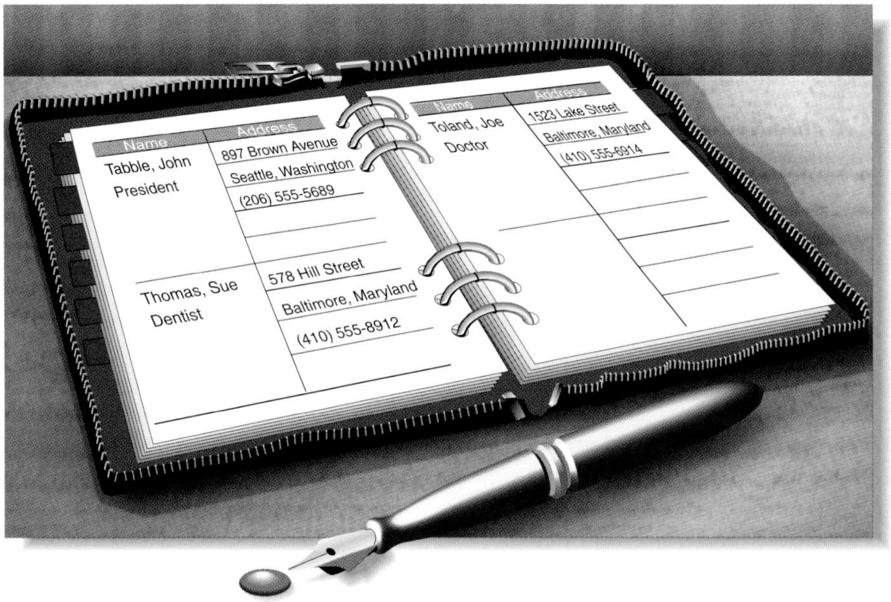

To create and keep track of business contacts, such as customers and suppliers, you may want to use Outlook with Business Contact Manager. For information on Outlook with Business Contact Manager see page 346. For information on creating business contacts with Business Contact Manager, see page 352.

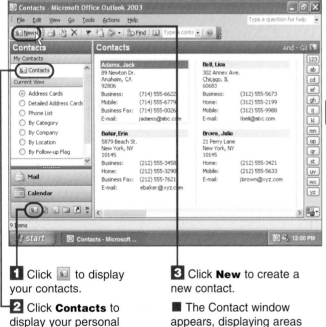

CREATE A NEW CONTACT

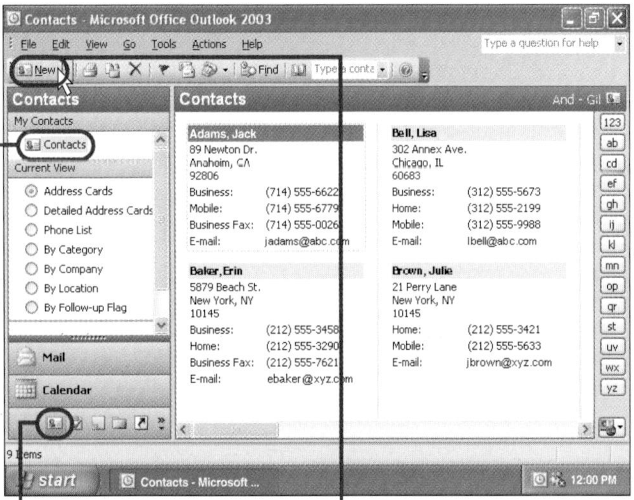

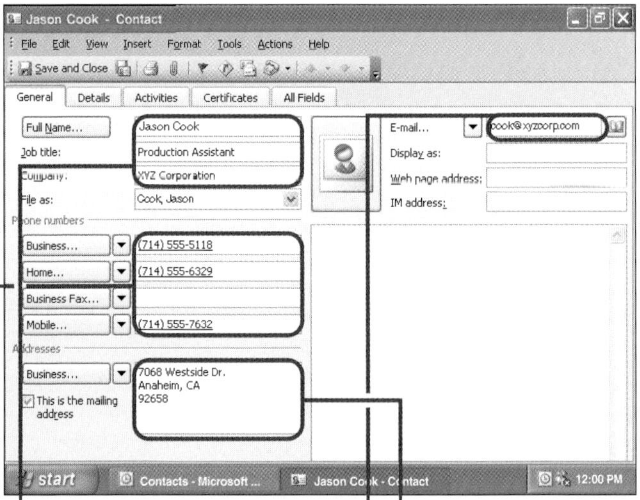

1 Click ![icon] to display your contacts.

2 Click **Contacts** to display your personal contacts.

3 Click **New** to create a new contact.

■ The Contact window appears, displaying areas where you can enter information about a contact.

Note: You do not need to enter information in every area.

4 Click an area and type the contact's full name, job title and company name.

5 Click an area and type the contact's business, home, business fax and mobile phone numbers.

6 Click this area and type the contact's address.

7 Click this area and type the contact's e-mail address.

Tip

Why did the Check Address dialog box appear after I entered an address?

If the address you entered is incomplete, Outlook displays the Check Address dialog box to help you complete the address.

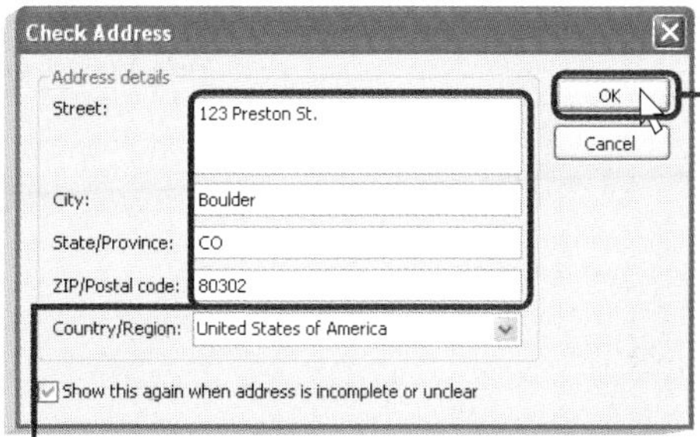

2 Click **OK** to confirm your changes.

1 To change part of the address, drag the mouse I over the part you want to change and then type the correct information.

Note: To type new information in a blank area, click the area and type the information.

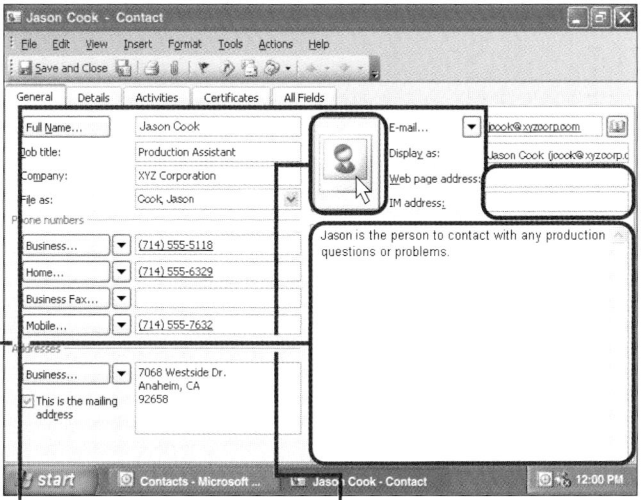

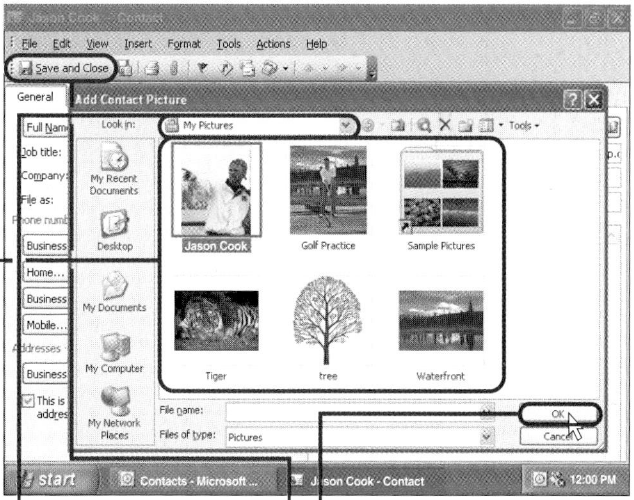

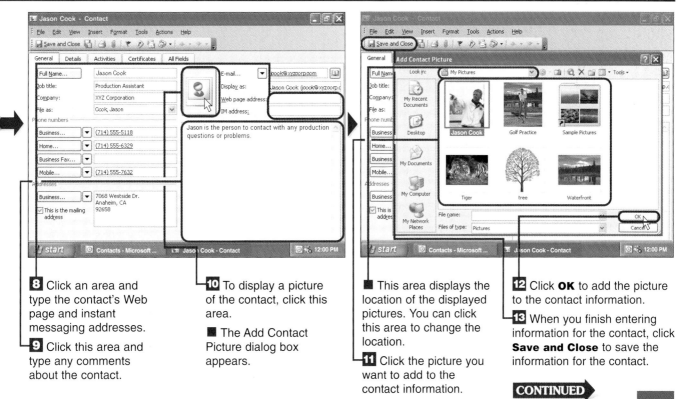

8 Click an area and type the contact's Web page and instant messaging addresses.

9 Click this area and type any comments about the contact.

10 To display a picture of the contact, click this area.

■ The Add Contact Picture dialog box appears.

■ This area displays the location of the displayed pictures. You can click this area to change the location.

11 Click the picture you want to add to the contact information.

12 Click **OK** to add the picture to the contact information.

13 When you finish entering information for the contact, click **Save and Close** to save the information for the contact.

CONTINUED

USING CONTACTS

You can change the way contacts are displayed on your screen or browse through your contacts to find a contact you want to work with. When information about your contacts changes, you can easily update the information.

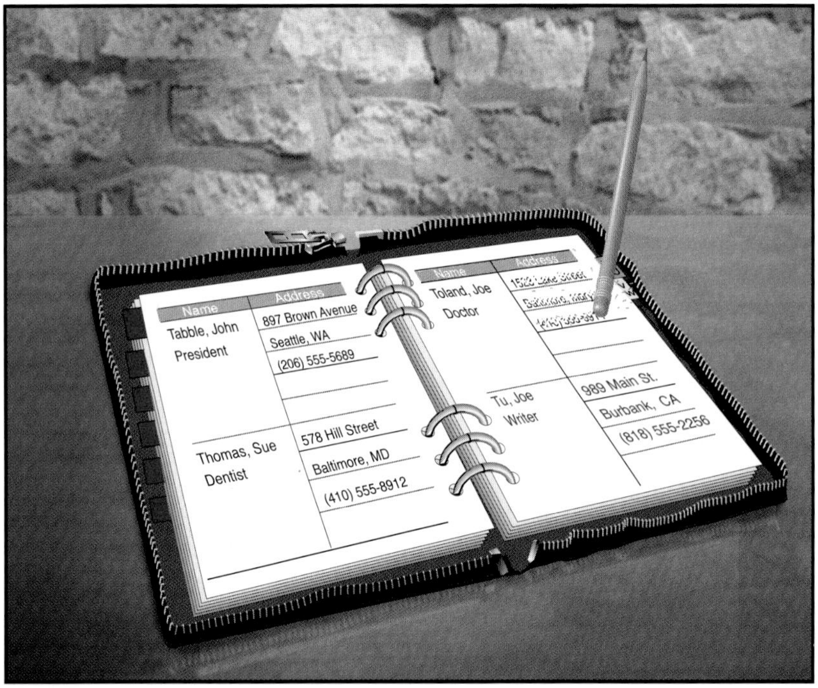

Outlook offers several different views you can use to display your contacts. For example, you can display additional details for each contact, organize your contacts into a phone list format or sort your contacts by company or by country.

WORK WITH CONTACTS

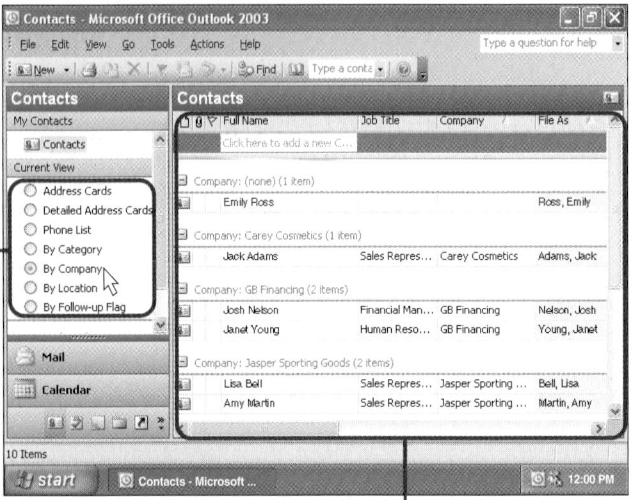

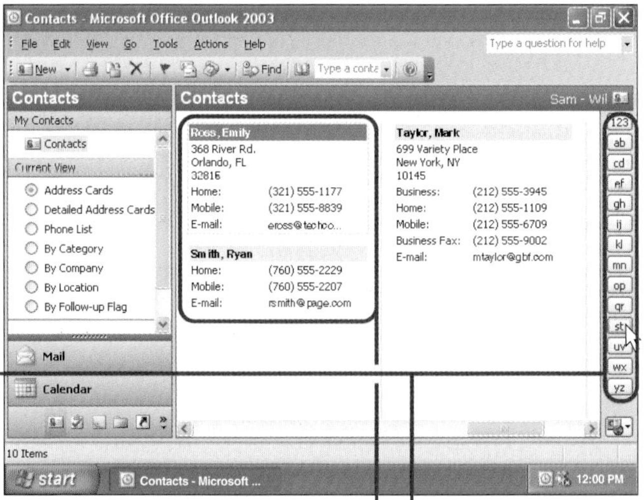

CHANGE THE VIEW OF CONTACTS

1 To change the way your contacts are displayed on your screen, click an option in this area (◯ changes to ◉).

■ Outlook displays your contacts in the view you selected.

■ To return to the default view, repeat step **1**, selecting **Address Cards**.

BROWSE THROUGH CONTACTS

■ These tabs allow you to browse through your contacts alphabetically.

Note: These tabs are available only in the Address Cards view.

1 Click the tab for the contacts you want to view.

■ Contacts beginning with the letters you selected appear.

Tip

How do I delete a contact I no longer need?

Click the contact you want to delete and then press the Delete key. Outlook places the contact in the Deleted Items folder. To view the contents of the Deleted Items folder, see page 311.

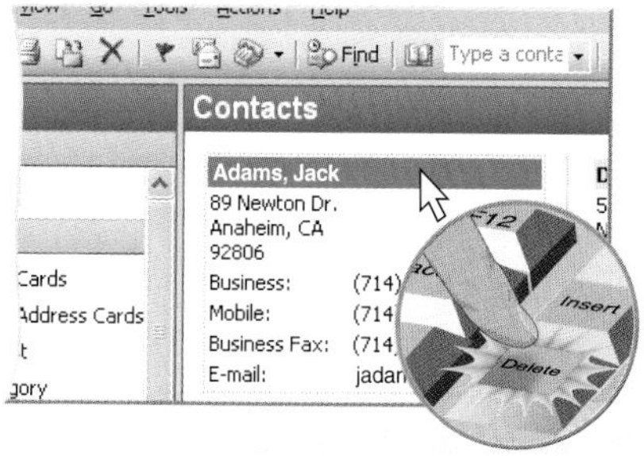

Tip

How can I later remove or change a picture I added for a contact?

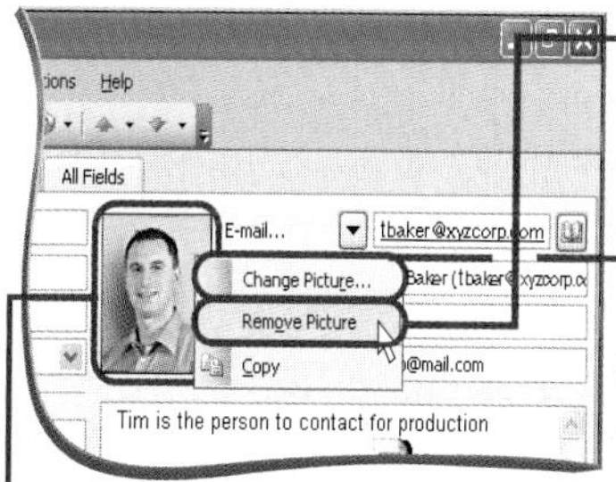

1 Double-click the contact to display the information for the contact.

2 Right-click the picture for the contact. A menu appears.

3 To remove the picture, click **Remove Picture** and then perform step **3** below.

■ To add a different picture, click **Change Picture** and then perform steps **11** to **13** on page 333.

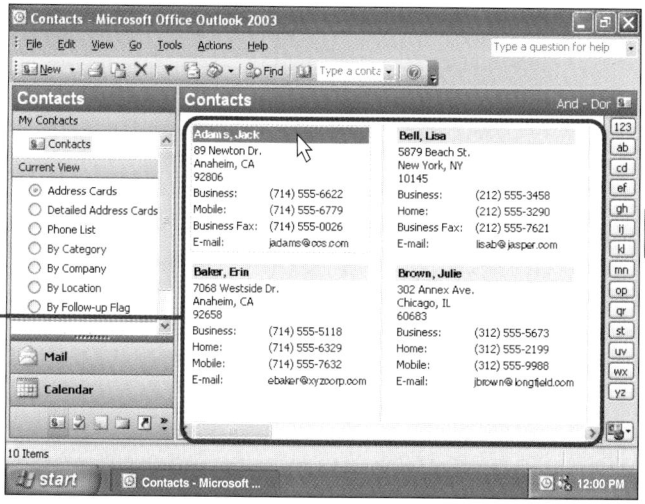

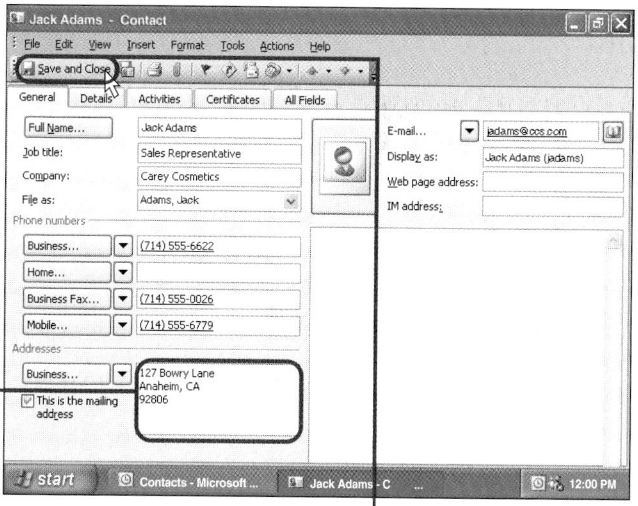

UPDATE CONTACT INFORMATION

1 To update the information for a contact, double-click the contact.

■ The Contact window appears, displaying the information for the contact.

2 Drag the mouse I over the information you want to change and then type the new information.

Note: To type new information for the contact in a blank area, click the area and type the information.

3 Click **Save and Close** to save your changes.

USING TASKS

You can create an electronic to-do list of personal and work-related tasks that you want to accomplish.

Outlook offers several views you can use to display your tasks. For example, you can choose to display only overdue tasks or only completed tasks in your task list.

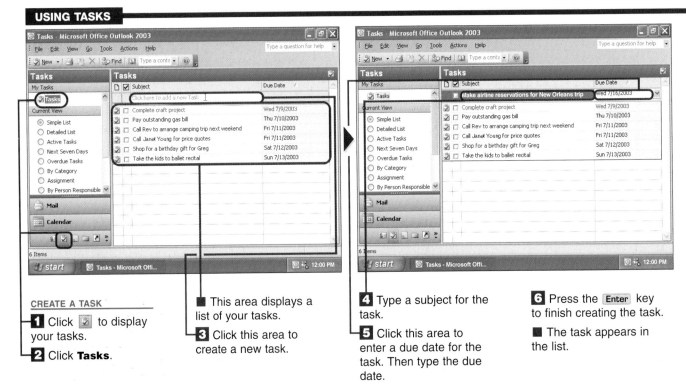

USING TASKS

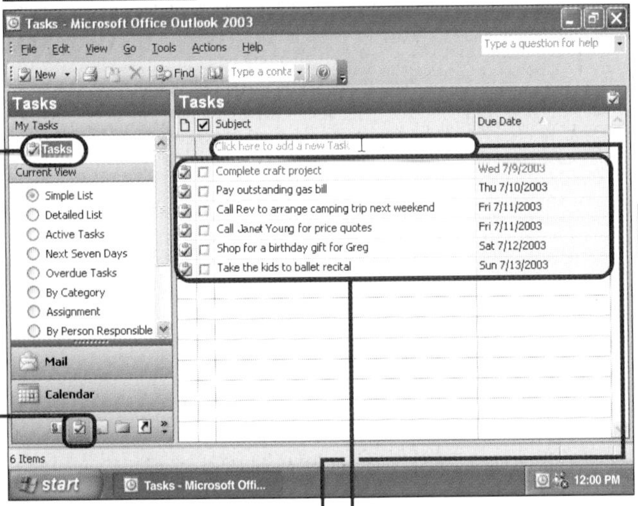

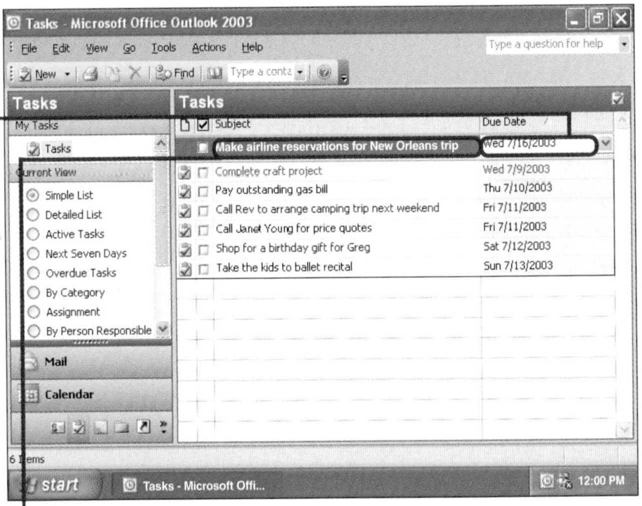

CREATE A TASK

1 Click the Tasks icon to display your tasks.

2 Click **Tasks**.

■ This area displays a list of your tasks.

3 Click this area to create a new task.

4 Type a subject for the task.

5 Click this area to enter a due date for the task. Then type the due date.

6 Press the Enter key to finish creating the task.

■ The task appears in the list.

Tip

Is there a quick way to enter a due date for a task?

Yes. Instead of typing a date, you can type a brief description of the due date, such as "Friday," "tomorrow," "next Thursday," "one month from now" or "New Year's Day 2004." Outlook will automatically change the text you enter to the corresponding date, such as Fri 7/11/2003.

Tip

How do I delete a task I no longer need?

To select the task you want to delete, click beside the task. Then press the Delete key to delete the task. Outlook places the task in the Deleted Items folder. To view the contents of the Deleted Items folder, see page 311.

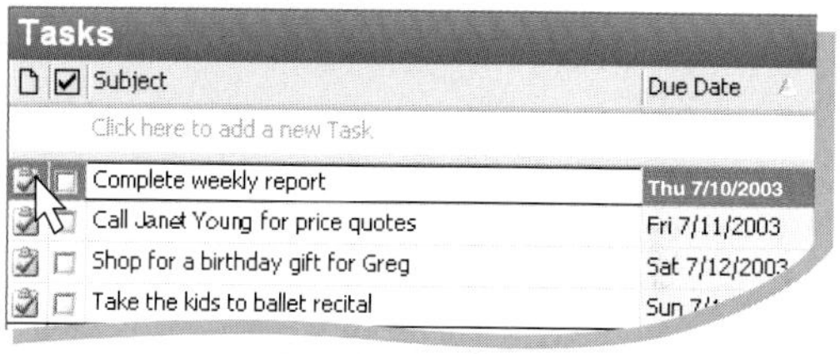

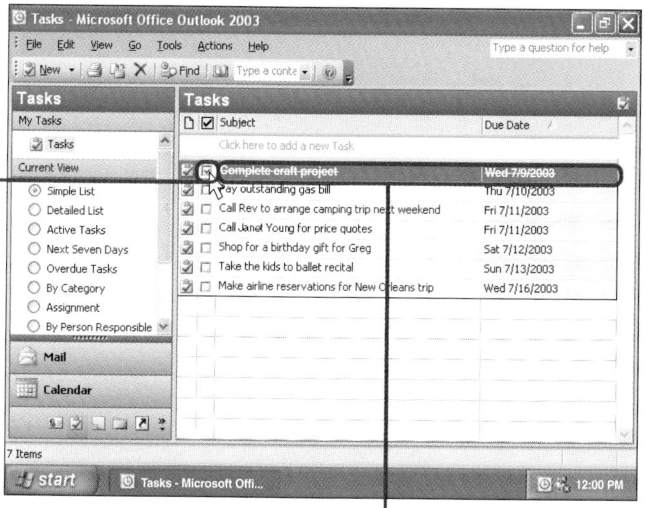

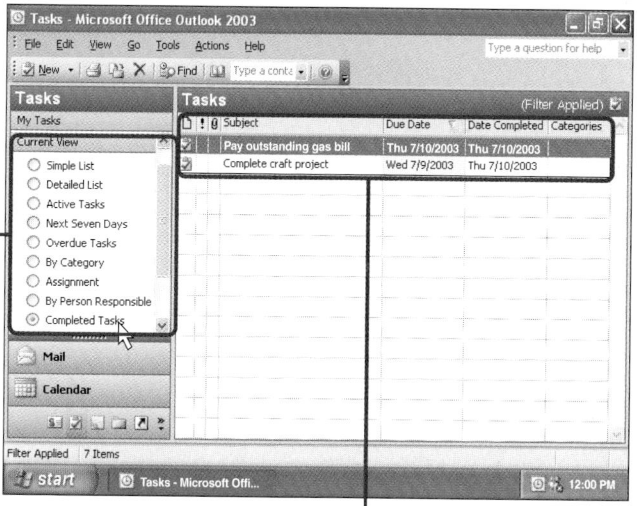

MARK A TASK AS COMPLETE

1 Click ☐ beside the task you want to mark as complete (☐ changes to ☑).

■ A line appears through the task to indicate that the task is complete.

*Note: To remove the line and once again display the task as incomplete, repeat step **1** (☑ changes to ☐).*

CHANGE THE VIEW OF TASKS

1 To change the way your tasks are displayed on your screen, click an option in this area (○ changes to ◉).

■ Outlook displays your tasks in the view you selected.

■ To return to the default view, repeat step **1**, selecting **Simple List**.

USING NOTES

You can create electronic notes that are similar to paper sticky notes.

Notes are useful for storing small pieces of information, such as reminders, questions, ideas and directions.

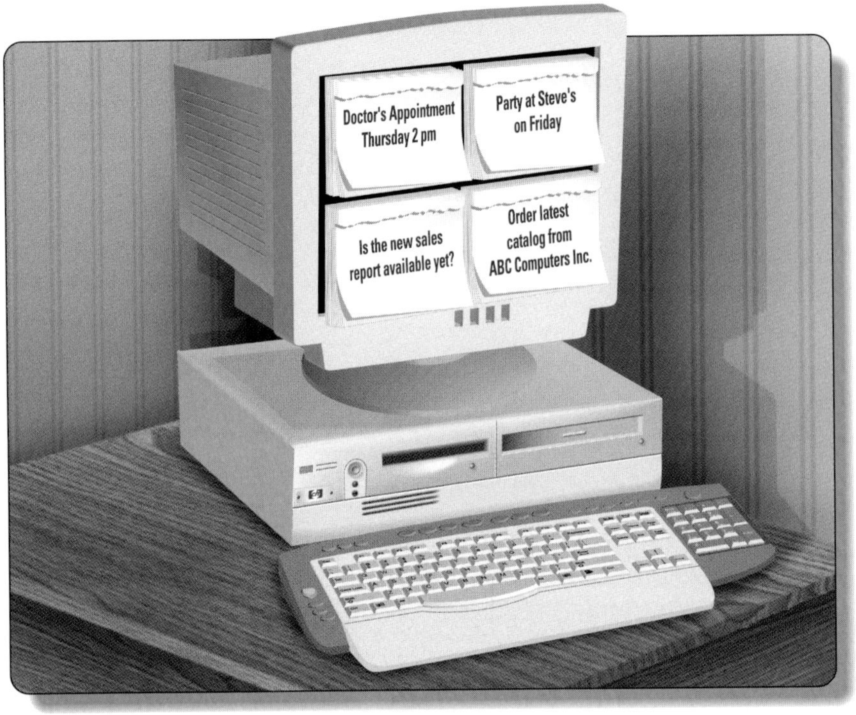

USING NOTES

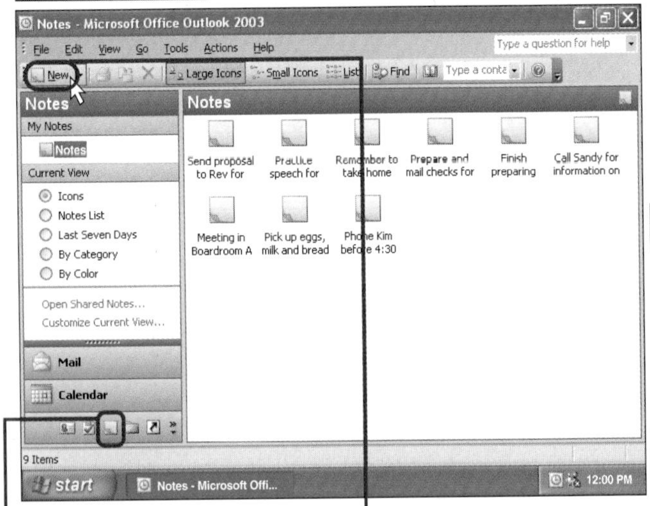

CREATE A NOTE

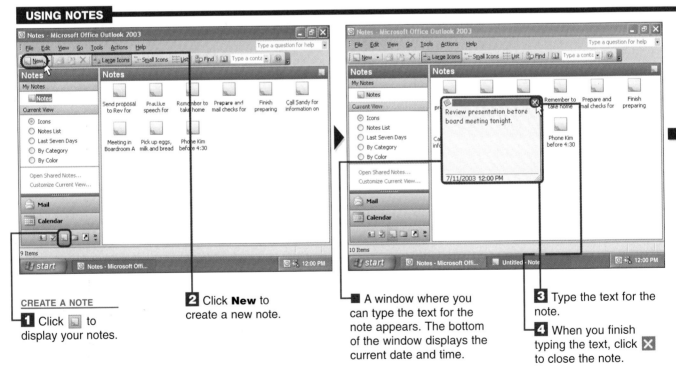

1 Click to display your notes.

2 Click **New** to create a new note.

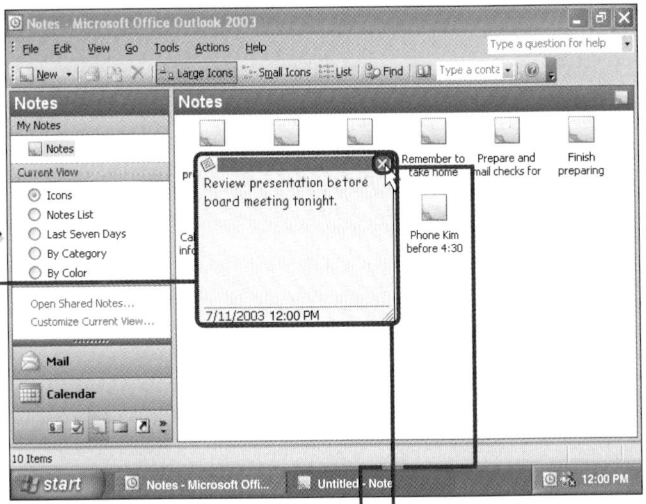

■ A window where you can type the text for the note appears. The bottom of the window displays the current date and time.

3 Type the text for the note.

4 When you finish typing the text, click ✕ to close the note.

Tip

How do I change the size of a note?

Position the mouse over the bottom right corner of the note (changes to ↘) and then drag the corner until the note displays the size you want. Changing the size of a note is useful when the note is too small to display all the text in the note.

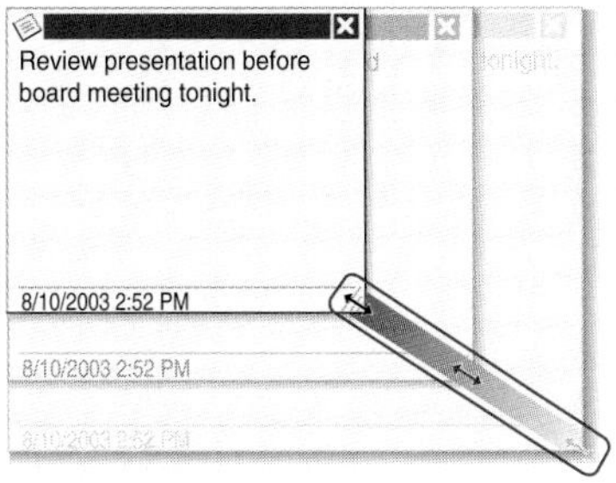

Tip

How do I delete a note?

To delete a note, click the icon for the note you want to delete and then press the Delete key. Outlook places the note in the Deleted Items folder. To view the contents of the Deleted Items folder, see page 311.

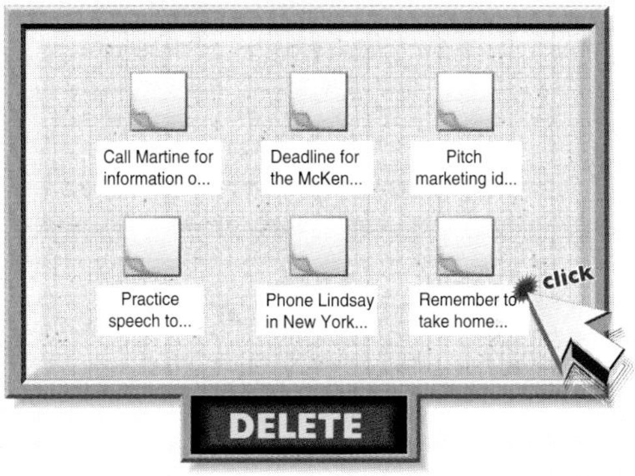

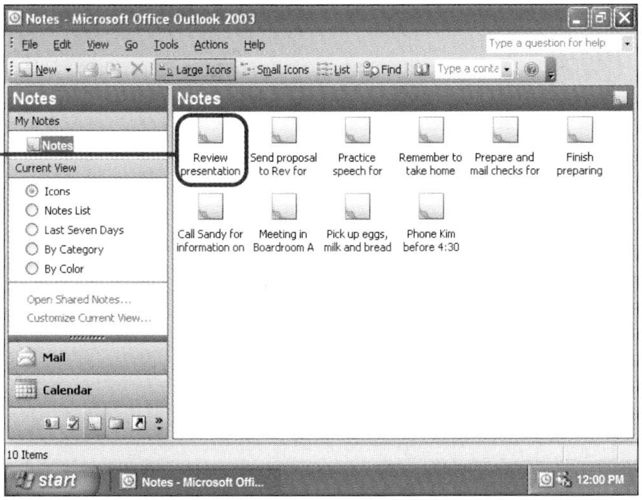

■ An icon for the note appears on your screen.

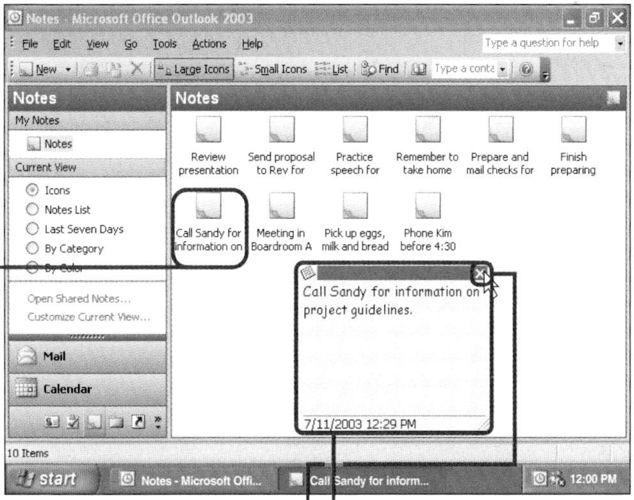

OPEN A NOTE

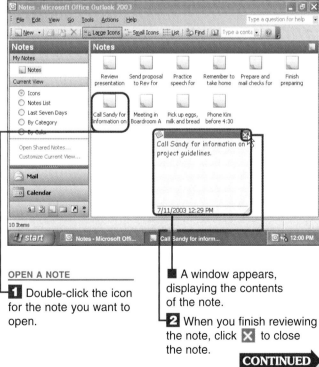

1 Double-click the icon for the note you want to open.

■ A window appears, displaying the contents of the note.

2 When you finish reviewing the note, click ✕ to close the note.

CONTINUED

USING NOTES

Outlook can help you organize and keep track of your notes. For example, you can change the color of your notes or the way the notes are displayed on your screen.

Changing the color of your notes can help you keep your notes organized. For example, you may want to display all your notes for a particular project in yellow, while your personal notes are displayed in blue.

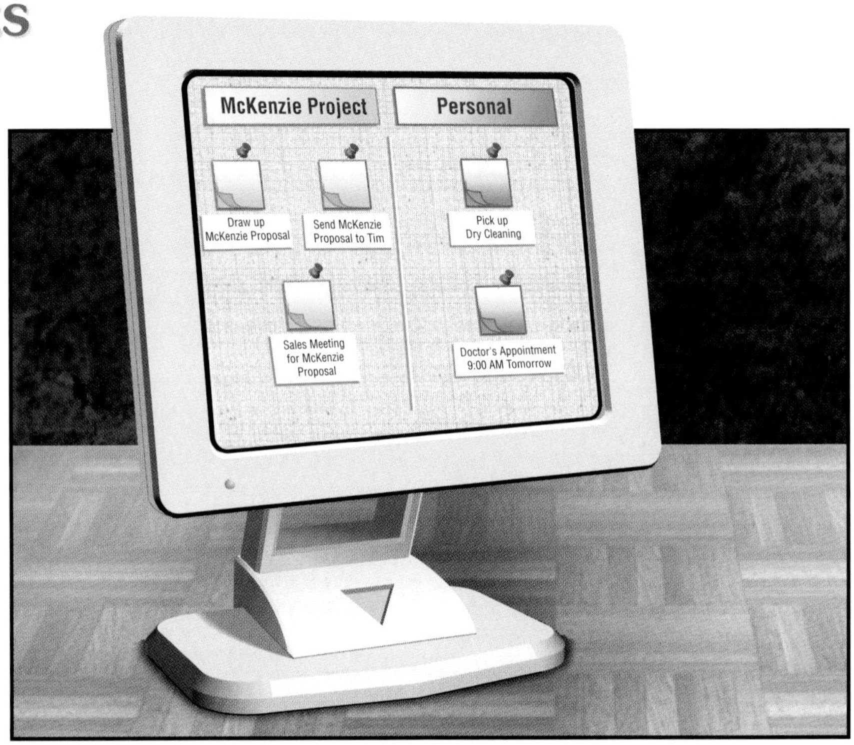

USING NOTES (CONTINUED)

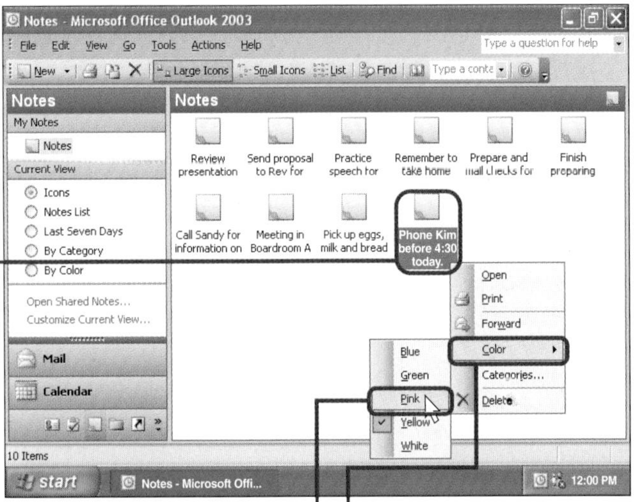

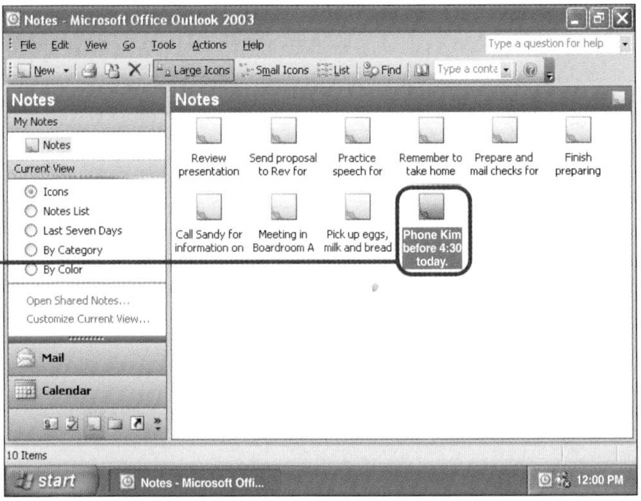

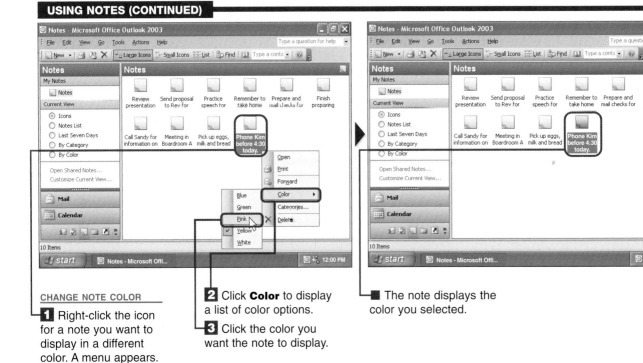

CHANGE NOTE COLOR

1 Right-click the icon for a note you want to display in a different color. A menu appears.

2 Click **Color** to display a list of color options.

3 Click the color you want the note to display.

■ The note displays the color you selected.

Tip

How can I arrange my notes on the screen?

Outlook offers several views you can use to arrange your notes on the screen.

Icons	Notes List	Last Seven Days	By Category	By Color
Displays each note as a large icon with the first few words of the note appearing below.	Arranges the notes by date. This view displays multiple lines of text for long notes.	Similar to the Notes List view, but this view displays only the notes you have created in the last seven days.	Arranges the notes by category. By default, notes are not assigned to a category.	Arranges the notes by color.

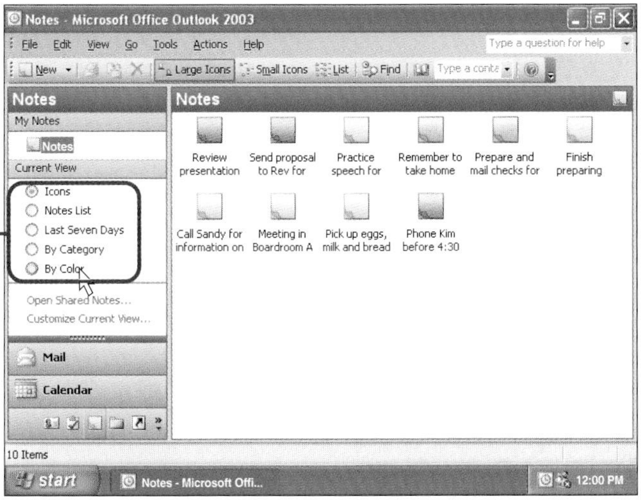

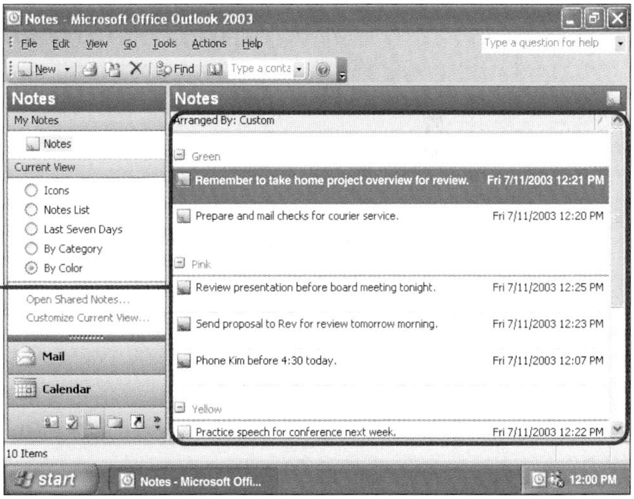

ORGANIZE YOUR NOTES

1 To change the way your notes are displayed on your screen, click an option in this area (○ changes to ◉).

Note: For information on the ways you can display notes on your screen, see the top of this page.

■ Outlook displays your notes in the view you selected.

*Note: To return to the default view, repeat step **1**, selecting **Icons**.*

USING THE JOURNAL

The Journal helps you keep track of all your activities in Office. Before using the Journal, you must choose which activities you want the Journal to record.

SELECT ACTIVITIES TO RECORD

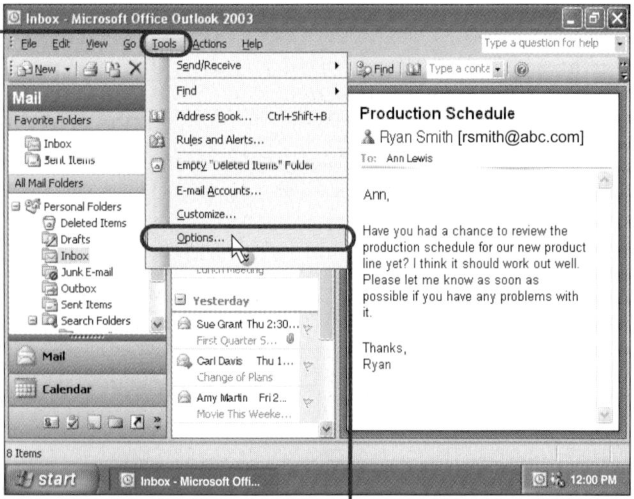

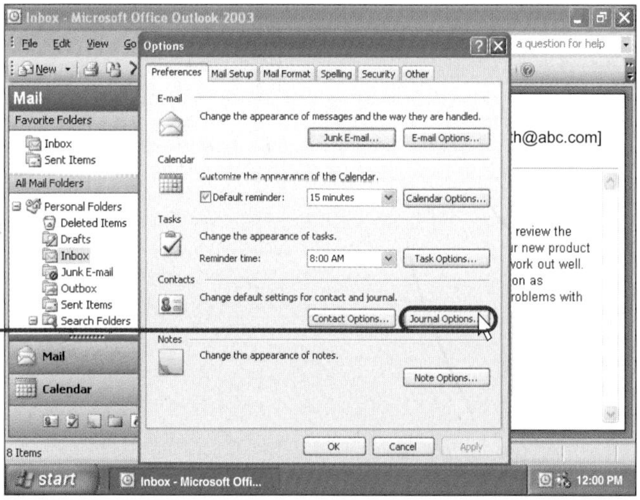

1 Click **Tools**.

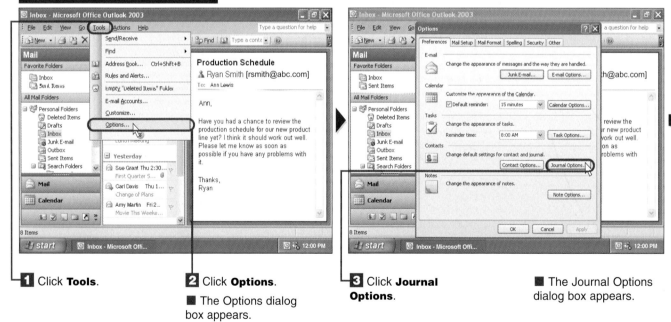

2 Click **Options**.

■ The Options dialog box appears.

3 Click **Journal Options**.

■ The Journal Options dialog box appears.

Tip

What activities can I have the Journal record?

You can have the Journal record your e-mail communications with people in your Contact list or files you save in programs such as Word, Excel and PowerPoint.

Tip

Why doesn't the person I want to record activities for appear in the Journal Options dialog box?

Only people that appear in your Contact list are available in the Journal Options dialog box. For information on working with the Contact list, see pages 332 to 335.

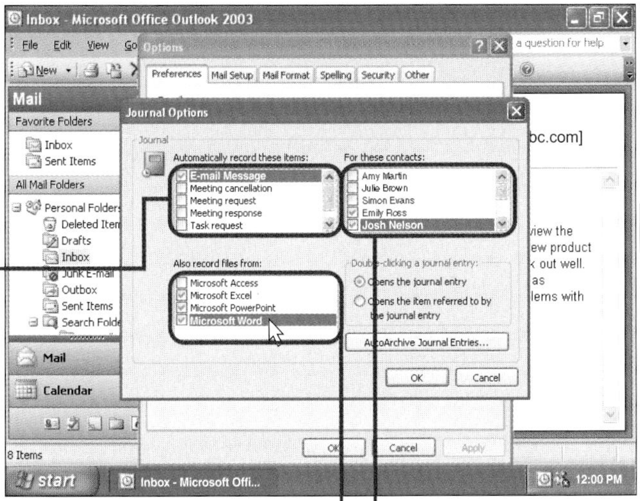

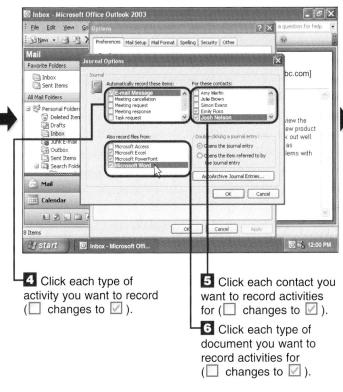

4 Click each type of activity you want to record (☐ changes to ☑).

5 Click each contact you want to record activities for (☐ changes to ☑).

6 Click each type of document you want to record activities for (☐ changes to ☑).

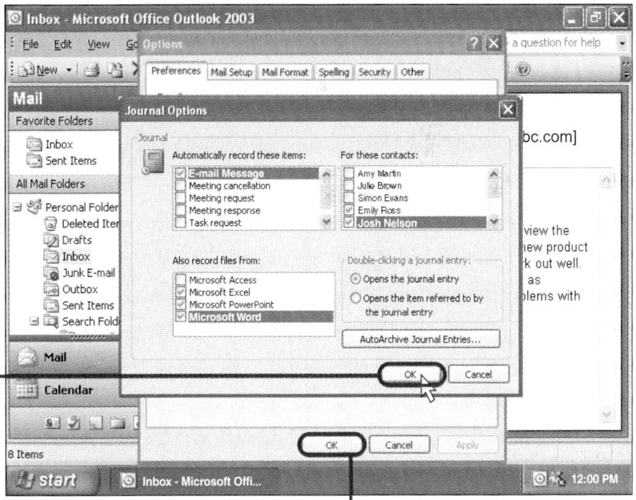

7 Click **OK** to save your changes.

8 Click **OK** to close the Options dialog box.

CONTINUED

You can use the Journal to view the activities you accomplished on any day.

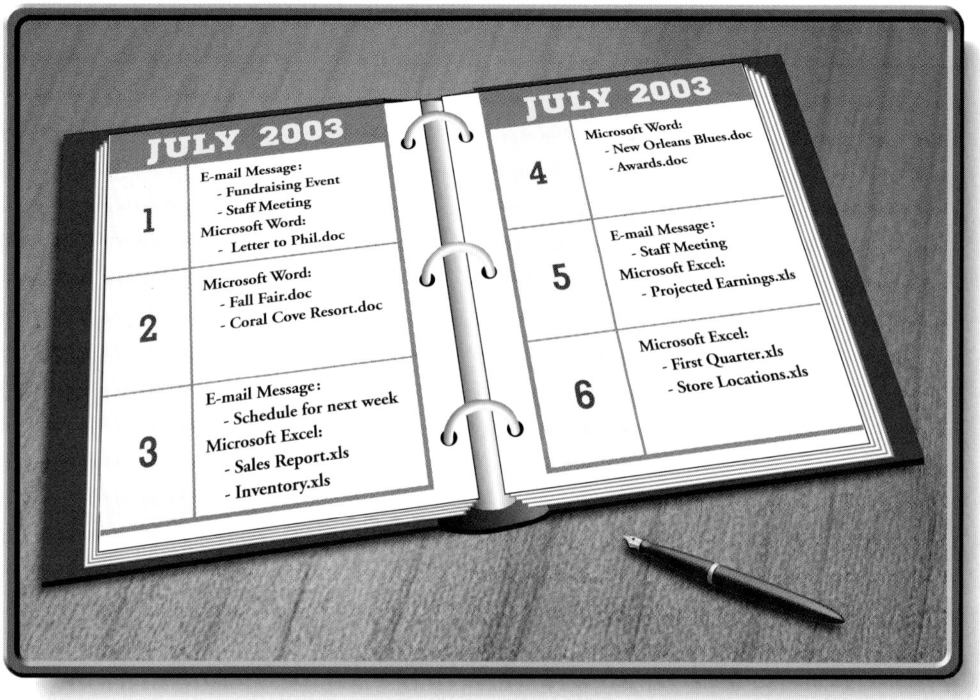

Before you can view your activities in the Journal, you must specify the activities you want to record. To specify activities, see page 342.

VIEW JOURNAL ACTIVITIES

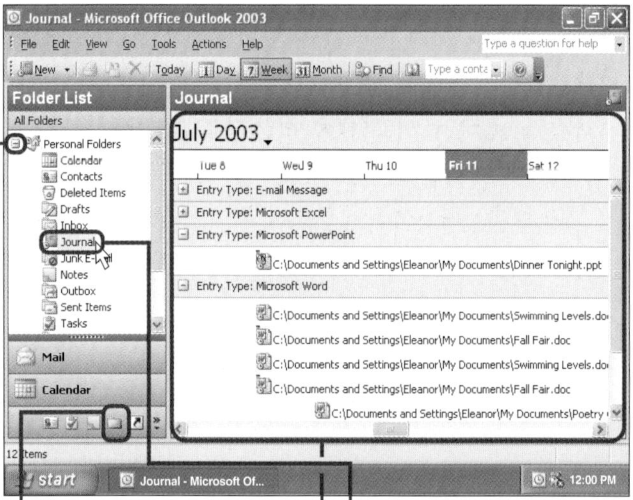

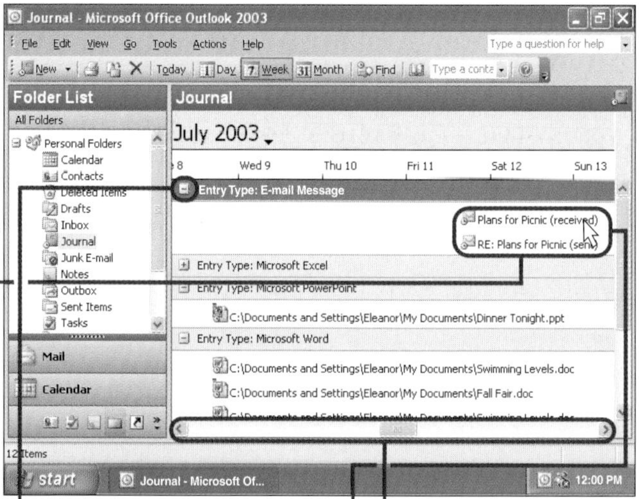

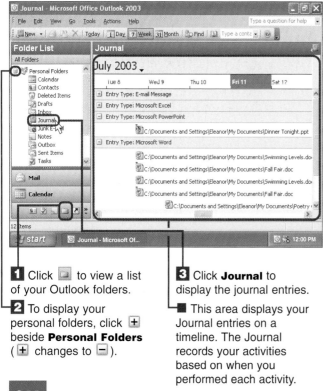

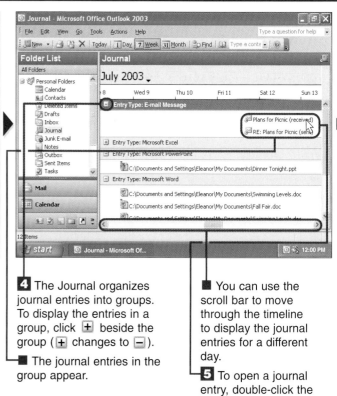

1 Click to view a list of your Outlook folders.

2 To display your personal folders, click + beside **Personal Folders** (+ changes to −).

3 Click **Journal** to display the journal entries.

■ This area displays your Journal entries on a timeline. The Journal records your activities based on when you performed each activity.

4 The Journal organizes journal entries into groups. To display the entries in a group, click + beside the group (+ changes to −).

■ The journal entries in the group appear.

■ You can use the scroll bar to move through the timeline to display the journal entries for a different day.

5 To open a journal entry, double-click the entry.

Tip

Can I change the amount of time the Journal displays on the timeline?

By default, Outlook displays the days of the week on the timeline. To change the amount of time shown on the timeline, click one of the following options.

1 Day	Displays the hours in the day
7 Week	Displays the days of the week
31 Month	Displays the days of the month

Tip

How do I remove a journal entry I no longer need?

To make the Journal less cluttered, you can delete a journal entry you no longer need. Click the journal entry you want to delete and then press the Delete key. Outlook places the journal entry in the Deleted Items folder. To view the contents of the Deleted Items folder, see page 311.

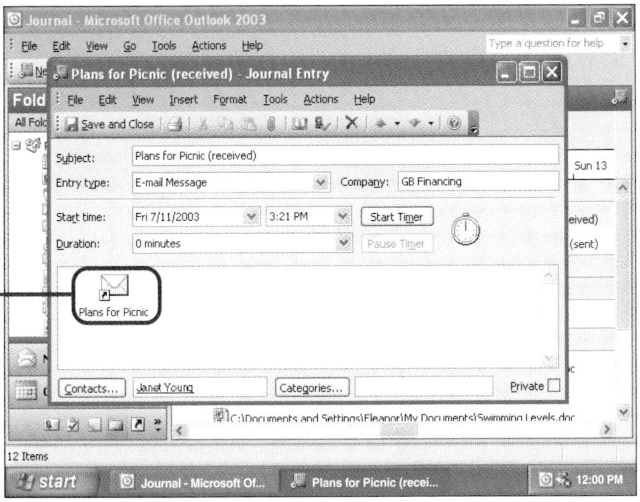

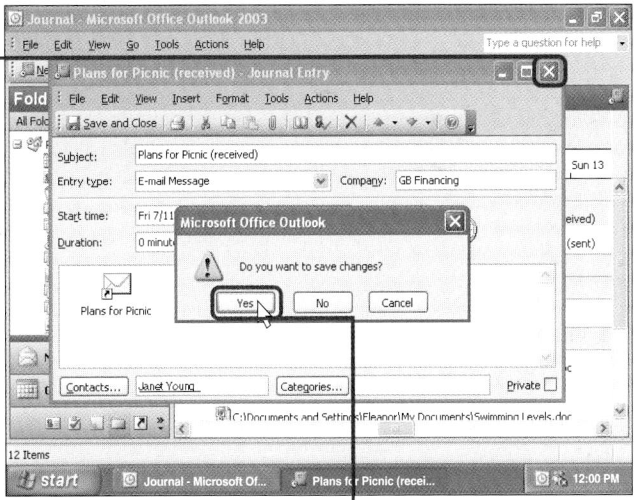

■ A window appears, displaying information about the journal entry.

■ To open the document or item, double-click the picture that represents the document or item. You can then work with the document or item as usual.

*Note: A warning dialog box may appear when you open a document or item. To continue opening the document or item, click **Yes** or **Open**.*

6 To close the journal entry, click ☒.

■ A dialog box may appear, asking if you want to save your changes.

7 Click **Yes** to save your changes.

OUTLOOK WITH BUSINESS CONTACT MANAGER

Business Contact Manager is an add-on to Outlook that allows small business users and salespeople to more effectively keep track of their accounts, business contacts and sales opportunities.

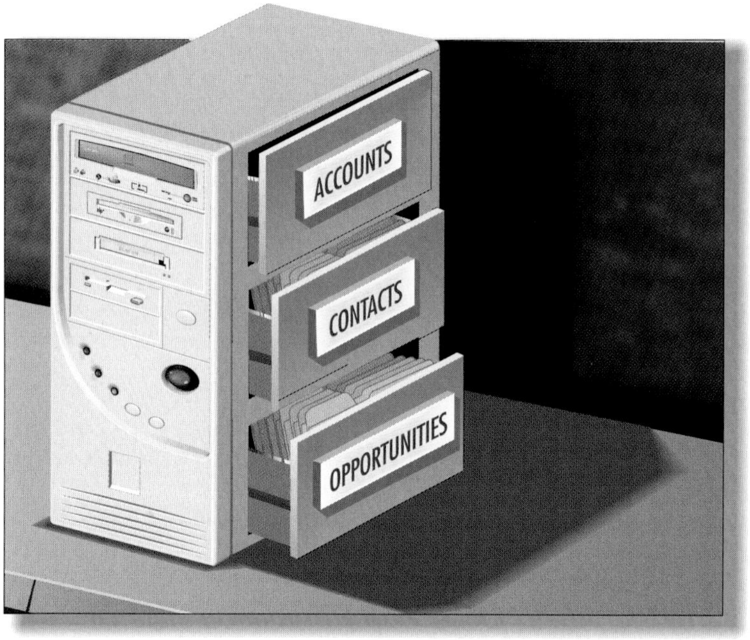

Outlook with Business Contact Manager provides a way for you to organize information about your business relationships and sales opportunities, together with all related e-mail messages, appointments, business notes and other items.

The information for an account, business contact or opportunity, along with all its related items, is referred to as a **record**.

Accounts

An account is a company or organization that you do business with. An account may be one of your suppliers or customers. You can link an account to a business contact you have created.

Business Contacts

A business contact is a person you do business with. You can link a business contact to an account you have created.

Opportunities

An opportunity is a sales lead or a potential purchaser of your products or services. You can link an opportunity to an account or business contact you have created.

E-mail Messages

You can link an e-mail message you have sent or received to an account, business contact or opportunity.

Appointments

You can add an appointment to the Calendar to remind you of an activity or meeting related to a specific account, business contact or opportunity.

Tasks

Creating a task allows you to keep track of a duty or errand related to an account, business contact or opportunity.

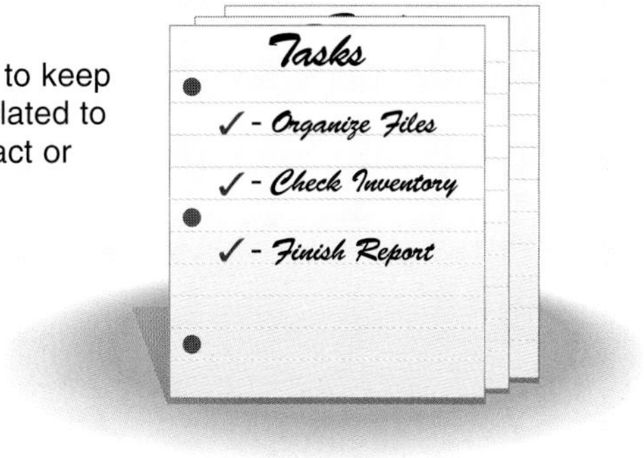

Business Notes

You can create a business note to store a small piece of information, such as a reminder, question or idea, for a particular account, business contact or opportunity.

Phone Logs

A phone log allows you to store information about telephone conversations related to a particular account, business contact or opportunity.

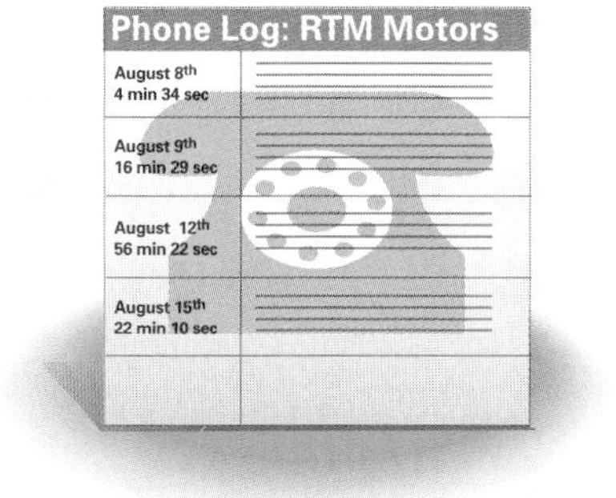

You can use Business Contact Manager to create an account for a company you do business with. Creating an account allows you to keep all the information for a company in one location.

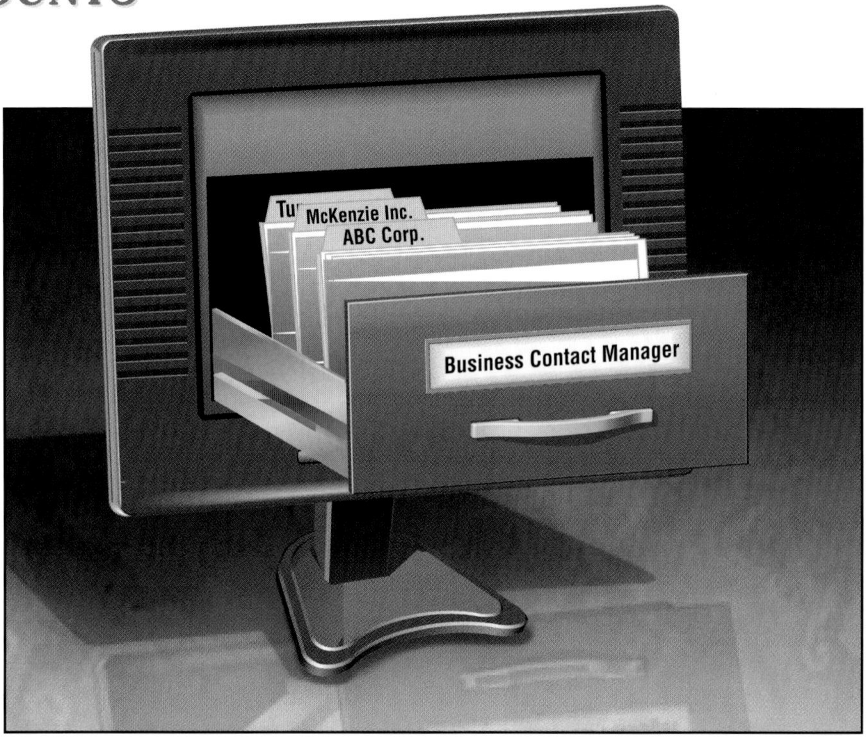

CREATE A NEW ACCOUNT

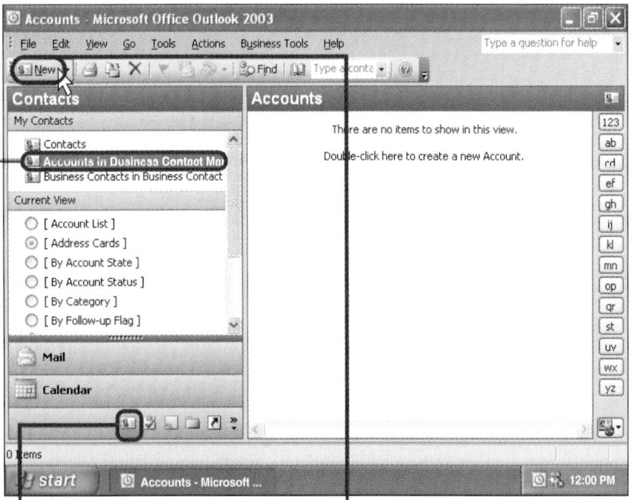

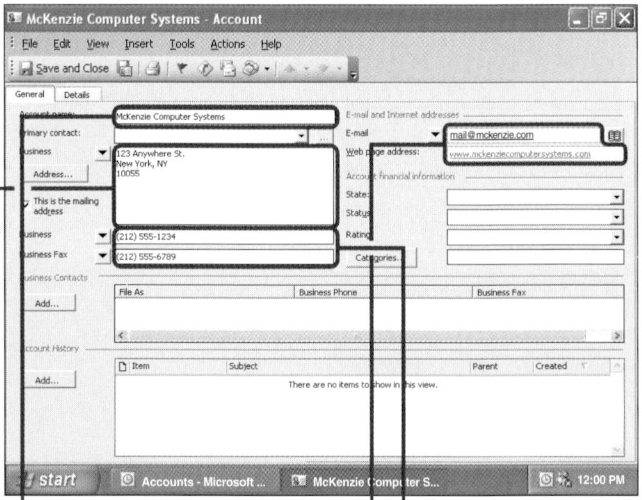

1 Click to display your accounts and contacts.

2 Click **Accounts in Business Contact Manager** to display your accounts.

3 Click **New** to create a new account.

■ The Account window appears, displaying areas where you can enter information about an account.

Note: You do not need to enter information in every area.

4 Click this area and type a name for the account.

5 Click this area and type the account's address.

Note: The Check Address dialog box appears if the address is incomplete. See the top of page 353 for more information.

6 Click an area and type the account's business phone and business fax numbers.

7 Click an area and type the account's e-mail and Web page addresses.

Tip

How can I enter a primary contact for the account?

After you create and save an account, you can specify a business contact that you most often work with for the account. You must first create the business contact as shown on page 352.

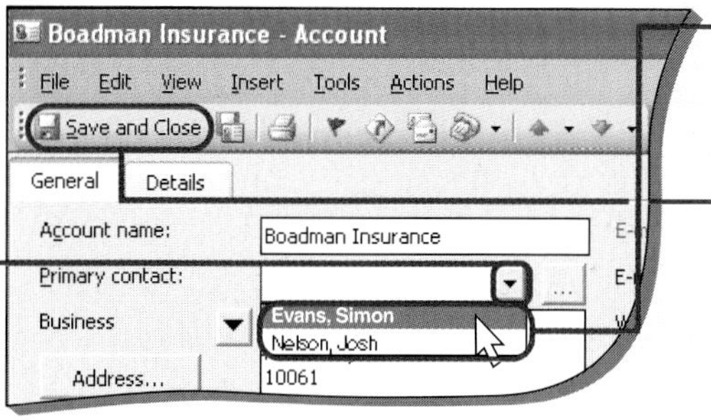

1 Perform step **1** on page 351 to view the account you want to enter a primary contact for.

2 Click ▾ in this area.

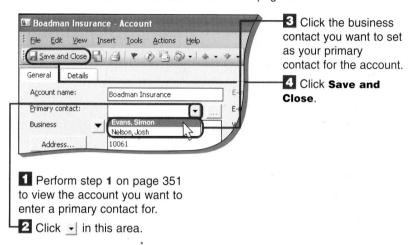

3 Click the business contact you want to set as your primary contact for the account.

4 Click **Save and Close**.

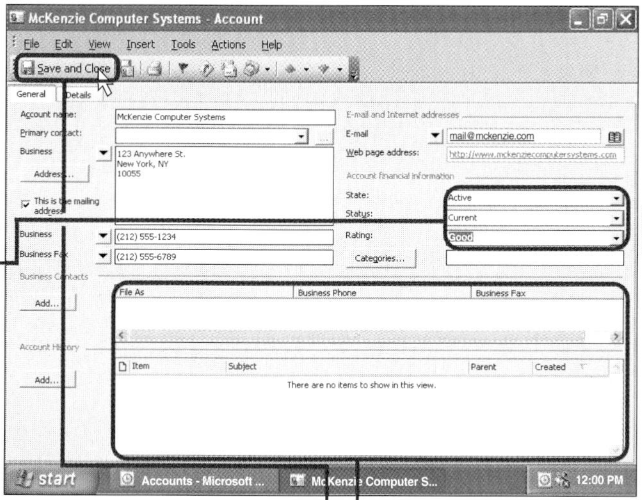

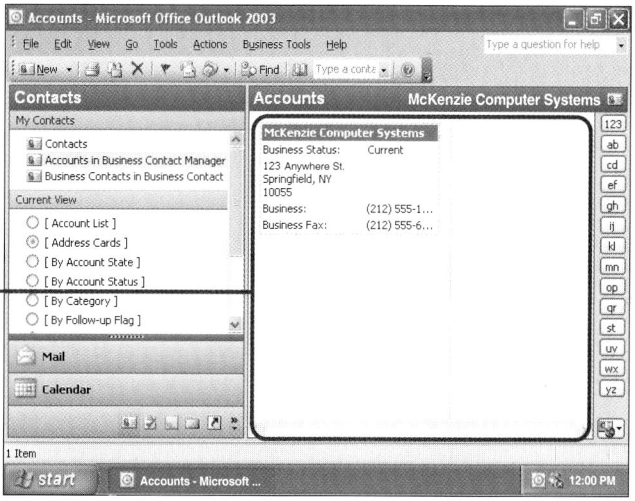

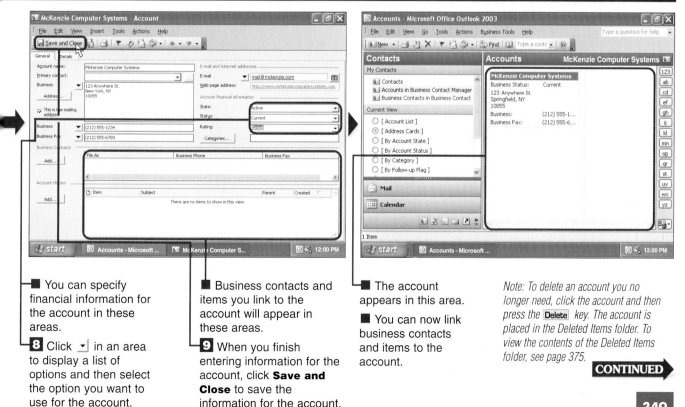

■ You can specify financial information for the account in these areas.

8 Click ▾ in an area to display a list of options and then select the option you want to use for the account.

■ Business contacts and items you link to the account will appear in these areas.

9 When you finish entering information for the account, click **Save and Close** to save the information for the account.

■ The account appears in this area.

■ You can now link business contacts and items to the account.

Note: To delete an account you no longer need, click the account and then press the Delete *key. The account is placed in the Deleted Items folder. To view the contents of the Deleted Items folder, see page 375.*

CONTINUED

USING ACCOUNTS

You can change the way accounts are displayed on your screen or browse through your accounts to find an account you want to work with. When information about an account changes, you can easily update the information.

WORK WITH ACCOUNTS

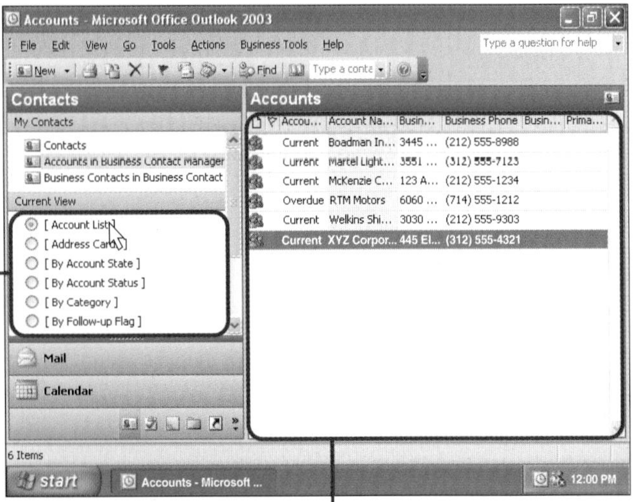

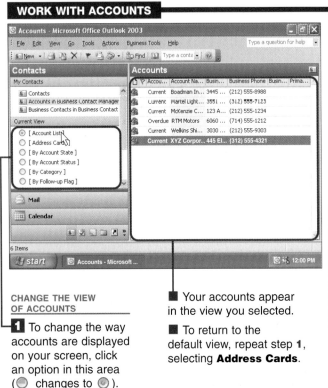

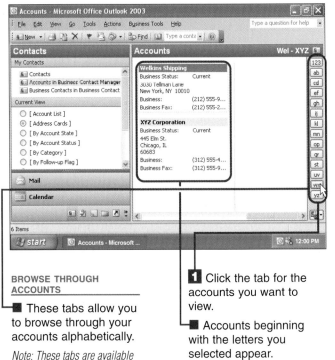

CHANGE THE VIEW OF ACCOUNTS

1 To change the way accounts are displayed on your screen, click an option in this area (○ changes to ◉).

■ Your accounts appear in the view you selected.

■ To return to the default view, repeat step **1**, selecting **Address Cards**.

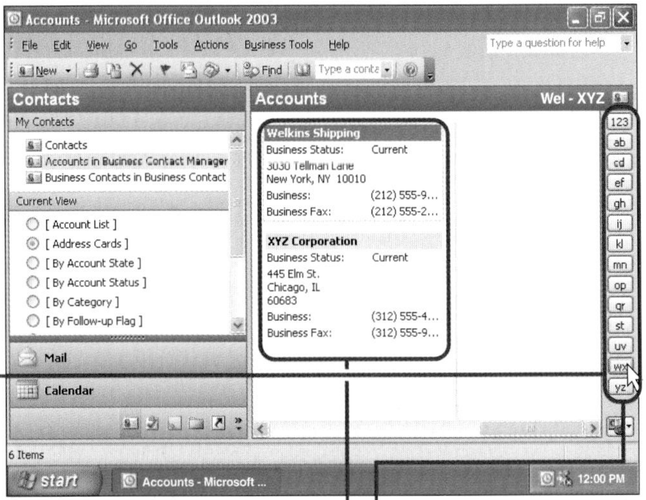

BROWSE THROUGH ACCOUNTS

■ These tabs allow you to browse through your accounts alphabetically.

Note: These tabs are available only in the Address Cards view.

1 Click the tab for the accounts you want to view.

■ Accounts beginning with the letters you selected appear.

Tip

What views can I use to display my accounts?

There are several views you can use to display your accounts. Common views include the following:

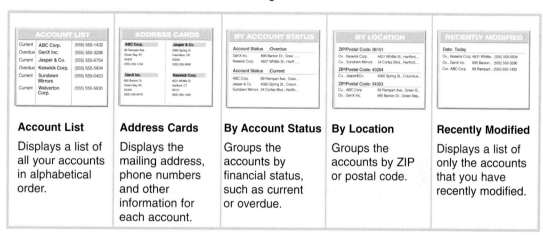

Account List

Displays a list of all your accounts in alphabetical order.

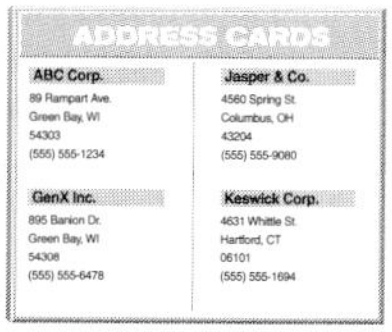

Address Cards

Displays the mailing address, phone numbers and other information for each account.

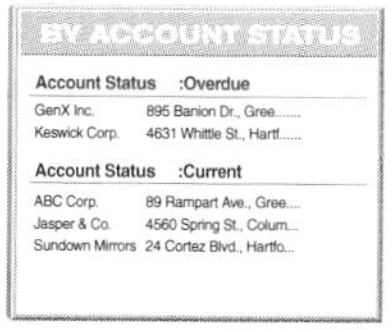

By Account Status

Groups the accounts by financial status, such as current or overdue.

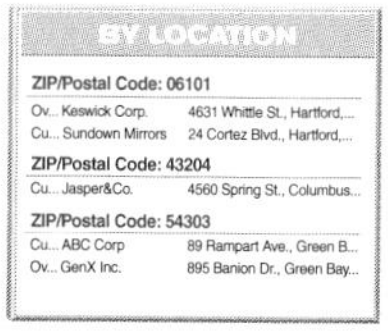

By Location

Groups the accounts by ZIP or postal code.

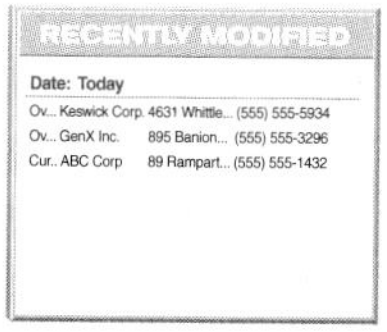

Recently Modified

Displays a list of only the accounts that you have recently modified.

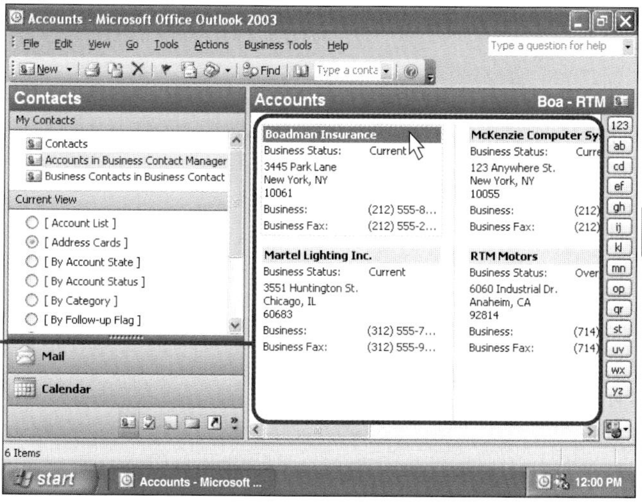

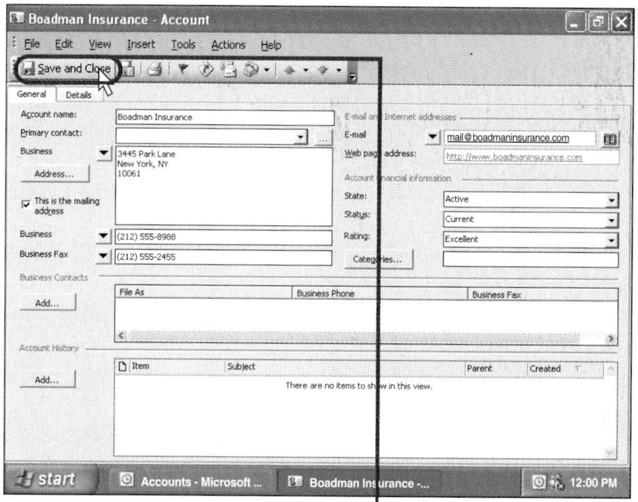

VIEW ACCOUNT INFORMATION

1 To view the information for an account, double-click the account.

*Note: To display all your accounts, perform steps **1** and **2** on page 348.*

■ The Account window appears, displaying the information for the account.

■ To update information for the account, drag the mouse over the information you want to change and then type the new information.

Note: To type new information for the account in a blank area, click the area and type the information.

2 Click **Save and Close** to save your changes.

You can use Business Contact Manager to maintain detailed information about your business contacts. A business contact is a person you do business with.

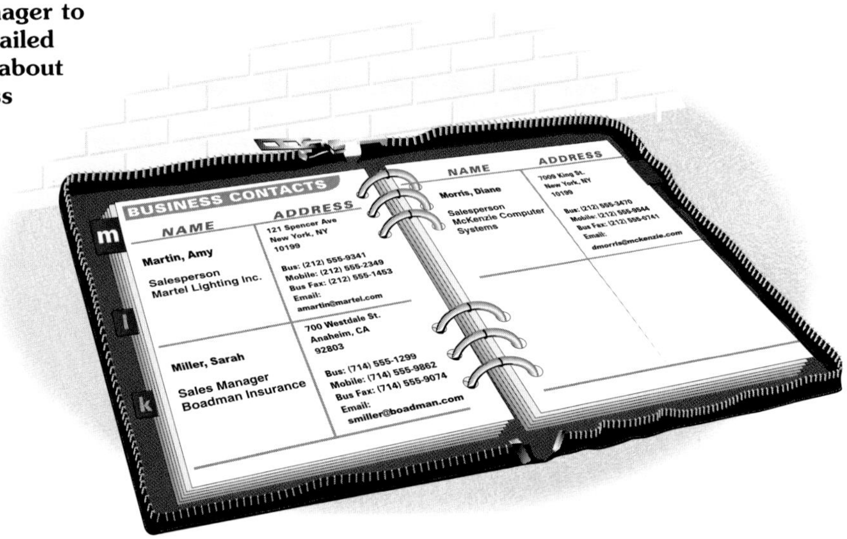

When creating a business contact, you can link the business contact to an account you have previously created. To create an account, see page 348.

USING BUSINESS CONTACTS

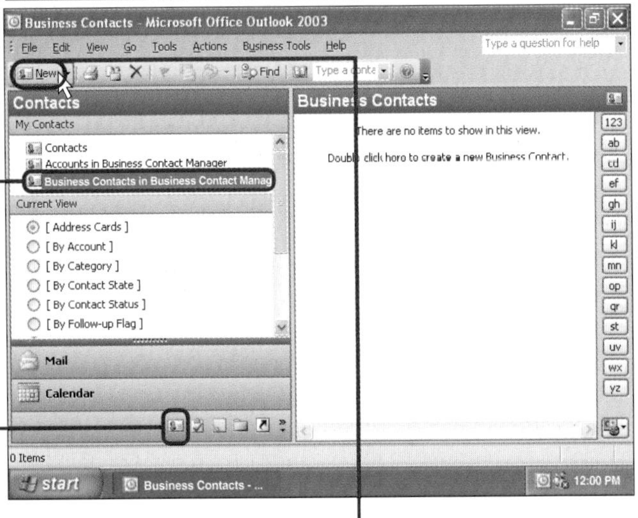

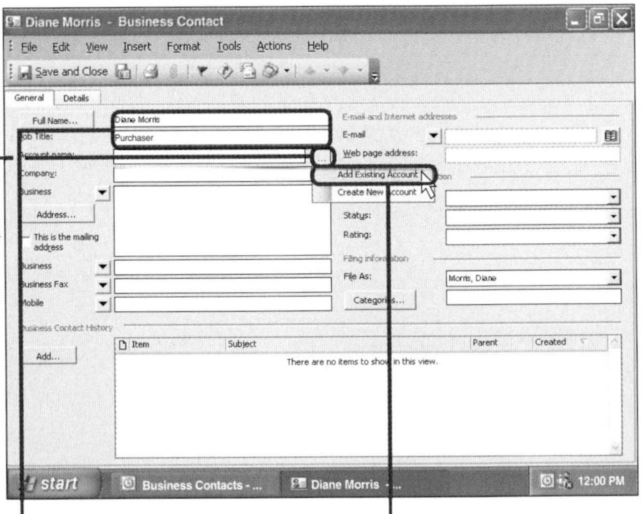

CREATE A NEW BUSINESS CONTACT

1 Click [icon] to display your accounts and contacts.

2 Click **Business Contacts in Business Contact Manager**.

3 Click **New** to create a new business contact.

■ The Business Contact window appears, displaying areas where you can enter information about a business contact.

Note: You do not need to enter information in every area.

4 Click an area and type the business contact's full name and job title.

5 To link the business contact to an account you have created, click [...].

6 Click **Add Existing Account**.

Tip

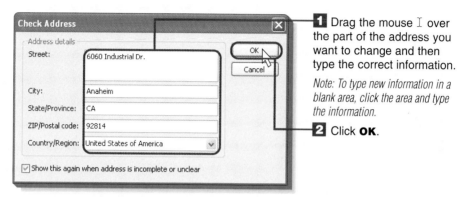

Why did the Check Address dialog box appear after I entered an address?

If the address you entered is incomplete, the Check Address dialog box appears, helping you to complete the address.

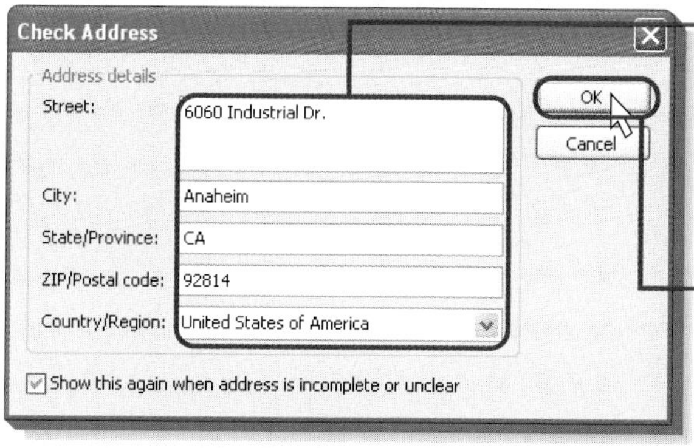

1 Drag the mouse I over the part of the address you want to change and then type the correct information.

Note: To type new information in a blank area, click the area and type the information.

2 Click **OK**.

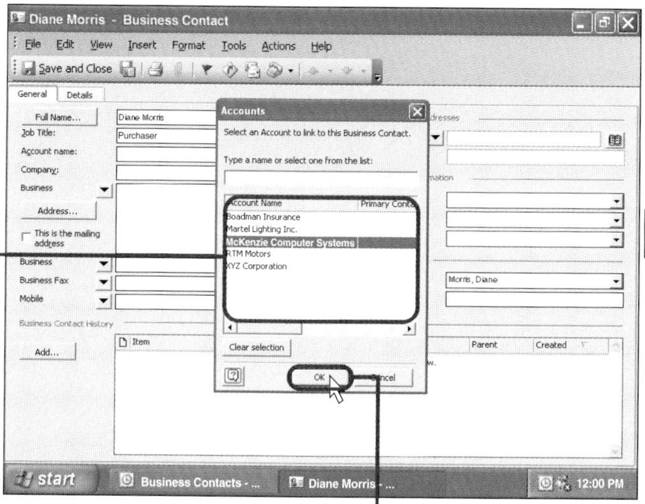

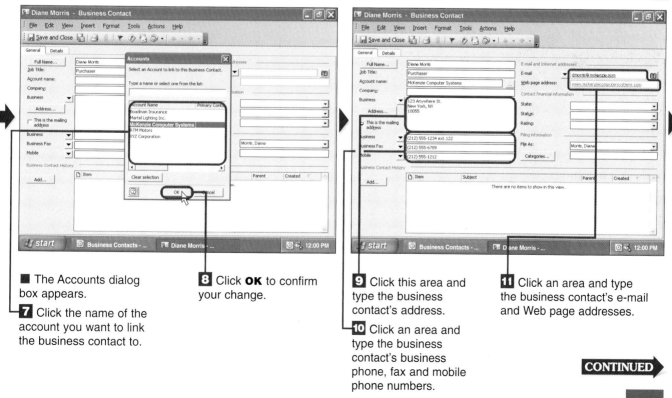

■ The Accounts dialog box appears.

7 Click the name of the account you want to link the business contact to.

8 Click **OK** to confirm your change.

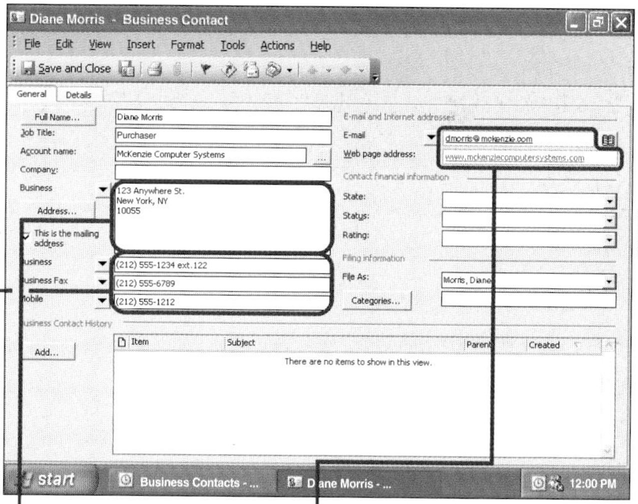

9 Click this area and type the business contact's address.

10 Click an area and type the business contact's business phone, fax and mobile phone numbers.

11 Click an area and type the business contact's e-mail and Web page addresses.

CONTINUED

USING BUSINESS CONTACTS

After creating business contacts, you can change the way business contacts are displayed on your screen or browse through your business contacts to find the one you want to work with.

There are several different views you can use to display your business contacts. For example, you can group your business contacts according to the accounts they are linked to, organize your contacts into a phone list format or display only the business contacts that you have recently modified.

USING BUSINESS CONTACTS (CONTINUED)

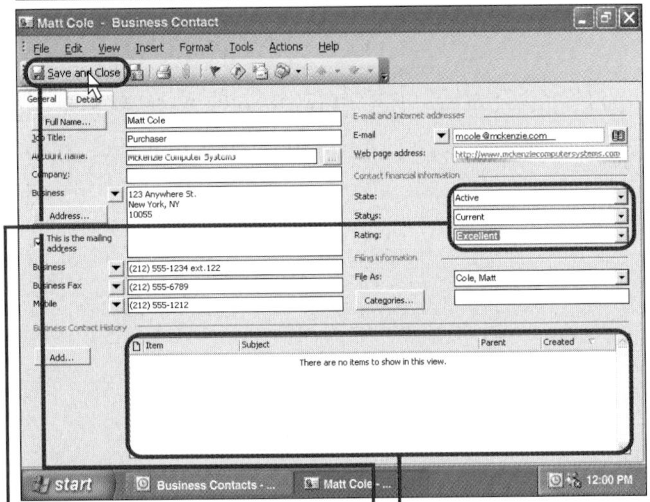

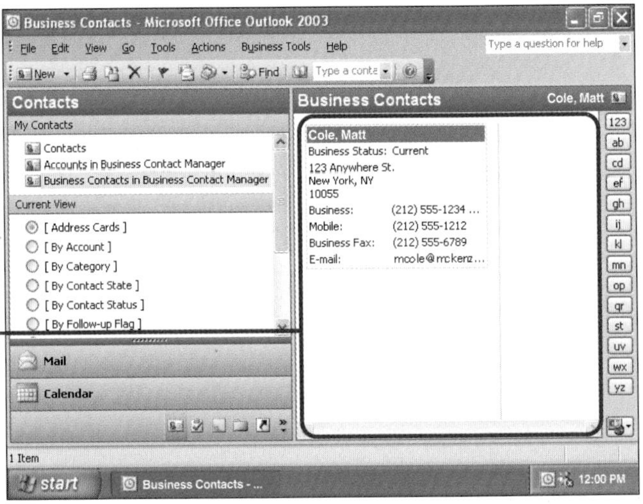

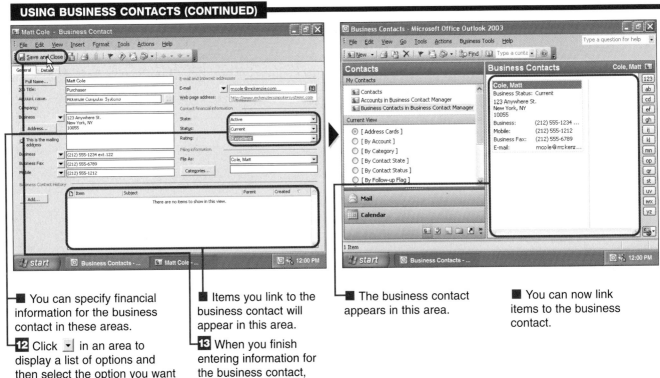

■ You can specify financial information for the business contact in these areas.

12 Click ▾ in an area to display a list of options and then select the option you want to use for the business contact.

■ Items you link to the business contact will appear in this area.

13 When you finish entering information for the business contact, click **Save and Close** to save the information.

■ The business contact appears in this area.

■ You can now link items to the business contact.

Tip

How can I link items to a business contact?

After you create a business contact, you can link items, such as business notes, tasks and appointments to the business contact. This allows you to keep all the information related to a business contact together in one location. For information on creating and linking items to a business contact, see pages 356 to 373.

Tip

How do I delete a business contact I no longer need?

Click the business contact you want to delete and then press the Delete key. The business contact is placed in the Deleted Items folder. To view the contents of the Deleted Items folder, see page 375.

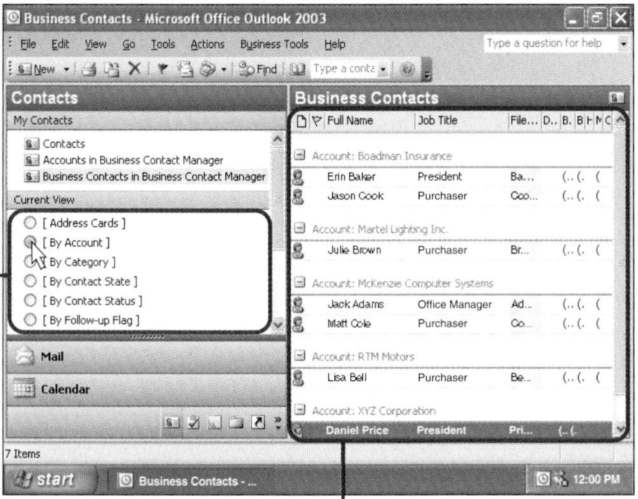

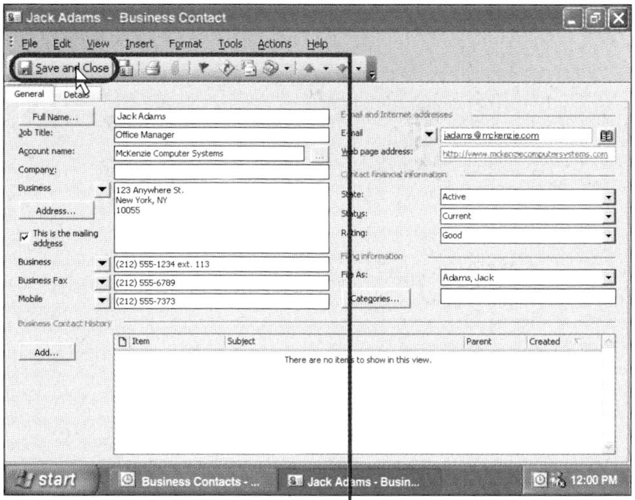

CHANGE THE VIEW OF BUSINESS CONTACTS

1 To change the way business contacts are displayed on your screen, click an option in this area (◯ changes to ◉).

■ Your business contacts appear in the view you selected.

■ To return to the default view, repeat step **1**, selecting **Address Cards**.

VIEW BUSINESS CONTACT INFORMATION

1 To view the information for a business contact, double-click the business contact.

*Note: To display all your business contacts, perform steps **1** and **2** on page 352.*

■ Information for the business contact appears.

2 Click **Save and Close** to save your changes.

USING OPPORTUNITIES

You can create an opportunity to store information about a sales lead. An opportunity is a potential customer or client.

After you create an opportunity, you can link related items, such as business notes, tasks and appointments, to the opportunity. This allows you to keep all the information related to an opportunity together in one location.

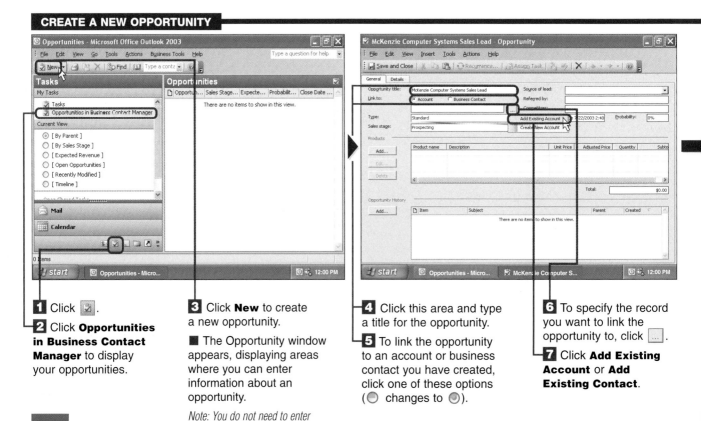

CREATE A NEW OPPORTUNITY

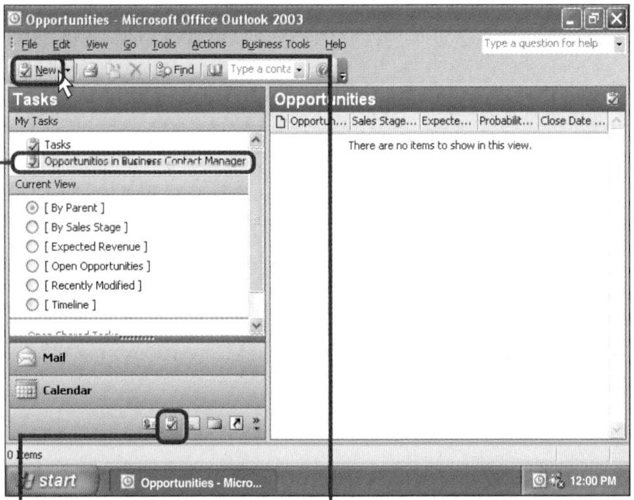

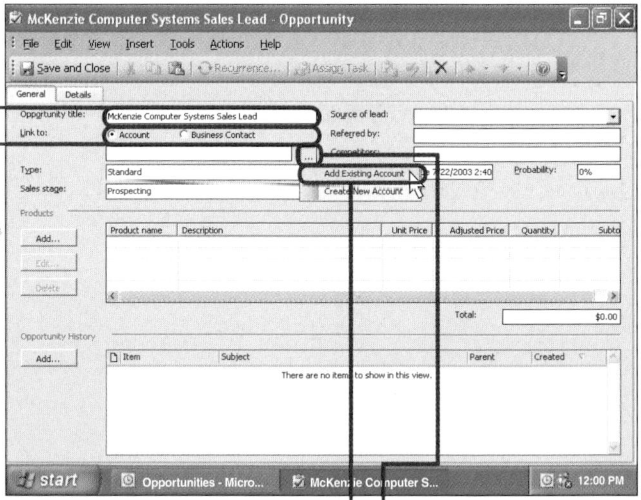

1 Click [icon].

2 Click **Opportunities in Business Contact Manager** to display your opportunities.

3 Click **New** to create a new opportunity.

■ The Opportunity window appears, displaying areas where you can enter information about an opportunity.

Note: You do not need to enter information in every area.

4 Click this area and type a title for the opportunity.

5 To link the opportunity to an account or business contact you have created, click one of these options (○ changes to ◉).

6 To specify the record you want to link the opportunity to, click [...].

7 Click **Add Existing Account** or **Add Existing Contact**.

Tip

How can I create a new account or business contact when I create an opportunity?

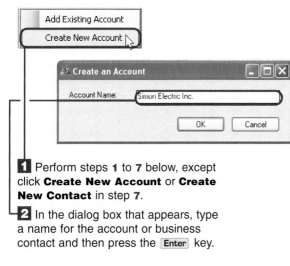

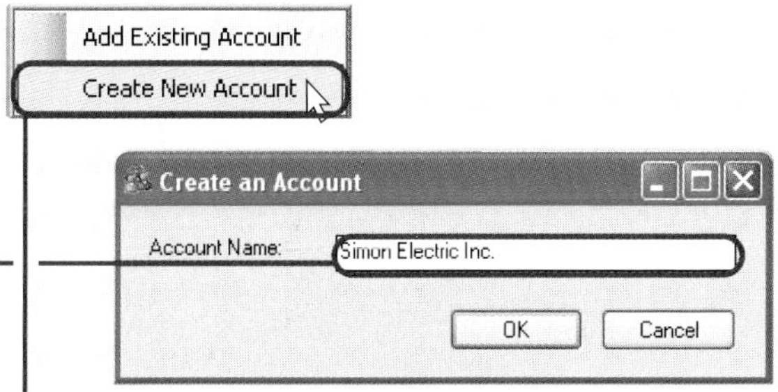

1 Perform steps **1** to **7** below, except click **Create New Account** or **Create New Contact** in step **7**.

2 In the dialog box that appears, type a name for the account or business contact and then press the Enter key.

3 Skip to step **10** below to continue creating the opportunity.

■ After you finish creating the opportunity, you can view and enter information for the new account (see page 351) or business contact (see page 355) you created.

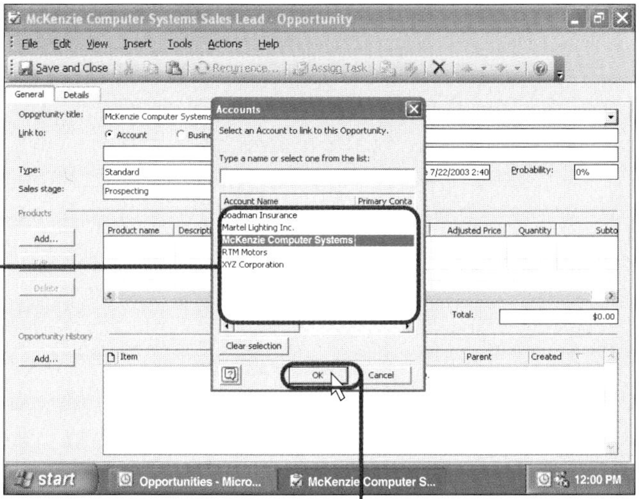

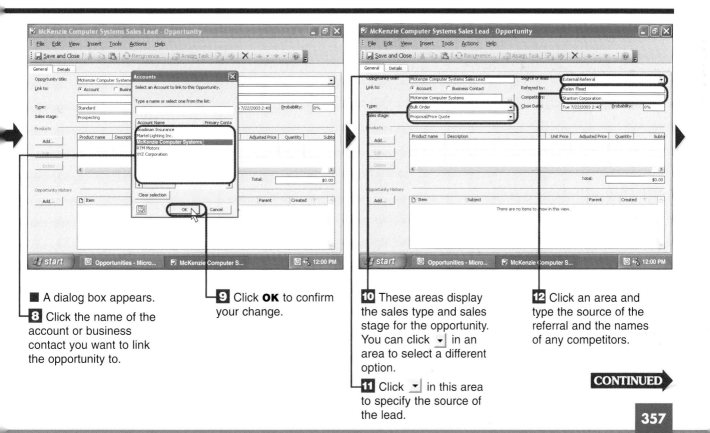

■ A dialog box appears.

8 Click the name of the account or business contact you want to link the opportunity to.

9 Click **OK** to confirm your change.

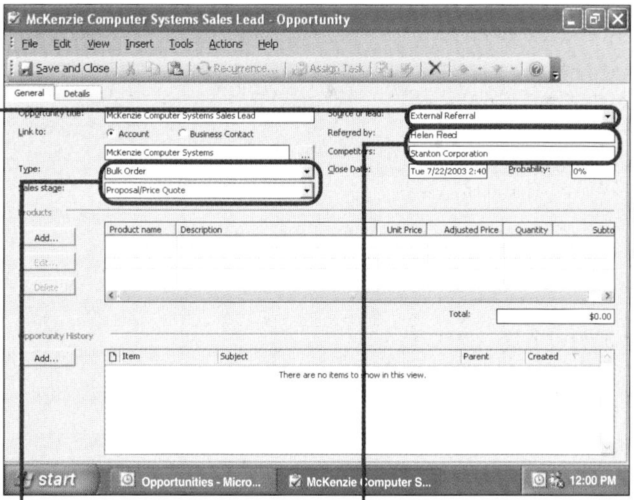

10 These areas display the sales type and sales stage for the opportunity. You can click ▾ in an area to select a different option.

11 Click ▾ in this area to specify the source of the lead.

12 Click an area and type the source of the referral and the names of any competitors.

CONTINUED

When creating an opportunity, you can specify a date when you expect to close a deal with the opportunity and a percentage to indicate the likelihood of closing the deal successfully.

If the opportunity is interested in purchasing your products or services, you can include information about the products or services.

CREATE A NEW OPPORTUNITY (CONTINUED)

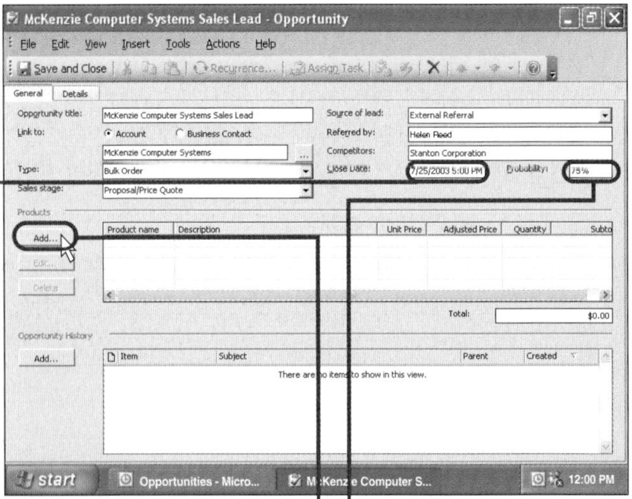

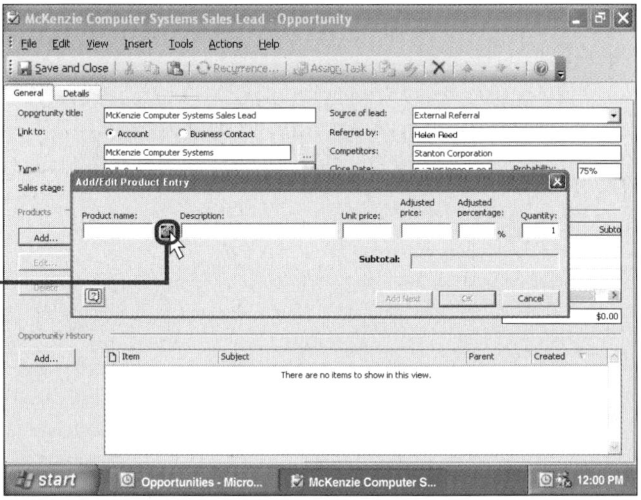

13 This area displays the close date of the opportunity. Drag the mouse I over the existing information and type the correct information.

14 Double-click the number in this area and type a percentage to indicate the likelihood of closing the deal successfully.

15 To specify a product that the opportunity is interested in purchasing, click **Add**.

■ The Add/Edit Product Entry dialog box appears.

16 Click ▣ to select a product from your product list.

Note: To create a product list, see page 362.

■ To add a product that is not in your product list or if you have not previously created a product list, refer to the top of page 359. Then skip to step **21** on page 360.

Tip

How can I add a product to my opportunity information if I have not created a product list?

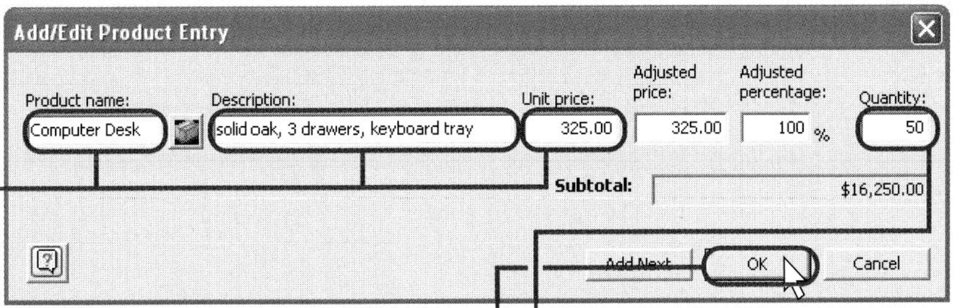

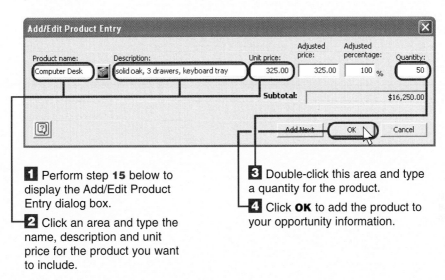

1 Perform step **15** below to display the Add/Edit Product Entry dialog box.

2 Click an area and type the name, description and unit price for the product you want to include.

3 Double-click this area and type a quantity for the product.

4 Click **OK** to add the product to your opportunity information.

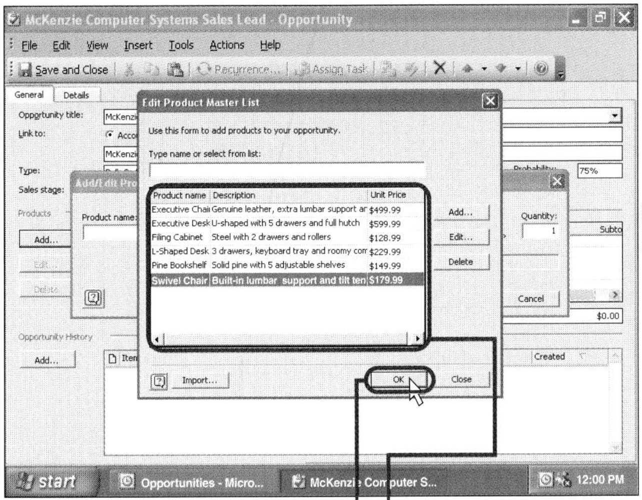

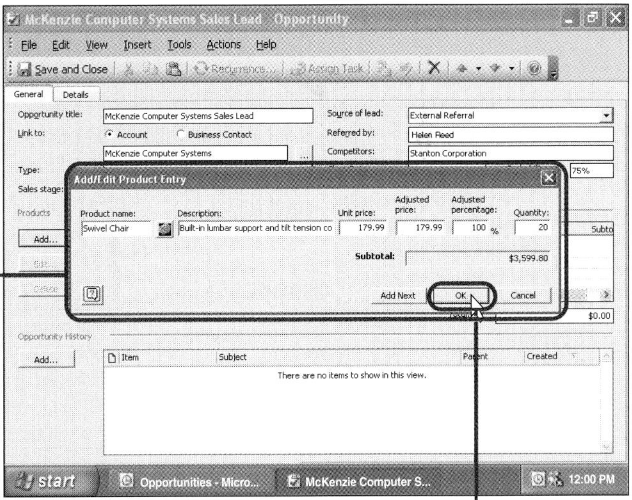

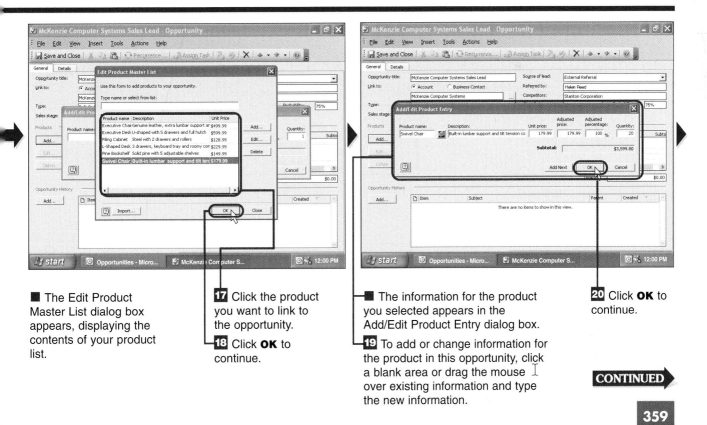

■ The Edit Product Master List dialog box appears, displaying the contents of your product list.

17 Click the product you want to link to the opportunity.

18 Click **OK** to continue.

■ The information for the product you selected appears in the Add/Edit Product Entry dialog box.

19 To add or change information for the product in this opportunity, click a blank area or drag the mouse over existing information and type the new information.

20 Click **OK** to continue.

CONTINUED

After creating an opportunity, you can change the way your opportunities are displayed on the screen.

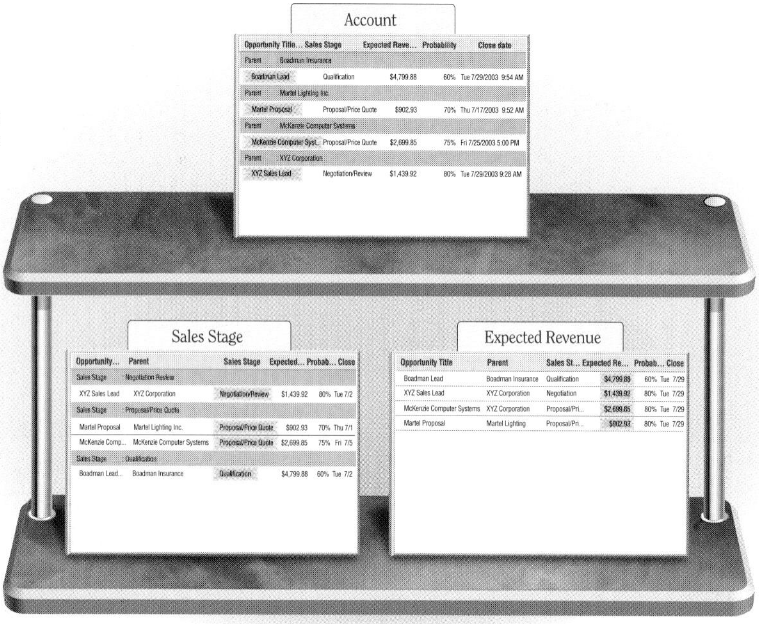

There are several ways to display your opportunities. For example, you can group your opportunities according to the accounts or business contacts they are linked to. You can also organize your opportunities by sales stage or expected revenue.

CREATE A NEW OPPORTUNITY (CONTINUED)

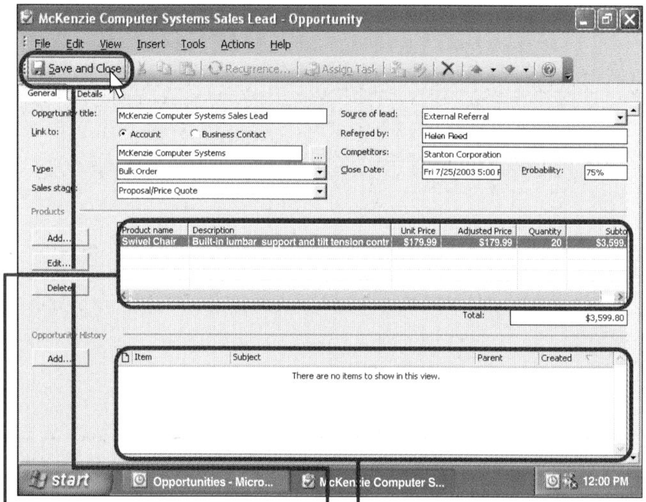

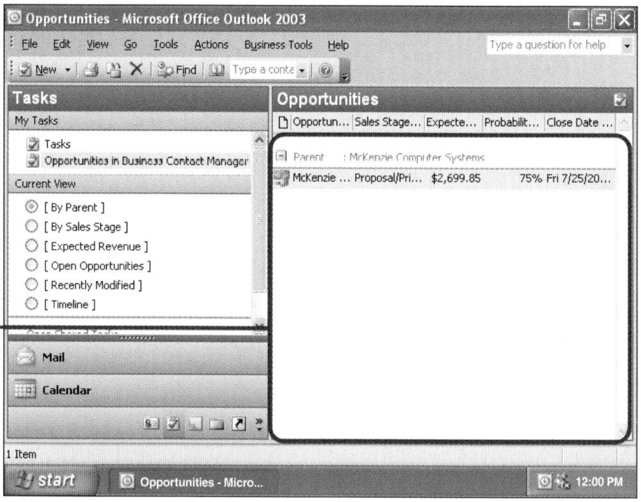

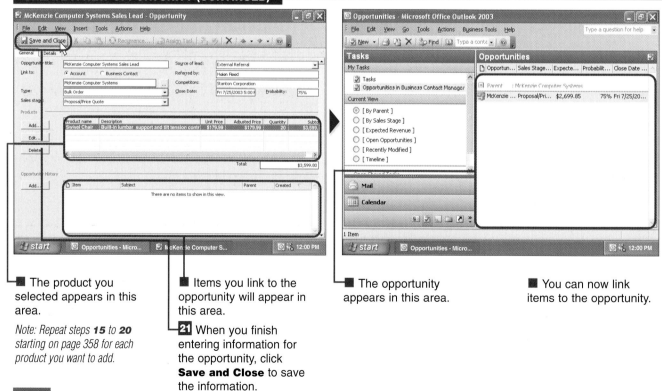

■ The product you selected appears in this area.

*Note: Repeat steps **15** to **20** starting on page 358 for each product you want to add.*

■ Items you link to the opportunity will appear in this area.

21 When you finish entering information for the opportunity, click **Save and Close** to save the information.

■ The opportunity appears in this area.

■ You can now link items to the opportunity.

How do I view the information and linked items for an opportunity I created?

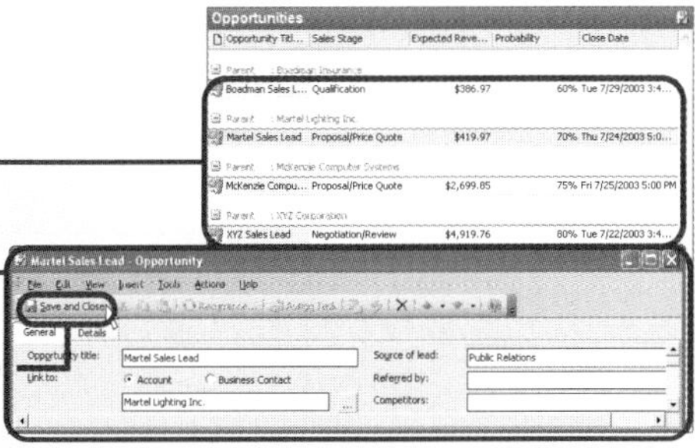

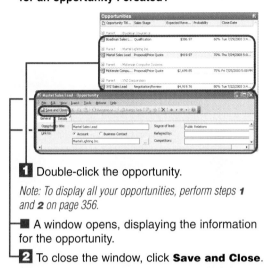

1 Double-click the opportunity.

*Note: To display all your opportunities, perform steps **1** and **2** on page 356.*

■ A window opens, displaying the information for the opportunity.

2 To close the window, click **Save and Close**.

How do I delete an opportunity I no longer need?

Click the opportunity you want to delete and then press the Delete key. The opportunity is placed in the Deleted Items folder. To view the contents of the Deleted Items folder, see page 375.

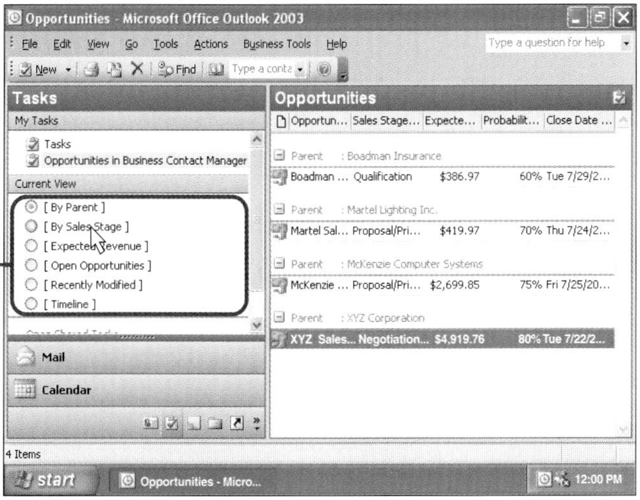

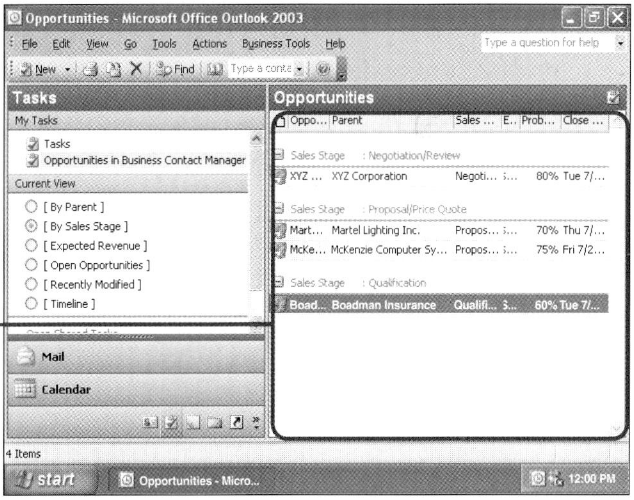

CHANGE THE VIEW OF OPPORTUNITIES

1 To change the way opportunities are displayed on your screen, click an option in this area (◯ changes to ◉).

■ Your opportunities appear in the view you selected.

■ To return to the default view, repeat step **1**, selecting **By Parent**.

CONTINUED

You can create a product list to store information about the products or services your company provides.

When creating an opportunity to store information about a sales lead, you can use the product list to quickly add information about products the opportunity may be interested in purchasing.

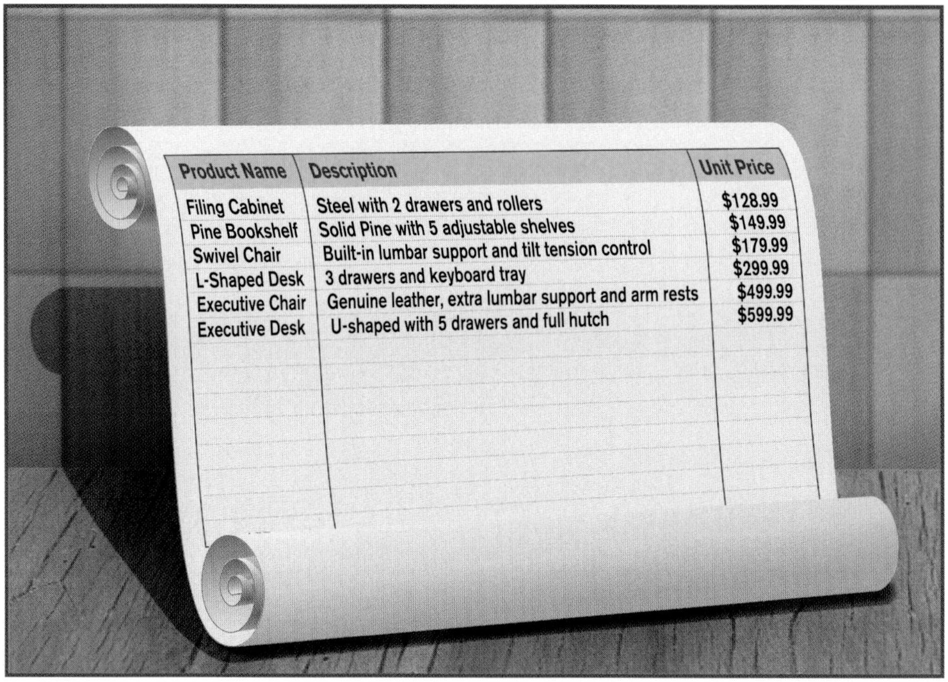

CREATE A PRODUCT LIST

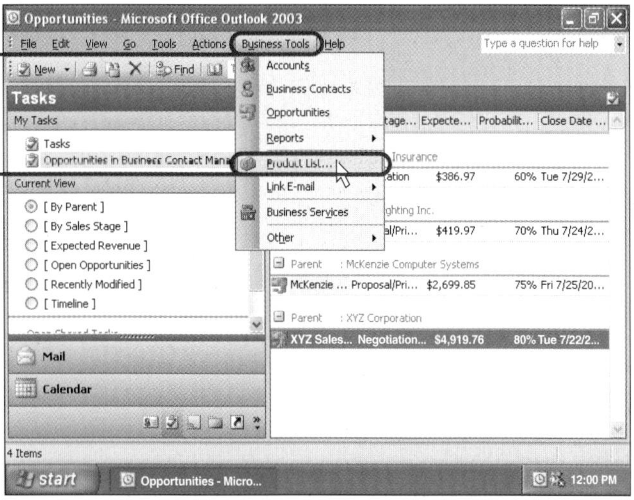

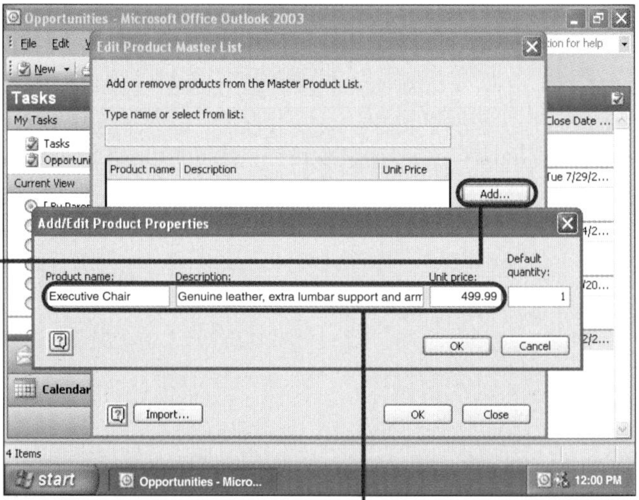

1 Click **Business Tools**.

2 Click **Product List**.

■ The Edit Product Master List dialog box appears.

3 Click **Add** to add product information to your product list.

■ The Add/Edit Product Properties dialog box appears.

4 Click an area and type the name, description and unit price for the product.

Tip

How can I edit information about the products in my product list?

To display the product list, perform steps **1** and **2** on page 362.

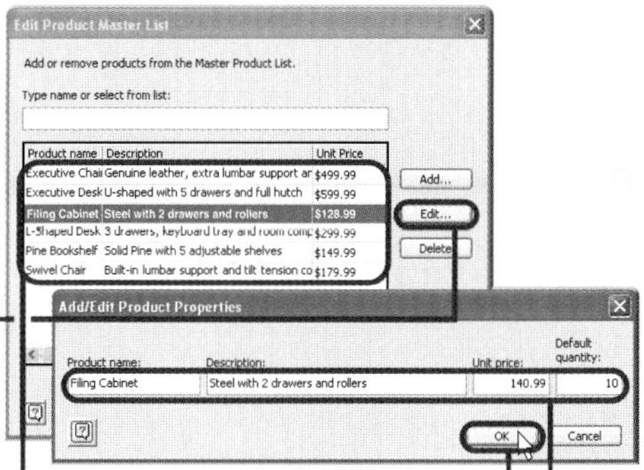

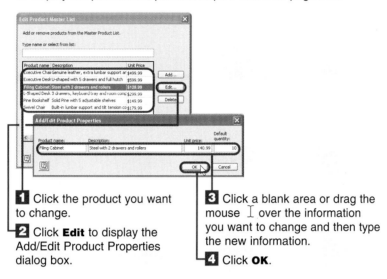

1 Click the product you want to change.

2 Click **Edit** to display the Add/Edit Product Properties dialog box.

3 Click a blank area or drag the mouse I over the information you want to change and then type the new information.

4 Click **OK**.

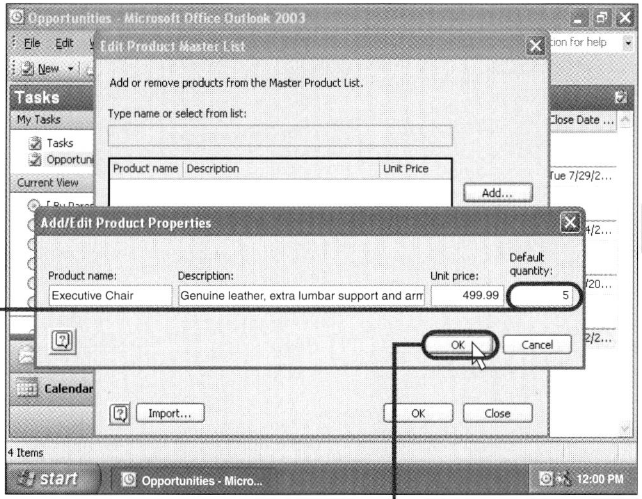

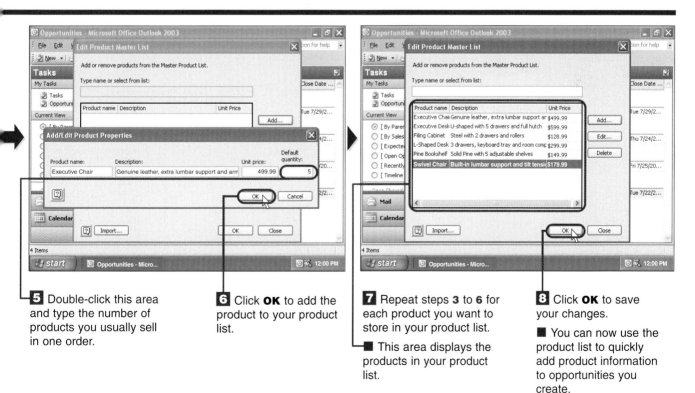

5 Double-click this area and type the number of products you usually sell in one order.

6 Click **OK** to add the product to your product list.

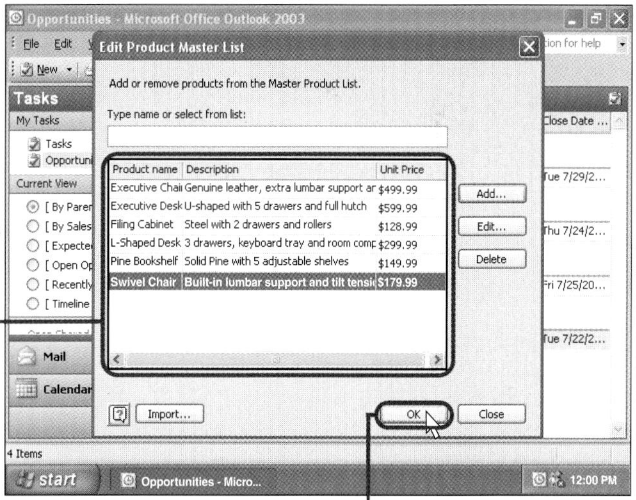

7 Repeat steps **3** to **6** for each product you want to store in your product list.

■ This area displays the products in your product list.

8 Click **OK** to save your changes.

■ You can now use the product list to quickly add product information to opportunities you create.

LINK AN E-MAIL MESSAGE

You can link an e-mail message you have sent or received to an account, business contact or opportunity.

Before you can link an e-mail message to a record, you need to create the account (see page 348), business contact (see page 352) or opportunity (see page 356) that relates to the e-mail message.

E-MAIL
To: Ann Lewis
From: Amy Martin
I received the price quote for the office furniture we are interested in purchasing. It looks fairly reasonable, but we would like to request a higher discount rate (20%) due to the high quantity we are purchasing. Please let me know if this would be possible.
McKenzie
Computer Systems

LINK AN E-MAIL MESSAGE

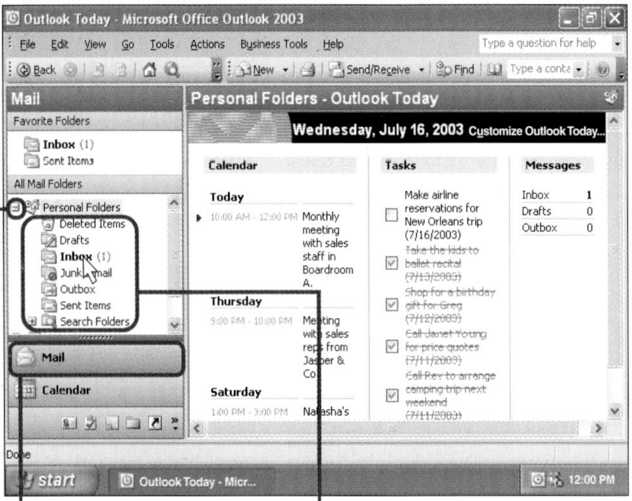

Outlook Today - Microsoft Office Outlook 2003
Mail
Personal Folders - Outlook Today
Wednesday, July 16, 2003
Calendar
Tasks
Messages
Personal Folders
Deleted Items
Drafts
Inbox (1)
Junk E-mail
Outbox
Sent Items
Search Folders
Mail
Calendar

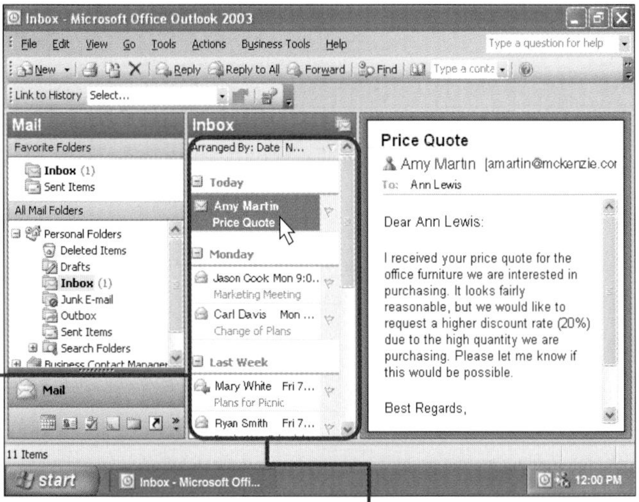

Inbox - Microsoft Office Outlook 2003
Mail
Inbox
Price Quote
Amy Martin
Price Quote
Dear Ann Lewis:
I received your price quote for the office furniture we are interested in purchasing. It looks fairly reasonable, but we would like to request a higher discount rate (20%) due to the high quantity we are purchasing. Please let me know if this would be possible.
Best Regards,

1 Click **Mail** to be able to read and work with your e-mail messages.

2 To display all the mail folders, click ⊞ beside **Personal Folders** (⊞ changes to ⊟).

■ The mail folders appear.

3 Click the folder that contains the message you want to link to a record.

Note: For information on the mail folders, see the top of page 311.

■ This area displays the messages in the folder you selected.

4 Double-click the message you want to link to a record.

Tip

How can I view an e-mail message I linked to a record?

You can view an e-mail message with all the other information for the account, business contact or opportunity you linked the e-mail message to.

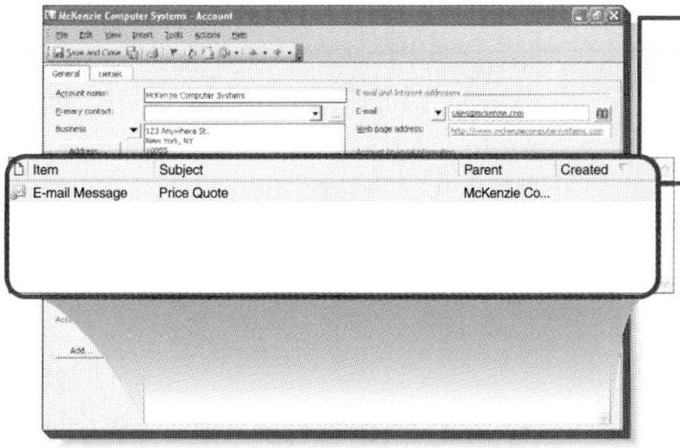

■ The e-mail message you linked to the account, business contact or opportunity appears in this area.

■ You can double-click the e-mail message to view its details.

1 Display the account (see page 351), business contact (see page 355) or opportunity (see page 361) information.

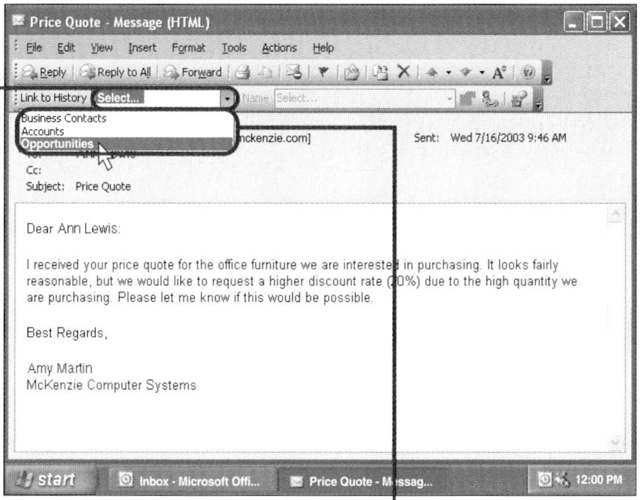

■ A window appears, displaying the contents of the message.

5 To link the message to a business contact, account or opportunity, click ▾ in this area.

6 Click the type of record you want to link the message to.

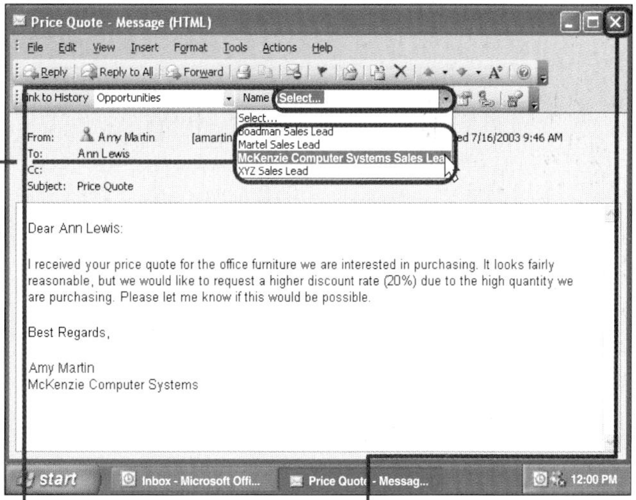

7 To specify which business contact, account or opportunity you want to link the message to, click ▾ in this area.

8 Click the record you want to link the message to.

9 Click ☒ to close the window displaying the message.

■ A dialog box appears, asking if you want to save your changes. Click **Yes** to save your changes.

SCHEDULE AN APPOINTMENT

You can schedule an appointment in the Calendar to remind you of an activity or meeting related to an account, business contact or opportunity.

Before you can schedule an appointment, you need to create the account (see page 348), business contact (see page 352) or opportunity (see page 356) that relates to the appointment.

SCHEDULE AN APPOINTMENT

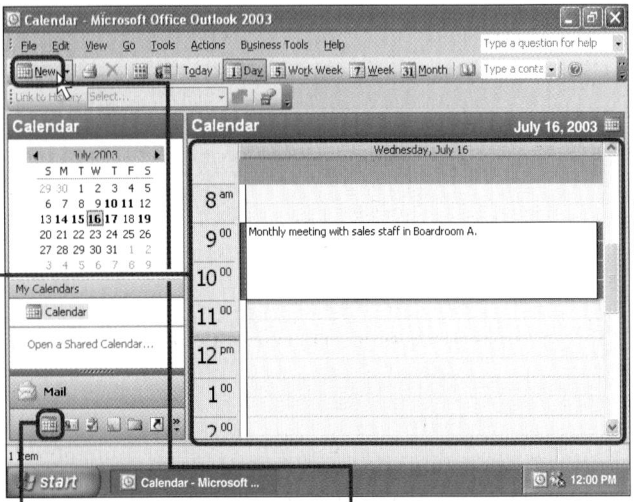

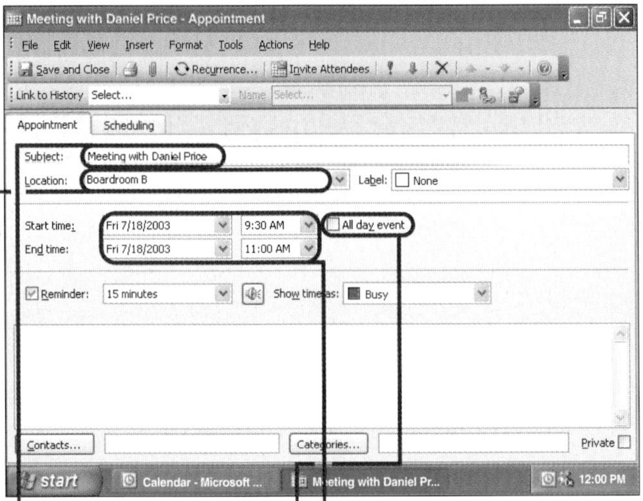

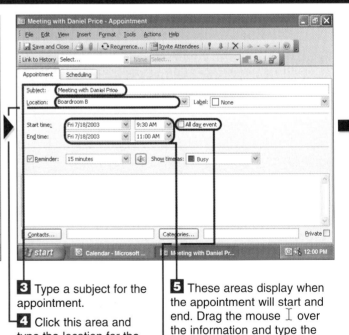

1 Click ▦ to display the Calendar.

■ This area displays the appointments for the current day.

2 Click **New** to schedule a new appointment.

■ The Appointment window appears.

3 Type a subject for the appointment.

4 Click this area and type the location for the appointment.

5 These areas display when the appointment will start and end. Drag the mouse I over the information and type the correct information.

■ To make the appointment an all day event, click this option (☐ changes to ☑).

Tip

How can I view an appointment with the other information for the record I have linked the appointment to?

You can view an appointment with all the other information for the account, business contact or opportunity you linked the appointment to.

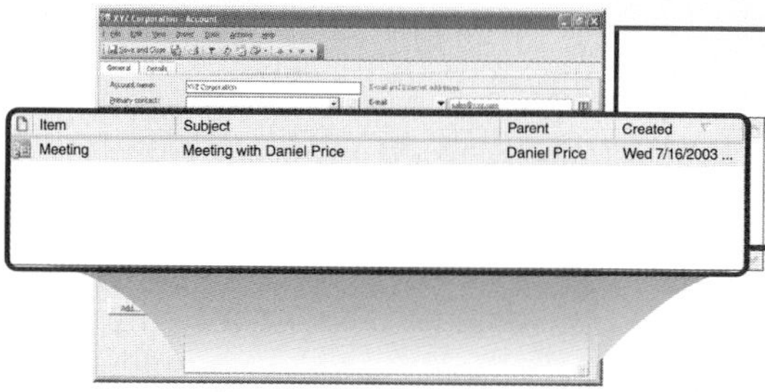

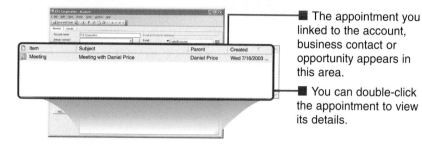

■ The appointment you linked to the account, business contact or opportunity appears in this area.

■ You can double-click the appointment to view its details.

1 Display the account (see page 351), business contact (see page 355), or opportunity (see page 361) information.

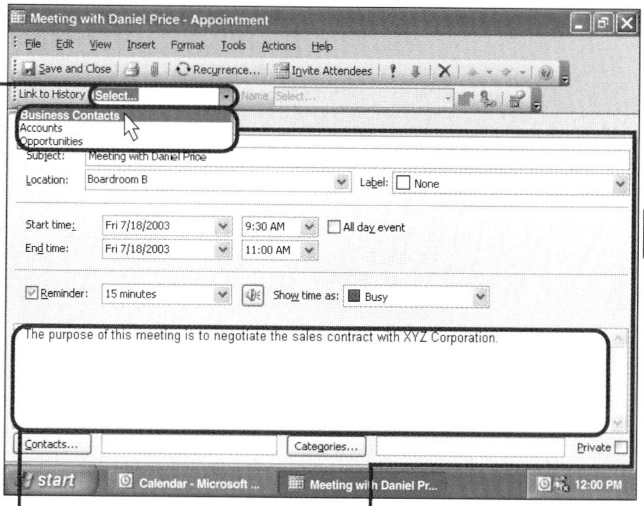

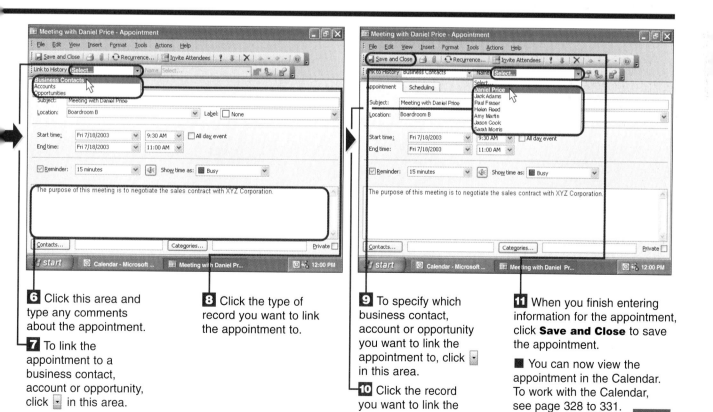

6 Click this area and type any comments about the appointment.

7 To link the appointment to a business contact, account or opportunity, click ▾ in this area.

8 Click the type of record you want to link the appointment to.

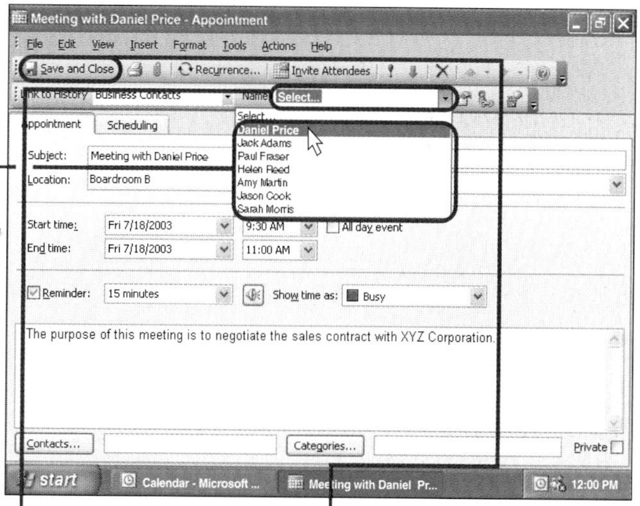

9 To specify which business contact, account or opportunity you want to link the appointment to, click ▾ in this area.

10 Click the record you want to link the appointment to.

11 When you finish entering information for the appointment, click **Save and Close** to save the appointment.

■ You can now view the appointment in the Calendar. To work with the Calendar, see page 328 to 331.

CREATE A TASK

You can create a task to keep track of a duty or errand related to an account, business contact or opportunity.

Before you can create a task, you need to create the account (see page 348), business contact (see page 352) or opportunity (see page 356) that relates to the task.

CREATE A TASK

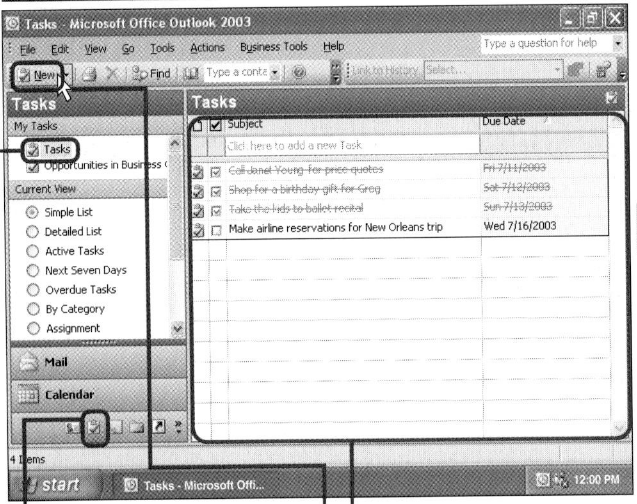

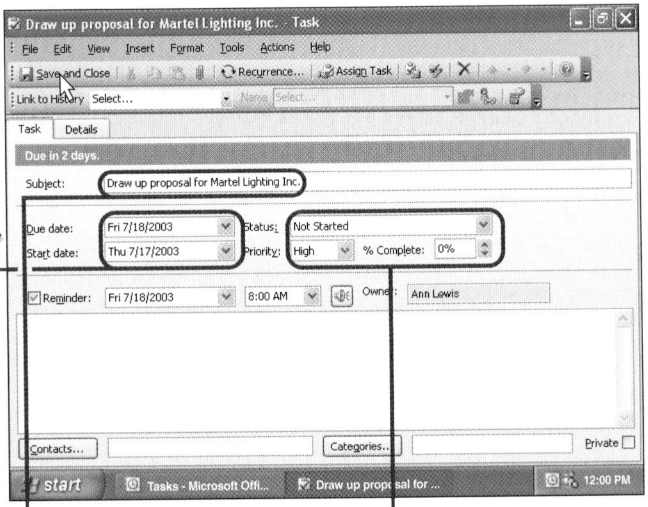

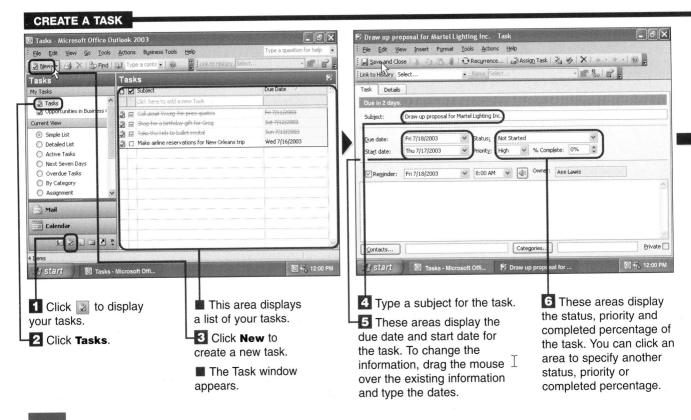

1 Click to display your tasks.

2 Click **Tasks**.

■ This area displays a list of your tasks.

3 Click **New** to create a new task.

■ The Task window appears.

4 Type a subject for the task.

5 These areas display the due date and start date for the task. To change the information, drag the mouse over the existing information and type the dates.

6 These areas display the status, priority and completed percentage of the task. You can click an area to specify another status, priority or completed percentage.

Tip

How can I view a task with the other information for the record I have linked the task to?

You can view a task with all the other information for the account, business contact or opportunity you linked the task to.

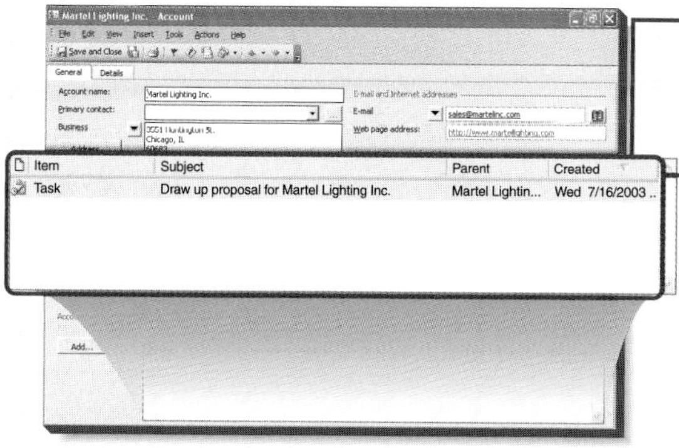

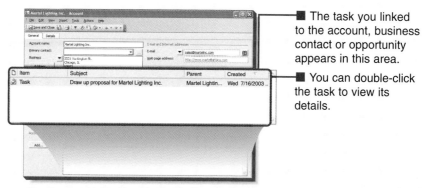

■ The task you linked to the account, business contact or opportunity appears in this area.

■ You can double-click the task to view its details.

1 Display the account (see page 351), business contact (see page 355) or opportunity (see page 361) information.

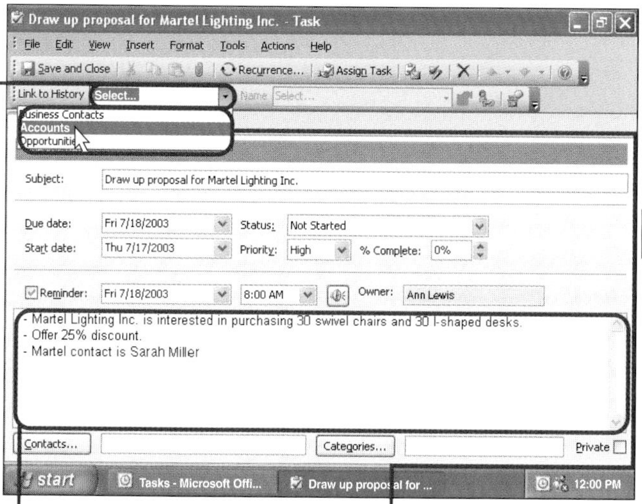

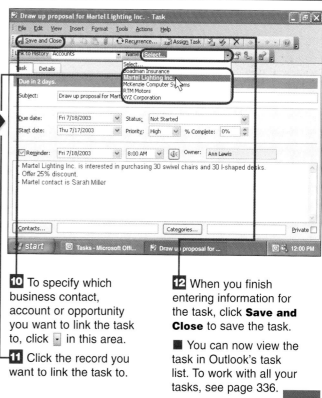

7 Click this area and type any comments about the task.

8 To link the task to a business contact, account or opportunity, click ▾ in this area.

9 Click the type of record you want to link the task to.

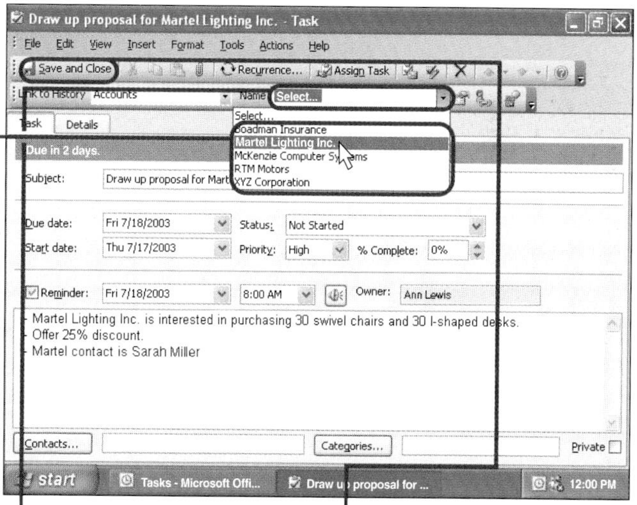

10 To specify which business contact, account or opportunity you want to link the task to, click ▾ in this area.

11 Click the record you want to link the task to.

12 When you finish entering information for the task, click **Save and Close** to save the task.

■ You can now view the task in Outlook's task list. To work with all your tasks, see page 336.

CREATE A BUSINESS NOTE

You can create a business note to store a small piece of information, such as a reminder, question or idea for a particular account, business contact or opportunity. Business notes are similar to paper sticky notes.

Before you can create a business note, you need to create the account (see page 348), business contact (see page 352) or opportunity (see page 356) that relates to the note.

CREATE A BUSINESS NOTE

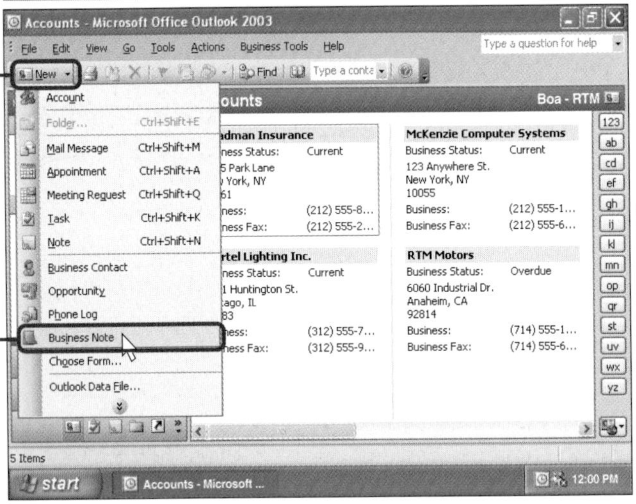

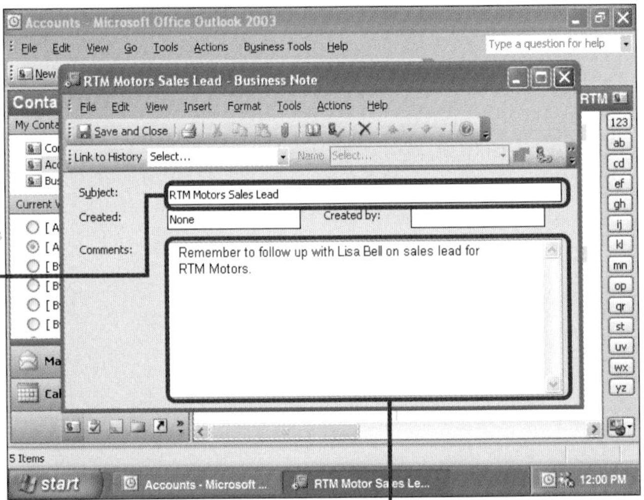

1 Click ▾ in this area.

2 Click **Business Note** to create a new business note.

Note: If Business Note does not appear on the menu, position the mouse ↖ over the bottom of the menu to display the menu option.

■ The Business Note window appears.

3 Click this area and type a subject for the business note.

4 Click this area and type the information for the business note.

Tip

How can I view a business note I created?

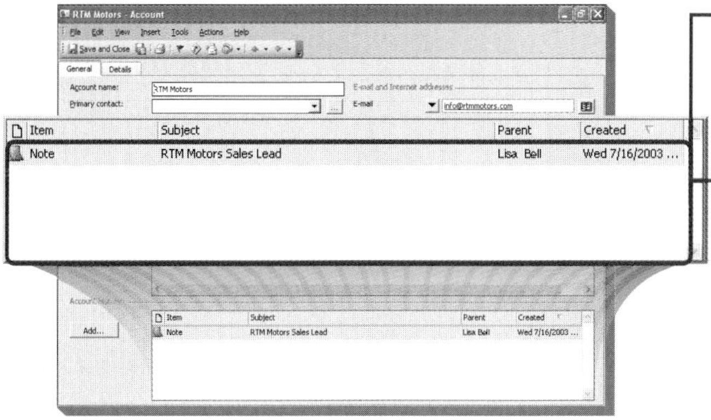

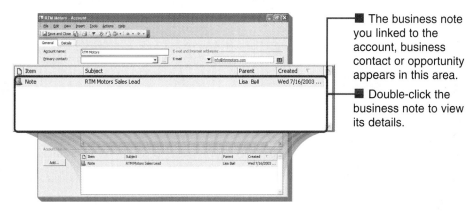

■ The business note you linked to the account, business contact or opportunity appears in this area.

■ Double-click the business note to view its details.

1 Display the account (see page 351), business contact (see page 355) or opportunity (see page 361) information.

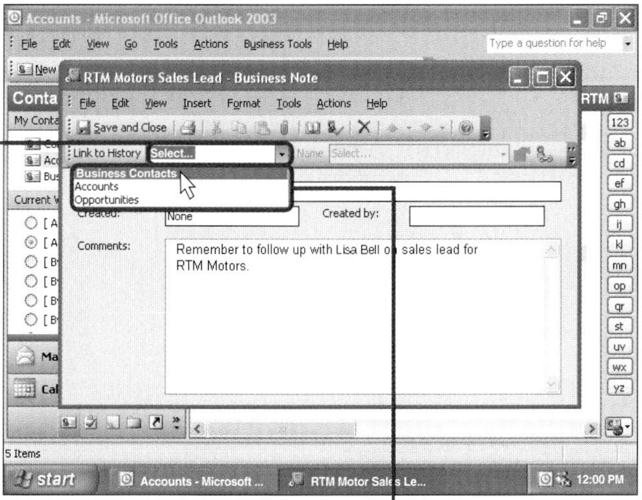

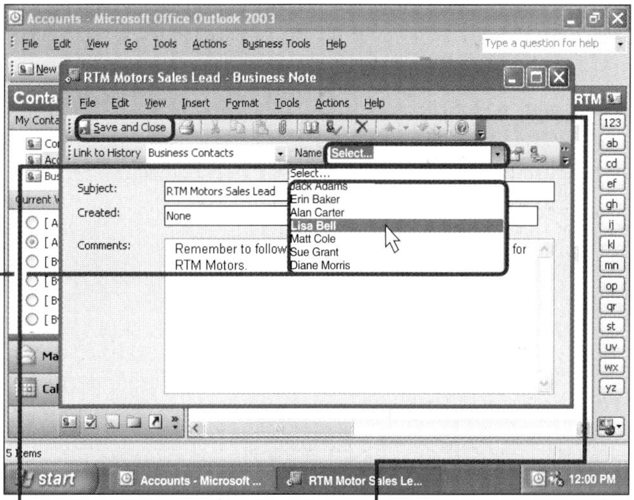

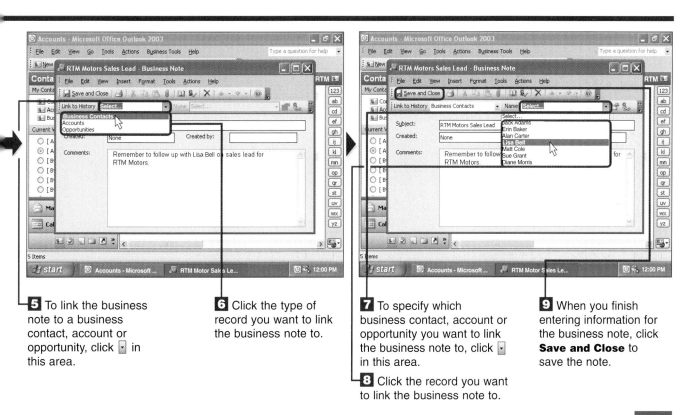

5 To link the business note to a business contact, account or opportunity, click ▾ in this area.

6 Click the type of record you want to link the business note to.

7 To specify which business contact, account or opportunity you want to link the business note to, click ▾ in this area.

8 Click the record you want to link the business note to.

9 When you finish entering information for the business note, click **Save and Close** to save the note.

You can create a phone log to record the amount of time you spend in telephone conversations related to a particular account, business contact or opportunity.

Before you can create a phone log, you need to create the account (see page 348), business contact (see page 352) or opportunity (see page 356) that relates to the phone log.

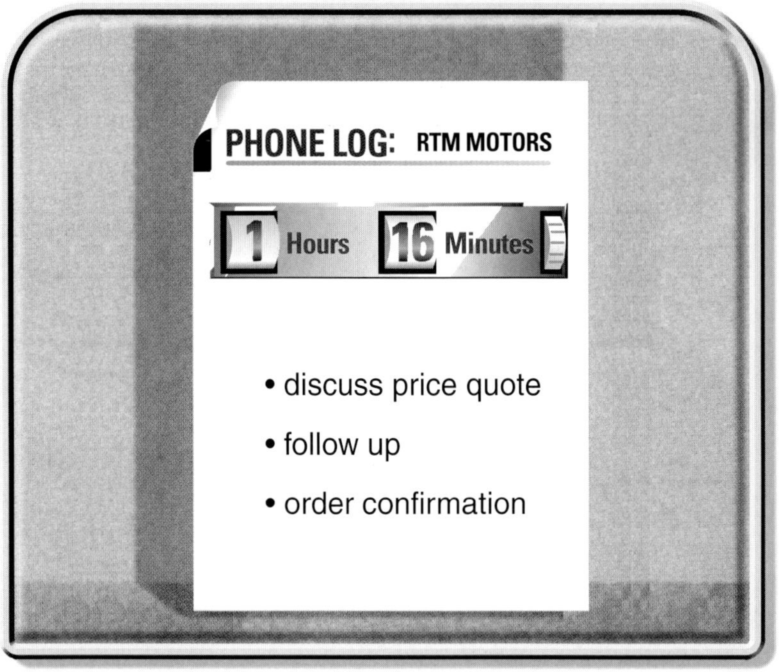

CREATE A PHONE LOG

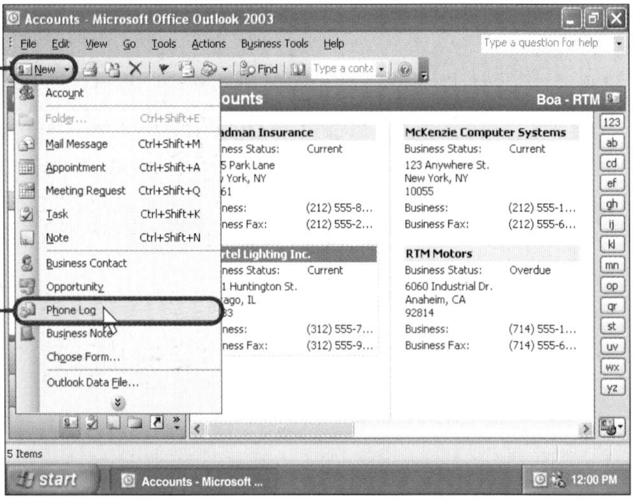

1 Click ▾ in this area.

2 Click **Phone Log** to create a new phone log.

Note: If Phone Log does not appear on the menu, position the mouse ↖ over the bottom of the menu to display the menu option.

■ The Business Phone Log window appears.

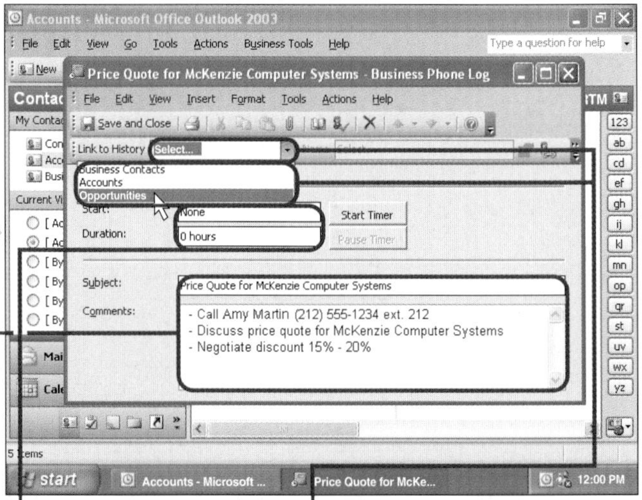

■ These areas will display the start date and time and the duration of the phone conversation.

3 Click an area and type a subject and comments for the phone log.

4 To link the phone log to a business contact, account or opportunity, click ▾ in this area.

5 Click the type of record you want to link the phone log to.

Tip

How do I use a phone log I created?

Each time you have a phone conversation, you use the timer in the phone log to record the length of the conversation. At the end of a conversation, you can pause the timer until your next conversation.

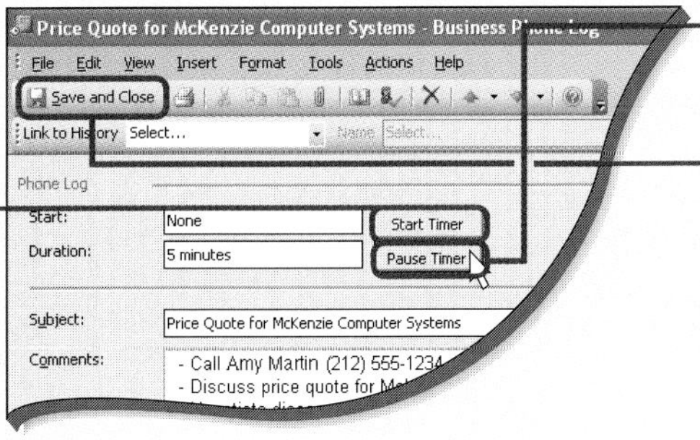

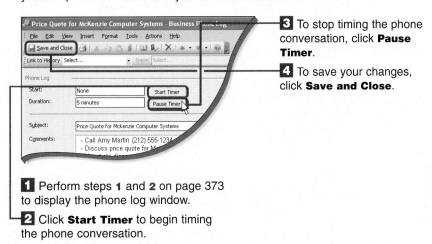

3 To stop timing the phone conversation, click **Pause Timer**.

4 To save your changes, click **Save and Close**.

1 Perform steps **1** and **2** on page 373 to display the phone log window.

2 Click **Start Timer** to begin timing the phone conversation.

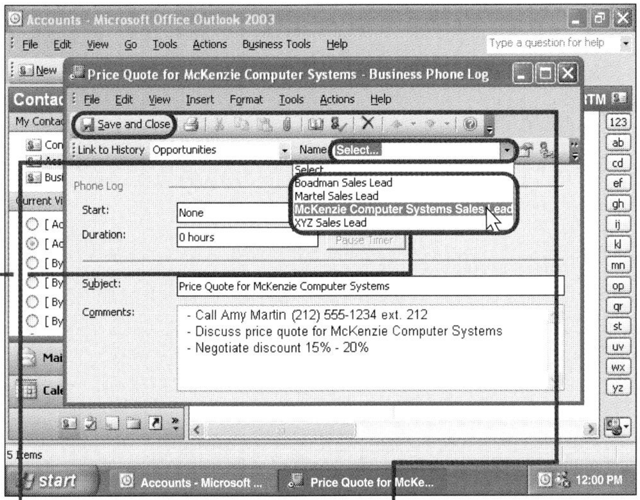

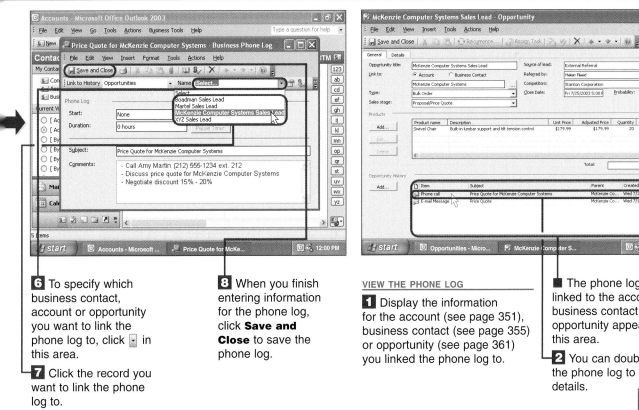

6 To specify which business contact, account or opportunity you want to link the phone log to, click ▾ in this area.

7 Click the record you want to link the phone log to.

8 When you finish entering information for the phone log, click **Save and Close** to save the phone log.

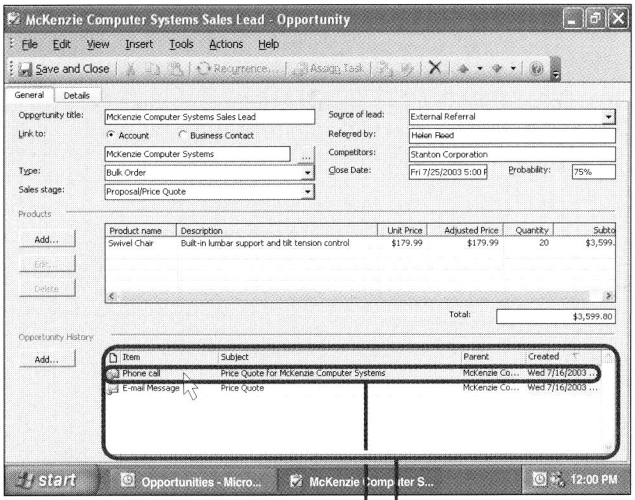

VIEW THE PHONE LOG

1 Display the information for the account (see page 351), business contact (see page 355) or opportunity (see page 361) you linked the phone log to.

■ The phone log you linked to the account, business contact or opportunity appears in this area.

2 You can double-click the phone log to view its details.

You can view all the business items you have created.

Business items include opportunities ( ), e-mail messages ( ), appointments ( ), tasks ( ), business notes ( ) and phone logs ( ) that you have linked to your accounts, business contacts and opportunities.

WORK WITH BUSINESS ITEMS

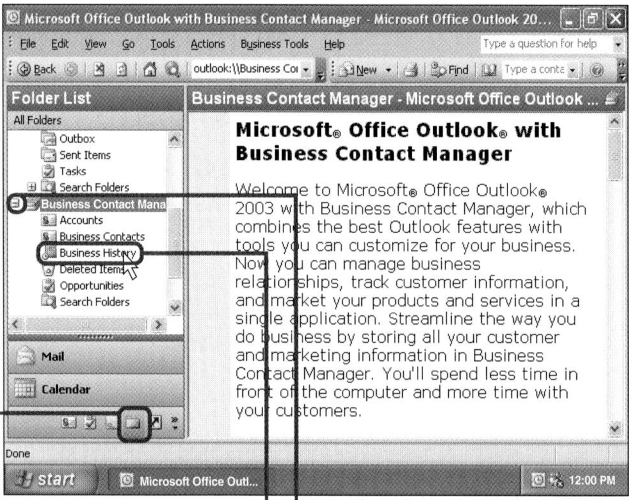

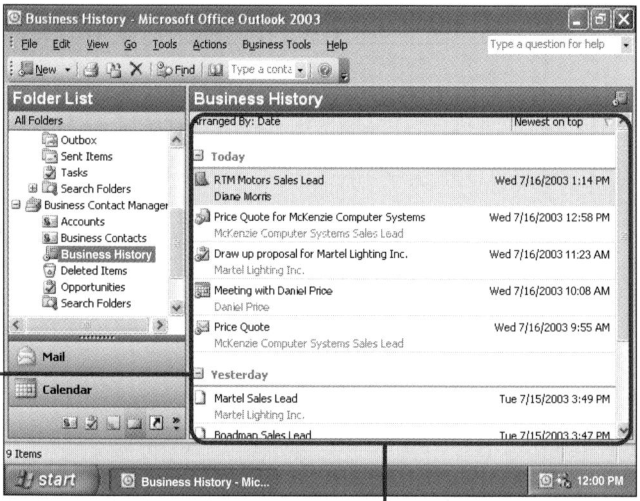

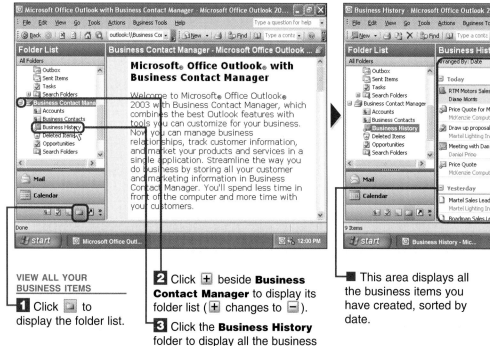

VIEW ALL YOUR BUSINESS ITEMS

1 Click ( ) to display the folder list.

2 Click (+) beside **Business Contact Manager** to display its folder list (+ changes to −).

3 Click the **Business History** folder to display all the business items you have created.

■ This area displays all the business items you have created, sorted by date.

■ To view the contents of a business item in the list, double-click the item.

Tip

Can I use the Business Contact Manager folder list to quickly view my records?

Yes. After performing steps **1** and **2** on page 374 to display the Business Contact Manager folder list, you can click one of the following folders to quickly display the records of interest.

Accounts—Displays your accounts

Business Contacts—Displays your business contacts

Opportunities—Displays your opportunities

Tip

How can I permanently delete business items I have created?

You can empty the Deleted Items folder at any time to permanently remove deleted business items from your computer.

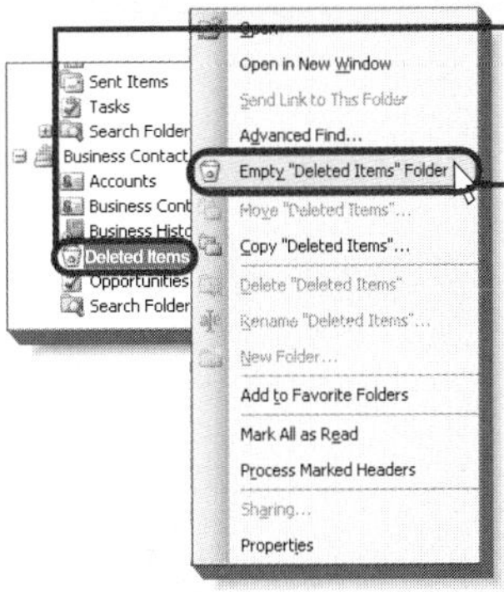

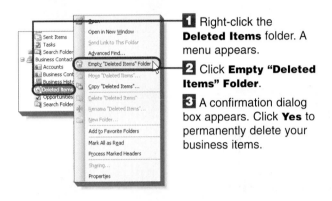

1 Right-click the **Deleted Items** folder. A menu appears.

2 Click **Empty "Deleted Items" Folder**.

3 A confirmation dialog box appears. Click **Yes** to permanently delete your business items.

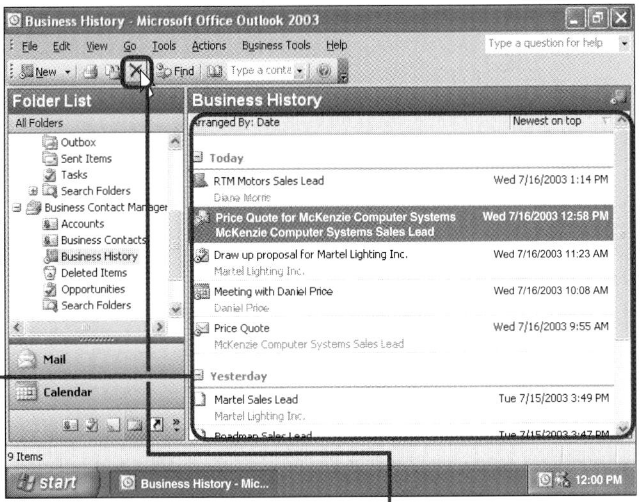

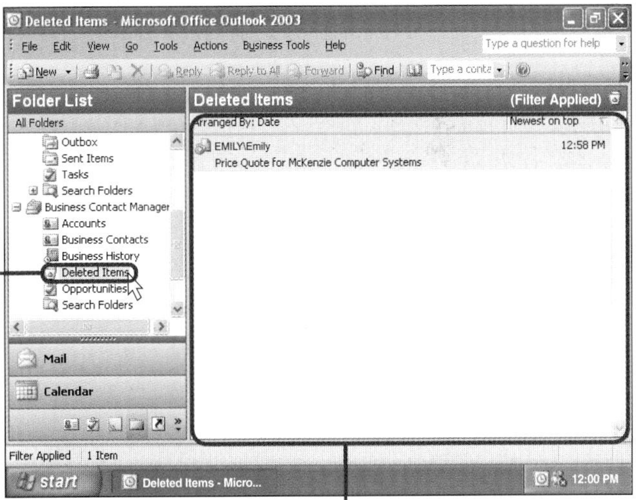

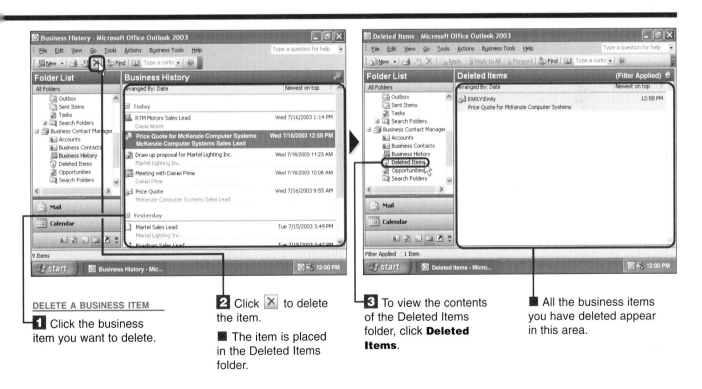

DELETE A BUSINESS ITEM

1 Click the business item you want to delete.

2 Click ☒ to delete the item.

■ The item is placed in the Deleted Items folder.

3 To view the contents of the Deleted Items folder, click **Deleted Items**.

■ All the business items you have deleted appear in this area.

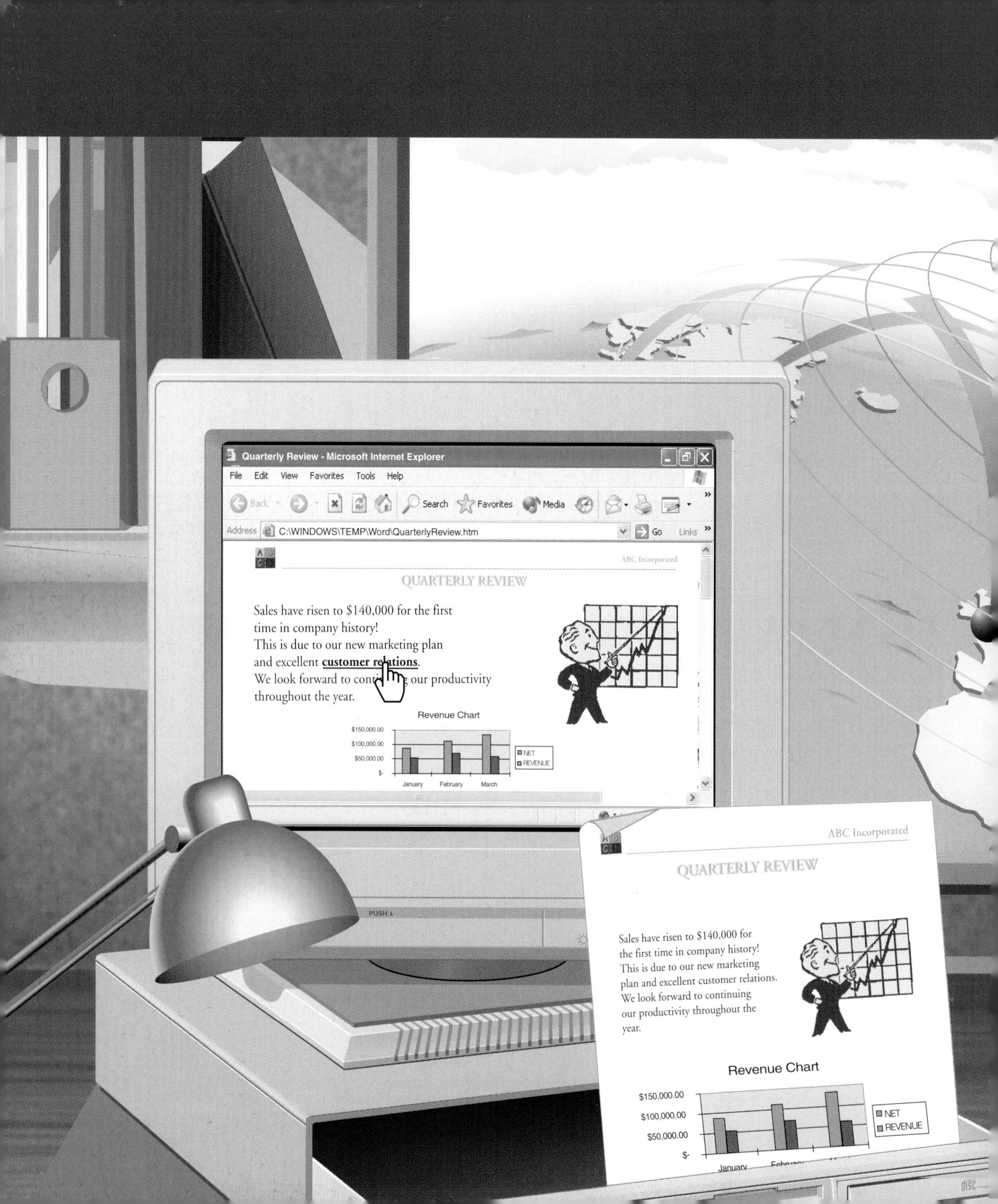
Quarterly Review - Microsoft Internet Explorer
File Edit View Favorites Tools Help
Back Search Favorites Media
Address C:\WINDOWS\TEMP\Word\QuarterlyReview.htm
Go Links
ABC Incorporated
QUARTERLY REVIEW
Sales have risen to $140,000 for the first time in company history!
This is due to our new marketing plan and excellent customer relations.
We look forward to continuing our productivity throughout the year.
Revenue Chart
$150,000.00
$100,000.00
$50,000.00
$-
January
February
March
NET
REVENUE
PUSH
ABC Incorporated
QUARTERLY REVIEW
Sales have risen to $140,000 for the first time in company history! This is due to our new marketing plan and excellent customer relations. We look forward to continuing our productivity throughout the year.
Revenue Chart
$150,000.00
$100,000.00
$50,000.00
$-
NET
REVENUE
January

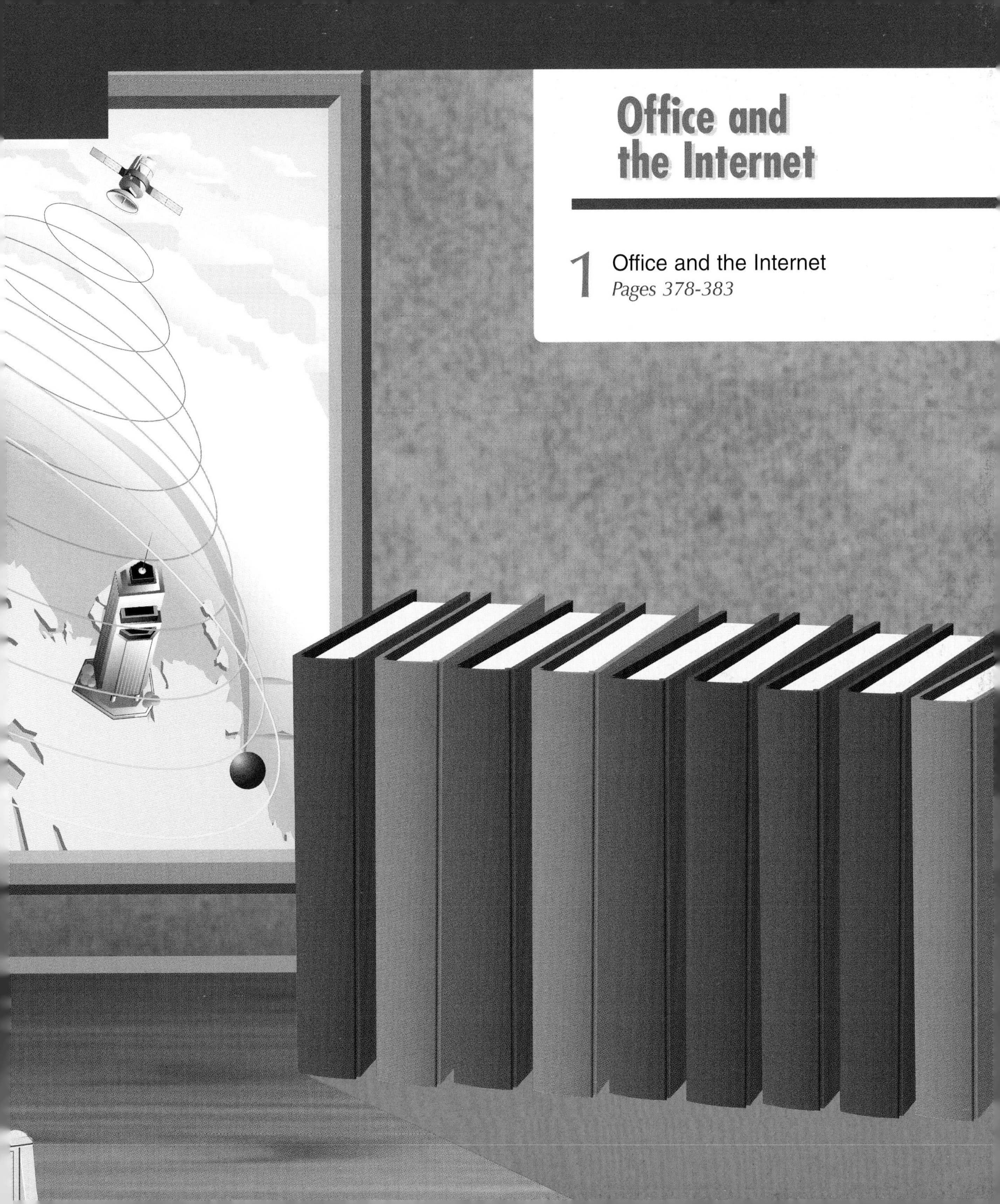

Office and the Internet

CREATE A HYPERLINK

You can create a hyperlink to connect a word or phrase in your file to another file on your computer, network, corporate intranet or the Internet.

An intranet is a small version of the Internet within a company or organization.

You can use the method shown below to create hyperlinks in Word, Excel, PowerPoint and Publisher.

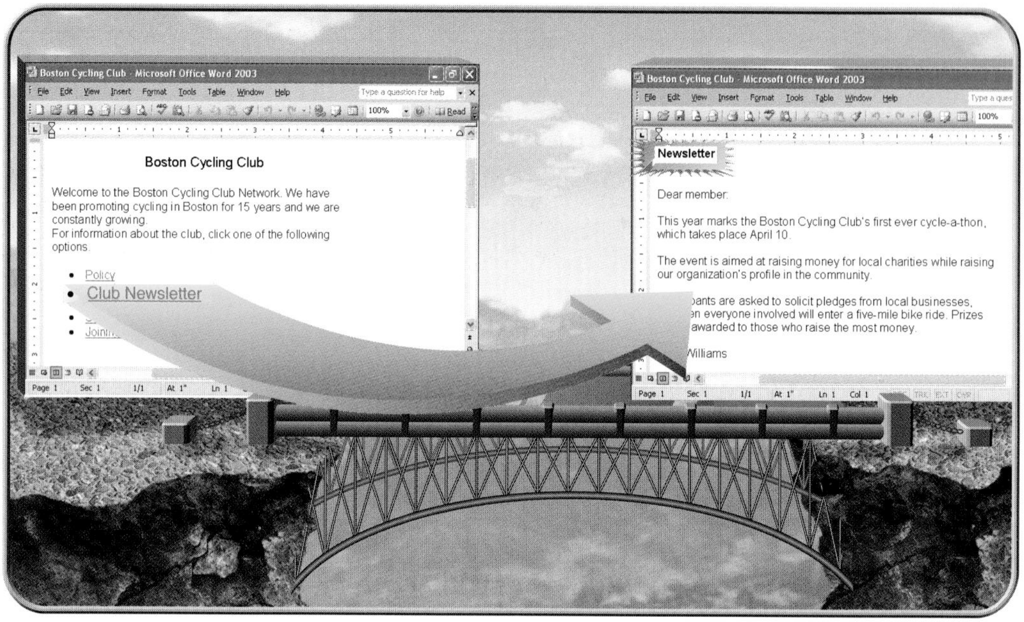

CREATE A HYPERLINK

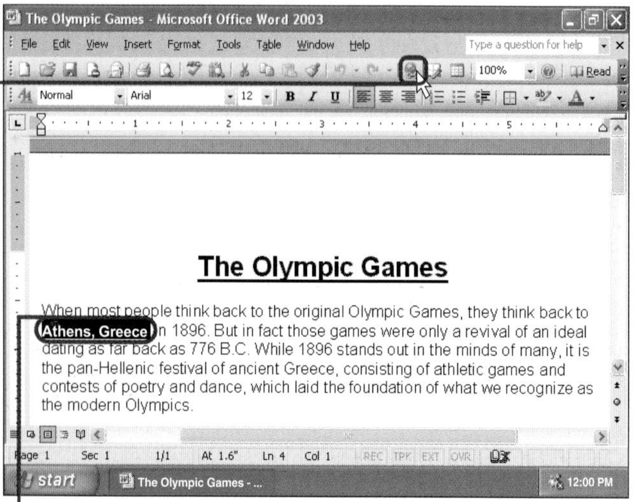

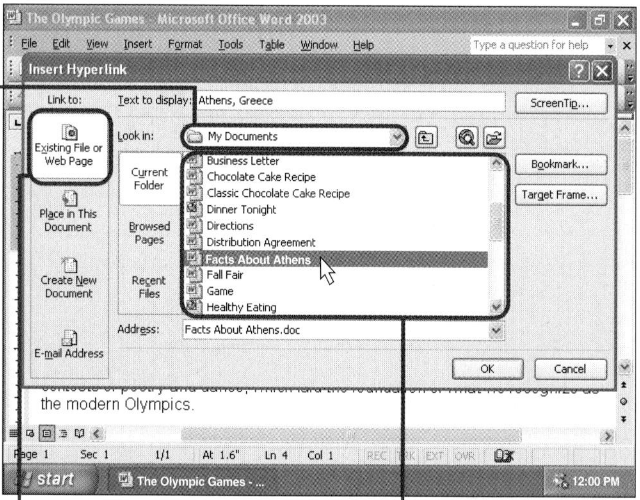

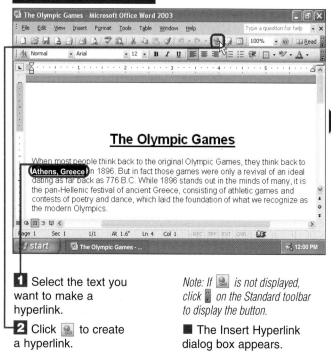

1 Select the text you want to make a hyperlink.

2 Click to create a hyperlink.

Note: If is not displayed, click on the Standard toolbar to display the button.

■ The Insert Hyperlink dialog box appears.

3 Click **Existing File or Web Page** to link the text to an existing file.

■ This area shows the location of the displayed files. You can click this area to change the location.

4 To link the text to a file on your computer or network, click the name of the file you want to link the text to.

Tip

Can an Office program automatically create a hyperlink for me?

When you type a Web page address in a Word document, Excel worksheet or PowerPoint presentation, the Office program will automatically change the address to a hyperlink for you.

Tip

Why does nothing happen when I click a hyperlink on a PowerPoint slide?

If you click a hyperlink while viewing your presentation in the Normal or Slide Sorter view, the file or Web page connected to the hyperlink will not appear. You must display your presentation in the Slide Show view to display the file or Web page connected to a hyperlink. For information on displaying a presentation in the Slide Show view, see page 175.

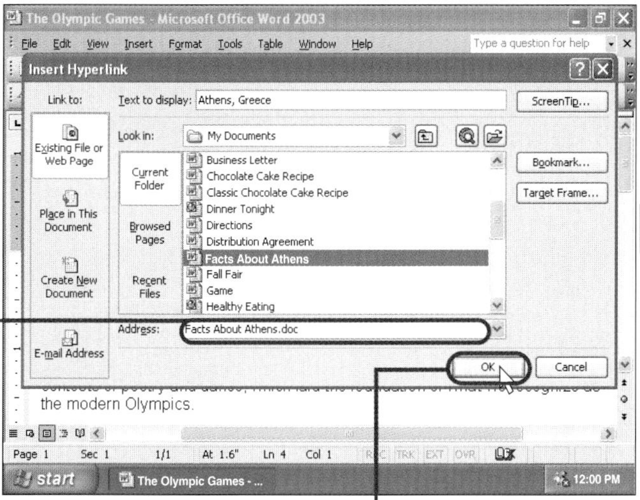

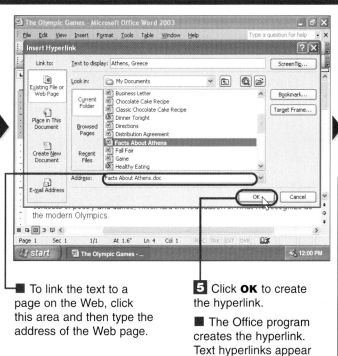

■ To link the text to a page on the Web, click this area and then type the address of the Web page.

5 Click **OK** to create the hyperlink.

■ The Office program creates the hyperlink. Text hyperlinks appear underlined and in color.

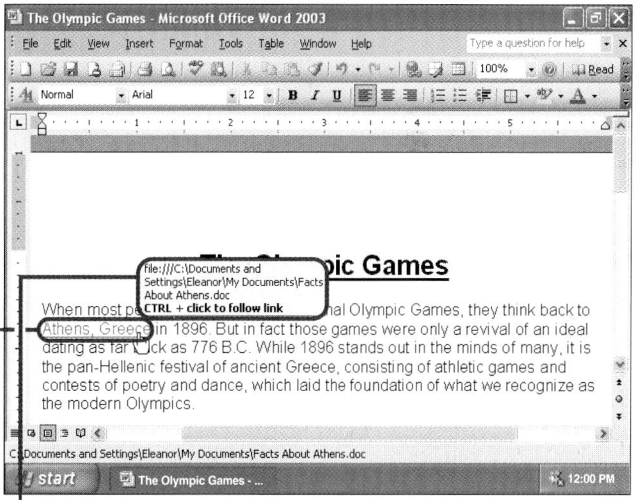

■ When you position the mouse pointer over a hyperlink, a yellow box appears, indicating where the hyperlink will take you.

■ To display the file or Web page connected to the hyperlink, click the hyperlink.

Note: In Word and Publisher, you must press and hold down the Ctrl *key before clicking the hyperlink.*

■ A warning dialog box may appear. Click **Yes** to continue.

PREVIEW A FILE AS A WEB PAGE

You can preview how an Office file will look as a Web page. This allows you to see how the file will appear on the Internet or your company's intranet.

An intranet is a small version of the Internet within a company or organization.

You can use the method shown below to preview a file you create in Word, Excel or PowerPoint as a Web page.

PREVIEW A FILE AS A WEB PAGE

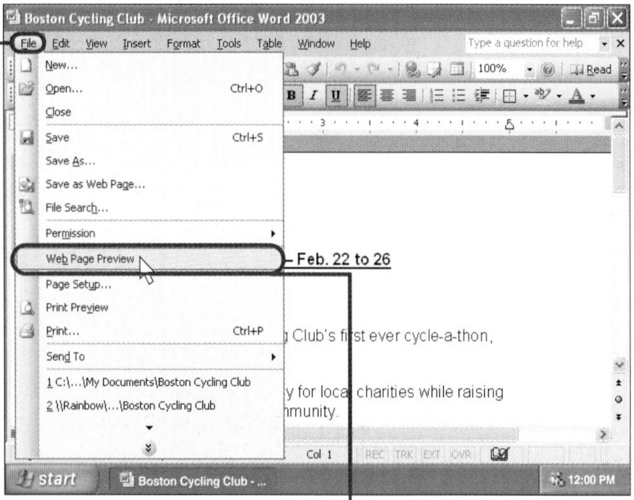

1 Display the file you want to preview as a Web page.

2 Click **File**.

3 Click **Web Page Preview** to preview your file as a Web page.

Note: If Web Page Preview does not appear on the menu, position the mouse over the bottom of the menu to display the menu option.

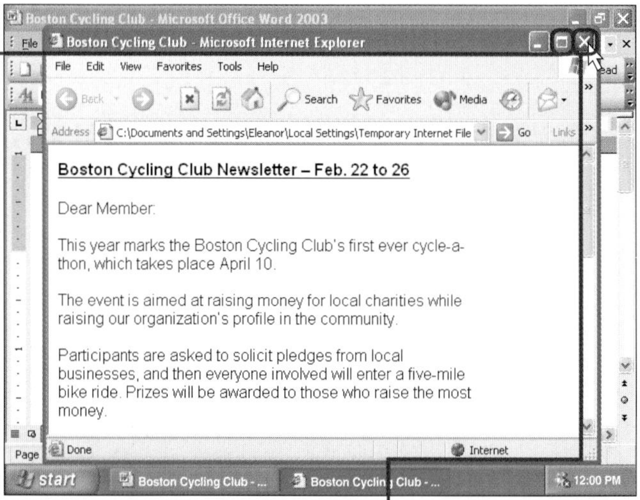

■ Your Web browser window opens, displaying the file as a Web page.

■ To maximize the Web browser window to fill your screen, click .

4 When you finish reviewing the file as a Web page, click to close the Web browser.

PREVIEW A FILE AS A WEB PAGE (CONTINUED)

Preview a Word Document

When you preview a Word document as a Web page, the Web page displays any formatting or graphics you included in your document.

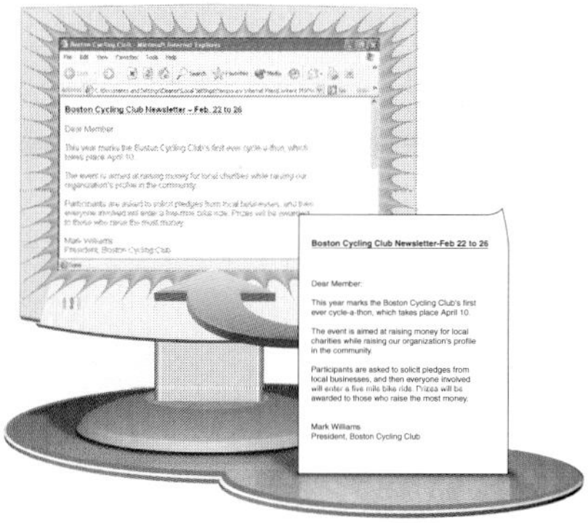

If your document contains multiple pages, all the pages in the document will be displayed on the same Web page. You can scroll through the Web page to see all the pages in the document.

Preview an Excel Workbook

When you preview an Excel workbook as a Web page, the gridlines that separate each cell do not appear.

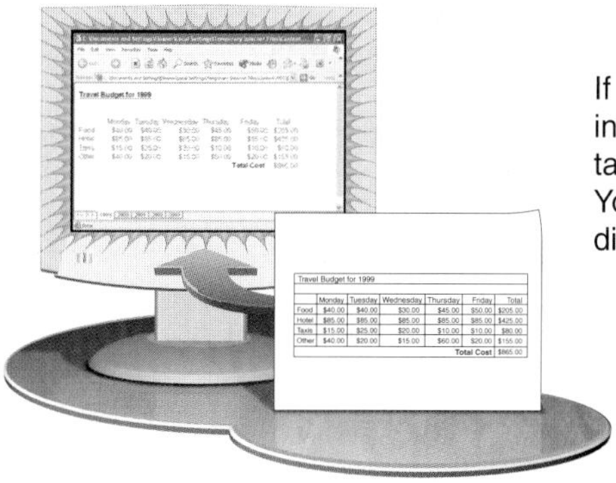

If your workbook contains data in more than one worksheet, tabs appear for each worksheet. You can click a tab to display a different worksheet.

Preview a PowerPoint Presentation

When you preview a PowerPoint presentation as a Web page, the Web page displays the title of each slide in your presentation and the current slide. You can click a slide title to display a different slide.

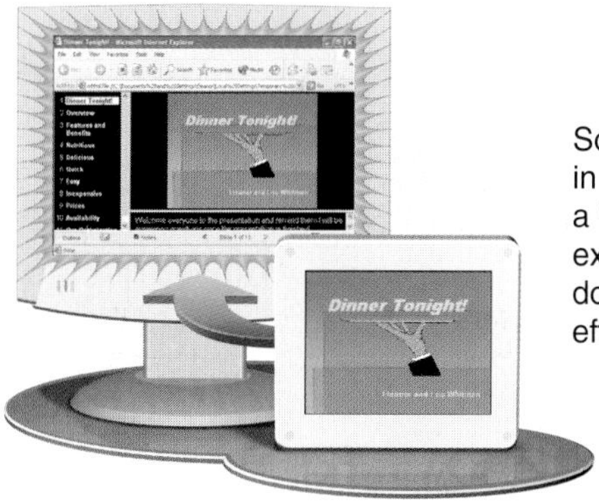

Some of the features available in PowerPoint will not work in a Web browser window. For example, most Web browsers do not support animation effects.

SAVE A FILE AS A WEB PAGE

You can save an Office file as a Web page. This allows you to place the file on the Internet or your company's intranet.

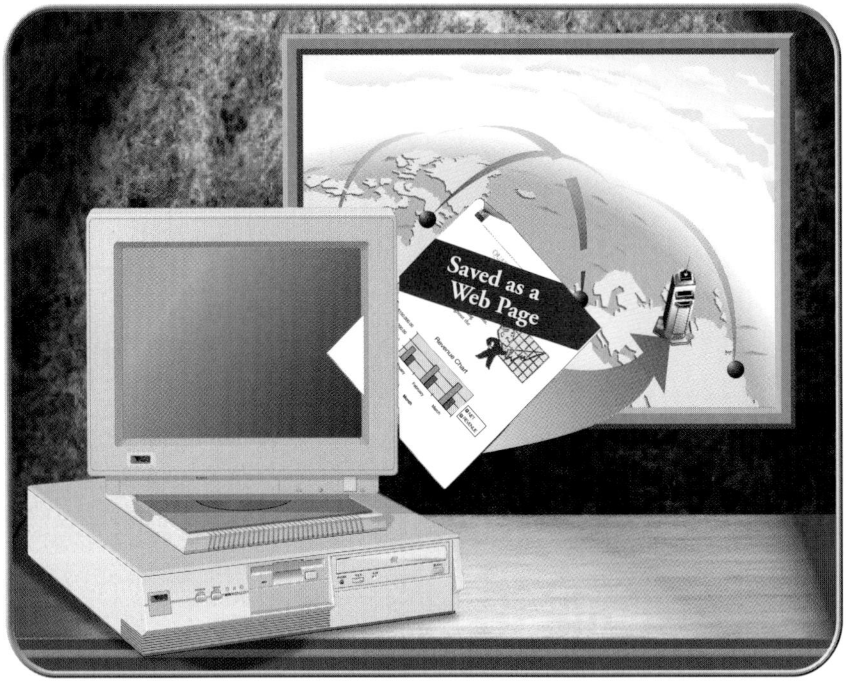

An intranet is a small version of the Internet within a company or organization.

You can use the method shown below to save a file you created in Word, Excel or PowerPoint as a Web page.

SAVE A FILE AS A WEB PAGE

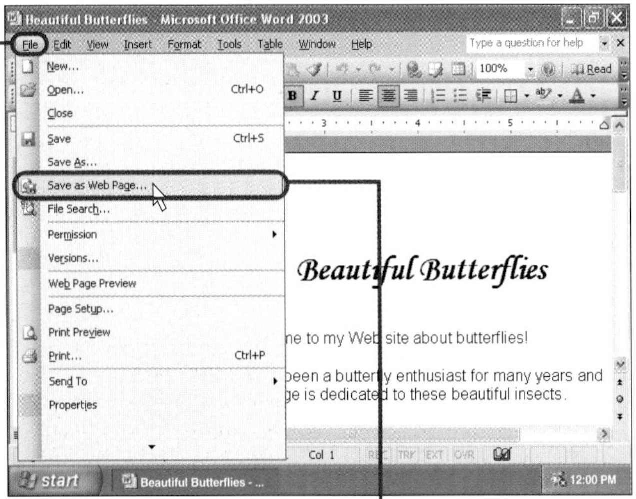

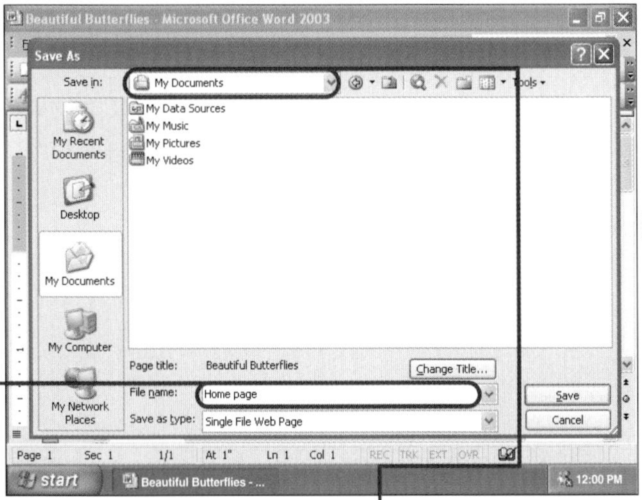

1 Display the file you want to save as a Web page.

2 Click **File**.

3 Click **Save as Web Page**.

Note: If Save as Web Page does not appear on the menu, position the mouse over the bottom of the menu to display the menu option.

■ The Save As dialog box appears.

4 Type a file name for the Web page.

■ This area shows the location where the Office program will store the Web page. You can click this area to change the location.

Tip

What is the difference between the file name and the title of a Web page?

The file name is the name you use to store the Web page on your computer. The title is the text that will appear at the top of the Web browser window when a person views your Web page.

Tip

How do I make my Web page available for other people to view?

After you save a file as a Web page, you can transfer the page to a computer that stores Web pages, called a Web server. Once the Web page is stored on a Web server, the page will be available for other people to view. For information on transferring a Web page to a Web server, contact your network administrator, Internet service provider or Web hosting service.

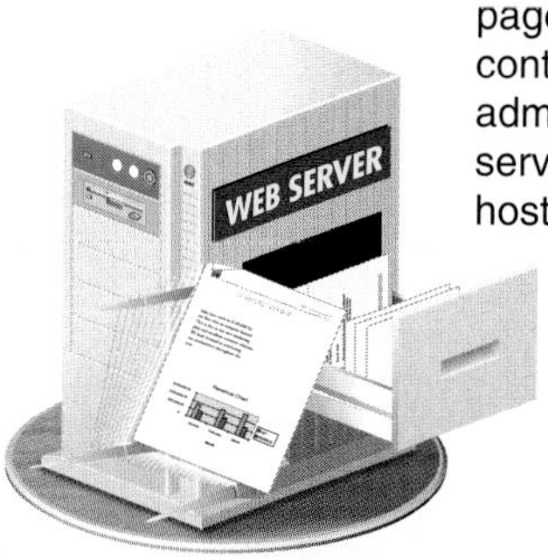

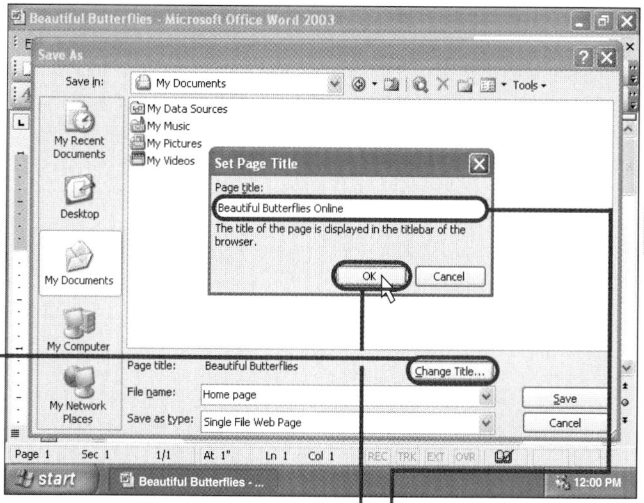

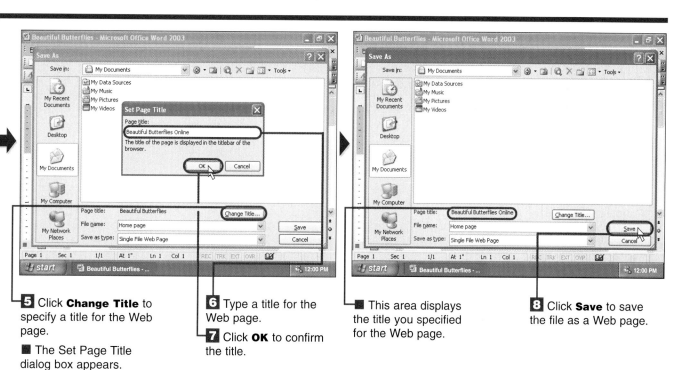

5 Click **Change Title** to specify a title for the Web page.

■ The Set Page Title dialog box appears.

Note: A default title may appear in the dialog box.

6 Type a title for the Web page.

7 Click **OK** to confirm the title.

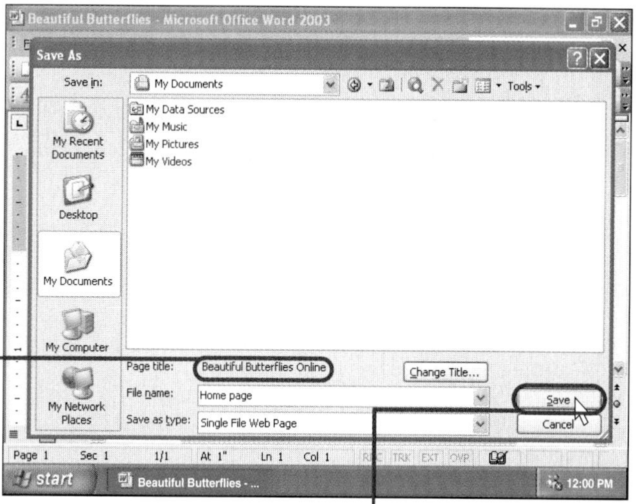

■ This area displays the title you specified for the Web page.

8 Click **Save** to save the file as a Web page.

INDEX

Numbers & Symbols

A

B

C

D

L

M

N

O

P

R

T

U

maran illustrated DOG TRAINING

MARAN ILLUSTRATED™ Dog Training is an excellent guide for both current dog owners and people considering making a dog part of their family. Using clear, step-by-step instructions accompanied by over 400 full-color photographs, MARAN ILLUSTRATED™ Dog Training is perfect for any visual learner who prefers seeing what to do rather than reading lengthy explanations.

Beginning with insights into popular dog breeds and puppy development, this book emphasizes positive training methods to guide you through socializing, housetraining and teaching your dog many commands. You will also learn how to work with problem behaviors, such as destructive chewing.

ISBN-10: 1-59200-858-5
ISBN-13: 978-1-59200-858-2
Price: $19.99 US; $26.95 CDN
Page count: 256

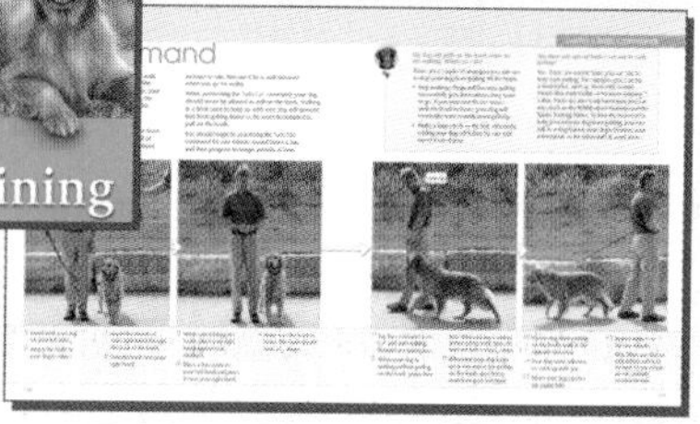

maran illustrated WEIGHT TRAINING

MARAN ILLUSTRATED™ Weight Training is an information-packed guide that covers all the basics of weight training, as well as more advanced techniques and exercises.

MARAN ILLUSTRATED™ Weight Training contains more than 500 full-color photographs of exercises for every major muscle group, along with clear, step-by-step instructions for performing the exercises. Useful tips provide additional information and advice to help enhance your weight training experience.

MARAN ILLUSTRATED™ Weight Training provides all the information you need to start weight training or to refresh your technique if you have been weight training for some time.

ISBN-10: 1-59200-866-6
ISBN-13: 978-1-59200-866-7
Price: $24.99 US; $33.95 CDN
Page count: 320

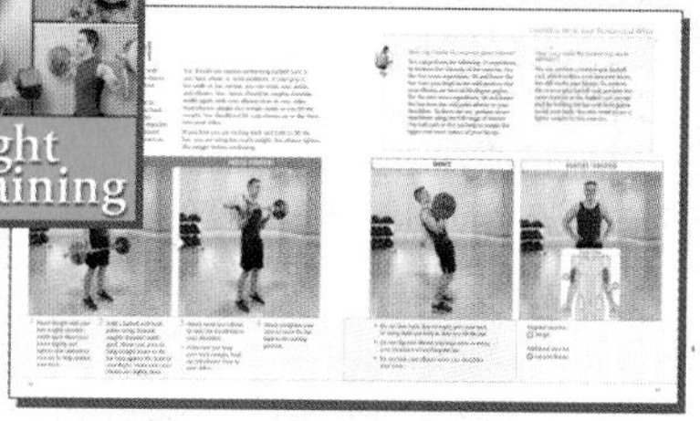

maran illustrated YOGA

MARAN ILLUSTRATED™ Yoga provides a wealth of simplified, easy-to-follow information about the increasingly popular practice of Yoga. This easy-to-use guide is a must for visual learners who prefer to see and do without having to read lengthy explanations.

Using clear, step-by-step instructions accompanied by over 500 full-color photographs, this book includes all the information you need to get started with yoga or to enhance your technique if you have already made yoga a part of your life. MARAN ILLUSTRATED™ Yoga shows you how to safely and effectively perform a variety of yoga poses at various skill levels, how to breathe more efficiently and much more.

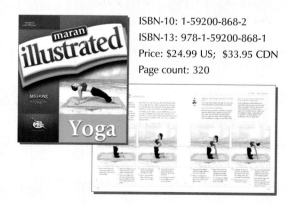

ISBN-10: 1-59200-868-2
ISBN-13: 978-1-59200-868-1
Price: $24.99 US; $33.95 CDN
Page count: 320

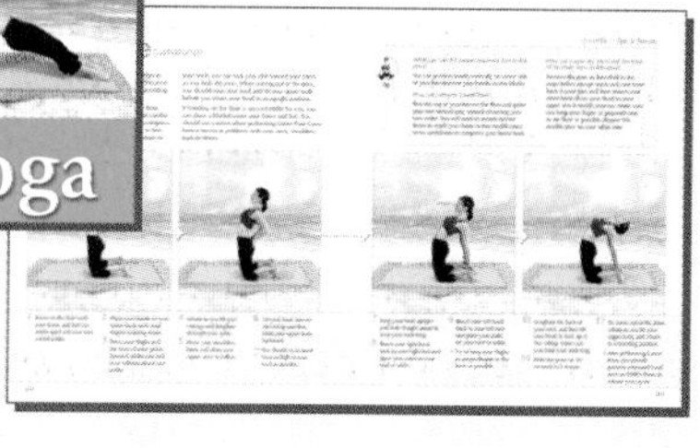

maran illustrated GUITAR

MARAN ILLUSTRATED™ Guitar is an excellent resource for people who want to learn to play the guitar, as well as for current musicians who want to fine tune their technique. This full-color guide includes over 500 photographs, accompanied by step-by-step instructions that teach you the basics of playing the guitar and reading music, as well as advanced guitar techniques. You will also learn what to look for when purchasing a guitar or accessories, how to maintain and repair your guitar, and much more.

Whether you want to learn to strum your favorite tunes or play professionally, MARAN ILLUSTRATED™ Guitar provides all the information you need to become a proficient guitarist.

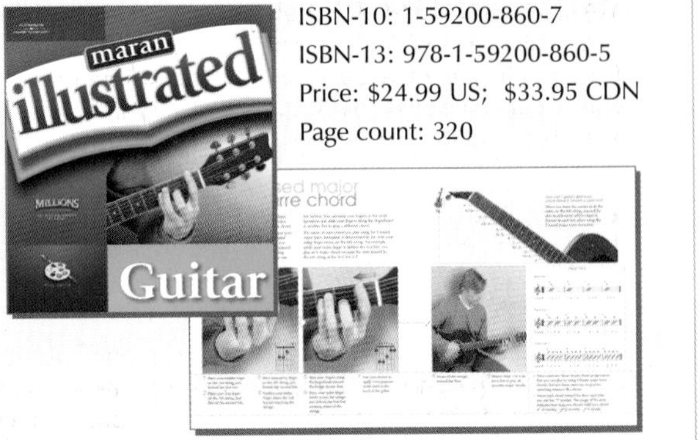

ISBN-10: 1-59200-860-7
ISBN-13: 978-1-59200-860-5
Price: $24.99 US; $33.95 CDN
Page count: 320

maran illustrated PIANO

MARAN ILLUSTRATED™ Piano is an information-packed resource for people who want to learn to play the piano, as well as current musicians looking to hone their skills. Combining full-color photographs and easy-to-follow instructions, this guide covers everything from the basics of piano playing to more advanced techniques. Not only does MARAN ILLUSTRATED™ Piano show you how to read music, play scales and chords and improvise while playing with other musicians, it also provides you with helpful information for purchasing and caring for your piano.

ISBN-10: 1-59200-864-X
ISBN-13: 978-1-59200-864-3
Price: $24.99 US; $33.95 CDN
Page count: 304

maran illustrated KNITTING & CROCHETING

MARAN ILLUSTRATED™ Knitting & Crocheting contains a wealth of information about these two increasingly popular crafts. Whether you are just starting out or you are an experienced knitter or crocheter interested in picking up new tips and techniques, this information-packed resource will take you from the basics, such as how to hold the knitting needles or crochet hook, to more advanced skills, such as how to add decorative touches to your projects. The easy-to-follow information is communicated through clear, step-by-step instructions and accompanied by over 600 full-color photographs—perfect for any visual learner.

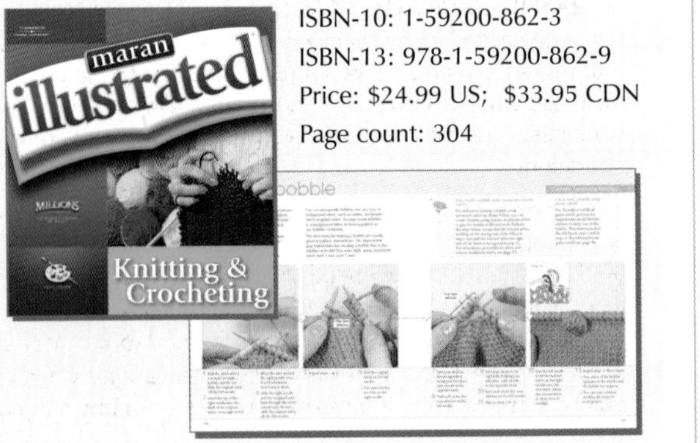

ISBN-10: 1-59200-862-3
ISBN-13: 978-1-59200-862-9
Price: $24.99 US; $33.95 CDN
Page count: 304

maran illustrated POKER

MARAN ILLUSTRATED™ Poker is an essential resource that covers all aspects of the most popular poker games, including Texas Hold'em, Omaha and Seven-Card Stud. You will also find valuable information on playing in tournaments, bluffing, feeling at home in a casino and even playing poker online.

This information-packed guide includes hundreds of detailed, full-color illustrations accompanying the step-by-step instructions that walk you through each topic. MARAN ILLUSTRATED™ Poker is a must-have for anyone who prefers a visual approach to learning rather than simply reading explanations.

Whether you are a novice getting ready to join in a friend's home game or you are an experienced poker player looking to hone your tournament skills, MARAN ILLUSTRATED™ Poker provides all the poker information you need.

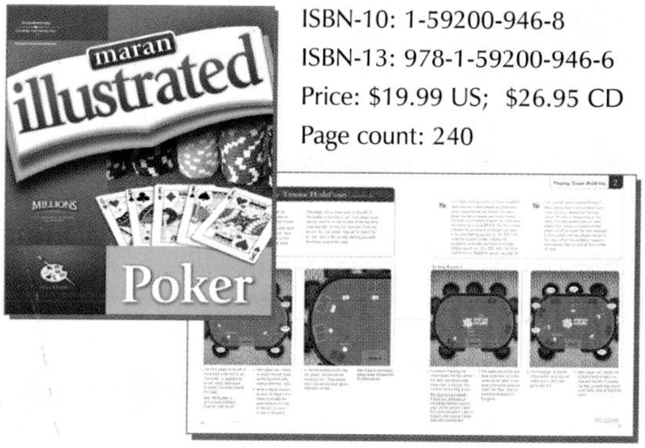

ISBN-10: 1-59200-946-8
ISBN-13: 978-1-59200-946-6
Price: $19.99 US; $26.95 CD
Page count: 240

maran illustrated SUDOKU

MARAN ILLUSTRATED™ Sudoku is an excellent resource for anyone who wants to learn how to solve Sudoku puzzles or improve their skills.

This book contains easy-to-follow instructions explaining how to play Sudoku as well as advanced puzzle-solving strategies. The colorful illustrations and step-by-step instructions are perfect for any visual learner. MARAN ILLUSTRATED™ Sudoku also contains over 100 puzzles and answers so you can put your new Sudoku skills to the test!

Whether you have never tried a Sudoku puzzle before or you are an experienced player, MARAN ILLUSTRATED™ Sudoku is the book for you.

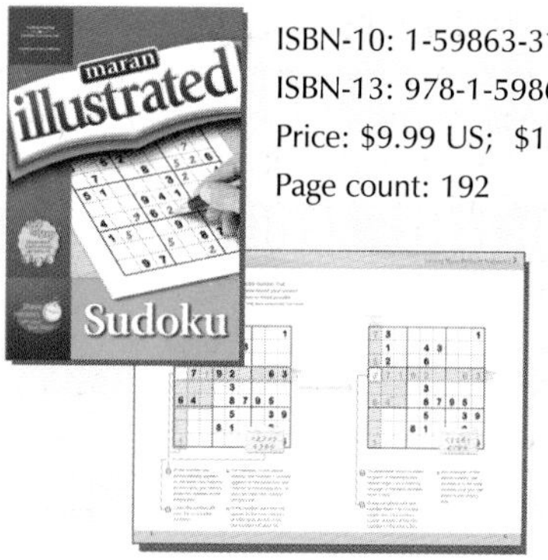

ISBN-10: 1-59863-316-3
ISBN-13: 978-1-59863-316-0
Price: $9.99 US; $13.95 CDN
Page count: 192

maran illustrated EFFORTLESS ALGEBRA

MARAN ILLUSTRATED™ Effortless Algebra is an indispensable resource packed with crucial concepts and step-by-step instructions that make learning algebra simple. This easy-to-use guide is perfect for those who wish to gain a thorough understanding of algebra's concepts, from the most basic calculations to more complex operations.

Clear instructions thoroughly explain every topic and each concept is accompanied by helpful illustrations. This book provides all of the information you will need to fully grasp algebra, whether you are new to the subject or have been solving quadratic equations for years. MARAN ILLUSTRATED™ Effortless Algebra also provides an abundance of practice examples and tests so that you can put your knowledge into practice. This book is a must-have resource for any student of algebra.

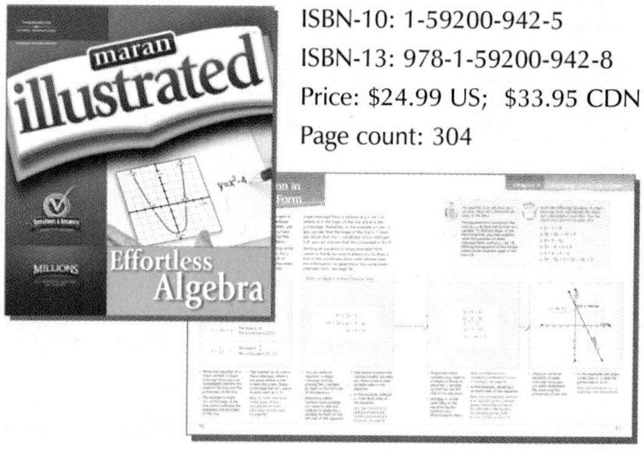

ISBN-10: 1-59200-942-5
ISBN-13: 978-1-59200-942-8
Price: $24.99 US; $33.95 CDN
Page count: 304